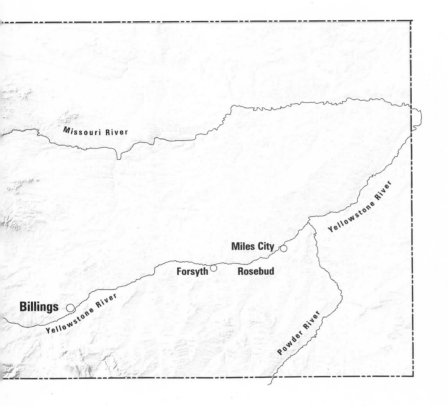

Missouri River

Yellowstone River

Miles City

Forsyth   Rosebud

Billings

Yellowstone River

Powder River

ONE
NIGHT
IN A BAD
INN

ONE
NIGHT
IN A BAD
INN

A TRUE STORY BY

CHRISTY LESKOVAR

PICTORIAL HISTORIES PUBLISHING COMPANY, INC.
Missoula, Montana

Library of Congress
Control Number 2005910601

ISBN 1-57510-123-8

FIRST PRINTING March 2006
SECOND PRINTING November 2006

PRINTED IN CANADA
Friesens, Altona, Manitoba

COVER & BOOK DESIGN
FRONTISPIECE MAP
Arrow Graphics, Missoula, Montana

PUBLISHED BY
Pictorial Histories Publishing Company, Inc.
713 South Third Street West, Missoula, Montana 59801
PHONE (406) 549-8488, FAX (406) 728-9280
EMAIL phpc@montana.com

FOR MOM AND DAD

Wherever men have lived
there is a story to be told.

—HENRY DAVID THOREAU

The bad inn lasts for only a night.

—ST. TERESA OF AVILA

ONE AFTERNOON ON
THE JEFFERSON SLOUGH

IT ALL STARTED when I heard that my great-grandmother was accused of murder.

There we were at Aunt Aila's, sitting in the living room, sipping tea, munching cookies, and visiting. After a little while, Aunt Aila got up and left the room. She returned with a large box. She said Sammy had sent it (my uncle). She set the box on the coffee table and opened it. She withdrew a large envelope from the box and from it a piece of paper which she passed to us. I had never seen such a paper. Printed in bold type across the top was "Descriptive List of the Prisoner." At the bottom were two pictures of a striking young man, one facing forward, the other to the side. I read quickly down the page. The crime was murder.

"Who was *this*?" I asked.

"Archie," Mom said, "Grandma's brother, your great-uncle."

My great-uncle?

Auntie Mary told us what happened. Oh, my. I hardly knew I had an Uncle Archie, now I knew why. Then she started talking about the fire and about finding the body and about Grandma T's mother being arrested. I was floored.

"Was that the time Mother told the man's fortune?" Mom asked.

"No, that was another time," Auntie Mary replied, another barn-burning story and another scandal. I had heard that one.

"I never heard any of this," said Mom.

"I was a middle-aged woman before I knew my mother lived in an orphanage," declared Aunt Aila in reply.

"Orphanage?" asked my brother, Jeff. "What was she doing in an orphanage?"

Nobody seemed to know.

I sat there listening to all this, hardly knowing what to make of it. These stories were incredible, and they were about my own relatives,

Grandma T's mother and brother, and this on top of all the other incredible stories Mom and Grandma had told me over the years. I knew from those stories that Grandma came from a notorious family, but I had no idea they were this notorious. I also knew that she had endured an unbelievably difficult life fraught with more hardships and horrors than one person can be expected to bear, and none of it her own doing. I was too shocked and overwhelmed by some of the more dreadful tales to ask questions, so I knew only snippets, and some of the stories were too awful to ask for more details; to do so would have seemed cruel. The important detail I did know was that she refused to have any part in filling that family closet full of skeletons nor did she wallow in those hardships. She knew she was captain of her own ship with regard to character. She chose to rise above it all, and she did. She was a remarkable lady. Now five years after she passed away to hear even more stories about her notorious family—it was a lot to take in during the span of one afternoon.

The next day I flew home, and as the days passed, Grandma and her stories sat quietly in the back of my mind, a pleasant I'm-here-for-a-reason memory that happily would not go away. Mom had been saying for years that someone should write all this down. She said it again that afternoon at Aunt Aila's. "Somebody should write a book about this," she said. "Oh, no!" said Auntie Mary. "Why not?" said Aunt Aila.

So I did.

First I had to find out the rest. I had no idea what I was getting into when I started. The research turned into quite a detective hunt and took me all over the country and to Europe. It was a tremendous amount of work, very difficult, and loads of fun, and I'm glad I did it. As I gathered family stories from everyone I could find, and read and researched and sought to learn about the places and times in which my grandparents and great-grandparents lived, and corroborate all I'd been told, and discover what I had not been told, the story only grew more interesting, much more interesting.

Here's what I found out. We begin with the fire.

PART ONE

The Forsyth Episode

CHAPTER ONE

IT HAPPENED during the first week of March 1913. Grandma was eleven years old at the time. She and her mother and brothers and sister were living in Forsyth, a small railroad and ranching town on the banks of the Yellowstone in Rosebud County, Montana. Her father, Arthur Hughes, still lived on the ranch, the land they had homesteaded eight miles west of town. On Tuesday of that week, Arthur hitched the horses to the milkwagon and drove into town. He stayed the night at the family home in Forsyth and returned to the ranch the next day. Before he left, he told Tom, their hired man, to come out on Saturday and help him with the fence. He said he'd be back in a few days with a load of hay for the cow.

The next was a normal day. Grandma and her brothers attended school. Her mother, Sarah, went to work at the Northern Pacific lunch counter. That evening Sarah and Tom played cassino until Tom went to bed. Sarah stayed up later and finished her mending by the light of the fire. Then she went to bed. It was after one o'clock.

Then on Friday, as they did every morning, ranchers across the valley pushed back their curtains and looked out at the day to see what Mother Nature had delivered during the night. In her fickleness, she had already brought snow, rain, and sleet that week. Today—nothing. It was clear. But as one of those ranchers peered across the prairie, where yesterday he had seen a house, today he saw a blackened patch of rubble.

Sheriff Moses went out to investigate. That's when he found the body and the rumors started.

THE MAN WHO lived in that burned down ranch house was my great-grandfather Arthur William Frederick Hughes. He was born at sea on March 16, 1871, aboard a clipper ship sailing across the South Pacific from Australia to Wales, the first child born to William and Mary Hughes, the former Mary Price. It must have been a fright-filled labor and delivery for Mary, her first child and born on a ship at sea no less. Why and for how long William and Mary were in Australia, I don't know.

Once in Wales, they settled in a house on Cross Lane in or near Llandovery, a quaint farming village on the northwestern edge of the Brecon Beacons in South Wales. It was a verdant, damp land of rolling hills and narrow valleys wrapped in perennial mist, lending an air of mystery to the place and perhaps providing fodder for all those legends and superstitions, of which there were many. Whether you cotton to such things and are convinced that bad luck is sure to come to those who fail to obey the decrees of superstition, or whether you dismiss all that and simply attribute life's misfortunes to life's misfortunes, Arthur's started very early in life.

By the time he was five years old, Arthur had three younger siblings. His mother had her hands full, so she sent him over the hill to live with his grandparents. He wasn't there long, maybe a year or two, when his grandparents died. For some reason, Arthur didn't go back over the hill to live with his parents; instead, he went, or was taken, to the dreaded workhouse, the paupers' refuge, said to be awful by design so as to discourage anyone from such a fate. The workhouse was to be no better than a laborer's dwelling: if no smoke came from the working man's chimney in the dead of winter neither should it from the workhouse. The old, the orphaned, the insane and infirm, the feeble-minded, all of the destitute lodged at the workhouse, as well as vagrants and some able-bodied poor. Some workhouses had crude beds pushed tightly together; in others, the sleeping space was simply an open area filled with straw surrounded by a curb or a wooden sleeping platform, not one for each person mind you, a community sleeping area, the only separation being of men and women.

Children such as Arthur attended school either within the workhouse or at the town school, and if he went to school in town, he walked there garbed in formless workhouse attire to serve as a constant reminder of his wretched station.

Whether these children should learn to read and write was a subject of debate in nineteenth century Britain. Were the poor to be educated, they might rise up as the rabble had in France, argued one side. It will only lead to rick burning. Why should workhouse children go to school when most laborers' children do not? Education would give workhouse children an advantage—it wouldn't be fair. Educate those children so they won't remain burdens as adults, argued the other side. Teach workhouse children only to read, not to write, came back as compromise. The countervailing argument, this from the Poor Law commissioners, was: children who learn to read should also learn to write. The debate ended in 1870 with compulsory education.

Arthur's mother learned to write. I don't know whether his father did. Of all the women in our story of her generation, Mary Hughes is the only one who learned how to write. I don't know about most of the men.

When Arthur was around ten years old, the workhouse apprenticed him to a family named Rees who employed him as a farm servant. He lived on their farm. At some point, Arthur was sent to a paupers' school for boys which was in another part of Wales. What was unusual about this school, for Wales at the time, was that it was a Catholic institution. There Arthur Hughes learned to read and write in English and Welsh, and he learned to be a stonemason and bricklayer. He was baptized a Catholic, though whether that was before or while he lodged at the school, I don't know. When he left the school, probably as a young teenager, he migrated to the coal-rich Rhondda Valley, a place he was certain to find work.

Around age twenty, Arthur succumbed to the lure of the New World. He secured a job caring for the children of a large family readying to make the passage. His pay for looking after the children during the voyage was his fare. They landed at Quebec on June 21, 1891. That October, Arthur entered the United States through Niagara and made his way to Wilkes-Barre, Pennsylvania.

Wilkes-Barre was a major town in eastern Pennsylvania's anthracite coal mining region. Coal fueled the economy in the nineteenth century and demand for it was great. Though it was found in many places throughout the country, anthracite coal was not; eastern Pennsylvania was the only place it was mined in the United States. Anthracite, also called stone coal, was particularly valuable because it burns cleaner and more efficiently than the more abundant bituminous (soft) coal. The Pennsylvania coal companies recruited Welsh coal miners because they were skilled at mining anthracite in Wales. Consequently, when Arthur arrived, Wilkes-Barre and its environs were full of Welsh people. It was the most Welsh town in America. Arthur easily found work as a stonemason.

By now, Arthur had grown into an attractive young man, his face adorned with a long, drooping, dark brown mustache, as was the fashion of the day. His blue eyes exuded youthful cockiness which deepened into confidence as his reputation as an accomplished craftsman grew.

After three years in Wilkes-Barre, Arthur decided to become an American citizen. His decision to set down roots was no doubt influenced by the financial opportunity the New World afforded him; however, he may have been moved not only by his head, but also his heart, and further enticed to stay by his friends the Thomases, more specifically, by their daughter Sarah.

The father, William Thomas, was born December 15, 1846, in Llantwit Major, a small, whitewashed town of narrow, meandering streets near the mouth of the River Severn in the very south of Wales. When grown, William migrated to the prosperous coal fields of South Wales. There the sometimes bartender, sometimes bricklayer, sometimes coal miner met Ann Price Davies. Ann, called Nancy, was the daughter of a mine superintendent and, in that class-conscious world, a giant step above William's station. Apparently this did not matter to Ann, for she married William anyway. Ann's father used his influence with the mining company to be sure his son-in-law advanced, and in time he did.

Ann and William first lived in Cymbach Aberdare, a place where it was said the people learned "to drink beer like water." Later they moved further south to Trebanog near Llantrisant, in the Rhondda Valley.

Babies came quickly: first Thomas, named for William's father, then Isaak, named for Ann's father, and on January 20, 1875, Sarah was born. She was named for Ann's mother. When Ann went to town to register Sarah's birth and was asked to sign the registry, she marked her X.

Though babies still came every sixteen months or so after Sarah—ten in all though only six would live to adulthood—they were all boys for a long time. For eight years, Sarah was the only girl, and she was her father's pet. She was also his favorite companion. When William came home from work, he would take her by the hand, and the two walked up the road to the nearest tavern. Little Sarah would sit by his side, and when he had a drink, she had a drink, of the same.

One theory is that the Thomas family's immigration to America was at Ann's behest. Ann Thomas was determined to raise a genteel lady in Sarah, but that was no easy task. She found her daughter to be a difficult, headstrong girl. The fact that the child was often intoxicated did not help matters.

The family would go to America leaving Sarah behind in finishing school. This would separate William from Sarah, thereby eliminating Sarah's opportunities to drink. After several years, the school would deliver a refined, tempered, young lady back to her mother. That was the plan.

William was the first to immigrate. He arrived in December of 1886. Ann joined him in Wilkes-Barre soon after bringing the three youngest children with her: Simeon, Joseph, and Mary Ann, ages nine, seven, and three. Eleven-year-old Sarah stayed behind in Wales to finish her schooling, as did her elder brothers, Thomas and Isaak, ages fifteen and thirteen. Sarah attended school in or near Brynmawr, so possibly that's where the family was living when they left.

While Sarah and her brothers continued their schooling in Wales, Ann and William and the younger three children settled into the middle strata of Pennsylvania's coal mining world.

Up, up, up at the top of this world were the coal barons. They owned the mines, were American born, lived in stone mansions and attended stone churches along Franklin Street. They were Episcopalians and Presbyterians.

Far below the coal barons, though far above the work-a-day miners, were the mine bosses of which William Thomas was one. They were mine superintendents, assistant superintendents, fire bosses, and so on. Many were Welsh. There was a special skill to undercutting anthracite with picks which the Welsh knew how to do since they mined anthracite in Wales. The American coal barons hired Welshmen to train their workforce; hence, the Welsh filled out the mine management ranks. They were Calvinist Methodists or Welsh Presbyterians which are two names for the same sect, one with a Presbyterian structure and Methodist theology. The Thomas family attended the Welsh Presbyterian Church in Wilkes-Barre, known as the big white church on the corner to its members and as the mine bosses' church to those who worked for its faithful. As late as the 1950s, services were held in Welsh.

Still well below in the economic strata were the miners who loosed the coal from the earth, carted it above ground, and sent it down the breakers. Many were immigrants from Poland, Ireland, Italy—generally Catholics—and also from Cornwall, Wales, and other European lands. The coal barons had their churches, the mine bosses had their church, and the miners had theirs. They were three distinct and separate worlds.

A year after Ann and William settled in Wilkes-Barre, Ann gave birth to another son, William George. At that time, it was the fate of many little boys in coal country to go to work at the colliery as soon as they were able. When the miners dug or blasted the coal loose from the earth, rock and slate came with it, and after it was carted above ground, these had to be removed. Boys as young as eight did this dirty work. They sat in a perennial cloud of coal dust plucking slate and rock from the coal as it bounced down the breakers. These children labored ten hours a day, six days a week, but this would not be the fate of William Thomas's sons. They would enter the workforce only after they finished their schooling. William George would not be a breaker boy, he would be a "scholar." In fact, as the rest of the family immigrated, and the children grew up, and Sarah's brothers went to work in Wilkes-Barre, for the most part, they did not work in the coal mines. Her sister, Mary Ann, became a teacher.

Two and a half years after he immigrated, William Thomas made his declaration of intention to become an American citizen. The next year sons Isaak and Thomas joined the family in Wilkes-Barre. The last to immigrate was Sarah, when she was around sixteen or seventeen years old. Arthur may have brought Sarah to America for the Thomases; he knew them in Wales. He and Sarah came to this country around the same time, though I don't know the exact date Sarah immigrated. As a child, she had urged Arthur to join her family when they went to America. "My father will get a job for you," she assured him, so possibly it was not the lure of the New World but the lure of Sarah Thomas that brought Arthur Hughes to America.

As for Sarah's sojourn at the finishing school, the school did its job, at least in part. When Sarah stepped off that train in Wilkes-Barre, Ann Thomas greeted a poised, impeccable in appearance, young woman who practiced social graces with the confidence of a well-bred lady—when she wanted to. Not the school, nor Ann, nor anybody else could suppress Sarah's wild nature. Sarah would not be tamed because she did not want to be. As unyielding as the most belligerent stallion, her will would not be bent by anyone.

"I told you not to drive that horse at top speed!" Ann Thomas scolded, finger wagging, every time Sarah returned after racing off like a Fury in the sulky through the busy streets of Wilkes-Barre. Wherever Sarah was going, she wanted to go fast. The sulky at top speed was her preferred mode of transportation, hardly a lady-like posture for a Victorian woman whose full skirts were to be always to the ground, never revealing a bit of—dare I say it—leg. However, when bedecked in her finest hunter green gown, hat, and cape, Sarah left the sulky behind and proudly drove the buggy led by her matched team of a mare and gelding. The jet black horses were outfitted as regally as their driver with long plumes affixed to their halters. Altogether the ensemble made a smashing appearance.

It was in Wilkes-Barre that Arthur began to court Sarah. They first met when he worked for the Thomases as their hired man in South Wales. Sarah was a rambunctious child then who lingered near the stables whenever he was working. Now she was a comely young woman, full of gaiety and fun. She was also a cultivated woman; as an accomplished vocalist, she had given her own concert. Arthur was enchanted, so much so that he may have fallen in love with a fictitious woman, succumbing to "the first mistaken impulse" of an "undisciplined heart" as Dickens put it, or did he delude himself into thinking she'd settle down once firmly ensconced in marriage and motherhood.

By this time, the Thomas family had lived for several years in a comfortable three-story home on the edge of town across the street from the Empire Mine. It was to this house that Arthur Hughes came to call to ask William for Sarah's hand. William said yes, Arthur could marry his daughter, and they were married on August 4, 1897, in the Thomas family home, the pastor of the Welsh Presbyterian Church presiding. Arthur was twenty-six and Sarah was twenty-two. They settled in a house on Northampton Street, a few blocks from the Thomases. Their first child was born ten months later on June 11, 1898. Sarah named him William George after her little brother who died of pneumonia the year before. She dutifully noted the details of her son's birth in the family Bible: it was on a Saturday at five o'clock in the morning.

Their second child, Hector Osiris Dundonald Warren, was born eighteen months later on December 9, 1899. He also arrived quite early in the morning. Sarah named him after a military commander who carried all or some of those names.

Their third child was my grandmother Aila Mae, born August 21, 1901. She arrived at the very convenient hour of four o'clock in the afternoon—even in the womb, she was considerate. As an adult, she would take great pains never to inconvenience anyone. Her name had three syllables beginning with a hard A and hard I and was pronounced A (as in say)–*EYE*–la. Sarah said she named her after an Armenian schoolmate in Wales. Another time she said she read the name in a book. Aila was the third child and first

Arthur and Sarah Hughes' wedding portrait,
Wilkes-Barre, Pennsylvania, 1897.

daughter born to the third child and first daughter. Sarah was very superstitious and she no doubt had a superstition about that.

One month after Aila was born, she and Hector and Bill were christened at the Central Methodist Episcopal Church in Wilkes-Barre.

Sarah's brother Isaak was also married, and he and his wife, Ella, had a two-year-old daughter named Catherine; however, Grandma never spoke of this little cousin which makes me think the Hugheses and Thomases didn't see much of them. She did mention Uncle Ike, but never Aunt Ella or cousin Catherine. Ella was born and raised in Pennsylvania and no doubt had lots of family around to occupy her time, but she was also Irish, and as such, it's a very good chance she was a practicing Catholic, meaning she and Ike would have been married in the Catholic church and their daughter baptized Catholic. To Sarah, this was anathema.

Since little Catherine wasn't in their lives, when Aila came along she was the first baby girl in a long time that the Thomases had all to themselves, there being no pesky Hughes in-laws around to compete for her affection, and they took full advantage of the situation. As she said herself, "I got more than my share of the good things of life."

Arthur, Hector, Sarah, baby Aila, and William Hughes,
Wilkes-Barre, Pennsylvania, 1902.

Two of Sarah's brothers: Tom, Ike, Sim, or Joe Thomas.

To put it mildly, they doted on her, and who wouldn't want to. She was adorable. She was also willful—a willfulness rightly directed that one day would serve her well. She never appeared idle, always alert and on the verge of something, ready to pounce or run or play. She inherited her mother's dark hair and dark eyes, and she was a beauty. She wore pretty clothes, had a nurse to care for her and lots of uncles to coddle her, and coddle her they did. Her favorite was tall, red-haired Uncle Tom, Sarah's eldest brother. Uncle Tom would come to the house, stand at the gate, and whistle. As soon as she heard him, Aila would burst out the door and scamper down the steps, shoes in hand, her socks black with coal dust. Tom would bend down and slip her tiny shoes onto her tiny feet. Then he would straighten and say, "Come along, Princess," and Aila would stretch up her arm, he'd take her by the hand, and they walked, rather Tom walked while Aila pranced, to the corner store where Tom bought a cigar for himself and a piece of candy for Aila.

Even more wonderful to Aila than Uncle Tom was her precious grandmother Ann Thomas. By the time Aila was old enough to remember, Ann was as round as she was tall, four feet ten, due to dropsy, but that did not slow her down one bit. Out she went and often. Two men carried her on a chair to and from the buggy. Ann knew practically everyone in the Heights, their Welsh neighborhood. She was a formidable woman who commanded authority. When she threw an order from the porch, those sons minded, as did everybody save Sarah. As talented and hard working as Arthur Hughes was, his ascent to foremanship was hastened by Ann Thomas's shear force of personality.

From the time Aila took her first steps, Ann was teaching and molding her to be a proper little lady. Aila was only too happy to emulate her grandmother.

"Come along, little gal," Ann would say whenever she readied Aila to go with her for a ride in the buggy. And when not going somewhere with her grandmother, one of Aila's uncles was scooping her up and lifting her onto his shoulders and taking her for a walk, or he was taking her for a ride on his horse, he'd prop her in front and away they'd go. The entire extended family picnicked together on the banks of the Susquehanna. Music was ever present, somebody singing or playing an instrument. Aila's world was filled with her grandmother, her uncles, and music. It's my impression that she was a spectator in her mother's life.

When Aila was around three years old, Arthur moved the family across the river to a little hamlet called Dallas, and while living there, on September 13, 1904, Sarah delivered twin boys. They named one Arthur Franklin and called him Archie; the other they named Ferdinand. Sadly, little Ferdinand died.

Then one day a few months later, Arthur up and announced that he was moving his family again, this time even further west—all the way to Montana! It might as well been the moon. Ann Thomas was aghast. How could he even think of taking her precious granddaughter off to that wild uncivilized place. She insisted that Arthur leave Aila behind with her. He wouldn't hear of it.

It was a sad parting for many reasons. Ann probably knew that she and her little granddaughter would never see each other again, and they didn't. Two days before Thanksgiving the following year, Ann Thomas died.

CHAPTER TWO

GRANDMA ALWAYS SPOKE fondly of those years in Wilkes-Barre—of Uncle Tom and Uncle Sim and Uncle Ike. "They were so good to me," she said, and especially of her beloved grandmother Ann Thomas, the "plump little lady" for whom she had the deepest affection and held in the highest esteem. "My grandmother expected everyone to remember their manners whether they were scrubbing floors or at a dinner party," she said approvingly. It's amazing that she remembered those years at all, she was so young when they left. Her life was happy there, and as such, it made an indelible impression.

She did tell me why her father had to leave Pennsylvania, but as for why he chose to go to Montana, she never said and I never thought to ask. Being from there myself, it didn't seem like an odd place to go, but for Welsh immigrants in Pennsylvania at the turn of the century, it might as well have been the moon with oxygen, especially where they first settled—in desolate, windswept, bitterly cold, blistering hot eastern Montana. The moon might have had better weather.

Since I never asked what drew her father to this remote, Godforsaken place, I can only guess. Perhaps it was the promise of free land. There was still plenty available on the northern plains in 1905, and most of it was in eastern Montana. The allure of the West may have captivated Arthur's imagination as well. The West—the mere sound of the name conjured adventure, the unexpected, untold opportunity for the hardy and enterprising. The compelling advertisements beckoned:

Good land cheap for homeseekers.

Whatever there is for the man who lives in the east, Montana offers him with almost usurious interest.

Larger than European kingdoms . . . its resources are so varied that mankind might well marvel at their magnitude.

It was late March of 1905 when my great-grandparents Arthur and Sarah Hughes with sons Bill, Hector, and Archie, and daughter Aila, my grandmother, packed up everything they had in the world, quit their home in Pennsylvania and journeyed to Chicago where they boarded the Northern Pacific bound for Montana. "I thought we were up, up, up there on the ladder of everything," Grandma reminisced with delight about their emigrant train car. There was a heater at each end and a kerosene lamp in the middle. Their animals rode in a car behind the baggage car. Arthur watered and fed them at every watering stop.

They ended their journey in Forsyth. Why Forsyth, I do not know. The tiny town was about the size of their Welsh neighborhood in Wilkes-Barre. Though small, it was modern. Some residents already had the telephone and that summer they would have electricity.

Forsyth began to sprout from the prairie around 1882 when the Northern Pacific crews arrived laying track en route to the coast. Back then everybody lived in tents and every other tent along Main Street was a saloon. One early settler spent his entire first night behind a cottonwood dodging bullets as crazed or drunken gamblers rode up and down firing their revolvers at anything that moved. That lasted until the U.S. marshal arrived and calmed things down. Now twenty-three years later, the Hugheses landed. It was a quiet week; the prior had seen a killing, a suicide, a forgery, a juvenile elopement, and two elections. Arthur settled his family in rented accommodations and began his search for land.

The West had been neatly divided into a grid of one-mile-square sections, that is, 640 acres each. Under the Homestead Act, Arthur could claim a quarter section. All he had to do was build a house, settle on the land, and cultivate it for five years. Having done that, and paid the twenty-two dollar filing fee, he would own the land free and clear. To the resilient, independent-minded Arthur Hughes, it must have been an irresistible offer. A whopping 160 acres would be his—a tract the size of which he never could have dreamed of owning in Wales.

After two months, Arthur found the quarter section he wanted. It was on the Howard Flat eight miles west of Forsyth, about a mile south of the Yellowstone. It was a good, workable piece of land, and all of it was usable. It was flat up to the low hills along the southern end and devoid of timber. There was no water, but Arthur had designs on how he could remedy that situation.

His decision made, on June 21, 1905, Arthur filed for his quarter section at the Land Office. Then he loaded his young family and their belongings onto their wagon and set out to build a new life on the frontier.

If my great-grandparents expected eastern Montana to be full of dense forests or one huge, nondescript, perfectly flat plain as far as the eye could see without a hill or tree in sight, they were surprised. It was neither. A lot of it was flat but there were hills aplenty, some high, some low and soft, others were angular shapes—rough outcroppings jutting skyward with earth seeming to grow out of them. There were no forests though cottonwoods hugged the Yellowstone, and on the hills a few tenacious ponderosa pines provided color and defiant proof that Mother Nature plants and flourishes at will, even between rocks. Here and there clusters of pale green sage adorned the land, and elsewhere, tall lanky grass reached for the dry summer sun—not the thick carpet of green grass that you see in rainy places—this was knee-deep grass that stood up proudly like wheat, and from a distance with a light breeze looked like gentle swells rippling across a lake, only instead of blue, these swells were green or gold, depending on the time of year, and instead of wet, they looked soft, as if God were running his mighty hand across Nature's velvet.

It was certainly different from any place they'd ever been, but Arthur and Sarah didn't go there to admire a land like none they'd ever seen. They went there to work and to live. Gone were the verdant hills of Wales and the dense forests of Pennsylvania's Wyoming Valley, their lush grassy floors well-watered by Mother Nature leaving the countryside neat and tidy. Not so in the West—this was a rugged untamed land, and everything was on such a huge scale. They must have been struck by the boldness and immensity of the place and the stark remoteness after living in an eastern city where their neighbor's house sat but a few feet away. The wide-open spaces denote limitless possibilities to one, desolation to another. As she rode into that nothingness, Sarah probably thought Arthur was taking her to the ends of the earth. That may have been his plan.

Two dray horses pulled the wagon on which the family rode. Tethered to it was the flatbed piled high with furniture. The other livestock were tied to the flatbed. As they left Forsyth, they may have passed a group of Northern Cheyenne who sometimes camped on the outskirts of town, their tepees staked in a cluster, ropes of drying meat hung in between.

It was a slow eight miles, plodding along on that dirt road, pulling a heavy load of furniture. After the Indians, they probably didn't see another soul the whole way. They certainly saw plenty of cattle and horses and sheep grazing and, quite likely, the white bottoms of frisky antelope leaping across the prairie.

After a few hours, Arthur turned the wagon off the dirt road toward the south. They rode a short distance through the tall grass toward a lonely dilapidated shack. Arthur stopped the horses in front of the shack. This was it. This was their new home. This was where they were going to live. It must have been some tirade that Sarah leveled at him when she saw the place. It was awful—it had no windows, no real door. They could see out through the cracks in the walls and the wind could blow dust and dirt in. For water, they would have to walk half a mile to Emmell's Creek with pails and pans, this with children only seven, five, and three years old, and a baby ten months. It was enough to make many a woman want to sit down and cry. I suspect Sarah's reaction was more peppery.

Their closest neighbor, who lived about a mile away, watched in amazement as the newcomers arrived. "We couldn't believe how they came in and just plopped down like that."

Arthur and Sarah climbed down off the wagon and moved their belongings and the children into the tiny shack, Sarah probably still chewing Arthur out in Welsh. Once they were settled, Arthur drove back to town in peace. He bought a load of lumber, returned to the homestead, and set to work building a corral and barn for the livestock they brought from Wilkes-Barre; these were four blooded horses, the two drays, and at least one milk cow. Arthur planned to build a house for his family, but that would have to wait. The barn came first. In taking care of the animals, he was protecting their future livelihood. "If we lose the animals we lose everything," he said. Apparently he thought his family was more resilient than the horses and cow.

Soon after they arrived in Montana, Arthur registered his brand with the State. It consisted of three symbols in a row: a bar (a horizontal line), a backward B, and an upside down triangle. This he branded on the cow's left rib and each horse's left shoulder.

Around the time they settled on the homestead, they started to run out of money. I don't know why. Perhaps Arthur had planned on a stone masonry job that didn't materialize, or he had done a job and didn't get paid.

Whatever the reason, as their money ran out, so did their food. With their situation looking bleaker and bleaker by the day and no obvious remedy in sight, suddenly out of the blue, a bright spot appeared in the form of a fellow named Jonas who showed up at the ranch with a recently slaughtered calf—certainly a welcome sight and plenty of meat to keep the Hughes family fed for a long while. All was fine until a nearby rancher discovered that one of his calves was missing. It was that calf. Now only days after Arthur settled his family in that shack in the hinterlands, he and Jonas were arrested for grand larceny and hauled off to the county jail.

They posted bond and Arthur rejoined his family on the homestead and resumed work on the barn. The trial would be in the fall.

Around the time Arthur finished the barn, Jonas skipped town. Since the two were on the same bond, Sheriff Northway threw Arthur back in jail. Now poor Sarah was alone on the prairie, living in a shack with four small children, and having to walk half a mile across the open range for water. Since the barn turned out to be nicer than the shack, Sarah moved the family into the barn.

Things grew desperate for Sarah and the children while Arthur was in jail. The county supported them for a time. After four long months, Arthur's trial date finally arrived. The judge instructed the jury that Mr. Hughes was on trial for stealing the calf, not for receiving stolen property. The jury found Arthur to be not guilty.

Now free, Arthur could build a proper home for his family. With an influx of cash from Sarah's parents, he paid a builder one hundred dollars to frame a twenty-one by twenty-four foot house, and he did the rest. He nailed boards to the outside in horizontal ship lap, used flint for coping, and finished the inside walls with lath and plaster. There were four small rooms on one floor and an attic. He bought an ACME cooking range and an ACME heater which he placed in the kitchen; both burned coal. He built a large fireplace to provide much valued light as well as warmth. Kerosene lamps provided light as well. He placed the showpiece of their furnishings in the front room which was also the kitchen. It was a wood-carved Murphy bed framed by two full-length mirrors. Aila slept in it, and when her little sister came along, she slept in it too. Every morning the bed was made and put up right away in case visitors stopped in to see it. Such large mirrors were a rarity in farm homes, so the bed became a popular attraction. Everybody wanted to see those mirrors, or see themselves in those mirrors.

Though dryland farming was being touted at the time, Arthur was wise to irrigate. "Land and water must go together," he said. Beginning at the west end of his property and making optimum use of the natural slope of the land, Arthur dug a ditch across the homestead to a spot upstream on Emmell's Creek. It was slow, arduous work with pick and shovel. He hired two men to help him. When they finally reached the end of the mile long ditch, they broke the earthen dam separating the creek from the ditch, allowing the healthy creek to flood the ditch, providing Arthur with ample irrigation water. Arthur would draw from this ditch using gravity to irrigate the rest of his land.

Arthur also hired a man to dig a well. He most likely did this before he built the house so he could be sure that the house would be close to the pump. Then he erected a windmill, and they were as well-fixed as anyone for water.

Arthur fenced their land, built stables for the horses (which he called a barn), built two more barns, an ice house, and a chicken house. He purchased a coal burning heater for the large barn to provide heat should he have to nurse a sick animal. He enlarged the kitchen, it being not only the room for cooking and eating but also for washing people and clothes. As Grandma said, "When it came down to it, you got up, you were in the kitchen." Later he piped water into the house.

As for crops, Arthur planted winter wheat, corn, and potatoes on ten acres, alfalfa for hay on another twenty acres, and used the remaining land to graze their stock. In time, he added chickens, geese, sheep, pigs, and more milk cows. I'm not sure whether they raised stock to sell or only for their own use. If to sell, theirs was a combination farm, meaning they raised and sold livestock and crops. Joseph Kinsey Howard, writing in the 1940s with the benefit of hindsight, concluded that a combination farm was the best, and possibly the only, way for a homesteader to make a go of it on the plains of eastern Montana.

Frontier wives such as Sarah had to be as clever and industrious with household affairs as their husbands were on the farm. They cut bottles to make jelly jars. They made soap; a common recipe was melted beef fat, lye, and wood ashes mixed together and left to set up in bread pans. The goose was to be eaten, but her feathers were never wasted; those went into pillows. A use and a reuse was found for everything. They were no-nonsense, get-to-work scrubbing the stove, scrubbing the clothes, scrubbing the children, and then pulling up carrots kind of women who labored from dawn until they dropped into bed well after dark. They weren't afforded the luxury of being frivolous or pampered. When one of the boys thought he'd get a rise out of his teacher by letting a mouse loose in the classroom, the intrepid young woman quickly and unceremoniously dispatched the creature with the fire poker.

Sarah planted a vegetable garden and grew herbs which she used for cooking and cures. She stored enough vegetables to last the winter in the twelve-by-fourteen-foot cellar Arthur dug a few feet from the house. Though theirs was a simple wooden farmhouse in the middle of the prairie, she kept it neat and clean and as pretty as she was able. "Very clean" and "immaculate" were the modifiers most often used to describe Sarah's house wherever she lived.

Putting up the hay was a typical chore for a homesteader, but there was something about the way Arthur did it that drew spectators. First he cut the alfalfa and let it cure in the sun. Then he and his help raked the hay into windrows, gathered it into shocks, loaded it onto the wagon, and drove to the barn. There they pitched the hay onto a belt which took it up into the loft and dumped it. Neighbors came to the ranch to see this belt. I don't know whether there was something unique about the contraption Arthur devised to power the belt or the curious neighbors were simply green honyockers who didn't know the first thing about putting up the hay and wanted to see how it was done. Farmers who had to buy hay in the spring complained about the high prices. Arthur and Sarah always had plenty of hay for their stock; they never had to buy any. Perhaps they even sold some.

One of Arthur's heavier chores was putting up the ice, and for that, he hired help. The men cut blocks of ice from the frozen creek and lifted them with huge pincers. It was a precarious and potentially deadly task if one of them slipped into the fast moving water below the ice. They loaded the ice blocks onto the horse-driven wagon or sled and drove to the ranch. There they stacked the ice in the ice house, layering straw or sawdust in between to keep the blocks from freezing together. They cut enough ice to last the summer.

Fences were few in the Yellowstone Valley when Arthur and Sarah and the children arrived in 1905. Most of the land was vast open range used by ranchers to graze huge herds of cattle, horses, and sheep. One nearby outfit boasted nearly seven thousand head of horses; the French cavalry was a

customer. In the early days, many of those ranchers made do with powdered milk, a milk cow seeming an inconvenient, unnecessary luxury. The
darned animal insisted on being milked twice a day at the same time. It tied
a rancher down. He needed his cowpunchers out attending to his livelihood, not home milking cows. Sarah would not make do with powdered
milk and no butter. She was accustomed to the best and she wanted the
best, even in the hinterlands. If his wife demanded fresh milk, other men's
wives probably wanted it too. Arthur recognized the opportunity and started
a milk business. Soon he added butter and eggs.

From time to time, a newly arrived homesteader would show up at
the ranch looking for Arthur. Word had gotten around that ol' Hughes
had the sixth sense for finding water. The newcomer would ask Arthur to
show him where to dig on his land, and Arthur would oblige, as he had
for the others. Otherwise, the stoic Arthur Hughes kept to himself.

Sarah, on the other hand, was anything but stoic and the last thing she
ever wanted to do was keep to herself. Even though there was always
work to be done with the chickens, in her vegetable garden, and around
the house, every now and then Sarah took time for a diversion, and one of
her favorites was going visiting.

From the doorway she would holler to Bill to ready the buggy. Then
she'd take off her apron, put on her hat, and march outside. She'd leap
into the buggy, whack the horse's rear, and she was off.

She'll be coming down that dirt road when she comes . . .

At a full gallop, she'd thunder down the dirt road to the Andersen/
Tadsen ranch house about a mile away, an immense cloud of dust following the high-speed buggy, evoking Elijah's fiery chariot departing for the
heavens. Sarah would race the horse right up to the house, and *whoa*, pull
back on the reins and bring the horse to a dead stop. No sooner were all
four hooves on the ground, Sarah would jump out of the buggy and yell,
MR. ANDERSEN!

And we'll all go to meet her when she comes . . .

Mr. Andersen came quickly whenever he heard Sarah yell, announcing
her arrival. He would greet her with a kindly, good afternoon, Mrs. Hughes,
and Sarah would return the greeting. Then he'd say something to bait her
like, what do you think you're doing racing that horse? And Sarah would

snap back something to the effect, what of it? I'll drive my horse the way I see fit! And they were off on their regular repartee of cussing each other out. "Could she cuss!" his granddaughter Mignon told me. After the two had just about cursed their teeth loose, to borrow a Twainism, Mr. Andersen would invite Sarah in for a cup of coffee. She would accept, and any family member within earshot of the cussing match would join them. Mr. Andersen's grandchildren would gather round the table and listen, so intrigued were they by the eccentric Mrs. Hughes, this Auntie Mame of the frontier. Mr. Andersen and Sarah would visit for awhile, and then as abruptly as she arrived, Sarah would thank him for the coffee, say goodbye, and gallop her horse and buggy back to the ranch, leaving her host and his family in a cloud of dust.

TWO YEARS AFTER they arrived in Montana, on Monday, August 12, 1907, Sarah gave birth to their second daughter, Sarah Eleanora Patricia Montana Hughes. She was sometimes called Sarah but usually called Patsy. When Patsy was born, Bill, the eldest child, was nine years old; Hector was seven; Aila, my grandmother, was almost six; and Archie would turn three in September.

That fall, Aila began first grade. She and her brothers attended the Andersen School, about a mile and a half from their home. There were four children in the first grade and only three or four in the sixth, seventh, and eighth grades combined. "It seemed when the boys got big enough to work on the farm they didn't have much time for school in those days," Grandma explained. All the children were in one room, so the eighth graders heard the first graders' lessons and the first graders heard the eighth graders' lessons, if there was an eighth grader that year. To say that a child in those days had a fifth grade education meant only that he had matriculated no further. A bright child could have picked up much more, being in the same classroom with older children and hearing their lessons year after year. Bill was in the fourth grade the year Aila started school. He was a precocious lad who couldn't understand why other children weren't as quick as he, and he was never reticent about expounding upon what he knew. And he was mean. Hector was much more popular. He was bright, amiable, and talkative. He could strike up a friendship with anyone. Everybody liked Hector.

*Andersen School. Aila is at left front, Bill is at far left, Hector is in the
second row, third from the right. The teacher is May Kendrick.
Rosebud County, Montana.*

Sometime after Aila completed first grade and had gone on to second,
she awoke one morning and was surprised not to see her mother in the
kitchen. She pattered into her parents' bedroom looking for her. Then
she saw them. A baby! Two babies! She scurried over to get a closer look.
Oh my, they were so tiny, so precious, each snugly swaddled, only their
round little faces beamed through. She reached out to touch one of them.

Aila, go fix breakfast for your brothers, said Sarah from the bed.

Yes, Mother.

After breakfast, Aila put on her boots, hat, coat, and mittens and ran
out the door. Bill and Hector were almost to the road. "Wait for me," she
hollered.

"If we wait for you we'll freeze to death," Bill retorted. Aila ran and
stumbled through the deep snow, almost disappearing at times behind
the drifts. Her brothers paid her no heed and walked ahead as fast as their
legs could carry them.

To merely say the children walked to school is to make light of what
could be a perilous journey. Aila was always tiny, even for her age. To get

to school, this tot and her brothers had to walk across the open range where cattle and horses trod, plus rattlesnakes and the occasional bobcat. Some families who lived much further from school waited until a child was eight years old before sending him because before then he was too little to be traipsing across the range that far by himself. No doubt, Arthur and Sarah gave the children strict instructions to stay clear of the horses and cattle when they walked to school. Rattlers were the biggest worry.

Apart from the critters, deep snow was an obstacle to surmount but even worse were blizzards. A rancher riding by in his wagon rescued a teacher on her way to a country school. He found her walking in circles; she was completely disoriented by the blinding snow. One little boy collapsed in deep snow on his way home, exhausted by the bitter cold. It was only by the grace of God that his father happened to see him fall and rescued him. Otherwise he'd have frozen to death.

Of the souls who endured the homestead experience, John Steinbeck wrote: "It is argued that because they believed thoroughly in a just, moral God they could put their faith there and let the smaller securities take care of themselves." It seems surviving the trek to school counted as one of the smaller securities.

My fingers are frozen, Aila lamented when she finally arrived at the log school house that day.

Come here, Aila, said the teacher, directing her to the stove and rubbing Aila's hands between hers in the warmth emitted by the burning coal.

Aila liked school. The lessons came easily to her. She didn't like the teacher who grabbed her by the arm one day and swung her like a rag doll, pulling her arm out of the socket. Aila remembered the incident with a scowl in her heart. How dare that teacher treat her so cruelly. This day, she quickly finished her assignment and sat quietly listening to the other grades' lessons, the same lessons she had heard the year before. Finally, school was out. She hurried home to see the twins. She couldn't wait to hold them.

No twins. No one said what happened.

ANOTHER YEAR BROUGHT another teacher. Aila was glad. She liked this one. First thing every morning and every afternoon immediately following lunch, the teacher strolled the aisles watching the children practice their Palmer Hand, her long full skirt covering all but the hem of her shoe.

One day after school Aila was skipping playfully toward home when she heard one of the girls taunting her, calling her a fattie. Fattie, fattie, you're a fattie, said the girl. Aila stopped. I am not fat! she retorted. Are too! said the girl. Am not! Are too! Am not! Are— That was enough. Aila ran straight at the girl and hit her over and over until the teacher came out and separated them.

After receiving a severe scolding, Aila walked home still seething in anger at the girl. Then something came over her. She hated it when her mother or Bill beat her and here she had done the same thing to someone else. She could have killed that girl, she thought, the rage in her was so deep. It terrified her. She would never do it again, she told herself. She would never hit another person, never.

WHEN THEY WEREN'T in school, Aila and her siblings helped their parents with household chores and on the farm. They fed the chickens, gathered eggs, milked the cows, helped put up the hay, churned cream to make butter, pumped water for morning in case it froze during the night, which was often. Whenever a dish broke, it was Aila's chore to pound it with a mallet into a mass of tiny grain-size pieces, and these went into the bucket of oyster shell for the chickens. Sarah supervised care of the chickens. She was very particular about fresh eggs.

Aila always looked forward to helping her father on the ranch because it meant time with him. She adored her father. The sun rose and set on him. "My father is the best stonemason in the country," she said. "My father is a crackerjack with animals," she said. Her father could do anything and do it better than anybody. She said it was from him that she learned hard work. She had great respect for the hard working. Those who weren't were a sorry disappointment.

She especially liked to help her father when it meant getting on her pony to do so. Arthur bought her a Welsh pony with all the trappings and taught her to ride. "You are supposed to ride like a grown up lady in a parade," he told her. He was proud of his little daughter. She could ride anything even as little as she was. He also taught her to shoot. At both shooting and riding he boasted she was expert. Annie Oakley is said to

Aila, Arthur, Patsy, Sarah, and Archie Hughes,
Hughes Ranch, Rosebud County, Montana, circa 1912.

have remarked that learning to shoot teaches a woman self-possession.
As a woman, Aila Hughes would embody that virtue in abundance.

In addition to her pony and all those other animals on the ranch, Aila
had a pet. No, not the usual cat or dog, though they did have a dog and
probably a cat too, to keep the mice down, but these weren't Aila's pets.
Hers was a piglet. When the pig had piglets, one became Aila's pet. She
brushed it, fed it, petted it. The piglet followed her around on the ranch.
Arthur built a little swinging door in the door to the house so the piglet
could go in and out at will. "Pigs are not dirty," Grandma said shaking
her finger, remembering her pet piglet. "If a pig has a clean place to live, a
pig is clean!" My impeccable grandma with a pet pig. That pig must have
had an immaculate place to live. A pig never had it so good.

Apart from such novelties, ranch life certainly had its perils. There
was the time the bull charged Aila's pony, while Aila was on the pony.
The bull rammed the pony's side, Aila flew into the air, and pony and
rider crashed to the earth. She was all right, just bruised and shaken up.
Mostly she was worried about her pony, that he would have to be put
down, but whatever his wounds, they were within Arthur's veterinary
skills. "My father took care of the pony," she said proudly, "so everything turned out all right."

And there were diseases, horrible lethal diseases now unheard of in this country. One year Aila got horribly sick. Her head ached, she burned with fever, her stomach ached. None of Sarah's home cures seemed to work. She just grew sicker and sicker, so sick that Arthur went to town for the doctor. The last time they sent for the doctor was when the mare couldn't deliver her foal. Aila had watched the poor animal cry in pain "in her horse language" as she called it. Arthur described Aila's symptoms to the doctor and he came out right away. She looked terrible. The doctor examined her, then he stood, looked at Arthur and shook his head regretfully and said, "It's typhoid fever. She'll never live." Aila heard him, and knowing my grandmother, those were fighting words. She did get better, but she was terribly sick for a long time. Her memories of being sick were of her father staying up with her during the night and having to learn how to walk again when she recovered.

After she had fully recovered and was active as ever, she walked in the house one day and asked her mother if she could have some milk. Yes, she could. Aila heated the milk on the stove and then sat down at the table to drink it. Aila, sit up straight when you drink that milk, Sarah chastened. Aila sat up straight and asked where her father was. Sarah said he went away on a job. What job? He's building the state capitol in Helena. (This was the enlargement of the capitol building.) The state capitol, where the governor works! Aila was in awe. The most wonderful man in the world just flew far above all prior pinnacles she had set for him.

Arthur returned from Helena with a beautiful velvet dress for Aila. She was thrilled. Sarah looked at the dress and looked at Arthur and demanded, "And what did you bring for Willie and Hector?" Arthur did not reply but instead stood beaming at his delighted young daughter as she hugged his gift and thanked him over and over. Sarah interpreted his lack of reply to mean he brought nothing for Bill and Hector. She yanked the dress from Aila's arms and threw it in the fire.

DURING ONE OF THOSE summers in eastern Montana, Aila saw her first airplane. It was a first for many in Rosebud County. It was at the fair or rodeo, some such big doings. Her mother said she could go as long as she took Archie and Patsy with her, so the three children climbed on her horse and went. It was quite a show with barrel races and women in beautiful clothes wearing great big feathered hats parading on horseback. Aila was delighted by all it, especially the beautiful clothes.

Then came the barnstormer. Imagine the first time you saw an airplane the pilot was flying loops and swerves and what not. The crowd must have gasped and gasped again. Then the pilot flew up, over the corral, something went wrong, and the plane fell straight down like a duck full of buckshot and crashed. The crowd shrieked and stampeded out of the stands. Aila pinned Archie and Patsy against the fence with her tiny body, terrified they'd be trampled to death in the rush. When the stampede finally subsided, Aila stepped back from the fence and released them. They were crying. They cried and cried all the way home and were still crying when they got home. Sarah scolded Aila that she could have done a better job watching them.

THE WINTER OF 1911 brought another kind of excitement to the valley when one of the neighbors accused another neighbor of cattle rustling. The alleged thieves, a father and son, lived down the road a couple miles from the Hugheses. Undersheriff Bitle went out to investigate and took a contingent of deputies with him. They staked out the place and waited for the suspects to appear, hopefully with a hot cow. They did appear, cow in tow, and a shoot-out erupted. When it was over, Undersheriff Bitle was dead. The fatal bullet was recovered, and it was immediately clear that it could have come from only one gun—the father's—and he was charged with first degree murder. His eighteen-year-old son was accused of starting the gun battle and was charged with manslaughter. A change of venue was requested and granted and the trials were moved to Miles City in Custer County. The father's was first. Legal prowess was much in evidence on both sides. The prosecution team included Rosebud County Attorney Charles Crum and Custer County Attorney Sharpless Walker. The defendant was represented by two lawyers: one a state senator from Red Lodge, the other from Billings. The jury concluded that the father was indeed guilty, but not of first degree murder. They decided instead for manslaughter, and he was sentenced to ten years in prison. The son was found to be not guilty. A reporter speculated that this was due to the sympathy-arousing (and probably tear-filled) testimony provided by his mother.

(The outcome of the Bitle murder trial is particularly interesting when juxtaposed against two events later in our story.)

BY 1912, THE Hughes family had lived on the homestead for seven years and ranch-life seemed quite normal to the children. Whether it ever seemed normal to Sarah is doubtful, even though both she and Arthur became quite adept at it. Life in Montana had certainly been a shock for her—living in a shack in the hinterlands after their comfortable life in the East. And they had to contend with Montana's notorious weather. Winters were long and severe. Temperatures dipped well below zero and stayed there. The bitter wind chilled a person to the bone and those feeble wooden farmhouses provided little shelter against it. Snow was plentiful and at times so deep they couldn't go anywhere for days. That second winter had been especially fierce. A rancher along the Rosebud lost almost half his cattle and most of his sheep.

Harrowing thunderstorms punctuated the hot summer months with lightning to ignite the parched grass. A light wind could sweep a prairie fire across a quarter section in minutes. And if dry lightning wasn't the menace, it was hail big enough to pound your crops to a pulp. Sometimes Mother Nature jealously held back her snow and rain. Drought set in three years before the Hughes family arrived and stayed for two. To make matters as bad as could be, the dreaded hoppers came with it and ate the range bare. They'd come again, as would the drought.

Those living in nearby Froze to Death Valley along Froze to Death Creek sent their children to Froze to Death School. Other place names denoted similarly dire events: Cannibal Island, Dead Man's Spring. The valley was so named after several Indians froze to death there. Legend had it a trapper lived on the island an entire winter eating raw meat. A train wreck killed three men and threw one into the spring. There was no Horn o' Plenty Gulch, no Never Starve Island. It was a hardy breed who came and stayed.

Even for an experienced farmer, which Arthur wasn't, farming was especially difficult in Montana because of the dry climate. A 160-acre tract was plenty of land to support a family in the East where it rains. Not so in the arid West. Here was a huge country, the United States, a land extending from sea to sea; the western half was hardly populated at all. The politicians in Washington conceived a plan to give away the land. Most of them had never spent much time there, if any. They hadn't tried to farm in arid country. Later Congress expanded the parcels to 320 acres.

A man named Campbell published a convincing pamphlet in which he maintained that there was no need to worry about the lack of water; if native grasses grew without irrigation, other crops would too, as long as the farmer followed his system. Some homesteaders believed the literature and did not irrigate—a ruinous decision.

And free land wasn't enough. A homesteader needed capital to get his farm going: to buy barbed wire for a fence, lumber to build a house and barn, and equipment to work the farm. One thousand dollars was recommended as startup capital. That was more than a year's wages.

Some homesteaders resorted to burning their fence posts for heat to survive the winter. No fence meant animals could wander over and graze on your crops in the spring. Congress added a provision to the Homestead Act to address homesteaders who went insane.

The pilgrims came together. The early settlers to the West came in wagon trains. When the homesteaders came, they came alone, and plopped down in the middle of a desolate prairie. It was a desperate existence. Tenacity was their virtue. Most didn't make it.

But the Hughes family did. Having fulfilled the requirement to better the land, President Taft granted Arthur a patent for his quarter section on February 23, 1912. All told, Arthur had spent $1,500 dollars proving up on their land. In June, Arthur sold the homestead to Sarah for a dollar. In August, Sarah "and Arthur Hughes her husband" sold the homestead to an Iowa man for $4,800. The family had turned their hard work into cash. Sarah bought a house in Forsyth for $500. It was a larger home on two lots on 8th Avenue, south of the tracks. Sarah and the children moved into that house so Bill could begin high school in the fall. The men who bought the homestead were absentee owners. Arthur continued to live on the ranch and care for the stock and crops. It was still known as the Hughes Ranch.

Arthur then turned his sights to cultivating another piece of land. He filed for eighty acres about a mile due east of the homestead. This was under the Desert Land Act. The land would be his after three years as long as he irrigated it and paid one dollar per acre per year for those three years. He didn't have to live on it.

Where so many had failed, my great-grandparents had cashed in their homestead, bought a comfortable home in town, had plenty of money in the bank, and were working another piece of land to repeat their earlier success.

Then there was the fire.

CHAPTER THREE

No one reported seeing the fire, just the aftermath. The house had burned to the ground, but only the house. The barns, the ice house, the chicken house, and the animals were untouched. Sheriff Moses sent for the coroner as soon as he found the body. While waiting for him to arrive, two little boys wandered by.

"Do you boys know who was staying in this house?" asked Sheriff Moses.

"No, sir," they replied.

"Did you see anybody around this house?"

"No, sir." The boys glanced curiously at the smolder and ruin and walked on.

William Moses had been sheriff of Rosebud County for a little over a year now. He was born in Texas. As a young cowboy, he rode north on a cattle drive up the Texas Trail to the Black Hills. He worked for several cattle outfits there, later dabbled in the mercantile business, and then ran for sheriff in Belle Fourche, South Dakota. He served two terms after which he moved his family to Montana to take a job as a detective and stock inspector on the Crow reservation. By that time, he had already lost three of his five children and his wife to premature deaths and had remarried. He was elected sheriff of Rosebud County in the fall of 1911. He was in his early fifties, wore a thick mustache, was small in height, and "nervy" when it came to pursuing lawbreakers, or so said the local paper.

Soon Coroner Frank Booth pulled up to the ranch in his car. He had lived in Forsyth for four years and owned the Furniture and Mortuary. Then the six men he had summoned to serve as jurors arrived. At least two of them lived near the ranch, meaning within a mile or two. One was Mr. Andersen's son-in-law, another had owned that huge horse ranching outfit, but by this time he had sold his herd.

Sheriff Moses led Coroner Booth and the six jurors through the soot and cinders to where the blistered corpse lay. They must have shuddered at

William Moses, Rosebud County Sheriff, 1912.

the sight of it. It was gruesome. Enough was left to tell it was a man, but not enough to tell who. The head was completely burned off as were the hands and feet and most of the arms and legs. Only a charred torso with the stub of one arm and one thigh remained. It had sunken deep into the bedsprings, and there was a loaded Winchester laying next to it. After the jurors had a good look, Coroner Booth sent them on their way. Sheriff Moses picked up the Winchester and removed the bullets. He handed the rifle and bullets to his deputy and told him to drive his car back to town. Then he and Coroner Booth pried the blackened body from the bedsprings and placed it in a basket. They covered it with a blanket, loaded it into Coroner Booth's car, and drove to Forsyth.

TOM ELLIOTT, their hired man, was the first one up that morning. The brawny Irishman pulled his flannel shirt and overalls over the winter underwear in which he slept. Then he went to the kitchen and made the fire. Tom was from County Down and had come to Montana through Canada about six years earlier. He had worked for several other ranchers before the Hugheses. He did chores for Sarah in town and helped Arthur on the ranch.

Aila was next to emerge from the bedrooms. She said to Tom, "My mother wants you to wake her at seven o'clock sharp." At said hour, Tom obediently walked to Sarah's bedroom door and called to her.

Sarah sat up and reached for the deck of playing cards on the table next to her bed. She quickly read her fortune, never one to linger over anything. Then she gathered the cards, returned the deck to its place on the table, got up, dressed, swiftly brushed her long, dark brown hair, wound it on top of her head, and pinned it in place.

By now everybody was up and in the kitchen. Sarah scooped flour into a bowl, added a pinch of salt, a scoop of sugar, and baking powder. She stirred this with a fork, cut in a generous chunk of butter, and then mixed in an egg and enough milk to make the dough hold together. She rolled out the dough to about a half inch thick, cut out rounds or wedges, and handed each to Tom who cooked the cakes on the griddle. Aila set the table and made and poured the tea.

After breakfast, the four older children walked to school. Bill was in the ninth grade at the high school. It was in the main part of town, north of the tracks. Hector, Aila, and Archie attended the grade school a few blocks from their house. Hector was in the seventh grade, Aila was in sixth, and Archie was in third.

Bill was the first family member to hear about the fire. He ran home as fast as he could to tell his mother. Sarah burst into tears and nearly collapsed. She went to the phone. Then she told Tom to ready the buggy, and they set off for the ranch.

Once they were well out of town, they saw the car approach. Coroner Booth slowed and stopped his car along side the buggy. Sarah pulled the reins. Sheriff Moses stepped out of the car and walked over to speak to her. He told her about the fire and about finding the body.

"Did you find his watch?" Sarah asked.

"No, ma'am," he replied.

Sarah handed the reins to Tom and told him to go to the ranch and water and feed the animals. She stepped down from the buggy and climbed into the car with Coroner Booth, Sheriff Moses, and the shrouded body remnant. She sat silently as they rode to town.

Coroner Booth drove to the morgue, and he and the sheriff unloaded the body. Then the sheriff left. Once inside, Frank Booth removed the blanket and allowed Sarah to view the body. She asked him to turn it over, which he did. I'll take him home now, she said. Coroner Booth said that wasn't possible. The body must remain in the morgue for the autopsy. At this, Sarah raised quite a fuss. She insisted on taking him home right then. Booth insisted the body stay put. Seeing she had no recourse, she left and walked home. Coroner Booth telephoned Dr. Huene.

Later that evening, Sheriff Moses went to Sarah's house. Tom Elliot answered the door and invited him in.

"It's rumored over there in town that Hughes met with foul play," Sheriff Moses said to Tom. "Do you think he had any enemies?"

Tom told the sheriff about an altercation Arthur had some time ago with a fellow named S——. Just then Sarah came down the stairs and entered the room. She exchanged greetings with the sheriff. Sheriff Moses said that Mr. Elliott was just telling him about some trouble her husband had with S——. He asked if she knew anything about it.

"Oh," she said, "everybody forgot about that long ago."

They talked some more and then Sheriff Moses said, "I need to take your hired man here, Mr. Elliott, to the jail."

"Why?" Sarah asked.

"He has been implicated in the fire. I'm taking him to the jail for questioning."

Sarah was visibly startled at this. Moses escorted Tom to the door and took him outside. Sarah walked to the door and called out anxiously, Tom, come back! Tom stopped and turned toward her. The sheriff took him by the arm and led him away.

Sheriff Moses questioned Tom at the jail but got nowhere. Tom denied knowing anything about the fire and the sheriff had no evidence indicating that he did. He had no choice but to release him.

Early the next morning, Sheriff Moses drove out to the ranch to look for evidence. He parked his car and walked toward the burned-down house. As he approached the house, he spied a watch in the gutter. He stooped down and picked it up. He walked slowly through the rubble and soot and charred chunks of wood, surveying all as he went, looking for clues as to how this might have happened. He walked toward the bedsprings where he had found the body. He looked around on the floor near the bed and moved the cinders out of the way to see what was underneath. Something caught his eye—a knife. He picked it up, turned it over in his hand, and examined it. Then he poked around some more. He found a few buttons; some looked like underwear buttons, others could have been from a vest. He kept looking. He pulled out his watch. It was almost time for the inquest. He put the evidence in his car and drove back to town.

He went directly to the courthouse where jurors, officials, and witnesses were assembling for the inquest. Coroner Frank Booth opened the proceeding: "Now begins the matter of the inquisition over the body of a person as yet unknown. Mr. Horkan will question the witnesses on behalf of County Attorney Beeman."

Sarah was the first to testify. She knew George Horkan. He had defended Arthur on the larceny charge. Mr. Horkan asked her how old she was. "Thirty-nine years," she said.

"How tall a man was your husband?" he asked.

"Well, by gosh, I don't know," she said.

"How old is your husband?"

"I think he is thirty-nine years old."

"Where was he born?"

"He was born on the Pacific Ocean. I thought he was born in Wales. He was one of twenty-four children. There were twenty-four up till yesterday. They are all scattered around the world. I only learned he was born on the ocean the other day."

"Was your husband home on last Wednesday night, March 5?"

"As far as I know he left our house to go to the ranch."

"Did your husband sleep out at the ranch every night?"

"Yes, sir. Ever since the boy came in."

"What boy?"

"Alfred Larson."

"Was he working for you?"

"Yes, sir."

"When did he quit."

"Three or four weeks ago. About three weeks, don't know exactly."

"Since then your husband has been sleeping out at the ranch alone?"

"Yes, sir."

"When was the last time you saw your husband?"

"Wednesday noon — I had dinner with him."

"Were you quarreling with him at dinner?"

"No, sir."

"Did he tell you whether or not he was going out to the ranch Wednesday night?"

"He told me that he was going out to the ranch and would be in yesterday afternoon with a load of hay for the cow."

"Did he tell you of having any trouble with anyone out at the ranch?"

"No, sir."

Horkan asked what trinkets her husband carried. She said he carried a knife and a watch—a silver watch, not very large.

"I hand you this watch and ask you to look at it and see if you can identify it."

"Yes, it is. Yes, sir, that is his watch."

"How can you tell."

"By the size."

"Did he have a knife?"

"Yes, sir."

"I hand you a portion of a knife and ask you to look at it."

"Yes, sir, it is the knife."

"Take it in your hand. What makes you so nervous when you look at it? Anything particular about it that recalls anything to your mind — I say is there anything particular about this knife which recalls to your mind anything?"

"It belonged to the best friend I ever had, it belonged to the best friend I ever had, the best friend I had carried it," she said.

"You never saw anyone use this knife on your husband?"

"No. My God, no."

"Are you positive that the knife belonged to your husband?"

"Yes, sir, I am positive."

Horkan asked what kind of underwear her husband wore and showed her a piece of underwear taken from the body.

"Yes, that is his underwear," she said.

He showed her a watch chain and keys. Yes, they belonged to her husband, she said.

"Did you know this man Thomas Elliott?" he asked.

"Only just that he is working for us. He has been in town doing the chores for me, then he would go out to the ranch every Saturday night and work out with Arthur."

"Did he board and room over at your house?"

"Yes, sir."

"Was he at your house Thursday night?"

"Yes, sir."

"How do you know?"

"Well, I will tell you for one thing, my boy stayed out late, and he and I were playing cassino that night."

"Did he sleep in the same room with your boys?"

"Yes, sir."

"Did he eat breakfast there the next morning?"

"Yes, sir, he got up and made the fire."

"Did he and your husband ever have any trouble?"

"No, sir."

"How much insurance did your husband have?"

"Sir?"

"How much life insurance?"

"Ten thousand."

"When did he take this insurance out?"

"After he sold the homestead. He had two thousand for a number of years. He had fifteen thousand when he first came here but could not keep it up."

"Do you know who is the beneficiary named in the insurance policy?"

"I don't. I haven't looked."

"Insured in the Montana Life I suppose?"

"Yes, sir, but I have never opened the policy since he got it."

"You say you didn't talk about getting this insurance out with your husband?"

"Well, he spoke some time ago that if he could get hold of some money he would insure himself again."

"You told him it was a good thing, I suppose."

"I did not. I told him it was money wasted."

"You viewed that burned body in the morgue?"

"Last night I looked at it and this morning when you were there."

"Was there anything about that body which conveyed to your mind that it was the body of your husband?"

"I cannot see anything, it was so burned up."

"Have you any theory how this thing happened?"

"None whatever. All I can think of is that the house took fire."

Horkan asked whether they kept coal oil out at the ranch. Sarah said yes they did, at the kitchen door or under the kitchen table.

"You have not heard of anyone having it in for your husband who would get away with him?"

"No, sir, not now I don't. I don't know of anyone. He never had any trouble. I was the only kicker. He never caused any trouble."

"Did your husband at any time make any statements that he was afraid someone would kill him?"

"Not for a couple of years."

"Before that time he was afraid?"

"Yes, sir."

"When?"

"Well, when Mr. R———— took a try at his life, you remember that time."

"Has he never gotten in any trouble out there in the last three or four months?"

"No, sir, not that I know of."

"Did your husband and S—— have any trouble?"

"That was old man S——. Alfred told me about it. I asked Mr. Hughes and he said it was nothing. Mr. S—— had a little too much drink, that is all. I could not get anything out of him. We never had any trouble with S——. They were always pretty good neighbors."

"Your husband as a general rule did not drink?"

"No, sir."

"Did your husband always carry a gun?"

"No, sir, never carried a gun."

"Did you keep a gun out there?"

"Yes, sir, we had a gun at the house."

"Have you told everything you know about his matter?"

"Everything that I know."

"You are not holding anything back."

"Nothing at all."

"And you have no idea at all as to how this thing happened, have you?"

"None whatever."

Mr. Horkan said he had no further questions for Mrs. Hughes. He escorted her to the door and summoned Tom Elliott. In answer to Horkan's questions, Tom said he was about forty years old and had been in Montana six years working around the stables. He said he came to Rosebud County the latter part of January.

"When did you go to work for Hughes?" asked Horkan.

"I went to board there when I came up to work on the ice," said Tom.

"That is, at the Hughes house in town?"

"Yes, sir."

"You were out at Hughes's ranch about seven o'clock Thursday evening?"

"No, sir."

"When Mrs. Hughes says you went out there Thursday night she is telling something that is not a fact?"

"Last Saturday I was out there."

"Is it not a fact that you and Mrs. Hughes went out there last Wednesday or Thursday?"

"No."

"She was not home Thursday night?"

"She was down at the restaurant working at the depot and she did not get home that night until about seven o'clock. She told me she was at the restaurant."

"And you went to bed pretty early that night?"

"About nine — a little after ten."

"And she was in the house that night, and you didn't do anything?"

"Nothing."

"Was there anyone else there?"

"The two little girls and the little boy were in bed; the two older boys were still up."

"You did not get up at all that night, and you did not notice any commotion around the house?"

"No, sir."

"So that if Mrs. Hughes says that you went out of the house that night she is telling something that is not a fact?"

"I did not get up."

"Have you had any conversation with Mrs. Hughes about this matter since it happened?"

"No. A little conversation came up last night. She said there was a rumor over in town that there must have been foul play."

"You have been in the house and around when Hughes was home a great deal?"

"Yes."

"Did he have any trouble with his wife?"

"No, sir."

"Did he have any trouble with you?"

"No, sir."

"Don't remember having a conversation with Mrs. Hughes in which she said she would like to get away with Hughes and get some of that insurance?" asked Horkan.

"No, sir."

"And if she testified to that she would be telling a lie?"

"She would be telling a lie."

"Have you any idea how this happened out there?"

"No, sir, I have not the least idea."

"Did he ever tell you that he was afraid anyone would try to kill him?"

"Not lately."

"When did he?"

"One day he told me that a man named S—— almost choked him. He threw him off and threw him in a pail of water. He got mad when Hughes was going to put him out and he pulled a gun on Hughes. He stepped into a room and by chance he had a gun there and told this man to get out. So he went out."

"How long ago was this?"

"About the sixth or seventh of February."

"Last month?"

"Yes, sir. He had been in here in the town and he rode out drunk, this Mr. S——."

"Which Mr. S—— did he mention?"

"The old man."

"Did he tell you what the trouble was about?"

"No, sir, he did not."

"Did Hughes ever tell you that he was afraid of S—— or anyone else would kill him?"

"No, sir, he did not. Just remarked that the man was drunk and did not know what he was doing."

Coroner Booth asked Tom if he ever knew of Hughes being drunk out at the ranch. Tom said no.

"What has been the relations existing between you and Mrs. Hughes — you are simply working there?"

"That is all."

"Never become any more intimate with his wife?" interjected one of the jurors.

"No, sir, I am sure of that — no, sir," replied Tom.

"What time did you get home on Thursday night?" asked Horkan.

"On Thursday night I was never out of the house," Tom said.

"And you are sure that Mrs. Hughes and yourself did not go out of the house from Thursday night until Mrs. Hughes went out Friday morning?"

"No, sir, I am sure about that."

"Did you hear the horses make any noise that night?"

"No, I tied the cow and horse both up that night to keep them from knocking the skin off, and they were both tied up the next morning."

"Do you know anything about Hughes having a gun?"

"Yes, sir, he told me he had and laid it on his bed on top of the cover."

"Did he ever tell you the reason why he did that?"

"He did not."

Horkan said he had no further questions for Mr. Elliott. Coroner Booth asked the jurors if they had any questions. All shook their heads no.

Bill testified next.

"State your name," Horkan asked.

"William George Hughes."

"How old are you, William."

"Fourteen."

"You understand the meaning of an oath do you?"

"Yes, sir."

"You understand that if you tell something that is not a fact you are committing perjury?"

"Yes, sir."

"That it is not only a violation of the law of the land but of God?"

"Yes, sir."

"And I want you to consider that."

"Yes, sir."

Horkan asked Bill about the days leading up to the fire: where was his father, where was his mother, where was Tom Elliott. Bill identified the watch, knife, and keys as belonging to his father.

"When was the last time you saw your father?" Horkan asked.

"Wednesday noon."

"Have you and your mother talked any about this matter this morning?"

"No, sir."

"And she told you about what testimony to give?"

"No, sir."

"What time did you go to bed Thursday night?"

"Between ten and eleven o'clock."

Horkan asked what time Tom Elliott went to bed. Bill said he heard his mother tell Tom to go to bed around one o'clock. Until then they had been playing cards. Horkan asked whether Tom Elliott got up that night after he went to bed. Bill said he didn't know. Did your mother and Elliott go away that night?

"No, sir."

"Had they done so would you have heard them?"

"I think I would."

Horkan asked whether his brothers heard anything. Bill said no.

"Did you have any horses in town that day?"

"A single buggy and one of the buckskins was in—brought in the day before by Hector."

"Did your mother ever talk to you about insurance?"

"No, sir, but she was looking up insurance papers this morning."

"Did she look up any yesterday and the day before?"

"No, sir."

"Did your mother say anything about how this happened?"

"No, sir."

"Have you slept out there with your father in the last month or so?"

"No, sir. The last time I was out to the ranch was January 6. I have not been out there since."

"But your father has been out there most of the time at nights?"

"Yes, sir."

"Were you over there at the house before the sheriff arrested this man Elliott last night?"

"I was in bed."

"Did you have any supper that night?"

"Yes, sir."

"What was the conversation about at supper?"

"I don't know that Mother talked about anything. She was all in pieces last night."

"Did you have any talk about getting insurance last night?"

"No, sir."

"Elliott was going away last night — didn't he talk about going away?"

"No, sir."

"Don't you remember he told your mother last night at supper that if he could get away he would pull out?"

"No."

"You never heard your mother talk with anyone about getting away with your father did you?"

"No, sir."

"Or did you ever hear any talk about anyone having it in for your father and would be liable to kill him?"

"No, sir, the only man I ever knew was R———."

Horkan excused Bill and called Alfred Larson. He was the boy who had worked for Arthur driving the milkwagon.

"How old are you?" Horkan asked.

"Fifteen years," Alfred said.

"Do you understand what an oath means?"

"No, sir."

"You know what it means to be sworn and testify in a courtroom?"

"Yes, sir."

"You know what will become of you if you tell a lie after you have been sworn?"

"Yes, sir."

Horkan asked Alfred about that altercation with S———: where did he live, what did he look like. "He was a short, dark complexion fellow. He came out with Hector, Mr. Hughes's son," replied Alfred.

"And what happened there?"

"Mr. Hughes and Mr. S——— had an argument."

"What did he do?"

"Well, all I know about it was that he is some relation to F——— and he came in there and he was about half drunk and Hughes rolled him out and put him on his horse and he started away."

"Did they have a fight?"

"I don't know."

"Where were you?"

"In bed. I got up and looked around the corner and saw him seated in the water pail."

"Had any gun been drawn?"

"Yes, sir. S—— drew his gun and Hughes took it away and got his Winchester."

"And he ordered him out of the house."

"Yes, sir. He had to roll him out as he could not stand up."

"And this man went away."

"No, he came back and got his half gallon of whiskey and his bottle."

"Was Hector Hughes there?"

"He came with S—— but went right back. He went back about a half hour afterwards."

"And he went back before this scrap started?"

"Yes, sir."

"Have you talked to Mrs. Hughes any the last few days?'

"No, sir, I have not been over there since last Tuesday."

"Hughes was in?"

"He was there."

"Did he say anything?"

"Yes, sir, he said the buckskin mare got killed."

"Did he say who killed it?"

"No, he said she was dead up there."

"You don't know anything about how this house got afire?"

"No, sir."

"And you have not heard any talk about it?"

"I have heard a number of people talk about it."

Horkan asked about the coal oil. Alfred said Arthur kept two cans and a jug of coal oil at the ranch.

"Where did he usually put his lantern when he came in in the evening?"

"Under the table in the kitchen."

"Did he always keep a light burning?"

"Yes, sir, all night long."

"Near his bed?"

"On a little stand."

"Did he always have a gun there?"

"He did. His gun lay along side of him when he slept there, a 38 Winchester."

"How did he sleep?"

"His head was to the north, and his bed was in the northwest corner."

"But did you ever notice how he slept?"

"He slept kind of curled up in a ball."

"Never noticed his sleeping on his stomach a great deal?"

"No, sir."

"Did he ever tell you that he was afraid anyone would kill him?"

"Well, he told me several fellows, but he didn't mention any names. I remember he told me there was a lot of people around there who would like to kill him."

"But he never told you who?"

"No, sir."

Sheriff Moses interjected, "Did you ever help Hughes while you were out there take wire off fences?"

"No, sir," said Alfred, "I have seen him take it off but I never helped him."

A few weeks before the fire, a rancher saw Arthur take some barbed wire off the fence at the ranch and snake it down the road to somewhere east of Emmell's Creek, which was where Arthur's desert claim was located.

Next up was Sheriff Moses. Horkan asked about his investigation at the Hughes Ranch.

"I went up there on the solicitation of the county attorney, Mr. Beeman. He said he had been informed that Hughes's ranch had been burned and there was a possibility that Hughes may have robbed this house of the doors and windows and other things and then set fire to the house. And I told him that I would go up and investigate and see if I could find out anything and also look into the house and go down and look over the premises of this desert claim on which he was fixing to build."

Sheriff Moses then described the scene and enumerated the articles he had collected.

"What was the position of this body on the springs?" Horkan asked.

"It was lying on its chest," replied the sheriff, "apparently in a natural position, that is, what was left of the remains. It was practically in the middle of the springs, the springs being burned down to the ground, it was lying in the center, and beside the remains was a Winchester rifle lying with the muzzle to the feet, and the gun was cocked."

"And there was a cartridge in the barrel?"

"Yes, sir, in the barrel."

The next to testify was the doctor who had performed the autopsy.

"Well, I examined the trunk of a human being thirty-four inches in length," said Dr. Huene. "The body was very much burned — arms burned off and the legs burned off with the exception of two thirds length of the thigh which was left. Upon opening the body, I removed the liver and the stomach, heart, and right kidney. Beside the stomach was evidence of fresh blood, and a great deal of blood there had been cooked. Both lungs showed air and on removing the left lung there was a large hole burnt in the posterior chest wall, about the eighth, ninth, tenth rib."

"What have you got to say about the clotted blood, doctor, and the discovery of the hole in the back of the body?" asked Horkan.

"Well, the blood would make you think the blood was there before the body was burned. I don't see how the blood would get there after the body was burned."

"From your examination, doctor, what have you got to say in regard to the man dying from the effect of smoke or fire?"

"Well, from the way you speak of the position in which he was found, you would think it was impossible that he died from the effect of smoke or fire."

"What have you got to say about the condition of the lung, would it carry the impression to you that he had died from the heat which he would be breathing in at the time?"

"There was too much air in the lung."

"It was then your opinion that the man was killed or had actually died before the burning of the body."

"That is what would be my impression, yes, sir."

"What have you got to say as to the dimensions of that gash or hole in the back?"

"You cannot say anything positive, for naturally the hole would not be as large when made as when we found it, on account of the fire getting into the rib and burning back in, but it must have been large enough to let fire get on the inside. It was not a puncture."

"A man in ordinary health, accustomed to sleep on his stomach would not keep that position when burning, would he doctor?"

"Not unless he was drugged or chloroformed, and if under chloroform he would draw his legs up, and if he was under the effects of morphine to make him unconscious, it would not destroy the reflexes."

"Well, doctor, you take a man who was a heavy sleeper, what effect does smoke have upon him?"

"Why he strangles, it is such an irritant."

"But it would naturally have a tendency to wake one up?"

"Well, if he did not suffocate and burn up. Even if he did sleep he would have to struggle in his sleep."

"In other words, it would be impossible for him to remain in the same position and smother to death."

"Yes, sir, it would be impossible."

"From your examination of the lungs there, the condition of the lungs did not show that the man inhaled fire?"

"He didn't inhale fire enough to singe the lung tissue."

"That would demonstrate the fact that he met his death from something other than fire?"

"Yes, sir, it would to me."

Horkan excused Dr. Huene and again called Sarah and asked her, "What was your idea last night in asking the coroner to examine the back of the body over there?"

"I just wanted to see it, that's all," she said.

"Did you have any particular reason?"

"No, no, I just wanted to see it all."

"Had you any special theory that he was hit in the back?"

"No, I was wondering, and just wanted him to turn it over so I could see it. I did not think it was burnt that bad. I never thought it was only a torso. I did not think it was burnt that bad, although Mr. Booth told me on the road that it was burned."

So ended the testimony.

The jury deliberated. They concluded the body was that of Arthur Hughes, and he met his death by foul or criminal means on the night of the fire.

Sarah stopped on her way home from the inquest to send a telegram to the Montana Life Insurance Company. Then she went to Frank Booth's Furniture and Mortuary to make the burial arrangements.

The body was moved to the Hughes home in Forsyth that afternoon. The funeral was held two days later. Arthur's Masonic Lodge sent a beautiful bouquet in condolence. It was a terribly sad, tear-filled day for Aila. Her beloved father and hero was gone. The *Forsyth Times-Journal* reported, "all that was mortal of Arthur Hughes was laid to rest in Forsyth cemetery."

Archie, Hector, Aila, Bill, Sarah, and Patsy, circa 1913.

The *Miles City Daily Star* called it the most dastardly crime since the murder last summer in Joppa.

Who wanted Arthur dead and why? Was there another brawl with S——? Had R——— come back to finish the deed? Was it a burglary gone awry?

The talk had already started with another suspect in mind.

"I went to Hughes's house in Forsyth between half past seven and half past ten the evening of the fire and the children said their mother and Elliott had gone out with the horse and buggy to the ranch."

"I heard Sarah, the day after the fire, at the Northern Pacific lunch counter, complain that she was very tired because she had been out driving very late the previous night and did not feel well. She acted so nervous."

"Sarah said she wasn't grieving much over Arthur's death, and when she got the insurance, she would get along a great deal better and have a much easier time of it than when Arthur was alive."

"Weeks before the fire, we heard Sarah say that Arthur was insured for *ten thousand dollars*, and he was worth more to her *dead* than alive.

She paid up the monthly installments on Arthur's life insurance several months ahead. She said she wanted to be sure the insurance was up to date because something might happen to Arthur."

Whether it was gossip embellished with every repetition or true, Sarah may have invited suspicion. She drank, and drank a lot. When she did, she was a torment. She beat the children—the small ones. She favored the older boys, especially Bill. Aila came home from school one day to find Archie a huddled mass in the corner sobbing. Sarah had beaten him with the whip. Aila picked him up and carried him away and rocked and soothed him. Hector protected the younger children when he was around. When Sarah was chasing Aila through the house with the buggy whip, it was Hector who grabbed the whip from his mother. If Hector wasn't there, Sarah beat Aila with the whip or whatever was handy. And if Sarah wasn't beating Aila, Bill was. This was no sibling rough-housing. Bill had a vicious mean streak. Once he tore after Aila with a board. Sarah stopped him that time. Hector also fended off Bill. He was just as big even though he was a year and a half younger.

And then there was the reason they left Wilkes-Barre.

Aila scampered into the house that day, probably after an outing with her grandmother, and ran from room to room, calling for her mother. She ran to her mother's room and stopped cold at the open bedroom door. There was her mother, with a man, on the bed.

When Arthur finished with the man, he was either dead or close to it. They had to leave, possibly as much for Sarah's indiscretion as for Arthur's beating a man to death. And there was the horrible shame of a cuckolded man.

They could have gone anywhere. As a stonemason, Arthur could have found work in any big eastern city, but if he needed to disappear, Montana was as good a place as any.

And if he thought hiding his wife in the wilderness would force a restoration of her virtue, it didn't work. From time to time, Arthur went away to work stone masonry jobs leaving Sarah to her own devices for weeks on end. Aila said she was never so happy to see one of her mother's men as the morning she watched her mother put rat poison in their oatmeal. Just then, this man walked in and Sarah became very much distracted. Aila got up and threw out the tainted food.

Sarah stopped at nothing to get money for drink. Such was the fate of Aila's pony. She sold it while Arthur was away.

Sarah would be gone for days at a time when she was on a toot. The children were left alone. Aila stayed home from school to take care of Archie and Patsy. She fed them the best she could, even when she was so little that she had to stand on a stool to reach the stove.

This time was different. Sarah packed a suitcase when she left.

Sarah and Tom arrived in Miles City with a chinook that blustery March day. The heavy snow delivered with the vernal equinox was quickly being blown dry. They walked from the depot to the Hotel Olive where they registered as man and wife. The next morning after breakfast, they walked down Main Street to the courthouse. Still garbed in her mourning black, Sarah discreetly asked the county clerk not to tell anyone, "especially no newspapermen," when they applied for the marriage license. It had been only three weeks since the fire. She used one of her middle names, Eleanor, as her first. Both she and Tom said they had been widowed.

That afternoon they went to the Presbyterian minister's home and were married. That evening they went to a show. Unbeknownst to either of them, Rosebud County Undersheriff John van der Pauwert had followed them to Miles City and had been lingering about, watching their every move. He watched them go into the theater and waited outside. The show ended. The crowd poured out into the street. As soon as Sarah and Tom came out, Undersheriff van der Pauwert stepped forward and arrested them for the murder of Arthur Hughes.

They spent their wedding night locked in separate cells in the Custer County jail. *"On Bridal Trip are Arrested for Murder in First Degree,"* screamed the front page headline. The next morning Undersheriff van der Pauwert took them back to Forsyth and locked them in the Rosebud County jail. They weren't there long. Sheriff Moses had to release them due to the lack of evidence.

But something as piddling as a lack of evidence was not enough to deter the newly elected county attorney. Henry Beeman went to work to build a case that would stick. Armed with innuendo and gossip, he filed a motion charging Sarah and Tom with the murder of Arthur Hughes. In addition to the talk, the evidence he cited was that Sarah had submitted a life insurance claim and that Sarah and Tom had married soon after Arthur's death. One witness claimed to have heard Tom tell Sarah that they shouldn't get married now as it would throw suspicion upon them. According to this witness, Sarah replied that they were both in the deal and equally guilty and it would be better if they were married, and as soon as they were married, they could sell all and leave the state.

Another point cited as contributing to the body of evidence was that both Sarah and Tom had positively identified the deceased at the inquest, when in fact, according to the transcript, no one identified the body. When asked whether there was anything about the body to identify it as that of her husband, Sarah had said, "I cannot see anything, it was so burned up."

The most compelling account came from the person who claimed to have been at the Hughes house in town on the night of the fire. According to this witness, Sarah and Tom were not there, and the children said they had gone to the ranch in the buggy.

It was enough to convince Judge Charles Crum. He issued a bench warrant, and Sheriff Moses promptly arrested Sarah and Tom for the murder of Arthur Hughes. They were arraigned the next day. Both pled not guilty. Judge Crum ordered that they be held in the county jail until the next term of district court which was five months hence.

The penalty for first degree murder in Montana was death or life in prison. Any murder was awful and caused a sensation, especially in a small community, but this was no run-of-the-mill murder. This was a *woman* involved in a *love triangle* accused of *murder*. It had all the makings of a real-life dime novel. Deadwood had Calamity Jane, now it seems Forsyth had Sarah.

CHAPTER FOUR

IF BEING ARRESTED for her first husband's murder wasn't bad enough, on the way to the county jail Sarah learned more startling news, this time about her second husband. Her distress grew even worse when Sheriff Moses showed her to her cell. She and Tom would be separated. Once locked in their respective cages they couldn't even talk to each other.

After Sheriff Moses left, Sarah summoned John, the jailer, to her cell and asked him, or more likely told him, to fetch her some writing paper and a pen and ink. John obediently poked through the sheriff's desk until he found the stationary. He gave Sarah several sheets and a pen and bottle of ink. She sat down and proceeded to pour out her heart to Tom.

Dearest Sweetheart

Why did you not tell me in Miles City you had a wife living. O God, Tom, it hurts more than I can tell you, but I will tell you Tom unless they can prove it let it go and do not say anything about it, because Tom never tell anybody that you told me today for I swore I did not know. O Tom I cannot let you go, you do not know nor you never will know how much I think of you. I could never give you up for no other woman on God's earth. . . I would give a good deal if they would put us together, O God Tom you do not know how lonesome I am without you. You have been the best friend I have had since the fire, and no matter what you have done Tom you are no worse than I am and you will find it out some day for I shall tell you something that you would never think of me, but I will tell you this much if there had been no fire Arthur and I was going to part as quick as school was out. He said he would never take care of me no more. He told me lots of times, Tom, when I would ask him for anything that he would soon leave, but he said he would never give me a divorce for he would make me live without it. But Tom for God sake don't think of leaving me. . . All I ask is be true to me and I will pass by the rest.

From your little Sweetheart
Sarah XXXXX

She again summoned John and asked him, or told him, to take the letter to Mr. Elliott.

Then she sat down and picked up her needlepoint. Her mind was racing. The boys—she needed to tell them what to do with the things at the ranch. She put down the needlepoint and hurriedly penned another letter.

Willie,

You folks must not come down here anymore because Moses was mad today when you want to see me. You must tell Mr. Tull, he will fix it for you. And Willie, tomorrow is Saturday. You must go to the ranch and bring in all the harness and tools and grain and bring them to town. Put them in the front room until I come out. And bring the chickens and geese and don't write no letters to nobody that Mamma is in here and you move everything Saturday and Sunday. And then you and Hector go to school for the rest of the term so you will pass for 10 year work. And don't forget the oyster shell for the chickens. Never mind, Mr. Tull will see that you little folks get what you need until I come home. I'll be home in about a month, and you two big boys sleep in our house and keep the key yourself, and don't talk to nobody about Mamma because you two are the only ones to bring me free. Remember, Willie, when you come here with Mr. Tull I will explain things to you, and I'll get the Insurance pretty soon and then we will be all right. Be true to Mamma because I will be out a long time before Tom, you read this with Hector and then burn it and don't dare tell no one you got it. But do what I told you. Don't forget the harness, saddle, tools, chickens, and geese and grain. You can move all in two loads on the cart. Take the boxes from the icehouse to pack the chickens in.

The Mr. Tull to whom she referred in the letter was Braz Tull, the lawyer she had hired to get her and Tom out of this mess. He was forty-two years old and had lived in Forsyth practicing law for two years. He was married, they had no children. A few months before this, a man sued Sarah and Arthur. He claimed they owed him money. Braz Tull represented the man doing the suing and won. Arthur had been involved in several debt-related lawsuits since they moved to Rosebud County. Whether he was the plaintiff or defendant, he always won, except in that one suit where he was named with Sarah. It was the only one in which Sarah was named and the only one he lost, and that was the one in which Braz Tull represented the opposing party. Perhaps that's why Sarah hired him.

I don't know whether Tom or Bill ever saw these letters, but the sheriff did, and he gave them to the county attorney who put them in the court file.

Sheriff Moses brought Tom to Sarah's cell occasionally and gave them a few moments together. This business about another wife still bothered her. She never had enough time to talk; she wrote to him again.

O Tom I wished you had not told me you was married in the Old Country. That was as bad as the arrest . . . but I do not believe I could stand many more shocks. Tom I wished I could die, honest to God I do, but never mind when the time comes I will have the marriage annulled. That is if they can prove you are married. They won't know anything about John Dunn unless you tell them, because honest to God Tom I could not live without you now, it was all right until I got in the family way, . . . and you know it old Boy we have made our bed, Tom, and we will sleep on it, come what may. People will talk no matter what we do anyhow. If you will have to go away Tom will you help me just the same to raise my babies, because Tom I will never be able to do it alone. Promise me that you will help me no matter where you go, I can easy move after you where ever it will be for that is what I will do anyhow, but if they will make any trouble you can easy promise to go away from me, anyhow you do not need to tell them that you have twisted yourself around my old heartstrings as tight as you have, for I will never tell, you are my all in all Tom and you know how much that means but don't tell them that I said I love you for I have told them I did not marry you for love because Tom I would never give Arthur away that bad. I'll tell you what Arthur done with me last Xmas. I sent word for him to eat Xmas dinner with us and you know nothing stopped him and he sent word in with Al Larson that he could not be bothered with us every holiday. The same Tom for the last 5 yrs he tried his best to be away and let me alone with the little ones. The only Xmas dinner he eat with me was the first one and that was the last one so you can see Tom how much I have been alone for 15 yrs so do you blame me for leaning on you so much, I want somebody Tom that will go with me once in a while. I am tired going alone, if he would go to town with me, from the ranch we was sure to quarrel before we would be a mile from the house. . . Arthur was away a week horseback up to Rancher and all that country he took Hector with him and I ask him if I could go, no it was too far he said he wouldn't bother with me. So Tom don't scold me for staying by you if you stay here 10 yrs I stay right in Forsyth with you, but I will do my best and get you out as well as myself, are you sure Tom that your wife is alive. Yet why don't you write and find out. I give the letter to Tull to mail, don't tell him nothing until you write to somebody in the old country and find out first. For Tom if your wife happens to be dead then the law could not touch you you see and we would not need to be married again because this one would stand good. . .

O God Tom to think what I have suffered this week and the last I never can tell you. O Tom to think that I must stay in here. Let me tell you Tom if I get out on Bail I believe I will send the children home and jump in the river with the baby for by that time Tom I will be big and every body will know what is the matter with me. Dear Tom I don't think I could let Lizzie Woods laugh at me Tom I could not stand it, and the babe will be yours when it comes you know that as well as I do, write and tell me Tom if I don't get the Ins are you willing to work and help me raise them Children for Tom you must remember they are all mine. . .

Tom, I wish you had told me that you had a wife I never would have married you although I would have kept you just the same . . .

From your little Sweetheart
& wife, Sarah

Sheriff Moses walked in just as John was delivering Sarah's latest epistle. He snarled at John, "I'll lock you up too if I catch you passing notes for her again!" Sarah remembered that the cards had portended an early marriage and a bereavement and that a young man would befriend them. She figured that was John.

Poor Sarah was really miserable now. John brought her a piece of apple pie for breakfast and it was no sooner down than it was back up again. In addition to the morning sickness, she was swollen. She told Tom in another letter that she would get some tobacco that day at noon.

CHAPTER FIVE

BY NOW IT HAD been two months since Sarah and Tom were arrested. School was out for the summer. Aila walked behind the house to where they kept the milk cow. They kept two cows at the house: one was tied up so it wouldn't wander off, the old cow that could hardly walk was left loose. Aila pulled a stool over to the one that was tied up and sat down. She squeezed and squeezed and squeezed until she had enough. She took the milk inside, warmed it on the stove, and gave a little to Archie, a little to Patsy, and that left a little for herself. She was about to go to the neighbor's house where she worked as a hired girl when a woman came to the door. She said her name was Miss Alderson and that she was the superintendent of schools. She told Aila that she was going to send her and her little brother and sister away to a place where they would be looked after. At that, Aila's little chin shot up, and with a confidence some grown women never possess, she replied, "We can stay right here. I can take care of my little brother and sister myself. I've been doing it all my life!" She was eleven years old.

The couple for whom Aila worked learned of these plans and urged Miss Alderson to allow Aila to stay and remain in their employ. Miss Alderson agreed as long as Aila went to school. Aila said, No, I must take care of my little brother and sister. Wherever they go, I must go, too. She steadfastly refused to be separated from Archie and Patsy.

Stone Matlock, the state deputy humane officer, arrived by train from Helena to take Aila, Archie, and Patsy to Twin Bridges. Those deciding such matters had concluded that Bill and Hector, then fifteen and thirteen, were old enough and industrious enough to take care of themselves and would be better off staying behind.

Miss Alderson handed the three children over to Mr. Matlock at the depot.

It was a long, lonely train ride. First they lost their father, then their mother was taken away, now they were being taken away, away from their family, away from everything that was familiar, into the unknown. The train kept going and going. Plains and hills gave way to mountains, huge mountains. Aila sat with her arms around Archie and Patsy and stared out the window listening to the melancholy sound of the train stamping away the miles, hundreds of miles.

Mrs. Shobe read the application for the new arrivals:

> The children are destitute.
> The address of the nearest relative, William Thomas, is Wilkes-Barre, Pennsylvania. The mother, Sarah Hughes, is now confined in the Rosebud County Jail awaiting trial for the murder of the father, Arthur Hughes.

Those poor, poor children.

They stepped down off the train onto the wooden platform at the Twin Bridges depot. The still snow-capped Tobacco Roots soared heavenward before them. A smartly attired woman approached. She smiled and greeted them and introduced herself as Mrs. Shobe. She said she was there to take them to their new home. One stranger had handed them off to another stranger who handed them off to yet another. At least they were together. Aila grasped Archie and Patsy by the hand, they said goodbye to Mr. Matlock, and followed Mrs. Shobe.

She led them to Main Street. After a short walk down Main, they turned and crossed the Beaverhead. A little way past the bridge, they turned right and left the road and walked toward a gigantic brick mansion. They walked past the mansion to a two-story red-brick house and went inside. Mrs. Shobe explained that the doctor would see them, and they would stay there for awhile. Then she said goodbye and left.

The doctor examined them and kept them quarantined for several days, as was the procedure for new inmates. All three children received a clean bill of health. The month before they arrived, the entire orphanage had been quarantined for three weeks because of a measles outbreak. A third of the children contracted the disease, and two died from it.

When their quarantine period was over, Mrs. Shobe returned and gave Aila, Archie, and Patsy orphanage clothes: one set for everyday and another for Sunday, the norm for many children of the time. Aila and Patsy donned the muslin dresses, black bloomers, and black, woolen stockings. Aila wound a broad, white ribbon around Patsy's head and tied a large bow on top. She tied a ribbon around her own head with the bow to the side; her long, brown braids hung down her back. Archie put on his suit of short pants, a shirt and tie, long socks, a coat, and a cap.

Then came the horrible news: they were to be separated. Tears burst forth. *Please* Mrs. Shobe, can't we stay together? Aila pleaded. "I can take care of my little brother and sister myself. I've been doing it all my life." Please, can't we stay together?

No they couldn't.

Still teary and clutching her hanky, Aila posed in the flower bed on the side of one of the red-brick buildings. A man propped Patsy on the heavy concrete ledge next to her. Archie stood at the foot of the stairs next to Patsy. The man took their picture.

Mrs. Shobe then led Aila to the mansion. This grand three-story Victorian edifice was the main house of the orphanage. The children called it the castle. Aila followed Mrs. Shobe up the wide staircase which led to the main door, and they went inside.

Aila, Patsy, and Archie Hughes,
Montana State Orphans' Home, June 1913.

Montana State Orphans' Home, main house,
Twin Bridges, Montana, recent photo.

The interior of the house was as Spartan as one would expect—clean, tidy, and functional. They walked up another flight of stairs to the big girls dormitory on the third floor. Mrs. Shobe showed Aila her bed and locker.

Another matron took Patsy to the small girls cottage and Archie to the small boys cottage. Each cottage was a two-story red-brick building with white trim. A covered front porch ran the width of each cottage. From the porch, one entered a long hallway which bisected the building. The matron's office and living quarters were on the right. A large play-room was on the left. The children slept upstairs. There was also a cottage for big boys and one for toddlers. The babies lived in the main house. A matron lived in each cottage and supervised the children.

The next morning the big girls matron woke Aila and the other girls at six o'clock. Aila got up, made her bed, dressed, and scrambled into line with the other girls. On the matron's order, they marched to the dining room on the first floor and stood along the wall. The bell rang, and each child moved to his or her assigned table. The bell rang, they sat. The bell rang, they said grace. The bell rang, they began to eat. Talking was not allowed during meals other than to say in a low voice, please pass the bread, and the like. On holidays, the children could talk during meals.

One of the cottages at the orphanage, recent photo.

After breakfast, the bell rang, they stood. The bell rang, they left for their assigned chores. When it was Aila's turn to feed the toddlers, she rose earlier to feed them before she ate breakfast. Patsy was too little for chores, so after breakfast and lunch she went to her cottage or the playground to play jacks or hopscotch with the other little girls. In the fall, she would begin first grade at the orphanage school. The school at the orphanage went through eighth grade. Older children attended high school in town.

The children were called to lunch at noon and to dinner at six. All ate in the same dining room at the same time. They were assigned to a table with children from their cottage or dormitory. The meal regimen was plentiful and the same every week. Tuesday was stew day. Bedtime was around eight or nine o'clock. They drifted off to the muffled sounds of new children crying themselves to sleep.

The orphanage was actually a ranch. The big boys did most of the farm chores. They raised cattle, pigs, and chickens; grew alfalfa, wheat, and vegetables. At the dairy, they pasteurized milk and made cheese, butter, and ice cream. Also on the premises were a slaughterhouse, laundry, sewing room, and electric power plant. For the farm boys, the chores were familiar, and it was a source of pride for many of them that they could close the gates, so to speak, and not need anything. The place was quite self-sufficient. Other than vegetable gardening, farm girls didn't work the farm at the orphanage though they had at home. What was expected of a girl on a farm or ranch was not expected of her at the orphanage.

Aila and the other big girls fetched soap in a bucket while it was still a warm, grey goo. They used it to scrub the stairs and clean the washrooms. The orphanage was kept immaculately clean by the children under the direction of the matrons. The big girls took turns rinsing diapers—a job they loathed. The girls helped in the kitchen. They visited on the back porch while shelling peas, snapping beans, and shucking corn. After they finished their chores they could play or read. In addition to their studies at school, the girls learned to sew, crochet, and tat; the big girls helped teach the little girls.

One reason for having the children perform these chores, other than necessity and not wanting them to be idle, was so they would learn how to do these commonplace tasks. Some children came to the orphanage as babies and knew no other life. I read an account of two little girls in a British workhouse who were invited to Christmas dinner by a local family. The girls meekly asked the mother if they could watch the meal being prepared. They had never seen such a thing. They were completely institutionalized.

Saturday was bath day. It took the entire day to bathe all the children. On Sunday mornings, Mrs. Shobe taught the children Sunday School after which they sang hymns. Mrs. Shobe was such a presence at the orphanage that some of the children thought she was the superintendent of the Orphans' Home. Actually, it was her husband who was the superintendent. Mrs. Shobe was the head matron. A woman who lived there as a little girl, at the same time as Grandma, told me, "Mrs. Shobe was a *real* lady."

After church services, the rest of Sunday was for play. The children roller-skated, jumped rope, played baseball and kick the can. On the playground, as in the dining room, the children were segregated according to age and gender. However, siblings could spend time together on Sundays. The big girls matron often took her wards for walks on Sundays. They scavenged for rubies along the river bank. Aila probably did not partake in this outing since Sunday was the only day she could spend time with Archie and Patsy, and even then, only for one hour. She must have lived for Sunday.

Others who resided at the orphanage around the same time as Aila, Archie, and Patsy said they learned a strong work ethic and self-discipline while there, and these sustained them through life. The staff enforced good manners; they taught the children to be polite and gracious. Part of the governing philosophy was to treat the children fairly and spend their "surplus energy" by keeping them busy. Otherwise, like adults, they were bound to start "pitying themselves" and get into trouble if allowed too much free time. Among the stated goals were: "To rear men and women into usefulness of lives, into a nobility of character and a highness of purpose"; to follow "higher principles of a pure morality and thus surround the children with the safeguards of wholesome teaching, good habits, noble aims and pure lives"; and to furnish "proper, mental food for their eager, young minds."

The Biennial Report for November of 1914 said: "The majority of our children have come from poverty-stricken homes, early in life they have been compelled to do things for themselves. This has sharpened their intellect, consequently they are absorbing more from the surroundings than a child of luxury would be able to do and when relieved of the necessity of self support they turn very readily to education if it is placed before them in an attractive manner." The report went on to caution: "Hardship is likely to drive them into an impure atmosphere."

The children did not talk about their family circumstances. Many felt ashamed for being in the orphanage. They thought they had done something wrong and that was why they were sent away. When they left, many closed the door on that chapter of their lives and never discussed it with anyone, not even with siblings who shared the experience.

That was certainly true of Grandma. She mentioned the orphanage to me only once. I was out of college by then. We were in the kitchen at Mom and Dad's. It was Thanksgiving, we were visiting as we prepared dinner. Grandma was seated at the kitchen table, Mom was at the stove making the gravy, and I was standing at the counter making the salad. I don't remember the context, but in the course of our conversation, Grandma turned toward me and said, "That was when I was in the orphanage." I stopped what I was doing and looked at her in astonishment. I was astonished by most things she told me about her life, but an orphanage? This was the first I'd heard about it, and it was the first Mom had heard about it too. It didn't dawn on me at that moment that I knew she hadn't been orphaned. Before I could ask her about it, somebody walked into the kitchen and sidetracked our conversation. Now dinner was ready, Dad carved the turkey, we promptly put the food on the table and took our places in the dining room.

I remember thinking, she might not want to tell us about the orphanage in front of guests, so I better wait and ask later, but by the time dinner was over and the company gone, I forgot. I never thought to ask, why were you in an orphanage if you weren't an orphan?

Like my grandmother, most of the children in the orphanage were not orphans. A boarding school or children's home would have been a more apt name. Later the name was changed to the Montana State Children's Home. Some children were there because they had been abandoned, some were taken there by the authorities because of neglect or abuse. Sometimes it was the parents who put their children in the orphanage, in some cases, only a few of their children. They simply could not take care of them. When they could, they took them home.

Parents were expected to pay a monthly fee while their children lived in the orphanage. Decades later it was ten dollars a month per child. I don't know how much it was in 1913. If after a year the parents had made no payments, the child could be adopted.

One former resident referred to it as life by the bells—a bell to go to breakfast, a bell to sit down, a bell to begin eating. Boarding schools were run in much the same way. The bells kept all to a schedule which provided structure—an obvious necessity in keeping a large number of children in line. At one elite boarding school in the Rockies, the boys were graded on how well they did their chores and had to wear shorts year round, even while playing ice hockey. The orphanage boys got to wear long pants in cold weather. It strikes me, thinking of boarding schools and the orphanage, the poor sent their children away because they had to, the rich sent their children away because they wanted to.

The orphanage staff was strict, but according to those who lived there back then, treated the children well. For the most part, the children did not misbehave. If they did, they were spanked or missed an outing or made to stand off alone. An errant big girl might be sent to sleep in the little girls cottage, humiliation being the punishment. The staff was forbidden from withholding a meal to punish a child. Corporal punishment could be used only as a last resort and each incident had to be reported to the board.

If material comforts were all that were needed for happiness, the orphanage children would have been jubilant. They were not. The plenty they missed was love—the love of parents. Even those who entered as babies knew its absence. The staff was instructed not to single out any child, so they kept their distance. Consequently, the children were starved for affection—no hugs, no tender tap, not the slightest embrace. A man who entered the orphanage as a toddler told me, when he was around ten years old, he got sick and had to be put in the orphanage hospital. One day while walking down the hall with the nurse, she put her hand on his shoulder. He said it meant the world to him.

At least the orphanage provided stability, a warm bed, and plenty to eat which was more than some children had before they came or after they left. The orphanage provided an out for parents in hard times. Their children would be clothed, fed, and educated while they got their feet on the ground—or got out of jail.

Chapter Six

A WORLD AWAY in New York City, a steamer docked on the East River. Sailors poured off the massive ship, the young ones restless and ebullient, the older men exhausted. A man calling himself John Price was among the latter. He went directly to a flophouse in the Bowery, an area which in those days was so rough even the prostitutes had fled. Yes, she had a room, the innkeeper told him. She was no doubt happy to rent to the likes of John Price, a reticent, quiet man, not one to come in drunk and wild at all hours. John dropped his duffel bag in his room and walked to a saloon for a tall beer and to get a line on where he might find work. He had decided to stay put awhile rather than work another voyage right away.

After a hearty dinner, John returned to the flophouse for a long, pacific sleep. In the morning, he wrote a letter, mailed it, and started looking for work.

A couple of weeks later he made his way to South Street, past the bustling fish market, to the Seamen's Church Institute. The moneyed and clerics of New York City had formed the Seamen's Church Institute in the mid 1800s, their purpose being to stop shanghaiing and civilize the sailors whose behavior in port was scandalous. The institute ran a large dormitory and chapel, stored a sailor's belongings while he was at sea, and collected his mail.

John walked up to the mail window and gave his name and asked if there was any mail for him. The man working at the mail window did a double take. He wasn't used to seeing a sailor walk up in a Stetson. Sailors didn't wear cowboy hats. He told John yes, he did have mail for him and handed John three letters and a telegram and said, "There was a fellow here looking for you a few days ago. He wanted to know if I'd seen you and if you had any mail. He wrote you a letter. It's here. He left his card. Here it is, *Charles Hayes, Lawyer.* He wants you to go see him at his office. It's over on Maiden Lane. And Mr. Deans said he wants to see you too. He's the assistant superintendent here. I'll see if he's in his office."

The man left the window and walked to Mr. Deans' office. John began to fidget. The man returned to the window and said, "Mr. Deans is not in, you can—"

"I have no time to wait," said John, "I'm going to Forty-second Street." And with that he left.

JENNIE HAYES was sitting in the parlor of her comfortable Bay Ridge home in Brooklyn with her cousin Thomas Jones that June day. Her husband, Charles, was at work in his law office in lower Manhattan. The burst of spring colors outside her window had done little to relieve her gloom. She was troubled over news of Sarah. She had urged Charles to do whatever he could to help her. Jennie and Sarah had grown up together in Wales and Wilkes-Barre and had corresponded since Jennie moved to New York when she married Charles. Jennie was convinced that Sarah was innocent. Of course she was innocent. Sarah could never do such a thing. These allegations were simply outlandish, too outlandish to be considered remotely possible. Jennie fingered the photograph of Sarah and Arthur and the three youngest children on the ranch in Montana. Arthur's wide-brimmed hat created a dark shadow obscuring his face in the picture. Jennie remembered him from Wilkes-Barre. Sarah looked thin. Her normally full face appeared gaunt. Life must be hard in Montana. She turned the picture over. On the back Sarah had written *Best Love for Chas & Jennie*.

A knock interrupted her thoughts. Edith, her maid, answered the door and led the visitor into the parlor. He was middle-aged, plainly dressed, and possessed a rugged, weather-worn face, the face of a man who had spent his life doing hard labor outdoors. He held a large hat in his muscular hand. He asked Jennie whether she knew Sarah Hughes of Wilkes-Barre, who was Sarah Thomas before. Jennie said yes, she did. He said he hoped she might have news from Sarah.

"You see," he said, "I am her husband, Arthur Hughes."

Jennie nearly dropped.

"Arthur Hughes!" she gasped. "How is it you are not dead?!"

She invited him to sit down and told her maid to bring tea. Then she and her cousin Tom listened stupefied as Arthur told them of his travels. As it turns out, while his wife was being hauled off to the county jail for his murder, Arthur Hughes had been on a ship bound for Buenos Aires.

After hearing the tales of the marvelous places he'd been, Jennie shook her head and lamented, "And poor Sarah in jail."

"What is she in jail for?" Arthur asked, sipping his tea.

"For your murder, of course," she replied curtly.

"My murder!" Arthur exclaimed almost spilling his tea.

"I am going to wire her that you are living," said Jennie. "Then the sheriff will have to let her go."

"She will get out all right," said Arthur gravely, putting down his tea, "even if I have to go back and suffer myself."

They talked some more. Jennie told Arthur what she knew about Sarah's situation. Perhaps she left out the part about Sarah marrying the handyman. Arthur listened, then he said goodbye and left.

When Jennie's husband, Charles, returned home from work that evening, he had barely removed his hat and coat when she blurted out the story of the remarkable visitation from the man thought dead.

"Why I nearly dropped dead when he told me he was Arthur Hughes!" she exclaimed.

Being a lawyer, Charles probably prodded her a bit as to how she could be so sure that this man was indeed Arthur Hughes, her friend's husband. After all, the authorities in Montana said he was dead and burned up in that fire. Did Jennie know this Arthur Hughes? She said she met him shortly after he and Sarah married. She had gone to Wilkes-Barre to visit her parents. She spent an hour with Sarah and Arthur on the square. She said she also knew Arthur when he was a boy. Charles asked what Mr. Hughes looked like. Jennie said when he came today he wore plain dark clothes, a shirt with no collar, and an overcoat. His hair was dark, his eyes were blue, and he wore a heavy beard and mustache.

But, dear, if this man wore a heavy beard and mustache and you last saw Arthur Hughes fifteen years ago, how can you be sure he was indeed Arthur Hughes?

"Because I remember," Jennie said confidently, "Arthur Hughes had a blue mark on the left side of his face to the left of his left eye, about the size of a fifty cent piece. This mark on his face came from the coal mines— from an explosion in the coal mines. A person couldn't help but notice it. I remember seeing it when I met him on the square and I saw it again today. I told him, 'You will be found out by that blue mark!'"

SHORTLY BEFORE THIS interchange in Brooklyn took place, Braz Tull received an urgent message from Sarah. He hurried over to the jail to see her. John unlocked Sarah's cell and placed a chair inside for Mr. Tull. He entered the cell and sat down. Once John was out of earshot, in a hushed, excited voice, Sarah told her lawyer that during the night, a man appeared at her window and told her that Mr. Hughes is alive!

Braz Tull then posted a letter to Mr. John P. Price, Seamen's Church Institute, New York City, inquiring as to the state of aliveness of Mr. Arthur F. Hughes of Forsyth, Montana.

ARTHUR LEFT THE flophouse after breakfast. He had finished one brick-laying job but hadn't yet found another. He walked down Bowery contemplating his next move. With Sarah's life in jeopardy, he was compelled to act. He must find a way to free Sarah short of returning to Montana. Going back was out of the question. A storefront caught his eye: Imperial Developing & Printing. He stopped, thought for a moment, turned, and went in.

"I want to have my picture took and put on one of these here postal cards," he told the photographer.

Arthur took his pose for a full-length photograph. He returned when the pictures were developed and paid twenty-five cents for two. The photographer was intrigued by Arthur. He looked like a farmer and not many farmers came around the Bowery. He was even more intrigued when he saw how Arthur signed his name in the receipt book: "Arthur Hughes, Forsyth, Rosebud County, Montana." He didn't have customers from the far West.

"How's business over there in Montana State?" he asked.

"There is nothing doing for your people, for picture men," Arthur replied. "They are too busy there stealing cattle."

After Arthur left, the photographer made another print of the curious stranger's photograph and placed it in the sample gallery in the window.

Arthur then went to Brooklyn to see Jennie Hayes. This time her husband, Charles, was at home. Arthur gave Jennie one of the picture post cards and said, "Please send this to Forsyth if Sarah is convicted and that

Postcard picture of Arthur Hughes.
IMPERIAL DEVELOPING & PRINTING, NEW YORK CITY

way all will know I am alive and there will be no choice but to free Sarah."

If she is convicted? So he was willing to let his wife sit in jail and stand trial for a crime he knew she didn't commit, leaving his three youngest children in an orphanage and the elder two to fend for themselves, and if his wife was convicted, then he'd do something about it? What a prize. And how he did he know there would be enough time after she was convicted? The last murder case in Rosebud County was dispatched post-haste without a trial and Arthur knew all about it. It happened exactly one year before. A young drifter from back east had wandered onto a ranch near Joppa and asked the woman of the house for something to eat. The woman fed him and gave him some chores to do. Later in the day she walked in and found him ransacking the house. He shot her twice and ran off. Her poor little boy came home from school and found her dead. A posse tore after the murderer and caught him. He admitted that he shot the woman, and then when arraigned in court, he pled not guilty. A fortnight later, a huge, masked mob stormed the jail. They disarmed the sheriff and his deputy, collared the accused, marched him down Main Street to the big cottonwood, and lynched him. The investigation found that he was killed by Persons Unknown.

Whether she knew about the lynching or not, Jennie wasn't about to wait for the trial. She immediately sent the post card with Arthur's picture on it to Forsyth.

THE DAYS PASSED, but time did not alter Arthur's plans. He remained steadfast in his refusal to return to Montana. On his next visit to the Hayeses' he asked, "What news is there of Sarah?"

"She is still in jail," replied Charles.

"Arthur, won't you go back to set her free?" pleaded Jennie.

"If she is convicted, I will go back," Arthur replied soberly.

Jennie started to ask where he was working, but Charles cut her off.

Arthur rose to leave. Charles walked him to the door. "Can I see you tomorrow?" Charles asked.

"Yes," Arthur replied, "where?"

"On Hudson, near Canal Street."

The next day the two men met as arranged in lower Manhattan.

"Arthur, how are you?" Charles asked.

"Well, I am worried," Arthur replied.

"Arthur," Charles said, "your wife's trial is in only a few weeks time. She could be sentenced to death. You can't get the insurance. Your wife is already married again to this man Elliott." Charles's intention in laying out the facts was to convince Arthur to go back to Montana. How reminding him of his wife's hasty nuptials furthered that end is a mystery to me.

"I don't care what happened," Arthur replied, "but if Sarah is convicted I will go there and give myself up."

"What are you doing? Are you working?" Charles asked.

"I can't make any money in bricklaying business. I am working on some of the lines."

"What do you mean?"

"I am working over here on some of the steamship lines on the East River."

Arthur turned to leave.

"When will I see you again?" Charles asked.

"Well, I don't know," said Arthur. "I will call."

Arthur remained a conundrum to Charles and Jennie. They never knew when he would appear at their door and whether he would ever return. He visited them again a week and a half after he met Charles at Hudson and Canal. Every time she saw him, Jennie's hopes were raised that he had come to say goodbye, he was leaving for Montana to free Sarah, and every time her hopes were dashed.

During one visit when Charles was not at home, Jennie asked, "Arthur, what happened on the ranch? How did that body get there and you living?"

"I went to the cemetery and got it."

CHAPTER SEVEN

BACK IN JANUARY, a few weeks before the fire, a sheepherder named John Kiernan was walking through the Northern Pacific Railroad yard in Forsyth. John was around fifty years old and single. The men on the switching crew recognized him and were puzzled by his behavior. He was not a drinking man, but he seemed drunk. He appeared to be in a daze. The crew continued their work. One of the men walked to the rear of a string of cars and found John face down on the tracks. He helped him to his feet and asked if he was all right. John didn't seem to want further help. He stumbled over to a caboose and sat down on the steps. After a few minutes, he stood and shuffled along next to the tracks. He seemed oblivious to the approaching locomotive rolling ever so slowly through the railroad yard. As the engine passed, John stumbled and fell against it. The force of the huge machine knocked him to the ground. He died.

As far as anyone knew, John had no family in Montana. His employer thought he had relations in the Old Country, and he knew John to be a thrifty, hard-working man and that he had put some money away. Coroner Frank Booth tried to locate relatives.

A few days later, John Kiernan's body was laid to rest in the Forsyth cemetery. The winter had been relatively mild thus far. Some years the ground froze so hard that the grave digger couldn't break it with a shovel and burials had to be postponed until it thawed. That was not the case this year, and John was buried.

Four days later, Arthur hitched the good mare to the milkwagon and drove to town. It was the middle of the night. He passed no one along the way. He rode clear across town and still saw no one. All were asleep. He stopped the wagon at the cemetery which was on the east edge of town, opposite the ranch. He left his horse and wagon at the entrance to the cemetery, picked up a shovel and railroad tie from the wagon bed, and walked the five hundred or so feet up hill to the back of the cemetery.

The cemetery was sparsely populated. Forsyth was a small and relatively new community, so not many people had been around to die. Rustic wooden crosses marked some of the graves, a few had headstones. All were covered with snow except one. There Arthur proceeded to dig. All was quiet save the sound of the shovel crisply cutting the frost-bitten earth. Arthur dug and dug and dug in the dark, bitter cold, as the mercury sank lower and lower. He kept digging until he was standing on top of the coffin. He pried the lid off. There lay John Kiernan. Had his people in the Old Country ever learned what happened next, they would have always begun this story with, "*Purrrr* Johnny Kiernan . . ."

How on earth Arthur got John Kiernan's body out of that grave is a wonder. It's a macabre thing to think about, especially when it was your great-grandfather who did it. It's hard to believe he could do such a thing—not the accomplishment of it but the bizarreness of the whole affair. Somehow, he did it—picked up John Kiernan's body, which was about the same size as he was, and heaved it or hoisted it out of the grave and onto the ground above. He put the railroad tie in the coffin, covered it with the lid, and refilled the grave. Then he picked up the body and carried it to the wagon. Fortunate for Arthur, it was a downhill walk. When he got to the wagon, Arthur dropped the body in the back, covered it with hay, and drove to the ranch. Again, he passed no one the whole way. At the ranch, he unloaded the corpse and buried it in the snow. There lay John Kiernan for three weeks.

Mother Nature is usually generous with snow in Montana. It comes early and stays late—except this year. There was a thaw that Valentine's Day. Everything melted, water was running everywhere. Of all the luck, a thaw just when you have a body buried in the snow. If it thawed too quickly, the river and creeks and ditches might flood and poor Kiernan float away—and after all the trouble to dig him up. And Arthur had to keep the body hidden from Alfred and anyone else who might stop by the ranch, like that drunk S——. My best guess is, he put the body in the ice house and covered it with straw. Wherever he put it, there lay John Kiernan for another three weeks. Six weeks Arthur kept that body.

JENNIE LISTENED dumbfounded as Arthur told her all this.

"How in the world did you carry the body to the house?" she asked.

"I really don't know how I got the strength," said Arthur. "First I put it on my back and then I took it in the wagon."

"How did the house get afire?" she asked.

"Well, I might as well confess to you, I done it all. And when I looked back from the hill, I could see the house burning for ten miles and I nearly went crazy thinking of what I had done, and I never dreamed that my poor Sarah could suffer for what I had done."

"How did you get away then?"

"I jumped the freight and then took a train to New York."

"Why didn't you come to see us then?"

"Because I was afraid you would give me away."

"Where did you go to?"

"To Saint Lucia and then to Buenos Aires on a steamer, and from there I came to you thinking I might hear something from Sarah. Before I came here I made up my mind to write a letter to a friend of Sarah's. I wanted to let Sarah know I was living. So I wrote a letter to Eleanor S. Thomas in Billings. This way Sarah would know that I am living."

It was after Arthur wrote the letter to Eleanor S. Thomas of Billings that Braz Tull wrote to Charles Hayes and asked him to look for John P. Price at the Seamen's Church Institute.

"Why did you do it, Arthur?"

"I had to get away from there. The sheriff wanted me dead. He had a number of lawsuits against me, and I won them all. Now I'm sorry I done it, now that poor Sarah is in jail."

"Well, what was your motive for doing it, Arthur? Was it to collect the insurance?" Jennie asked.

"As long as I got away I don't care what happened, if Sarah got it or not. If Sarah got the money she could educate the children as she pleased."

"Did anyone know of your plans?"

"No."

"Did Sarah know?"

"Sarah is innocent of any wrong that I done. She did not know what I was going to do. I will wait now and see what they do with Sarah, and if they convict her, then I will go back and face the music."

"Will you ever go back and live there?"

"I will see Sarah sometime or other, I hope."

First Jennie hears that her childhood friend is in jail for killing her husband.

Then said dead husband appears at her door. Now said dead husband tells her that the man everybody thought died the night of the fire didn't die the night of the fire but instead was some poor soul he dug up and put there. Whatever Arthur's troubles were, he was the perpetrator of this mess. Jennie's loyalties and sympathies rested squarely with Sarah.

"I am going to tell all to save Sarah," she declared. "I knew right along she was innocent."

"Yes, she is innocent," said Arthur soberly. "If I had known all this, I never would have done it."

"It's too late now," snapped Jennie. "We must tell the truth to save Sarah!"

CHAPTER EIGHT

MURMURINGS IN FORSYTH sharpened. How could Hughes have been killed in his own home without a struggle? How could you tell whether there was a struggle if the house burned to the ground? The debate went on between the "he's dead" camp and the "he's alive" camp.

In August, Sarah sold the house in Forsyth for five hundred dollars which was what she had paid for it. Before vacating the house, Hector and Bill collected those possessions dear to their mother—the family Bible, family pictures, Aila's silver baby spoon.

With the house sold, the boys had to find somewhere to live. Fifteen-year-old Bill found a job on a ranch near the town of Rosebud, a few miles east of Forsyth, and he boarded there. All I know about Hector, who was thirteen, was that he lived near Howard. That was near their homestead, so perhaps he stayed on the ranch and cared for the animals. He could have lived in the large barn; it had a coal stove.

Around this time, Braz Tull called on County Attorney Henry Beeman at his office. Henry Beeman had lived in Rosebud County since he was a boy, with brief interruptions to attend college and law school. He was forty-three and married with two children. Five years before this, he represented a man who sued Arthur. Arthur won, Beeman lost. He was now in his first term as county attorney.

Braz Tull told Henry Beeman that he had received some startling news about the Hughes case by way of New York City. He said witnesses there claimed to have seen Arthur Hughes alive.

This certainly caught Henry's attention. He was firmly in the "he's alive" camp but he had no proof. He needed material proof—Arthur Hughes in the flesh.

Who were these witnesses, he asked, and how did Braz know they were reliable, and how could they be sure this man in New York was truly Art Hughes, the Art Hughes who was supposed to be dead and burned up? Braz proposed that they have these witnesses deposed by lawyers in New York to establish their credibility and get the full story. Henry agreed.

Still the question remained, if this man in New York who claimed to be Arthur Hughes was in fact he, then who was dead and burned up in the ranch house? Did Hughes kill him? Were Mr. and Mrs. Elliott in on it? Braz said he had reason to believe that a grave had been molested in the Forsyth cemetery and that was the body burned up in the fire, not Mr. Hughes.

Braz and Henry then reviewed the death notices for the weeks leading up to the fire. Two men had died. They told Coroner Frank Booth about the alleged grave robbery and asked that those two graves be exhumed. The next day Coroner Booth told the grave digger to dig them up. He and Henry and Braz stood by and watched. The grave digger dug and dug until he emptied the first grave. He pried the lid off the coffin. The body was there, touched only by nature. Then the grave digger dug up the second grave, John Kiernan's. In the coffin, he found a railroad tie, but no John Kiernan.

Nevertheless, Sarah and Tom remained locked up, accused of murder, while the still alleged dead man did odd jobs around New York City.

Another person whose interest was piqued by this new information was O. W. McConnell of Montana Life. He was investigating Sarah's life insurance claim.

ARTHUR AGAIN CALLED on Jennie and Charles Hayes at their home in Brooklyn. Judging from his rough suit of clothes and haggard visage, Arthur's circumstances were deteriorating the longer he stayed in New York. Jennie listened while Charles told Arthur the latest news.

"Your wife's lawyer, Mr. Tull, is arranging for depositions to be taken here in New York to prove that you are alive," explained Charles. "I will represent Mr. Tull at the hearing. We will take testimony from Mrs. Hayes, her cousin Thomas Jones, and others."

Arthur was pleased to hear this. His efforts to prove from a distance that he was alive, and his wife did not kill him, were about to receive the sanction of a legal proceeding. That should satisfy the authorities. Then he could leave and know Sarah was free of the gallows.

Now it was early September. Court convened in Forsyth. Sarah and Tom were present with their lawyer, Braz Tull. Judge Charles Crum set the date for their murder trial for September 29 at ten o'clock. Sheriff Moses escorted the two back to their jail cells.

On the other side of the state in Twin Bridges, Aila, Archie, and Patsy began the new school year at the orphanage. Aila was in the seventh grade, Archie was in fourth, and Patsy was in first. Soon after school started, the autumnal equinox dropped two feet of snow on the town.

As the snow fell in Montana, across the country in New York, witnesses and lawyers gathered in an office on John Street in lower Manhattan to determine whether this man in New York who claimed to be Arthur Hughes was in fact the man Sarah and Tom Elliott stood accused of murdering. County Attorney Beeman had hired the New York law firm of Parker, Davis, Wagner & Walton to represent the State of Montana. The firm assigned Roy Robinson to the case. Charles Hayes represented the defendants, Sarah and Tom.

The first witness was the owner of the photography studio where Arthur had his picture taken. The two lawyers quizzed him about his enterprise. Then the photographer, Joseph Victor Ray, testified. Charles Hayes showed him a picture and asked, "In June last, did a man whose picture is represented by the photograph here shown you Defendants' Exhibit A call upon you?"

"Yes, sir," replied Mr. Ray.

"And did he at that time give you a card or write something on a card which is here shown you?"

The photographer pointed at the card and said, "I remember this name, 'Arthur F. Hughes.'"

"Had you seen him before?"

"No."

"Did the man shown here on Defendants' Exhibit A for identification pose for that photograph?"

"Yes, sir."

"Was he alive?"

"Certainly."

Roy Robinson asked, "How many people had their picture taken at your place on an average each day?"

"Sometimes four or five, sometimes about twenty-five or thirty."

"From four or five or from twenty-five to thirty, and you remember each one of those persons that appeared before you?"

"I can't remember all of them. It is impossible to remember."

"Well, how many can you remember?"

"I can remember a few. I can remember this one because he was from the West."

"Is that what impressed this man upon you?"

"Yes."

"How long was he in the gallery having his picture taken?"

"About fifteen to twenty minutes."

"Did he say what he is doing here in New York?"

"No. I didn't ask him."

"You would not be able to remember this man if it was not for the fact that he was from Montana, is that the reason you remember him?"

"Yes."

"You would not remember him otherwise?"

"If I would see him I would remember him."

Roy Robinson asked Joseph Victor Ray whether he had noticed any marks or scars on this man's face. He said no. Any marks on his hands? No.

"As he is posed in the photograph, you could see his left hand distinctly, can't you?" asked Mr. Robinson.

"Yes, sir," said Mr. Ray.

"Did you notice any deformity of the fingers?"

"I didn't notice."

"Do you notice it now?"

"Yes, sir."

"What is the deformity?"

"He has a broken finger."

Mr. Ray was excused and Charles Hayes summoned Emil Stromberg from the Seamen's Church Institute.

"Did you ever have occasion to see the person represented by this photograph Defendants' Exhibit A?" Charles asked.

"Well, this picture looks like a man who represented himself as John P. Price," said Mr. Stromberg.

"And where did he so represent himself?"

"Because he came into the Seamen's Church Institute and I was in the post office there."

"Was that 25 South Street this borough?"

"Yes."

"And you had charge of the mail?"

"I have charge of the mail."

"Did you notice anything about his left or right hand?"

"No."

"Did you receive any mail for Price?"

"Yes."

"And did you deliver it to Price?"

"Yes."

"And was the man to whom you delivered the mail the man shown by this photograph Defendants' Exhibit A?"

"The face looks like him. Of course he had a hat on."

"So far as you can recall, that is the man to whom you delivered that mail?"

"Yes."

"What mail was there? Was there anything in the name of Mr. Tull?"

"There was something from Mr. Tull."

"Do you remember Mr. Tull's address?"

"I don't remember his address, but it said, 'Forsyth, Montana.'"

Roy Robinson asked, "How long have you worked down at that Seamen's Church home?"

"I have been connected with it for nearly seven years."

"I have lived in New York a good many years," said Roy Robinson, "and I have never before this week heard of the Seamen's Church Institute. Therefore I ask you how a stranger in New York City from Montana could find the Seamen's Church Institute?"

"I don't know."

"Was this man represented by these photographs a sailor?"

"No."

"He didn't have on a sailor's suit?"

"He had on a farmer's suit."

"Your institute doesn't have anything to do with farmers?"

"No."

"Do you have any other people applying at your place for mail other than sailors?"

"We don't receive any mail except for sailors."

"How did it happen that you delivered mail to a farmer?"

"Because we didn't know he was not a sailor until he called for the mail."

"Are the people who call for mail usually in sailor's clothes?"

"Yes."

"How many times did you see this man?"

"I only saw him once."

"He only called once for his mail?"

"Once."

"You have never seen Mr. Price since?"

"No."

"Did you see any marks on his face which would identify him?"

"No."

"You had a good look at his face?"

"No."

"Were the fingers of his left hand mutilated in any way?"

"Not that I know of. They looked like normal hands. I didn't pay any attention to his hands."

Jennie Hayes testified next. She recounted what Arthur told her about digging up the body and setting fire to the house.

"Did he say anything about collecting insurance money?" asked Roy Robinson.

"Yes," she replied, "he said he has five children and if Sarah got it she could educate the children as she pleased."

"Do you expect to see Arthur Hughes again?"

"I may and may not see him again."

"Do you know where he works?"

"I do not."

"Why didn't you ask him where he works?"

"Charles would not let me ask too many questions."

"Have you no idea where he could be found?"

"No."

"Why didn't you notify the district attorney's office?"

"Because I didn't want any trouble in my house."

"You could have had a detective outside of the house."

"Well, I don't want any trouble around my house at all."

"Do you think if we brought Arthur Hughes here he would be dangerous?"

"Mr. Hughes would not be a dangerous man to come and testify here. He is not that kind of a man. I think he would harm nobody."

Charles Hayes then made a statement as a witness after which Roy Robinson questioned him.

"When did you first see Sarah Hughes, now Sarah Elliott?"

"I never met the lady in my life," said Charles.

"When did you first see Arthur Hughes?"

"About June 13 or 14, 1913."

"Before you first saw Mr. Hughes on June 14, 1913, had you gone to the Seamen's Church Home at 25 South Street and inquired about him?"

"Yes."

"When was that?"

"Early in the month of June, prior to Hughes calling at my residence, I called at 25 South Street and there saw Mr. Stromberg who was a witness here today."

"How was it that you called at that address?"

"I got information from Mr. Braz D. Tull, of Forsyth, Montana, to inquire at the Seamen's Church Institute for John P. Price. I complied with his request and inquired there. There were some letters there for Price, and Mr. Stromberg said that he would give the letter that I had left and which I had written to this man Price if he called."

"Is that the first time you interested yourself in the case?"

"I was interested in the case prior to that because Mrs. Hayes had known Mrs. Hughes for some years, who is known now as Sarah Elliott in this case, and we were interested in her welfare, thinking that she was innocent of any crime."

"Was the first visit to the Seamen's Church Institute the first time you did anything active in the case in New York?"

"I had advised Mr. Tull with regard to defendants' interests, thinking that there had been a real murder of Arthur F. Hughes, and I only gave him the benefit of my legal knowledge."

After the depositions were completed, Roy Robinson sent a telegram to County Attorney Beeman advising him that the testimony of these witnesses was not sufficient to prove that the man who claimed to be Arthur Hughes was indeed the man believed to have been murdered on the night of the fire. The alleged Arthur Hughes must appear and be deposed. County Attorney Beeman agreed and Roy Robinson so advised Charles Hayes. It must have taken some doing, but Charles managed to persuade Arthur to appear. Three days after the first depositions were taken, lawyers and staff again assembled in lower Manhattan, and this time Arthur was there.

Charles Hayes began the questioning: "In the case entitled 'State of Montana versus Thomas Elliott and Sarah Elliott,' now pending in the court above entitled, the defendant, Sarah Elliott, and her co-defendant are charged with murder in the first degree for the murder of one Arthur F. Hughes, the husband of Sarah Hughes, now known as Sarah Elliott. The murder is alleged to have taken place in Rosebud County, State of Montana, in March last. Do you know Arthur F. Hughes, who is referred to in this proceeding?"

"Yes, sir," Arthur replied, "I am the man. I am Arthur F. Hughes myself."

"How long did you reside in Rosebud County, Montana?"

"About eight years."

"Are you the husband of Sarah Hughes, who is known by the name of Sarah Elliott?"

"Yes, sir."

Charles asked Arthur what was his father-in-law's name? William T. Thomas. What was his mother-in-law's name? Ann Thomas.

"Is your father-in-law alive?"

"Yes, in Wilkes-Barre."

"Is your mother-in-law alive?"

"No, she died four or five years ago in Wilkes-Barre."

"What day of the week was your first child born on?"

"I think it was on Saturday, I am not sure, ten months and eleven days after we were married."

"How many children do you have?"

"Five, three boys and two girls."

"All living?"

"Yes."

"Will you look at Exhibit D, for identification—a photograph, and state whether or not it is a photograph of you, there shown, and who else?"

Pointing at the picture, Arthur said, "Myself, my wife, my youngest boy, and Aila and Sarah."

"Where was that photograph taken?"

"It was taken in my own yard at the Howard Flat."

"Where?"

"Rosebud County, Montana."

Charles asked Arthur to describe the ranch and to tell where he went after he left Montana.

"Have you returned to Forsyth since March last?" Charles asked.

"No," Arthur replied.

"What interest have you in this matter?"

"To save my wife from unjust political punishment."

"What is your reason for not going there in person?"

"Powerful interests there among public officials and elsewhere will do me and railroad me at all events."

"Was there any murder on the night of the fire so far as you know?"

"No, there was no murder."

"Did you murder anybody?"

"No, sir."

Roy Robinson asked, "Mr. Hughes, what does the 'F' in your name stand for?"

"Frederick," Arthur replied.

"Where were you born?"

"There is no positive fact where I was born, except between Australia and Pennsylvania. I was born on the high sea."

"When did you go from Wilkes-Barre to Rosebud County, Montana?"

"We got into Rosebud County on the third of April. It is seven or eight years ago, 1905, we went direct from Wilkes-Barre."

"Where are you living now?"

"I decline to answer on advice of counsel."

"Where are you working now?"

"I am not working now."

Roy Robinson asked Arthur how tall he was, what shoe size he wore, what hat size, what glove size, what collar size, what shirt size, what coat size, what trouser size.

"Do you know who set fire to your farmhouse last March?"

"I refuse to answer on advice of counsel."

"Do you know the body of what man was found in the ruin of the house?"

"I refuse to answer on advice of counsel."

"Do you know why the house was set fire to?"

"I refuse to answer on advice of counsel."

A photographer took a picture of Arthur from the elbows up holding his left hand near his face so his mutilated fingers showed prominently in the picture. The tips of the index and middle fingers on his left hand had been cut off in an accident. Then the photographer took a picture of those assembled for Arthur's deposition.

After the pictures were developed, Charles Hayes put the photographer under oath and asked, "Was the picture of the man showing his mutilated hand produced from the negative and not retouched in anyway?"

"Yes."

Those assembled for the deposition, left to right.
Mary Lokitz, stenographer; Arthur D. Strahl, commissioner;
Solomon J. Rosenblum, onlooker; Roy M. Robinson, attorney for the State;
Charles S. Hayes, attorney for the defendants; Arthur F. Hughes.
New York City, September 1913.

Arthur Hughes showing his mutilated fingers.

"Were the people photographed alive?"

"Yes."

The pictures and transcript were sent to Forsyth.

CHAPTER NINE

SHERIFF MOSES STEPPED off the train in Manhattan and went directly to police headquarters. There he saw Deputy Police Commissioner Dougherty and informed him of his purpose in the city. His next stop was the Pinkertons to hire a detective. From there, a short walk through the canyon of towering skyscrapers called Nassau Street took him and the Pinkerton man he had hired to the law offices of Parker, Davis, Wagner & Walton. The secretary directed them to Roy Robinson's office. O. W. McConnell of Montana Life was already there as were New York police detectives Lennon and Brown. Detective Lennon reported that he and his partner had tapped Charles Hayes's office phone, and one of their men was shadowing him.

Roy Robinson read aloud the latest communication from County Attorney Beeman. On these instructions, the group devised a plan and agreed to rendezvous every morning at Mr. Robinson's office at eleven o'clock.

After the others left, Roy summoned Charles Hayes to his office. He told Charles that they must have another hearing with this man who claimed to be Arthur Hughes of Forsyth, Montana. Some witnesses said he was Arthur Hughes, another said he was John Price. After all, this could be a ruse set up by Mr. and Mrs. Elliott to cover up their crime. Roy said he had more questions for the alleged Arthur Hughes and that he had scheduled another deposition for Friday, October 3, at four o'clock. Charles said he would arrange to have Mr. Hughes there.

The day before the deposition was to take place, O.W. McConnell went to see Charles Hayes at his Maiden Lane office. McConnell told Charles that he was investigating Mrs. Elliott's life insurance claim for her first husband, Arthur Hughes. He said that he had heard some intriguing rumors about Mr. Hughes being alive and living there in New York City. That would be good news for his wife since she could hang if she did kill him. In any event, he said Montana Life was only interested in clearing up this claim. He said he understood that Charles knew this man who claimed to be Arthur Hughes and asked if he could arrange a meeting. He offered to pay Charles for his trouble. Charles agreed, and the fee was set at fifty dollars. Charles was to bring Arthur to the front of City Court the next day, Friday, October 3, at one o'clock. McConnell would bring Senator Edwards with him to identify Arthur. (Senator Edwards was a state senator from Forsyth.)

Charles sent a message to Arthur telling him about the two meetings on Friday—one with the insurance man and one with the lawyer. Arthur replied that he would appear for both.

That evening Charles noticed someone following him when he went home from work.

The next morning, Friday, Arthur rose, shaved, and dressed and ate breakfast. Before leaving the flophouse, he sat down and penned this letter.

My dear Sarah,

My ship sails tonight or tomorrow for parts unknown you shall hear later and it will be some time before I will be able to see you. You had better try and send Aila May and little Pat to Jenny Hayes. Hayes wants Aila May themselves and they have a good place for little Sarah. I think it is the best for you to do but you do what you think is best you must use your own judgment. I am very sorry you ever wrote to your family at Wilkes-Barre your sister could do you no good.

I remain yours
Arthur

It is puzzling that Arthur didn't propose sending the children to Sarah's family in Wilkes-Barre. And what did Sarah's sister have to do with this? Anyway, Arthur put the letter in his coat pocket and left to meet Charles.

At noon, the same cast of characters assembled at Roy Robinson's law office—the lawyer, the sheriff, the detectives, and the insurance man. At a quarter to one, McConnell left for his one o'clock rendezvous with Charles and Arthur. The Pinkerton and police detectives followed him.

McConnell found Charles at the agreed spot in front of City Court. Charles was alone, Arthur was not with him. Charles appeared apprehensive. He told McConnell, "I know I'm being shadowed, and I know that the sheriff from Forsyth is in New York."

"Montana Life has not requested a warrant for Mr. Hughes," McConnell assured him.

"Where is Senator Edwards?" Charles asked.

"He hasn't arrived. I will identify Mr. Hughes from the photographs."

Charles left McConnell and walked across the street. The police detectives followed him. Charles found Arthur in front of the *World* building. As he was telling Arthur what McConnell had said, the detectives approached and demanded, "Are you Arthur Hughes?" and they arrested him.

Charles ran back across the street to where McConnell was standing. "They're arresting Mr. Hughes!" he cried. McConnell feigned surprise. The two men hurried over to the detectives and with emoted indignation McConnell demanded, "Who in —— are these fellows who are arresting Mr. Hughes?"

CHAPTER TEN

A FLURRY OF telegrams flew across the wires to County Attorney Beeman:

> I HAVE SEEN ARTHUR F HUGHES. NO MISTAKE IN HIS IDENTITY.
> MRS HUGHES IS CERTAINLY NOT GUILTY OF MURDER.
> —O W MCCONNELL

> HUGHES ARRESTED, MOSES WILL LEAVE WITH HUGHES WHEN
> REQUISITION SIGNED.
> —PARKER, DAVIS, WAGNER & WALTON

> HAVING SOME TROUBLE ABOUT PAPERS BUT THINK WE WILL GET
> MATTERS ARRANGED. HUGHES SAYS HE IS AFRAID HE WILL BE
> LYNCHED.
> —WM MOSES

The October 4 *New York Times* headline read: "'DEAD' MAN IS HERE
... BETRAYED BY BIG HAND ... HE SAYS—REMARRIAGE OF HIS
'WIDOW' ANNOYED HIM." The *World* article of the same day led: "HE
WOULDN'T STAY DEAD AFTER WIFE MARRIED ANOTHER." Both
reporters fixated on the size of Arthur's hands as the final clue to bring his
arrest. The *World* said his hand was the size of a ham. The *Times* said when
detectives found a man with hands of immense proportions encircling a
glass of beer in a Park Row saloon, they arrested him. Arthur did have
muscular hands, he was a stonemason after all, but it was the mutilated
finger tips that distinguished him. And he was arrested on the street, not in
a saloon. I suppose the saloon vignette made for more colorful reading.

The protagonist of these news stories was immediately taken to
magistrate's court, conveniently across the street from where he was nabbed.
Sheriff Moses, Roy Robinson, and O. W. McConnell had prepared a laundry list complaint of arson, grave robbery, and insurance fraud to keep
Arthur tightly locked away until Sheriff Moses could obtain extradition.

Sheriff Moses then took the train to Albany to see Governor Sulzer. A
few years earlier, the governor of New York was also named Hughes, Charles

Evans Hughes, the son of a Welsh immigrant father and American mother. Hughes resigned his governorship when President Taft appointed him to the Supreme Court in 1910. Grandma said Charles Evans Hughes was her paternal grandfather's cousin. I haven't been able to confirm the relationship. I do not doubt my grandmother's veracity. She has a very reliable record. If anything she tended to downplay things. I don't know about the veracity of whoever told her this. However, she seemed to be able to distinguish truth from tale and was always careful about what she said. It would have been a curious irony had he still been governor.

The new governor, Governor Sulzer, promptly signed the extradition order, and Sheriff Moses returned to New York. Arthur was placed in his custody, and they left on the next train west.

EARLIER IN THE WEEK in Forsyth, a crowd gathered at the courthouse expecting the start of Sarah and Tom's murder trial. To their disappointment, the clerk announced that it had been postponed.

Three days later, the newspaper included a front page teaser hinting that news may be coming in the Hughes saga. "When the facts are made public," the story read, "the history of the affair will make up one of the most remarkable stories which has yet found its birth in this section of the state."

Even with no murder trial that week, there was plenty of other business for the court to attend to, and it soon became clear to the county clerk that the old courthouse simply would not do. Rosebud County had a brand-new beautiful stone courthouse which was much larger. The clerk insisted that the county officers be allowed to move in. Judge Charles Crum agreed, and he ordered the construction foreman and county superintendent to turn over the keys. The county superintendent insisted he had no key. The construction foreman refused to turn over his keys and promptly locked himself in the new courthouse and everybody else out. He wanted to be paid and feared, if he turned over his keys, his outstanding bill would not be paid which was a realistic worry since the county coffers were bare. Judge Crum wasn't having any of that. He ordered the county superintendent and construction foreman thrown in jail for contempt. Sheriff's deputies broke a window at the new courthouse and climbed inside to hunt down the fugitive construction foreman and his

Rosebud County Courthouse, recent photo.

keys. Another deputy went to arrest the county superintendent. The moment the deputy arrived, the county superintendent discovered, yes, he did have a key, and gave it to the deputy. The county clerk et al. moved into the new courthouse while deputies continued to search the building for the runaway construction foreman. They finally found him squirreled away in the attic. After much coaxing, he climbed down and was summoned to explain himself before Judge Crum.

Meanwhile, the editor of the *Forsyth Times-Journal* launched a frontal assault against those he believed responsible for the county's dire financial straits. With his rallying cry "let in the light," he charged that the county commissioners had used their offices for private gain and on foolish projects like building a bridge where there was no road, and in doing so, they had sent the county tumbling into financial ruin—a situation the politicians planned to remedy by imposing a draconian tax increase on the populace. One commissioner hurriedly placed his assets in his wife's name.

To their relief I'm sure, when Arthur arrived, he shoved the construction foreman and the county commissioners and their controversy clean off the front page. He took it all. The enormous, banner headline bellowed:

Arthur F. Hughes Located and Arrested in New York City
Graphic Story of Events Leading to Discovery and Capture

Sheriff Moses Will Bring Him Back
to Face a Charge of Conspiracy to
Swindle Life Insurance Company

Story of Body Graveyard Robbery,
Arson and Detective Sleuthing Has
Dime Novel Backed Clear Off Boards

The lengthy, detailed account, which covered the entire front page, very thoroughly ran down the whole story, including that bit about Arthur telling the photographer in New York that they are too busy stealing cattle out there in Montana. The ire of the reporter at this assault on local pride came through quite clearly in the article.

Out in Twin Bridges at the orphanage, Mrs. Shobe removed the leather-bound ledger from its place on the shelf. She opened it to H, Hughes, Aila, Sarah, and Arthur. Next to "Father" she neatly drew a slash across each letter in the word "dead" and next to it wrote "living." I don't know what happened next, but I imagine she summoned Aila, Archie, and Patsy and said something to the effect, children, we have news of your parents. Your father is alive.

I wonder how Bill and Hector learned the news—at one moment to be overjoyed at hearing the unthinkable, their father thought dead was alive, and then to learn about the grave robbery. It had to be humiliating for them. I can picture Bill's employer sliding the paper across the dinner table and saying, looks like your father is alive after all, and in big trouble.

Besides the mammoth newspaper story, there was a bumper crop of gossip for the boys to overhear. Did you know that John Kiernan was playing cards with Arthur Hughes the night he was killed in the railroad yard? The facts needed no embellishment but got it anyway.

The day Arthur arrived in Forsyth, the murder charge against Sarah and Tom was dropped, and they were both promptly charged with bigamy—Sarah because of Arthur, and Tom because of the alleged wife in Ireland. They remained in jail.

Before locking Arthur in his cell, Sheriff Moses took him to see Sarah. She looked up from her needlepoint only long enough to say, "Nothing doing, Arthur, no home, no children, no money," and returned to her stitching.

Arthur probably didn't have much to say to Tom, nor Tom to Arthur. I wonder if they were in the same cell.

Judge Charles L. Crum, circa 1904.
PHOTO COURTESY OF THE CRUM FAMILY.

That afternoon, October 14, 1913, Sheriff Moses took Arthur, Sarah, and Tom to the courthouse to be arraigned before Judge Crum. Arthur's case was first. The clerk read the charge, "Arthur F. Hughes is charged with the crime of removal of a dead body of a human being from its place of sepulture without the authority of law on the twenty-second day of January, 1913."

"HOW DO YOU PLEAD?" demanded Judge Crum.

"Guilty, sir," replied Arthur.

Sentencing was the next day.

"MR. HUGHES," boomed Judge Crum, "YOU HAVE BEEN INFORMED AGAINST BY THE COUNTY ATTORNEY ON THE CHARGE OF REMOVING A DEAD BODY OR THE BODY OF A HUMAN BEING FROM ITS PLACE OF SEPULTURE IN THE FORSYTH CEMETERY. You were duly arraigned, WAIVED the benefit of counsel and time in which to plead, and ENTERED YOUR PLEA OF GUILTY, and this morning was set as the day for the SENTENCE OF THIS COURT TO BE PASSED. Have you at this time, MR. HUGHES, any legal EXCUSE to offer why the JUDGMENT and SENTENCE of the court should NOT be pronounced?"

"No, sir," replied Arthur.

"As I recall the FACTS in connection with this matter," Judge Crum orated, "this is perhaps one of a NUMBER OF CHARGES which may be URGED AGAINST YOU BY THE PROSECUTION. The only charge to which you have pled GUILTY and which has been URGED AGAINST YOU BY THE PROSECUTION is the particular charge of REMOVING A BODY FROM A CEMETERY, and that is the CHARGE upon which the court must SENTENCE YOU at this time.

"The court is of the opinion, MR. HUGHES, that during the LAST SIX MONTHS, or since this crime was committed, that YOU perhaps have had as much GRIEF as the OTHER PARTIES who are supposed to have been CONNECTED WITH THIS OFFENSE. There is one LESSON in life which you have apparently OVERLOOKED, and that is: THAT IT DOES NOT PAY IN THE LONG RUN TO VIOLATE THE LAW. And I hope that when you are THROUGH with the term of sentence that I shall be COMPELLED to give you in the STATE PRISON that you will look at life from a DIFFERENT ANGLE and attempt to lead a DIFFERENT COURSE.

"It is the judgment and sentence of the court, MR. HUGHES, that you are GUILTY AS CHARGED in the information and that you be confined to the STATE PRISON AT DEER LODGE AT HARD LABOR FOR THE PERIOD OF TWO YEARS, and you are remanded to the custody of the sheriff to carry out the sentence."

He also ordered Arthur to pay the cost of his prosecution.

Sheriff Moses took Arthur to the depot, and they boarded the next train west to Deer Lodge which was some 350 miles away in the southwestern part of the state. From the time Arthur arrived in Forsyth from New York, to the time Sheriff Moses delivered him to the custody of Warden Frank Conly at the Montana State Prison, was three days.

We now go back to the day our three defendants were arraigned and pick up Sarah's tale. Seeing a large audience forming in the courtroom, she waived the reading of the charge. The clerk handed a copy to Braz Tull. It read as follows,

> That one Sarah Hughes, late of the County of Rosebud, State of Montana, on the twenty-seventh day of March, A.D. 1913, at the County of Custer and State of Montana, committed the crime of bigamy. That . . . Sarah Hughes, then and there, did knowingly, wilfully and feloniously marry one Thomas Elliott, the said defendant being then and there, the lawful wife of another person, to-wit; Arthur F. Hughes, then and there living, the marriage of the said defendant, Sarah Hughes, and the said Arthur F. Hughes not having been annulled, dissolved or pronounced void by the judgment of any competent court, but then and there subsisting, as the defendant well knew, and the said Arthur F. Hughes not then and there being absent from the said defendant for five successive years . . .
>
> All of which is contrary to the form of the statute in such case made and provided and against the peace and dignity of the State of Montana.

It was a full day for our Sarah. In the morning, her supposed-to-be dead first husband shows up, by lunchtime the capital offense waged against her by the State is dropped, and now at mid-afternoon she is charged with a new felony as is her new husband. She needed time, or her lawyer needed time, to enter her plea. Judge Crum DEMANDED that she appear before him the following day at ten o'clock to do so.

The next day, before an even larger crowd, she pled not guilty. Judge Crum set her trial date for two weeks hence and her bail at two thousand dollars. It may as well have been two million. Sarah returned to her jail cell.

Braz Tull subpoenaed Arthur to testify on Sarah's behalf, so Sheriff Moses got back on the train and returned to Deer Lodge to fetch him, and once again, Arthur took up residence in the Rosebud County jail with Sarah and Tom.

And, yes, let's not forget Tom Elliott. Shall we say *poor* Tom Elliott? It's hard to say. Was there a Mrs. Thomas Elliott still living in Ireland? Tom said no. A jury would decide.

As for the Mrs. Thomas Elliott living in Forsyth, the situation was more complicated. Two husbands were present, in the flesh. The question for the jury would be: did Sarah know Arthur was alive when she married Tom?

The crescendo begun with a fire-ravaged ranch house, a charred body in its midst, would climax with Sarah's bigamy trial. Great theater had come to this whistle stop. Murder was awful, but bigamy, a *woman* charged with bigamy, that was tantalizing.

All who could squeezed into the courtroom including newspapermen from far and wide. Reporters came all the way across the state from Butte which was over three hundred miles away. At center stage sat our Sarah, the fallen debutante turned farm wife turned grieving widow turned accused murderess turned accused bigamist—or was she the abandoned wife and mother turned unwitting, unknowing bigamist meaning not a bigamist at all. At stage right sat husbands number one and number two: one a grave-robbing, house-burning, death-faking, family-deserting, #&!!@ chip off the ol' block; the other—unlucky, mixed up with the wrong woman, or a rake with a family on every continent who took advantage of a distraught believed-to-be widow. The supporting players, Braz Tull for the defense and Don Smith for the prosecution, took their places. And at stage rear presiding high above the lot, decked in his decorous black robes, sat the Honorable Charles L. Crum. Whether there was a hero or heroine, victim or villain in this drama, would be in the eyes of the jurors, and the audience.

Don Smith represented the State for County Attorney Beeman. He made his opening statement and then called eight witnesses, one of whom was Sheriff Moses. (Unfortunately, the trial transcript was destroyed and the other court records and newspapers didn't recount what those particular witnesses said.) The State rested.

Braz Tull moved for a directed verdict of not guilty. This the court did not do.

Braz Tull then called Arthur and Clerk of Court Muri as defense witnesses. Arthur testified that Sarah knew nothing about his digging up that body. He wanted her to think he was dead, so he put the body in the house, torched it, and left. She had no part of it. He said he did it because he wanted his wife and others to believe he was dead. Before the fire, he told Sarah that he was going away and would never return. He insisted that Sarah was innocent of any wrong he had done.

Court adjourned.

On day two, the courtroom was again full of spectators, including many women. Seeing Sarah's husbands seated together added to the buzz, only to be abruptly silenced when Judge Crum entered the courtroom. "Hubs sit side by side," wrote the *Butte Miner*.

Don Smith again called Arthur to the stand. In his cross examination, Smith presented the English translation of the letter Arthur wrote to Sarah the day he was arrested in New York. He attempted to show inconsistencies between Arthur's testimony and the letter. According to gossip outside the courtroom, Arthur testified that he and his wife had intended to separate but he did not want to leave her unprovided for, that's why he did what he did, and he planned to divide the insurance money later. To this, peals of laughter erupted in the courtroom.

Bill and Hector were subpoenaed as defense witnesses but were never called.

Sarah then testified on her own behalf after which the defense rested.

Don Smith called Arthur to the stand for a second cross examination. Sheriff Moses and another witness testified in rebuttal. The State again rested.

The jury left the courtroom while the lawyers and Judge Crum agreed on their instructions. Those instructions were given in writing and the jurors retired to the jury room to begin deliberations. Court adjourned.

On October 31, day three of Sarah's trial, the jury came back into court. No, they hadn't reached a verdict yet. They asked that the testimony of one of the witnesses be read to them. It was. They returned to the jury room.

This was also the first and last day of Tom's trial. Jury selection, trial, and verdict were accomplished in one day. Eight witnesses testified for the State after which Braz Tull, Tom's now court appointed lawyer, moved for a directed verdict. Judge Crum instructed the jury to return a verdict of not guilty. The jury withdrew to the jury room, deliberated briefly, and returned to court with a verdict of not guilty. The prosecution had failed to prove the existence of another Mrs. Thomas Elliott in Ireland or elsewhere. After seven months in the county jail, Tom Elliott was a free man.

Now it was Saturday, November 1, day four of Sarah's trial, and the jury was still deliberating. Judge Crum ordered them into the courtroom which was again filled to capacity with spectators. Has the jury reached a verdict? he asked. The foreman said no, the jury was still unable to reach a verdict. Judge Crum asked, if with more time, could they agree? The foreman said no. To this, I imagine murmurs rippling through the courtroom, and the judge pounding his gavel demanding order. Judge Crum excused the jury. The newspaper reported that after the first twenty-four hours the jury was six to six, later it was seven to five in favor of conviction. After sixty hours of deliberation, two still held out for acquittal.

Braz Tull conferred in whispers with Sarah and then rose to address the court.

"Your Honor," he said, "my client wishes to withdraw her plea of not guilty and enter a plea of guilty." Louder murmurs and the judge again demands order.

"DO YOU HAVE ANY LEGAL CAUSE TO SHOW WHY JUDGMENT SHOULD NOT BE PRONOUNCED AGAINST YOU?" demanded Judge Crum.

"No, sir," Sarah replied.

"SARAH HUGHES has been DULY CONVICTED in this court of the crime of BIGAMY," roared Judge Crum. "It is therefore ORDERED, ADJUDGED, AND DECREED that the said SARAH HUGHES be PUNISHED by IMPRISONMENT at HARD LABOR IN THE STATE PRISON OF THE STATE OF MONTANA AT DEER LODGE FOR THE TERM OF TWO YEARS, and that she PAY the costs of this prosecution."

And with a slam of the gavel, court was adjourned.

Well. He certainly threw the book at her. A year later, a Rosebud County woman was convicted in Judge Mendenhall's court for shooting and killing a neighbor's horse she found grazing on her unfenced land. The woman was fined forty-five dollars, less than the price of a horse, and ordered to pay the costs of prosecution. She was given no prison time. One juror said they went easy on her because she was a woman. He said, had the accused been a man, they would have given him the limit. Killing another person's livestock was punishable by one to ten years in prison, whereas bigamy was punishable by up to three years in prison or a fine of up to two thousand dollars. No prison time for the horse killer and two years for the bigamist—quite a difference in sentences meted out to two women, especially considering the disparity in punishments dictated by the penal code. Here was Sarah, a mother with five children and a hung jury, and Judge Crum didn't even count the seven months she had already spent in jail as time against her sentence, and some of that time was while she was charged with a crime the authorities knew didn't happen.

In the vein of crime does not pay, the *Forsyth Times-Journal* closed this tale by predicting that other charges would be urged against Sarah and Arthur after they were released from prison, and that the Hughes family, now separated, would never be reunited.

CHAPTER ELEVEN

"HE MEANT TO stay there for the rest of his life, believe me he did," Grandma said forlornly, referring to her father and the homestead, "but things didn't work out very well. My mother was a butterfly . . ."

Were her parents in cahoots? Was the butterfly a bigamist? I have racked my brain over that question and continue to do so to this day. If Sarah knew, why didn't she say so? Maybe she did but nobody believed her. Maybe she didn't know where Arthur was until he wrote to Eleanor S. Thomas in Billings. And who was this Eleanor S. Thomas of Billings? When I first read that name, I thought, it's an alias for Sarah. Her maiden name was Sarah Eleanor Thomas. However, Sarah wasn't in Billings nor could she get there. She was in jail.

Putting the homestead in Sarah's name seemed a preemptive step in Arthur's disappearing act, but then they sold the homestead. Then he made a payment and commenced work on another piece of land—the eighty acre desert claim. Why? I looked at that land. It's all hills, big hills. To keep it, he had to irrigate it. Either he decided to disappear after he filed for that land, or he claimed it to provide proof that he had a stake in the community and wouldn't leave voluntarily.

If Sarah was in on the scheme, why did she marry somebody else? It predictably did heap suspicion upon her. She was shocked and distressed to hear about Tom having a wife in Ireland and said, had she known, she never would have married him. I initially took that as evidence that she was not in on the ruse. But what's good for the goose isn't necessarily good for the gander. In one of her missives to Tom she wrote, *"no matter what you have done Tom you are no worse than I am and you will find it out some day for I shall tell you something that you would never think of me."* Could she have been referring to Arthur being alive and her married again?

The simplest way to look at it is to assume that everybody told the truth. Arthur said Sarah was innocent. Then why did she plead guilty in the end?

Arthur's desert claim, Rosebud County, recent photo.

Perhaps she felt it was no use, her goose was cooked no matter what she said, and she wanted it over. That's how the newspaper reported it.

I don't know what became of Tom Elliott. And as for the baby, I found no record of a baby born to Sarah that year with the surname Elliott or Hughes in Forsyth or Deer Lodge. She could have miscarried the child, but absence of a record doesn't mean the child was not born. Years later, Bill told Patsy's daughters that he had a half brother named Frederick. However, those cousins and Grandma said they never knew whether to believe anything Bill said.

Grandma told Mom and my aunts that her father was away, and the barn burned down. The body of a dead transient was found in the barn. Then a neighbor started a rumor that the body was her father, and her mother had killed him. Later somebody from Forsyth saw her father working in another town and told him that his wife was in jail for his murder, so he came back.

Well, we know there was a fire. It was the house, not the barn. There was a man in the house. How he got there and the fact that he was already dead were missing from the story, as was the fact that Arthur did not come back of his own accord. Grandma was in the orphanage when the story unfolded, thanks be to God. At least she and Archie and Patsy were spared the embarrassment of the rest of the spectacle. It's just as well if they didn't know the whole of it.

How I found out what actually happened is almost as interesting as what I found out. But to paraphrase my grandfather, that story is enough to fill a volume all its own, and perhaps one day it will.

THERE CAN BE no doubt that Sarah was mighty steamed over the way all this turned out. Now what do you suppose an angry, highly superstitious woman would have done to those she blamed for her unhappy fate? And I don't mean Arthur. Before we quit Rosebud County, I will tell you what I know of what happened, and you can draw your own conclusions.

The next year, 1914, the Great War started in Europe. War prosperity came to eastern Montana, and Mother Nature quickly squelched it with a drought, devastating the plains for years. Then came the locusts, then the gophers, then the wind to blow away the topsoil. No, this wasn't ancient Egypt even though one of the characters was named Moses.

In 1918, the Yellowstone flooded wreaking widespread damage throughout Forsyth. Coroner Frank Booth got the worst of it. His Furniture and Mortuary was completely destroyed. The next year a flash blizzard killed four members of one family. Yes, a flood and a killer blizzard during a drought. That wasn't a curse, it was simply life on the plains. Hardy souls rode out the Horseman. Others left the state forever. I find it interesting that Sarah and Arthur managed to time their altercations around the droughts.

And then there's the sad tale of what happened to Sheriff Moses.

Sheriff Moses took Sarah and Arthur to prison in early November 1913. That December, a few days after Christmas, his wife left him. She asked John Burgess, who was one of Sheriff Moses's deputies, if she could stay with him and his wife. This obviously put Burgess in an awkward position. He and William Moses had known each other for years, since their Dakota cattle driving days. John Burgess told his wife, Martha, that Mrs. Moses was leaving her husband and had asked to stay with them. Martha Burgess was uneasy about sheltering a truant wife, but she acquiesced. A few days later, Mrs. Moses filed for divorce.

Needless to say, Sheriff Moses was in a very bad mood over his wife's leaving him. He and Burgess confronted each other on the street in Forsyth. It had something to do with money Moses owed Burgess for official business. They got into a fistfight and Moses knocked Burgess to the ground and grappled for his gun. A Forsyth policeman broke up the fight and arrested Sheriff Moses. He pled guilty. Then Burgess reportedly followed Moses with his six-shooter. Another time, Moses allegedly barked at Burgess to "quit harboring that —— woman" or he'd kill him. Another confrontation took place in the jail within earshot of a prisoner. That time, Burgess supposedly threatened to kill Moses. On yet another occasion, Sheriff Moses took Burgess's badge away for public drunkenness.

Now in mid January, a saloon keeper complained to Sheriff Moses that "Burgess pulled off an old fashioned tea party" in his saloon the night before, meaning he coaxed a patron into dancing "to the tune of his revolver." That afternoon Sheriff Moses went to the town of Rosebud to hold a sheriff's sale. While there, he hired a dray and ordered the driver to take him out to the Burgess place. Once they neared the house, Sheriff Moses told the driver to stop and wait for him. Moses climbed down from the dray and walked up the hill toward the house. The dogs started to bark. Martha Burgess looked out the window to see what the dogs were barking at and saw Sheriff Moses. She looked over at her husband. He was dozing in the chair. She didn't bother to wake him. Instead, she met Moses at the door herself and greeted him with the "business end" of her Winchester.

"You can't come in," she said.

"I don't want to," he replied. "I'm looking for your husband. I have a warrant for his arrest."

"Oh," she said. She walked over and woke her husband and told him that Billy Moses was there to see him. He got up and came to the door. Sheriff Moses told him that he was under arrest for the saloon incident. John Burgess said he'd go with him but he needed to get his coat first. He went back into the house and picked up his coat. He also grabbed two six-shooters.

Martha Burgess slipped on her sweater and followed her husband outside onto the porch. "I'm going with you," she said.

"No, you're not," said Moses.

"Yes, I am," she said. She was still holding the Winchester, now at her side, business end down. "You come, too," she told Slocum, their hired man. Just then her rifle went off and fired through her shoe. Everybody jumped.

"That was an accident, Billy," she said.

"What do you mean? Give me that gun —— —— you," said an angry Sheriff Moses, and he grabbed her left arm. Then another shot fired, another, another, another—all from John Burgess's gun. Slocum grabbed his hands and told him to quit shooting. Martha Burgess had been shot in the chest. Sheriff Moses was face down on the porch—dead. Three bullets had hit him, two after he was already down, one through the back of his neck. His revolver was underneath him. One chamber was empty, though if fired that afternoon, it didn't hit anybody.

The gunshots drove the drayman's team wild. He struggled to regain control of his horses and then drove as fast as he could into town for a doctor. By the time he returned, a crowd had gathered below the Burgess home, and John Burgess was keeping all at bay with his gun, threatening to shoot anybody who came close. "Don't do any more shooting; you've done enough," said his wounded, bleeding wife from the porch. After some coaxing, Burgess allowed the doctor through to attend to her. As he stepped onto the porch with the doctor, Burgess reportedly looked down at the dead sheriff and said, "You ——ed ol' cuss, you're just where you ought to be."

John Burgess was arrested for the murder of Sheriff Moses and locked in the Rosebud County jail. He was so terrified of being lynched that doctors said he was on the verge of a nervous breakdown. Judge Crum agreed to a change of venue. Prisoner and trial were moved to Miles City.

The trial began three months later. Competing legal teams waged a fierce war of attrition, calling over one hundred witnesses. In the end, it came down to the character of the deceased. Was he a peaceable or violent-tempered man? It depended on whom you asked. Some witnesses said he had been quarrelsome since way back. Others said they knew him to be peaceable. One witness called him turbulent and when asked, "What do you mean by turbulent?" he said, "Don't know, too big a word for me."

The former county attorney from Belle Fourche, South Dakota, where William Moses had been sheriff before moving to Rosebud County, testified that Moses had a good reputation as sheriff. A defense lawyer from Belle Fourche testified that Sheriff Moses was "quarrelsome" and "overzealous" in going after criminals (this from a defense lawyer). He said that he and Moses had words over a case and Moses pulled his revolver on him. When asked whether he had ever heard of Moses actually shooting anybody, he said no.

Martha Burgess testified that after her gun went off, Moses grabbed her arm and drew his gun and fired it and then her husband fired his gun. In later testimony, she recanted. She said she didn't see Moses shoot his gun.

A lodger at the Burgess home testified that shortly before the shooting, he overheard Burgess tell his wife, "I'm going down to where he's holding that sale and say, 'Billy Moses, you're a dead man.'"

Then John Burgess took the stand. He said Moses hadn't been himself since the Hughes trial—crazed he was, and mad. His wife's leaving him threw him further into a rage. Burgess said Moses threatened him for meddling in his family affairs. He feared for his life. He said that day on the porch, Moses pulled his revolver and poked it in his ribs; he then pulled his gun and shot in self-defense. And he said, after thirty years on the range, he believed there could be only one reason why Billy Moses, who owned an automobile, would come to his house in a dray: he intended to carry a body back with him.

Not guilty, said the jury.

Such was the end of the end for the sheriff who arrested Sarah.

As for the judge who threw the book at her, you'll learn about his fate later.

CHAPTER TWELVE

A VERITABLE DOOR slams shut at this part of our story. As you might expect, no details of Sarah and Arthur's sojourn at the Montana State Prison were passed down in family lore—nor was the fact that they went to prison. Though I have no first-hand, day-to-day accounts of their stay, what I was able to learn, I found quite interesting.

Grandma said, after leaving Wilkes-Barre, "We moved from place to place." I understood the reason to be because her father kept beating the rakes with whom her mother was carrying on and they had to leave, or were run out of town is probably a more apt way to put it. The philanderer-beating being dramatic enough, I never thought to ask Grandma where "place to place" was, and she was probably relieved that I didn't.

Sarah and Arthur entered a modern prison in Deer Lodge, Montana, that fall of 1913. The prisoners had completed construction of the new cellblock the year before. The women's quarters were five years old. It was a small building, separate from the men, within the same rampart-enclosed citadel. Decades later, the women moved into another facility and that building became maximum security for the men.

When Arthur arrived he was photographed, showered, and his head and face shaved. Thereafter he would shower once a week in cold or tepid water, per prison rules. His clothes were burned and he was given a cadet gray woolen prison uniform. Prisoners wore stripes only as punishment. He was photographed again and deposited in his cell.

Assuming Arthur lodged in the new cellblock, his six by eight foot cell had running water and a flush toilet, which many of the prisoners' homes didn't have. The old cellblock, which was still in use, had no such amenities, just buckets.

A metal cot hung from the cell wall on top of which lay a mattress and wool blanket. The other simple furnishings were a wooden table, a cupboard, and a stool.

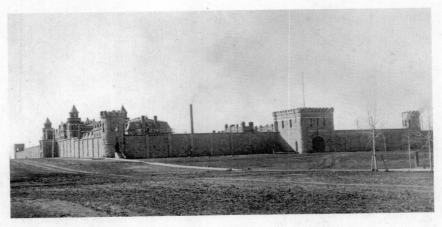

Montana State Prison, Deer Lodge, Montana, circa 1912.
MONTANA HISTORICAL SOCIETY, 950-012

Arthur woke at six o'clock every morning to the sound of the bell. He dressed, made his bed; washed his face, neck, and hands; shaved; swept and tidied his cell. The doors opened. All marched in line to breakfast. Strict silence was maintained. Only necessary speech in a low voice was permitted. Lunch was at noon. Dinner was at six or just before dark in winter. The meal regimen was hearty and the same every week. Tuesday was stew day.

There were around six hundred inmates in the prison while Sarah and Arthur were incarcerated. The vast majority of them were single men, American-born, first offenders, and to use Warden Frank Conly's words, "made good" after they left, meaning they never came back. And while living within the walls, most were idle.

Nearly half the men did nothing all the time and many did nothing much of the time in the way of work. A sentence of X years hard labor usually meant ½ X years doing next to nothing. The State Board of Charities and Reform implored Governor Stewart to find work for these men. "Idleness is the curse of the man behind bars, " wrote the board. "Work is the great reformer." The prisoners must acquire the habit of working. Work will help them become "objective-minded." This did not fall on deaf ears. The towering, no-nonsense Frank Conly, a former prison guard who was then the longest serving warden in the country, creatively sought work for the prisoners to keep them busy and teach them a trade. He believed that work was necessary to set the convicts aright, for those who were rightable. He contended that a large number of them were not of sound mind.

Prisoners slaughtered and butchered cattle for the prison's meat supply and to sell to the State Hospital for the Insane at Warm Springs and to the State Tuberculosis Sanatorium. Convicts apprenticed with a plumber at Warm Springs, learned barbering in the prison barber shop, and worked at the brickyard down the street. They made bridles, brooms, socks, and underwear, the latter three items for prison use and to sell to Warm Springs.

Frank Conly, Warden of the Montana State Prison.
MONTANA HISTORICAL SOCIETY, 941-566

A lucky, well-behaved convict, after serving some time within the walls and showing himself to be responsible, left the prison to work as a trusty on road crews, logging crews, or ranches. The prisoners vied for this work because it was outside the walls and trusties could earn more good time. It was the privilege of only a select few. Road crews lived seventy-five to a camp. They cleared the land by day with pick and shovel under the supervision of three unarmed guards. The prison had a band; the road crews had a piano.

Arthur worked as a trusty though I don't know what he did.

Warden Frank Conly saw correct penal theory as that of parent and child, teacher and student. "The prisoner must be encouraged to think along elevated lines," he wrote. He believed that the prisoner's downfall was due to the lack of a moral code. He said it was vital to reform to awaken "the moral sense of the criminal which would show him the futility of the violation of the law." To that end, Protestant church services were held every Sunday and a Catholic Mass at least once a month.

Judging by his correspondence and meeting minutes, Warden Conly saw women inmates as a nuisance and no great threat to society, so why keep them any longer than necessary. They were a perturbation in his smooth-running operation. Responding to a woman seeking the prison matron job, he wrote: "In reply to your letter, we have only one female prisoner and we are trying to get rid of her." That was after Sarah left. He sought early parole for one, the only reason given—she's a woman. For another, his reason was: she isn't like the rest in here who are prostitutes. (Prostitution was their occupation, not the crime for which they were imprisoned.)

During the time Sarah and Arthur resided in the prison, most of the inmates were thieves—larceny, burglary, and robbery being the crimes of choice. There was only one "removal of a dead body of a human being from its place of sepulcher" and one bigamist.

When Sarah arrived, she was placed under the charge of the matron. She was washed, as were her clothes which were returned to her, though she wore prison garb. Sarah then moved into her cell in the small, smelly, women's building. Fumes wafted into the cells from the sewer lines that ran underneath.

There were never more than four women prisoners at a time while Sarah was incarcerated. The numbers being so few, the limited talking rule may have been relaxed a bit for the women. If not, that restriction would have been rough on our Sarah. I can imagine the matron telling her to stop talking and Sarah in her innately superior attitude snapping back, what of it! I'll talk if I want! She must not have been too incorrigible; she did earn good time.

Sarah's two sorority sisters that first month were Sandra and Mildred. (Those aren't their real names. I've given the other felons pseudonyms.) Sandra, a thirty-seven-year-old black woman from Nashville, had worked as a domestic in Butte until she was convicted of grand larceny. She probably stole to feed her morphine addiction, a habit for which the bowels of Butte's Chinatown provided ample feed. She began her sentence seven months earlier, so she was probably through the ravings by the time Sarah arrived.

Sandra was paroled and replaced by another thief, Lydia, a twenty-year-old domestic. In June, Maria joined the trio, this grand larceny felon a pregnant, twenty-three-year-old, mulatto actress. When Maria's time drew near, the warden sent her to the hospital and Governor Stewart commuted her sentence so that by the time she delivered her baby, she could be paroled.

Then came Laura. She had been sentenced to ten years for stealing ten dollars from a man with whom she was out drinking. Warden Conly said she went crazy in prison, so he sent her to Warm Springs. After she settled down, the hospital returned her to the prison. At the next Prison Commissioners meeting, Warden Conly asked that she be released. He was afraid she'd go crazy again. Governor Stewart pardoned her on the condition that she leave the state forever.

The last to join the crew was Rena, a nineteen-year-old music teacher convicted of forgery.

Of the six women whose sentences overlapped with Sarah's, four were from Butte, all but one were sentenced to one or two years, and all were American-born except Sarah. And of the lot, the most sordid tale was Mildred's.

This thirty-two-year-old housewife from the Midwest was accused of rape for abetting the rape of her twelve-year-old daughter. Charges were filed nine months after the fact, which would indicate that the little girl had a baby, which caused the county attorney to investigate, there being no doubt that a crime had been committed. A twenty-six-year-old married man was charged with raping the girl. Several incidents were alleged, but he was charged with rape on one particular day, presumably nine months to the day before the baby was born. Witnesses said the girl's mother, Mildred, was present in the cabin and in the barn when the rapes occurred. The instructions to the jury were specific: Mildred wasn't charged with knowing her daughter was being raped and doing nothing to stop it, but for advising and encouraging the rapist. The charge did not state whether Mildred benefitted financially, however the newspaper alluded to such. Mildred maintained her innocence. The jury convicted her, after which the accused man pled guilty to rape.

Mildred and Sarah shared something else in common besides having daughters the same age—their husbands were also in the prison. Mildred's husband, whom I'll call Fred D——, the little girl's stepfather, had been convicted of grand larceny for stealing a mare. The crime came to light when he tried to sell the animal several months after he stole it. He pled guilty and was sentenced to eight years in prison.

It just occurred to me, if Mildred's daughter was sent to the orphanage she would have been in the big girls dormitory with Aila.

I imagine the women prisoners complained mightily to each other about why they were there and how unfair it all was. Sarah must have known why Mildred was sent up.

As for what work these women did while in the prison, in prisons in the West at the time women prisoners sewed prison uniforms, cleaned the warden's quarters, and cooked. Sarah was not a violent offender nor was she a thief. The warden had two daughters, so his wife probably didn't want Mildred in their house. Sarah was good at whatever she put her mind to, including cooking. She could have been the warden's cook. He and his family lived across the street from the prison.

CHAPTER THIRTEEN

THE WEEKS PASSED for Sarah at the prison, for Arthur wherever he was working as a trusty, and for Hector and Bill on ranches in Rosebud County. For Aila, Archie, and Patsy, their days at the orphanage were filled with school, chores, and play. Now it was cold and snowy, soon it would be Christmas. The children were asked to select between two gifts. Each child got what he or she picked. Santa Claus was the big mining company in Butte.

In February, the next epidemic struck. Within three months, the orphanage saw 150 cases of measles, chicken pox, and mumps spread through a population of 172 children. Some of the children contracted all three diseases. The next winter twenty-eight children were stricken with scarlet fever. I have a vague and unreliable recollection that Grandma said she had scarlet fever.

In the spring, eighth graders across Montana, including those at the orphanage, took the State Eighth Grade Examination. Aila would take the test the next year, in 1915. I couldn't find the test she took, but here's a sampling of questions from the 1920 test:

> Give the historical setting of two of the following selections: Paul Revere's Ride; The Storming of the Bastille; William Tell and the Apple; Song of Marion's Men; the Skeleton in Armor.

> Write a letter to one of the candidates for the legislature or for a state or county office asking how he stands in regard to a certain measure that may be of vital interest to your school, community or county.

> Land sold at the rate of $1900 for 12 acres would cost how much for 75¾ acres?

> A woman having $500 can lend it on a personal note at 6% interest or place it in a savings bank at 4% interest compounded semi-annually. Which will bring the greater return the first year?

When did Poland become independent? To what nation had she been dependent?

Where would you advise a stranger to settle in Montana if he wished (a) to raise flax? (b) Corn? (c) Fruit? (d) If he wished to invest in oil lands? (e) If he wished to get work in a coal mine? (f) In a copper mine? (g) In a fish hatchery? (h) If he wished to investigate a large irrigating project?

Frequent reference is made at the present time to the Monroe Doctrine. What is the meaning of this famous doctrine? Do you believe in it? Give reason for your answer.

Explain (a) Fugitive Slave law, (b) Emancipation Proclamation.

What were some of the mistakes made by the North after the Civil War in the reconstruction of the South?

Tell the difference between direct and indirect taxation. How does the federal government obtain its revenues?

That was from an eighth grade test. The children were only thirteen or fourteen years old, and for the most part, grade school children didn't have homework back then, at least not much, and a teacher might have more than one grade in a classroom.

That summer, Aila's teacher, Miss Dragstedt, and another teacher organized a dance routine for the Fourth of July parade. They tried out the oldest girls first but soon grew frustrated because they couldn't find enough girls who could learn and remember the steps.

"Ila," said Miss Dragstedt mispronouncing Aila's name, "we'll have to put you there. If you can't do it, I don't know what we'll do. You're the last good looking girl we have to try out. You can dance. I've seen you dance and skip along these halls."

"Oh, I'm so fat. They wouldn't want me," said Aila who was never fat.

"Oh, yes," said Miss Dragstedt, "your turn will come."

The girls were to dance on a flatbed in the parade. Miss Dragstedt showed Aila the simple steps to what Aila described as a drill dance. The other girls forgot their steps or turned the wrong way. Aila readily learned and remembered the steps, so Miss Dragstedt decided that she would lead the dance. On the day of the parade, Aila climbed aboard the flatbed, the music started, and she led the dance. It was a resounding success. The crowd applauded enthusiastically. To Aila, the approbation was wonderful. She had experienced nothing like it and thought it was the most marvelous experience of her young life. "I lived for that sort of thing," she said.

MEANWHILE IN Deer Lodge that same summer, long before she was eligible for parole, Sarah began the wheels turning to get her children back.

> The State of Montana
> Bureau of Child and Animal Protection
> M.L. Rickman, Secretary
>
> Helena, Montana, August 12th, 1914
>
> Hon. Waller Shobe, President
> State Orphans' Home
> Twin Bridges, Montana
>
> Dear Mr. Shobe:
>
> I have a letter from Mrs. Hughes, who is now in the State Prison, asking me if she can have her children after she secures her release. I spoke to Governor Stewart about her request and he thinks that the children should be returned to her. I suppose they are still at the Orphans' Home, but it will be best not to give her a definite answer until I have heard from you.
>
> Very truly yours,
> M. L. Rickman
> Secretary

Arthur wrote, too. He asked that the children be turned over to their mother.

A prisoner was eligible for parole after serving half his minimum sentence. Upon release, each received fifteen dollars worth of clothes and five dollars. To put five dollars in context, miners earned $3.50 per day; three meals and a bed for the night in a boarding house cost a dollar.

Every month the State Board of Prison Commissioners, which consisted of the governor, the attorney general, and the secretary of state, who at the time were Sam Stewart, Dan Kelly, and Dell Alderson, met to review Warden Frank Conly's parole recommendations. Throughout Arthur and Sarah's incarceration, month after month up to the November 1914 meeting, the board paroled all the prisoners recommended by

Warden Conly with two exceptions: one man hadn't served half his sentence so was ineligible, and the other was about to be deported. Taking a broader sweep, looking at the meeting minutes from 1912 to 1916, all recommended by the warden were paroled except one who had violated a suspended sentence and two lifers—the board wanted to look into those further before deciding. It was rare that the board did not follow the warden's recommendations for parole, and in those rare cases that they did not, the reason was provided in the minutes.

Now it was November of 1914. Sarah had served twelve months, which was half her sentence, and Arthur had served almost thirteen months, a little over half his sentence. Warden Conly wrote his monthly letter to the board, this time recommending eighteen prisoners be paroled. The names were listed in alphabetical order except for three which were tacked on the end as if an afterthought. Those were Arthur Hughes, Sarah Hughes, and Maria P———.

On November 6, 1914, the board met. They paroled all but the last three. Maria had not served half her sentence so was denied. The minutes gave no reason why Arthur and Sarah Hughes were denied parole.

At the December 3 meeting, Warden Conley recommended fourteen prisoners for parole including Sarah Hughes. He did not list Arthur. The board paroled all but Sarah. No reason was written in the minutes.

Then on December 18, 1914, the State of Montana gave my great-grandfather a suit of clothes, five dollars, and his freedom. After serving fourteen months of his two-year sentence, Arthur was released unencumbered. He was not paroled.

"Expiration of sentence under Rule 119" was written in the prison log as the reason for Arthur's discharge. This was written above the words "Parole expires" which were crossed out. An inmate with a two-year sentence could earn three months good time. Under Rule 119, a prisoner who worked outside the walls as a trusty could earn an additional ten days off his sentence for every month. Every month of what? If the rule meant every month of his sentence minus good time, for Arthur, who had a two-year sentence, good time would cut his sentence to twenty-one months, ten days per month would be 210 days which is seven months. Seven months under Rule 119 plus three months good time equals ten months off a twenty-four-month sentence, so fourteen months, which is the amount of time Arthur served. Arthur must have worked as a trusty through most, if not all, of his sentence, so even though he was "in prison," he spent hardly any time actually in the prison compound. Perhaps someone needed some stonework done.

The board met again on December 22. Warden Conly recommended nine prisoners for parole, this list sans Sarah. The board paroled all who were recommended and then instructed the clerk "to prepare the usual form of parole for the case of Sarah Hughes."

Twice Warden Conly recommended her for parole, twice the board denied her, and when she wasn't on the list, the board paroled her. Maybe she was cooking for somebody other than the warden. And as for Arthur, why recommend him for parole, deny parole, and then release him? What is most puzzling to me is that treatment of these two was so different from the other inmates who, when recommended, were paroled unless ineligible and the reason was provided in the minutes. So what happened? That, dear reader, remains a mystery. Believe me, I tried to find out, but to no avail.

Three days later, on Christmas day, the matron gave Sarah new clothes and five dollars. She escorted Sarah to the tower—the conduit in and out of the prison. The guard up in the tower lowered the key on a rope. The guard below unlocked and opened the door. Sarah stepped across the threshold she had entered fourteen months earlier and regained her liberty.

Arthur was waiting for her.

PART TWO

Straight to Butte

CHAPTER FOURTEEN

MY OTHER GRANDMOTHER said in those days, "When you moved to Butte you lost your reputation." Sarah and Arthur didn't have a reputation to lose. At last they found a town where their indiscretions, if not unnoticed, would blend in with all the other shenanigans.

Sarah and Arthur went directly from prison to this wide-open mining camp grown into a city. Civilization had descended but the lawless spirit of a camp remained. It was a raw, hard drinking, hard living town where the saloons never closed and literacy was well above average. Visitors from the East were shocked by the debauchery they witnessed there. One called it "simply an outpost of hell." Butte was at once cosmopolitan and reckless. Gambling and prostitution, though illegal, persisted unfettered while the stores sold the finest china, the women were fashionably dressed, the miners' homes were well-kept and nicely furnished, the likes of Caruso and Chaplin performed there, and you could find any cuisine from a Cornish pasty to a Chinese noodle parlor to a butcher selling kielbasa to a kosher market.

Butte, Montana, sits a mile high in the Rocky Mountains on an immense deposit of mineral wealth, the "richest hill on earth," a boom town where the ore never ran out. Raucous mining camps were aplenty in the West, but Butte outlasted them in ore and wildness. Early photographs show a town gray and grim—a cluster of mine yards wrapped in a crazy quilt of tiny houses, each clutching closely to the nearest mine, and a little further from the mines, stately Victorians, and sandwiched in between, a bustling uptown with wide boulevards and modern everything. At night she was called "the glittering hill," but as night's veil lifted, any weary miner who woke up, rubbed his bleary eyes, looked around at the town and exclaimed, "Why, she's turned ugly!" needed only look up to see Montana high and handsome embracing her. The East Ridge soars to eight

Butte. Note the home in the foreground with the latice work
above the porch and behind the house—a mine dump.
© WORLD MUSEUM OF MINING #2927B

thousand feet forming the Continental Divide, the Pintlers zigzag across the western horizon, and the Highlands to the south tower to over ten thousand feet and are snow capped all but a few weeks of summer. One can feel very small at the foot of such mountains, invincible on top, and in both places, in awe of the Creator.

If winter was severe in Montana, it was downright arctic in Butte. A person stated the temperature as above or below—simply saying the temperature was forty degrees was not specific enough. Mother Nature sent snow any month she pleased, even on the Fourth of July parade. Such conditions taxed the abilities of the most ardent and tenacious gardener attempting to beautify the tiniest corner of Butte's visage. Much of the native plant life was long dead, killed by the old arsenic-spewing, open-hearth smelters, by this time shut down due to local uproar. The most common yard was unadorned dirt. She was a rugged gal she was, attempts to spruce her up were readily foiled. Despite her bleak appearance, she was not another faceless town. Butte had life, and her citizens loved the tough old girl just the way she was.

She was born out of gold, panned by the first prospectors in Silver Bow Creek around 1864. That was placer mining where the ore is found mixed in sand or gravel and the miners use water to separate it. By the early 1870s, the placer claims were dwindling and Butte was fast becoming a ghost town. There were fifty people left, no stores, and two saloons. Then silver mining picked up. That was quartz, meaning underground, hard-rock mining.

The West was a land pregnant with opportunity where Everyman could strike it rich. All were equal in that regard, even a poor boy from Ireland. Marcus Daly immigrated to America when he was only fifteen. He traveled west to the Comstock, worked hard, and distinguished himself. Though unlettered in geology and engineering, the warm, gregarious Irishman had a nose for mining and for business and he advanced in the mining company.

In 1876, Daly's bosses, the Walkers, sent him to Butte to look for silver. He recommended they buy the Alice Mine, which they did. Daly managed the property, he owned stock in it, the mine prospered, and so did he.

In 1880, Daly sold his interest in the Alice and bought the Anaconda silver mine. There's often a story behind the curious names of these mines, and this one came from a news story the original claimant, Michael Hickey, read while fighting for the North in the Civil War. "Grant will encircle Lee's forces and crush them like an anaconda," wrote Horace Greeley. Hickey liked the name and chose it for his mine. Daly chose it for his new company.

Two years after Daly bought the Anaconda mine, Thomas Edison electrified New York City. That very same year Marcus Daly found copper in the Anaconda, an immense deposit of rich copper, the biggest ever found in the world. Providence was smiling on Marcus Daly and he was smart enough to know it. This marvel called electricity would soon light the rest of the country and then the world, and the world needed copper to do it.

Legend has it the sly Daly kept his find quiet and closed the Anaconda. What were people to think other than that the mine had played out? After all, Butte was a prosperous silver town and the Anaconda was a silver mine. Then Daly bought the adjacent mines, the Neversweat and the St. Lawrence, for a song and opened all three mines mining copper along with the sizable deposits of silver and gold imbedded in the tremendous copper vein.

Transportation was essential to Daly's success. When plans for the railroad were being completed the debate was: would the train go to Butte or to Helena? Helena was considered the center of commerce in Montana, but

Butte won. In a delightful show of characteristic hubris, the *Butte Weekly Miner* conceded that eventually a branch line might extend to Helena and to "San Francisco and other insignificant villages on the Pacific Coast." A Utah and Northern workman drove the last spike in the line to Butte just months before Daly discovered his copper bonanza.

If what I just described sounds simple, it wasn't. Though all seemed to be aligning in Daly's favor, embarking in the copper business was a bold move. At that time, the ore had to be shipped all the way to Wales or Baltimore for processing, and it takes tons of ore to yield pounds of copper. Transportation costs readily gobbled up profits. The decision to dive headlong into the copper market required a huge capital outlay to build a large concentrator and smelter nearby. Daly's partners, James Ben Ali Haggin, George Hearst, and Lloyd Tevis, had that kind of money. They owned America's greatest gold and silver mines: the Homestake in South Dakota and the Ontario in Utah. In fact, it was Daly who prodded George Hearst into buying the Ontario. Even so, when the plucky Daly presented his copper proposal to them, Hearst and Tevis changed the subject. Haggin steered the conversation back and firmly decided in favor of Daly. With their financial backing, Marcus Daly built his concentrator and smelter a few miles west of Butte, and he built a town to go along with it, which he called Anaconda.

Ten years later, Congress ended government purchases of silver to back the dollar. The bottom fell out of the already declining silver market. Silver towns became ghost towns. Providence had indeed smiled on Marcus Daly and on Butte, for Butte was now a copper town. By 1895, one quarter of the world's copper came from the Butte mines. In the next three years the Anaconda reaped profits of thirteen million dollars, half of which was paid in dividends. By 1905, Butte had the largest payroll per capita in the world and the miners were among the highest paid industrial workers in America. Butte was booming.

Sarah and Arthur's legal travails made the front pages of the Butte papers a year and a half before they settled there. However, nothing Sarah or Arthur did could compare with the skulduggery immortalized as the War of the Copper Kings. Butte was home to Marcus Daly's powerful adversary, William Andrews Clark, a dour school teacher from the Midwest who mined the miners and the ore and made himself a millionaire. The two woke up one day and decided they hated each other. They sparred over business dealings, the location of the state capital, and Clark's political ambitions. Though both were Democrats, when Clark ran for the territory's congressional seat, Daly plotted to beat him, ostensibly because the Republicans seemed more amenable to his logging on public lands. Daly's shift bosses inspected ballots, and some of Daly's men must have forgotten that they had already voted because they voted again. About the only thing that didn't happen was the election day miracle of the dead rising to vote. Clark lost.

Then in 1889, Montana became a state (and enacted the secret ballot, the first state to do so). In those days, U.S. senators were elected by the state legislatures. Montana's first legislature was evenly split between Democrats and Republicans with several house seats in dispute. The Senate convened but the Democrats refused to show. Warrants were issued to force them to Helena. Some fled the state. The House Democrats and House Republicans met separately. When the Democrat senators were finally rounded up and hauled to Helena, they still refused to meet with the Republicans, so the parties met separately. The Republicans elected two senators and the Democrats elected two senators, one of whom was William Andrews Clark, and four men claiming to be Montana's two senators traveled to Washington and knocked at the U.S. Senate's door expecting admission. The Republican-controlled Senate kept the Republicans and sent Clark and his fellow Democrat packing.

Clark ran again for the Senate. Daly supported another Democrat. The legislature voted day after day. The field was crowded and no winner emerged. Bribes were alleged and saw inflation as the voting continued. Detectives dug for dirt to aid in the art of persuasion. The legislators voted and voted. No one gained enough votes. When the last day of the session came, they still hadn't elected a senator. They gave up, adjourned, and went home. The Republican governor appointed a Republican to the Senate, but the senators in Washington refused to seat him. They wouldn't accept a gubernatorial appointment made simply because the legislature failed to act. Montana would have to make do with only one senator.

The next time, Clark had to be coaxed into running. Daly was now in cahoots with the titans of Standard Oil, and Helena businessmen feared they were set to take over the state. They convinced Clark to run. He agreed and this time he was absolutely determined to win. "We'll send the old man to the Senate or to the poor house," said his son. Clark put his machine in motion, and what a machine it was.

Though Clark already owned the *Butte Miner* and Daly owned the *Anaconda Standard*, both sought to expand their spheres of influence to the rest of the state. Clark would buy an editor, and Daly would follow closely behind and buy the paper. As the voting began in Helena, rumors of bribes abounded. The legislature formed a committee to investigate the allegations. A Kalispell legislator stood before the committee and showed them an envelope stuffed with thirty $1000 bills which he said Clark's lawyer had given him to purchase his vote and two others. Other alleged bribes were alleged to be even more. Clark's *Butte Miner* called his accuser a "moral leper" and "well-paid harlot." A Midwestern newspaper ran a political cartoon declaring the $1000 note: "The kind of bill most frequently introduced in the Montana legislature."

Day after day, the voting continued, the field shrank, and in the end, Clark was elected to the Senate and men of humble means returned home thousands of dollars richer.

Daly wasn't about to give up. The Senate could still refuse to seat Clark. The day Clark took his seat in the Senate, Montana's other senator, Senator Carter, presented memorials signed by the governor and others alleging that Clark had bribed his way into office. The Senate Committee on Privileges and Elections convened to investigate. They called witness after witness, and in the end, they voted unanimously to declare the election null and void and recommended that Clark be rejected by the full Senate. But before the full Senate could vote, Clark resigned.

Meanwhile back in Montana, Clark's men artfully coaxed the governor out of the state, leaving the Clark-friendly lieutenant governor in charge. As soon as Clark resigned, the acting governor appointed him to the open Senate seat. This made Clark an *appointed* senator instead of an *elected* senator, so the election nullification didn't matter. The hoodwinked governor hurried home as soon as he learned the news and appointed another Democrat to the Senate, and once again, Montana sent two men to Washington for the same Senate seat and the senators faced the decision of whom to keep and whom to throw back. They adjourned before considering the question.

By the time the next legislative elections came around in 1900, Marcus Daly was on his death bed. He died before the legislature convened to elect a senator. With his rival gone, Clark won without scandal. He served one term and didn't run for reelection. Twelve years later, the Seventeenth Amendment to the Constitution was ratified requiring direct election of senators, and if you didn't already, now you know part of the reason why.

Clark was reported to have said, "I never bought a man who wasn't for sale." Neither did Fritz Heinze, the dashing young bachelor from New York who dazzled Butte's ladies and bamboozled the men. He arrived in 1889 after Daly and Clark were well-established and wildly rich, and his ambitions soared just as high. Though a bright, well-educated, mining engineer, Heinze sought his fortune through litigation and chicanery. In an early scheme, he leased a mine. The owner said he could keep most of the profits from the low grade ore, so Heinze mixed waste rock with the high grade ore, making all of it low grade, and himself rich.

Heinze's favorite ore extraction method required a judge and a newspaper—he owned both. Butte citizens called him a "courthouse miner." If he didn't invent the frivolous lawsuit, he certainly took the practice to new depths. Perhaps his most inventive litigious escapade was the time he tracked down the daughter of a deceased man who had sold his mine to the Butte and Boston Company. Heinze had himself declared the girl's legal guardian and executor of her father's estate. Then he insisted that her father had not been of sound mind when he sold the mine, therefore she owned it, and by extension, he controlled it.

Marcus Daly had absolutely no use for this shameless eastern sharpie. He called Heinze a "blackmailer" and a "thief." When Daly joined forces with Standard Oil executives Henry Rogers and William Rockefeller (John D.'s brother), Heinze's greatest foe swelled into a behemoth. The confident young man would not cower. There was no limit to his audacity or imagination. The writer Joseph Kinsey Howard called him one of few men "able to make the mighty Standard Oil Company sweat blood." He tied the mines, the mining companies, and the courts in knots for years.

The crux of his main battle was over apex mining law which said that a vein belonged to the owner of the land where the vein apexed, that is, broke through the surface. The owner could follow the vein even if it passed below someone else's surface claim. The trouble was the veins under Butte were jumbled and fractured. Whether this was a continuation of that vein was not clear and was hotly contested. The debate went to court. Expert after expert testified for weeks using elaborate models and charts to prove ownership of the lucrative ore. All the while, Heinze's judge napped off and on, tobacco juice drooling down his gray fuzzy beard, and miners in litigant properties skirmished underground.

The war ended with Heinze selling for millions and agreeing to drop his incessant litigating. By age forty-five, the fast-living tycoon had lost his wife, lost most of his fortune, and died.

BY THE TIME Sarah and Arthur arrived in Butte in 1915, the dust had settled on the War of the Copper Kings. Only Clark remained. Most of the mines were consolidated into the Anaconda Copper Mining Company, known as the ACM or simply, the Company. The economic slump caused by the outbreak of war in Europe was ending and the war boom beginning. Arthur easily found work. He and Sarah also found the town to be full of single men—miners needing room and board. They took in boarders.

Butte was an anomaly in Montana, an island surrounded by land, a tightly drawn industrial city full of ethnic enclaves in the midst of massive cattle and wheat ranches. The mines were a magnet for immigrants. Italians populated Meaderville; Slovenes, Serbs, and Croatians settled in McQueen and East Butte; the Irish filled Dublin Gulch and overflowed it; the Finns lived in Finntown, the Chinese in Chinatown; Cornwall's Cousin Jacks and Cousin Ginnies clustered in Centerville and Walkerville (actually a separate town); Germans and Scandinavians congregated on the Flat, and betwixt and between lived a hodgepodge of Greeks, Lebanese, Scots, French, Hungarians, and more. Those with money resided on the West Side. There was a Welsh church on Dakota Street but no Welsh neighborhood. When Welshmen learned that there was a boarding house run by a Welsh woman, they gravitated to Sarah's. In the early days, all her boarders were Welsh.

By far the most dominant ethnic group in Butte was the Irish—an Irishman named the town, an Irishman named the creek, an Irishman started the Company, an Irishman opened the first saloon. Mom's perky history teacher, Sister Genevieve, said the Irish told friend and kin, "Don't stop in the United States, go straight to Butte!" Most were from Cork; however, there were Irish from throughout Ireland in Butte. A small contingent hailed from County Antrim in the north, and one of those was my grandfather Peter Thompson.

CHAPTER FIFTEEN

THOMPSON IS NOT an Irish name. It does not begin with O' meaning "grandson of" or Mc meaning "son of." It is a Germanic patronymic name, so either Peter Thompson's people came to Ireland from somewhere else, or they adopted an English equivalent when the English tried to force the Irish to drop their Irish names.

They, rather he, came from somewhere else—Scotland.

The first of our Thompsons to set foot in Ireland was naturally Adam. He was Peter's great, great, great, I don't know how many greats, grandfather and was a commissioned officer in the British army. He settled in County Waterford where he met and married Bridget Waters.

A descendant of Adam and Bridget named James Thompson married Grace McCauley. She was a teacher. They lived in County Antrim in the north. Grace was a Catholic but she agreed to become Protestant when she married James. They had four sons: Peter, James, and John, and Sam. Grace raised the children Protestant until her son John was sixteen. That was the year the bell called her home—she wanted to be Catholic again. Grace returned to her faith and her sons became Catholics also.

Grace's son John married Martha Kinny and here the Thompson blood mingled with "the best blood in Ireland" according to my Irish aunts, though they never said why.

Martha and John had a son, and then another, and then another, and then another, Sam, born October 12, 1869. After four sons, Martha was pining for a daughter. She grew Sam's reddish brown hair long and kept it in curls so at least he'd look like a girl. Lucky for Sam, a girl came along, he could be a boy.

We momentarily leave the Thompsons and turn to the other vigorous branch of this bountiful tree—the Gribbens. The Gribbens grew out of Irish sod, as it were, going back to some year BC when the Celts arrived and they, liking the lay of the land, stayed there, to again paraphrase my grandfather. They weren't called Gribbens then. Fixed surnames wouldn't come along for centuries, not until the reign of Brian Boru around 1002 AD. Gribben is a derivation of O'Gribin, a name originating in Donegal in the northwest of Ireland.

Hundreds of years after the Celts came and stayed we find a forlorn Denis Gribben. His beloved wife, Bridget, has just died and her tiny baby too. A carpenter by trade, Denis built a simple, wooden coffin and laid both mother and babe in this their last earthly shelter. Now poor Denis faced the daunting task of raising his six children alone. He managed well enough until what history calls the Famine came along, more aptly called the Great Hunger. The worst of it was in the west. Men drove carts piled high with food through the countryside and would give a hungry person something to eat if he'd swear allegiance to the Church of England. Denis Gribben would not. He heard about work in the coal mines near Ayr, Scotland. He thought he could do better there so he sold all, took his family, and went. His youngest child, also named Denis, was a little boy when Denis took him to work at the coal mine. Young Denis's job was to open and close the mine door. The miners grew fond of the lad and taught him to read though not to write.

When young Denis grew up, he returned to Ireland and there he met Jane McDonald. Denis and Jane fell in love and decided to marry. When the appointed day arrived, all assembled in the McDonald family home and waited. A knock came in the dead of night. Jane's father opened the door and greeted a man he called Mister in the open and Father once inside. The nuptials accomplished, Denis and Jane Gribben lived with Jane's parents in their small stone house in the townland called Magheralane near Randalstown, County Antrim, in the north of Ireland.

This stone house was a freehold, meaning it was rent free, which was no small blessing. The acre of land on which it sat was in the midst of verdant, perpetually damp farmland and had been Jane's mother's dowry. Jane's father was a stonemason and he built the house. He also built the stone school house at the top of the lane.

Denis and Jane Gribben's first child was born June 24, 1868. They named her Rosetta for Jane's grandmother and called her Rose. Rose was followed by nine siblings: John, named for Jane's father; Denis; Jane who died when she was only two; Mary; Bridget, named for Denis's mother; Elizabeth Ann, called Annie; Margaret Jane, called Maggie; Sarah, who died when she was not yet one; and Hugh, who lived three days.

The McDonald/Gribben house at Magheralane, near Randalstown,
County Antrim, Ireland. Though public records say Jane's maiden name
was McDonnell, the family says the name is McDonald.

Like his father, Denis Gribben was a carpenter and he worked diligently at it, and when his sons grew up, they would become carpenters
too. Denis gave Jane everything he earned and she managed the family
finances. When the grocery money ran short, Jane bought what she needed
on credit until Denis's next pay day. He never knew of the shortfall. The
children never did without.

The tiny farm on which Denis and Jane raised their family was within
the six counties that would one day be called Northern Ireland. Looking
back on those years growing up on that farm, their daughter Bridget said,
"Our politics and religion kept us strictly in the minority groups, but we did
not suffer any discrimination from the majority who were our good neighbors and loyal friends. It is true my father could not vote because his shortage of acreage made him ineligible, but he and my brothers held the good
jobs which were given them by members of the majority groups. The people
who operated the firm where my father and brothers worked were bred and
born Scotch, and in addition, they had an extra supply of sagacity. If a man
were intelligent, industrious, and capable, they hired him regardless of his
politics or religion. They were the businessmen who invested their money
in factories, bleach greens, and railroads." She went on to say they were not
the types who kept prejudice alive.

Their most memorable neighbor in Magheralane was an imposing, fierce woman they called Big Rosie. Big Rosie and her husband had lived in America, earned and saved a lot of money, and returned to Ireland. Big Rosie would storm into the house from time to time and tell Jane what for. "You're spoiling those children," she would scold Jane. "They shouldn't be playin' and carryin' on as they do. They should be scourin' the tin cups with the ashes and you must slap them until they do!"

I never heard how Jane responded other than to ignore Big Rosie. Jane wasn't one to slap her children.

Even without Big Rosie's chides, the children did help their parents. They cut grass for hay and tilled potatoes on their tiny farm and did household chores. They dug up chunks of peat moss to burn in the hearth. Bridget in particular relished being in the moss, for it meant she was also in the purple heather.

One day when Jane went to town, the girls decided it was an opportune time to put on a show. The only place they had been was to church, so their show would be Mass. One was promptly draped with a blanket as the priest. They stacked benches, the choir mounted, and the show began. The priest sang, the choir sang, all with tremendous enthusiasm, until the door burst open and Big Rosie flew in. "You shouldn't be up there singin' and carryin' on when yur pur mother is away to town. You should be scourin' the tin cups with the ashes!"

Jane sent her children to school as soon as she thought the child could manage the lessons. The teachers at this small country school weren't particular about checking a child's age since they needed the students. Bridget was so small when she started that her brother Denis had to carry her there on his back. Once the children mastered the three R's, they quit school to work for pay to help support the family.

Rose, being the eldest, was the first to leave school to work for pay. As a little girl, she most likely did babysitting and housework. When grown, she became housekeeper for the Webbs. They owned the linen mill in nearby Hollybrook House. The Webb's mill finished the fabric which involved stretching the linen on vast bleach greens. Linen was to that part of Ireland what copper was to Butte, so working in the home of one of the linen lords was a good job for a young woman like Rose, and she must have made a favorable impression on the Webbs, for in time they would hire three of her sisters: Bridget as the governess, Annie as the maid, and Mary to assist the French cook.

It wasn't long before the tall, ruddy, blue-eyed handyman at the Webbs caught Rose's eye. "Leave the gate open," she'd say, "Sam will be by," and Sam Thompson would be by, and seeing the gate open, went in to see the lovely housekeeper, Rose. He chased her until she caught him.

Rose's father was already sick with consumption, so Sam had to deal with Jane to ask for Rose's hand. The first time he asked, Jane sent him away. He came back and asked again. She sent him away. I don't know how many times he came back and she sent him away. Eventually she gave in and consented to the marriage. Sam Thompson did not have a trade as did her husband, her sons, her father, her brothers, and her uncles. They were carpenters and stonemasons. They and their forebears had built bridges all over the north of Ireland and Scotland and they built St. Macanisius Church. Without a trade, it would be very difficult for Sam to support a wife and children. There were plenty of suitable young men with trades whom Rose could marry, but Rose Gribben had made her choice and time had not dissuaded her.

Sam and Rose were married on January 3, 1892. Sam was twenty-two and Rose was twenty-three. Rose's brother John was Sam's best man. They moved to Glasgow and Sam worked on the docks, though not for long. The dock workers went on strike. They then returned to County Antrim and lived with the Gribbens.

That December, their first child was born. They named her Ellen Elizabeth and called her Nellie. Their second child was also a girl. They named her Mary Teresa and called her Mary.

A son arrived on September 4, 1895.

"He's to be called Denis Malachy," said Rose as Jane picked up the tiny three-day-old baby and left for the church with Sam. Sam's brother Peter and Rose's sister Bridget went with them. They were to be the baby's godparents.

Once at the church, when the priest asked the child's name, before Sam could speak, Jane blurted out, "Peter Joseph." She had decided that Sam would like to have his first son named for his favorite brother.

When they returned home after the baptism, Jane handed the tiny baby to Rose and said flatly, "There's Peter Joseph for you."

A few days later, Jane went to town to register Peter's birth. When asked to sign the registry, she marked her X.

Rose and Sam's next child was also a boy.

"He's to be called Denis Malachy," said Rose as she sent him out with Sam and Jane. This time the name survived the child's baptism.

Sam and Rose and the four children then moved in with Sam's uncle Paddy Kinny, a bachelor living in Farlough, a townland about a mile up the road from Magheralane. Paddy was known in family lore for helping defend the pope against Garibaldi. After they moved, little Peter missed his grannie Gribben terribly. One day he wandered off to find her. Somebody spotted him toddling along the road and scooped him up and took him back to his uncle Paddy's.

John Francis was born next, and then Margaret Jane, called Jenny, bringing the count to six children. The year was 1900. The change in century would bring a change of doors and floors.

Sam heard about a job on the trams in Belfast. It paid more money, so he decided to move his family from the country to the city. They rented a small two-bedroom house on Carmoney Street in North Belfast. The rent was two shillings a week. Soon a house with three bedrooms became available around the corner for another six pence. They were country people and wanted to keep their country ways which meant having the boys and girls in separate bedrooms, so they moved into the three bedroom house at 17 Carntall Street, off the New Lodge Road. The neighbors thought Rose was out of her mind—another six pence a week just so the boys and girls could sleep in separate rooms.

The Thompson children observed a curious sight that first Sunday. A crowd of children marched up the street, growing larger and larger as it passed every house, until en masse they entered St. Patrick's Church. Thereafter, the Thompson children would join the procession every Sunday.

Soon after Sam uprooted his family for this job on the trams, he decided he didn't like it. He found it boring. He quit after one week and went to work heaving coal on the docks.

Jane Gribben traveled to Belfast to visit Rose whenever she was able. With her, she brought bolts and bolts of fabric to make clothes for the children. Though Jane did not want her daughter to marry Sam Thompson, once they were married she made the best of it and was always kind to Sam, so kind that he used to remark to the children, "If there's somebody tried to please me, you can call your grannie Gribben." The naming of his first son was a prime example.

Their next child was another boy, Patrick Joseph, and then came twins, Martha and Jimmy.

They now had nine children, the eldest of whom was only eleven. Needless to say, Rose had her hands full. In the family portrait taken that year, she is holding the two babies in her arms, surrounded by the rest of her children. It must have been a rare interlude of sitting still, there always being a diaper to change, a baby to feed, a toddler to keep out of danger or mischief. (I wonder why Sam isn't in the picture.) To lighten her load, if only a wee bit, Rose sent baby Martha to live with her mother and sisters in Magherlane. (Her father had already passed away.) Rose also sent ten-year-old Mary to live with the Gribbens, but that didn't last long. Mary grew weepy and homesick, so Jane sent her back home.

Peter began school at St. Malachy's shortly after they moved to Belfast. Rose dressed the irrepressible lad in the requisite long socks; short, grey pants; white shirt and collar; green, black, and white tie; and navy blue blazer. His elder sisters, Nellie and Mary, attended school in the same

The Thompson family, 1904. Back row left to right: Mary, Rose, Nellie. Middle row: Pat, twins—Martha and Jimmy, Jenny. Front row: John, Peter, Denis.

building but were taught separately, the boys by the Christian Brothers and the girls by nuns. Tuition was a penny a week.

The years passed for Peter as for any boy like him. The Christian Brothers saw that he learned and behaved in school. Summer was filled with play, and year round Peter and his siblings helped their mother.

Peter was a precocious child. He read every minute he could. When he wasn't reading, he was talking. When he wasn't reading or talking, he was fighting. Someone somewhere taught him to box, and he got plenty of practice on the rough streets of North Belfast. Whether it was simply his nature, or due to sectarian and labor troubles, or both, whatever the reason, this boy, Peter Thompson, grew to have a monstrous chip on his shoulder.

He had a permanent shadow in his brother Denis. Denis adored his older brother. He wanted to be just like him. Anything Peter would do, Denis would do. If Peter boxed, Denis boxed, if Peter danced, Denis danced, and when Peter swam in icy Belfast Lough, Denis dove right in after him. "A couple of daredevils they were," their youngest sister told me shaking her head and laughing.

An abrupt change came to Peter's life when he turned twelve. He would now go to school one day and work in the Whitehouse Spinning Mill the next. They called this "going to the half time." The weeks he worked two days, he earned two shillings. The weeks he worked three days, he earned two shillings ten pence. He gave his wages to his mother.

Peter's first job at the linen mill was to sort the flax fibers that would be made into thread or yarn. Nellie and Mary worked there as doffers. They replaced the full spindles of thread with empty spindles and while doing so were constantly pelted with water as the wet flax spun. They worked in their bare feet, standing in puddles of water, and were filthy and soaked by the time they walked home through gloomy, chilly, damp Belfast after their nine-hour work day. They hated it. It was made worse by children who didn't have to work in the mill and taunted them as they walked home.

The headmaster of Peter's school came to the house as soon as he learned that Peter was going to the half time. He pleaded with Rose to let Peter stay in school full time. Peter is a clever, intelligent boy, he said, with an education he can make something of himself. There must be a way to keep him in school full time.

No, there wasn't, Rose replied flatly. She would not make an exception for Peter no matter how much the brother pleaded, and plead he did, but to no avail. Like his sisters, Peter would work in the mill. They needed the money. Peter already knew how to read and write and do arithmetic. He would get all the education he needed with half-time school. Rose believed if you were a poor boy from Belfast, you'd grow up to be a poor man from Belfast, and you should be happy with that, and there was no cause to strive for more. Whatever your lot in life, that was good enough.

Rose's brother John did not share her view. He wanted to better his situation and he knew how.

He went to America.

CHAPTER SIXTEEN

HOWEVER, HE DIDN'T go straight to Butte. He stopped in Anaconda first.

On September 3, 1901, thirty-one-year old John Gribben arrived at the Port of New York aboard the *Oceanic*. He then took the train across the country to Anaconda, Montana, where the Company was building its huge new reduction works—the biggest in the world. John's carpentry skills were much in demand, and he went right to work. When his work there was done, he moved to Butte.

He rented a flat on East Broadway with the County Antrim family who had made the voyage with him. They were Hugh and Rose Ann and their mother Catherine. As the story goes, Rose Ann was about to wed some ne'er do well in Ireland, so the family spirited her out of the country to spare her this unhappy fate. Hugh and Rose Ann's brother John had preceded them to Montana. He lived with them too, as did another Antrim man, Alfred Mulholland. On hearing their Antrim brogue, the neighbors assumed the newcomers were Scottish.

When John Gribben arrived, Butte, Montana, was the most Irish town in America, though some in Anaconda dispute that claim. In addition to financial opportunity, John found Butte to be a lively bastion of Irish nationalism. He joined the Robert Emmet Literary Association and quickly became an active and influential member. The namesake of the organization had led the 1803 rebellion and was executed for it by the British, making him a martyr for the Irish cause. The Emmets were the Butte wing of Clan na Gael, an Irish-American organization that recognized the Supreme Council of the Irish Republican Brotherhood as the legitimate government of Ireland. Their existence was known, but their proceedings were secret. Meeting minutes identified members by number, never by name. The Emmets also played an anti-defamation role. They knew the best way to smash the harmful stereotype of the Irish being a bunch of feckless drunks was to prove it wrong. A man had to be literate and well-behaved to join. Public drunkenness and fighting were grounds for expulsion. The Emmets provided sick and death benefits for their members and raised money for their IRB brethren. They took advantage of the U.S. government program to sell excess rifles to rifle clubs. The Emmets' rifle club was Company A of the Irish Volunteers of America. They drilled and practiced preparing for the day they would return to the old sod to fight for an independent Irish republic.

Through his membership in the Emmets and the Ancient Order of Hibernians, John became acquainted with the men who did the hiring in Butte. Members gave preference to other Irishmen, especially to affiliated Irishmen. John's connections would prove beneficial not only to himself but to the other family members who would follow him to Butte.

Despite an enduring affection for his native country and an active interest in her political future, John Gribben had no intention of going back to Ireland, not to live. He had come here to stay, and he wasted no time in becoming an American citizen. He made his declaration of intention only a few months after he arrived.

John Gribben was a big man both in physical stature and character. He was serious and collected, thrifty and generous, and always dignified. In Ireland, he rose to foreman of the carpentry shop and made good wages. After his father died, John became head of the Gribben household, and according to his sister Bridget, if she or her sisters wanted anything, John made sure they had it. He treated them with the deference befitting the ladies they were. John did his best to help his married sister, Rose, and her family also. In fact, John and his siblings—all of them—gave part of their wages to Rose to help support Sam and her and the children.

In 1906, John planned a trip to Ireland to visit his mother, but for some reason connected to the San Francisco earthquake, he didn't go and decided to wait until the next year. Unfortunately, Jane Gribben passed away before he could get there, so instead of John going to Ireland, he sent tickets for his four maiden sisters, Mary, Bridget, Annie, and Maggie, to come to Butte. And they did not sail in steerage, John brought them second class, aboard the *Cedric*.

Their ship landed at New York on June 15, 1907. While passing through Ellis Island, each woman was asked for all sorts of information—her age, her occupation, her hair color, her eye color, her height, her destination, and so

John Gribben around age 33.
ELITE STUDIOS, BUTTE, MONTANA

on. Who paid for her ticket? Her brother John. Did she have fifty dollars with her? Yes. Between the four of them, that was two hundred dollars, what a miner made in two months if he worked seven days a week. I wonder if John sent that too and the money for the train tickets which cost at least forty-eight dollars each, depending on the class of service.

Once off Ellis Island and in Manhattan, the Gribben sisters went directly to Grand Central Station and boarded the train west. They rode and rode and rode, watching the great expanse of land pass by outside their window. Will it never end? More plains, now mountains, they must have thought they were going back of beyond, which in a way they were, but it didn't matter. Wherever it was, there would be Johnny.

Their train rolled into Butte with a snow storm—in mid June. They stepped off the train onto the cold, snowy platform and threw themselves at Johnny. It had been six years since they had seen him and they nearly devoured their brother in joyous greetings. Once they settled down, John led his sisters through the depot and outside to the waiting cab. They piled in, and the cab jolted up the steep hill as the wheels got stuck and unstuck in the snow, eventually making its way to their home on East Broadway. The house had two flats. John and his sisters lived in one, the rest of the Antrim contingent lived in the other.

Butte had to be a bit startling for the Gribben sisters, possibly even a shock. These women had lived all their lives in the quiet pastoral Irish countryside, and now here they were, settling into a rapidly growing industrial city well on its way to one hundred thousand people, and Butte was anything but pastoral and as rambunctious as any Wild West legend ever painted. The hustle and bustle and noise of city life must have been unsettling for them. Yet, Johnny had told them to come and so they had, trusting he knew best. When recollecting the adjustment, Bridget said, "At last, we breathed free air."

Less than two weeks after they arrived, Bridget was working. "Getting jobs had never been one of our problems," she said. "We just did not know how to worry about that." She even enjoyed the luxury of leaving a job that didn't suit her for one that did. First she did housekeeping and cooking; then she worked at Gamer's making candy. In no time, she and her sisters were settled into jobs they liked and would keep: Bridget as a clerk in the china department at Hennessy's, Annie as a seamstress at Madame Paumie's Parisian Dye House, and Maggie as a maid at the Thornton Hotel. I never learned what Mary did. My guess is she attended

Uptown Butte around the time John Gribben arrived. Broadway looking west.

© WORLD MUSEUM OF MINING #3949

Uptown Butte, circa 1900.

BUTTE-SILVER BOW PUBLIC ARCHIVES, PH018256

The Gribben's flat on East Broadway.

to the cooking, cleaning, and washing for the five of them, which was itself a full-time job, and it was work Mary enjoyed and was good at.

Every Sunday after Mass and breakfast, the four sisters walked into the prairie until they saw green. They found abundant green only a street-car ride up the hill at the Columbia Gardens. It was a beautiful amusement park filled with expansive lawns, immense ornamental flower gardens, a carousel of elaborately carved, brightly painted wooden horses, a fright-filled roller coaster, an arcade, and a huge dance pavilion with a dampened wooden floor. It was as beautiful a park as graced any great city and a comely refuge from a gritty mining town.

About a year after the Gribben women arrived, the town saw some unusual excitement. A man named Dawson had built an airplane and word was he was going to fly it. Hundreds flocked to see him do it. He knew how to build it, he knew how to fly it, he just didn't know how to land it. Every time he tried, the plane crashed and broke. He repaired it, went up again, tried to land, the plane crashed and broke. This went on until he ran out of money to fix it.

One of John Gribben's chief interests
at that time was seeing those four sisters of
his married off. When they arrived in Butte
in 1907, Mary was thirty years old, Bridget
was twenty-nine, Annie was twenty-six,
and Maggie was twenty-three. Four years
later, the weddings began in quick succession. Mary's was first. She married Walter
Breen, an immigrant from County Wexford
who was a widower in his fifties with grown
children. Walter was nearly twenty years
older than Mary and was foreman at the
copper tanks (the precipitator plant), which
was a very good job. John Gribben knew
Walter through the Emmets and Hibernians, so it is likely he introduced them,
though if with a match in mind, I don't
know. Walter was a firebrand when it came
to Irish politics and some of his ideas were pretty radical.

*Mary and Walter Breen
with daughter Molly and
baby Walter, 1916.*

The other three Gribben sisters wed the men next door. Maggie married Alfred Mulholland, Bridget married the neighbor John, and Annie
married John's brother Hugh.

In the middle of all his sisters getting married, John Gribben wed Annie
McStravick. John was forty-two and Annie was twenty-three.

Sadly, the two women who married men nearly twenty years their
senior were to leave their husbands widowers with young children. Mary
Gribben Breen died after only twelve years of marriage. Annie McStravick
Gribben died fifteen years after she and John wed.

Annie and Hugh were never blessed with children. After her sister and
sister-in-law passed away, Annie shuttled between the two widowers' homes
to help look after their children.

Maggie and Alfred had no children either. Maggie had been in poor
health since she fell into the hearth as a child. She died five years after
they married. She was only thirty-two. After she died, Alfred sent her
wedding ring to Rose. Rose had pawned hers.

I've gotten ahead of myself. We return to days when Mary and Maggie and
Annie McStravick are still very much alive and not everyone is married yet.

CHAPTER SEVENTEEN

NO DOUBT, Rose Thompson missed her siblings in America, but she had her own burgeoning brood to keep her occupied. Food on the table, her family around her, Rose was content. She reared her children on good food and good stories. She didn't want any of them to marry, none whatsoever. "You're like a mother hen," Sam said, "you want to keep them all under your wings." It was true. Her second youngest daughter would say to her one day, "Ma, you're a strange woman. While some women want to hold on to their sons, you wanted to hold on to your daughters as well."

After the twins, Sam and Rose had another daughter. They named her Bridget. Two weeks before her second birthday, little Bridget died. Rose was never the same. She was hospitalized for some time. Peter summed up the situation by saying, "My mother went to bed and never got up."

The next spring Rose, now forty years old, delivered another baby girl whom they named Rose Ann and called Rosie. The year after that, yet another daughter arrived, their twelfth child. They named her Bridget and they called her Bridget, until she started school.

On her first day, while calling roll the teacher exclaimed, "Bridget Thompson! What are you doing named for a Swedish saint? Don't you want to be Irish?!"

"*Yes*, Miss McNeill," replied Bridget.

"Then you will be *Brigid*!"

From then on she was Brigid.

THE NOISE LEVEL and general air of excitement instantly escalated whenever Peter, Denis, and John burst into the house after a long day working at the mill. This day Peter bounded up the stairs to the boys' room,

Peter Thompson, age fifteen, Belfast, 1910.

grabbed his book, and dropped onto the bed. He could already hear a row starting downstairs between Denis and Nellie. For many years now, the austere, aloof Rose had assumed the role of Irish dowager, the lady of the manor without the manor, so to speak, and Nellie ran the household. Nellie started baking the bread for the family when she was seven and had been running the household since she was twelve. She was now eighteen and still worked in the mill, now as a weaver. Denis resisted sibling authority with vigor. Nellie was just his sister even if his mother did put her in charge, even if she was the eldest. Who was she to boss him. John, the next younger than Denis, was thoroughly devoted to Nellie his entire life. For John, whatever Nellie said went, no questions. As for Peter, I don't think Nellie dared tell him what to do. Though small in stature, Peter's physical strength was evident and became even more apparent as he grew into manhood. From his confident demeanor and the deference his siblings paid to him, everyone knew when Peter Thompson entered the room and knew that he was the eldest son of the Thompson clan. Nellie wasn't about to boss Peter.

Denis was going on again about Darwin to shock his mother and to bait Nellie. "*You* were once a whelk," he proclaimed boldly, then he laughed and laughed until he nearly fell off his chair. Nellie wasn't amused at being told she used to be a sea snail and shot back with a fiery rebuttal. Denis then leapt from chair to chair pretending to be a monkey. This got the rest of the children going, not about Darwin, but laughing at Denis or going on about whatever they normally quarreled. When the noise level reached fever pitch, Rose bellowed in her husky voice, "Me and these two wee 'uns are goin' to room by ourselves and every hearn shall hang by its own tail!" That was her way of saying, I've had it, we're away, you're on your own.

Peter was too absorbed in his book to care about the ruckus downstairs. His sister Mary had sent it to him. He couldn't wait to finish it. He quickly devoured every book he got. The last time he saw Mary they were on the pier and their father was pinning a sign to her coat that said TO BUTTE. She was teary, she didn't want to go. Now she was with their aunts and uncle in Butte. He hadn't written yet to thank her for the book. His aunt Bridget had sent him a book too. He hadn't written to thank her either, so he put the book aside and wrote to Mary.

17 Carntall Street
Belfast
6-8-1911 [Aug 6]

To Miss Mary Thompson

Dear Mary

Just a few lines at present to let you know that we are all well. I am still working at Whitehouse and I guess I am just tired of it. I am laying your share since you left she paid me for a while but took it of me again. All the boys in the Mill are asking for you. Corny and John Egan are always asking for you. P. O'Rork says he was going to go out to you but as you would not send him a Post Card he says he will not go. I was very pleased with your books, papers and caps also the P.I. you sent me. Tell my Aunt B. that I was greatly pleased with the Book and watch she sent me and that I will write to her soon. As you know I was never keen on writing letters so that is why I delayed expressing my gratitude so long. John has never heard the end of that last P.I. you sent him and he says if he were near you there would be bloodshed. My mother says she was dreaming about writing letters all week but I guess if she keeps on like this you will never get this you never get it. My mother is going to get the five boys photos took on the one card soon. I guess I would be real pleased if you would send me a few more books. Nellie has got her photo took and is going to send you one. I am glad you were pleased with my last one. Joe Slavin has give Nellie no peace since she went there about Paddy McLarnon. Nellie says she wished you were here to see John in the meal hour. At present I don't see any loophole of escape out of the spinning room for me. There was a great lot of fighting in the town at the 12th of July. J. McAnespie and Christine was asking for you. Give my best to my aunts and uncle and the relations I have not seen.

I Remain Dear Mary
Your Brother
Peter Thompson

Peter did escape the spinning room, and then he escaped all together. He went to Butte.

Chapter Eighteen

Actually his mother told him to go, so he went. It was February of 1914 and Peter was eighteen years old. He and his chum Jack Thompson (no relation) sailed from Belfast to Liverpool where they boarded the *Cedric* bound for New York. His aunt Bridget had sent him money for the crossing and for the train ticket. He also had fifty dollars in his pocket, presumably at least some of that, if not all, came from Aunt B too, which undoubtedly was pooled from all the family members in Butte.

Aunt B was delighted to welcome her favorite nephew and godson to Butte. Peter had a charming, bewitching presence about him. He had a way of drawing others to him without trying, and I think he was probably

East side of Butte, shows only a few of the mines.
© WORLD MUSEUM OF MINING #2764F

oblivious to the fact that he had this trait, gift, power—I'm not sure what to call it. His striking good looks with that perfectly groomed dark brown hair and those piercing blue eyes, plus that unflinching confidence, were certainly part of it, though not all.

Peter moved into the flat on East Broadway with Aunt B and her husband and the rest of the Gribbens. By now, the Antrim contingent had swelled to eleven adults in two not very large flats. Soon they would all move. Uncle John Gribben purchased a two-story house with four flats on Montana Street. He and his wife, Annie, her brother, Paddy, and Peter moved into one of those flats; Uncle John rented out the other three. Aunt B and her husband took over operation of a boarding house on East Quartz Street; Aunt Annie Gribben and Peter's sister Mary lived with them and helped with the cooking and cleaning.

Uncle John and his sisters had high hopes for their newly arrived nephew. Peter was quick, intelligent, interested in everything. Though also impetuous and pugnacious, Peter was blessed with abundant God-given talents and boundless energy. In America, those talents needn't be stifled, and the potential fruits of that energy were limitless. The mines paid well, when the mines were going. Metal demand rode a roller coaster

Pennsylvania Mine.
© WORLD MUSEUM OF MINING #3963

and, with it, the mines and the livelihood of the miners. This bright lad needn't live that way. With more education he could get a steady job. Uncle John decided to send Peter to the Butte Business College, as he had Mary. Until then, Peter could work in the mines.

"The hill" as it was called, the mountainside on which Butte sat, was dotted with gallows frames, each towering majestically over a mine shaft. If you've never seen one in person, it's a black iron skeletal structure 125 feet high. One side is perpendicular, the other is slanted, together forming a right triangle with the ground. There is a platform near the top on which workmen stood to service the great wheel over which the cable ran. Metal cages hung underneath, each the size of a small closet, big enough to hold about six men uncomfortably. The cages were lowered into the mine to depths of over two thousand feet by a cable that ran from the cage, up the gallows frame, over the wheel, to the engine house. Seen from a distance, the gallows frame forms a graceful profile, the long sloping side evoking the train of a lady's evening gown, but it does look like a gallows, so the name fits. It is ominous, as dangerous as the mines were, to be lowered into them by something that looked like an instrument of death. It's no wonder those miners played hard, drank hard, and then filled the churches on Sunday (if not they, their families). They knew every day in the mine could be their last.

I remember Grandma telling me a story about a man she knew in Butte. I don't remember his name nor the context. I asked, "Whatever became of him?"

"Oh, he was killed in the mines," she said matter-of-factly.

"How *aw*ful!" I said with a shocked expression.

She smiled and with a dismissive wave said, "Dear, men were *always* being killed in the mines." She wasn't making light of the situation. It was just the way life was, no reason to be shocked. She had no choice other than to learn to live with it, and so she had. Yet it seemed to make her sad to think of it, not doleful, simply resigned to an unhappy fact, as she had learned to be about so many unhappy facts.

A couple weeks after he arrived in Butte, Peter went to the Company employment office to apply for his rustling card. A rustling card was a work permit issued by the mining company. This was relatively new. Before rustling cards, the union enjoyed sole control over who worked in the mines. Now the Company had a say in the matter. The rustling card was a bone of contention for some miners because they thought the Company could blacklist them and deny the card, thereby denying work. A couple years earlier, the Company fired five hundred Finnish miners. Some believed they were fired because they were Socialists. It was shortly after the great Finn firing that the Company started requiring the rustling card.

Peter easily obtained his card. On his first day of work in the mines, he joined the large group of men standing near the gallows frame at the West Colusa. There was still plenty of snow on the ground making the bright sunlight even brighter. No matter how cold it was in Butte, the sun came out and stayed out, quite a contrast from gray, gloomy Belfast. Peter stood there, no doubt squinting and shivering in the bitter cold, shifting from foot to foot, waiting his turn to go down into the mine. Now he was at the front of the line. He stepped into the cage with several other men, somebody shut the door, and the hoist operator lowered them deep underground. Though it was freezing above ground, it could be as hot as one hundred degrees Fahrenheit underground, depending on the mine, and the deeper you went, the hotter it got. The rock was even hotter. By the end of his shift, Peter's clothes were soaked through with sweat. He left the mine the same way he entered, in the cage. By the time he reached the top, he was enveloped in a cloud of steam as the cold air hit him and the other men in the cage. Years earlier on really cold days, and that could mean thirty below, and that was the high for the day, the miners' wet clothes froze as they walked home. The mining companies

The cages at the Belmont.
© WORLD MUSEUM OF MINING #1025

Miners at work underground.
BUTTE-SILVER BOW PUBLIC ARCHIVES #PH018246

lost a lot of miners on the way home, so to speak, to pneumonia, so they built rooms where the men could wash and change into dry clothes after their shift. The "dry" was already in place when Peter started to work in the mines.

Each miner used to take three candles into the mine. While working in areas not lit by electricity, he would affix a lit candle to his cap or to the rock so he could see what he was doing. Around this time, candles were being replaced by carbide lamps. In either case, men went about their work underground wearing an open flame on their heads or carrying one.

Though Peter worked in the mines, he never actually mined. He worked as a nipper fetching tools for the miners, and he drove the motor which transported cars full of ore on the mine's underground railroad. Mules were still used for this purpose, but motors were replacing them.

In addition to getting his rustling card, Peter joined the Butte Miners' Union. Butte was then a closed shop. Peter soon discovered that dues weren't all he owed the union. He was also obligated to pay strike relief for Michigan miners who had been on strike for months. The assessment grew and grew and grew until it was up to a day's pay a month. Disgruntled Butte miners complained that the assessment was becoming excessive. Rumors percolated that the striking miners weren't getting the money. This intensified dissatisfaction among some miners over what they perceived to be the union boss's soft reaction to the rustling card requirement, and there were those who grumbled that the union wasn't doing much to improve working conditions.

The mining companies and the union had lived together amicably for decades, since the Butte Workingmen's Union came to be in 1878, but by the spring of 1914, a rift had cut wide and deep between appeasers and hard liners vis a vis the union's posture toward the Company. There were rumblings that the Company actually controlled the union.

Then in early June, a charismatic man named Muckie McDonald convinced a group of miners at the Speculator, which was not a Company mine, to break from the union. Over four hundred men followed his lead in refusing to show their union cards at the start of their shift. In accordance with union rules, the mining company refused to let them work. Word of the renegades buzzed across town to the Miners' Union Hall. The next day a committee of six armed union men descended on the Speculator. Sheriff Driscoll caught wind of the situation, and he and his deputies were able to stave off trouble. It wasn't to last.

The next day was June 13, Miners' Union Day, one of Butte's biggest holidays. The annual fete began with a parade followed by family picnics and mucking and drilling competitions at the Columbia Gardens. All were tests of skill and speed. The drilling contest was scary to watch. One man held a long drill bit against a block of granite while his partner swung a huge sledge hammer back over his shoulder and bang, struck the bit. The man turned the bit a quarter turn, his partner struck it again, turned it, struck it, turned it, struck it. They did this at what seemed to be lightning speed. The audience watched in breathless anticipation, should he with the hammer miss the drill bit.

The family arranged to meet and attend the festivities together. Peter and Uncle John may have been in the parade. They would join the rest of the family later and go up to the Columbia Gardens together. Aunt B and Aunt Annie and the rest of the family found a good vantage point from which to view the parade and waited. The faint music steadily grew louder and louder, now the marchers were coming into view. A fine parade it

Columbia Gardens, Single Jack Drilling Contest.

© WORLD MUSEUM OF MINING #150

John Gribben, right front, flanked by his niece Molly Breen and his sister Annie on the steps of the Silver-Bow County Courthouse. Note the dress shirts, vests and ties under the spruce clean overalls.

was. Bands played festive airs and marched in splendid uniforms: first the
ACM Band, then the Montana State Band. The Irish Volunteers fife and
drum corp marched proudly behind the Irish flag. Officials rode horseback. Every working group imaginable paraded ensemble: clerks, teachers, butchers, teamsters, construction laborers. Just about everybody in
Butte was organized, earning the town the well-deserved nickname "the
Gibraltar of unionism." According to one prominent lawyer and politi-
cian of the time, even the chimney sweeps were organized when there
were only two of them.

The parade continued cheerily and normally until, all of the sudden,
rocks flew from the crowd at one of the men on horseback—Bert Riley,
the president of the Butte Miners' Union. His horse balked. More rocks
flew. Riley spurred his horse and rode toward the grandstand. Men ran
into the street and tried to block his way. A voice yelled, "Lynch him!"
He drew his revolver.

The crowd scattered and a mob formed. The parade devolved into a
riot. Men pulled another man from his horse and beat him. The horse was
spooked and stampeded. Rioters pushed a policeman through a storefront plate glass window. An all out brawl between the police and the
mob spread destruction and mayhem throughout uptown Butte.

Then the mob ran up North Main Street to the Miners' Union Hall.
They stormed the building and started throwing everything they could
pry loose out the windows: papers, typewriters, chairs, desks, doors, carpets, even the piano. Mayor Duncan was away, so the acting mayor, Frank
Curran, hurried to the scene. He stood in a second floor window and
urged the mob to stop. They threw him out the window. Fortunately, he
landed on a pile of carpets and suffered only broken bones. Police Chief
Murphy closed the saloons. When there was nothing left to throw out the
windows, the mob had nowhere to go but home.

Meanwhile, Union President Bert Riley and the rest of the union hier-
archy took sanctuary in Sheriff Driscoll's office. The sheriff deputized as
many men as he could; he issued each a Colt revolver and bullets. They
stood guard at the courthouse, rumored to be next on the mob's destruction agenda.

When relative calm returned, Riley slipped out of town. Rumors surfaced later that he was in Helena. He was advised not to return to Butte.
Within days, Muckie McDonald had organized a new union.

Onlookers watch the mob trashing the Miners' Union Hall, June 1914.
© WORLD MUSEUM OF MINING #419

News of the Butte mutiny and insurgent union quickly reached Charles Moyer in Denver. He was president of the Western Federation of Miners. The Butte Miners' Union was its Local No. 1 and by far the federation's largest and, until now, most peaceful local. In fact, Butte union men had been instrumental in starting the federation. Moyer caught the next train to Butte.

Once in Butte, Moyer held a meeting of union loyalists in the battered shell of the Miners' Union Hall. A hundred or so miners attended the meeting while hundreds, some reports said thousands, milled around outside in the street. The view from the upstairs windows was a veritable sea of caps. Those outside shouted a jeer now and then at the men inside. Otherwise, the crowd was restrained. Two accounts said Muckie McDonald circulated cards to men in the crowd that read: *"Fellow workers, in the name of your new union, keep peace and go home."* Considering his later actions, this is puzzling. Whether implored to leave or not, the crowd stayed.

While the meeting was underway inside and the crowd was milling around in the street outside, a miner named Bruneau entered or was about to enter the Miners' Union Hall. Accounts differ as to exactly where he was, but what is undisputed is—he was shot. In an instant, guns appeared in the windows and Moyer's men were firing on the crowd in the street. The crowd scattered. Amidst the whir of lead, one bullet hit a railroad clerk who just happened to be walking home from the post office across the street. He was shot dead.

The sight of the dead man, shot through the head, lying in his own blood, further provoked those outside. They fired back at the hall. In the midst of this gun battle, a drunk stumbled out of a saloon and strode up the street through the hail of bullets, impervious and unscathed. Soon the mob noticed that no one was shooting back. Several men ran to the rear of the building. It was empty. Moyer and the others had escaped.

The mob then ran to the nearby West Stewart Mine. At gunpoint, they forced the shift boss to hand over the dynamite. They came back and set their charges. Getting rid of the union wasn't enough, the symbol of the union had to go too. Pistol shots rang out, the fuse was lit, and BOOM! The two-story brick building shook but remained standing. The windows in the Federal Building across the street shattered. Women in the crowd of on-lookers fainted. Flying debris hit several men. Merchants hastily nailed plywood over their store windows as if preparing for a hurricane. More dynamite, more pistol shots, the fuse lit, BOOM, and the building shook but still stood. They tried again and again and again, all night. Finally, in the morning, another blast, and the Miners' Union Hall started to crumble, and then topple. Part still stood, but most was a pile of rubble.

There was another story in the Butte papers a few days later; however, for the local citizenry it paled in comparison to the goings on in their own town. Some Serbian nationalist named Gavrilo Princip shot and killed the Austrian archduke and his wife while they toured Sarajevo. It was the third headline on the front page of the *Butte Daily Post* that June 29, 1914, right after "President Wilson will not send Troops to Montana Now" and "Villa abandons his campaign on Mexican Capital." The assassination created some excitement in Butte's sizeable Serbian community, but that's all. Butte herself was a powder keg and she had her own battle ground to clean up. The war discussed in newspapers around the state was "the war in Butte."

Reverberations continued throughout the summer. Muckie McDonald and his cohort rounded up miners who refused to join the insurgent union. They put them on trial in kangaroo court and then sent them out of town, warning them never to return. And when they weren't deporting miners,

The blown-up Miners' Union Hall, June 1914.
© WORLD MUSEUM OF MINING #1736

McDonald and his men stood on street corners urging direct action. Invade stores and warehouses, they said, take what you need.

A deranged Finnish miner attacked Mayor Duncan with a knife. Duncan drew his revolver and shot him in self defense. The man died two days later. Duncan was so upset about it that in the middle of his city coming unhinged he decided to take some time off.

Once he was back at work, business leaders and Sheriff Driscoll urged the mayor to call in the National Guard. He refused. He didn't think it was necessary. The businessmen then turned to Governor Stewart. This is an insurrection, they said. Mayor Duncan assured the governor that he had everything under control. Sheriff Driscoll said not so, the situation was too dire for his deputies to handle, troops were needed.

Then in August, trouble makers blew up the rustling card office at the Parrot Mine. Then dynamite exploded at the water company reservoir.

Governor Stewart had had enough. He declared martial law, called in the National Guard, and made prison warden Frank Conly provost marshal of Butte.

Worst of all, the saloons were closed for a long time.

Martial law in Butte, September 1914, first day, Lieutenant Anderson,
Company H of the Montana National Guard, at Main and Granite.
BUTTE-SILVER BOW PUBLIC ARCHIVES PH018398

Martial law in Butte, 1914. Company D, Montana National Guard.
BUTTE-SILVER BOW PUBLIC ARCHIVES PH018398

Fingers pointed in every direction. The Socialists blamed the Butte
Miners' Union—they accused the union bosses of graft and of being
stooges for the Company. Muckie McDonald blamed Moyer and his
Western Federation of Miners. Moyer blamed the IWW. He insisted that
the Industrial Workers of the World, called the IWW or Wobblies, had

sent hundreds of operatives to Butte to cause trouble as part of a conspiracy to take over the federation. He and the Butte press believed that Muckie McDonald's new union was a front for the IWW; two of McDonald's lieutenants were Wobblies. Moyer had attended the first meeting of the IWW but found them too radical for his tastes. The Wobblies exhorted class struggle. They saw government as a pawn of the capitalists and they sought to overthrow capitalism and seize the means of production through revolution. Their weapons were sabotage and direct action. As wild and woolly as Butte was, it had been spared the bloody strikes that plagued so many mining towns. The Wobblies looked on those years of harmony between the Butte Miners' Union and the mining companies with contempt. Of the destroyed Miners' Union Hall, one Wobbly operative said, "'Here Lies the Remains of 36 Years of Peace and Prosperity'; the working men of Butte should be ashamed of those thirty-six years." The IWW wanted only one union to exist—theirs.

Some believed that leaders in the mob who started the trouble at the Miners' Union Day parade were detectives hired by the Company to infiltrate the union. A Department of Justice report written years later said, "The union faction whose doings provoked the trouble in 1914 had long been company controlled."

Some maintained that those setting the charges that blew up the Miners' Union Hall could not have been miners because it would not have taken men trained to use explosives so long to blow up a building. One account said it took eleven tries, another said twenty-six. However, the term "miner" was often used rather loosely to indicate anyone who worked in the mines. That included nippers, muckers, motormen. Not all mine workers used explosives.

So who were the culprits? Were they Wobblies seeking power through chaos? Were they detectives planted by Company bosses fearing a Wobbly takeover of the union? Those theories are not mutually exclusive. Were they simply disgruntled miners who turned into a mob? People do crazy things in a mob they would never do alone or with one or two others. The answer remains a mystery. Perhaps a piece of the truth is to be found in all those assignments of blame.

Whoever the cause and whatever their motives, it spelled the end of the Butte Miners' Union. The Company entered the breach and declared open shop. It refused to recognize any union, old or new. And it was the end of Butte's first Socialist mayor. Mayor Duncan was impeached

Hugh and Annie with niece Rosemary.

and removed from office, as was Sheriff Driscoll. Muckie McDonald was sentenced to prison on kidnaping charges for deporting miners.

There were lively discussions and strong opinions expressed among the Gribbens and their in-laws and friends regarding these events. Annie Gribben's husband-to-be, Hugh, was a city alderman. He had been appalled by the firing of those five hundred Finnish miners two years earlier. He called it a "cowardly and dastardly" act. A shoemaker by trade, Hugh was elected on the Socialist ticket in 1911, the same election in which Lewis Duncan was elected mayor, but by this time Hugh had left the Socialist Party. Not long after he was elected, Montana's Socialist Party became embroiled in its own troubles. It had to do with fears that Wobblies were infiltrating the Party and consternation over Mayor Duncan ignoring Central Committee recommendations for city appointments. The Central Committee had chosen a Wobbly as street commissioner, and Duncan refused to appoint him. Further acrimony developed over a part of the Butte charter that was allegedly pushed through by Wobblies. Hugh didn't come out in support of the Wobblies, nor against the disputed parts of the charter, nor in favor of the Wobbly as street commissioner. It seems Hugh's position was, I'm not for this Wobbly fellow, but party rules say we must follow the Central Committee's dictates on city appointments, and rules are rules. Shortly after that, Hugh parted company with the Socialists but remained an alderman.

As for Hugh leaving the party, he was a Catholic, and a priest told him he couldn't receive communion as long as he was a Socialist. The Church objected to socialism for a number of reasons, one of which was the Socialists exhorted class struggle, which promotes envy, a capital sin. Whether Hugh left the Socialist Party because of the Church's opposition, or because of these problems within the party, or a combination thereof, I don't know. And whether he still called himself a Socialist or later rejoined the party, I don't know either. I do know that Aunt Annie was in quite a huff about his not being able to receive communion.

AFTER TWO MONTHS, Governor Stewart lifted martial law, and Frank Conly returned to his post as warden at the state prison in Deer Lodge. Shortly thereafter, he released Arthur Hughes and paroled Sarah.

Peter Thompson had before witnessed violence and turmoil in response to dispirited labor. During the coal heavers lockout in Belfast, shortly after he started to work in the mill, the British government sent the army to patrol the streets while no fewer than nine British warships anchored at the mouth of Belfast Lough. (One wonders what sort of naval juggernaut the British government was expecting from the coal heavers.) The police mutinied in support of the strikers.

In Belfast, the trouble started because the workers wanted a union and the employers didn't. In Butte, the mob attacked the union, a union recognized by the mining companies. This was indeed a puzzlement.

Despite the turmoil, Peter worked steadily in the mines until August when half the mines shut down due to the interruption in world commerce caused by the outbreak of war in Europe. Even though many of the mines stayed down for the rest of the year, Peter resumed work at the West Colusa in September and there he remained for the next eighteen months. That first year he earned $3.50 per day. The next year his pay went up, averaging $3.83 per day; the year after that it was $4.40, and it kept going up. A bed for the night and three meals in a boarding house cost a dollar a day, leaving a single man with three quarters of his pay as disposable income–no taxes were withheld back then, so what he earned he took home. A thrifty man could easily save money to buy a house when he married, or to bring another family member to this country, and Peter did save, and he dutifully sent money to his mother to pay the passage for the next Thompson to immigrate.

Like his uncle John, Peter also wasted no time in becoming an American citizen. Only a few months after he arrived, he made his declaration of intention to do just that. As did all immigrants petitioning for citizenship at that time, Peter had to renounce allegiance to any foreign sovereign, in his case George V, and he had to swear that he was not an anarchist nor a polygamist nor did he believe in the practice of polygamy.

By mid 1915, Peter had sent enough money to his mother to pay the passage for the next Thompson to immigrate, and that July, Peter's father sailed to New York aboard the *Arabic*. It must have been with much trepidation and many prayers that Rose and the children bid Sam goodbye. Just two months earlier, a German U-boat had torpedoed the British luxury liner *Lusitania* off the coast of Ireland. More than one thousand passengers and crew perished, including 128 Americans. It's amazing to think of now, the passengers knew the U-boats were out there, the threat was real and present. The German government publically warned that any ship flying the flag of Germany's enemies was marked for destruction. Intrepid travelers read the warnings and got on those ships anyway. As for Sam's ship, the *Arabic* arrived safely in New York and returned safely to Liverpool, but that would be the last time she did. On her next voyage to New York, she was sunk, without warning, by a German U-boat.

Sam Thompson had no trouble finding work in Butte thanks to his in-laws' in-laws. His wife's sister's husband Walter Breen arranged a job for him at the copper tanks where Walter was the foreman. All Sam had to say about it was, "I don't know what I'm gettin' the wages for."

Peter had occasion to go to the depot the month before his father arrived. As usual, it teemed with people coming and going. Amid the throng, his eyes fell on a young girl, a beautiful dark-haired girl. He was transfixed. She was the most beautiful girl he had ever seen. There was something about her, something enchanting. He watched her make her way through the crowd. She had a child on each hand. They must be her little brother and sister. A tall man led them through the crowd. He must be their father.

Peter watched the girl until she left, and he knew, whoever she was, she was the one.

CHAPTER NINETEEN

AILA WAS AT the age when girls seem to grow up overnight. The child Arthur had left behind two years ago was long gone. In her place was a beautiful young girl wearing maturity born out of the responsibility she had assumed for her younger brother and sister. She was overjoyed to be with him again.

The three children followed their father out of the depot into the busy street. There were people everywhere, the town pulsed with energy. They turned and crossed the street and started walking up the hill along the bustling sidewalk, dodging people as they went, hearing strange languages spoken, smelling unfamiliar foods cooking, perhaps hearing the tinkling of a tinny piano as they passed a saloon and the clang, clang of a streetcar climbing up the hill. It must have seemed exciting to thirteen-year-old Aila and a bit intimidating to the younger two. It was all so strange and so fast paced compared to their lives until then. Father, what is that? Aila surely asked, looking up at a huge gallows frame, and as soon as he explained, What is that? pointing at something else. She had an insatiable curiosity and this new town burst with things to be curious about.

Butte looked a little like Wilkes-Barre in that the houses were close together and close to the street in compact neighborhoods. Where part of Wilkes-Barre was on a hill, this town seemed to be on the side of a mountain, which it was.

They walked several blocks up the hill to the corner of Ohio and Platinum on the edge of the Cabbage Patch. Written histories say this shanty town in the center of Butte was full of thieves, drunks, drug addicts, and retired prostitutes and was ruled by a king and queen not necessarily related to each other. Some of the ramshackle cottages were built out of dismantled pine grocery crates. A person would claim to own a shack and thereby demand rent from the occupants who wouldn't pay and later claimed to be the rightful owners since, after all, they hadn't paid rent. When a person died, the neighbors often stripped the house for kindling wood. And as in Mrs. Wiggs's burg of the same name, every winter Butte's Cabbage Patch residents could rightly say, "The thermometer's done fell up to zero!"

While riding around town one day, I remember Grandma pointing at a green house and saying, "*That's* where I lived in the Cabbage Patch." It stuck in my mind—a green house, the Cabbage Patch. "I *liked* the Cabbage Patch," she said resolutely with a characteristic nod for emphasis. "You couldn't find nicer people." Mom asked whether the house had a floor. No, she said, it had a dirt floor. I suppose when released from prison, one can't be too fussy about where one takes up housekeeping.

Arthur led the children into the house. As soon as she stepped inside, Aila whiffed the familiar scent of goose grease. Two men were sitting at the table playing cards. She recognized their language though she didn't understand it. It was Welsh. Her parents often spoke Welsh to each other and always did when they quarreled.

Hector and Bill were there too. Dear, dear Hector—Aila embraced her big brother, she was thrilled to see him.

The men playing cards stayed for dinner. Aila kept expecting them to leave. They were still there in the morning. Sarah explained that they were boarders and they lived with them. Aila came to understand that the men paid her mother for this privilege.

Sarah put Aila right to work. She cooked and cleaned and made beds for the boarders and did their laundry. Butte was a twenty-four hour town. Those working day shift ate breakfast at the boarding house, and Sarah and Aila sent them to work with full lunch buckets. After their shift, the boarders stopped at a saloon for a boilermaker (a shot and a beer), and then walked home to the boarding house, ate dinner, and then many went out again.

Besides her chores at home, Sarah insisted that Aila get a job. Aila, you must get a job to bring me money, Sarah demanded. Seeing that her mother's wrath had not dissipated in the two years they'd been apart, and knowing that if prompt action was not taken to satisfy her decree a sharp whack across the head would ensue, Aila quickly found a job. The Methodist minister and his wife hired her to be their maid. Their house was across town up the hill, almost in Walkerville. She worked there every day. The worst of it was emptying the pots. She hated that part of the job.

Sarah, Patsy, Aila Hughes, circa 1915.

Aila began high school that fall. After making breakfast and preparing the lunch buckets for the boarders, she walked across town to Butte High School. That first semester she took English, algebra, geography, and Latin, and sang in the chorus. After school, she worked at the minister's home. Her pay went to her mother.

By the end of the year, Arthur had achieved enough of a financial footing to move his family out of the Cabbage Patch. They moved further up the hill to a house on Gaylord Street. I suspect it had a floor.

Aila had been reunited with her family for several months now and was settled into her new life of high school, chores, job, and making new friends, and the old life of dodging the wrath of her mother and Bill. Even though she was away from the house much of the day between school and her job, Aila still looked after Archie and Patsy and protected them as best she could. She tried to shield them from beatings by their mother and Bill. Hector protected Aila; he was forever kind and good to her. Bill was as mean and cruel as ever. The two boys were as different as night and day and so were Aila's feelings toward them. For Bill, she felt antipathy. She'd just as soon never mention him nor give him a thought, for all such thoughts were very unpleasant. She always spoke of Hector with warmth, her love and fondness for him visible in her eyes. She used to say his name with the cadence of a ditty to which she tapped the beat with her hand. It began as an adagio with two half notes for Hector Osiris, then sped to an allegro with two eighth notes for Dun-donald followed by two quarter notes, a quick crescendo and brief rubato on Warren and slight decrescendo on Hughes. H e c t o r - O s i r i s - Dun-donald *Warren* Hughes. Hector came right after her father in her youthful pantheon of heros.

One cold winter morning in February of 1916, Aila made breakfast as usual and when all sat down to eat, Hector was missing.

Where is Hector? she asked.

He's sick, Bill retorted.

After breakfast, Aila went to Hector's room. He was all doubled up in bed. What's wrong, Hector? she asked.

It hurts, he groaned.

Aila, go to school, said Sarah brusquely as she walked past her and sat down on Hector's bed and started to administer one of her home cures. Aila, go on, Sarah repeated.

Hector looked awfully sick. Aila worried about him all day. When she returned home, she went to his room. He looked terrible. Later he was even worse. He was nauseous and feverish. She remembered her bout with typhoid fever. She pleaded with her mother to send for a doctor. Sarah scoffed at the idea. That time you were sick on the ranch the doctor couldn't do anything. What good are doctors.

Sarah concocted another herbal cure and gave it to Hector. It didn't help. With every hour, Hector became sicker and sicker. He could barely move and was in excruciating pain.

Please, Mother, Aila pleaded, we must get a doctor for Hector!

Sarah was sure it would pass and kept administering her home cures. Hector only got worse. The pain intensified. He began to vomit. Finally, somebody sent for a doctor. The doctor came and examined Hector and

Hector Hughes.

rushed him to St. James Hospital for emergency surgery, but by the time the doctor opened him, it was too late. His appendix had already ruptured and peritonitis had set in. There was nothing anyone could do for him.

Poor Hector languished for three days in the hospital. During that time, he was baptized by a Catholic priest. Finally, his beleaguered body gave out, and he died. He was only sixteen years old. Since he died a Catholic, he was buried in blessed ground at Holy Cross Cemetery. That must have been Arthur's doing. Sarah was enraged.

Aila was heartbroken. She returned to school downcast, mourning the loss of her dear, dear brother. One of the teachers who had been "very fond of Hector" to use Aila's words, found her walking between classes and called her aside. "It's your fault your brother died," the teacher scolded. "You should have done more to convince your mother to call the doctor! You could have saved him! It's your fault he died!"

CHAPTER TWENTY

BACK IN BUTTE's early days when the camp was bursting her seams into a town, respectable women—wives and mothers—joined their husbands in the rip-roaring settlement and brought their civilizing influence with them. Like an incorrigible stallion, kicking and rearing to throw a stubborn rider, Butte tried to shake off all efforts to civilize her. Nevertheless, the women were undaunted. Churches and schools were the first order. As the town grew into a city, the professions proliferated. By 1890, the citizenry included a cadre of women whose husbands' incomes afforded them domestic help, which in turn afforded them leisure time. To fill that time, and to cultivate their intellects and improve the social and moral conditions of the camp cum city, such women formed literary clubs. The first was the Homer Club.

The Homer Club met every other Monday afternoon. Membership was limited to twenty-five and later expanded to thirty women. They lived on the West Side. A candidate for membership had to be recommended by a member and approved by the entire club. The women began by studying the *Iliad* and the *Odyssey*. As the years went by, they studied other works of literature, the arts, and current affairs. Birthday luncheons were festive occasions with gourmet meals and elaborate table decor. The club endures to this day.

In the fall of 1916, recent discussion topics had included *The Picture of Dorian Grey* by Oscar Wilde, Jack London's works, and the solar system. When the appointed date and time came for the November meeting, all arrived promptly at the Cole residence. The Coles lived well into the West Side, about as far from the Cabbage Patch as a house could be and still be in Butte. Mr. Cole worked in the general office of the Company. Once all were seated, Mrs. Cole's daughter entertained the ladies with a piano recital of Franz Listz's "Liebestraum." Then the chair called on Mrs. Downey to present the day's topic. She spoke for twenty minutes, without notes, about trade relations with South America. After she finished, an orderly discussion commenced. A woman could speak only when recognized by the chair and was addressed as Mrs. _____, first names were not used. They discussed the kinds of goods desirable for trade with South America, appropriate tariffs, long term credits, the importance of the merchant marine to facilitate the economic shipment of goods, and the success Germany had enjoyed in trading with South America before the war.

The discussion closed and the meeting turned to parliamentary matters. One of the members moved that Miss Aila Mae Hughes be named the Homer Club's delegate to the Vocational Congress to be held at the Montana State College in Bozeman later that month, and that the club pay all her expenses. The motion was seconded, voted, and passed.

How did these well-to-do women from the rarefied world of West Side literary clubs even know of the existence of this girl from an East Side boarding house with two ex-convicts for parents. There was literally a line between those two worlds—it was called Montana Street—figuratively, there was a gulf.

There was something special about Aila, something intangible. She had it all her life. I loved her dearly, she was my grandmother and always special to me, but it is often difficult to see the remarkable in the familiar. Mom saw it. She knew her mother was remarkable and said so. I can't fully describe that special something Grandma exuded but I saw it in the way others reacted to her, even strangers. The combination of her beauty, her subtle, delightful charm, and the depth of her innate goodness made many want to help her, and others to take advantage of her. Yet, my question remains, how did the Homer Club members even know about her? She was a bright, disciplined student, that alone made her a fitting candidate for the Vocational Congress. My guess is a teacher at Butte High recommended her. It's one of many things I didn't know about to ask.

How she convinced her mother to spare her those few days is another mystery. She did go. That cold, snowy November morning Aila boarded the train for Bozeman. The *Butte Miner* devoted an ample portion of the Sunday society page to the event with large pictures of the four girls from Butte. Aila must have been thrilled to see her picture so prominently displayed in the newspaper, and on the *society* page, and it was such a sweet picture.

The purpose of the Vocational Congress was to introduce high school girls to various fields of employ and encourage them to make plans for higher education and for a particular vocation. There was a vocational congress for boys in February.

Jeannette Rankin had just been elected to Congress by the people of Montana. She was the first and at that time the only woman in Congress. Montana women had the vote, though not all women in the country did. Her election surely added further excitement as girls from throughout the state gathered in Bozeman. Miss Rankin had visited the orphanage while Aila was there.

Now in Bozeman, Aila settled into her room and then went to the tea for the delegates. After the tea, she and the other girls listened to welcoming

Butte Miner, November 26, 1916.

speeches and then attended the formal reception. For the next three days, she listened to speakers on a variety of vocations including medicine, science, journalism, music, agriculture, writing, education, business, home economics, and law enforcement. (Of particular interest to me was the title of the speech on writing: "Genius or Hard Work." Indeed.) In between speakers, the girls were entertained by piano recitals, the Men's Glee Club, the Treble Clef Club, and soloists, and each day the delegates sang in assembly. The girls also had the opportunity to meet with the college department heads.

This was in 1916 and Aila was fifteen years old. By the time the congress ended, her head must have been spinning with the world of opportunities presented to her. This experience surely helped foster her desire for a world beyond the boarding house, beyond her violent household, and possibly cemented her desire and resolve to become a teacher.

Now the three stimulating days were over and she was on the train back to Butte, back to school, back to emptying pots at the minister's home, and back to steering clear of her mother when she was drunk.

Soon after she returned home, Aila decided to look for a new job and she found one. Gamer's hired her to wash dishes. It was a restaurant and

Montana Street looking north from Mercury.
© WORLD MUSEUM OF MINING #2050

confectionary in uptown Butte. The manager fired her after only a few days. Apparently she didn't wash the dishes well enough to suit him. "It was the nicest thing he could have done for me," she said because then she applied for another job, this one at Symon's. It was a large department store. The manager who interviewed her probably read her seriousness and self-possession as maturity and confidence. He thought she was older than she was and she didn't enlighten him. She was also very pretty.

We'll put her in the millinery department, he concluded.

She completed her training and began her first day waiting on customers. The manager pointed out a particular hat and remarked that it had been in the store for quite some time. It was very expensive. A woman walked in. Aila politely greeted her. The woman said she didn't have a specific hat in mind. Aila asked if she would you like to try this one, and gestured toward the heretofore un-sellable hat. The woman agreed to try it on. She sat down in front of the mirror. Aila carefully placed the hat on the woman's head. She adjusted it and arranged the accouterments to be most becoming. The woman bought it.

Aila was one of those women who is born with a sense of style. She knew what hat and how worn would most flatter her customer. She often modeled the hats for them. When a woman saw Aila wear the hat, she naturally wanted it because she wanted to look like Aila. Aila knew the perfect angle at which a hat should sit on her head to accentuate her natural beauty. She could wear a napkin and make it look stylish. She was in her element.

She planned to go to college and needed to save money to pay her way. She already had a scholarship. Mom and I talked with her many times about the scholarship but neither of us ever asked how she won it. I assumed she won it in high school, but it turns out she was in the eighth grade at the orphanage. Somebody at the orphanage, Mrs. Shobe or her teacher, must have encouraged her to enter this contest. It was the sewing competition in the "County Championship in Industrial Contest." I think she made a corset cover. She won and went on to compete at the state fair in Helena. She won there, too. Her prize was a scholarship for one year at the Montana State College in Bozeman.

Still, that was for only one year. She would need more money to finish college. She tried to save a little from what she gave her mother, but it was a discouraging endeavor. Sarah regularly rifled through Aila's room and took all the money she could find. The more money Sarah could get, the more whiskey she could buy. Not satisfied that she was getting everything Aila earned, Sarah learned on which day Aila was paid and marched to the store manager's office.

"My daughter Aila Hughes works here and I want her pay," Sarah demanded with open outstretched hand.

"You didn't do the work, you don't get the money," replied the store manager indignantly.

At this Sarah raised quite a fuss, peppered with fiery expletives no doubt. No matter, the store manager would not yield. Sarah finally gave up and stormed out.

When Aila arrived at work, the manager told her about Sarah's visit and her demand and his response.

"Go ahead and give it to her," Aila said forlornly, "she'll get it anyway."

Which she did, and it went to drink.

Aila did her boarding house chores in the morning before school and worked at Symon's after school. In addition, she joined the debate team and became an officer of the Homesteaders of Butte. She and her mother were as different as day and night but one trait they shared was they were both social urbanites and very happy to be living in a metropolis. Though Aila was intensely private, she relished being out and about with people and hearing all the news. Her favorite diversion was dancing, and there were lots of opportunities to go dancing in those days. Sometimes the girls went as a group, as did the boys, sometimes they went as couples. Even if a girl went with a date, she danced with other boys. Young men and women generally didn't date exclusively until marriage was imminent.

One day a man called Frenchy invited Aila to a dance. He was one of their boarders. Arthur forbade her from going to dances. He didn't approve, she was too young, and if a young man wanted to call on his daughter, the young

Aila, Patsy, and kids from the neighborhood.

man better speak to him first. But that was an Old World custom and he had a New World daughter. He was night shift that week so he wouldn't know.

Aila told Frenchy that she'd love to go to the dance. He asked if she could bring a friend for his friend Peter Thompson. She said she would.

The four arrived at the Winter Garden on Montana Street and jumped right into the festivities. Aila didn't want to miss one dance. She'd dance all night if the orchestra and her partners could keep up with her.

Early in the evening, Peter asked if he could dance with Aila and the two couples switched partners. Aila smiled demurely at the handsome Irishman as he took her by the hand and led her to the dance floor. They danced the schottische or polka or whatever the next dance was.

Frenchy never got his date back.

PART THREE

The Story of a Soldier

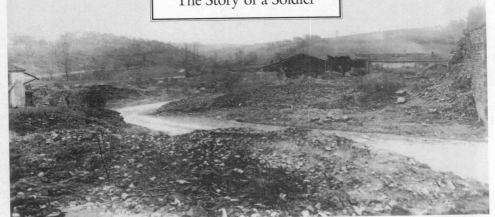

CHAPTER TWENTY-ONE

"JUST WHEN PEOPLE [were] saying, 'Peace and security . . . ,'" history quietly closed the chapter called the nineteenth century with its Age of Romanticism and Victorian Era. And ruin did fall on them. Jumping to the second decade, the new century came in like a thief in the night.

In only six years beginning in 1914, the Great War killed ten million soldiers, sailors, and airmen; millions more suffered its deprivations—hunger, homelessness, disease, and the crippling and disfiguring scourges of industrial warfare; kingdoms toppled; empires were crushed; Marxist revolutionaries seized one of the world's largest nations and set the stage to spread their errors; a deadly influenza struck with a vengeance, taking fifty million lives in a matter of months—the most lethal malady to strike mankind for its swiftness and magnitude; men in their twilight years declared peace and drew new borders for lands they'd never seen, the consequences of which they would never know; and as the turbulent second decade closed, the bleak pall of economic depression enveloped the globe.

It was as if the world was a dollhouse full of carefully placed figurines. A group of naughty children came along, picked it up, turned it upside down, shook it violently jolting all from their places, and then grabbed as many figurines as they could and threw them in the fire. I wonder whether it seemed as climactic at the time as it does now. To those touched by it all—the war, the influenza pandemic, the social upheaval—and they were legion, did it seem the Four Horsemen were galloping across the landscape of history, or did the burdens and changes simply creep up on them, even though in quick succession, and they in the midst unable to see the totality.

Those first twenty years included Grandma's first nineteen. They've been called a lost generation, those who came of age during the First World War. I think it was the historians who lost them, so overshadowed are they by the Civil and Second World War eras, though not for want of captivating, poignant drama. The pace and breadth of change they witnessed was staggering.

It was a time of hot or cold. People spoke clearly, often eloquently, said what they meant and meant what they said, exhibiting a clarity of thought that today is so often wanting. Before fighting a war, the government declared it. When you fought a war, it ended. Someone won, someone lost, and then you went home.

In Butte, the years of mine ownership by colorful, self-made men were over. Marcus Daly had sat along side the nipper and the mucker at Sunday Mass and knew them by name. He never forgot his humble roots. Historian Michael Malone wrote, "so long as he (Daly) ran the Anaconda, it treated its employees better than most corporations of the time." William Andrews Clark built the splendid amusement park called the Columbia Gardens for the citizens of Butte. Though ruthless toward each other, Clark and Daly had not been so toward their men. They believed a contented workforce was a productive workforce. By the time the war began, Daly had passed away and Clark had sold most of his Butte properties.

Now the lion's share of Butte mining was consolidated into the Anaconda Copper Mining Company. The name innocently chosen for a mine and then a company had become a self-fulfilling prophecy. The Anaconda devoured its competitors, owned several Montana newspapers, and wrapped itself around the state's electricity producers forming a single power company presided over by the Anaconda's president. Mining and its attendant industries provided most of the jobs in the state and within mining, the mighty Anaconda stood as king of the hill. The largest mining company in the world controlled Montana's industry, electricity, and press, and held the state in a firm grip. The Company wielded such power that back in 1903 during those legal battles with its nemesis Fritz Heinze, after Heinze's judge ruled against it in a dubious suit, Company bosses shut down the mines, holding the livelihoods of fifteen thousand men hostage as it were, and ordered the governor to call a special session of the legislature to pass the Fair Trials Law which would allow a litigant to dismiss a judge. The politicians did as told.

The miners were squeezed in the middle while Heinze and the Company and his other foes skirmished in court. Mines under litigation were closed by court injunction. Thousands of miners were thrown out of work. Butte was a one-shop town, so everybody's fortune rose and fell with the decisions of the Company and, at that time, the courts. When the miners weren't working, they weren't spending in the shops and saloons, and as a result, the entire local economy suffered. This battle between titans with the working man paying the price, coupled with the Company's hold on state government, gave fodder to that new force gaining ground—the Socialists. Butte, Montana, was one of the largest cities in the country in which the Socialists rose to power. In 1912, twenty-eight percent of Butte voters chose the Socialist candidate, Eugene Debs, for president.

Dismayed by corrupt businessmen, corrupt politicians, and corrupt judges, Montana's suffragettes looked to another solution—woman. With her high moral standards, woman must raise society from the abyss. She must take a more active role. She must vote. While the suffragettes successfully expanded the voting rights of Montana women to full suffrage, the Women's Christian Temperance Union with others succeeded in voting the state dry. Though soundly defeated in Butte, Prohibition passed by wide margins in the rest of the state. It did little to reduce drinking, and much to increase law breaking.

Enforcement in Butte wasn't enthusiastic. A Butte jury would find its collective mind in a welter when asked to rule on a bootlegger named O'Leary who shot at four Prohibition agents while being sentenced in federal court. He pled insanity. He said he was despondent over a lost love, and was in financial straits, and had a split personality. A Helena jury convicted him.

The few bootleggers who did get locked up in Butte turned the jail into a men's club. They sent out for groceries, kept a keg of whiskey tapped, played that scandalous jazz music on the phonograph, and walked around the jail in bedroom slippers—all for a look-the-other-way fee of a dollar a day, the price of a room in a boarding house. Butte, Montana, held the distinction of leading the nation in illicit alcohol consumption per capita. It was rumored that during one month alone, more than a hundred carloads of grapes rolled into the depot.

Before Prohibition, any woman seen in a saloon, other than to retrieve an errant husband, was a prostitute or believed to be. Respectable women did not frequent saloons. In 1907, this convention was codified, the purpose being to protect the respectability of young women. A woman could drink and buy liquor, but she had to buy it from the back door or send her husband or son for it. Under Prohibition, men and women drank together in speakeasies. There was no law to keep women out since the places were illegal anyway. So much for protecting young women.

Besides handing organized crime a lucrative business, Prohibition opened the door to normally law abiding citizens ignoring a law they saw as silly. The dominos of its unintended consequences are still falling.

And in Europe, war started over some "foolish thing in the Balkans" just as Bismark had predicted.

The heir to the Austrian throne, Archduke Franz Ferdinand, and his wife, Sophie, were riding in an open car through the busy streets of Sarajevo that day in late June of 1914. The couple had traveled to Bosnia to review military exercises in this recently acquired land; Austria-Hungary had annexed Bosnia and Herzegovina only six years earlier. Before the trip, the archduke had been warned of hostile sentiments in Bosnia against Austrian officials. His security force sent an advance team. They didn't speak the language and they didn't know the city. Six armed assassins easily entered Sarajevo and stood ready along the archduke's route. The first assassin heaved a bomb at his car. One account said it bounced off; another said it landed on the floor and the archduke promptly tossed it out. It exploded under the car behind him. A disgusted archduke was reported to have chided the burgomaster: "We have come here to pay you a visit and bombs have been thrown at us. This is altogether an amazing indignity!" He scuttled his speech making and ordered his driver to take him to the hospital so he could visit his injured aide under whose car the bomb had exploded. En route, the archduke's driver missed a turn and stopped. Nineteen-year-old Gavrilo Principe stepped forward and fired twice. One bullet killed the archduke, the other killed his wife.

Yet another royal assassination. The archduke and his wife were the fourth and fifth members of the Austrian royal family to be assassinated during the reign of Emperor Franz Joseph.

The assassins were captured and interrogated. As it turned out, they were members of the Black Hand, a secret society of Serbian nationalists that sought to unite all Serbs, including those in Bosnia and Croatia, then part of Austria-Hungary. Members took a death oath. Though they were Austrian citizens, they said their orders came from Colonel Dimitrijevic, the head of Serbian military intelligence, and their weapons came from the Serbian army arsenal.

Naturally, the Austrians were enraged to learn all this. Even before the assassination, Austrian officials firmly believed that Serbia had designs on those parts of the Empire inhabited by Slavic peoples. Only the year before, Serbia had expanded her borders in the Balkan Wars. The Austrians were never able to prove whether Dimitrijevic was acting as a rogue on his own or on behalf of a rogue government, but it didn't matter. Proof or no proof, they were convinced that the assassins were agents of Serbia and this was only one of many intrigues intent on wresting Bosnia from the Empire. And behind Serbia, Austria saw Russia.

The time had come to punish and subdue the troublesome beast to the south.

They moved quickly. The Austrian foreign minister, Count Berchtold, dispatched his emissary to the Austrian ambassador in Berlin. Upon receipt of Berchtold's instructions, the ambassador conferred with Kaiser Wilhelm. The kaiser assured the ambassador that Russia was unprepared for war and that Austria could count on Germany. The kaiser then left on vacation. A pity the diplomats and cabinet ministers didn't do the same.

Emboldened by the kaiser's support and his assurance that Russia would not get involved, on Thursday, July 23, 1914, less than one month after the assassination, the Austro-Hungarian Empire laid a series of demands at the tiny Kingdom of Serbia's door and gave Serbia only forty-eight hours to respond. At such a moment, any nation, especially a small one at odds with a large one, would want to consult with her allies. That was difficult. Britain's ambassador to Serbia was sick, Russia's had just died, France's had had a nervous breakdown, and France's president and foreign minister were at sea. Knowing all this, the Serbian prime minister left town for his country home. During the night he thought better of it and returned to Belgrade to deal with the note.

Serbia ended up agreeing to all the demands save for those which encroached on her sovereignty, specifically the demand that Austria-Hungary supervise Serbia's investigation of Serb complicity in the assassination. The moment she sent her reply, Serbia mobilized her army and began to evacuate Belgrade.

With the world's greatest military might—the Imperial German Army—firmly in her court, a confident Austria-Hungary denounced Serbia's reply and declared war on Tuesday and bombarded Belgrade on Wednesday.

Russia immediately mobilized her army in support of Serbia. Germany insisted that Russia cease mobilization and gave her twelve hours to do so. This Russia did not do. On Saturday, Germany declared war on Russia.

Russia was in an alliance with France and Britain—from the east and from the west, Germany faced a potential foe. Now that Russia had shown her card, Germany turned to France and demanded that she convey her intentions. France provided no assurance that she would stay out of a Russo-German war. On Monday, Germany declared war on France.

Germany's plan was to knock France out of the war quickly and then deal with Russia. Germany intended to invade France through Belgium and so informed the tiny nation. Belgium was a neutral country and that neutrality was guaranteed by treaty, a treaty to which Prussia, now part of Germany, was a signatory. Belgium held fast to her neutrality and replied to Germany with a resounding no—she refused to allow invaders to cross her border.

One looming question remained—what would Britain do? She threw down the gauntlet. Britain would not stand by while Germany invaded a neutral, and diplomatic chivalry aside, she could not allow her great naval rival to seize the Channel Ports.

Germany invaded Belgium anyway. A match was lit to the dry kindling that was Europe, *and they all fall down.*

Britain declared war on Germany; Austria-Hungary declared war on Russia and Montenegro; France and Britain declared war on Austria; Montenegro declared war on Austria and Germany.

The pope died.

Austria declared war on Belgium and Japan; France and Britain declared war on Turkey; Portugal declared war on Germany; Bulgaria declared war on Serbia; Greece declared war on Bulgaria and Germany; Turkey declared war on Romania; Italy declared war on Austria, Germany, Turkey, and Bulgaria, and on and on and on. The European combatants brought their colonial powers into the fray, and America would enter the slaughter at what turned out to be the eleventh hour. Before it was over, twenty-eight nations were at war, each for her own reasons, and Austria's Balkan crisis was lost in the dust. It was madness.

A Montana paper opined that if the crowned heads of Europe make it to heaven they'll manage to start a fight between the angels.

If only those crowned heads and their cabinet ministers could sit down to a civilized game of bridge to settle their disputes. Whoever wins this hand gets Alsace-Lorraine, whoever wins the next gets the Dardanelles. It's a shame it doesn't work that way. The stakes are too high.

Germany had no quarrel with Belgium. She was simply in the path the German war plan dictated the army take to avoid France's well-fortified frontier. Belgium's King Albert emerges as a heroic personage in this woeful drama. A reluctant monarch, as so many are who rule not by choice but out of duty because of the family they were born into, he read a plethora of subjects from coal mining to military matters to religion and lived an impeccable life. This monarch, who did not want war, actually led his troops. Under his command, the Belgian army valiantly fought the German invaders but was completely overwhelmed. They were nineteenth-century warriors fighting a twentieth-century war machine into which all the wonders of the industrial age had been poured. A seemingly endless stream of German infantrymen swept through the tiny country—a neutral, an innocent, with absolutely no connection to Austria's spat with Serbia. Even in their heavily fortified stone forts, the Belgians were helpless against the mighty German siege guns.

News of atrocities spread: against individuals—the summary executions of Belgian civilians, more than six hundred men, women, and children in Dinant alone, lined up and shot by German troops, the youngest, a three-week-old baby boy named Felix; and against civilization—the sacking of Louvain and burning of its world famous library. Irreplaceable lives and irreplaceable works were wiped from the earth for the unpardonable crime of being in the way.

A tired Belgian officer returned to his billet one evening and sat down to dinner with his host's family. Naturally, talk of the war ensued. His host, a local historian, mentioned the role flooding had played in slowing invaders during earlier wars. Flooding. Water and mud. It seemed so obvious. Tiny Belgium could unleash a weapon against which the formidable German army had no recourse. Much of that part of Belgium is below sea level; a system of locks kept it from flooding. The Belgians found the carefully hidden keys to the locks, waited for the tide to start coming in, and then opened the locks. They let the water come in and in, and when the tide was about to start going out, they closed the locks, thereby flooding the lowlands and creating a swamp between the Channel Ports and the River Yser. Just when all seemed lost for poor little Belgium, German infantrymen looked down and saw water begin to rise at their feet. If they continued to advance, they would be slowed considerably by the soft mud and even risked drowning—on farmland. Some did drown. Though

Belgians fleeing the fighting, 1914.
COLLIER'S PHOTOGRAPHIC HISTORY OF THE EUROPEAN WAR

the Germans fought on into France, they were kept south of the Channel Ports, leaving the vital gateway for the British army open. Contrary to the German war plan, no German soldier would brush the Channel with his sleeve.

The Allies were able to stop the rapid German advance short of Paris, but not the war, not yet, not for a very long time. Both sides literally dug in. They built tremendous trench systems stretching from the North Sea, across Belgium and northeastern France, all the way to Switzerland, facing off like two massive football teams. There they would duke it out for four long bloody years.

And this, the Western Front, was only one of several fronts in this horrible World War.

SO HOW DID OUR characters faraway in Montana learn about the war's beginning? Did the news arrive as simply a distant altercation of little interest or did they immediately recognize its magnitude? I'd say they immediately recognized its magnitude. All Uncle John and Aunt B and Peter had to do was glance at the headlines. The entire front page of the

Butte Daily Post was covered with dramatic war news the day after Austria declared war on Serbia:

> Austrian guns fire on Servian capital
> Army of every European power being massed
> European stock exchanges suspend operations
> France prepares for the worst
> NY market only one to hold firm
> 7 great European capitals in flutter

Another headline read: "Hopes that private correspondence between Kaiser and Czar would avert wider war." Three of those crowned heads, Kaiser Wilhelm of Germany, Czar Nicholas's wife Alexandra of Russia, and King George of England, were cousins, all grandchildren of the late Queen Victoria.

When the war began, some European officers and politicians predicted it would last months; others said years. In November, just three months after it started, the Twin Bridges weekly, the *Madison Monitor*, presaged:

> The war will not end until Germany has been crushed by overwhelming numbers. When she lies prone in dust, mangled in every limb and bleeding at every pore, the allies will dictate the bitter terms of peace. Their price may be the life of the German Empire. Before the end comes, Germany will have slain so many of her enemies that every family in England, France, Russia and all their colonies will have crepe on their doors. These bleeding wounds will cry for vengeance, not offer mercy or justice. The scars are so deep that the price of peace will stagger the world.

From the accounts I read of the genesis of the First World War, then called the Great War or the World War, my overwhelming sense is that events got away from the principals—as if some invisible force was moving through the lives of powerful men, a force of death and evil. Not that they were evil, but that evil made use of them. Even our language so indicates—war broke out—as if it happened by itself, which, of course, it never does.

A book published in 1910 insisted that war was an anachronism. Because of global dependency on one another for trade, developed nations would never again go to war, to do so would be futile. The cost was too great. No one would start one. The implied premise was that leaders would never again act foolishly, or greedily, or lust for conquest, or oppress their people, no evil men would rise to power. Reason, benevolence, and wisdom would reign all round. The thesis became very popular. Who would not want to believe it? The book was titled *The Great Illusion*, and that it was, and is.

In other quarters, a sense of foreboding preceded the war. It even touched down in sparsely populated Madison County, Montana, where one regular newspaper column was titled "News from the Outside World Gathered for Madison People." The year before the war began *The Madisonian* ran a political cartoon that showed a robust helmeted soldier of fierce mien already waist deep, wading ever further into deeper waters. He was *Europe*. Blood dripped from his drawn sword. He carried the shield of *militarism*. The swirling waters through which he trod were *battleships, standing armies*, and in the largest letters, *TAXES*. The dove of *peace* flew overhead, behind the warrior, well out of his sight, he'd left it behind.

Meanwhile in France, debate raged over *les pantalons rouge*, part of the traditional and revered French soldier's uniform. Red pants made sense when war was fought at close range with smokey muskets. The soldiers needed to be able to tell who their comrades were so they wouldn't shoot the wrong men. With long range artillery, red pants spelled bull's-eye. The British had already adopted the dull but safer khaki. I think the controversy over doing away with red pants more than anything illustrates how unprepared some of the combatants were for the incredibly destructive power of modern weaponry never before used in large scale war. The elite of the French officer corp went into battle wearing white gloves.

Though the United States was officially neutral, American companies sold goods to the Allies, i.e., Britain, France, etc., and American bankers extended credit to those nations for the goods they purchased from American companies. Being able to trade, or rather buy, was especially critical to Britain because she imported most of her food, two-thirds of it when the war began. By 1916, trade with the Allies more than tripled, while trade with the Central Powers, i.e., Germany, Austria-Hungary, Turkey, etc., dropped precipitously, down to next to nothing. The dramatic increase in trade with the Allies far and away offset the loss of trade with the Central Powers. The Germans were certainly free to buy whatever they wanted from American companies, but it was difficult to get it to Germany because of the British blockade, and President Wilson was much more vocal in his opposition to Germany's blockade of Britain using submarines than of Britain's blockade of Germany using mines. As you might expect, the German government was quite unhappy about this. Kaiser Wilhelm was so mad he refused to receive our ambassador for months.

Many in Butte, this city of immigrants, saw it the same way as the kaiser and called it a sham neutrality. They saw trade as support, especially trade on credit, and thought we were supporting the wrong side. Naturally, German immigrants sided with the Fatherland. The Finns were unhappy that we were supporting those on the same side as Russia, the country that invaded their homeland a hundred years earlier. The Socialists hated the war. The way they saw it, the working man fought and the capitalist gained. The Irish saw any enemy of England as a friend of Ireland. Marchers in Butte's 1915 St. Patrick's Day parade carried the flags of the United States, Ireland, and Germany.

John Gribben and his fellow Emmets certainly had strong opinions about the war. One of those Emmets was Jeremiah Lynch. Jeremiah had immigrated from County Cork, worked in the mines, and then attended law school in Chicago. He was beginning his law practice in Butte around the time John Gribben arrived. John and Jeremiah became lifelong friends and rose to leadership of the Emmets. Jeremiah was now a district court judge.

As early as 1909, Jeremiah told the Emmets that war between England and Germany was imminent. Germany was furiously building a navy to surmount Britain's supremacy over the seas. "England's distress will be Ireland's advantage," he declared. Two years later, Jeremiah predicted war between Germany and France. "The Irish will wait for England to show her hand and take the other side," he said.

When war finally came, hopes among the Emmets soared.

"This would be an opportune time to strike a blow in

Judge Jeremiah Lynch

the old land," said John Gribben, soon to be elected secretary general of the Emmets. "There are enough good men back there yet to do something. The freedom of Ireland is at no distant date." John believed German defeat of England would surely bring Ireland's liberation. Jeremiah agreed. "Ireland will never know prosperity until the English yoke is shattered," he declared. German naval superiority over England was without question in his mind, especially the submarine. "A few more of the English navy will see the bottom in short time," he portended. Belgium and France didn't seem to enter into the equation.

Meanwhile in Belfast where Rose Thompson and the rest of her children still resided, the Ulster Volunteer Force was purchasing arms and making plans for a provisional Ulster government should Home Rule be granted to Ireland. Home Rule would bring rule by the majority in Ireland, meaning Catholics. This was anathema to the Ulster Unionists. To some in England, it spelled the beginning of the end of the British Empire. A Home Rule bill had passed the House of Commons more than once only to founder later. A group called the Irish Volunteers sprang up to oppose the Ulster Volunteer Force. Now two underground armies prepared for war: the Nationalists who sought independence for Ireland and the Unionists who sought to preserve the status quo which meant remaining part of Britain with no Home Rule. Germany helped both sides. War in Ireland would surely distract Britain from war on the continent. Home Rule legislation again passed and fizzled, but civil war in Ireland was not to happen yet. When Britain went to war against Germany, Irishmen joined the British army to fight the Germans instead.

Chapter Twenty-Two

IT WAS TOO exciting to resist.

Pancake Tuesday, 1915, the war had been on only a few months. At a mere five feet three inches tall, Denis Thompson filled the room. He was the life and soul of every party, at least he thought he was and that made it so. He flew into his chair at the dinner table with the usual verve.

"What's for afters?" he asked as Nellie plunked a huge stack of pancakes on the table. Then with great aplomb, he pulled a slip of paper from his pocket and waved it with a laugh, "You'll get a shilling a day, Ma. Your son will make money for you! I'll have to leave it to you, I can't keep it!"

Rose shrieked, which caused little four-year-old Bridget to run from the house in terror.

"You cannot go," she said firmly.

Denis leaned across the table toward her and even more firmly said, "If you do not let me go I will go from here and never come back."

She was beaten. However, he was just a teenager, only seventeen, which was underage, and he looked it. On Rose's orders, Nellie signed whatever was necessary for him to enlist. John joined up too. He was even younger, he had just turned or was about to turn sixteen, but he didn't look as young. He was taller and didn't have a baby face like Denis.

After they were officially enlisted in the British army, Denis did nothing but fuss and complain about his uniform. It was much too big. Rose told Nellie to hire a tailor to fit it for him. Here he was, a poor boy from North Belfast, a lowly private with a tailored uniform, anything for Denis.

On seeing his elder brothers so handsomely bedecked in their army uniforms, eleven-year-old Jimmy exclaimed, "Ma, I want to go! I want to go!"

"You're too young," barked Rose. The next morning Jimmy refused to go to school. He said he had to drill for the army. Nellie said no he didn't and marched him to school.

Denis and John were assigned to the Royal Irish Fusiliers of the 16th Irish Division. There were two regiments of Irish Fusiliers. Later in the war, after suffering horrible losses, they were combined into one. The 16th was the Irish Catholic division of the British army. All the Irish Volunteers (that is, the underground army preparing to fight for an independent Ireland) were assigned to the 47th Brigade. The other brigades came up short, especially the 49th which included the Royal Irish Fusiliers, so when the 16th Irish Division left for England and then France, the 49th Brigade stayed behind in Ireland to build up their ranks.

When December rolled around, Denis and John were still in Ireland. They had been training with their regiment for several months and Denis was getting quite bored with it all. One day, he and rest of the soldiers in his unit were standing on the platform in Dublin waiting for their train. Waiting, always waiting, it was the bane of the young soldier, especially for a live-wire like Denis. On this particular day, Denis had had quite enough of all this waiting around, and when he saw the train for Belfast pull in, he bolted and hopped on it. One of his chums went with him. Nobody saw them in time and the train pulled out with the two runaway soldiers on it.

Denis and his chum stepped off the train in Belfast, very pleased with how clever they'd been, and gleefully walked down the platform with every intention of going home to visit their families, that is, until they saw the police escort waiting for them at the end of the platform. The policemen handcuffed Denis and his accomplice and took them to Victoria Barracks near the Thompson home on Carntall Street.

A man who worked at the prison named John McCann was a friend of Nellie's. Many a young man around Carntall Street knew, or wanted to know, the beauty Nellie Thompson. She was a spirited young woman. Soft, auburn curls framed her pretty, ever smiling face, her brown eyes glistening with merriment. She flitted about the house reciting poems and singing as she did her chores. Rumor had it she had a sweetheart in the merchant marine named Jimmy. Since he was just a sweetheart and away so much, there might be a chance for another young man, so many a young man hoped. John went directly to see her after Denis was incarcerated.

"Your Denis took French leave and is in the barracks' prison," he told Nellie.

Our Denis! A bold one he is! she must have thought. After he insisted on enlisting, and my mother didn't want him to, and I had to sign for him,

Nellie Thompson

and I went to all the trouble and expense of having his uniform tailored, and now on French leave.

John continued, "He isn't going back to Dublin until after Christmas, so I'm going to let your Denis home over the Christmas period, for I know you've a mother who'd make him come back."

"We'll see to that!" Nellie said.

After John left, Nellie reported to her mother all she had been told about Denis. As she did, there was a knock at the door. She answered it. Before her stood a terribly distraught woman. Nellie invited her in.

"I'm the pur mother of the boy taken prisoner with yur Denis," she bewailed. "Oh, Mrs. Thompson, they'll send them to Harborhell. Harborhell, Harborhell. They'll send them to Harborhell. Harborhell, Harborhell."

Rose looked at the woman, and then looked at Nellie. What was this woman carrying on about? Her Denis could take care of himself. She could not understand why this woman appeared at her door in pieces. And what was this Harborhell she was crying about?

It was a military prison and Denis didn't go there. He spent Christmas at home with his family. I don't know whether the other boy did or not. The two returned to Dublin after Christmas and were incarcerated at Portobello Barracks. After they'd been there a few days, Rose sent Nellie with the other boy's mother to find out how the two troublemakers were faring.

"What are you doing here?" Denis demanded when he saw that his visitor was Nellie. "Am I not able to look after myself? I don't need my sister looking after me. Whatever the prison can give, I'll take it."

Apparently Peter wasn't the only Thompson with a monstrous chip on his shoulder.

Seeing her brother was no worse for his confinement, Nellie returned to Belfast and reported to her mother.

When his prison term was up, Denis rejoined the regiment and soon after left for the trenches of France. As far as I know, Denis and John were in the same regiment. It was typical for the British army to keep siblings and friends together. That was an incentive to sign up. You could go with your chums. The error of that practice would soon prove painfully clear.

I'm told there is a picture of the regiment though I've never seen it. The men are marching in France. All are in strict military formation except one, Denis Thompson, who is waving to the cameraman.

CHAPTER TWENTY-THREE

WE JUMP TO the year 1917. Again, it is June. What is it about June? American troops are landing in France and in Butte. The image in my mind is of troop trains passing one another at the depot—troops arriving to make Butte safe for mining while Butte men leave to make the world safe for democracy. It didn't happen quite that way, but close. We back up to events earlier in the year.

Germany's plan to break the stalemate on the Western Front was to starve Britain out of the war. With torpedoes, Germany would attempt to do to Britain what Britain had been as yet unable to do to Germany with her naval blockade.

Germany looked across the sea and saw an immense nation supplying the enemies of the Fatherland, a nation unprepared to enter this European war and with no interest in doing so. The idea of America going to war in Europe was simply not in the main. Mexico and Japan were the American foreign policy headaches of the day. President Wilson followed a speak loudly and carry a small stick doctrine. He threatened to break diplomatic relations should Germany sink American ships; however, he put no might behind that threat.

It is a simple school yard principle: bullies don't hit someone they think will hit back. The German high command didn't believe the professorial American president, more at home in the library than as commander-in-chief, would pull the trigger. And if he did, he didn't have much of a trigger to pull. In size, the American army was on par with Romania's, nothing more than a bothersome gnat, a nuisance to be waved away, not even important enough to crush. "They will not even come because our submarines will sink them," proclaimed Admiral Capelle before the German parliament. "America from a military point of view means nothing, and again nothing, and for a third time nothing!" There was no Yamamoto to warn the German commanders: you are awaking a sleeping giant.

The debate in Germany about widening the U-boat campaign to all out unrestricted submarine warfare was widely publicized. Americans read about it in their newspapers. So it surely did not come as a complete surprise when late on the afternoon of January 31, 1917, the German ambassador to the United States, Count von Bernstorff, presented a note to Secretary of State Lansing that said, beginning at midnight, Germany will fire without warning on any ship traveling to or from the enemies of the Fatherland.

To be precise, the Germans would allow one American ship to one British port once a week. Otherwise, this constituted a submarine block-ade of nearly the entire North Atlantic. International law dictated that combatants warn a merchant ship and allow passengers and crew to board lifeboats before sinking it. No more. Now German U-boats would fire on anyone without warning. The message was loud and clear: America, cease supplying our enemies, and if you do not, we will find you, and we will sink you. President Wilson responded by severing diplomatic ties.

Earlier in the month, British and American operatives had intercepted a telegram from German Foreign Minister Arthur Zimmerman to the Ger-man ambassador in Mexico City. It said that Germany was about to com-mence unrestricted submarine warfare, and should this provoke the United States into war, the German government was asking Mexico, and proposed Mexico ask Japan, to ally with Germany in war against the United States. Mexico was to "reconquer" Texas, New Mexico, and Arizona, the said be-ing accomplished with "generous financial support" from Germany.

Trouble from south of the border was not unthinkable in 1917. Only three years earlier, U.S. Marines clashed with Mexican forces at Vera Cruz in an attempt to stop a German arms shipment to the Mexican dictator. In 1916, Pancho Villa and his cohort invaded New Mexico and murdered several Americans; President Wilson sent troops led by General John "Black Jack" Pershing into Mexico to hunt them down. And now in 1917, here was Germany plotting to foment war between the United States and Mexico.

As inflammatory as the Zimmerman telegram was, Wilson kept it quiet and tucked it away for the time being, but when the Senate balked at his plan to arm American merchant ships and threatened a filibuster, he pulled the Zimmerman telegram from his quiver and released it to the press. It made headlines across the country and predictably served to inflame anti-German sentiments first fueled by the sinking of the *Lusitania*.

And to add more fuel to the fire, by the end of March, four American merchant ships were at the bottom of the sea, sunk by German U-boats.

On April 2, 1917, President Woodrow Wilson addressed Congress. These actions by the German government constitute an act of war against the United States, he said in many more words. "The present German submarine warfare against commerce is a warfare against mankind." Even clearly marked hospital ships and ships carrying relief to "the sorely bereaved and stricken people of Belgium . . . have been sunk with the same reckless lack of compassion." He said the German government planted spies in our midst, even before the war began, and they have attempted to "stir up enemies against us at our very doors."

Two days later on Wednesday, April 4, the Senate took up the war resolution. They deliberated for over twelve hours. Several foreign dignitaries watched and listened from the gallery. At eleven o'clock that night, the roll call began. A grave pall fell over the chamber as each man was called by name and answered with his vote. All but six voted yea, and they sent the resolution to the House. On Thursday, debate began there. Member after member rose to denounce Germany or denounce both sides. One very loud dissenting voice came from Washington Republican William La Follette. He claimed that we were never truly neutral. From the very beginning we favored Britain's side in the war. We never objected to Britain's naval blockade of Germany while we vehemently objected to Germany's blockade of Britain. Britain had laid down mines in the North Sea, mines that sank three American ships. "Is a life lost by the destruction of a vessel coming in contact with a floating mine less dear than one lost on a vessel sunk by a torpedo fired by a submarine?" he asked. "Is the water less cold or wet?"

Speech after speech, fifty in all, for and against, continued well into the night, well past midnight, until finally, in the wee hours of that Good Friday, the members of the U.S. House of Representatives entered their own Gethsemani. They had to decide. They had to vote. They voted to send the nation to war. Republican Jeannette Rankin of Montana was one of fifty House members who voted nay. "I want to stand by my country," said the only woman in Congress, "but I cannot vote for war."

Once awakened, the lumbering giant was overwhelmed by the task at hand. There were just over 100,000 men in the American army and their biggest gun was a medium machine gun. The ferocious, insatiable beast called the Western Front was devouring men by the millions. In a single battle, the Battle of the Somme, one million casualties fell. One hundred thousand Americans would hardly be noticed. The beast could crush them with one swipe of his mighty paw. General Pershing, Commander of the American Expeditionary Forces, called for a one million man army to start and ultimately three million. This America could easily provide. However, training those men and equipping them with guns and ammunition, boots and blankets, horses and trucks, food and tents, and doing it quickly, was a monumental order. What troops Pershing could spare he needed to send to France immediately to boost the Allies' morale, to keep them going until the rest of the American army arrives. The Allies must know that America is in the fight in deed not only in word. If he sends the regular army now, who will train his new troops? There were many heart attacks in Washington DC that summer.

CHAPTER TWENTY-FOUR

AILA AND ARTHUR and Sarah and Peter and Uncle John and Aunt B and the rest of Butte read the dramatic news in the paper that Good Friday morning. "U.S. IS AT WAR WITH GERMANY" declared the huge banner headline. Below it was a picture of twenty-three young men from Dillon on their way to the war. Also in the paper was Congresswoman Jeannette Rankin's statement that she could not vote for war.

Then at noon, the stores closed and stayed closed until three o'clock, as they did every Good Friday.

Eighteen-year-old Bill Hughes was one of the first in line when the navy recruiting office opened in Butte the day before the House voted. The following week he was inducted into the U.S. Navy at the Salt Lake recruiting station and soon left for Mare Island.

The war gobbled up copper as fast as Butte's miners could free it from the ground. The mines ran three shifts. Immigrants poured into the city. Sarah had no trouble finding boarders and now she had room for well over a dozen.

"My mother was a butterfly, my father was a workhorse. He never gave her any peace," Aila said referring to the hotel. In many Welsh families, it was customary for the wife to handle the family finances. Such was the case in the Hughes household. Arthur dutifully gave his pay to Sarah, and she expected her children to do the same. So if the butterfly decided they would buy the hotel on Parrot Flat, that indeed is what they did.

It was an enormous, three-story brick building at 415 Kemper Street, near the gate of the Pennsylvania Mine. It had thirty-three rooms, twenty-three of which were bedrooms. Aila must have gasped when she saw the place—the thought of all that cooking and cleaning and laundry, plus school, plus working at Symon's. Imagine washing sheets for twenty-three beds with no washing machine, just a tub and some soap and a clothes stomper, and then towels and table linens and clothes for all those people.

Sarah, Patsy, Aila

"Do you know how to cook?" Sarah asked one of the boarders shortly after she took over the place.

"Yes, ma'am," he said.

"Well, you better do some or you'll forget how."

Sarah's was probably the only boarding house in Butte where the boarders cooked dinner. They'd walk into the kitchen and see Sarah attempting to do something with a roast and say, "Come on Ma Hughes, we'll do it, we'll do it." Soon Sarah was sitting at a corner of the table having a glass of beer with one of the men while another man peeled potatoes and carrots, yet another prepared the roast for the oven, and another cut thick slices from the loaves of bread Aila had baked early that morning. Arthur would walk in on this scene and later express exasperation with his wife for sitting around like a grand duchess while those who paid to be waited on worked. "*I'm* the kitchen chef," she responded.

"Oh, we had the best food in that boarding house," Aila recalled with delight. "The boarders could come and cook their own country style dishes. I learned more about food in a few months in that boarding house!"

The boarders who cooked received no consideration on their bill. Sarah charged as high a price as any boarding house in Butte.

Sarah spent over $1,500 outfitting the place, the same amount of money Arthur spent proving up on the homestead. How well it was furnished to begin with, I don't know. Once completely furnished by Sarah, there was a large leather couch, chiffonier, dresser, and player piano in the front room which doubled as a bedroom when necessary. The dining room had an oak side board and two oak tables and could seat twelve. Each bedroom had a brass or iron bed (most were brass), an oak dresser, a table and chair, and a rocker. The bedrooms also had slop jars and wash stands. The house had at least one bathroom with a toilet. There were two kitchens.

Despite Butte's harsh climate, Sarah succeeded in growing a garden in the back-yard. She grew herbs in tin cans in the kitchen window. She adorned the front room with potted ferns. The table tops she decorated with her handiwork. Never did she sit with an empty lap, she was always crocheting or embroidering, and singing Welsh hymns as she did. Sarah would accept only one condition for the house—spotless, but it was not for her to keep it so. Needle-point and gardening were Sarah's idea of work.

"Aila, you've had enough schooling. I need you here to cook and clean!" said Sarah.

Aila and Sarah Hughes.

Aila wanted to go to school, she wanted to go to college, she wanted to be a teacher.

"You can't go to school until you've finished all your work here," was Sarah's idea of compromise. So Aila got up at four o'clock every morning to finish her chores in time to go to school. She was in her second year at Butte High, and she almost never missed school. Every day after school she worked at Symon's.

A woman named Sylvia told me, when she was a little girl growing up on Parrot Flat, she could always count on a bowl of soup from Mrs. Hughes. She was the same age as Patsy; she remembered Patsy and Mrs. Hughes as being full of fun, but she thought Aila was boring, so serious, always working or reading. Sylvia's mother, on the other hand, didn't care who was full of fun and who was boring. She saw impeccable behavior and comportment in Aila and held her up as an example for her daughter to emulate. "Now Aila wouldn't do that," she would chasten.

Patsy Hughes

Most of Sarah's boarders at Kemper Street were unmarried miners. Many were young and footloose and changed mines often. A man left a particular mine because he got in a fight with the shift boss or he just didn't like the shift boss so he took his turkey and rustled work elsewhere. (His turkey was his bag of clothes.) When he changed mines, he often changed boarding houses so he could live close to the mine. As a result, boarders came and went.

Arthur worked at the Original Mine the entire first year they were in Butte. Now he was working at the Pennsylvania Mine through a Welsh or Wilkes-Barre connection or both and had been there over a year. All the men in Anna Hughes's Boarding House worked at the Pennsylvania or Tramway Mine. Why, you might ask, was Sarah Eleanora Patricia

Arthur Hughes in the alley behind their boarding house at 415 Kemper, 1916.

Hughes running an establishment named for Anna Hughes? Sometimes Sarah went by Anna, sometimes Sarah Ann, sometimes Eleanor, sometimes Mary, sometimes May, sometimes Ellen, sometimes Patricia, sometimes Sarah. Those are just the names I found written down. She may have used others. In the school records for the children, under the parents' names she was Anna, then Sarah, then Sarah, then Anna. Arthur was always Arthur. The butterfly flitted from notion to idea to notion, never resting on one for long; among those landings were a variety of names. She collected names like baubles. Whichever the butterfly fancied at the moment she picked up for the day. To those around the neighborhood and the boarders she was known as Ma Hughes or the more formal Mother Hughes.

Peter's father, Sam Thompson, lived briefly at 415 Kemper. "He didn't stay long," Aila said. "He didn't like the way the kitchen was run or something." Perhaps he didn't like to cook.

CHAPTER TWENTY-FIVE

AMERICA'S ENTRY into the Great War was certainly a sad turn for the Irish in Butte. Their new country was aligned with their old enemy. Lively political discussion burst forth whenever the Gribbens and Thompsons and their friends gathered. "I don't care who wins the war as long as England gets beat!" was Sam Thompson's oft expressed sentiment even though he had two sons in the British army. Peter did not share his father's sentiments. Like many of his generation, he dove headlong into the culture of his new country and had little interest in the politics of the old.

Reactions expressed among the Irish at their fraternal organization meetings ranged from subdued to unhinged. The Emmets had been reticent about speaking openly about the war since March of 1916 when a fellow Emmet warned them to be on the lookout for a Scotland Yard detective in Butte. The Hibernians, on the other hand, could not restrain themselves.

"There is not one Irishman in the United States that would fail Old Glory in time of need, but I hope that everyone that goes across the water to the trenches will never get back," declared Brother O'Leary. Like the Emmets, the Hibernians provided sick and death benefits for their members; however, they were more fraternal than revolutionary. Politics was the purview of their brother Emmets, but this shock over their adopted country supporting their mortal enemy was too much to take, simply beyond the pale.

"I deeply regret," said Brother O'Meara, "that the country for which our race has done so much good for should welcome such a renegade as England has sent to our shores—namely Count Balfour [the British foreign secretary]. We should all strive to be part of that government which is our house, and though the medicine is hard, still the directions say take it."

"We must guard our speech," chastened Brother Fitzpatrick. He then stood and recited the Gettysburg Address.

The meeting closed with good news about the division's treasury.

John Gribben and Jeremiah Lynch were also Hibernians. After the declaration of war, John made remarks of a "patriotic character" at one of the meetings. Jeremiah declared, "Long before the war is over, our race will shine out above them all as types of true citizenship, and it will be men of our stripe who will do the battling in the trenches."

The Emmets made no public anti-war pronouncements, so in that, they took the hard medicine and tacitly supported their adopted country. A radical Irish group called the Pearse Connollys did not, and they found political soul mates in the cantankerous Wobblies. The day after the United States declared war on Germany, posters appeared around town that said, "Enlist, Morgan Needs You." A fringe paper editorialized that, "There is no reason . . . why we should play the game of powder ring for Wall Street or sacrifice the lives of American youth and manhood."

Nevertheless, patriotism prevailed and overwhelmed these pockets of cynicism. Whether in favor of going to war or against it, now Congress had voted, the die was cast, it was time to get behind the war effort. Mayor Maloney asked the Pearse Connollys to cancel their parade commemorating the Easter Uprising, and they did. "Every drop of patriotism should be devoted to our country," said the mayor.

Now June approached and, with it, draft registration day. Erring on the side of caution, Secretary of War Baker sent an additional fifty men to supplement the National Guard troops already stationed in Butte.

Registration day was to be a holiday. The mines would shut down, businesses agreed to close, and the saloons would be closed by order of Mayor Maloney (as requested by the Feds)—some holiday.

Newspapers and posters notified men of their obligation to register for the draft. All men ages twenty-one to thirty were required to register. "It does not matter if you are blind, deaf, dumb, legless and armless; if you are in jail or a minister of the Gospel; if you are white, black or yellow; if you have conscientious scruples against war, or if you are a citizen of Germany, Senegambia or other land," you must register. Exemptions would be worked out later. The newspaper listed the questions the men would have to answer when registering. The article explained that men would be asked their date of birth. Now we know, said the article, men don't go about with the year they were born in their heads, so simply subtract your age from 1917 and that will give you the year you were born.

It sounds incredible. How could a person not know the year he or she was born? Birth certificates, marriage certificates, naturalization papers, and other documents I found listed several different dates of birth for Arthur, Sarah, and John Gribben. Apparently, the exact date a person was born wasn't a particularly important piece of information in those days, an approximation would do.

Aila always listed her correct date of birth and so did Peter, but his sister Mary insisted that he was born a year later than he was. Maybe it started with the draft.

Peter, you're only twenty, you don't need to register for the draft, I can imagine her saying.

Mary, I'm twenty-one, I'll soon be twenty-two.

No, Peter, you were born in 1896.

I was born in 1895.

Peter was right. Perhaps it was wishful thinking on Mary's part.

Besides registration instructions for the men, the *Butte Miner* ran a notice appealing to women: "Why not enter a trade where you will release men for national service? Remember to demand the same wages as men, for it is not patriotism to lower the standard of wages but appeal to the patriotism of the employer to train you into the new trade rather than a man."

Anti-British circulars were distributed throughout town urging Butte men not to register, for to join the army was to support England, the nation which "riveted the chains of slavery around Ireland." Orders went out to arrest anyone who spoke against registration or incited others not to register.

Despite the circulars, on Tuesday morning June 5, 1917, Butte men, including Irishmen, including our young Irishman, Peter Thompson, dutifully lined up at the draft offices to register for the draft. That evening with registration still underway, Finns, Wobblies, and Pearse Connollys marched in protest of the draft. Depending on which newspaper one read, registration went beautifully, without a hitch, a splendid show of patriotism, one attempted disturbance was swiftly nipped in the bud, one protester yelled, "Kill the cops," protesters who resisted arrest were clubbed—that from the *Butte Daily Post*. According to the *Miner*, tensions raged, soldiers stood guard with bayonets fixed at the corners of Main and Broadway and Park and Main; Butte was virtually under martial law.

The day did have its lighter moments. If some men in 1917 didn't know their date of birth, they surely didn't know how tall they were. When asked, a burly six foot plus Montenegrin replied, "I don't know, maybe five feet. I tall enough to fight anyhow." One man asked that he be moved to the top of the list. He had just gotten engaged and was having second thoughts. Being drafted seemed a deft escape. Another man did not claim an exemption for being married, even though he was, and told the registrar that he thought he was well-suited to trench warfare. When asked why, he said, "Oh, I've been married for four years and am in good training. I'm particularly adapted for the handling of small bombs. I've been ducking frying pans, rolling pins, and flatirons for such a long time that a ten-inch shell whistling over my head wouldn't bother me a bit."

Since the boarders were occupied with the draft, and assuming Symon's stayed open and Aila was at work, Sarah probably cooked dinner that evening. She always had a pot of soup on the stove. It was easily embellished into stew by adding chunks of meat and more potatoes and carrots. Patsy set the table, placing the cutlery and dishes just so with a folded napkin next to each fork, just as Aila had taught her, and Sarah had taught Aila. No matter how she behaved otherwise, Sarah insisted that mealtime be civilized and well-mannered.

The men poured into the house at the usual hour. One thing they were fastidious about was meal time. A wave of chatter ascended the stairs and then descended and trickled into the dining room. Indulge me a moment while I imagine their dinner conversation.

Did you register? asks a Welshman as he sits down at the table across from a Cousin Jack.

I did, stood on line for hours. I've a brother already in it.

Nothing doing, says another man. I didn't come here to be fighting European wars.

What are they fighting for over there? asks a youth with an American accent.

Well, you see this fellow killed the Austrian archduke, answers the Welshman.

Why he'd do that? asks the youth.

Something about Serbia, he's a Serb, replies the Welshman, as if that explained everything.

How'd that start a war?

Austria was mad at Serbia.

Who are we mad at?

Germany.

Germany? Why?

Because Germany invaded France. We're going to help the French and the British fight the Germans.

We are? But what have they to do with Austria and Serbia?

They're all fools! Sarah interjects as she serves the stew.

We're going to help the French who got in it on account of the Russians who got in it on account of the Serbs. The British got in it on account of the Belgians, explains the Welshman.

The Belgians?

The Germans invaded Belgium and they want no part of war so the British got in it to kick 'em out.

These men could well understand this. It was a familiar scene in any Butte saloon: you hit my friend then I hit you, then your friend will hit me, then another of my friends will hit the fellow who hit me, and so on. It was the unspoken code of honor—standing by your friend even if it bloodies your face.

So we're going to help the French help the Russians who got in it to help their friends the Serbs, concludes the youth.

I think the Russians are getting out of it. Aren't the Russians getting out it?

No, they're still in it. Their czar quit but they're still in it.

But what about the Serbs? asks the youth. Who's helping them?

I think they've already been beat.

Who?

The Serbs.

Then what are they fighting for over there?

Aila was home from work by now. She listened but kept her opinions to herself. "He said he kept us out of war," she said later with disdain, referring to Woodrow Wilson's reelection campaign. No, he didn't, and she never forgot. "Don't ever vote for an incumbent," she told me many times.

President Wilson's opponent in said election was Charles Evans Hughes. Hughes stopped in Butte during the campaign, as did all presidential candidates. I wonder if the family told anyone about Arthur being related to him. For a person in Butte, Montana, to be related to the

Republican presidential candidate—that would have been scandalous, on par with grave robbery, if not worse. Back in Forsyth, that would not have been the case. On Rosebud County's first election day in 1902, many strange new faces appeared at the polls to vote the Democrat ticket. Sure enough, the Democrats won. When it was discovered that those new faces came all the way across the state from Butte to vote, the election was declared a fraud and a new election was held. This time only Rosebud County voters voted, and lo and behold, the Republicans won.

Now it was Wednesday. Draft registration with all its attendant brouhaha was over. The next two days passed quietly. The police rounded up a few dozen slackers who failed to register for the draft. All those arrests were without incident. On Friday, the electricians voted to strike against Montana Power. There was a brief article on the front page of the paper about the dire food situation in Germany.

The next day, Saturday, Aila rose early, as usual, before everyone else. The house was cold. Winter had lingered late that year. There had still been two feet of snow at the Columbia Gardens on Easter. She dressed, put up her hair, and wrapped herself in a heavy sweater. The men on day shift would be up soon and ready for a hearty breakfast. Aila walked to the stove and removed the ash box and carefully carried it out the back door and dumped the ashes. The sun was just peeking over the East Ridge. She was accustomed to seeing steam billow up from under the gallows frames across the hill, but this morning, a dense pillar of black smoke was emerging from one and forming an ominous dark cloud against the dawn sky. She had heard the sirens during the night.

She walked back into the kitchen, slid the ash box into the stove, and threw a few chunks of coal on the fire. Then she filled the large kettle with water. It took all her strength to lift it onto the immense restaurant-size stove. The house was quiet save for the click, click of her heels as she walked to and fro across the kitchen floor. She cut thick slices of bread and laid them out on the table, slathered each with butter, topped each with a slab of meat, then another piece of bread, and wrapped each in paper. These were for the boarders' lunch buckets.

Some of the boarders were nice, some she didn't care for at all. There was one in particular whom she loathed. He was called Mitch. She slept in the cook's room off the kitchen and one wall was no wall at all, just a sheet hanging from the ceiling. One day this man invaded her room as she was beginning to dress. She screamed. Another boarder ran to her rescue and, to use her words, throttled him.

I don't know how she first learned about the fire. My guess is one of the boarders came in with a newspaper. She hears the door shut, looks over, the man walks into the kitchen, she says good morning. He sits down at the table and begins to read. She glances at the paper as she walks past him to retrieve the eggs. From behind her pince-nez she sees that it is marked EXTRA.

What has happened for there to be an extra? she asks.

Fire at the Granite Mountain.

How bad is it?

Real bad. All the North Butte and Company helmet men are there.

All the Company men?

The news must have struck her with a jolt. That meant her father was there. Arthur was on the rescue squad at the Pennsylvania Mine which was owned by the Anaconda Copper Mining Company. The Granite Mountain was owned by the North Butte Mining Company. Arthur's regular job was above ground. He went underground only when called for a rescue.

She starts to crack the eggs into a bowl.

Were any men killed? she asks.

Yep, lots.

She turns and looks closer at the headline: "DISASTER . . . MANY LOST." Below is a long list of names in bold type.

Says here two men burned up in the cage trying to get out.

I wonder if the memory of that burned body in Forsyth flashed through her mind and left with a shudder.

How did it happen? she asks, scooping flour into another large bowl.

Says a lamp might have exploded. Nobody knows for sure.

Lost in her own thoughts and worries, she adds salt, sugar, and baking powder to the flour and works in lard. She mixes in enough milk to form a dough, flours the counter, pours out the dough, kneads it quickly, rolls it out, and cuts biscuits. Then she opens the oven door and sticks her hand inside to feel if the oven is hot enough. It is, and in go the biscuits.

It was a somber breakfast all over town that morning. This drove every-day worry about work in the mines dramatically to the fore. Aila didn't have much time to read the newspaper with her very full schedule, but if she did peruse this EXTRA after cleaning up the breakfast mess, she would have seen a two-line item in bold type added just minutes before the paper went to print. It said that one of the rescuers had already perished. He had been a foreman at the Diamond Mine.

The North Butte with its Granite Mountain and Speculator shafts was one of the largest and most modern mines in Butte. Miners referred to both shafts together as the Speculator; hence, history has at times called this the Speculator Fire. Both the Anaconda and North Butte had safety first programs, and that year the North Butte Company decided to make their mine even safer by installing a fire suppression sprinkler system which, from what I've been able to ascertain, was not a typical feature of a hard-rock mine in 1917.

By early June, the only thing left to do on the sprinkler system was to install a water tank at the 2600-foot level of the Granite Mountain. To make room for the tank, and as a further fire prevention measure, the main electrical transformer on that level was to be moved several hundred feet back from the shaft. Before that could be done, an additional length of electrical cable had to be laid. On Friday morning, June 8, four electricians, three ropemen, two shaftmen, and one hoistman undertook this task. The lead-sheathed cable was 1200 feet long and weighed three tons. The men secured it to the hoist cable at intervals with hemp rope, and then the hoistman began the tedious work of slowly and carefully snaking the cable down the shaft. The lower end was almost at the 2600-foot level when the cable became twisted and the job stalled. The men cut some of the rope lashings and tried to untwist the cable. It was still twisted. They cut more, more until two hundred feet of cable was free of the lashings. Then they saw the heavy cable begin to slip. They scrambled out of the way and made it just in time before the entire three-ton cable broke loose and came crashing down the shaft.

The electricians went down to investigate. They found that the cable had taken quite a beating in the fall and was damaged beyond use. By now, they and the rest of the crew had been on the job for eighteen hours. The exhausted men reported what happened and went home.

As the cable had plunged down the shaft, it whipped against pipes and timbers and broke the water line which supplied the 3000-foot level. Men drilling on that level couldn't work without water, so they went home.

Later that night, the assistant foreman went down to investigate the damage. He took three men with him. They found the tangled mass of cable about fifty feet below the 2400-foot level. Half of the lead sheathing had been torn away in the fall exposing the frayed, oil-soaked insulation underneath. One of the men moved his carbide lamp closer to find the end of the cable. His lamp found it.

The oil ignited and then the timbers. The mighty fan bringing fresh air into the mine fanned the flames and quickly swept fire and gas through the shaft. Miners smelled danger and bolted. The Granite Mountain connected to several other mines at that level, so there were many exits; however, miners who didn't know where the fire was didn't know which shaft was safe. Over four hundred men were working underground at the North Butte that night. Even without the burning timbers, the burning oil from the cable could produce enough poison gas to kill a vast number of them, if not all.

The entire region's fire and rescue apparatus sprang into action. Fire fighters poured water down the shaft. The Company summoned all their rescuers and made all their resources available to the North Butte. The Bureau of Mines man on the scene summoned rescue cars from Red Lodge and Colorado Springs.

Every hospital was alerted, physicians flocked to the mine, ambulances stood by. All the undertakers in town were notified. As the news spread, families and friends ran up the hill. They massed at the mine gate, begging entrance, anxiously awaiting any news, any sight of a loved one emerging from the mine. Men and boys ran around the vertical wood plank perimeter fence searching for knot holes through which they could see into the mine yard. The area became so clogged with on-lookers that the National Guard had to cordon off the mine to allow rescue and first-aid workers to get to their jobs unhindered.

Now poison gas was sweeping into adjacent mines—the High Ore, the Diamond, and the Badger—in some places through leaks at closed doors. All those mines were evacuated as well as other adjacent mines.

Arthur caught the streetcar up the hill to the North Butte as soon as he received word. He and the other rescuers would have to enter the mine through the Speculator shaft and adjacent mines because the Granite Mountain shaft was now impassable—the collar had caved in from the heat and force of the fire fighting water. Arthur stood by with the twelve other men from the Pennsylvania Mine rescue squad, each with a breathing apparatus helmet and flashlight in hand. They split into two or three

Mine rescuers, "helmet men," 1917.
WORLD MUSEUM OF MINING #1217

groups. Those orchestrating the rescue gave Arthur and his team specific instructions as to where to search and what time to be back. Between the extreme heat down in the mine and sheer exhaustion from carrying out the injured and the dead, rescuers could easily fall victim to the disaster. If they were not back at the appointed time, another team stood by and would be right down after them.

Once down in the mine, Arthur could barely see through the smoke and steam. He and his fellow rescuers groped along the rails for direction. They found men dazed from the gas and hurried them to the cages so they could be taken quickly up to good air. One miner saw the silhouettes of creatures with big, bulky heads creeping toward him, and in his delirium, they looked monstrous. He was so terrified that he turned to run back into the gas laden drift. Those big-headed creatures, the helmet men as the rescuers were called, managed to catch and subdue him and take him to the cage and out of the mine. Doctors stationed at the 2200-

foot level of the Speculator and at the top of the shaft administered immediate first aid before sending the stricken men to the hospital. One delirious miner thought the doctor was trying to poison him and refused the coffee he offered. Another poor man didn't know his own name when he got to the hospital.

Rescuers found other miners prone, still grasping their lunch buckets. They checked for vital signs. Finding none they left the bodies and continued to search for survivors. The shaft cave-in had blocked gas and smoke on the lower elevations making rescue work down there even nastier and more perilous. Helmet men asked to go down to the 3000-foot level to search for survivors, but those in charge wouldn't let them. It was much too dangerous.

Fire fighters poured more water down the shaft. Mine fires were tenacious. The 1889 fire in the St. Lawrence was still burning behind bulkheads. When fire ignited in the High Ore-Modoc two months before the Granite Mountain Fire, miners had escaped through the Granite Mountain shaft. The North Butte mine was shut down for nearly two weeks then for fear of gas, and that fire was still burning. The men had built bulkheads to seal it off. Now when miners smelled smoke and gas, some figured it was from the Modoc and again tried to escape through the Granite Mountain shaft and ran directly into the fire.

One of the Pennsylvania Mine rescue squads found the assistant foreman who had investigated the dropped cable. It was believed to be his lamp that started the fire. After the fire started, rather than escape and save his own life, he ran through the drifts as fast as he could to alert as many miners as possible as to where the fire was so they could flee in a safe direction. He was with two other men when the rescuers found him and all three were unconscious. The rescuers took them to the cage. They managed to revive the two. The assistant foreman died.

Pennsylvania Mine rescuers then went down to the 1800-foot level of the Badger. They were walking toward the Speculator when one of them bumped into a concrete bulkhead. The intake valve on his breathing apparatus started to leak and he collapsed. The others rushed him out of the mine. They feared he was already gone. Fortunately, doctors at the Murray Hospital were able to revive him.

While the rescuers continued searching underground, family and friends above ground waited anxiously and prayed. A little tow-haired newsboy stood outside the *Anaconda Standard* office peering up at the list of dead and missing. He asked a newspaper man entering the office, "Say mister, I can't read that up there. Somebody said my daddy's name is there. Will you tell me?" The man perused the list. "Yes, sonny," he replied, "your daddy still is in the ground." The little tyke turned, his load of Extras tucked under his arm. A man reached for a nickel to buy one. Then suddenly realizing the import of what he'd just been told, the boy dropped the papers and ran up the hill.

After each one-hour shift in the mine, Arthur rested in good air above ground with the other members of his squad until called to go down again. The rescue would take days. At some point, the boss sent Arthur and his squad home to get some sleep.

Utterly exhausted, Arthur took the streetcar down the hill to Kemper Street. He walked around to the alley and entered through the back gate. A ghastly stench permeated his clothes. Aila saw her father through the window. Her heart was in her throat. Two helmet men had perished in the Pennsylvania Mine fire the year before. That was only a few weeks before her father went to work there. Now more dead. Thank God Father was not one of them. She watched her mother carry a bucket of water and soap and clean clothes to him. Thank God he wasn't dead.

After some rest, Arthur reported back to the mine and resumed his role in the rescue. Thirty miles of drifts and crosscuts and some fifteen miles of stopes, raises, and manways had to be explored to search for survivors and collect the dead. Other than the two men who were burned up in the cage trying to escape, the rest died of asphyxiation from inhaling carbon monoxide and tar-laden smoke. The intense heat down in the mine accelerated decomposition causing the bodies to turn a grisly black and blue and to swell. Some swelled so much that the skin split. A few helmet men buckled under the strain of beholding the ghastly sight. They had to wrap bandages around at least one body to keep the flesh from falling off. They tied the ravaged bodies onto ladders and hoisted them out. Some of the dead were so horribly disfigured that family members were never able to identify them.

The rescue would continue for eight days with 175 men taking part underground, plus those above ground orchestrating the rescue, plus doctors, nurses, and ambulance drivers attending to the injured. The coroner set up a makeshift morgue in the mine yard.

On Sunday morning, the timekeeper's list showed three dozen men still unaccounted for. Word went out again: all men working at the North Butte the night of the fire should report to the timekeeper. The only hope alive was that some men had escaped through other shafts and had not notified the timekeeper. Any men still underground at this late date must surely be dead, but the helmet men would search until they found them so at least their loved ones would have the consolation of giving their beloved a proper funeral and burial.

To make matters even more depressing, a bitter June blizzard blew into town.

Then came a startling development—the hoist engineer received the accident signal—nine bells. No one could believe it. It came from deep in the mine. A team of helmet men went down to investigate. They found twenty-five men barely conscious—but alive!

Shortly after the fire started, a group of twenty-nine miners tried several avenues of escape but were driven back by gas at every turn. A nipper named Manus Duggan led them into a blind drift, and at his insistence, they built a bulkhead and sealed it with their clothing. There they would wait until the gas outside cleared or rescuers arrived. They spread out and periodically altered their positions to take advantage of every precious oxygen molecule available in the closed drift. They rapped continuously on the air pipe and rails to signal their presence. They played cards, sang, and prayed, and waited. After several hours, they ran out of water. After twenty-four hours, neither match nor carbide would burn. After thirty-

Manus Duggan, one of the heroes of the Granite Mountain Fire.
WORLD MUSEUM OF MINING #2820

six hours, nearly all the oxygen was gone. Desperate and teetering on delirium, they broke down the bulkhead. Those able to walk picked up those too weak to move and they half crawled, half walked to the Speculator shaft, a quarter mile away. When they finally reached the shaft, one of them managed to ring the signal bell, then he collapsed, as did the rest, and waited for death. The helmet men arrived first. All were saved except four. In their delirium, Manus Duggan and three others had taken a wrong turn. It would be days before their bodies were found. Stuffed in his pocket was the letter Manus had written to his pregnant wife. Like others waiting behind the bulkhead, as he breathed the last oxygen molecules into carbon dioxide, knowing he may die then and there, his thoughts went not to himself but to consoling his wife and asking her forgiveness for any pain he may have caused her. "I want a hero," begged the poet Byron. Here's one.

The next day one of the helmet men insisted that he had seen another makeshift bulkhead, but he had a difficult time convincing the powers that be. They thought he was delirious from exhaustion and had imagined it. Nevertheless, they sent a team down. Sure enough, they found ten men behind a bulkhead. Unfortunately, some of them were already dead. Shift Boss Jim Moore had been their leader. He had periodically tested the air outside the bulkhead to see if it was clear. He wouldn't allow his men to risk testing it. He too wrote a consoling missive to his wife. As they were being rescued, he perished.

The lifeless bodies of two other shift bosses, Ben Tregonning and George Gorrie, were pulled from the mine. Like Jim Moore, they died exerting "almost super human effort" trying to save their men.

Several helmet men were overcome and had to be hospitalized. So many heros.

So ended a week in Butte, Montana. It began with the National Guard quelling an anti-draft demonstration and ended with the worst hard-rock mining disaster in American history. One hundred and sixty-three men were dead, an entire infantry company's strength, killed not by the gas and flamethrowers of the Germans, but by the gas and fire of the mine.

"In those days, they were always carrying out the miners," Grandma said, "and taking them to the cemetery," she added quickly. In the twelve months ending June 30, 1917, three hundred and twenty-seven sons, brothers, husbands, and fathers died in the Butte mines, half of them in the Granite Mountain Fire.

Funeral for victims of the Granite Mountain fire, 1917.
Miners are leading the procession on Park Street.
WORLD MUSEUM OF MINING #1897

An express carload of caskets arrived from Spokane. Grieving families prepared to bury their dead. Helmet men recovered still more bodies.
Then another labor volcano began to steam. More troops came. By the end of the month, the first American troops had landed in France.

CHAPTER TWENTY-SIX

I MUST QUALIFY that last statement before continuing with events in boisterous Butte. June of 1917 marked the arrival of the first *American army*
troops in Europe. Long before we entered the war, thousands of American men had joined Canadian, British, French, and Italian armed services
and had been fighting, driving ambulances, and flying bombing raids in
the Great War. One New Jersey man in the British army was punished
several times for "Yankee impudence."

Malcontents used the Granite Mountain disaster as yet another stone
to hurl at the mine operators. A new union sprang up, this one called the
Metal Mine Workers Union. Safety is substandard, the leaders said, wages
are too low relative to Butte's cost of living.

On Monday, just three days after the fire started, the new union called
a wildcat strike. Buzz percolated that professional agitators, namely the
IWW, were behind it. Strike leaders denied any affiliation with the IWW
even though the new union's vice president was a Wobbly. William
Andrews Clark declared he'd sooner flood his mine than recognize an
anarchist union. Mayor Maloney said, "If the IWW's start things in Butte,
the city of Butte is going to finish in the lead and when we're through an
IWW will stay as far away from this city in the future as a railroad train
can carry him." Police Chief Murphy claimed that some of the agitators
had never been in a copper mine. Some Butte men who did mine took a
dim view of going on strike while men were still entombed in the Granite
Mountain. Some saw attempts to force a shutdown of the mines during
wartime as treason.

Rumors of German provocateurs entered the mix. That was not a far-
fetched notion. The year before, German saboteurs had blown up fifty
million dollars worth of shells, high explosives, and dynamite on Black
Tom Island in New York Bay, munitions that were to be loaded onto

ships bound for France or Britain. The explosion was so great that it disintegrated the entire island, blew out windows in Manhattan, gouged holes in the Statue of Liberty, and woke up people as far away as Maryland.

In Butte, the electricians who had voted to strike against Montana Power now insisted that the miners' demands be met. If not, they would strike against the mining companies. Boilermakers, blacksmiths, and machinists walked out as an endorsement of the electricians, but not of the Metal Mine Workers Union. By the end of June, thousands of men were on strike, crippling the mines and threatening the war effort.

The opportunity to join the smeltermen's union was presented to the miners. If they did, that union would send them back to work immediately. The men voted against joining.

Labor discord competed with patriotism for primacy in the hearts and minds of Butte citizens that summer. Thousands of Serbs pledged their commitment to the war effort, which meant mining should continue. It is "no time to talk of wages when men are fighting for freedom," their spokesman declared. "Come what will . . . we will not be swerved by the IWW." A Serbian army officer came to Butte to recruit Serb expatriates who were not drafted into the American army.

Fourth of July 1917. Broadway at Dakota looking east.
The giant elk was there for an Elk's convention.

Though the strikers did not picket, Company thugs found and intimidated them. Arthur did not join the strike. He worked steadily at the Pennsylvania Mine. Peter worked through the strike at the Original. Sam Thompson left the West Colusa a few days after the strike began. He applied at the Emma three days later but did not go to work there for six months.

Bill Hughes was already back in Butte, his navy career having been very short lived. Two months after he joined, the commanding officer of the USS *Huntington* discharged him with an ordinary discharge for "disability not in line of duty (not due to own misconduct) in accordance with ship's medical survey," whatever that means. Bill worked through most of the strike at the Pennsylvania Mine.

Warnings of escalating violence soon reached Congresswoman Jeannette Rankin in Washington. She supported the strikers. Anaconda executive Con Kelley blasted her for coming out against the Company before she had all the facts. She sought an audience with President Wilson. She wasn't able to see him; however, his secretary told her that the president was monitoring the situation. Butte had become the nation's hotbed of unrest and the war desperately needed that copper. The miners asked President Wilson to appoint Congresswoman Rankin as mediator in the strike. He did not. Rankin's solution to the miners' grievances was government takeover of the mines. Congress never considered her bill but did outlaw strikes that could impede the war effort.

Now rumors flew that Germany was financing the IWW.

Police raided a Finn boarding house and confiscated guns and knives. Years later a report surfaced in the newspaper which said that "enemy agents and the IWW" had plotted to burn Butte and destroy the mines during the war but these intrigues had been thwarted by the Secret Service.

In mid July, the IWW brought in one of their big guns. Frank Little railed against country, Company, and capitalism in anti-war speeches before anybody who would listen. He called the soldiers "Uncle Sam's scabs in uniform." He said, "If the federal government takes over the mines we will make it so hot for them they will not be able to send any troops to France." His career as a Butte orator lasted only two weeks. In the dead of night on Thursday, August 1, six Persons Unknown wearing kerchiefs over their faces entered his boarding house. They claimed to be officers, of what, they didn't say. The terrified innkeeper directed the masked men to Frank Little's room. They grabbed Little, took him outside, threw him in their car, drove off, stopped, tied him to the back of the car, and dragged him to a railroad trestle south of town. There they beat him, then carried or pushed him up onto the bridge, tied one end of a rope to the trestle and the other end around his neck, threw him off the bridge, and disappeared into the night. The calling card pinned to his underwear read: "<u>OTHERS</u> <u>TAKE</u> <u>NOTICE</u>! FIRST AND LAST <u>WARNING</u>! 3-7-77."

The numbers were the familiar calling card of the vigilantes. No one knows for certain what the numbers meant, but they are believed to be the dimensions of a grave: three feet wide by seven feet long by seventy-seven inches deep. At the bottom of the card was a series of initials; the first, an L, was circled. The rest were presumed to be future targets, and it was easy to guess who they were. The crime was never solved.

It was the first lynching in Butte in nearly fifty years. A Pinkerton detective named Dashiell Hammett said he was offered five thousand dollars to kill Frank Little. He declined. A crusty, old Butte miner told me, "It was our men who killed Little." I pressed him for names. He just grumbled and said how much he hated the IWW.

Ten days after Frank Little was lynched, the American army arrived to occupy Butte. The next month Butte's first quota of conscripts entrained for Camp Lewis.

By now, Peter Thompson had lived in Butte for three and a half years. Two summers had been filled with labor unrest and violence with three mine disasters in between. In 1914, there were riots and the Miners' Union Hall was blown up and martial law. In 1915, five hundred pounds of dynamite exploded at the mouth of the Granite Mountain Mine, blowing seventeen men to atoms. In 1916, the Pennsylvania Mine fire killed twenty-one men, and now in 1917, the Granite Mountain disaster with a lynching close on its heels. So why not go off to war?

These days Peter was living at Mrs. O'Keefe's boarding house on East Park Street. He often stopped to see Aunt B on the way home from work. This was one such day. He let himself in the front door and walked into the kitchen. Hello, Aunt B, he said in his soft, lyrical voice as he set his lunch bucket on the counter. Aunt B smiled and said, Hello, love. It always lifted her spirits to see her favorite nephew. Aunt B was now thirty-nine years old and had been married four years. She had just given birth to her second child, Harry, a few weeks earlier. Her first child, John Denis,

Aunt B
HOWES NEW STUDIO, BUTTE, MONTANA

died when he was only one month old. Peter peeked in on baby Harry while Aunt B busied herself making the tea. She turned up the fire under the kettle and asked Peter how his day was. Peter chatted incessantly about this and that as she put out the cups and saucers and milk and sugar and waited for the water to boil. Then she spooned tea into her brown, earthenware teapot, filled it with boiling water, and let it steep, all the while smiling and listening to Peter. He was probably telling her about a book he just read. Peter was an avid reader and enjoyed talking about what he read and she enjoyed listening to him. She didn't have much time to read these days, what with running a boarding house and a new baby. She poured the tea. Peter spooned sugar into his cup, poured in some milk, and stirred it, still chattering away. Then he told Aunt B that he had gone to the army office that day. Did you? she said. "Yes, the man told me if I join I'll get my second papers right away, so I did."

He was referring to his citizenship papers. Peter already had his first papers, meaning he had made his declaration of intention to become an American citizen. If he joined the army, the waiting period would be waived. Besides, it looked like a good fight and he didn't want to miss it.

I wish I knew what Aunt B's reaction was to this news. Did she see going off to war any more dangerous than work in the mines? Considering what had just happened at the Granite Mountain, and what happened the year before and the year before that, maybe not.

Going off to war certainly fit Peter's pugnacious personality. He'd stand up to anybody and was always ready for a fight should it be called for in his mind. Such provocation could include someone looking crosswise at him or saying he couldn't be Irish with a name like Thompson and definitely included someone trying to cheat him at cards.

And besides, this was an honorable fight, a war to end all wars. Why the president himself said it was a war to make the world safe for democracy. What could be more honorable?

Chapter Twenty-Seven

Fears that due to all that clamorous anti-war sentiment Butte would not fill its conscription quota did not come to fruition. Montana men volunteered in droves, nearly twelve thousand, considerably more per capita than any other state. Volunteers more than made up for slackers. Montana would send eight percent of its total population to fight in the Great War, far and away more than any other state. In absolute numbers, Montana would send more men than Colorado, Florida, Maine, Oregon, Rhode Island, North Dakota, and South Dakota, all of which had larger populations than Montana, some considerably larger.

Montana's draft quota was erroneously high due to a wildly exaggerated population estimate. Somebody in Washington DC arrived at the crazy idea that nearly one million people inhabited the state. That number was so preposterous as to be laughable if it didn't involve sending so many men to their death. Fewer than half a million souls inhabited the Treasure State. In proportion to population and as a percentage of men mobilized, more Montanans would die in the First World War than from any other state.

As for the nation, twice as many American servicemen would die in a year and a half in the First World War than in the decade-long Vietnam War. As sad and tragic as the deaths were in Vietnam, imagine the shock of all those deaths times two scrunched into a year and half and the lion's share in only a few weeks.

In mid-September, the second contingent from Butte readied to entrain for American Lake, Washington, where the army was building a new training post called Camp Lewis. Peter joined the rest of the fresh conscripts at the auditorium the day before they were to depart. His chum Ray Coughlin was there too; he had volunteered at the last minute. Another chum, Gordon Reid, was one of the first called in the draft. Mayor

Maloney gave each man a pass for entrance to parties and shows through-out Butte. They were the toast of the town and they made the most of it. The prediction that the soldiers would sing "Yankee Doodle" in Berlin on the Fourth of July became a popular send-off.

The festivities climaxed the following evening. The recruits paraded through town to the Northern Pacific depot accompanied by Spanish American War veterans, Governor Stewart, Senator Clark, labor contin-gents, a Greek society, the Croatian St. Phillip and St. Jacob Society, Serbs, Boy Scouts, and the Orphans' Home Band. If Aila, Patsy, and Archie were there, they no doubt recognized some of the boys.

The crowd cheered the men as they marched. They were already heros in their eyes though none had as yet even picked up a bayonet. Once at the depot, pandemonium erupted. Anxious family members sought their beloved soldier for last minute hugs and kisses. Women fainted in the crush and were passed overhead through the checkroom window. One frenzied woman beat her way through the horde wielding a closed um-brella. Peter's sister Mary and her husband and his father and his aunts and uncles were surely there. The men boarded their assigned cars. Red Cross volunteers handed each a comfort kit. Family members cried and waved, the soldiers-to-be waved and cheered, the whistle blew, the wheels turned, the train slowly pulled out of the depot, and they were off on their grand adventure.

Adventure was what many a young man thought of war then. Ro-manticism had held sway when the nineteenth century turned her final page. She would accompany the boys over there, but would she return, or be trampled to death at the bottom of a filthy trench. As the American novelist and war ambulance driver John dos Passos put it, this generation was raised "during the quiet afterglow of the nineteenth century, among comfortably situated people who were confident that industrial progress meant an improved civilization, more of the good things of life all around, more freedom, a more humane and peaceful society." They had not from their earliest days drunk in "the brutalities of European politics with their breakfast coffee" as would their children who would go off to fight a generation later.

Romanticism had accompanied the boys across the Channel as well; however, by 1917 she was all but smothered. For nearly two years, Peter's brothers Denis and John had endured the grisly reality of the grand adventure in the trenches on the Western Front, where as the German writer soldier Erich Maria Remarque wrote, life was "simply one continual watch against the menace of death." And that death was delivered by new and horrible weapons, the most unnerving of which was poison gas. Poison gas as a weapon of war was unheard of before German scientists and generals plucked it from Pandora's Box for the First World War. A deserter warned British officers about German plans to use it, but they didn't believe him. They didn't think anybody would stoop to such a thing. It violated the rules of warfare and they thought it was logistically impossible.

The first gas attack came on a beautiful, sunny, breezy April day in 1915 in the Ypres salient in Flanders. German artillery gunners had been shelling the center of town for forty-eight hours. Then the guns stopped. There was a brief silence. Then a rumbling sound emanated from the German lines, then a hissing sound, then low, greenish-yellow clouds swept across no man's land, all the way to the Allied lines and lasted for fifteen minutes. The Reverend O. S. Watkins was working in a hospital near Ypres and described the aftermath: "No human courage could face such a peril . . . there staggered into our midst French soldiers, blinded, coughing, chests heaving, faces an ugly purple color—lips speechless with agony . . . It was the most fiendish, wicked thing I have ever seen."

Gas casualties were legion in that first gas attack because the Allied soldiers had no protection. Until masks could be designed, manufactured, and issued to the troops, British soldiers were told to roll up a piece of wet cloth, stuff it in their mouths, and breath in through their mouths and out through their noses. Primitive masks then arrived. Robert Graves, a British officer and poet, said he received ever changing instructions on how to use the mask. Another British officer poet, Siegfried Sassoon, wrote of a training class in which the instructor explained that "gas was still in its infancy." Sassoon noted that most of them were "dead or disabled before gas had time to grow up."

Denis and John were doused with chlorine gas in their first battle. By then, poison gas had been in use for a year, and the soldiers did have gas masks. Irish soldiers standing on the firing step with their masks firmly in place watched the eerie greenish-yellow chlorine clouds billow toward them across no man's land, and below the clouds, the running legs of German infantrymen. British machine gunners fired on the approaching troops. German soldiers who survived the deadly sprint across no man's land leapt into the British trenches. Fierce hand to hand, bayonet to bayonet fighting ensued, ending with the Irish soldiers repelling the Germans, and many from both sides, of course, dead.

Two days later, the Germans attacked again with gas. This douse was especially heavy, and whether some of them didn't put on their masks quickly enough or the masks didn't work, gas casualties were horrendous. Irish soldiers fell three deep on the firing step, the agony and terror they suffered in their last moments fixed for eternity on their faces. Then the wind changed and sent the gas over the German lines.

In August of 1916, Denis and John's division joined the offensive on the Somme which was already well underway. It would later be called the First Battle of the Somme. The day the battle began, July 1, 1916, nineteen thousand British soldiers were killed—in a single day. It seems every author has used the same simile to describe the aftermath—cordwood, they stacked them up like cordwood—ninteeen thousand dead men. Siegfried Sassoon called it "a sunlit picture of Hell." It was during this battle that the British introduced their new weapon of war: the tank.

To reach the front, the 8th Royal Irish Fusiliers had to walk through a narrow trench, the floor of which was covered with dead soldiers. Once in position, they attacked. The German forces tried to circle around and cut them off. Wounded soldiers being carried to the rear were easily picked off. Then British artillery shells began to fall on the Irish soldiers. The firing mechanisms were worn causing the guns to fire short, but the gunners didn't know it for some time.

Battles in the First World War went on for months. The Somme lasted nearly five, and at the end of this prolonged meat grinding, little had changed other than a lot of young men were dead or maimed. At its farthest point, the British line had advanced only seven miles.

While at the front, Denis and John and their fellow soldiers lived in the trenches amid the unwelcome company of hefty trench rats, pervasive cooties, and snails that oozed through the dirt walls when it rained, and it rained a lot. Their boots became clods of muck. Wet and cold was their normal state. The air was musty and dirty. Humor was an essential ingredient to guard against outright going insane or falling into despair, especially when the shelling started. Canadian artilleryman Coningsby Dawson wrote, "If unconscious heroism is the virtue most to be desired, and heroism spiced with a strong sense of humor at that, then pretty well every man I have met out here has the amazing guts to wear his crown of thorns as though it were a cap-and-bells."

In the middle of one fight, some Welsh Fusiliers leaned a dead comrade against the trench wall until they had time to bury him. His arm had been outstretched when he was killed and it reached clear across the trench. As the Welshmen passed by, they pushed the stiffened arm out of the way and retorted, "Out of the light you old ———! Do you own this bloody trench?" Others shook the dead hand and said, "Put it here, Billy Boy." They were gritty coal miners and somewhat hardened to the daily prospect of death.

During lulls between the carnage, soldiers holding the line from the trenches stood guard and waited, watched for Gerry should he attack, repaired what needed fixing, and at night tried to glean what they could from the enemy while patching wire. They were always wary of snipers, day or night. Now and then a human limb protruded through the muddy trench wall. Death surrounded them. Life in a mud hole. Filthy, miserable, unnerving, and dull—this was war in the trenches: a war of waiting, interrupted by terror.

John learned soldier talk. Denis came down with trench fever. He was sent home to Belfast to recuperate after which he returned to the trenches. Their division was now assigned to the British Fifth Army.

When relieved from the line, John and Denis billeted in French villages. It was the lap of luxury compared to living in the trenches. There, well behind the lines, they drilled, played sports, enjoyed what the French villages could offer, and the French merchants enjoyed the soldiers' money.

Then they returned to the trenches and waited. Darts landed in the Irish lines with a message from Gerry. It referenced the Irish domestic situation and urged the soldiers to desert.

The war was supposed to be over in months. It has lasted years. There is no end in sight. The French army is demoralized. Soldiers mutiny. What is next? French General Petain answers: We will wait for the Americans.

German General Ludendorff does not wait. In March of 1918, he attacks the British Fifth Army at the Somme. They have not yet recovered from the Third Battle of Ypres, also called Passchendaele. German gunners hurl one million shells on the British lines, one fourth of them gas shells, including mustard gas. It is the fiercest artillery bombardment thus far. Hours of brutal, relentless, accurate artillery and gas wipe out the

British front line. Storm troopers wielding ferocious flamethrowers pour out of the German trenches and bound across no man's land. The 16th Irish Division counter-attacks but is horribly outnumbered—several German battalions against a single British company. The British Fifth Army collapses. In only days, the Germans take 70,000 prisoners and inflict almost 200,000 casualties. General Ludendorff then turns to Flanders. His objective—to seize the Channel Ports and cut the British supply route. It is there that British General Haig makes his now famous proclamation: "Every position must be held to the last man: there must be no retirement. With our backs to the wall, and believing in the justice of our cause, each one of us must fight on to the end." Their backs to the sea, twenty-five miles from Dunkirk, die if they must, they would hold the line, they would not retreat. The British army held.

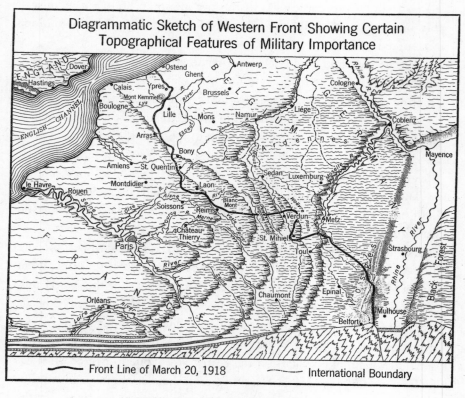

AMERICAN ARMIES AND BATTLEFIELDS IN EUROPE, P. 4.

JIMMY SAVAGE RODE past the Thompson home on his bicycle day after day. He wished to spare Mrs. Thompson this news. After a week, he could wait no longer. The young postman went to the door and knocked. Nellie answered it. He said he had a card for her mother. Nellie thanked him and took the card and gave it to her mother. Rose looked at the card. She turned it over. At the top it said "I am Prisoner of War in Germany." Below were three options: "I am well," "I am wounded," and a third that was illegible. The last two options were crossed out. It was from the Limburg prison camp and was signed Denis Thompson.

John had been wounded and was being invalided home to recuperate. Peter would soon set sail for France. She had three sons in the war. Rose Thompson was not an overtly religious woman, but she clutched those beads and now more than ever she stormed heaven to demand, implore, beseech protection for her sons. Losing one of them was not to be considered.

Dear Mother,
    Just a few lines to let you know I am well hoping this finds all at home the same. I was bad for a few days last week with fever but am pleased to say I am alright again. I am just beginning to wonder if you have received the other cards and letter I have wrote. Remember me to all at home especially Rose and Bridget. Don't forget to let me know how John is also the McAnespies. Tell Nellie Jim Blake was taken prisoner along with me. I will draw to close hoping to hear from you soon.
                    From your son
                    Denis

Europe poured an entire generation into this prolonged war of attrition: aristocrats and laborers, poets and farmers, miners and bankers. Siegfried Sassoon wrote that if the war lasted much longer, "we should be coming to the trenches every day by train like city men going to the office."

France alone mobilized eight million men for the Great War. By the time it was over, more than half those men were dead or wounded, as were more than half the Germans, half the Russians, half the Romanians, and half the Austro-Hungarians. "Dead" is quite clear, but "wounded" can sound benign and fortunate, we are relieved that at least they weren't killed. We think of wounds as something familiar, a broken bone or a deep cut, but wounds in war can mean having your leg blown off, having a chunk of your face shot to pieces, being blinded by shrapnel, having your nerves worn raw by relentless bombardment, being reduced to "permanent human wrecks," maimed for life.

It was the first mechanized war. The scientist stood behind the soldier, safe from bullets and bombs, while feeding him new and more effective means of killing and maiming before the other fellow could kill or maim him. And the war was not limited to soldiers, sailors, and airmen. Unspeakable crimes were committed against Belgian civilians, crimes documented by the perpetrators themselves. Menacing zeppelins dropped bombs on London. A seemingly invisible gun fired on Paris from seventy-five miles away, an unheard of range. From Serbia alone, while 45,000 soldiers were killed, 650,000 civilians perished from hunger, cold, and disease. Even worse was the Armenian genocide in which hundreds of thousands of Armenian men, women, and children were massacred outright or marched into the desert and left to starve by the Ottoman Turks. To think civilians watched the Battle of Bull Run unfold. This time there was no audience. All were prey.

Correspondent Irvin Cobb wrote of the war: "It's too big to comprehend . . . No man can grasp it all . . . No man can take in completely the horrors, the splendors, the suffering and the glory of it . . . I have an impression locked up inside me, but I shall never be able to give it to others . . . Here you get a Gettysburg for breakfast, a Chancellorsville for lunch, Waterloo for supper, and to make a good measure, they throw in a Sedan around tea-time."

Adversaries fought from dirt ditches, bursts into no man's land were met with annihilation, advances were measured in yards, and into this quagmire—the Americans.

CHAPTER TWENTY-EIGHT

PRIVATE FIRST CLASS Peter Thompson was sworn in as an American citizen on June 1, 1918, at Camp Lewis. He was assigned to Company E, of the Second Battalion, of the 362nd Regiment, of the 181st Brigade, of the 91st Division, known as the Wild West Division. The 91st drew from the western states of California, Idaho, Montana, Nevada, Oregon, Utah, Washington, and Wyoming, and the Territory of Alaska, hence their nickname. His regiment's motto was *arma tuentur pacem*, arms are the guardian of peace.

Twenty-seven percent of the soldiers in Peter's company were foreign born (which was probably close to what it was in Butte). They were from Austria, Hungary, Mexico, Sweden, Canada, Italy, Russia, Montenegro, Norway, Wales, Ireland, Greece, Turkey, Germany, Bohemia, and England. We were at war with some of those countries making their native sons enemy aliens, and some of them spoke hardly any English and their level of education was so low that the company commander deemed teaching them and forming them into soldiers for a combat regiment in the time allowed was impossible. He recommended several Austrians be discharged or transferred, and two he recommended be interred. However, many enemy aliens remained in the company. One was German-born but had already become an American citizen.

Training with bayonet, Camp Lewis.
FORT LEWIS MILITARY MUSEUM

In the middle of their training at Camp Lewis, a bit of a scandal erupted regarding Peter's brigade commander. This fifty-five-year-old general, a West Point graduate, caused quite a stir when it was discovered that he had been out drinking in a hotel room, to the point of intoxication, with several junior officers. Not only was such intemperate behavior unbecoming to an officer and a gentleman, it was also illegal, Prohibition having already passed in the state of Washington. The army wanted to avoid a scandal for a number of reasons, one of which was this general was a popular speaker in promoting the war effort, but as time went on, it became apparent that this was no brief flight of intemperance, but a pattern of decided intemperance—the man was a drunk—and this was manifesting itself in sloppiness in his command. He was sacked.

To replace him, the army summoned fifty-nine-year-old General John B. McDonald from his comfortable post at the War Department. This distinguished looking, silver-haired officer was a native of Alabama and a graduate of the Academy.

Peter's battalion commander, Captain Henry Edmonds, began his military career as a buck private long before the war started. He went to Camp Lewis as a corporal to help with the training. He thought he had really arrived when he made sergeant. Before the war was over, he would be a major.

Brigadeer General John B. McDonald,
Commander of the 181st Brigade.
NATIONAL ARCHIVES AND RECORDS ADMINISTRATION, SC9584

AFTER EIGHT MONTHS of training at Camp Lewis, Peter and the rest of the Wild West Division prepared to entrain for New York. As he readied to leave, Peter wrote to Aila and closed his epistle with, "Now remember all this, Aila, because we'll talk about it when the war's over."

Another busy soldier sent three letters: one to his dearest love, another to his best girl, and the third to the only girl he ever loved. The censor mixed them up when depositing the letters in their envelopes. If that soldier survived the war, he may not have survived his return.

Private First Class Peter Thompson,
taken before the 91st left for France.

Peter Thompson and Ray Coughlin, Camp Lewis.

Peter (right) and another soldier at Camp Lewis.

Peter at Camp Lewis.

Gas mask practice, Camp Lewis.
FORT LEWIS MILITARY MUSEUM

One third of the men in Company E. Peter is in the front row, the fifth from the left.
Generally, company strength in the First World War was 256 officers and men;
however, in the 362nd Regiment, company strength was smaller,
ranging from 145 to 228. Company E was the second smallest company
in the regiment with 150 officers and men.

The soldiers of Company E assembled for a photograph shortly before they left Camp Lewis. Peter is easy to pick out; he is by far the shortest man in the company, probably in the regiment, possibly in the division. He barely met the height requirement for enlistment and didn't meet the weight requirement. A man had to be at least five feet one inch tall and weigh 128 pounds. Peter was five feet three inches tall and weighed 115 pounds.

The trains took the soldiers back through Montana. Butte citizens eagerly awaited them at the depot with gifts of fruit, lemonade, doughnuts, cigars, and magazines. The saloons closed half an hour before the troop trains rolled into town and reopened half an hour after they left.

The soldiers were greeted warmly in every town throughout their cross country trip, leaving them with the feeling that an undivided nation was truly behind them as they headed off for war.

They detrained near New York City and waited at Camp Merritt for their next orders. While they waited, sight-seeing and flirtations with local girls distracted those soldiers who could get passes into New York. Several men in Peter's regiment, including his chum Gordon, came down with the measles. Gordon would miss the war. Some companies were spared the measles outbreak completely, but Peter's was really hit hard—one third of the 150 men in Company E were quarantined and put on detention, including a few noncommissioned officers. I don't know what they did to be put on detention. Perhaps whatever it was also gave them the measles. They stayed behind at Camp Merritt, but some would rejoin the regiment later in France.

After five days at Camp Merritt, the healthy soldiers boarded river boats at Alpine Landing and cruised down the Hudson, past the sights of Manhattan, into New York harbor. When the Statue of Liberty came into view, the spirited young soldiers broke into a chorus of, "And we won't come back 'till it's over, over there!" I know it sounds like a scene from a Jimmy Cagney movie but they really did sing it.

Whenever I hear "Over There" I think of the doughboys, which made me wonder, why were the American soldiers in the First World War called doughboys? There are several theories, but from what I read, the name came from General Pershing's campaign into Mexico in 1916 to chase down Pancho Villa. The cavalry became covered with dust—*adobe* dust. There goes an adobe, a-do-be, a dough-boy.

Peter and his fellow soldiers disembarked the river boats and boarded the huge *Empress of Russia* and steamed out of New York harbor on July 6, 1918. Their ship zig-zagged across the Atlantic in the largest convoy to date, protected by a flotilla of destroyers and cruisers, fourteen ships in all, painted with bizarre random lines and ferocious teeth. The wild design was no cubist rendering but camouflage—a multi-colored object being harder for the U-boats to spot against the horizon than a huge solid-colored object. Airplanes flew ahead to scout the way off shore.

The ship was filled to the brim with soldiers. It had been provisioned in China and the soldiers speculated that the rations had been around the world a couple of times already. The lower decks stunk of hard boiled eggs. To avoid the stench, many slept on deck in the open. Peter and his chums sneaked in a few hands of panguingue until they were caught and punished for gambling. With card betting suspended, they bet on how many kittens a pregnant stowaway cat would produce.

Lieutenant Whitney of the machine gun battalion thought he would spend his time aboard ship writing lengthy letters home, but after reading the censorship rules, he concluded that about all he could write was "it is a nice day and the ocean is full of salt water," and he wasn't sure whether even that would pass.

One diligent sergeant brought a large bottle of ink with him, certain he would find none of the indispensable fluid in France. During the voyage, he learned that the army issued tablets which when mixed with water made ink as good as that in his heavy bottle. So he heaved the superfluous liquid overboard which, on its way to the Atlantic, met the face of one of the Chinese cooks. Thereafter, pies cost the soldiers a whopping dollar and often were devoid of filling.

Their ship managed to make her way through the U-boat infested waters without incident and arrived safely at Liverpool on July 17, 1918. While waiting on the dock, Peter watched pallid men, women, and children, their clothes disheveled, their hair matted, disembark from another ship. They had been bound for America when a German torpedo sank their ocean liner.

Once assembled, the doughboys marched four miles through the cobblestone streets of Liverpool to Knotty Ash Rest Camp. Children ran along side them shouting, "The Yanks are coming!" Women and old men lined the road waving handkerchiefs in welcome, some offering a teary "God bless you" to the passing soldiers as they marched swiftly and confidently, enjoying the attention.

After two nights, the soldiers entrained for Southampton. There, under cover of darkness, they boarded ships and slipped across the Channel. Though seaside towns were under a blackout and there was no moon, through the darkness the soldiers could make out the remnants of sunken ships cast onto the shore by the tide.

They arrived at Le Havre the next morning and marched to camp where they enjoyed a substantial meal—a welcome change. Rations had been sparse during the month-long journey. With satisfied stomachs, they bedded down in tents. For the first time, they could hear the faint boom of the guns at the front.

In the morning, they marched to the train station. They were astounded at how puny the boxcars looked compared to those back home. "A cattle car here would hold one Texas steer!" exclaimed a Wild West doughboy. *Hommes 40—Chevaux 8* was written on the sides of the boxcars. The soldiers called them sidecar Pullmans and thought it funny that five men equaled one horse. They lined up to be sure it was so. To be specific, five *enlisted* men equaled one horse. The officers rode in coaches.

Several trains were required to transport Peter's regiment. Peter boarded the Company E train. I don't know which train it was. There was more than one company per train. The boxcars were crowded, so the men took turns sleeping on the floor. Around midnight near Bonnieres, a village halfway between Rouen and Paris, the first troop train was switched onto a siding to let a freight train pass. There they waited.

Whether negligence or sabotage, who knows. The switch was not switched back. The freight train diverted onto the same siding. Danger lights flashed, the brakeman signaled, but to no avail. The freight train's engineer ignored the warnings and traveling full bore at sixty miles per hour crashed into the stopped troop train. The engine careened through boxcars full of soldiers. Cars piled on cars and splintered like match boxes. Men and limbs and wood flew in every direction. Seven cars were smashed before the freight train rolled to a stop. Soldiers in undamaged cars were jolted forward and thrown on top of one another. They scrambled to their feet, slid the doors open, jumped off the train, and ran to the rear. They frantically climbed through the wreckage to rescue the injured only to have a fellow barely alive say, help him over there, he's in worse shape than I am. Doctors hurried to the injured. Soldiers scribbled down the last words of those about to die and led the priest to the dying. After they had done all they could for the injured, they gathered the dead. Thirty-two men from Peter's regiment "went West" that night, sixty-three more were maimed. Five thousand French civilians turned out to attend the funeral and burial and adorned the graves with flowers.

Another Montana soldier should have been on that train but wasn't. Bill Lake started to feel poorly in New York but didn't let on because he didn't want to be left behind. While on board ship, his measles came on with a vengeance. He was still sick when they arrived in Liverpool and was ordered to stay behind to recuperate while the rest of the regiment left for France. The machine gun company took the brunt of the train crash and Bill Lake was in the machine gun company. His best friend in the regiment was killed. Measles may have saved his life.

The rest of the trains continued on to their training area at Montigny Le Roi in the Haute Marne region of eastern France. Peter's company billeted in the villages of Bonnecourt and Freecourt. They slept wherever they could: in barns, chicken houses, and makeshift barracks. The French villagers warmly welcomed the doughboys and were intrigued by whatever the tall foreigners were doing, and the soldiers were equally intrigued by them. "Everything seems so old and ancient in France," wrote one private in a letter home. "Even the humans live to be about one hundred years old." The soldiers took note of an unusual mark of distinction outside the villagers' homes—a pile of manure—the more manure, the more animals, the wealthier the family. A frequent observation made by the doughboys about the inhabitants of those homes was the dismal condition of their teeth. Another was the stark absence of young men in the villages, only old men and boys were left.

Soon after they settled in, officers dispatched the soldiers of one entire battalion to sweep and clean the streets. The French villagers looked on stunned.

For the next several weeks, Peter trained with the rest of the 91st Division on the pastoral, undulating landscape of Haute Marne while farmers worked the surrounding fields. War remained an abstraction.

It was now August and it was hot, very hot, especially for a young man from Butte, Montana, and Belfast. Wearing those "tin hats" with the sun blazing down on them, one soldier said it felt like he was "wearing the kitchen stove" on his head "with the fire drawing well and the coffee boiling over."

While they were training one day, a truck convoy passed heading east, toward the front. The small trucks were full of men. More trucks passed, still more, and more, and more. Hours later, Peter and his fellow soldiers sat down on the grassy fields and ate lunch. More trucks passed. The soldiers resumed their drills. The same convoy still passed. Still later, they sat on the verdant field to rest, and watched the last truck in the convoy disappear over the horizon.

Days later, another convoy passed, just as long.

When they weren't training, the doughboys were a boon to the local economy. Not able to understand French, when they purchased an item they simply slapped a fistful of francs on the counter and let the merchant take what he wanted. They soon learned not to do that. Peter bought a small French-English dictionary to help him wade through the language barrier. American officers in another division arranged to take French lessons from a local teenage girl. Her mother attended as chaperone. Whenever one of the officers made a mistake of grammar or vocabulary, the girl swatted him with a switch.

Where in proximity to one another, comradery quickly developed between the French soldiers and jocular Americans. One lieutenant explained, "You see, we think the French are crazy, and the French know damn well we are." According to Floyd Gibbons, a newspaper man who arrived with the First Division, the French view of Americans derived chiefly from silent movies and dime novels, and I suspect from Buffalo Bill's Wild West Show. Americans were expected to gallop through town on a wild bronc, not holding on while not falling off, fire their revolvers willy nilly, then dismount, eat dinner, and for dessert, pelt each other in the face with cream pies.

Let's digress for a moment and check in on Denis.

11 August 1918

Dear Mother

   Just a few lines in answer to your ever welcome letter. I was pleased to see by it that all at home were well as this leaves me well at present. I received 4 parcels last week from the Red Cross. One was from Lady Carson and there was one from you. The first chance you get of sending me a parcel send some socks and a shaving gear and some wool and needle. I will come to a close hoping to hear from you soon.

From your son
Denis

And a week later,

18 August 1918

Dear Mother

   Just a few lines to let you know I am well hoping this finds all at home the same. If you can will you send me a pack of cards also some books. Have you got any idea how long this war is going to last. As regards what kind of work I am dong it is just ordinary labor about a yard

_____

_____

_____

to hear from you soon.

From your son
Denis

(The last three lines were blacked out by the censor.)

Faraway from where Peter trained on a farmer's land, Denis the city boy was helping another farmer harvest his crop. Denis thought he was in Holland and so approached the farmer about escaping. Denis was not in Holland. Nevertheless, the German farmer, his wife, and his daughter, especially his daughter, took a liking to our ever animated, ever cheerful Denis. When Denis was sent back to the prison camp, the farmer begged him to return after the war. He would gladly give Denis a job, and hoped Denis would become his son-in-law.

September 1st, 1918

Dear Mother

Just a few lines to let you know I am well hoping this finds all at home the same. Send me Paddy McAnespie's address. I hope he is well also Harry. I was dreaming about being at home the other day and Peter was there also Paddy McLaverty and Davie Holmes. I will draw to a close hoping to hear from you soon

From your son
Denis

We return to Peter and find him still training in Haute Marne. The 91st has just set out for three days of maneuvers. Rumor has it this will be the end of training after which they will be sent to the trenches in a quiet sector.

On day two, maneuvers were abruptly halted. We're pulling out, Peter's commander said. To where, they didn't know. Must be big, went the buzz, nobody would cancel maneuvers otherwise. Their attitude was, we came here to do a job, let's go do it.

Sunday morning at Montigny le Roi, Haute Marne, where members of the 91st Division were quartered in the homes of French villagers.

U.S. ARMY MILITARY HISTORY INSTITUTE, SC-31864

Men of the 362nd Regiment starting their hike to the zone of advance,
Dammartin, Haute Marne, France, September 4, 1918.
U.S. ARMY MILITARY HISTORY INSTITUTE, SC31870

Peter stuffed his overcoat, blanket, shoes, clothes, and shelter half into his pack. It weighed sixty pounds, more than half what he weighed.

A field clerk delivered their orders: the regiment was to march to Chauffort. They loaded those sixty pound packs on their backs, formed a column, and set off. Their cavalcade presented a picture of the old century meeting the new. Soldiers with puttee-wrapped shins sat on the buckboards of horse-drawn covered wagons reminiscent of the wagons that carried their grandparents to the American West, but in this particular wagon train, only the drivers rode, everybody else walked, or to use one of Aila's expressions, used "Shank's mare." Motorized trucks carried still more rations and ammunition.

It was now early September. The bright, summer sun warmed the soldiers in their woolen, olive drab uniforms and made them hot as they marched into midday. They would start marching on the hour, stop at ten minutes to the hour, rest, and start again on the hour. Twenty-four kilometers later, they reached their destination. They looked for shade and, whether finding it or not, dropped to rest. Then their commander received another message. The order to march to Chauffort was a mistake. They were supposed to march to Chalindrey, which was in the opposite direction from where they had started and just as far. Much cursing of the anonymous, erring field clerk ensued.

The next day they marched back the way they came and beyond. It was another sunny, summer day until less than an hour into the march when the heavens opened. They marched and marched, in the rain, through the mud, up the hills. Their sixty-pound packs grew heavier and heavier as they became water logged. A few men collapsed on a steep climb but caught up at the rest stop. Even so, the men whistled and sang as they marched.

Fully outfitted doughboy with one of those sixty-pound packs.
FORT LEWIS MILITARY MUSEUM

Mademoiselle from Armentières, parley-voo,
Mademoiselle from Armentières, parley-voo,
Mademoiselle from Armentières
She hasn't been kissed in forty years,
Hinky, dinky parley-voo.

I don't know which songs they sang that day but that was a popular one. Another was,

We don't want the bacon,
All we want is a piece of the Rhine.

In between songs, they shouted catcalls at passing troops. They carried the joviality of a group of pals going off to camp. More than half the men in Peter's regiment were from Montana—miners and cowboys—the carefree, happy-go-lucky sort. Sure his work was dangerous, but he did it with no one looking over his shoulder and that he liked. Every day he beat death was triumph.

Rain continued throughout the day. Trucks and wagons became stuck in the mud. Soldiers were called out of their column to push them out. At last they arrived in Chalindrey and joined the rest of their brigade. They camped in pup tents for the night. Their next march wasn't so long, just to the train station.

When their train arrived, the aroma left by the previous passengers made their identity unmistakable. Peter's battalion commander insisted that the

French station master have the boxcars cleaned before the men boarded the train. The indignant station master mumbled something in French—such a fuss over a little horse manure. While Frenchmen grudgingly cleaned the boxcars, a cowboy found a piece of chalk and wrote "Powder River to Berlin" in huge letters across the side of one of the cars. This piqued the curiosity of the other soldiers, and they asked about it.

"What? Never heard of the Powder River?" replied the bow-legged cowboy. "Why it's the greatest little body of water in the world. It's a mile wide and an inch deep!"

Said to begin "nowhere . . . and end in much the same fashion," this beloved river of Montana cowboy lore was thusly christened by a drunken cowboy while removing the dust from his throat after a month-long roundup. Knowing he would have to cross the Powder River, he sold his mare that couldn't swim. When he reached the river, he discovered that he had sold his mare for nothing. The river was nothing more than a contiguous collection of puddles. Yet the more he drank, the deeper and wider the river got, and the wilder his exuberance for it grew, as did the exuberance of the other cowboys. Years later in faraway France, the Montana cowboys' enthusiasm for the scrawny waterway was so infectious that it even captivated the miners

The Powder River, a recent photo.

and city men. Their nickname was born. Ever after, the regiment would be known as the Powder River Gang.

> Wild and wooly, full of fleas.
> Fight and frolic, as we please;
> Powder River—let 'er buck!
> Wade across it you're in luck.

The soldiers boarded the cleaned-out boxcars and traveled north. They detrained near Houdlaincourt and billeted there. It was Sunday, a rest day. After Mass, Peter and his buddy Ray and some other soldiers enjoyed a refreshing swim in the canal.

The next evening they set out on foot. They marched at night to hide their presence from German pilots. The boom of the guns grew louder and louder as they inched closer to the war. Officers sternly ordered the men to sterilize their drinking water. Before daybreak, they stopped in dense woods on the slope of a muddy hill. After much confusion in the dark, they finally figured out where they were supposed to be. Peter dropped his pack and lay down. He tucked his gas mask under his head and immediately fell asleep.

After a few hours, he awoke. The brilliant sun pierced through the leafy branches in narrow shafts. It was pleasantly cool in the woods. He heard a gentle lulling hum. I wonder if he recognized it. He saw a group of soldiers standing along the edge of the woods peering up at the sky. He walked over and joined them and looked up. So these were the flying aces of legend. He watched the planes swoop and dip, then a puff of smoke, then another. He could hear the faint tat-tat-tat-tat-tat of machine gun fire.

Almost as attention grabbing as the aviators was the sight of their new commander—Colonel John Henry Parker. He strode through the camp sporting the ribbons of the Distinguished Service Cross, awarded for extraordinary heroism. This fifty-one-year-old Missouri native and graduate of West Point earned his nickname "Gatlin' Gun" Parker while manning said gun on San Juan Hill during the Spanish-American War. He called himself "an artist with a machine gun." He would be the only American infantry officer to ride into battle in this war on horseback. In a war with long range artillery, high on a horse was the last place one wanted to be, but that didn't seem to bother Gatlin' Gun Parker. Once an artillery bombardment opened up on an American battalion in transit; the troops were

Colonel John Henry "Gatlin' Gun" Parker, Commander of the 362nd Regiment.

NATIONAL ARCHIVES AND RECORDS ADMINISTRATION, SC56637

thrown into confusion, everybody diving for cover in ditches along the road. Parker saw what was happening and calmly rode up—on his horse. Everybody else was diving for cover in ditches, and there was Parker, sitting high in the saddle. He slowly walked his horse up and down the line, while artillery shells exploded all around, and periodically stopped and talked to the men, encouraging them on, bracing them up not only with his uplifting words but with his blatant fearlessness and outright defiance of danger.

Everything about Gatlin' Gun Parker was extraordinary and conspicuous. A strapping figure of a man, he was a leader sure to spur a young soldier's imagination. If war was a great adventure story, Parker was its dashing hero. Every inch of his six foot three inch frame exuded grit and purpose. He looked and acted the part and was just the man to lead a band of fearless miners and cowboys.

CHAPTER TWENTY-NINE

GENERAL PERSHING HAD anticipated that the American army would be ready by 1919; however, by the spring of 1918 the situation was growing desperate. The German army was advancing rapidly toward Paris. The French government was preparing to evacuate. Recognizing the dire need, General Pershing threw what American troops he had into the fight. British nurse Vera Brittain wrote of her first glimpse of them. It was earlier in the year during the massive assault on the Somme, the battle in which Denis was captured and John was wounded. Untold numbers of wounded men poured into her field hospital in northeastern France. She had never seen anything like it. For the first time she feared the worst—that they actually might lose the war. Then she learned that Paris was being shelled. Then news came that the Germans were already in the suburbs of Amiens. If the Germans took Amiens, they'd drive a wedge between the British and French lines—the result would be catastrophic. Night time air raids rattled her already threadbare nerves. Then she read General Haig's bold pronouncement about no retirement and fighting to the end, and she was buoyed by it. Then a day or two later, while walking back to her ward,

> I had to wait to let a large contingent of troops march past me along the main road that ran through our camp. They were swinging rapidly towards Camiers, and though the sight of soldiers marching was now too familiar to arouse curiosity, an unusual quality of bold vigour in their swift stride caused me to stare at them with puzzled interest.
>
> They looked larger than ordinary men; their tall, straight figures were in vivid contrast to the under-sized armies of pale recruits to which we had grown accustomed. At first, I thought their spruce, clean uniforms were those of officers yet obviously they could not be officers, for there were too many of them; they seemed, as it were, Tommies in heaven. Had yet another regiment been conjured out of our depleted Dominions? I wondered, watching them move with such rhythm, such dignity, such serene consciousness of self-respect. But I knew the colonial troops so well,

and these were different; they were assured where the Australians were aggressive, self-possessed where the New Zealanders were turbulent.

Then I heard an excited exclamation from a group of Sisters behind me. "Look! Look! Here are the Americans!"

I pressed forward with the others to watch the United States physically entering the War, so god-like, so magnificent, so splendidly unimpaired in comparison with the tired, nerve-racked men of the British Army. So these were our deliverers at last, marching up the road to Camiers in the spring sunshine! There seemed to be hundreds of them, and in the fearless swagger of their proud strength they looked a formidable bulwark against the peril looming from Amiens.

U.S. Marines drove the German army from Belleau Wood. American infantry divisions fought at Chateau-Thierry and Cantingy; together with the British and French armies they stopped the German advance. Paris was saved.

Before this, General Ludendorff had been dismissive of the Americans—these upstarts from a yet-to-be civilized nation. A communique from his commander at Chateau-Thierry told him otherwise: "Personnel must be called excellent . . . The various attacks of the Marines were carried out smartly and ruthlessly. The moral effect of our fire did not materially check the advance of the infantry. The nerves of the Americans are still unshaken."

It is the depth of folly to underestimate one's adversary.

After successful fighting into the summer, and with the German advance decisively stopped, and more and more American divisions arriving in France by the day, French General Ferdinand Foch took stock of the situation, and he smelled blood. Now was the time to strike the fatal blow. Under his command, the Allies would launch a major assault along the entire Western Front, from Verdun to the sea. With one colossal sweep, they would drive the German army out of France and Belgium, cut the German supply lines, and end the war *en fin*.

General Foch had only recently been named supreme allied commander. Before the spring of 1918, there had been no commander over all Allied forces. It was chiefly at British General Haig's insistence during the spring disaster on the Somme that one somebody should take charge of this war. The politicians agreed and picked Foch. Until then, the British fought here, the French fought there, the Russians, the Belgians, the Italians, each fought their own wars against Germany, Austria, Turkey,

General Ferdinand Foch and General John Pershing, July 22, 1918,
at Pershing's summer quarters, Val des Ecoliers, Chaumont, France.
NATIONAL ARCHIVES AND RECORDS ADMINISTRATION, SC14592

and so on. Had one somebody been in charge from the beginning and the
Allies made a concerted effort to beat Germany, the undeniable strongman
of the enemy forces, would the war have lasted so long? And had there
been no supreme allied commander in 1918, and the American army,
though tremendous in strength, thrown into a helter-skelter conflict,

would the war have ended so quickly? We'll never know. The fact was, now they were together, under one somebody named Foch. In consult with his generals, he would decide who would attack and when and where. At last, the war had a boss.

By September of 1918, there were sufficient troops in France to comprise an American army. Foch wanted to feed American regiments and companies into French and British divisions, using them as replacement troops, but Pershing said no. Americans will fight as an American army. There were several reasons for Pershing's position. He worried that low morale among Allied troops could infect the gung ho Americans, and in his words, "The nationals of no country would willingly serve under a foreign flag in preference to their own." He also believed that the presence of a new adversary would have a debilitating effect on the enemy's morale. Pershing held his ground, though the price was steep. He was forced to put an inexperienced, poorly equipped army in two huge, back-to-back engagements. First, the American army must reduce the German salient at St. Mihiel, and then quickly after, that same army must launch the largest offensive in American history between the Argonne forest and the Meuse river, the most difficult sector on the Western Front. This required moving 600,000 men with 2700 guns and supplies sixty miles on three narrow dirt roads and be prepared to attack in less than two weeks. The logistics were staggering. Time did not allow General Pershing to equip the army with American tanks, artillery, and airplanes, so these he bought from the Allies, though still not enough. At the eleventh hour he learned that the 150 British tanks he had been promised would not be available. Bemoaning this deficiency because the tanks could have greatly reduced infantry losses, Pershing wrote after the war, "As usual, the American soldier discounted the odds placed against him and carried the day by his dash and courage."

For four long years, the combatants had fought a stalemate from the trenches punctuated by massive prolonged assaults resulting only in carnage and in no strategic gains. General Pershing strongly believed that to win the war, the Allies must break out of the minutia of siege warfare. If there be carnage, victory must result. Hit the enemy hard with overwhelming strength, run him over, and keep going until you crush him. The French battle plan for St. Mihiel was three hundred pages long, Pershing's was fourteen, the difference—trench warfare versus open warfare. The American First

Army would fight in the open, on the battlefield, not from the trenches. Once engaged, it did not stop until the war was over.

Another factor contributing to the copious detail of the French battle plan was that French commanders tended to micro-manage the battle from afar; whereas, the American practice was to give orders which allowed initiative on the part of subordinate officers to do what made sense in response to the ever fluid situation on the ground once the fighting started. Even a French division commander—a general—had to request permission just to move his command post forward, and it could take hours to get a reply.

Pershing counted on a "self reliant infantry."

AT ONE O'CLOCK on the morning of September 12, 1918, the big guns began to fire on the German lines at St. Mihiel. The 91st Division waited in army reserve. Peter sat on a hill with his regiment under drizzle and mist and watched the war. Even if he could sleep with all the noise, who would want to. What a show it must have been as the massive guns thundered, lighting the night sky. Several German officers committed suicide that night. The notes they left said they were utterly discouraged now that the Americans were in the war, and they would rather die than be defeated.

At five o'clock that morning, the American infantry jumped off behind a rolling artillery barrage. They cut swiftly through the barbed wire entanglements or threw chicken wire over the top and ran across. The Germans were in retreat, burning all as they went. Within hours, the army had achieved its objective—the salient was flattened. The "dagger pointed at the heart of eastern France" was smashed. The citizens of St. Mihiel were liberated. It was over so fast that the 91st was not called into battle.

French officers were amazed by the speed with which the American infantry passed through the barbed wire entanglements of no man's land. One French officer on surveying the scene after the battle concluded that the Americans were able to get through quickly because they had long legs and big feet.

CHAPTER THIRTY

PETER'S REGIMENT moved out after dark to a waiting convoy. It would take 15,000 trucks to transport the entire 91st Division, and it was only one of nine American divisions to enter the line at jump-off in the next bout, and that didn't include divisions held in reserve. And these divisions were huge. Mobilization had been swift and enormous without time to train enough officers for normal size divisions. Some had 28,000 men, nearly twice the size of a European division. The 91st had 20,000. It boggles the mind to think of orchestrating movements of such masses of men in secret. All travel on open roads had to be at night with no lights.

The rickety trucks bounced along the pot-holed narrow dirt road, each driver keeping his eyes closely fixed on the faint vehicle ahead lest he stray from the road. The forty mile trip took hours. The truck would stop—another traffic jam. The truck started again. Stop, start, stop, start. Another stop. An officer poked his head into Peter's truck. This is where we get out, he said. They were at Remembercourt. It was the first village Peter saw that had been shelled. His battalion bivouacked in the woods. They slept and rested. Once day was well gone, they moved out on foot. They passed white crosses along the road. They marched and marched and kept marching. It was by far their longest march thus far. Some soldiers tossed their blankets to lighten their packs. They arrived at Jubrecourt exhausted. They spread out to find shelter amid the crumbling wrecks of what was left of the village. The wells in one abandoned town had been poisoned by German troops. Sterilizing would do no good, water had to be trucked in. The men were appalled. Poisoning seemed downright unchivalrous to them. They weren't ones to back down from a fight, but there were rules. Poison didn't enter into a fair fight.

Now they were only three kilometers from the front. Unexploded shells were scattered about the landscape. While eating breakfast, the soldiers heard a shell scream overhead. They tensed. It landed behind them. Ah, the Boche missed again, joked a doughboy. They all laughed. The Germans lobbed gas shells on them that night. Nobody laughed at those.

The next day a German pilot flew over and dropped a bomb on them as they stood in mess line. Not one hungry soldier moved from the line. Even before they were battle-hardened, their stomachs reigned supreme— or was it their pride. Anti-aircraft gunners fired at the German plane. Some men were injured by falling debris.

Night after night, howitzers and long range guns on mighty caissons rolled toward the front and before dawn disappeared into the woods or under camouflage. This created even more excitement among the young soldiers.

They set out again. The closer they moved to the front, the more difficult the marches. They tripped and stumbled across the battered land. This was the Verdun sector where in 1916 the French had stubbornly defended the city against an unrelenting German siege for nearly a year. French soldiers were buried alive in collapsing trenches under mountains of dirt hurled on them by massive artillery explosions, the only evidence of them visible, the points of their bayonets sticking up through the dirt.

Dawn approached. Peter's regiment stopped their march and camped in pup tents in the woods. They nursed their blistered feet. Gas alarms sounded throughout the night. Gas rattled them. With every alarm, the men quickly put on their masks and took them off as soon as they heard the all clear. Some tried to sleep with their masks on. The masks made their faces hot and uncomfortable. It began to rain. The already damp ground beneath them became saturated. "Two

Doughboy outfitted for gas attack.
THE U.S. ARMY 1890–1920

hours of rain will produce more mud to the square inch in France than anywhere else in the world," wrote one soggy soldier in a letter home— and he was from rain-soaked western Washington. In some places, they sank to their knees in mud. Just moving around became a struggle.

By now, American soldiers had replaced almost all the French troops in what was now the American sector. To hide his identity from the enemy, one American officer donned a French jacket and hat before he approached the front line trenches to inspect no man's land. On the way back, he passed a French officer seated at a linen-draped table under a tree. The Frenchman greeted him and handed him the menu and asked if he would you like to join him. The American, eying the repast, replied no thank you, he had already eaten.

Officers ordered their troops to keep conversation to a whisper lest the Germans hear English spoken. Two hundred German shock troops raided the sector to the right of the 91st in an attempt to capture prisoners whom they could interrogate to find out what was afoot. Colonel Parker ordered: "NO AMERICAN OFFICER OR SOLDIER WILL—UNDER ANY CIRCUMSTANCES—ALLOW HIMSELF TO BE CAPTURED."

Such was the prelude to the Meuse Argonne Offensive.

Miles ahead of the American soldiers were the railroad lines that supplied the German army. Their objective was to cut that supply route, thereby crushing the entire German war effort in France. To reach those vital rail lines, the doughboys would have to overcome several nearly impregnable German lines of defense equipped with six hundred artillery emplacements plus machine gunners, snipers, and minefields. The Germans began to fortify this region as soon as they achieved a foothold in France in 1914, and they had used every topographical feature to their advantage. It was the most difficult and defendable terrain on the Western Front. All advantage went to the defender. The American First Army would have to completely overwhelm him or be pounded into oblivion.

The area through which the Americans were to attack was bounded on the west by the heights of the Argonne Forest, which rose three hundred feet above the valley, and to the east by the River Meuse, a river easily missed, cached behind its bushy banks. Between the Argonne Forest and the Meuse lay a rippling terrain, an earthen tablecloth not yet pulled taut. Long, smooth swells of earth followed one after the other with forests, dense brush, and hills sprinkled throughout. In springtime when not war torn, those swells are swathed in brilliant yellow mustard and thick green grass, the kind of vivid pastoral scene immortalized by the Impressionist painters. These normally picturesque swells gave the enemy splendid vantage points from which to fire down on advancing troops and were so frequent that the Americans would have to pass over them, becoming easy targets. Across the river to the east was more high ground full of German guns.

In short, the American First Army would attack through a dense forest and swell-ridden valley into which hundreds of German guns were pointed, and they would do so for twenty-two miles.

Lloyd's of London laid odds at six to four that the war wouldn't be over before June of 1919.

Hills throughout the valley provided more high ground for German guns. At dead center loomed Montfauçon, a wisp of a hill by Montana standards, but the highest ground in the Argonne and prominently placed to provide the well-fortified and organized defender both a view of the entire assaulting army and a position from which to hurl artillery shells in every direction. From the stone church on top, lookouts enjoyed a panoramic view of the region. They could see all the way to Verdun. It was now late September. Recognizing the daunting task they faced, French General Petain doubted the Americans would make it to Montfauçon by Christmas. General Pershing planned to take it on the first day.

The 91st Division was assigned to the V Corps which was at the center of the American line. The 91st took the left wing, placing it between the heights of Argonne Forest and Montfauçon. The advance would be to the north. They would face the 117th German Division, veterans of the Carpathian campaign in the east, and the First Prussian Guards, the German army's elite and considered among the best of Germany's first class shock troops. Any self-respecting Berlin hostess would be sure to include a Guard officer at her parties. These battle-tested, well-armed German troops sat poised expecting an attack on September 25 in the direction of Metz.

The day before the battle was to begin, the signal battalion joined the V Corps. They would learn their duties during the fighting. Peter's regiment never received nearly the signaling apparatus they needed. They were woefully short of motor vehicles and horses to move troops and ammunition and to take wounded to hospitals. What horses the regiment did get were half starved and could barely walk. Their Pioneer Platoon, detailed for small engineering jobs, had only shovels for tools. Only sixteen men in each company were issued automatic rifles. Though several men had been thoroughly trained on Stokes mortars, none were provided. The joke around the regiment was—are we to bite the Hun with our teeth?

They did have rifles, bayonets, grenades, plenty of machine guns, and loads of ammunition. And as for *elan*, enthusiasm, grit, determination, boldness—all of this was in abundant supply throughout the Wild West Division, and especially in its wildest regiment—the 362nd. Many of them thought like Shakespeare's Henry that those abed at home would one day "hold their manhoods cheap" for having missed the coming fight. In more current language, an American captain from another division said, "Here I am in France at the head of 250 men and horses and the guns and we're rolling up front to kick a dent in history. The poor unfortunate that ain't in this fight has almost got license to shoot himself."

And as for how long the fight was going to last, the Wild West men were much more optimistic than Lloyd's of London. "Heaven, hell, or Hoboken by Christmas," was their motto.

Peter's platoon commander gathered the men and told them to pre-

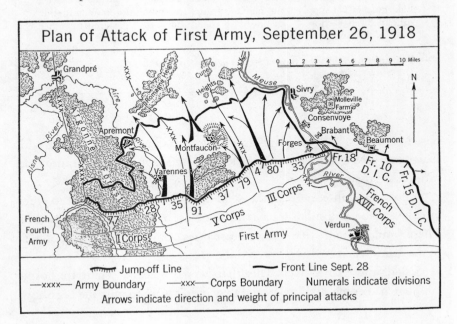

AMERICAN ARMIES AND BATTLEFIELDS IN EUROPE, P. 172.

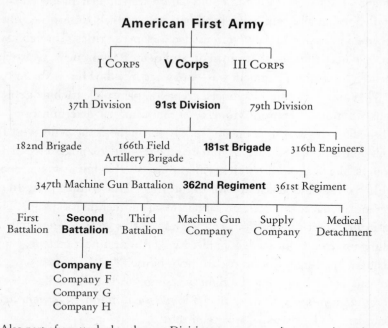

American First Army

I CORPS   **V Corps**   III CORPS

37th Division   **91st Division**   79th Division

182nd Brigade   166th Field Artillery Brigade   **181st Brigade**   316th Engineers

347th Machine Gun Battalion   **362nd Regiment**   361st Regiment

First Battalion   **Second Battalion**   Third Battalion   Machine Gun Company   Supply Company   Medical Detachment

Company E
Company F
Company G
Company H

Also part of or attached to the 91st Division were a gas regiment, an air service squadron, an engineer train, a signal battalion, a sanitary train (ambulances, field hospital), a supply train, military police, an ammunition train, a mobile ordnance repair shop, a machine shop truck unit, a mail detachment, other field artillery units, and several French officers.

The units in bold type show Peter's chain of command.

pare light packs. Take no blankets, no overcoats, no half shelters, he said. Leave everything behind but bring slickers and as much ammunition and rations as possible.

Untried and ill-equipped, the Wild West Division was about to enter what was to be, and still is today, the bloodiest battle in American history. There would be more than 100,000 casualties, roughly the number of men in the army when America entered the war.

Sick or injured men feigned health to keep from being sent to the hospital. They had come all this way and they didn't want to miss the Big Show.

Chapter Thirty-One

Once upon a time in the kingdom of Burgundy there lived a beautiful queen named Kriemhilde. One day Kriemhilde's brother, King Gunther, a bachelor in want of a wife, left for faraway Isenland to woo Brunhilde. Now this was a rather delicate maneuver. To win Brunhilde, a suitor had to compete with her in athletic games. If he won, he won her. If she won, she slew him. We know that since Brunhilde was still a maiden, all had lost and perished. Still, Gunther was determined. With help from his friend Siegfried of Netherland and Siegfried's magic cloak, Gunther won the competition, at least that was how Brunhilde saw it, and Gunther and Brunhilde were married. They returned to Burgundy where Siegfried wooed and married Gunther's sister, Kriemhilde. Kriemhilde mocked her sister-in-law, Brunhilde, with tales told to her by Siegfried. This greatly distressed Brunhilde and angered her loyal vassal, Hagen. Hagen then tricked Kriemhilde into telling him where Siegfried's weakness lay, and with this information, Hagen slew Siegfried. The heartbroken and vengeful Kriemhilde then married Etzel, King of the Huns. To avenge Siegfried's death, she provoked a battle between the Huns and Burgundians, killed Gunther and Hagen, and in the end, one of the Huns killed her.

And it was for this bloody lot that the Germans named their lines of defense.

The German entrenchments in the Argonne were denser than in other parts of the Western Front because of the proximity of the rail lines. The trenches were timbered, well-protected by barbed wire, and covered by gunners hidden behind concrete emplacements and by camouflaged machine gunners who were protected by snipers and bomb throwers. First the 91st would face the Hagen Stellung—the first fallback line of defense for the German army. Next came Volker, a Burgundian vassal and minor player in the *Nibelungenlied.* And finally, they would face Kriemhilde, the bitter queen who brought all to a bloody end through her gossip and revenge.

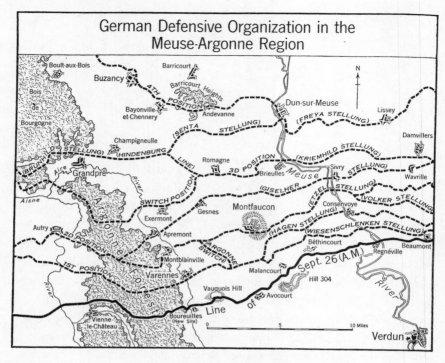

German Defensive Organization in the Meuse-Argonne Region

AMERICAN ARMIES AND BATTLEFIELDS IN EUROPE, P. 170

Late on September 25, 1918, Peter's battalion (the Second) took their position at the front. They would advance behind the First Battalion.

The commander of the 91st, General William "Wild Bill" Johnston, a fifty-six-year-old Ohio native who began his military career as a paymaster's clerk, issued the following order: "The 181st [which included Peter's regiment] and 182nd Brigades will push forward for the corps objective line, rendering mutual support to each other and to adjacent divisions, but not delaying their own advance by waiting for adjacent divisions. After reaching this line, the advance of each Brigade will continue to the Army Objective without waiting for the advance of divisions on the right and left."

More succinctly, 181st Brigade Commander General McDonald ordered: "Must not halt until Epinonville."

At 1:00AM on September 26, 1918, the thunderous artillery barrage erupted—the biggest thus far of the war. The earth trembled in response. German gunners returned the volley. Peter sat with the other soldiers of his company on the reverse slope of a steep hill, and there they waited,

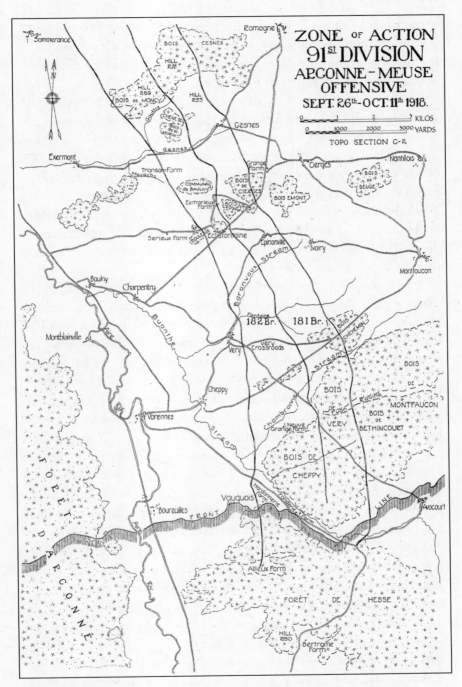

ZONE OF ACTION
91ST DIVISION
ARGONNE - MEUSE
OFFENSIVE
SEPT. 26th – OCT. 11th 1918.

TOPO SECTION G-2

STORY OF THE 91ST DIVISION. HILL 288 AND CHARPENTRY ADDED BY ARROW GRAPHICS.

about to face "all the horrors of the ages" as Winston Churchill put it: poison gas, rapid fire artillery, tanks, flamethrowers, widespread use of machine guns, bombs dropped from airplanes—all firsts of the First World War, a war in which R.I.P. came to mean "rest in pieces."

Shell after shell screamed overhead. Soldiers said words couldn't describe the show of power. After nearly four hours, the firing slowed, the artillery shortened its range and resumed rapid fire onto the German front line trenches. Then the guns dropped smoke and skunk gas shells. The smoke mixed with the heavy morning fog to form a thick curtain between the opposing armies.

In the middle of this, just before jump off, a runner ran up and delivered a note to Colonel Parker. It was from some army bureaucrat who demanded immediate remittance of fifty-six cents for a comb Parker's orderly had lost three years earlier.

At 5:30AM, the order came down the line to fix bayonets. Peter slid his blade in place. At 5:55AM, he climbed the hill and went over the top.

Like thoroughbreds at the races, their pent up energy finally released, the soldiers whooped and hollered, the cowboys yelled, "Powder River!" as they burst into no man's land. A rolling artillery barrage led the way. Most of the barbed wire entanglements had been flattened by the bombardment. Soldiers cleared what was left using wire cutters, axes, and bangalore torpedoes (long metal tubes filled with TNT). Every bit of ground had been torn asunder by the shelling. Not a blade of grass was left. The soldiers slowed to a walk and walked around craters as deep as ten feet. They had to take five kilometers of woods before they reached the valley leading to Epinonville. They entered the first, Bois de Cheppy. All the limbs had been blown off the trees reducing the forest to pathetic sticks protruding from the ground. Half an hour into the advance—they saw no sign of the enemy. The German front line trenches lay just ahead. They approached with bayonets at the ready and found the trenches empty, caved in from the shelling. Now an hour into the advance and still not a German in sight, not a live one anyway. The sun rose. It was cold and foggy. There was so much metal on the battlefield that their compasses were thrown off. Platoon leaders had trouble keeping direction. Troops crossed in and out of each others sectors. An hour and a half into the advance—still no Germans. They continued apace through the second woods. They crossed the German second line trenches. Machine gun block houses and concrete dugouts lay in ruins from the shelling. Hagen had put up no fight. They were now well beyond no man's land. Though shelling had preceded their advance, there was some vegetation between shell holes. Tree trunks still held limbs. The brush was thick enough in places to make passage difficult. There was supposed to be a road. It was on the map. No road could be found. It must have been blown up. They advanced on paths and railroad beds. Tension started to ease. The men joked that they would walk all the way to Berlin like this with no one in the way.

At two hours into the advance, they entered the third woods, Bois de Chehemin. Suddenly, the tat-tat-tat-tat-tat of a German machine gun fired at their right flank. The Company I commander was hit. One of his men was shot and killed. Men from Peter's battalion swooped over the nest, wrested it from the Germans, and claimed the regiment's first trophy: twenty *kamarades*. Most were old men and boys and seemed relieved to be captured. A young private turned to lead them to the rear. His commander saw what he was doing and barked in his ear: get *behind* them!

Now they were in the war. Sharp cracks from sniper rifles and incessant machine gun fire came from an invisible enemy hidden in the woods, and the woods were full of them. The soldiers dove into shell holes to escape the snipers. Once they eliminated that particular menace, they emerged to continue the advance. The sixteen men in Peter's company carrying automatic rifles spent an inordinate amount of time trying to un-jam their weapons. They were an old French issue and jammed repeatedly. The Enfield rifles, carried by most of the infantry, jammed when the least bit dirty and soon they would be dirty all the time. The soldiers relied chiefly on their bayonets and grenades to mop up the woods. Five different kinds of hand grenades were issued to the doughboys. Some they had never seen before.

The bayonet would become their "best friend," but bayonet-to-bayonet fighting was gruesome. As one Wild West soldier described it, all that remained were "little heaps of bleeding bodies." And as for artillery, "one minute there may be two or three specimens of perfect manhood, the next minute nothing but raw carcasses or groaning wounded with stumps for arms or legs." Men were "mangled to pieces by shells" and "the less said about" it the better.

By mid morning, the fog had burned off. The air was full of observation balloons and airplanes, though not many Allied planes, and they didn't seem to deter the Germans.

An hour or so later, the three forests were behind them, and the soldiers faced the long, wide, ridge-cut valley leading to Epinonville. Peter's battalion reorganized in a ravine and advanced to fill a gap in the line. A burst of machine gun fire came from their right. The men dropped to the ground and pulled themselves forward. Colonel Parker strode up and down the line, puffing his pipe.

Now a sniper was firing on Peter's battalion. Sergeant Dykes grabbed a machine gun—no more sniper.

Then all of the sudden the American artillery barrage stopped. German resistance stiffened. Shrapnel and high explosives rained down on Peter's battalion from Montfauçon, ahead and to the right, and from Eclisefontaine, ahead and to the left. Epinonville was sandwiched in between. From the ridge ahead, they faced implacable machine gunners. Heavy guns along the heights of the Argonne Forest to their left fired on them as well. The powerful explosives ripped open the earth, hurling decaying bodies from their graves. A horrible stench wafted across the battlefield.

It turns out their artillery was diverted due to some mis-communication. As a result, there was no bombardment to pave their way into Epinonville. The regiment resorted to their one pounders and machine guns to batter the well-fortified town. This dissipated counterfire somewhat though the troops still endured a tremendous double enfilade plus frontal fire. The First Battalion crossed the ravine which led to the town and entered Epinonville around 6:30PM, suffering heavy casualties as they went. Though the town had been badly damaged, there were still plenty of buildings standing to hide machine gunners and snipers. Snipers were there in force in the northern part of town and machine gunners were firmly ensconced along the flanks. The doughboys crept along, taking cover from the wreckage, tossing a grenade into each building as they passed. They captured many prisoners and guns.

They had advanced much further than the troops on either flank and this left them in a precarious position.

"You must keep contact with us and give us enough runners. Tell Decuis for Gods sake to get busy and do something and get busy and connect us up with Brigade—do something with his signal contraptions or quit."

It soon became clear that the flanking troops were not about to catch up. The forward battalion was exposed by quite a distance, leaving the troops in danger of being pinched off by the enemy. They were ordered to stop the advance for the night and dig in. They did as ordered. The forward battalion formed a line along the southern edge of town.

By now, the troops had been on the move for twenty hours, most of that time fighting. The men dropped. Cook wagons were nowhere to be seen. They devoured cold rations. Peter's battalion slept in the German trenches they had taken hours earlier that afternoon. German shelling continued throughout the night though lighter than it had been.

Peter's battalion commander, Captain Edmonds, tried to find the regimental command post. He never did. The order he received said, "Be on the alert," author unknown.

It rained hard that night.

"Men are continually getting shot and there is no medical aid available whatever. Can you send up relief?"
No ambulances could get through. Nothing could get through. Cook wagons and artillery caissons were stuck in the mud, miles behind. Batteries, ambulances, and supplies for three divisions were trying to advance on one muddy beat-up road but were caught in the infamous traffic jams of the Argonne that General Pershing took a beating over from the French. Engineers had to build a road as the army advanced. It was impossible for anything on wheels to keep up with the infantry.

"Can't we do something to get the wounded evacuated sooner?" barked Colonel Parker by field message.

It was still raining. Before dawn, Peter's battalion advanced on Epinonville. Again there was little or no artillery to clear their way. Again they faced the triple threat of unrelenting machine gun and sniper fire from the front and heavy artillery from Montfauçon on their still exposed right flank. Enemy artillery intensified. No matter, these rough hewn cowboys and miners ignored the bullets and bombs and pushed ahead. They crossed the valley and advanced on the town. They jumped over the First Battalion to take the lead and battered the town with their one pounders and machine guns. Men were continually being shot. Two officers were down, one dead. There was still no medical aid to speak of for the wounded. Those wounded who could, kept on. Those who couldn't simply lay against a tree or crawled into an abandoned dugout and tried to hold on until help or death arrived.

"Can't we evacuate the wounded faster?" Parker demanded again by field message.

General Johnston kept asking for ambulances too. None had arrived. It sickened him to see his own men, wounded in the legs and unable to walk, crawling along the road in search of a hospital. Those who did make it to hospitals found them over-crowded and rushed, one so much so that the staff flatly refused to render any reports; they were simply too overwhelmed by the number of wounded. The 362nd's regimental surgeon made no reports the entire time they were fighting in the Argonne. It makes me wonder if the statistics compiled after the war un-der-reported the number of wounded. We hear of the "fog of war," but I'd say the chaos of war is more like it. (The fog of war is what writers grope through trying to figure out what hap-

Major General William H. Johnston,
Commander of the 91st Division.
NATIONAL ARCHIVES AND RECORDS
ADMINISTRATION, SC95582

pened.) How could anyone possibly keep track of how many men were wounded in the midst of all that chaos. And of course, there were men like my grandfather who wouldn't fess-up to being wounded, and others who refused to go to the hospital because they didn't want to be separated from their unit.

Despite the heavy casualties, the troops fought on, painstakingly isolat-ing those blasted machine gun nests, one by one. A group of nine Wild West soldiers captured forty prisoners. Snipers captured twenty more. Colonel Parker stopped a group of prisoners as they were being escorted to the rear.

"WHO ARE WE FIGHTING UP THERE?" he barked.

His interpreter quickly translated the question and response: "Two regiments of the Prussian Guards in the Bois de Cierges and Bois Emont, north of Epinonville, and a regiment of German artillery in the Bois de Beuge, sir."

Parker growled at the prisoners and sent them on their way. Those three woods were on an east-west line north of Epinonville. Prisoners also said some three to six thousand fresh German troops had just arrived and with considerable artillery.

Now the Wild West men were finally getting some help from their own artillery. They doggedly fought on, continuing their advance on the town. Then suddenly the Allied artillery range shortened and started shelling the regiment. The men stopped, confused. They were being hit by German guns from the front and American guns from the rear. It rattled their nerves to be fired on by their own guns. Men yelled, *"Raise the artillery!"* as if anyone could hear them above the roar.

Parker dashed off a message: *"Our artillery is shooting short one kilometer or more by now. Please stop it—they are causing as many casualties in our support line as the Boche is in front."*

Frantic officers shot rockets to signal the gunners to increase their range, but still the American shells fell on the regiment.

"Our artillery is shelling short and hitting our own support line. STOP IT."

General McDonald pulled them back to get them out of the line of fire. The artillery gunners finally received the message and increased their range. Even so, the men stayed put, understandably afraid to move in case the guns started shelling short again. Then out strode the irascible Gatlin' Gun Parker, clenching his pipe in his teeth, brandishing his cane. His presence boomed over the battlefield. He ordered the men forward. They went.

They fought on into Epinonville, tossing a grenade into each house, dealing with those they met face-to-face with the bayonet or taking them prisoner. It was a bloody, grueling, hard-fought fight, but by afternoon, they occupied most of the town. They were relentlessly pushing the Germans back, suffering horrible casualties as they did, when an officer arrived with the message: *"Fall back behind Epinonville and dig in."*

Fall back?

Parker bristled. He said he could not accept such an order unless it was in writing or told to him directly by a superior officer. He sent a message to General McDonald saying his men were already in the right half of Epinonville and to pull them back "would be suicidal."

Despite his objections, the order flew right over his head directly to his battalion commanders, and to his great astonishment, he saw them withdrawing. He ran up to the front and told them to stop, which they did, but by the time he stopped them they were already on the southern edge of town, the area the First Battalion had held during the night. He ordered his battalion commanders not to withdraw any further except on "a direct order from General Pershing" delivered in person, and if any-one so much as mentions withdrawing—ARREST HIM!

He then went to see General McDonald.

"We have to withdraw," McDonald said, "the artillery are going to shell Epinonville on orders from the Corps Headquarters."

"I will not withdraw!" Parker responded. "Please give me your map."

McDonald handed him the map. Parker marked the position of his troops and wrote:

Chief of Artillery:

This map indicates my exact line, which will be held. If a single American shell falls on that line I will personally kill those who fire it.

John H. Parker
Colonel commanding 362nd Infantry

McDonald told him to send the map to the artillery and hold his position.

Meanwhile, German airplanes flew in low and fired on Peter's battalion. The men shot back with machine guns and rifles. The pilots fired rockets to indicate the American position. German artillery gunners adjusted their range accordingly and pounded the troops.

While waiting out the artillery barrage, Colonel Parker saw troops in the sector to their right going to the rear. When the barrage slowed, he sent a message to the commander of those troops saying: *We are going through Epinonville, can't you come back and drive with us? Our right flank is exposed. We are going through.*

I don't know whether Parker received a response. He ordered the regiment to advance, and they did.

German gunners were now deluging Epinonville with shells. General McDonald ordered an enveloping attack—they'd squeeze the town in a giant pincer grip. Peter's regiment attacked from the east. His battalion in particular took heavy machine gun fire from the woods on their ever exposed right flank. They forced the Germans out of Epinonville and from the orchard beyond, driving the Prussian Guards "like a flock of sheep" to use Colonel Parker's words. The two regiments closed the pincer and forced the Germans further back, all the while taking considerable losses. They had yet to see an ambulance.

"Can't we evacuate the wounded faster?" Parker scribbled again on a field message and stuffed it in a runner's hand.

Every time the Wild West doughboys pushed them back, the German gunners took their guns with them and quickly found another splendid vantage point from which to fire on the soldiers. About a hundred Germans began to cross a clearing toward them. The regiment's machine gunners mowed them down.

Heavy artillery and machine gun fire still pelted Peter's battalion from Bois Emont on their open right flank. The artillery had done nothing to silence those guns. The troops turned to the right and tried to attack the gunners hidden in the woods, but they were too few to overtake them.

"Am 400 yards and can't make it. It is full of machine guns and they have me enfiladed from both sides. Every time a man sticks his head up, he is a casualty. The artillery has not bombarded the woods," reported Captain Edmonds, Peter's battalion commander.

German General Ludendorff was throwing more and more troops into the battle, and he had a lot more at his disposal now that the Eastern Front was gone. Early in 1917, just before the United States entered the war, Russia tumbled into chaos. There were bread shortages and strikes, and on the Ides of March, Czar Nicholas abdicated. The next month the Germans helped Lenin return to Russia. Lenin believed that a humiliating Russian defeat would further his plans for revolution. In October of 1917, his band of Bolsheviks took over the Russian government and within six months sued for peace and pulled Russia out of the war, effectively surrendering to Germany. This was a crushing blow to the Allies. In the blink of an eye, the Eastern Front was gone, freeing fifty German divisions for fighting elsewhere. Now in September of 1918, Ludendorf was taking full advantage of the situation. While the Allies were benefitting from a great influx of fresh though green, well-fed though ill-equipped American troops, the Germans were benefitting from an influx of experienced though battle-worn, well-armed though hungry troops. (By then, the British blockade was taking its toll on the German people and their food supply.)

The divisions on both flanks of the 91st fell back. The Wild West men did not. They steadfastly held their position despite the intense enemy fire. Then, to their relief, they saw an olive drab wave emerge from well behind on their right. It topped the crest of a ridge and calmly and steadily swept forward. The sun broke through the clouds. The regiment breathed a sigh of relief. At last, help was coming to silence those guns in Bois Emont and fill out the line along their right flank. Then, just as calmly and steadily, the wave reversed course, swept up the ridge, down the opposite side, and slowly disappeared to the rear. Peter and the other men watched in disbelief, all the while enduring fierce shelling from their right. Colonel Parker turned to his orderly and growled, referring to his own men, "These roughnecks will stick till hell freezes over!"

Despite their wide open right flank and getting next to no help from those vaunted airplanes and hardly any artillery support, and when they did get it twice it hit them, by afternoon the regiment had advanced well past Epinonville. They found well-appointed dugouts: glasses of beer left unfinished on a table, a fur coat—it would have come in handy on these cold nights. Finally, they occupied the hill that was the corps objective for the day. The division now held a line extending from Bois des Bouleaux, up north of Eclisfontaine, north of Epinonville, all the way to the southern edge of Bois Emont, which wasn't even in their sector. They had made great progress. Then at 5:00PM, General Johnston received a message from the corps saying the artillery was about to pummel the Charpentry-Eclisefontaine road to help the 35th Division advance. The 91st was past that road. They'd be right in the line of fire. By the time Johnston received the message, the barrage was to begin in only thirty minutes. There was no time to protest. He had no choice but to pull his men back.

Peter's regiment occupied the northern heights of Epinonville ridge for the rest of the day and night. They were hit almost continually from the front and both flanks with high explosives, shrapnel, sneezing gas, tear gas, and phosgene. The division two over to their right took Montfauçon.

At one point, machine guns, snipers, artillery, and airplanes hit Peter's regiment all at once. *Would be nice to see some of our planes up there helping us out.* German shelling increased during the night with plenty of phosgene in the mix. This gaseous shrapnel turned the very air they breathed into a means of torture and death. It caused the lungs to fill with water, drowning the victim. Being blown to atoms was definitely an easier way to go. Fortunately, their gas masks protected them from phosgene, but nothing could protect them from high explosives. And diving into a shell hole to escape snipers and machine gunners could mean diving into a large puddle of water tainted with mustard gas and the ensuing blistering burns. Casualties fell continually. It was cold. They took blankets from the German dead.

Colonel Parker's order for the night read as follows: *"Regiment goes into alert bivouac . . . Feed your men tonight the best you can . . . If they come over tonight use the bayonet. Do not endanger lives by promiscuous shooting. This is a bivouac in arms. If the 2nd Battalion is forced to fall back it will fall back on the line held by 1st Battalion, which will be held—use the bayonet. Don't let your troops get out of hand—rest. The Army artillery will shell the Boche through a line north of Eclisefontaine Bois de Beuge."*

General Johnston congratulated his troops on their progress and notified the corps commander that the 91st had advanced farther than the divisions on the right and on the left.

A heavy gas attack came. They hurriedly slipped on their masks. It dissipated. They took off their masks. There were continuous calls for the mask throughout the night. Peter may have tried to sleep with his mask on. He couldn't see his own hand through the mask in the dark, he could barely breath. I suspect he hardly slept.

For the second night, the 91st was a bulge in the line, and within the 91st, Peter's regiment was a bulge in the bulge. Their right flank had been "in the air" to use Colonel Parker's words since the first night of the battle. Their left flank had been closed but was now wide open. Their next major obstacle would be Kriemhilde. The bitter queen would prove much more obstinate than her vassals Hagen and Volker.

Again it poured—another night of rain, high explosives, shrapnel, gas, and little sleep. The rain was relentless.

BEFORE SUNRISE, the 361st Regiment was ordered to the front. Peter's regiment, the 362nd, followed. As the 361st reached the front they were blasted by enemy fire and recoiled from it. Again they tried to attack and were blasted back. General McDonald saw this and went up to the front. He placed himself at the center of the line, and with all the troops watching, the silver-haired gentleman took off his hat, waved it in the air and shouted, "COME ON, MEN. DO YOU WANT TO LIVE FOREVER?" and he went forward, and they followed him. They stubbornly drove through the valley beyond Epinonville and into Bois des Epinettes. They fought through and cleared the woods. High explosives landed close by and pelted them with mud. They were already caked with mud from lying in it. German pilots fired on them, now snipers. A gas attack came, it cleared, then another, it cleared. Allied observation balloons tumbled from the sky in flames.

The 35th Division, on their left, withdrew. They dropped so far back that they were south of the 91st Division's guns and ration dump at Very, land the 91st took on the first day. The 37th Division, on their right, also straggled well behind. German soldiers in Bois Emont attacked Peter's regiment from the right. The doughboys fought back and drove the Germans out of Bois Emont, which wasn't even in their sector. Those gunners likely moved into Bois de Cierges, for when the soldiers reached those woods, they found the enemy there in force. They followed the 361st to the middle of the woods until they were hung up by fierce artillery and persistent sniper fire.

Then a message arrived saying the 37th Division had taken Cierges, the town due east of the northern edge of Bois de Cierges, which would mean they had caught up with the 91st. Colonel Parker wasn't convinced. After dark, he took a patrol and reconnoitered the area. He searched for three hours, skirting the German front line, and found no sign of the 37th in Cierges and no sign of the 37th nor the enemy even south of Bois Emont, which was south of Cierges. The fact was, the 37th Division was one kilometer behind the 91st. General Johnston asked the corps commander to order the 37th to advance.

The 35th Division also remained far south. So still, the 91st stuck out in the line far ahead of the flanking divisions. Peter's regiment successfully repelled German soldiers attempting to encircle them from the rear.

The Wild West doughboys now held a booty of hundreds of German prisoners and scores of enemy guns. One former German POW said he ate better as a prisoner of the Americans than he had before or since. The prisoners ate the same rations as the soldiers. The Wild West soldiers saw the German prisoners as men like them, there to do a job. Their attitude was reminiscent of a neighborhood football game: each man tries to hit the opposing fellow as hard as he can, and when it's over, they go have a beer together. When he's "the enemy," he's an abstraction, the amorphous "them." An abstraction—the Hun—killed Belgian civilians. When he's the fellow to whom you give rations in the prison yard, he's a fellow like any other, and you don't know him enough to quarrel with him. You shot at each other because it was your duty, and you wanted to get him before he got you or your buddies.

During the night, Peter's regiment moved ahead to occupy the sector held by the 361st which by this time had been completely "cut to pieces" and needed relief. Just getting there was an ordeal. They sank to their ankles in mud.

Isn't it enough to fight this war . . . do we have to fight it in this rain and mud?

Enemy artillery intensified during the night.

They tried to sleep in shell holes and foxholes. Some soldiers lay in as much as six inches of water.

THEN CAME September 29. A chill wind swept through. At daybreak, the sun came out. It was a beautiful, sunny Sunday.

Peter crawled out of his waterlogged hole. He was soaked through. The wind chilled him to the bone.

Cook wagons and trucks carrying ammunition and guns were still stuck in muddy traffic jams miles behind.

The soldiers tried to clean their rifles. The bolts were clogged with muck.

At 7:00AM, Peter's battalion attacked in the first wave. They fought on to capture the rest of Bois de Cierges which was still swarming with enemy gunners. Artillery and machine gunners at a farm on the northern edge of the woods pummeled them mercilessly. One old soldier named Harold Meyer, when asked whether the enemy troops were well-trained and well-armed, replied simply, "And how!"

Nevertheless, the regiment pressed on. They discovered comfortable dugouts and houses which appeared to be officers' quarters, well-stocked with wine and beer. The Germans had settled into the area with no intention of leaving—ever. By midmorning, the doughboys had fought their way through the gas-laden woods all the while enduring ferocious artillery and gas shells from the front and the right.

The forward troops emerged from the northern edge of the now cleared woods. Before them lay an open field leading to the town of Gesnes. The field was cut by three soft ridges and was completely bare. Nowhere could a soldier seek cover. German machine gunners lined the flanks. Enemy artillery gunners hidden on densely wooded hills north of Gesnes were delivering tremendous frontal fire. A concrete pill box cached high on one of those hills provided German lookouts with a view of every inch of the valley leading to Gesnes. They could see all the way to Epinonville. Phone lines ran from the lookouts to the artillery gunners.

Colonel Parker sent scouts and sharp shooters to reconnoiter the western half of Gesnes. They found it was defended by two regiments of Prussian Guards backed by machine gunners and considerable artillery.

The First and Second Battalions attacked in a line. Companies E and F led the Second Battalion. (Peter was in Company E.) Heavy enemy fire stopped them at the crest of a knoll north of the woods. They attacked again, and again were repelled by heavy fire. To continue the advance without artillery support would be slaughter. The men held their position along the northern edge of the woods and waited for the artillery. They were double enfiladed by German machine gunners and pummeled by the worst artillery ever from the front. The regiment's machine gunners fired back but it was like tossing pebbles at boulders.

"Where is the —— artillery?" demanded Colonel Parker.

"Somewhere in France, sir."

"Get an artillery officer up here!"

General Johnston asked the 35th Division commander to stop his retreat to protect the 91st's lines of communications. He said he could not.

Around noon, Johnston saw the lead brigade of the 37th Division on their right retire from a hill just north of Ivoiry two kilometers back. By 12:30PM, enemy artillery was overshooting Peter's battalion and enemy snipers were firing on them from the rear.

At 1:00PM, the summoned artillery officer arrived and reported to Colonel Parker that the long-promised guns were still several miles away. By 1:30PM, German troops were massing on the regiment's wide open left flank. They attacked. The regiment's machine gunners shot them.

All this time, the 37th Division was pestering the corps commander to order the 91st forward. They insisted the 91st was not on their flank and was behind them, when in fact, the 91st was not on their flank because they were so far ahead. A colonel in the 37th was misreading his map.

Just to be sure, Colonel Parker again reconnoitered the zone directly on their right and found that the 37th was still far behind the 91st.

At 2:00PM, an officer from the 37th reported to General Johnston that his brigade "could not continue" and they had retired to Ivoiry, which Johnston had already seen them do.

Also at 2:00PM, Colonel Parker reported in person to General McDonald: "The position in front of the western half of Gesnes is defended by two regiments of Prussian Guards, backed by machine guns enfilading the ground from all directions and by the heaviest artillery concentration I have yet seen. The positions can be taken by these regiments if it is desired to pay the price, which will be very severe loss. Artillery preparation should be made if possible. The regiment is in position and will attack when ordered. The positions of the enemy's machine guns and artillery are as indicated on the sketch herewith."

He also told McDonald that the 37th was far behind them, leaving their right flank wide open.

Parker then returned to the regiment. At 2:50PM, he received a phone message from General McDonald: "Our division states that army held up because the 181st hasn't taken its objectives. Capture Gesnes regardless of cost. Artillery will be at 3:10PM, attack at 3:15PM, artillery doesn't have sufficient ammunition for a rolling barrage."

The order originated at the corps. General Johnston asked for support. He received no reply.

Colonel Parker requested that the attack be pushed back to 3:40PM to allow time to circulate the order. He ordered his troops not only to take Gesnes but to take the ridge half a kilometer beyond the town. Gesnes was in a deep ravine and he was sure they'd be heavily gassed. It wasn't a good place to stop.

By 3:50PM, the American artillery barrage had not started. Whether there ever was the promised five minutes of artillery fire is disputed. Some official histories say there was. Men in Peter's regiment, including Colonel Parker, said there was none. Others said it was minimal and completely overwhelmed by the German barrage.

Where is our artillery support? How can the Germans have so many shells? How can they know our position?

With the flanking troops several kilometers behind them and no artillery support, to advance meant certain massacre. But if ordered to advance, they would advance, and he would lead them. This would be Parker's charge.

> Not tho' the soldier knew
> someone had blunder'd:
> Theirs not to make reply,
> Theirs not to reason why,
> Theirs but to do and die . . .

The corps commander, who ordered the attack, must have learned the true situation because he rescinded his order, but it was too late.

The First and Second Battalions massed at the front ready to jump off in wave formation. Wielding his pearl-handled revolver, Gatlin' Gun Parker led the charge.

> Cannon to the right of them,
> Cannon to the left of them,
> Cannon in front of them
> Volley'd and thunder'd;
> Storm'd at with shot and shell,
> Boldly they rode and well,
> Into the jaws of Death
> Into the Mouth of Hell . . .
> —Alfred, Lord Tennyson

> The order came to advance,
> Capture the town we must!
> The Colonel said we'd do it, too,
> We'd do it by God, or bust.
> "Powder River, Hook 'em cow"
> This was their war cry yell
> And it means, we'll never stop, this side
> Of the fiery brink of hell.
> —Lieutenant E. L. Clerc, 148th Infantry
> Liaison Officer with the 362nd

"Powder River! Let 'er buck!" they whooped and hollered like wild men and dashed onto the open field into an inferno of bullets and bombs, gas and shrapnel.

Earthen geysers erupted across the battlefield. A continuous sweep of German machine gun fire from three sides and brutal artillery mowed the soldiers down like densely placed figurines in a shooting gallery. The lines thinned rapidly. Peter ran on through this hail storm of lead and explosives.

Man after man fell. It is the mystery of war and of life: why does one man fall and another man stand? Four men are together, one steps a few feet away, a shell kills the other three. Why? Only God knows.

Pilots and lookouts in the tower beyond Gesnes signaled German gunners. The gunners adjusted their aim to the first ridge just as the doughboys topped it, and like a giant, merciless scythe, swept the ridge, cutting the men down, treating the wheat as chaff. In less than an hour, half of the men were down. A German pilot flew over and signaled the artillerymen as the soldiers approached the second ridge. Again, the gunners adjusted their range and pounded the regiment. Those who survived the third ridge came upon a German tank on the descent. The Americans shot the crew, commandeered the tank, and turned the mighty gun on a German machine gun nest.

Peter crept along the bank of the road leading to Gesnes, shell after shell exploded all around him, fellow soldiers were blown to bits, the wounded screamed out in agony. It is impossible to imagine what it does to a man's soul to witness such carnage. Peter was a boxer. He boxed at Camp Lewis. Boxing was a gentlemanly way to fight. A man faced his opponent straight on and won with his cunning and his fists. This kind of fighting—bringing a man's entrails out with a bayonet, throwing grenades into a ruined building to blow the limbs off a man you can't even see—this was a dastardly way to fight. But if you didn't stick him with your bayonet first, he'd stick you, and if you didn't throw the grenade first, he'd blow your limbs off.

I asked Grandma, "What did Grandpa Peter say about the war?"

"Kill or be killed! Kill or be killed!" she said with intensity, and that was all she said.

When we read that men were blown to bits, it is tragic but abstract, words on a page. It seems the more extreme the tragedy, the more unreal. We cannot begin to comprehend it. But to Peter, they weren't faceless casualties, statistics in a book. They were Doug and Harry, Seth and John and Elijah and Fred, another Harry, Joe, Angelo, Al, Jim, Mervin, Elwood, Charlie and Ed and Amen and George and another Fred and Howard and so many others. Most were privates, just like Peter.

Though the carnage was nonstop, so were the acts of bravery—the sergeant who though severely gassed and wounded maintained his command and insisted others be attended to first; the private who, while his company was swept by machine gun fire, crept forward alone and slithered stealthily up to those blasted machine gun nests, and with a few well-aimed grenades, put the gunners out of action and singlehandedly captured four Germans and two machine guns; another private who, seeing the enemy about to open fire, warned his company commander, which drew attention to himself and cost him his life; and so many other stories we'll never know because the witnesses are dead.

Colonel Parker was hit in the leg with shrapnel but kept on. He was hit again, this time in the left arm, now shrapnel in the other leg, he collapsed. Gesnes was just ahead. He tried to get up. He couldn't. He looked at his troops attacking the town "regardless of cost" and complained bitterly that he couldn't go with them. "Just see them go!" he said to his orderly. He crawled into a muddy shell hole for cover and turned command over to Lieutenant-Colonel James Woolnough. He quickly marked a map showing the enemy machine gun and artillery positions. He gave the map to a runner and told him to take it to General McDonald. Then he told his orderly to burn the rest of his maps and orders lest the land be taken back by the enemy.

The troops entered Gesnes and began to sneeze uncontrollably. German gunners were pouring gas shells into the town. It was soon full of gas. Undaunted, the Wild West doughboys donned their masks and drove the enemy from the town with their bloody bayonets. Kill or be killed. Kill or be killed.

At 5:00PM, Colonel Parker received a message from one of the company commanders: *"HAVE TAKEN GESNES. NEED HELP."*

Parker dashed off a message: *"Captain Tracy reports taking Gesnes, send him support at once, he needs help."*

There were no reserves left in the regiment. Every man standing was in the fight. They had far outpaced any phone line. The only communication was by runner, and every time an officer sent one, he just had to hope and pray he'd make it, and there was no way of knowing how long it would take.

Peter's battalion was now scattered and thin. So many officers had fallen. The troops tried to reorganize. With or without officers, they advanced. Ignoring the lack of support on their flanks, they doggedly fought on past Gesnes, up the slopes, smashing the German defenses as they went. They struggled up to the base of one of those fire-spewing hills. With barely a pause, one of the cowboys yelled, "Powder River! Let 'er buck!" and they dashed up the hill like wild men, diving into ditches for cover. The German soldiers panicked and fled at the sight of these crazed Americans charging their line. Seeing the German troops flee, the Americans quickly scrambled after them. Those who didn't get away ran out with hands raised yelling, "*Kamarade! Kamarade!*" and became prisoners. The Germans who fled left their wounded behind but hastily pulled their guns with them and resumed firing on the regiment. They did leave some heavy artillery behind and those guns the doughboys captured.

Not only had the Wild West men taken an enemy stronghold well north of Gesnes, they now stood firmly at the American army's first objective.

And in their sights lay the vengeful Kriemhilde.

General McDonald sent a runner with a message to General Johnston: "*The 181st Brigade has reached its objective.*" Good news, yes, but a mixed blessing. The general pondered what to do. Conditions surrounding his division had grown even more perilous. The divisions on both flanks were still falling to the rear. Besides the added danger their retreat placed on his infantrymen, the field artillery brigade, though still far behind and trying to advance, would soon be exposed to enemy fire from both flanks, and the division's communications wires could be cut. General Johnston received a message from the 35th Division saying they were falling back and were almost to Baulny, several kilometers behind the 91st. Johnston sent an urgent message imploring the 35th Division commander to stop his retreat and cover the 91st's artillery and communications lines. He replied that he could not. Johnston sent a message to the 37th Division commander telling him that the 181st Brigade was at the army objective and urging him to order his troops forward to Bois Emont.

"*Can't you move up and cover our flank?*"

The response: "No, we have no more fight in us."

With the 35th Division so far behind, General Johnston feared an attack on his left flank could easily wipe out the artillery. He had no choice but to deplete his reserves. He sent a machine gun battalion and a battalion of engineers to Serieux Farm to cover the artillery and the communications line. It sounds ridiculous—sending the engineers to protect the artillery, but with no help from outside his division, he did what he had to do.

The Wild West Division now held an eight kilometer salient, almost three times the length their line was supposed to be. It reached well into the sector to the left and extended two kilometers ahead of the American line and miles ahead of the flanking divisions. It stretched all the way from Serieux Farm, up through Bois de Morine to the summit of Hill 255 one kilometer northwest of Gesnes, and down to Grange Farm. Within this salient, the 181st Brigade, with Peter's regiment at its apex, had driven a mile deep spike into the German defenses. They were four kilometers ahead of the 74th Brigade (37th Division) on the right and six kilometers ahead of the 70th Brigade (35th Division) on the left. Only scouts of the 37th Division had reached Cierges which was south of Gesnes—a fact substantiated by a general who was an observer at the battle. Now flanking fire was shooting them from behind. The German troops need only scurry to the center and surround them.

Darkness encroached. They stopped the advance and dug in to form a line of resistance, all the while enduring heavy artillery and machine gun fire. Fractured units attempted to make liaison with each other. They were determined to hold their position. To do otherwise was unthinkable.

Colonel Woolnough assigned those officers he could find still standing to approximate sections of the line and ordered them to take command of whatever troops were there regardless of company or battalion.

By this time, the corps commander had an accurate assessment of the situation. Peter's regiment was so far ahead of the rest of the army that they were in imminent danger of being surrounded and pinched off by the enemy.

The corps commander sent the order to General Johnston, who sent it to General McDonald, who sent it to Colonel Parker: "The Division Commander sincerely congratulates the 1st and 2nd Battalions on the brave grand event, but in view of the serious situation in which this battalion is left, it is inadvisable to hold its present position tonight. Send forward a battalion to cover the withdrawal of troops and draw them back to a position in rear that can be safely organized for defense, particularly against counter attack and flanking. Organize this position and hold. Call on Davis for assistance and after withdrawal is accomplished his battalion will help carry out the wounded."

Both Parker and Woolnough were opposed to the idea of withdrawing. Parker sent a message back saying the regiment could hold its position and requested that the order to withdraw be revoked and support be sent to them. Then Woolnough and several other officers picked him up and carried him a mile back to Grange Farm where the wounded were being collected.

Shortly after that, Colonel Woolnough received a verbal order to withdraw. He was uncertain as to the authenticity of the order and as to whether Parker's message had been received, so he sent his intelligence officer, Captain Carlos McClatchy, with a message requesting that the 362nd Regiment be allowed to hold their position and that support be sent to them.

General Johnston agreed and made exhaustive pleas to the corps commander that his troops be allowed to hold their ground and that support be sent to them, but it was to no avail. Later that evening, Captain McClatchy returned with the order—they must withdraw.

The message reached Peter's battalion late that night.

Withdraw. But we're at the objective, we did as ordered. Withdraw. We took Gesnes regardless of cost, we did it, we reached the army objective. Withdraw. So many dead, so many wounded to take this ground, and now we must give it back? They weren't men to walk away from a fight. Retreat was not in their western blood.

Well after midnight, the remnant of a splintered, bedraggled regiment began marching back over conquered land amid the heart-rending moans of their wounded brethren strewn across the battlefield. They picked up and carried all the wounded men they could. Patrols would go back and search throughout the night and collect the rest of them. It was raining again and cold. They carried the wounded on stretchers across the ripped, pock-marked earth, through wire, across ditches, over hills. The rain turned to sleet. Stretcher bearers slipped in the mud, stretchers broke, dropping the poor wounded soul, sending him to new levels of agony. The woeful moans filled the darkness between artillery blasts and machine gun fire. And they had to withdraw. Men wandered dazed and bewildered through the wreckage. They were spent by the carnage they had just lived through, exhausted from four days in battle with next to no sleep, little food, soaked to the skin, boots water logged, no overcoats, no blankets, no shelter, no woolen underwear, in the cold and rain. Adrenalin had heretofore suppressed the physical effects of what they'd endured. Now men were spitting up blood from being gassed. They began to drop from exposure and exhaustion. And they had to withdraw.

After collecting the wounded, the dead would be next. The battlefield was covered with them. Chaplains organized search parties. It would be ten days before they could reach all of them.

American graves in the Argonne, men of the 91st buried near Very.

NATIONAL ARCHIVES AND RECORDS ADMINISTRATION, SC53096

Gesnes—the aftermath.

U.S. ARMY MILITARY HISTORY INSTITUTE, SC38542

WHEN PETER'S BATTALION assembled the next morning, of the 773 men who began the attack on Gesnes, only 133 appeared. Of the entire regiment, only 500 men were present when General Johnston reviewed the troops that morning. (They left Camp Lewis with 2928.) At noon when an official tally was made, only 845 men were found ambulatory and still effective. In addition to the dead and wounded, some men had simply gotten lost in the chaos and would in time make their way back to the regiment. Some had been taken prisoner by the Germans though not many, only two from Peter's company.

In a two-hundred-yard stretch, search parties found one hundred dead American soldiers. One hundred lives for two hundred yards, only to withdraw, and not because they couldn't overcome the enemy, but because the flanking divisions had "no more fight in them." Two yards of dirt for one man's life, then given up. Only in the currency of war could this be possible. The horror of the great adventure was sobering.

In a few days, General Pershing would replace the corps commander.

The skeletal remains of the regiment now lay exhausted at the position they had held at daybreak the day before, Peter's battalion on the northern edge of Bois des Epinettes. As ordered, they dug in for defense. Outposts still held Bois de Cierges, Bois de Baulny, and Tronsol Farm.

They settled into shell holes and dug foxholes. They fought in the mud, ate in the mud, slept in the mud. German gunners moved to the high ground and shelled the entire division constantly from 10:00AM the day after the attack on Gesnes until 8:00PM the following day. After five days in battle, still no ambulances had arrived. The soldiers put the wounded in shacks and dugouts to get them out of the rain.

So many dead, so many officers dead or wounded, made platoon organization impossible. There were simply not enough men.

At long last, some ambulances finally arrived but not nearly enough to evacuate all the wounded. Soldiers put wounded men in any vehicle they found going to the rear. The ambulance carrying Colonel Parker was hit four times by enemy fire despite the red cross on it.

The rolling kitchens finally caught up after struggling across the muddy beat-up land and thick brush. Shells landed all around and killed one of the cooks. Nevertheless, the determined cooks served up a hearty meal of stew and coffee. While the soldiers stood in line, a shell landed nearby and sprayed them with mud. Nobody moved. It was their first hot meal in five days.

A young private wandered back to the regiment after being holed up in Gesnes for more than twenty-four hours.

Patrols advanced to within five hundred meters of Gesnes and encountered no Germans but took some rifle fire. Even during that horrid withdrawal, the Wild West men had managed to capture several pieces of German artillery and a tank, making it as difficult as possible for the Germans to reestablish a stronghold in Gesnes.

The divisions on either side of the 91st were relieved.

For one hundred hours, the 91st Division would hold the line enduring poison gas, shrapnel, high explosives, machine guns, and air raids. They received no orders to attack. Some soldiers had drunk water from shell holes and streams and now had dysentery. The shelling intensified, the diarrhea intensified. Peter lay in his foxhole. He shifted and tried to lie with just one side on the ground as the rain slowly filled the hole with water. Ah, it's useless. He lay back in the puddle. Sleep was impossible.

The Germans retook Hill 255. Enemy patrols pushed forward. American patrols were dispatched and found machine gunners in the vicinity of Gesnes. A German battery moved in on their left. They watched a German plane tumble from the sky in flames; it was close, only a half mile away.

With no overhead cover, they were clearly visible to the enemy and suffered heavy losses under merciless shelling. Peter's buddy Ray Coughlin was shot. Orders arrived at 10:00PM on the third day that said be ready to advance in the morning. However when morning came, the new divisions on their flanks, the First and 32nd, were not yet in place, so there was no attack. Enemy fire quieted considerably during the night. It resumed around 10:30AM when German gunners opened up with the fiercest barrage thus far. It continued all day until 8:00PM, and they used a lot of gas.

During those one hundred hours holding the line, the Wild West troops were hit by twenty-eight German bombing raids covering the entire division. German gunners shelled division headquarters, the artillery brigade, and the engineers, all of whom were south of the infantry. A bomb exploded in front of the brick cottage occupied by General Johnston. The division command post took a direct hit, killing those manning the message station plus a runner and a liaison officer. In only one hour, 35 men were killed and 115 were wounded.

In the middle of all this, an exasperated young private jumped out of his shell hole and exclaimed in disgust, "Gee whiz, this war is getting on my nerves!" and climbed back into his hole.

Engineers hurriedly rebuilt the Very-Epinonville plank road so trucks carrying rations and ammunition could reach the infantry and ambulances could evacuate the wounded. German gunners found them and destroyed their work.

On October 4, nine days after the battle began, the Wild West Division was finally relieved. Peter's battalion remained in the line several hours after the rest of the regiment had left. For some reason, no one showed up to relieve them. Finally, hours later, the relief troops did show up, and Peter and his fellow soldiers rejoined the regiment and marched back to Bois de Cheppy where they feasted on a glorious hot meal of steak, potatoes, hot cakes and syrup, and coffee. They tried to scrape off the mud. A few were able to shave and bathe in chilly Chambronne Creek. They dropped and slept as German planes flew overhead. The luxury called sleep was cut short by orders to march to rest billets.

They marched and marched, dreaming of sleep in billets far from the guns, out of the rain. Then suddenly, Peter's regiment stopped. Slowly the column of soldiers turned around as the order passed down the line.

Wild West doughboys with captured German guns—relieved to be relieved. October 5, 1918, northwest of Bois de Cheppy.
FORT LEWIS MILITARY MUSEUM

The rest of the 91st continued marching to rest billets in the rear. The 181st Brigade, which included Peter's regiment, was now attached to the First Division and ordered back to the front.

Nearly all the regiment's automatic riflemen were dead or wounded and their rifles lost. Hardly any grenades were left. Most of the companies were at less than half their original strength, some significantly less. They had been in the line for eight days—four days fighting, four days holding the line—in appalling conditions with no woolen underwear, no change of clothes, soaked to the skin, in the cold, in the rain, under incessant shell fire, with hardly any hot food, and now deprived of rest. But war is war. They started a ten mile march back up the road they had just marched down. It was raining. It was dark. It was cold. The narrow, muddy road was a mess with traffic jams. Trucks and wagons kept getting stuck in the mud causing all traffic to come to a complete standstill. Peter and his fellow soldiers would march a few feet and then have to stop and wait for fifteen or twenty minutes until the road cleared; march, stop and wait; march, stop and wait. It was unnerving. They passed three piles of dead horses and many American graves.

They bivouacked at Eclisefontaine and waited for orders, all the while under heavy shell fire. Twenty-four hours passed with no food. The rolling kitchens were lost in the traffic mess.

The next morning before dawn they marched to the position they had held eight days earlier. That same unyielding German artillery and machine gun fire pummeled them, much of it coming from one densely wooded hill. American artillery gunners fired at it but missed the guns due to the lack of airplane observation.

On October 8, they were ordered to advance to a position between two hills beyond Gesnes (Hills 255 and 269) but not to attack. When Peter's brigade approached the position, they found the hills still occupied by the enemy. General McDonald asked for orders. The order came—attack. Later but too late, another order came—do not attack. In between receipt of those two orders, they attacked alone, with no support. They were pelted with shells and machine gun bullets. They captured several prisoners including a German officer who spoke perfect English. In the middle of this fire-fight, a telephone rang and a faraway voice asked: "Have you a pot of glue that you can send back to me to paste some maps?"

It was impossible to advance further. They dug in on the hillside.

It was raining again and miserable. There was a light frost that night.

The next day the order came for a general attack. After futile artillery preparation, Peter's regiment attacked one of the hills. It was 150 to 200 feet high and crowned with several German machine gun nests. The German gunners pinned the soldiers down in a clump of trees near the base. Then suddenly, one of them yelled, "Let's get 'em!" and several doughboys stormed up the hill yelling, "Powder River!" and were quickly followed by several hundred. They captured seven machine gun nests without losing a man. Stanley Kerr, an old soldier from the machine gun company, called it "a crazy yelling strategy . . . we could have been slaughtered if the Germans had kept their heads."

French, Australian, and German eyewitnesses spoke of being amazed by the boldness and dash of the American soldiers. One of those witnesses remarked, had the Americans been more careful, more would have survived. They didn't go over there to be careful. They went there to win the war.

The brigade took and occupied the two hills and continued their advance to the next one. The three hills formed a triangle with the one they now faced, Hill 288, at the apex. Thick undergrowth kept them to the road and paths which were covered by German gunners. They followed a thicket-lined serpentine path to a long densely wooded ridge. A heavy fog drew in and enveloped them. The fog mixed with smoke. They could barely see. They left the path and groped forward through waist-high underbrush. Powder fumes burned their eyes. Ahead was Hill 288. They could see at least three machine gun nests on the slope. German artillerymen blasted them with high explosives, now gas. Peter quickly donned his mask. Between the mask and the fog and the smoke and the gas, he was nearly blinded. The yellow gas hung low, trapped by the dense foliage. It was slow to dissipate. They were only four hundred meters from German trenches, but they didn't know it. It was a new trench system, dug since the battle began, so not on their aerial maps. German artillerymen poured more high explosives and gas on them. They crept forward still. Their mud-caked olive drab uniforms and those bug-eyed gas masks gave them the appearance of giant two-legged insects creeping through the forest. They began to make out barbed wire entanglements ahead. The machine gunners pounding them were behind that wire; they covered all approaches. All three battalions attacked but were repelled by those gunners. They attacked again and again and again and every time were repelled. All day they fought and lost many men doing so. They couldn't advance. They wouldn't retreat. They dug in while the shelling continued.

Around dawn, they moved out. German and American artillery shells screamed overhead. The Germans dropped sneezing gas. On went the masks. All clear, the masks came off. Then the firing stopped, leaving an eerie quiet. They crept along, past many dead. Invisible machine gunners broke the silence and pummeled them. German generals were throwing more and more reinforcements into the fight. They made a formidable opponent. The Wild West doughboys fought through the barbed wire only to face more guns hidden in the woods.

Word came that the First Division would be relieved, and Peter's brigade was now assigned to the 32nd Division. They had fought for four days, held the line under constant bombardment for another four, marched to the rear, rested for one day, marched back to the line and rejoined the fight, all the while the flanking troops were relieved.

Did somebody forget about us?

Though completely exhausted, they renewed the attack the next morning but were pinned down by German gunners firmly ensconced on the heavily fortified hill. It proved an indomitable obstacle. Allied artillery gunners came to their aid and bombarded the hill for fifty-minutes nonstop. When it was over, the machine gun battalion commander led a patrol to examine the results. Unfortunately, the enemy guns were still intact.

Finally late on the night of October 12 somebody did remember them, and Peter's brigade was relieved.

They began their march to the rear, past Gesnes, past Epinonville. Their adrenalin spent, only pride kept them standing. They camped in pup tents near the brick pile that had been Avocourt, back near jump off, and savored a long longed for hot meal. The next morning they continued their forty-five kilometer march. It was grueling. Wounded men plodded along with the aid of makeshift canes, up hills, down hills, through the mud. General McDonald tried to get trucks to transport his men. No trucks. They kept marching, marching. One officer was in such bad shape that he was tagged several times for evacuation, but he wouldn't leave his men. He hobbled along. The order came down to shave every day. They kept marching. General McDonald fell ill and was confined to his bed. That night they bivouacked in the woods under pouring rain. In the morning they resumed their march. Soon the war was behind them. Civilization once again

Epinonville—the aftermath.
U.S. ARMY MILITARY HISTORY INSTITUTE, SC98718

prevailed. Buildings stood intact, well-fed animals grazed, flourishing crops appeared ready for harvest. They marched through towns absolutely full of soldiers, no room even to bivouac. They kept marching. Finally after five days march, they arrived at rest billets in Revigny. They began to drop. Some men were hospitalized for exposure. The rest of the 91st was already gone. That evening they too would board trains.

CHAPTER THIRTY-TWO

DENIS TURNED and saw a little boy beckoning him from outside the fence. He smiled and walked over to him. Seeing German children broke his heart. They were so gaunt and threadbare. Denis asked what a wee boy was doing there. The little boy held up a piece of bread and pointed at Denis's chest and said something in German. Denis put his hand to his chest and looked down and then looked at the boy. He asked what he wanted. The boy pointed again and said something in German and held up the piece of bread. Denis looked down at his chest. Is it this wee button you want? he asked, pointing at one of the buttons on his uniform. The little boy nodded rapidly and smiled. Denis yanked the button off his uniform and handed it to the boy. The boy gave Denis the crust of bread, said *danke*, and scampered off.

20/10/18

Dear Mother
      Just a few lines in answer to your very welcome letter which I received a few days ago. I was pleased to see by it that all at home were well as this leaves me well at present. Peter presently being behind time I hope he likes France as well as I did. I was at home this time twelve months ago enjoying myself with P. McAnespie. I hope it doesn't be long we all meet in Carntall St. I am looking forward to that day. I will write a letter next week. With best love to all.
                                 From your son
                                 Denis

He posted the card with the Red Cross and returned to his cot. He picked up the Bible the chaplain had given him and began to read. By the end of war, he would read it nine times.

On his next visit to the Red Cross, he received a letter from home. He asked the Red Cross man for a sheet of paper and an envelope and then went back to his cot.

Geschrieben den <u>27/10</u> 1918

Dear Mother

Just a few lines in answer to your ever welcome letter which I received about a week ago. I was pleased to see by it that all at home were well as this leaves me A.1. I hope Peter and John are well. If you have got any photos of them send me one. I should like to see them with a uniform on. I wrote to Father about a month ago. As regards to what kind of work I am doing I am at present working with an electrician. I should like to get my photo taken also but I have got no chance. I haven't been at Limburg since May. I am out in a small working camp. I don't think Red Matthews will be kept here long as all the Red Cross men get sent home. I was pleased to hear of Willie getting his ticket. Also of Johnnie Butler been back in Belfast. When you told me about P. Kelly's man getting his commission. I didn't get [a package] for about three weeks. I thought it was Annie Man. Tell all about there I was asking for them. With best love to all

From your son
Denis

Limburg was a special prison camp for Irish prisoners of war. The Germans had separated the Irishmen from the rest of the British prisoners in an effort to persuade them to form an Irish Brigade that would fight in the German army against the British. The Germans also allowed Sir Roger Casement to visit the prison and try his hand at recruiting Irish prisoners for the cause of Irish independence. Both the Germans and Casement met with little success. When Casement approached the soldiers, they tore up the recruiting forms and threw them in his face and said, "In addition to being Irish Catholics, we have the honor to be British soldiers." After his fourth try, Casement wrote to a friend: "I will not return to Limburg to be insulted by a handful of recreant Irishmen." Casement was eventually found out and was executed for treason for his role in the 1916 Easter Uprising in Dublin.

In May of 1915, two years before Denis was captured and before the United States entered the war, former U.S. senator Albert Jeremiah Beveridge toured German prison camps as a neutral observer. Prisoners told him that they were fed regularly but didn't get much meat. French soldiers said things were all right considering they were prisoners. A British soldier complained that they couldn't get jam. The German captors complained that the British prisoners complained all the time. Prisoners who received money from home could buy food and clothes at the prison canteen.

The Germans doled this out at ten marks per week to prevent the soldiers from spending it foolishly.

Later in 1915, the Wittenburg prison camp became so disease ridden that the Germans surrounded it with machine gunners and dogs and abandoned it. After being roundly criticized by neutrals, they returned and improved conditions.

An American prisoner of war from Peter's regiment said that he had been treated well by the Germans, better than the British and French soldiers. I don't know what conditions were like for Denis at Limburg. According to his sisters, Denis never complained about the prison camp, but then none of them, John, Denis, or Peter, would talk about the horrors they experienced in the war.

By now, John had recuperated from his wounds and returned to France. As before, he dutifully sent half his pay to his mother, but sometimes diversions got the best of him. This day he wrote: *"Dear Mother, I'm off to the front. I'm broke. Could you send me a shilling?"*

As for Peter, while he and his brigade were marching to rest billets, General Johnston received a coded message from headquarters which said: *"Two American Divisions are at the disposition of the King. The 91st with artillery and the 37th without artillery."*

The news spread rapidly through the Wild West men, including those in the hospital. General Johnston stopped some of them on the road. They exchanged salutes. He glanced up and down at their uniforms and demanded, "Why are you men wearing bedroom slippers?"

"We've come from the hospital, sir."

Hospital inmates were bolting from their beds, stowing away, walking, riding, doing whatever they could to join the 91st for the Big Show in Flanders. I imagine nurses chasing after them and crying out, you can't leave yet, you're wounded!

Peter Thompson may have been one of those escapees. It would be in character for Peter to flee a hospital to join a fight. He was shot, he had a bullet hole in his chest, but I don't know whether it happened in the Argonne or Flanders, and I don't know whether he was hospitalized for it. He also had scars from burns on his back. Grandma said those were from gas. I suppose that would have been mustard gas.

One fourth of the division's men, including two hundred officers, had fallen as casualties in the Argonne leaving the 91st with fewer than fifteen thousand of its own men able to go to Belgium. That means after only two weeks in battle, five thousand men from the 91st were dead or wounded. In the first nine days alone, the casualty count came to *five hundred men* killed or wounded *each day*; that amounts to more than two entire companies per day dead or wounded. In Peter's regiment, more than half of the Montana men were already casualties. In his entire brigade, all the field officers but one were casualties.

An officer in Peter's regiment named Farley Granger, who was wounded at Gesnes and now able to walk only with a cane, insisted that he would go over the top with his men in the next bout. He did and was the only original officer of his battalion able to do so.

Thirty-five hundred untried replacement troops were added from the 85th Division, most of them Midwesterners. Their average service time was four months; some had only a few days of training before they shipped out. Another five hundred men were assigned to the 91st but were influenza casualties and stayed behind. The men of the 85th were billeted in towns separate from the 91st to prevent the Wild West men from being exposed to the Spanish influenza—the other horrible enemy in this horrible war. Imagine, five hundred otherwise healthy young men from one division all down with the flu at the same time. And this was no run-of-the-mill flu. It killed as surely as bombs and gas. At its worst, the lungs filled with fluid, depleting the poor soul of oxygen to the point that he turned a grisly dark blue and died, not unlike the effects of phosgene. Back home, the flu was so bad that draft calls and almost all training had to be stopped. More than 40,000 American servicemen both at home and abroad would die from the Spanish flu and flu related pneumonia—the equivalent of two entire divisions wiped out by the flu.

Trains rushed the Wild West troops northward nonstop to Flanders. Peter's brigade left so quickly that there was no time to issue winter underwear or replace arms and equipment lost in action.

The trains took them to Ypres, or near it. Even after the devastation they had already fought through in France, the soldiers were dumbstruck by what they saw as they stepped off those trains. The destruction was unspeakable—only ruins enough to tell there had been a town, and a large town at that. Though Peter had certainly read about it in the newspaper, words could not begin to describe what happened there. Ypres was bombarded mercilessly early in the war. Her citizens watched in horror as the majestic tower of Cloth Hall, there since the Middle Ages, burned, crumbled, and collapsed. Their huge, glorious cathedral, everything—reduced to rubble. After it was over, a man on horseback could see clear across the town, so flattened was it by the shelling. Beyond Ypres, desolation extended to the end of every horizon, and the horizon was very far off on this very flat land. All was quiet. The battle had moved east. The soldiers formed a column and set off.

The devastation grew worse as they marched across no man's land. Shells had left enormous craters, much larger than any they'd seen in the Argonne. There were shell holes within shell holes. Entire towns had been obliterated, the only proofs of their existence, the crude sign posts erected by British soldiers.

The Ypres salient had been the site of some of the most intense fighting of the war, where the British and Germans "just locked horns and fought in their tracks." As they marched, Peter and his fellow soldiers surveyed the wastes of war littering the landscape: decaying horses, smashed tanks, downed airplanes, wrecked caissons, broken cannons, shattered pill boxes, bullet-riddled helmets, the only order to the place—row upon row of crosses marking the dead. Away from their column, they saw not one living thing, not plant nor animal nor human, on the brown, barren, beat-up earth. One wonders, did those famed poppies come up red from all the blood spilt there.

Part of Peter's regiment marched to Moost and sought billets among the ruins. Orders for the rest of the regiment sent them to Passchendaele. They marched to where the map said Passchendaele should be but no town could be found.

An interpreter asked a French sentry, "*Ou est Passchendaele?*"

"*Ici*," he replied dryly, pointing to the ground at his feet.

Through the darkness they could barely make out the red tint of pulverized bricks covering the ground. The town had been blown to dust. This was where Denis and John had fought in the Third Battle of Ypres, also called Passchendaele. When the battle began, the rain began. Both were relentless and would last for months. The water table in that part of Belgium is high, only inches below the surface in some places, and much of the land is below sea level. Exploding shells dug tremendous craters opening underground springs, and nearly every inch of land was penetrated by the shelling. Between the water from above and the water from below, Flanders became a deadly morass. The mud that had slowed the German invaders now consumed British soldiers. Horses pulling artillery caissons sank to their breasts. Men sank to their knees, or sank completely. Wounded British soldiers crawled or fell into shell holes for cover. Before they could be rescued, the shell holes slowly filled with water, and they slowly drowned. I suppose the same was true for German soldiers. British soldier Edwin Campion Vaughan wrote in his diary of taking cover in a shell hole and being sucked into the mud. He laid rifles on the mud above the hole and summoned every ounce of strength he could to hoist himself on top.

Despite the impossible conditions, the battle continued for more than three months. When the generals finally decided to call it off, the line had moved only five miles, and half a million men were dead or wounded and tens of thousands missing—swallowed in Flanders mud or blown to bits. As he marched across that land, I wonder if Peter knew the whole of what his brothers had endured there.

The doughboys camped that night in the open, there being not the semblance of shelter or cover anywhere.

In the morning, they continued marching northeast and left no man's land. They were now behind what had been the German lines throughout the four-year stalemate. Fields were green, the devastation was markedly less, though evidence of war still presented itself in damage to villages and farmhouses. After ten miles, they stopped near Roulers. Dead soldiers lay all over the ground—and pieces of dead soldiers—French and German. Their first duty was to bury them. After the soldiers finished that grisly task, they sought billets among ruined farmhouses and barns. At nearly every crossroad in the midst of the rubble, they saw broken statues of the Virgin Mary and battered crucifixes—the downtrodden Christ, so emblematic of this downtrodden people, ravaged by war. Few buildings could be occupied. Most of the men slept on the ground in tents.

Officers began to train the replacement troops. This was difficult because the division was woefully short of officers owing to the Gesnes massacre. They had received no replacement officers. As it turned out, there wasn't much time to train the new men anyway; in only a few days they would be back in the fight. The officers issued winter underwear and ammunition to the troops.

Private Peter Thompson was promoted to corporal.

They marched closer to the front. Crossroads had been mined and were exploded before the troops approached. Belgian civilians, who hid in their cellars when the battle passed through, had by now emerged and were repairing the damage to their homes and farms. The soldiers passed farmers tending their fields, trying to carry on with their lives and ignore the war while the deep boom of cannons bellowed from the front. The main crop in the area was turnips. Belgian farmers sold a lot of turnips to the 91st. According to one Wild West doughboy, that's all they ate for two days.

Wild West hospital escapees continued to arrive. By the armistice, one thousand would rejoin the division by rail, car, or foot.

The 91st and 37th American Divisions now prepared to enter the battle with the French army along side Belgian and British forces, all under the command of King Albert of Belgium. They were driving the Germans back at the northern end of the Western Front while the American army did the same at the southern end and the French and British took the middle (American divisions were fighting in those armies as well). The Wild West troops would remember the coming fight as the Battle in the Turnip Patches. There is a charming photograph in the regimental history of a grinning doughboy standing in his foxhole. A quaint farmhouse and windmill provide the backdrop. He looks more mischief maker than warrior having dug a hole in a turnip patch. One would never know that a war was being waged behind the photographer's back.

As they readied to go into battle, the regiment received an encouraging message from Colonel Parker, written from his hospital bed in Bordeaux. He was no longer their commander, but they would always be his men. He praised their achievements in the Argonne and boasted that "no Regiment of any Division or any service at any time has ever done better in its first combat." He said he was "proud to have received a share of the injuries" and encouraged them to apply the lessons which they "bought and paid for by lives and wounds" and to collect from the enemy "the price he has not yet paid."

They also received commendation from General McDonald for "their gallant conduct" and "indomitable will."

For three days and three nights, German gunners shelled the troops continually with high explosives and gas, including mustard gas. German planes raided the entire division. British and French pilots swooped in and forced the German bombers back. The proximate threat of the enemy had a "tonic effect" on the men. By the time they entered the line, morale was at fever pitch.

Rail lines at Waereghem, Belgium, destroyed by mines before the Germans retreated from the city. Soldiers are from the 316th Engineers, 91st Division.
NATIONAL ARCHIVES AND RECORDS ADMINISTRATION, SC30898

On the night of October 30, the Wild West Division relieved French troops at the front. They were outside the town of Waereghem, twenty kilometers south of Ghent. The order to enter the line came with little notice, allowing no time for officers to reconnoiter their position. Jump off would be before dawn; the drive would be to the east. The terrain ahead was open with farmhouses and small patches of trees sprinkled throughout. The land rolled ever so slightly banking softly toward the River Scheldt (the Escaut in French), twelve kilometers from jump-off. Directly ahead on the banks of the river lay the town of Audenarde, an ancient fording point going back to Roman times. Audenarde would be the second largest town taken by American forces during the First World War, the largest being Chateau Thierry.

And fifty kilometers due east of Audenarde was Brussels.

The men dug in throughout the turnip patches along the Waereghem-Steenbrugge road and waited for zero hour. Peter's battalion was at the vanguard on the left side of the regiment. Throughout the night German gunners pounded them with high explosives and poison gas. They were

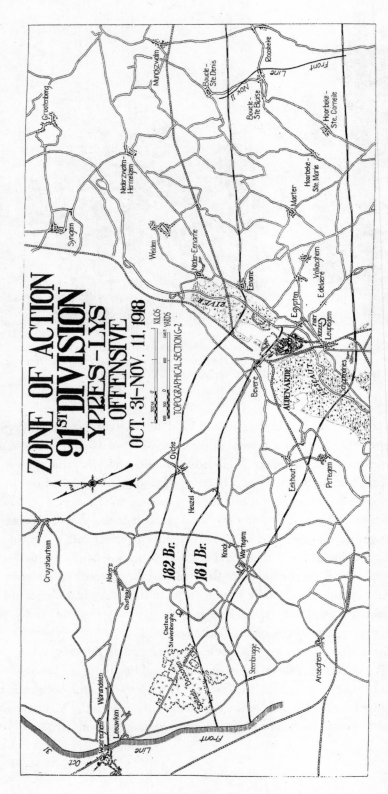

ZONE OF ACTION
91ST DIVISION
YPRES-LYS
OFFENSIVE
OCT. 31–NOV. 11, 1918

TOPOGRAPHICAL SECTION G-2

STORY OF THE 91ST DIVISION. STEENBRUGGE ADDED BY ARROW GRAPHICS

half buried in dirt and turnips thrown up by exploding shells. Enemy artillery intensified. Several men were killed.

The Allied artillery barrage began at 5:30AM on the morning of October 31. Five minutes later, the division jumped off. Peter's company was completely disorganized. Their commanding officer had not returned from the battalion command post. They had no orders and they didn't know their objective. As they saw the rest of the line jump off, they hurriedly fixed bayonets and jumped off too. Sergeants led their platoons forward and scrambled to show new recruits how to fire their rifles. Enemy artillery intensified to the fiercest ever.

At the center of their sector was Spitaals Bosschen, a long low ridge on which sat several farms surrounded by thin, scanty woods. Heavy barbed wire entanglements along the base of the ridge protected enemy machine gunners hidden in those farms. The order of battle for the 91st was for the two brigades to take the woods in a pincer grip, the 182nd from the north and the 181st (Peter's brigade) from the south. Allied artillery gunners dropped smoke shells along the ridge to blind the enemy to the advancing infantry. Peter's brigade attacked and was squeezed between enfilading fire from both flanks: the machine gunners in Spitaals Boschen and artillery at the Chateau Anseghem. Ferocious artillery from the front blasted them as well. Peter's battalion took the bulk of the flanking fire from Spitaals Boschen and were pinned down under heavy fire from three sides. After four hours into the advance, they had progressed only one hundred yards and were suffering heavy casualties.

Nevertheless, the troops took a collective breath and pressed on at the price of many lives. They ran along hedges, keeping their heads down, and darted behind farmhouses to escape enemy fire. They searched each house for snipers and machine gunners. A group of soldiers ran down into the cellar of one farmhouse looking for Germans and to their startled amazement found a terrified Belgian family instead. When the Belgians realized these soldiers were their liberators, the women flew at the doughboys and hugged them voraciously, bubbling over with what must have been thanks, though the soldiers couldn't understand them.

As in any war, or anything for that matter, not all civilians were of the same mind. There were reports of Belgians signaling German gunners. Two Belgian men said German soldiers had forced them to man machine guns. To further complicate matters, an American lieutenant reported that

German soldiers were disguising themselves as Belgian civilians. It was confusing for the Americans because to them Flemish and German sounded the same making it sometimes difficult to distinguish friend from foe. There had been no civilians in the Argonne.

While on his way back to his unit after delivering a message, a runner named Private Simkins saw a house crumbling under explosives with three women and an elderly man inside. Dodging sniper bullets, he ran into the house and carried out one of the women, ran back for the next, carried her out, and the next; when he went back for the man, he was already dead.

The Wild West men fought on, and by early afternoon, they reached their first objective, the heights just beyond Spitaals Boschen. By evening, the mopping up troops had cleared the woods. Wounded soldiers and civilians were quickly evacuated by ambulance. This terrain was much more easily traversed than in the Argonne.

Darkness began to fall. The officers halted the advance for the night. Peter's company dropped back to near Steenbrugge. They had advanced to the objective, which was two kilometers further ahead; however, the adjacent French division had not made it that far, so the Americans dropped back to maintain liaison with the French.

The land where Peter stopped for the night was flat as could be. There was no cover anywhere, not even a reverse slope behind which they could hide, so the soldiers dug trenches in which they could take cover for the night. By this time, they must have learned the fate of Lieutenant Closterman, Peter's company commander. He and his orderly had been hit by an artillery shell while returning from the battalion command post with the orders for the day. Both later died.

German artillery gunners and machine gunners kept firing at Peter and his fellow soldiers as they dug their trench and settled down into it. There they would wait and try to rest until they received orders to advance. An artillery shell exploded nearby and threw dirt on them, then another, another, the barrage was relentless. The Germans seemed to have an infinite supply of shells and bullets. The noise was deafening, the air musty, laden with dirt thrown up by exploding shells. Some men can sleep through anything, but Peter wasn't sleeping. He peered over the top of the trench out into the battlefield in the direction of the Germans. He saw Sergeant Arnold Pratt out there. Peter watched him, and then suddenly, the sergeant lurched and fell to the ground. He'd been shot and was lying there helpless, fully exposed to enemy fire. Without thinking, Peter scrambled out of the trench and ran to him, and with shell after shell exploding all around and machine gun bullets whizzing by, Peter knelt down and bandaged his wounds. Then he got up, grabbed Sergeant Pratt, and though Pratt was nearly twice his size, Peter singlehandedly dragged or carried him back to the trench. Once at the trench, Winks Brown helped Peter pull Sergeant Pratt down into it. He was very badly wounded and had to be evacuated to a hospital, but he was alive. Peter had saved his life and at grave risk to his own. He would later tell his sister Nellie, "I only did it because I hated him."

THE NEXT MORNING found the Wild West men invigorated for the battle ahead. After their baptism by fire in the Argonne, they were hitting their stride as a division. Their objective for the day was to drive the Germans across the river. Before dawn, they attacked. Peter's regiment, this day in support, followed the lead regiment of the brigade. German artillery gunners kept firing at them from the Chateau Anseghem ahead and to the right. As in the Argonne, their right flank had been exposed almost since their first day in battle. German gunners on the high ground beyond the river clearly viewed the advancing troops and fired accurately. As for the German infantry, they seemed to be fighting a rear guard action, burning all as they went.

Belgian civilians in Wortegem, almost halfway to Audenarde, ran upstairs to their second floor windows and watched their liberators approach. They thought they were British. As the troops entered the town, the Belgians rushed down into the street. It was then they discovered that the troops were American. Women and elderly men lined the road, smiles beaming through their tears, waving handkerchiefs in greeting and gratitude at the soldiers as they marched through town. Women rushed forward and pressed apples, sandwiches, and cigars into the soldiers' hands and offered them cups of coffee and milk. The soldiers were pleased to get it. The Belgians said the German infantry was retreating and had taken all able-bodied men with them.

Then the Germans started shelling the town again, and that sent the Belgians scurrying back into their cellars.

The Wild West men continued to advance rapidly despite the artillery bombardment and machine gunners and snipers firing from farmhouses. They halted on the outskirts of Audenarde. It was the largest town in the area and had suffered little damage from the war until now. The River Scheldt (Escaut) ran through the middle of Audenarde, south to north, so it was directly in the path of the troops. They would have to cross it to take the entire town. German artillery gunners at Fort Kezel on the high ground across the river were blanketing the entire area with shells.

Officers dispatched patrols to reconnoiter the west side of Audenarde. The soldiers slipped into town and found the streets eerily empty. They crept along, on the look-out for any sign of the enemy, . . . then CRACK! A sniper. They quickly took cover. One of the soldiers tossed a grenade in the direction of the shot. They continued on, and . . . CRACK! Another sniper from another direction. Snipers were unnerving. They never took snipers prisoner. Through the shadows in a second floor window one of the doughboys saw the faint silhouette of a machine gunner and hurled a grenade his way. They continued to creep down the street, turned a corner, and were surprised by a German patrol. They fought it out in the street. Another German patrol entered the fray and the street fighting intensified. An American officer hauled a machine gun up to a second floor window and began firing on the Germans below. Unbeknownst to him, while he was firing out the front of the house, three German snipers were in the attic firing out the back at another American patrol.

An intelligence officer searched the pockets of a wounded German soldier and found this message: "Early tomorrow we must be ready to meet hostile attack. Opposite our sector lies the 91st American Division. For each prisoner brought in the division will give 18 days extra leave."

So they had a bounty on their heads. The troops took this as an esteemed compliment from a formidable opponent.

The patrols then reconnoitered the river. The Scheldt split into three canals as it cut through Audenarde. The Germans had blown up all the bridges leaving nowhere to cross. Stones from the collapsed bridges had dammed the shallow waters, flooding the west bank. The engineers found one bridge that looked like it might be made passable with minimal work, but every time they tried to get near it, those invisible machine gunners and artillerymen opened up and drove them back. The French division on their right attempted to cross the river on rafts but were forced back by those same tenacious artillery gunners. Houses directly in the path of Peter's brigade offered excellent cover for enemy machine gunners and snipers. That path was also protected by the artillery gunners at Fort Kezel. A secret crossing directly ahead of where they stood was impossible. The troops settled in for the night outside of Audenarde while their officers contemplated a forcing of the river.

BY MORNING, they had decided. The officers had learned that the 37th Division on their left had crossed the river on fallen trees and light footbridges thrown down by their engineers. General Johnston requested permission for his troops to enter the sector of the 37th and cross the river there. Permission was granted. That night, the division would march north, cross the bridges erected by the 37th, then march south, launch a frontal attack on Fort Kezel, and take the east side of Audenarde.

As for that day, they would take Audenarde west of the river. They searched every house for machine gunners and snipers. All the stores had been looted. They came upon two enormous craters left by mines. By evening, the doughboys occupied all of Audenarde west of the river and had posted guards at all the bridgeheads. As in Wortegem, ecstatic Belgians emerged from their cellars to heap gratitude on their liberators in the form of food and wine.

Around 6:00PM, German artillery gunners resumed firing and heavily shelled the town.

After nightfall, the Wild West men began to march north, but before they could cross the river, this message arrived: "The corps to the north is not ready to cross the river, a further advance is postponed."

It was November 3. The troops were mystified. They thought the real fight would be forcing the Scheldt. Why stop now? And of all places, why stop in a heavily populated area putting all those civilians at risk. General Johnston was mystified too. He wanted to press on and take all of Audenarde and keep going. Instead, the French commander ordered him to send the 91st to rest billets back near jump off. French divisions extended their lines to cover the sector that had been held by the 91st.

Once at rest billets, the soldiers launched their next campaign—this one against the cooties. Advantage went to the cooties.

Rumors of an armistice bubbled through camp and were summarily ignored. They had heard such before. German pilots pestered them with air raids.

During the days that the French occupied Audenarde, German gunners bombarded the town severely with high explosives and poison gas. Many civilians were killed by the gas.

After five days, the French Army of Belgium renewed the advance. The 91st was called back to the front. Their orders were to cross the Scheldt at Audenarde and wage a frontal attack on Fort Kezel. Detailed plans were drawn for crossing the river. It would be a difficult operation to accomplish in secret and required precision.

In the midst of this planning, startling news arrived—the enemy had vanished. Engineers quickly threw foot bridges across the river. Infantry patrols were dispatched. They searched and searched but could find no Germans. French cavalrymen galloped far into what they believed to be German occupied land, but they found no Germans.

Two days earlier, the American army had cut the rail line near Sedan. Word was the troops were hanging their wash on the Hindenburg Line. Bulgaria had surrendered; though buttressed by Turkish and German

316th Engineers, 91st Division, placing an abutment for a bridge
over a canal in Audenarde, November 10, 1918.
NATIONAL ARCHIVES AND RECORDS ADMINISTRATION, SC39442

troops, the Bulgarians had simply walked away under an onslaught of French, British, Greek, Serbian, and Italian forces. They'd had quite enough of this war. The British had just defeated the Ottoman Turks in Palestine. The Italians had defeated the Austrians. The German people were rioting in the streets for lack of food. The German navy mutinied. Now the German army was retreating in disorder across the entire Western Front, "running like jack rabbits" as one lieutenant put it.

Marshal Foch ordered a general attack. The 182nd Brigade scurried across the river in pursuit of the enemy and overtook them.

The order for November 10 read: "Maintain contact with the enemy. Attack tomorrow at ten o'clock."

Peter's regiment reentered the line four miles east of Audenarde and prepared to attack in the morning.

During the night, General Johnston received this message:

On account of delay in delivery of ammunition, operations foreseen for this morning, November 11, will be postponed until further notice. No action will take place the morning of the 11th.

Then in the morning, the French liaison officer arrived with this message:

Hostilities will cease along the whole front from Nov 11–11h (French time); Allied troops will not pass the line attained to that date and hour until further orders, report exact location of line. The line of outposts reached at that hour will be held. Communication with the enemy strictly forbidden until receipt of orders sent to the Army Commanders.
FOCH

General Johnston ordered the 91st to advance only if there was no opposition and to hold their position at 11:00AM.

They advanced as far as Boucle St. Blaise, and there they waited and prayed they would live until eleven o'clock. Those last two hours were horrible. German gunners were hurling every shell they had at them, as if a prelude to a major offensive. The doughboys couldn't tell whether their artillery was doing the same.

Peter and the rest of them sat there under the shelling and waited, and waited, and waited, until at last it came: the eleventh hour, of the eleventh day, of the eleventh month.

And the firing stopped.

CHAPTER THIRTY-THREE

THE TROOPS STAYED in Audenarde for several days. Under a low sky and heavy mist, Peter and his fellow soldiers cleaned the streets of war debris. Officers helped restore civilian government.

Belgian refugees trickled through town pulling two-wheel farm carts piled high with their belongings. At last, they were going home.

The convent near the church received daily attention from the soldiers due to a persistent English-speaking sister named Sister Mary Monica. The wounded had been moved into cellars during the shelling and were now being brought back up into the convent which was serving as a makeshift hospital. Sister showed the soldiers the room where German troops had killed their own officers.

Some of the soldiers billeted in the convent, and Peter was one of those. He was quite impressed.

To care for the sick, of course the sisters needed food to feed them. The hospital had money to buy food; the difficulty was in finding food to buy. For this, Sister Mary Monica bypassed the soldiers and went right to the top.

> Convent des Bernardines
> Rue Haute 8
> Audenarde
> Nov 21st 1918

> Sir
> In the name of our Rev Mother General, who has overtaxed her strentgh, and is ill with a bad cold, which I hope will not be serious, I take the liberty of making an appeal to your Excellence the General for our sick and old people.
> The Commission at the head of the Hospital are willing at any cost to supply us with nourishing food such as fresh meat and condensed milk. We address ourselves to you, Sir, to know where we could be furnished with them.

Your former kindness and Rev Mother General's anxiety for the
needs of sick have urged us to trouble you again. Hoping, Sir, that you
will pardon us.
    I remain yours respectfully in JM
                            Sister Mary Monica

General Johnston replied that army regulations did not allow him to
sell food. He suggested that she contact relief agencies still at work in
Belgium, and he promised to bring up the matter with the American officer assigned to Belgian army headquarters.

The soldiers made more attempts to rid themselves of the irrepressible
cooties at a factory the Germans had converted to a delousing facility.

King Albert arrived unannounced. He visited General Johnston and
expressed thanks for helping to liberate his country. He then called on
the burgomaster. One of the division's bands quickly assembled and played
the Belgian and American national anthems. The music drew out civilians
from their cellars who until now had not been convinced that the shelling
was truly over.

Belgian families dug up the china and silver they had buried when the
war started and used it to entertain American officers. "The people here
are certainly tickled to death to see us, and they can't do enough for us,"
wrote one grateful officer in a letter home. "The major and the four cap-
tains had dinner, soup, chicken, potatoes, one of those rich gravies that
the French make, cheese and fruit and black coffee in real black coffee
cups, some treat, linen on the table, silver and china . . . There we were
dirty and muddy and buggy at that shining spotless table . . . It was a long
cry from eating out of a tin dish in a muddy shell hole to silver and linen."

A detachment from the 91st left Audenarde temporarily to join French
troops with General de Goutte at Aix-la-Chapelle. They marched to the
cathedral and presented arms and colors at Charlemagne's tomb. A band
played the "Marseillaise" and the "Star Spangled Banner." General de
Goutte then delivered a blistering speech about the menace of Germanic
tribes throughout the centuries.

New orders arrived. The division marched toward the Rhine, in the
rain. After two days march, General Pershing changed their orders, and
they marched toward Brussels. Now when they marched over the cobblestone streets of large towns, they paraded at attention with flags unfurled
and bands playing. Belgians hung their flag from their windows and

Men of the 91st in front of the battered city hall in Audenarde, November 12, 1918.

U.S. ARMY MILITARY HISTORY INSTITUTE, SC39449

General McDonald entering the church of Notre Dame de Pamele for the Te Deum service. Te Deum is an ancient Latin hymn reserved for occasions of great joy and thanksgiving. Audenarde, Belgium, November 15, 1918.

U.S. ARMY MILITARY HISTORY INSTITUTE, SC59427

cheered the troops. Every night the soldiers billeted such that they could take offensive positions at a moment's notice.

While marching one day, the soldiers passed a set of sign posts. One pointed west, one pointed east:

1914—Uns Vaterland Muss Grosser Sein—nach Paris
Our Fatherland must be greater, this way to Paris

1918—Us Vaterland Caput-nach Berlin
Our Fatherland is caput, this way to Berlin

In another place, Peter saw a sign that said, *Gott mitt uns*. Underneath he wrote, *we got mittens too.*

They billeted west of Brussels while King Albert triumphantly reentered the city. This was to be their farthest point east. The rest of their marches would be west, toward home.

AMERICAN
YMCA

ON ACTIVE SERVICE WITH
AMERICAN EXPEDITIONARY FORCES

Dec 3rd 1918

My Dear Mother,
    Just a line to let you know that I got your most welcome letter a couple of days ago. I wrote John a letter today also. I guess he is still in France somewhere. Well I am not somewhere any more. I am now in a little Village in Belgium called Grammene. This is the last place we were fighting up on the Flanders front. We are going to go from here to Dunkirk in a couple of days. We are going to walk as it is about 60 miles. We expect we will be about a week getting there. I put in a request for a furlough today whether I will get it or not is the question now. If I do I will be home by Christmas anyway. Is Dennis home yet? I hope he is not as bad as the papers are saying some of them are but at the best he will be alive I hope.

                    Your loving son,
                        Peter

Peter stuffed the letter and a few francs in an envelope and mailed it. He never sent an empty letter to his mother.

The next day they set off.

Dec 4th 1918
River Lys

My Dear Mother,
We started our march to the seaboard today. We left Grammene at 7 o'clock this morning. We arrived in Meulibeke at 12 noon. The distance we marched was about 15 kilometers. We thought we had a good PC [post of command] at Grammene but this one here had it charted off the map. I have a feather bed with a stove in our room and a cooking stove to boot. Some class to the Unit's officers. Thanks to Coughlin we will have another good night's rest. Anyway that helps on the hike. We left Meulibeke today and hiked for 5 hours and arrived at Hooglide. We expect to leave here at 3 o'clock tomorrow morning.
Your loving son,
Peter

They continued their march and stopped west of no man's land, not quite as far as Dunkirk.

A French priest arrived with the troops who liberated Denis's prison camp. He asked Denis his name and where he was from. When Denis said he was from Belfast, the priest exclaimed, "Belfast! The poor boy, he's lost his mind. A boy from Belfast named Thompson and he thinks he's a Catholic."

"But I am a Catholic!" Denis insisted and with a quick burst of energy he enumerated all the Catholic churches in Belfast.

Soon after, Rose received that long awaited card. At the top was printed: MY ADDRESS WILL BE RECEPTION CAMP, SOUTH CAMP, RIPON. Written below was:

Dear Mother
I am well.
From Denis

The letters were small and faint, not his usual bold script, obviously written by a weak hand. It looked as if he was falling down the page as he wrote. Doubtless, Rose had heard rumors . . . he must be weak from hunger . . . No, her Denis was fine, he was fine, that was that, and he was coming home. They were all fine. Her three sons had survived the war and with all their limbs and senses, thanks be to God.

PETER MADE his way to his billet, careful to stay on paths and roads lest he sink in the mud. His billet was one of the elephant huts built by the British. It had a plank floor. A piece of arched corrugated metal formed the sides and roof. He shared the hut with twenty-nine other soldiers from his company. It was raining the day they arrived and it rained almost nonstop the entire month of December. Living so many days in sight of no man's land, with its devastation and massive graveyards, under interminable rain and mist and low clouds, the world looked gray and dismal. Their job was done, they just wanted to go home. The days seemed long with little to do. Moving about in the mire was precarious. Some days training was impossible. They sat and waited in their huts under the constant ping, ping, ping of rain tapping the metal roof. This prolonged inaction after having their lives spared gave much time for reflection. They thanked God they were alive. Rumors of ship-out dates formed the basis for bets. The latest rumor was that they would be sent to Russia as a cavalry division.

The soldiers pooled their money to put on a Christmas party for the children of the village. What money was left over after buying gifts for the children, the soldiers gave to the poorest families.

The day after their rain-soaked Christmas they learned that they were not going to Russia, but to France, and then home! Doubly good news was that they would go by train. They had already marched 150 miles in Belgium and 115 miles in France.

Corporal Peter Thompson was promoted to sergeant.

When Peter's regiment reached their billets in snow-covered La Ferte Bernard, about forty kilometers from Le Mans, they learned, yes, they were going home, but not yet. They would have to wait their turn. Their excitement melted with the snow. It was disappointing news for most, but not all. Peter still hoped for a furlough to Belfast. He sat down, pulled paper from his pocket, and wrote to Denis.

Sgt. Peter Thompson
Co. E 362nd Inf.

Knights of Columbus
OVERSEAS SERVICE

ON ACTIVE SERVICE WITH
AMERICAN EXPEDITIONARY FORCES

A.P.O. 776 A.E.F

DATE 7-2, 1919
[February 7, 1919]

My Dear Brother,

Just a line to let you know that I got your most welcome letter last night also the picture and I must say that old Harry is looking good and natural. I must write him a letter. I sure am in a hell of a fix don't know what to do. The division is giving 14 day passes to Italy and Great Britain and I have put in for one but there is only so many men allowed to go every day and as we are just about to go to the States I don't know whether I will be able to go or not. I had a letter from John last night. He never said anything to me about him going to the Rhine. What is all the strike about back there and who is striking? I guess it is as bad as the one in 1907. Gee we sure had some great times old James Savage and myself those days.

I don't know whether Father will be able to send for you and John or not. I think they have passed a law in the states where they will not allow any immigration for 2 years. I don't know if they passed the law or not but I know they were working on it.

This country sure is the nuts. It has been raining here for the last week and a man has a hell of a time keeping clean when he has to wade in mud to his knees every time he goes outside. Glad to see that everyone at home is feeling good as this leaves me fine and dandy. I am most liable to be home any day now. Gee I have been saving my franks for a long time to go home on and sure will be disappointing if I can't get home. Write soon.

Peter

Censored by _____

More rumors of ship-out dates came and went. "If waiting made us sick we would all be dead," wrote one bored soldier in a letter home. The officers did their best to keep the men occupied and distracted from severe bouts of homesickness. The soldiers trained and drilled in the mornings and competed in athletics during the afternoons. Peter fought in the regiment's boxing match. The feisty Irishman entered the ring to cheers and hoots and hollers. Then his opponent stepped into the ring. He was one of the biggest men in the regiment. At five feet three inches tall, Peter barely came up to his chest. Peter didn't flinch. He threw one powerful punch at his opponent's heart, and the giant "went down like a poled ax" to use Peter's words.

General Pershing ordered each regiment to put on a horse show. That kept the cowboys occupied for awhile. A few soldiers formed a theatrical group called the Powder River Gang. They performed for the rest of the 362nd and then toured the other regiments. The soldiers formed debate clubs, some took classes in the evenings organized by the chaplains, still others kept to the usual evening entertainment of cards and dice and chasing the local girls. A few officers attended European universities.

General Pershing came to La Ferte Bernard to review the division. Seeing the dismal condition of their foot apparel, he declared that the men who took Gesnes should have better boots. Soon they did.

Colonel Parker also visited the regiment. He had recovered from his wounds and was now assigned to a post in Paris. While recuperating in Bordeaux, he wrote this in his summary of operations:

> I did not see in the whole regiment a single case of cold feet nor a single yellow streak. For a regiment that had no previous experiences in action whatever we only desire that it be said that we took every objective assigned to us at the moment ordered and never gave an inch of ground that we had taken regardless of the cost.

No doubt he expressed the same to his men when he saw them that day in La Ferte Bernard.

> They that had fought so well
> Came thro' the jaws of Death,
> Back from the mouth of Hell . . .
> When can their glory fade?
> O the wild charge they made!
> All the world wonder'd.
> Honor the charge they made!
> —Tennyson

Years later when the army set out to write the history of the war, Parker did indeed "honor the charge they made" in that he jealously guarded the story of these heroic men, and in no uncertain terms, even crossing swords with George Marshall. General Johnston did the same. He took Pershing to task for glossing over the accomplishments of the 91st in his book. (General McDonald had already passed away.) Colonel Woolnough still expressed bitterness over what happened at Gesnes. In letters written by all three men, even though a decade had passed, the passion in their voices came through loud and clear as they described what happened, the splendid accomplishments of their men, what went wrong.

At some point, I don't know whether in Belgium or France, Peter found his brother John and they were able to enjoy a few beers together.

After reading everything he could find, Peter had plenty of time to think. I suspect his mind drifted to good times with family and friends. Rosie and Brigid were toddlers when he left Belfast. Now they were in school. He wrote to Aila. I wonder whether he had a picture of her. And there was his dear aunt B. It was her birthday. It took him a few days, but he did get around to writing to her.

> Sgt. Peter Thompson
> Co. E 362nd Inf.

Knights of Columbus
OVERSEAS SERVICE

ON ACTIVE SERVICE WITH
AMERICAN EXPEDITIONARY FORCES

A.P.O. 776 A.E.F

DATE 20 Feb 1919

My Dear Aunt,

I am almost ashamed to write to you but hope you will regard this letter as a kind of yearly good thing which does not even come on its schedule time. I should have written I know but hope you will understand and therefore save me the trouble of making excuses. I am still alive and feeling better if possible than I was when I left Butte. So that in itself is a blessing. I saw lots and have had lots of experiences since I left. When I get back I will be able to give full vent to my usually abnormal gift of talking. I saw lots of action more in fact than wanted but since I suffered nothing I am not sorry. I have covered more country on foot than most ordinary folks cover in a train in a life time. I believe I have walked all over France twice and Belgium. I guess I have seen some of the most historical places in the world. Towns, churches, shrines and most everything else that is historical. I have worshiped in churches that were built in the 9th and 10th century and hid behind statues that are thousands of years old from German artillery fire and do you know Aunt B. most of these old places where I was when you trace their history back for 9 or 10 centuries you always find that the founders of the towns were Celts. Which gives a present day Celt a kind of a self pride and of course makes one proud of his forefathers. I was in one town in Belgium in fact we fought our way into it and fought in its main streets called Audenarde. It is a very historical place. The town itself was founded in the . . . century by Celts but they not liking the lay of the land left it. There is a river there called the Escaut [Scheldt]. There was an old bridge crossing the river but the Germans blew it sky high and left us to swim the river. There is some very beautiful sculpture in the streets of the town. Most of the statues were gifts of different Kings and Dukes. There is a very beautiful church there called the Church of St. Walburga. It was first built by a Norman Prince who captured the town in the 9th century. It was finished in the 11th century. I could not begin to tell you what the town was like nor its full history, the town has a history of its own which could fill a volume. I lived for a week in a convent which was built in the 15th century and it sure was some place. I spent most of my time exploring it but as there was some sisters still in it I did not get doing all the exploring I would have liked to as one could not very well disturb the sisters. They kept a hospital there and the Germans had gone and left some of there wounded there. The name of this town was Oycke. A funny thing that happened there was there is a plain between the towns of

Oycke and Audenarde. In 1708 the French and Austrians fought on this plain and the French won. On the same day in 1918 we defeated Germans on the same plain.

At present we are in France and quite close to us is another old historical town, this town lives mostly on its tourists, that is the American tourists who come there every year. The town was closed up until the American government took it over for a leave area for us troops.

The town itself was founded in 57 BC and of course was built by Celts. It was inhabited by Celtic fishermen, privateers and pirates who grew rich with the plunder accumulated in their various raids on England and other nearby countries. They built a wall around the town which still stands. It is in most places about 40 ft high and 20 ft thick. The town itself was built on . . . You can see what a stronghold it is. Especially in those days when they fought with spears and so forth. Anyway the town was besieged a thousand times by the British but never was taken. It has been a seaport of renown for 1,000 years and the Romans used it as a watering place. The town itself was one of the few places that the Romans never captured. The people had a republic when the Romans ruled Gaul. The sailors of this town were among the boldest explorers after the discovery of America and a son of the town has the privilege of being the first man to explore the St. Lawrence and is given credit for discovering Canada. I stood in the church on the place where he knelt to receive the Bishop of St. Malo's blessing before he set sail for Canada in the year 1535. There is built right on top of the town a monastery. The town looks funny it raises straight up in a funnel shape and the monastery is a very beautiful building and sits right on top. I have a picture of it would like to send it to you but it is too big. I will try to get it home. Right out from the town is another very remarkable piece of architecture. There is a round rock out in the bay it raises up in a gradual slant for 200 feet and is surrounded by quicksand and right on top of it is a church the church or monastery was founded by St. Aubert in the year 709 by the order of Archangel Michael so legend says. The name is Mont St. Michel. This place also has a history all its own which would fill a volume . . . I could go on talking forever on the wonders of the place but will have to stop as it is getting quite late and Coughlin is making some hot chocolate and that is something I can't afford to miss. Anyway, there is a couple of towers built in the town by Queen Anne and on one of them is her inscription which reads "Grunt who will, so shall it be . . . such is . . . good . . ." What it means I don't know maybe the people of the place did not like the idea of her building the towers. I hope to see some other places before I go back to the states amongst others I would like to see that very historical place called Ireland but I think my chances are slim. We expect to leave for America most any time. I wonder if you will find time to read this rather lengthy narrative but I know you would love to see these places yourself and I am sure are glad that I am getting a chance to do so.

How is "The Baby" hope he is well. Also John and all the rest of the family. How is my father behaving himself. Hope yourself is in the very best of health.

Your loving nephew, Peter

Censored by _____

(The . . . in the letter is for words I couldn't make out.)

Denis and Peter Thompson, March of 1919.

At the beginning of March, Peter's request for furlough was finally granted. He sailed to England, boarded the train to Liverpool, and from there, sailed to Belfast. He spent two weeks with his mother and siblings and visited his granddad in Randalstown. Nellie's cooking had already put flesh back on Denis's slight frame. The two brothers tooled around Belfast with their chums. Rose sent them to have a picture taken in their uniforms. John was still with the British army on the continent.

When it was time for Peter to go, Rose told him, Send me a card to tell me you've arrived. He said he would and bid her goodbye. Then he stooped down and kissed Brigid and Rosie goodbye.

While waiting for his train in London, he bought a post card and wrote on the back,

Mother
Leave here in a few minutes everything ok so far. I forgot about the shoes.
Peter

The front of the post card showed two little boys. One was kneeling at his bed, hands folded, head bowed, saying his night prayers. The other boy was slipping his arm into his pajama top while saying to the praying lad, "Don't pray to be gooder, 'cos the good 'uns always dies young!"

PART FOUR

For Better or for Worse

Chapter Thirty-four

"Be nice to him and he'll give you something," Sarah whispered to Aila as she picked up the tray. It wasn't dinner time and meals were at the table, not in the boarders' rooms, but her mother told her to prepare a tray and take it to him. She climbed the stairs and walked down the hallway to his room. She called to the man from outside the door. He opened it. He wasn't wearing a stitch. She dropped the tray and bolted.

She ran down the stairs, and as she rounded the corner, a sharp slap across the face nearly knocked her flat.

WHO DO YOU THINK YOU ARE, YOU STUPID FOOL? Sarah yelled. DON'T YOU KNOW I NEED THAT MONEY!

Aila picked up the laundry basket and went outside. She swore to herself every time her mother yelled at her and humiliated her that if she ever had children, she would never yell at them or ridicule them, and she would never ever beat them.

She asked Patsy to help her take the laundry down. Patsy obediently left whatever she was playing with and hurried over to help her big sister. Aila pulled the clothes pole out from under the clothes line, and she and Patsy took the laundry down and folded it. A little girl who lived across the alley opened the back gate and asked if Patsy could come out and play. This little girl's father had died and the family lived on the pittance her mother earned taking in laundry. She came home with Patsy every day after school and Sarah saw to it that she had a bowl of soup and a piece of bread to eat.

Aila, can I go play? Patsy asked.

May I go play, Aila corrected.

May I?

Yes, you may, but first help me with this last sheet.

The sheet folded, Patsy scampered out the back gate into the alley to join the girls. Aila may have heard them sing this little ditty as they played:

There was a little bird and its name was Enza. We o-pened the window and in-flu-Enza.

Sickness and death were on everyone's mind. The army was attacking in France. Lists of men killed in the fighting appeared in the newspapers. A terrible flu was going around. Someone Aila knew had just died from it. The schools were closed, as were theaters, churches, and dance halls, all closed by order of the Board of Health.

In late September of 1918, the Silver Bow County Board of Health reported little contagious disease. Then suddenly, in early October, the dreaded Spanish influenza struck like a thunder clap. Within days, hundreds were sick and scores were dying. Three hundred new cases and twenty deaths were reported in Butte in a single day, and those were only the reported cases. The actual number was believed to be much higher. A family member would get sick, then another, then another, soon all three were dead.

There couldn't have been a worse time for an epidemic. Public assemblies were limited as much as possible, but war work had to continue. Closing the mines could not be considered. The war needed copper. Red Cross volunteers gathered to make bandages and slings for the soldiers; now they also made hospital masks. Barbers fumigated their premises every night and wore masks. All in contact with the public were told to wear masks. The Board of Health asked that more streetcars be used to alleviate crowding. They ordered businesses to close. When some didn't, they threatened to call out the troops to force them to close.

If you feel a sudden chill, go home and go to bed, advised health authorities. Open the windows. Sneeze and cough into a handkerchief. The newspaper reported that the only places open in Seattle were the cemeteries and predicted Butte may soon be closed up tight.

This was happening at the same time the 91st was attacking in the Argonne and Flanders. Two brothers from a family who ranched down the road from the Hugheses in Rosebud County joined the army and fought in France. Another brother stayed behind. The two who went off to war lived. The one who stayed home died of influenza. Such stories were repeated across the country. A husband went off to fight and lived; his wife died of influenza. Another soldier languished in a field hospital, his siblings at home did the same, all three perished from the virus. There is some kind of providential lesson there. Poison gas, bombs, and bullets we know to fear, but the flu? Young healthy adults aren't supposed to die of the flu. In 1918, they did—in droves. Twice as many Montanans died in the influenza pandemic as were killed in the war. Even with all man's industrial genius, nature proved the more efficient killer.

The influenza passed through Butte like a viral tornado, hitting this household, missing that one, hitting yet another, weaving a destructive course with the force of a Biblical plague. It mercifully skipped over 415 Kemper Street, at least in its lethality. Since school was closed (I don't know whether Symon's was closed), Aila spent more time at the boarding house. She hurried to pick up the mail every day hoping to find a letter from Peter. She read his letters and then burned them. She didn't want her mother to know. Days passed, now weeks, and no more letters came. She read the newspapers. She knew the army was attacking.

USS Tampa is Sunk
Fearful Death Struggle on West Front
HUN DEFENSE BACKED BY ENERGY OF DESPERATION
PEACE PROPOSAL IS REJECTED
10 officers and 106 enlisted men go down as victims of German
    submarine attack
Spanish malady is epidemic in Butte
Flaming towns mark Hun Retreat
Pershing's Yanks Facing Violent Opposition but Enemy is in Confusion
Transport sinks in storm after collision off coast of Scotland, probable
    loss 372 American soldiers
ARMISTICE IS UNLIKELY
Cases of flu increasing
NO PEACE WITH AUTOCRACY

A cartoon showed the kaiser hog-tied on a platter. The German people were handing him to the Allies.

NO IMMEDIATE PEACE SEEN IN ENEMY NOTE

Peter's name didn't appear on the casualty lists. Surely he didn't have time to write letters during the fighting. Aila was not one for false hopes. She didn't see the cup half full or half empty, she saw this much water in the glass. She was a realist. She was not prone to conjecture. Peter may be all right, he may not. Through the boarders and neighbors, she learned that this man was wounded, that one was killed, but no news of Peter.

Another day while doing her chores on one of the upper floors of the boarding house, Aila was startled to see one of the boarders step out of

Aila

his room in front of her and block her path. Excuse me, she said politely, and started to go around him. He grabbed her by the shoulders and tried to push her into his room. She struggled to get away but couldn't. She reached up from her tiny four feet eleven inch frame and dug her finger-nails into his face and scratched. He shrieked in pain and surprise, put his hands to his bloody face, and in the same instance, stepped back, and went tumbling down the stairs.

He learned his lesson and so did Aila. After that, she kept a hat pin in her hair. The hat pins she used were two or three inches long with a tear-drop pearl end. The pin was thick and stiff enough to poke through straw or felt. She could inflict damage with it if necessary.

She told me that story sixty years later with utter contempt in her voice. "Don't push a man," she said, "he's too strong. Grab his thumbs and pull them back, like this." Here was my dear little grandma, as sweet a picture of graceful femininity as one could find, telling me how she learned to protect herself in her own home.

As wild and wooly as Butte was, women were safe on the streets. The only reason Aila was accosted in her own home was because Sarah told the boarders her daughter was on the menu. The going rate for a working man's whore was one dollar, the same as one day of room and board in the board-ing house. I can't help but wonder if Sarah got the idea from Mildred. Re-member Mildred? She was the woman in prison with Sarah who had been convicted of aiding and abetting the rape of her own daughter.

Around the time the United States entered the war, the Montana attor-ney general ordered the line closed (Butte's red light district). Aila re-ferred to his ilk as "one of those goody, goody politicians," her voice dripping with disdain, a tone she reserved for meddling politicians who she thought were up to no good. The line was along Mercury and Galena Streets, far from 415 Kemper. Do you suppose it ever occurred to the attorney general that when he closed the line the prostitutes would not leave a boomtown full of single men, and would not suddenly become clerks at Hennessy's, but instead would move into hotels and boarding houses throughout town where they would carry on their trade around children who otherwise never would have met a prostitute? Well, that's what happened. Some moved to 415 Kemper. The word around the neigh-borhood was Sarah was running a brothel. Of course Aila refused to join their profession, despite intense pressure from her mother. Even so, she was always kind and polite to the prostitutes, as she was to everyone. They in turn liked her. They probably felt sorry for her, seeing the abuse she endured from her mother. They would invite her to their rooms for tea. She always said the same thing about them: "They were very *clean*."

While Aila was fending off aggressive boarders, others were waging their own home front battles during the war. At the center of one of the loudest was someone quite familiar to Arthur and Sarah—Judge Crum.

Charles Crum was born in 1874 in Indiana. He read the law with a lawyer in Oklahoma and passed the bar. In 1906, he moved his family to Rosebud County hoping the dry climate would benefit his wife's frail health. They homesteaded twenty miles or so west of Forsyth. When his wife's health did not improve, he moved his family into Forsyth, and there he practiced law. In 1910, his wife died. Charles was then thirty-six years old and had five young children ranging in age from one to thirteen. He hired a housekeeper to care for the children.

He ran for county attorney, served one term, and then ran for district court judge and was on the bench when Arthur and Sarah's cases came before the court and still was when we entered the war.

In June of 1917, shortly after we declared war on Germany, President Wilson signed the Espionage Act which said in part

> Whoever, when the United States is at war, shall willfully make or convey false reports or false statements with the intent to interfere with the operation or success of the military or naval forces of the United States or to promote the success of its enemies and whoever . . . shall willfully cause or attempt to cause insubordination, disloyalty, mutiny, or refusal of duty in the military or naval forces of the United States, or shall willfully obstruct the recruiting or enlistment service of the United States, to the injury of the service or of the United States, shall be punished by a fine of not more than $10,000 or imprisonment for not more than twenty years, or both.

Zealous citizens and prosecutors vigorously sniffed out suspected offenders. One such zealot was Rosebud County Attorney Felkner Haynes, and in October of 1917, he made his first catch—a local rancher named Ves Hall. Hall's crime? That he said he'd sooner leave the country than be drafted, and it was okay to sink the *Lusitania* if it was carrying munitions, and he hoped Germany would win the war, and he said Wilson was a crook and a tool of Britain and Wall Street. He made these utterances in conversation at a saloon or picnic or some such place. For this, Felkner

Haynes brought charges against him under the Espionage Act, specifically for making and conveying "false reports and false statements with the intent to interfere with operation and success of the military" and for attempting "to cause insubordination, disloyalty, mutiny, and refusal to duty in the military . . . and obstruct recruiting."

The case went to federal court in Helena. Judge Crum testified as a character witness on Ves Hall's behalf. After hearing the evidence, Judge George Bourquin ordered a directed verdict of not guilty. He did not believe such comments uttered in the hinterlands would jeopardize the army in beating the Germans, and he did not believe the authors of the Espionage Act intended to prosecute chit chat.

Needless to say, Felkner Haynes was very unhappy about this verdict. He was also unhappy with Judge Crum for taking the opposing side in that he testified on Ves Hall's behalf. And it suffices to say that Crum was unhappy with Haynes for bringing the charges in the first place. It was a volatile mix of two strong personalities, and right after the trial, flint and powder came together and fireworks flew. According to Judge Crum, Haynes accused him of being "pro-German" and threatened there'd soon be a killing in Rosebud County over the Hall case. Crum fired back calling Haynes an "infamous liar" and "a thief" and "a perjurer" and other "vile names." At that, Haynes jumped up and came at Crum, and Crum pulled his revolver on him.

He probably shouldn't have done that.

Though no actual *gunshots* were fired that day, the whole brouhaha was far from over. Many state politicians were incensed at Judge Bourquin for finding Ves Hall not guilty, but since Bourquin was a federal judge, there wasn't much they could do about it other than to complain, and complain they did, and complain some more. However, out in Rosebud County, there sat Judge Charles Crum, a defense witness in the Hall case and a district judge known for giving full vent to his bombastic nature in loudly expounding his strong sentiments against American entry into the war. He did this even after we declared war on Germany. When chastened, he declared his allegiance to the United States. Nevertheless, his nemesis, Felkner Haynes, interviewed witness after witness and assembled a bundle of damning affidavits.

According to these sworn statements, Judge Crum said the government had no right to compel its citizens to fight Great Britain's war. He called it a Wall Street war and said Wilson was the hireling of J.P. Morgan, and the president and congress were induced to declare war on Germany to protect loans made by American bankers. One affiant alleged that while in court one day, Judge Crum made a speech to the jury saying directly or by inference "that this was a rich man's war to carry out a rich man's purpose, and that it was being intended and carried on to acquire more territory for the British Empire, and the acquisition of certain German possessions, to reclaim Alsace-Lorraine for the French Republic, and to obtain certain Austro-Hungarian territory for Italy and Japan."

Judge Crum was by no means alone in his opinions about the war. A professor at Smith College expressed much the same view in a book, but he waited until after the war was over to publish it. However, whatever one can say about the causes, intrigues, and motivations that led to the First World War, as Clemenceau put it, one cannot say that Belgium invaded Germany.

Affiants speaking against Judge Crum also claimed that he said if he were of draft age, he would resist, and he would not allow his son to return to this country and be shipped off and murdered on foreign soil, and that England would save her own men and send Americans, as she had sent Canadians, to be butchered on the front lines. He allegedly advised several men not to comply with the draft laws. That probably sealed his fate.

And there was that bit about him pulling his gun on Felkner Haynes.

Haynes delivered these affidavits to Governor Stewart who in turn forwarded them to the state legislature, many members of which were already loaded for bear over the Ves Hall case. A group of citizens from Roundup filed a resolution in defense of Judge Crum, but it didn't help. The legislature impeached him.

While this was going on, one of Judge Crum's sons was dying of cancer. He received the articles of impeachment at his son's deathbed. This news on top of the anguish he was already suffering over his son's condition, plus the physical exhaustion of keeping his court schedule while going as often as he could to Miles City to be with his son, drove the judge to a breakdown. His lawyers advised him to resign, believing in his weakened condition he could not withstand the ordeal of a trial. He followed their advice and resigned. The legislature put him on trial anyway. There was only a prosecution—no defendant, no defense lawyers, no defense witnesses, no opportunity to challenge the veracity of his accusers. He was convicted and removed from an office he no longer held.

One month later, his son died. Judge Crum then went to Mexico, stayed there for awhile, returned to Forsyth, and moved his family to North Dakota. He resumed his law practice, but the impeachment cloud would never leave him. He fell into despondency and drink and died an embittered man.

Such was the fate of the judge who threw the book at Sarah.

MEANWHILE IN BUTTE, agitators clashed with authorities throughout the war. A young career officer named Omar Bradley, late of the Academy, had been training with the 91st at Camp Lewis and was champing at the bit to get to France and experience war. Instead, he was sent to Butte. It was forty below the day he arrived. He called it a wild frontier town. He wrote in his autobiography that almost everyone packed a gun. His noting this seemed to indicate he found it extraordinary, even for the times.

Rumors of a general strike surfaced in March of 1918. The Pearse Connollys asked Captain Bradley for permission to hold a St. Patrick's Day parade. As long as state and city officials agreed and it was not unpatriotic, Bradley said yes, he would allow the parade. City officials said no parade. Governor Stewart said no and asked Bradley to prevent the parade. Rumors of an impending riot circulated. Several thousand gathered anticipating a parade. Wobblies massed in the streets with brass knuckles and knives. Captain Bradley spread his soldiers through town with rifles loaded and bayonets fixed. The show of force dispersed the gathering storm. Fifty men were arrested.

Despite pockets of trouble here and there, by and large patriotism flourished among Butte citizens throughout the war. A priest named Father Cotter told the Hibernians that their loyalties must stand firmly with their adopted country. "Receiving the benefits and blessing which she holds out to us," he said, "we are ever ready to remain loyal to her, to sacrifice ourselves if necessary for the principles for which the United States stands." General Pershing's brother came to town to launch the fourth liberty loan campaign. The Red Cross held a fruit pit drive. It is our patriotic duty to eat fruit and save the pits. In Butte and across the country, Americans collected peach, apricot, and cherry pits, and walnut shells. They were needed to make charcoal for gas masks.

The society page noted that Miss Aila Hughes hosted "a merry party on Wednesday evening . . . The rooms were prettily decorated in the national colors as well as those of our allies. The evening was pleasantly spent in music and dancing." One gentleman and several young ladies rendered solos. Refreshments were served at midnight.

That summer Aila had another job in addition to working at Symon's and the boarding house. She was secretary and bookkeeper

Arthur Hughes at the top of the stairs with several boarders. 415 Kemper Street, Butte, Montana.

for a man named Thomas Thomas (not Sarah's brother). He owned the Surprise mine just south of their house. Arthur was the general manager, but he didn't work there long. Within a couple of months, he was again working for the Company at the Pennsylvania Mine.

Then in September, just as our troops were flattening the salient at St. Mihiel, the IWW called a wildcat strike against the mines. Other unions refused to endorse the strike (this in the Gibraltar of unionism). Police, private detectives, and military intelligence agents raided the offices of the IWW, the Metal Mine Workers Union, and the *Butte Bulletin*, a firebrand labor paper run by admirers of the Bolsheviks, the publication of which had been banned by the State Council of Defense. The *Bulletin's* editor, "Big Bill" Dunn, was arrested and charged with sedition.

The raids threw fuel on the fledgling strike. More miners walked out. Wobblies intimidated and beat up miners going to work. Undeterred, Arthur continued to work. Sam Thompson didn't.

A deputy sheriff attempted to arrest a man for seditious talk. An altercation ensued which resulted in the deputy badly beaten and the man shot dead.

A group of women descended on U.S. District Attorney Burton Wheeler at his office. They said their husbands wanted to work and demanded protection so they could get to work. They said they'd come back with a thousand women if that's what it took to get his attention.

Wheeler summoned two IWW leaders to his office and accused them of being paid detectives. One admitted it was so. Then a very public war erupted between Wheeler and ACM lawyer Dan Kelly. This wasn't a first for these two; both Democrats, they ran against each other for attorney general—Kelly won, and they sparred in court—Kelly won that one too. Now once again, they swung their caissons into place and began to fire.

Kelly accused federal officials, i.e., Wheeler, of failing to enforce the law thereby making Butte a haven for the "radical element," i.e., the IWW. Wheeler blasted back saying, while it is true that the IWW called the strike, "They were encouraged to do so by the paid agents of your company." Kelly returned the volley. He called Wheeler a slacker and a liar and said if his accusations were true that the ACM hired men to disrupt mining thereby impeding war production, it was Wheeler's job to prosecute such people. He said, yes, the Company had obtained information on the IWW from men who happened to be "present at those meetings," but the idea that the Company would incite behavior that cost the Company millions was "too absurd for consideration," and these "so called strikes . . . have really been efforts to obstruct the proper conduct of the war."

A federal mediator arrived. The miners went back to work. The strike lasted two weeks.

Then the influenza hit, and the Wobblies fell out of the newspapers.

One month later, WAR ENDS covered the entire front page of the *Miner*, and in the more optimistic *Butte Daily Post*, PEACE.

Butte celebrated the armistice for three days and three nights. The troops stayed.

CHAPTER THIRTY-FIVE

By THE SPRING of 1919, soldiers were returning home from France across the country. Butte soldier John Troup summed up the sentiments of many of them when he said, "I wouldn't have missed the experience for one million dollars and would not want to go through it again for ten million." They were in between worlds—glad to have the horror behind them, yet they missed the comradery and excitement. Forever changed, now they had to find, or resume, their places in the world. That was especially difficult in 1919. Four years of war demand ended overnight. Economic uncertainty persisted while details of the treaty were debated. There was no GI bill for those men, just sixty dollars and a train ticket home.

"Keep away from the large cities," a U.S. Employment Service pamphlet cautioned them. "Almost every large city in the country has unemployed men walking the streets, many of them ex-soldiers . . .

"You left the United States during a period of great industrial activity with high pay and positions easy to find. After the signing of the armistice conditions changed. The industries of the country are in a period of readjustment, pay is not so high and positions are not so easy to find . . . It is best if you go back to the work you did before . . .

"Many of us have had our minds unsettled by the war and it is going to be difficult to settle down. You know what has always happened to drifters . . ."

The situation was especially bad in Butte because of changes in how copper was sold during the war. Before the war, the mining companies had a purchase contract in place before they mined, meaning they mined sold ore. The War Industries Board took over sale of copper during the war and reversed this practice, so the companies had to mine first and then sell. As a result, the mining companies were left with tremendous stockpiles of unsold ore when the war ended. The price of copper plummeted and production with it. Miners jostled each other in line at the mines vying for coveted jobs. Soon the city of Butte was broke.

Earlier in the year, in February, the Company cut day's pay from $5.75 to $4.75. A wildcat strike was called the next day. Picketers blockaded entrances to the mines, effectively shutting them down. Strikers roughed up any man they saw carrying a lunch bucket. Troops came—the 44th Infantry from Fort George Wright near Spokane. Their commander declared that law and order would be maintained. The soldiers broke up the pickets. Several strikers were wounded in the process. Soldiers raided IWW headquarters and Finlander Hall. A mob marched on the *Butte Daily Post*. One man was bayoneted.

Dynamite exploded under the home of a miner who insisted on working through the strike and had been threatened for doing so. The familiar vigilante calling card, 3-7-77, was left on his porch. Whether or not this was connected to the strike was not known. The police didn't think it was.

The strikers complained that the cost of living had risen with wages and didn't drop commensurate with the drastic wage cut. Mining executives and the local army commander tried to persuade merchants to lower their prices. It's because of the Department of Agriculture that prices are so high, complained one wholesaler. Strikers surrounded the streetcar barns and bullied the drivers into not taking the cars out. The Silver Bow Trades and Labor Assembly endorsed the strike. The Army and Navy League also voted to endorse the strike but later rescinded their endorsement. They said the meeting had been packed with radicals and didn't truly represent their organization. The electricians also endorsed the strike but later rescinded their endorsement. Other unions voted against endorsement or never took up the issue.

Calls went out for a general strike. There was a general strike in Seattle that same month. More troops came. Streetcar service resumed. The miners went back to what jobs there were. Some troops left. The strike lasted ten days. Arthur worked through it at the Berkeley.

In response to pleas for higher wages, the mining companies initiated the practice called contract mining. Contract miners were paid by how much ore they mined, so the faster and harder they worked to get "the rock in the box," the more money they made. Day's pay men were paid for the day regardless of what they did. At the North Butte Mining Company, contract miners earned an average of $7.25 per day while the cost of production dropped forty percent.

Yet, discontent over day's pay being lowered continued to fester. On the Fourth of July, there was a big victory parade, and a strike was called. Early the next morning, the ACM pay office was dynamited. Later in the day, an IWW convention convened.

Meanwhile, the mining companies negotiated new contracts with several craft unions. The miners still had no recognized union; however, as part of those agreements, day's pay was raised back to $5.75.

IN THE MIDST of all this labor turmoil, Peter Thompson was mustered out of the army and returned home to Butte. The family was overjoyed to see him. Judging by portraits of him in his uniform just before he left for France and right after the war, they had bid goodbye to a boy and welcomed home a man. He went from house to house visiting everyone. When he walked into his aunt Mary's house, his little six-year-old cousin Molly scampered into the room, and he bent down and swooped her up into his arms.

And, of course, he went to see Aunt B.

Peter, you sound like an American, she exclaimed. He had lost his brogue, only a slight lilt remained.

Fourth of July Victory parade, 1919.
BUTTE-SILVER BOW PUBLIC ARCHIVES, PH01858

The family greets the returning hero at Aunt B's in May of 1919. Aunt B wrote on the back: "Peter just returned from France, helped save democracy." Back row left to right: Peter's aunt Mary, Peter's sister Mary, Nell Coughlin (Ray's sister), Aunt B. The woman seated in the middle is Walter Breen's sister. Peter is in front with all the children. The extended family had welcomed at least one baby a year from 1912 to 1918 (the exception being 1913). Peter became an uncle for the first time while he was away and is no doubt holding his nephew Gilbert.

I am an American, Aunt B, Peter replied. I've my papers to prove it!

Those high hopes the Gribbens had for Peter were reignited the moment that exuberant, enthralling presence reentered their lives. Peter could charm the birds out the trees. He was intelligent. He read insatiably. Bulfinch's *Age of Fable* was a favorite and he often quoted from it. There was always a penny dreadful, as his sister called them, tucked in his back pocket. He had the Business College education thanks to Uncle John. Veterans had priority for what jobs there were. There was a job for Peter at the post office. It was a *steady* job. That meant it was a *good* job—there would be no up and down as in the mines. But Peter didn't want the post office job. He wanted to work in the mines. He went to work at the Tramway.

And, of course, he went to see Aila. I can only imagine their first meeting.

Aila steps outside to sweep the front porch. The sun is bright. Clumps of snow line the road. Out of the corner of her eye she spies a familiar figure. She recognizes that gait—the long, confident stride of a man a foot taller, hands thrust in his pants pockets, head held high, hat pushed back— the very picture of a man ready to take on the world. She feigns preoccupation. He says hello and climbs the steps. She brightens. A smile slips over her lips. They exchange pleasantries. He makes a date with her.

Yes, he was right to wait for her to grow up. She had grown even more beautiful while he was away. Hers was an elegant, quiet beauty. Her dark brown eyes, alert and bright, sparkled against her fair, flawless complexion.

She looked serious and studious, so grown up really with those pince nez resting on her nose. Yes, she was the one. However, marriage was for the future and of no immediate concern to Peter. I don't think he informed her of her future plans. I suspect the thought that she might marry somebody else never entered his mind. Why would any girl marry another man if she could marry Peter Thompson?

Sergeant Peter Thompson

Debate, Girls' Club, Athleta

AILA HUGHES
"Hughie"
"Great on rebuttal speeches"

WILLIAM HUGHES
"Bill"
"Takes a general interest in everything"
Speaker, Debater, and Swimmer

Aila and Bill's photos in the 1919 MOUNTAINEER, *the Butte High yearbook.*

As for Aila's intentions, she would graduate from high school in less than a month, completing four years of school in three and a half years. In the fall, she planned to go to college and become a teacher.

Her brother Bill was now almost twenty-one years old. He would also graduate in June. Based on his age, Bill should have graduated from high school three years earlier; however, he missed at least one year of high school while his parents were in prison because he had to work to support himself. He resumed his studies when the family reunited in Butte. Then he left school to join the navy. After the navy discharged him, he again returned to school. Then the schools closed during the influenza epidemic. When the schools reopened, he resumed his studies. Many boys, then and now, would never have returned to school after being on their own. Bill resumed his studies not once but three times. He was a voracious reader and spoke with authority on a variety of subjects. Erudite, well-read, committed to finishing his education, one would think he was a young man with plans.

A few days before graduation, the headline of a small article at the top of page five of the *Butte Miner* read:

BRIDE'S FATHER STARTS ACTION
Son-in-Law is Charged with Perjury in Allegation that
He Declared 15-Year-Old Girl to be 18 Years of Age

It was Bill. Bill and a girl I'll call Eloise had been secretly married for three months. She lived with her parents, and he with his. When her father found out, I don't know how he found out, he accused Bill of a lot of things, but as for specific laws broken, he had Bill charged with perjury for swearing under oath that Eloise was eighteen when he applied for the marriage license.

Despite the perjury charge, Bill managed to graduate from high school with Aila. Now that he was out of school, Sarah chastened him to get money for her all the more. Bill had worked off and on in the mines since he was eighteen, never for more than a few weeks at a time, usually for only a few days. He worked as a streetcar operator for awhile and possibly other places. Sarah insisted that he get money for her. I don't know whether she cajoled or merely suggested that he could get money even if he didn't have a job. Archie said she made that quite clear to both of them. "Our mother taught us to steal," he said.

In addition to cajoling her children into dubious methods of securing cash, or trying to, Sarah had her own creative guiles for getting money. She conducted seances at the boarding house. I don't know whether she charged an up front fee or the money making was part of the show. I can picture the participants sitting around a table in a dim, candle-lit room. Sarah summons the dead. There are three knocks. That's the dead calling, your dead relative come to tell you your long lost cousin is in desperate need of money. Your dead relative says you must send the money, you must, you must send it right away. It is dangerous to anger the dead, you must do as they say. Where does your cousin live? Chicago? Not any more. You don't know where? The spirits will tell me, just leave the money right here on the table, five dollars will do it, and I'll send it to your long lost relative.

Arthur had been working at the Berkeley Mine since January. He left there in May and went out of town to work a stonemasonry job. He told Aila he would be back in time for her high school graduation, and he was. Around that same time, he was injured and couldn't work for several weeks. By July, he had recovered and returned to work at the Pennsylvania Mine.

Aila still had her regular chores at the boarding house in addition to working at Symon's, but now there were fewer boarders for whom she had to cook and clean. Earlier in the year when labor troubles reignited amid the depressed metals market, Sarah's boarding house business dropped off drastically. By summer, she was down to only two or three boarders. The mining companies gave preference to married men and her boarders were usually single. Sarah may have believed in those silly seances, but apparently she did not believe in rainy days because she never saved for one, and she spent money whether she had it or not. She bought on credit, and before the hard times, the merchants seeing a thriving business at 415 Kemper certainly had reason to consider her a safe risk. But with Arthur out of work for several weeks, and the boarding house business dwindling, and the butterfly's propensity to spend and not save, Sarah was now in a financial pickle. It was

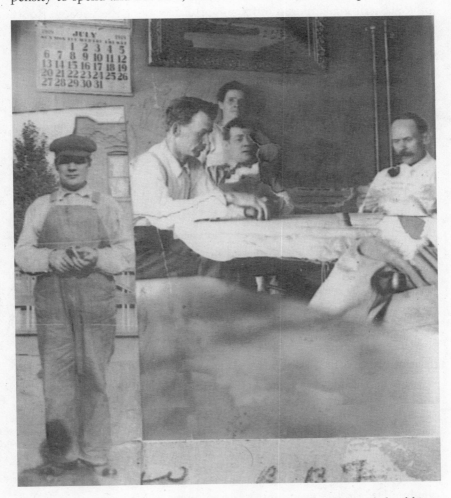

Card game in the boarding house. Arthur is in the middle, Sarah is behind him. Inset picture is of Arthur.

inevitable that her creditors would soon come calling. By August, they had started to circle, and within a span of six weeks, our Sarah was embroiled in three lawsuits and hired a different lawyer for each.

Sarah had faced litigation before, and she was definitely one to put up a fight. In a weird way, I think she enjoyed the high drama of it.

The first to sue her was Montana Mattress. Sarah was in debt to them for $1550 worth of bedding, furniture, curtains, linoleum, mirrors, and the like.

Six weeks later, the owner of the Moxom Café, Mr. Simeon, sued her. That mess started two years earlier when a man named Richard Richards offered Sarah a half interest in six mining claims along the Tobacco Roots. The price was one thousand dollars. Sarah said she had no money, but Mr. Richards didn't see that as an obstacle. He sold the mining claims to her for a dollar and took her promissory note for one thousand dollars. The note was secured by two mortgages: one on the house and one on the furniture. The catch was—Sarah didn't own the Kemper Street house. Mrs. Dougherty owned it. Sarah was buying it, but the deed was still in Mrs. Doughtery's name. Sarah wouldn't actually own it until she had paid for it in full, which she had not yet done. Richard Richards promptly sold the promissory note to another man, who promptly offered it to yet another man, who said he wanted to buy it but didn't have the money and then acted as a go between to sell it to another man—Mr. Simeon. Now two years later, Simeon discovered that Sarah had been "in debt to various and sundry persons . . . and was insolvent" when she mortgaged the house and she didn't own it nor anything else. To sue her was akin to trying to drain a dry well, but he did it anyway. Sarah responded that she never entered into an agreement with this man who was suing her nor with the man who sold him the note, which was all true. Then she launched a cross complaint against Richard Richards saying the mining claims were worthless and he knew it, she had been defrauded. That case didn't go anywhere because Richard Richards was nowhere to be found. Simeon then gave up on Sarah and sued the man who sold him the worthless note. He lost.

After Montana Mattress filed suit but before Mr. Simeon, Ellen Dougherty sued Sarah. Actually, she sued Sarah and Arthur.

Mrs. Dougherty's complaint stated that while Sarah had made payments on the house from July of 1916 to April of 1919 (each more than one hundred dollars per month), her payment in May was a few dollars short and she didn't pay in July and August. Therefore, Mrs Dougherty demanded the house back. Sarah said she'd burn it down first. Mrs. Dougherty got a restraining order to keep Sarah from damaging the house.

Sarah responded by saying she had paid faithfully for nearly three years, but due to the labor troubles in Butte, she couldn't find enough boarders to keep the house profitable, plus Arthur had been injured and was out of work for a few months (it was a few weeks), and one of her sons had suffered a prolonged illness (Archie), and because of all this, it was impossible for her to keep up the payments, and this was due to circumstances beyond her control, and she shouldn't be punished for it.

The purchase price of the house was $5000. Sarah had been making payments to Mrs. Dougherty through the bank and had assumed two mortgages of Mrs. Dougherty's. To date, Sarah had paid a total of $3514.88 in monthly payments. In addition, Sarah claimed she had spent $1479.31 in improvements to the house. She said the furnace had been inoperable when she moved in, but she didn't know it until the cold weather came. She had to have the furnace repaired, plus the chimneys and roof. She had also purchased radiators, faucets, a toilet bowl, windows, door locks, and did electrical wiring. All told, she had spent $4994.19 in payments and improvements.

Mrs. Dougherty amended her complaint to allege that while Sarah occupied the house the furnace had been demolished by explosives, water had been left to freeze in pipes and had damaged several radiators, a toilet had been removed, windows had been broken, locks had been removed, hinges had been taken off doors, electrical fixtures were missing, plumbing had been removed, and the house was in a general state of disrepair and was not clean. For all this, she claimed damages of $1440.

The house was put in receivership, and Sarah and Arthur were ordered to vacate the premises. They refused. Sarah argued that she couldn't make payments on the place if she wasn't living there running the boarding house. They were held in contempt of court and ordered thrown in jail. Arthur was not jailed. He and Aila and Archie and Patsy and their boarders continued to live in the house while this dragged on. Whether Sarah was jailed, and if so for how long, I don't know. In January, she was living at 415 Kemper with the rest of the family and had seven boarders.

Arthur filed a motion asking that he be dismissed from the case. This was all his wife's doing. He had nothing to do with it. Sarah filed papers saying this was so. The boarding house was her enterprise, her husband had no part of it, she alone had entered into the agreement to buy it. Nevertheless, poor Arthur couldn't get out of it.

Then Mrs. Dougherty claimed that back in 1916, three years after she bought the house, she was then a widow and a real estate man came to see her and urged her to sell the house. He said that Mrs. S. Anna Hughes would like to buy it. He presented the papers to her which she signed. It was only then, so she said, that she realized that Mrs. S. Anna Hughes didn't have the money to pay for the house and she wanted to undo the sale. Then Arthur Hughes rented a room from her, and she didn't know he was connected with Mrs. S. Anna Hughes, and then Sarah moved in with him, and they took possession of the house, and Sarah told her, if she reneged on the deal, she would sue her.

Mrs. Dougherty also insisted that Sarah had earned plenty of money running the boarding house. She could have easily paid her bills but instead had squandered her profits on "riotous living and for unnecessary items and for dishonest purposes." Sarah was famous for her parties, or infamous, depending on your perspective.

The trial date approached, and Judge Lamb was assigned to the case. Mrs. Dougherty filed an affidavit to disqualify him. Then Judge Jackson was assigned to the case. Mrs. Dougherty filed an affidavit to disqualify him. Then Judge Law was assigned. Sarah filed an affidavit to disqualify him. In the end, Judge Winston heard the case. He ruled in favor of Mrs. Dougherty and ordered Sarah and Arthur to pay her $827 plus 8% interest. Needless to say, they didn't, or couldn't, pay, so the court ordered the sheriff to seize property amounting to $827 plus interest, but there was no property to seize. Months earlier, another judge had ruled in favor of Montana Mattress and ordered Sarah to return the furniture.

Sarah's litigation maelstrom dragged on for over a year. We now return to the month her spate of lawsuits began. Montana Mattress has filed suit. Mrs. Dougherty and Mr. Simeon are still waiting in the wings. Sarah is pestering Bill to get money for her.

Late on the night of August 18, 1919, a masked man garbed in overalls, a brown coat, and checkered cap entered the Cooper House on Talbot Avenue. He pulled a revolver from his pocket and ordered the couple behind the bar and two patrons to throw up their hands. Motioning with his revolver, he ordered them to stand against the wall across from the cash register. They did as told.

"Take whatever you want, just don't shoot anybody," cried the terrified woman.

"I never had trouble with any woman, only my wife," the robber snarled back.

He walked over to the cash register, placed a sack on the counter, and stuffed all the money from the register into it. Then he walked over to the owners and customers with his revolver still pointed at them. He ordered the two patrons to give him whatever they had. The two men emptied their pockets into the sack. The robber backed his way to the door, opened it, slipped out, and vanished into the night.

He ran to his room at the boarding house. Thirty minutes later, the police joined him in that room, and with him, they found the sack of money, the loaded revolver, and fifty-three bullets.

One of the policemen asked him his name. He said it was Harry Randolph, but of course, it was Bill.

They arrested him. He said he didn't do it and pled not guilty. While awaiting trial, his marriage to Eloise was annulled and her father dropped the perjury complaint.

Bill's trial began in October. Judge Lynch presided. The two saloon customers he had robbed, H. J. Elliott and Joseph Jackson, testified. The trial ended in a hung jury. Two weeks later, there was a second trial. This time the jury convicted Bill of robbery.

The jury deferred to Judge Lynch for sentencing. Robbery was punishable by one to twenty years in prison. Bill's lawyer, Mr. Beadle, reminded Judge Lynch that Bill was young, only twenty-one, and that he had volunteered for the navy in the Great War, and there was some doubt as to his guilt since there had been a hung jury in the first trial. Judge Lynch noted Bill's military service and gave him a sentence at the lighter end of the scale: two to five years hard labor at the Montana State Prison in Deer Lodge. He was sentenced on Saturday, November 1, six years to the day and date after his mother was convicted of bigamy.

CHAPTER THIRTY-SIX

OF COURSE Aila was mortified by all this. Her friends knew about Bill's illegal marriage and the robbery. How could they not know? It was in the newspapers, and on the front page, and gossip traveled faster than newsprint. The humiliation of scandal after scandal, the physical beatings and ridicule she endured from her mother, the debauchery she witnessed, the licentiousness her mother tried to force her into—it was enough to drag any soul into the mire. But not this soul. She wouldn't let it. Aila Hughes rebelled. From a very young age, she charted a different course. "I was not going to live like that," she said flatly, "I decided I was going to be a *lady*," and from this conviction, she never wavered. The image that keeps coming into my mind is of the Phoenix rising from the ashes. Indeed, out of this ash heap of scandal and debauchery emerged no mythical bird but a rose—an exquisite blossom, beautiful and delicate in appearance, yet hardy and resilient enough to withstand the bitter cold of sorrow and blistering heat of adversity. The thorns protecting her were innate goodness and a willful nature rightly directed, also called fortitude. Aila Hughes would not allow what she grew up around to determine the kind of person she would be. She knew her own mind and would never follow the crowd just because. In fact, if the crowd was going a certain way, that alone gave her reason to think twice.

She lived life deliberately. She refused to fall slothfully into the patterns around her. It was as if the fear of going the way of her mother was so great that she wouldn't allow herself the slightest infraction, for it might open a crack in her soul, then a tear, then a gouge, then a gaping hole to let in filth and wantonness. No, it would not happen. She would not let it. And to free herself from Sarah's cloud, she had to be beyond reproach. "What a man thinks of himself, that it is which determines, or rather indicates, his fate," wrote Thoreau. She saw herself a lady, and that she was.

Aila, age seventeen. One of her high school graduation portraits.
ZUBICK ART STUDIO, BUTTE, MONTANA

While some boldly proclaim that they are making the world a better place, others quietly, steadfastly work at bettering themselves, and in doing so, they do better the world. Aila Hughes worked at bettering herself: bettering her speech, bettering her mind, bettering her style, bettering her veneer. She read books on etiquette. She observed the elegant West Side ladies, how they dressed, how they carried themselves. Being a lady meant being kind and considerate, well-behaved, modest, polite and gracious. It meant following the golden rule, never raising her voice, holding back harsh words. It was the highest ideal ever before her, something forever worked toward, the perfection of which could never be attained because the standards she set for herself were so high.

Sarah taught Aila what she had been taught at finishing school and by her own mother. There was a proper way to set a table. There was proper behavior at table. There was a proper way to stand—back straight, shoulders back, head up, hands behind or at her side. There was a proper way to sit—back straight, shoulders back, feet together with one foot slightly ahead of the other or ankles crossed, palms up, one in the other resting gently on her lap. It was to appear natural and effortless, as we see none of the painstaking labor of the artist, only the resulting masterpiece. Aila saw this not as a way to put on airs—that wouldn't be ladylike—but out of respect for decorum and courtesy toward those around her. She strove to be an embellishment to the world. She was well-spoken and chose her words carefully. Her diction was impeccable—not forced and affected, but effortless and natural. She turned simple penmanship into a thing of beauty. She worked at mastering the art of being a lady, both inwardly and outwardly. For her, that was the pinnacle.

Judge Lynch offered to send her to law school. Aila appreciated his offer; however, she didn't like having somebody else decide what she should study. She wanted to be a teacher. A man offered financial help for college. She politely declined. "You never know if there are strings attached," she said.

Now comes another I-wish-I-had-asked-more parts. I knew Grandma planned to go to college and I knew she had a scholarship to the Montana State College in Bozeman. She and Mom and I talked about it many times. Naturally, I assumed that she planned to go to Bozeman. I never thought to ask: where were you going to go to college? As it turns out, her high school transcript was never sent to Bozeman. It was sent to Radcliffe.

As the date she was to leave approached, she had to tell her mother. With all the courage she could muster, she drew a deep breath and announced: Mother, I'm going away to college.

Sarah scoffed at her. You aren't going anywhere, she said. You are going to stay right here and help me run this house.

Aila insisted that she was indeed going away to college. Sarah said no, she wasn't and she didn't want to hear another word about it.

Aila said, Mother, it's all arranged. I am going to go.

Sarah erupted. NO, YOU ARE NOT! YOU ARE GOING TO STAY RIGHT HERE AND WORK!

But, Mother, if I go to college, I can get a steady job, a good job, I can become a teacher.

A TEACHER?! YOU HIGHFALUTIN LITTLE FOOL, THINKING YOU CAN BECOME A TEACHER, WHO DO YOU THINK YOU ARE, YOU'LL NEVER AMOUNT TO ANYTHING, YOU ARE NOT GOING ANYWHERE, YOU COULD MAKE PLENTY OF MONEY FOR ME RIGHT HERE IN THIS HOUSE IF YOU WEREN'T SO HIGH AND MIGHTY. IT'S YOUR JOB TO STAY HERE AND HELP ME AND WORK!

Mother—

With that, Sarah jumped up and ran out of the kitchen and into Aila's bedroom. Aila followed her.

Mother! she gasped. Sarah was pulling Aila's clothes out of the closet and ripping each to shreds.

YOU ARE NOT GOING ANYWHERE! Sarah screamed. YOU WILL STAY RIGHT HERE!

Mother, *please*, Aila pleaded and tried to take the dresses before her mother could tear them up.

YOU LET GO OF THAT! Sarah yelled and she yanked the dress out of Aila's hands and threw her daughter against the wall of the closet. Aila's head banged against one of the protruding nailheads on which she hung her clothes and she sank to the floor in a heap.

Having torn to shreds every piece of clothing Aila owned, save the clothes on her back, Sarah left the room, left her sobbing daughter with bleeding, throbbing head, and stormed out.

CHAPTER THIRTY-SEVEN

A FELLOW NAMED Jim Winston moved into the boarding house. He was from New York, the state not the city. He was twenty-five years old and worked as a motorman in the mines. He was different from the other boarders. He didn't "want something" from Aila, he simply enjoyed being around her.

He began to court her. He gave her a broach. He got a marriage license. Then something happened. I don't know what. I thought perhaps he was killed in the mines, but he wasn't. Whatever the reason, they didn't marry. I can't help but wonder if Sarah had something to do with it. She didn't want Aila to marry at all. She wanted her to stay and take care of her.

EXACTLY TWO MONTHS later, in mid April of 1920, Butte seethed again. The IWW called another wildcat strike. They distributed circulars throughout town which demanded a six-hour day, a raise to seven dollars a day, abolition of the rustling card, abolition of the contract and bonus system, and release of all political and industrial prisoners in the entire country.

Other Butte unions refused to endorse the strike.

On the first day, several hundred picketers lined North Main Street and the Anaconda Road. They stopped men carrying lunch buckets and sent them home. Those who wouldn't be turned back so easily, they beat up. Wobblies dragged miners off streetcars to prevent them from going to work. When one streetcar conductor refused to let the ruffians on board, they broke down the door and dragged him and five others off the car and beat them up. One man suffered three broken ribs and cuts to his face. Another man told the local Bureau of Investigation agent that the IWW threatened to kill him if he went to work.

A woman named Mrs. Cundry came upon picketers beating up a boy and threatened to shoot them if they didn't stop. She reached into her pocket and they bolted. Later she complained to a newspaperman, "I don't see why it is that a bunch of these foreigners can stand there on the hill and tell an American citizen that he can't work. Every time my husband and my boy come off shift I go to meet them and walk home with them, I am that worried but my husband says that no IWW can tell him whether or not he will work." When asked about her gun, she said, "I never shot a gun in my life and I am scared to death of a revolver, but they didn't know that."

Some men took a circuitous route around the picketers and managed to get to work. Arthur was one of those. No matter what was going on in Butte, strike or no strike, Arthur worked. Lord knows they needed the money, especially considering his wife's pecuniary habits.

Though Arthur went to work that day, many men didn't, or couldn't. If this continued, the smelters in Great Falls and Anaconda would be affected. Governor Stewart asked for troops.

That night Wobbly-led "dry squads" prowled hotels, cigar stores, pool halls, and soft drink places (the Prohibition euphemism for saloons) and demanded that Prohibition and gambling laws be enforced while the strike continued. I can only imagine how bizarre that must have seemed to the people of Butte—to be invaded by a bunch of teetotaling anarchists. How weird.

The sheriff and mayor issued a joint proclamation stating that those who wanted to work should be allowed to do so and that protection would be provided to be sure they could. Sheriff O'Rourke tried to hire more deputies. His forces were overwhelmed by the number of picketers.

The next day the Company hired several deputies to guard the mines. The guards and Wobbly picketers brawled throughout the day. The guards severely beat up several picketers. Later that afternoon, the picketers massed at the Neversweat Mine on the Anaconda Road. Sheriff O'Rourke hurried to the scene with several deputies. The picketers insisted that he arrest the mine guards who had done the beating. He said he would investigate and that it was his job to protect everybody. He implored the crowd to disperse. They didn't. Then the shoving started, and the punching, and rock throwing, and then somebody yelled, "Look out for that man in the window, he's going to shoot!" Shots rang out. One bullet grazed a deputy. Then a flurry of gunfire erupted. It lasted only seconds but was long enough for fifteen men to be wounded, six of them seriously.

The initial shots were believed to have come from a nearby boarding house. The ensuing investigation found no evidence to support or discount this. The investigation also found that the mine guards had fired their guns, but the policemen and the sheriff and his deputies had not. The Wobblies said they had been protesting peaceably, and without warning, the guards started shooting at them.

Four companies of troops arrived. The miners went back to work.

In reporting on these events, the *Anaconda Standard* took a dim view of the fact that many of the picketers were foreign born, had lived in this country for several years, and had never applied for citizenship.

A few days after the affray, a man named Thomas Manning died of gunshot wounds. He was believed to be one of those shot on the Anaconda Road; however, during the inquest over his death, at which 101 witnesses testified, not one remembered seeing him on the Anaconda Road the day of the shooting, and no one knew how or when he was brought to Finlander Hall after he was shot. Acting Coroner Doran asked the lawyers representing the IWW to produce witnesses who could attest to Manning's whereabouts on the day of the shooting. None appeared.

The autopsy showed that Manning was killed by a .32 caliber pistol. The mine guards, sheriff deputies, and policemen carried shotguns and heavier caliber handguns. The jury concluded that a Person Unknown shot him.

It also came to light during the inquest that many of the Wobbly picketers had traveled to Butte from throughout the West with the sole purpose of instigating a strike. These itinerant protesters said they had never worked in the Butte mines and one said he had never worked in a mine anywhere. They testified quite candidly that the purpose of the strike was to seize the mining properties. Had their demands been met, they said they would have presented even more onerous demands.

Signs were now posted at Company properties that said in effect: IWW need not apply.

Later that year, the Wobblies discovered a highly placed mole in their ranks. He was a Thiel detective. After his cover was blown, an informant for the Bureau of Investigation (now the FBI) reported: "Everybody suspects everybody now. If they only knew who are the stools and how many of them there are, they would sure be a dismayed bunch. To think that so many of their supposed best men are paid agents makes me laugh every time I think of it."

Arthur worked steadily at the Pennsylvania Mine through the duration of the strike. Sam Thompson worked at the West Colusa. Peter was working at the Pennsylvania in February. I don't know where or if he was working that April when all the trouble happened. If he was in Butte, he wasn't working at an ACM mine. He sometimes worked for the North Butte and he may have worked for other mining companies. I wasn't able to find those records.

In June, Peter went to work again at the Tramway Mine. He worked there eleven days and then went to work at the Speculator. Around that time, he and his father bought an old car together. Sam didn't know how to drive, so Peter drove him wherever he wanted to go. That summer, Peter drove to Seattle to see his sister Mary and her family who were living there temporarily. He stayed with them for awhile and worked on the docks.

CHAPTER THIRTY-EIGHT

PETER'S BROTHER John was now home in Belfast. One day during a meal, Denis reached across the table for the sugar, and before he could get it, Nellie snatched it away. Sugar was scarce and she imposed her own rationing. Denis picked up his cup and hurled it at her in retaliation. It crashed against the wall. "Who do you think you are only three years older and lifting the sugar!" he scolded. Nellie just shrugged him off. Jimmy bounded up the stairs to report to Rose, "It was only a cup broke, Ma."

The two youngest children, Rosie and Brigid, were now ten and nine years old. Often they came home from school to find a boisterous crowd filling the kitchen with laughter and chatter. The shy little girls would try to sneak past Denis and John and their chums. Denis would see them and call them over and the two would obediently detour to their big brother. Denis would ask the girls what they learned at school that day, and the two would dutifully relate the high points of their lessons. Now give us a wee poem, he'd say, and Rosie and Brigid would whisper to each other and then stand at attention as one of them performed the recitation. The poems always had a moral, like the one about the proud cat . . .

A very small cat wore a very big bow.
She thought she was lovely, so stuck- up, you know.
She danced 'round the room like a black, furry ball,
With her nose in the air and no manners at all.
Well, one day I tell she gave no more airs,
She tripped on her bow and fell down the stairs.
Her mother was sorry, but what could she do?
Pride must have a fall, we all know that's true!

The young men would applaud, and Denis would send his little sisters on their way. Rose would hear them and call out, now come give me a wee poem.

Denis and John each received a war bonus from the British government. Rose told Nellie to take them to buy a suit of clothes and overcoat with it. "And go to the market while you're out," she added, "and buy some wee herrings and some wee eggs and a bit of beef, not a bit near the shoulder for it does all the work."

Nellie said she would and left with her mental shopping list and two brothers in tow.

They walked into the men's clothing store. Denis tried on a suit and stood before the mirror for some time admiring himself from all sides. John, a head taller but much shyer, tried on his suit.

"What do you think?" the salesman asked John. "Don't you want to look in the mirror?"

"There's my mirror," John replied gesturing at Nellie. "Whatever she says."

Brigid and Rosie Thompson, ages ten and eleven, in the school yard at St. Malachy's, Belfast, Ireland, 1920.

They bought their suits and overcoats and left the store. Once outside, Denis shook his head in disgust at John. "You're never going to change. You're never going to change," he said, referring to John's undying deference toward Nellie.

When they returned home, John told Rose, "Mother, I think I'll stay in the army." He intended to join the Royal Guard.

"No, you'll not stay in the army," she said. "It's too dangerous. You and Denis are to go to Butte with your father and Peter."

So they did.

IN BUTTE, the summer of 1920 passed in relative calm and waned quietly into fall. Then the mines slowed down. The robust metals buying in the first quarter appeared to be a false start. Buying stopped. The price of copper dropped; wages and supply costs were the highest ever and stayed high. The worst was yet to come. The cold weather settled in.

During her evenings at home, Aila sat in the rocker next to her bed, snugly wrapped in a heavy quilt, and read. She relished her evening respite after a long, labor-filled day of chores at home and work at Symon's. Every spare moment at home, of which there were very few, she spent reading in her room. After reading a poem that she particularly liked in a magazine, she would pick up the scissors and clip it out and put it in the large envelope in which she kept all the other poems she had collected. She was an American girl, chock full of all the can-do that embodies, with a Welsh soul. She adored poetry. Her Celtic mind delighted in bending itself around verse, pondering the veiled meaning, bathing in the beauty of the words and ideas. Even the few letters she penned she wrote more in stanzas than sentences. I found dozens of poems she had clipped and I've included some in this narrative where I thought events might have inspired her to keep that particular one. Several were about perseverance.

Bill was paroled that November after serving one year in prison. He served less time for armed robbery than his mother did for bigamy. Warden Conly seldom wrote a comment on a prisoner's dossier, but on Bill's he did. "Tough kid," he wrote. Shortly after Bill returned home, Arthur left. Aila said, "My father left and came back three or four times, then he left and never came back." This was that time. Aila was nineteen, Archie was sixteen, Patsy was thirteen.

Sarah. Aila wrote on the back, "Don't you ever think of her anymore, Daddy, that you don't even write to her?"

One evening Aila picked up her senior year *Mountaineer* and pasted this card inside:

The Philosophy of Life

Did it ever occur to you that man's life is full of crosses—and temptations? He comes into the world without his consent, and goes out against his will, and the trip between is exceedingly rocky. The rule of contraries is one of the features of his trip. If he is poor, he is a bad manager; if he is rich, he is dishonest; if he needs credit, he can't get it; if he is prosperous, everyone wants to do him a favor. If he is in politics, it is for graft; if he is out of politics, he is no good to the country. If he doesn't give to charity, he is a stingy cuss; if he does, it is for show. If he is actively religious, he is a hypocrite; if he takes no interest in religion, he is a hardened sinner. If he gives affection, he is a soft specimen; if he cares for no one, he is cold blooded. If he dies young, there was a great future for him; if he lives to an old age, he missed his calling.

I was shocked when I read that. It's the most cynical thing I've ever read. I couldn't imagine my sweet little grandma being so cynical. Yet as I thought about it, how could she not be? She had her whole life in front of her and only abuse to look forward to at home. Her father had abandoned her, her mother tried to sell her. One avenue of escape had already been thwarted by her mother, maybe two. Nevertheless, she managed to keep a glimmer of hope. In that same *Mountaineer*, she pasted a what-people-did-that-day column she had clipped from the newspaper. It read: "Miss Aila Hughes and Miss Elizabeth Cassidy returned from a teachers' meeting in Billings."

She hadn't given up.

Aila, Sarah, and Patsy.
The men are probably boarders.

AFTER SEVERAL MONTHS in Seattle, Peter returned to Butte and went to work at the Badger Mine. The army had been looking for him almost since he was discharged. The Republic of France had decorated him with the *Croix de Guerre* with gilt star for saving that man's life in Flanders. When the recruiting officer finally tracked Peter down and attempted to give him the medal, Peter told the officer that it wasn't only he who saved that man; Winks Brown helped him pull the man into the trench. Peter asked whether Winks Brown received a medal. The officer said he didn't know. Peter declared adamantly that he would not accept the medal unless Winks Brown received a medal too.

The officer did some investigating and found out that Winks Brown had not been decorated. He had not run out of the trench to save the man, exposing himself to enemy fire, as Peter had.

Years later, the newspaper reported that when Marshal Foch visited Butte during his tour of the United States shortly after the war, he tried to give Peter the medal, but Peter wouldn't accept it because Winks Brown had not been decorated. I tried to confirm this in newspaper articles written at the time of Marshal Foch's visit. Lengthy articles in the Butte papers reported what was going to happen during his stop in Butte but said little about what actually did happen. Soldiers were asked to appear in uniform. It is easy to imagine that Marshal Foch may have recognized those soldiers on whom his country had bestowed so high an honor. No matter, Peter would not accept the medal from anyone, not even Marshal Foch, unless Winks Brown was also decorated. The recruiting officer gave up and left the medal at John Gribben's house; Peter was living there in one of the flats with his father and his sister Mary and her family who by then had returned from Seattle.

As for Winks Brown, his real name was Wingfield Brown. He was from Philipsburg, about sixty miles from Butte. He was two years older than Peter, born in 1893, and was studying law at the University of Montana when we entered the war. During the assault on Gesnes, he took a machine gun bullet in the chest, right above his heart. After the war, he returned home, finished his law degree, ran for county attorney of Granite County, and won. He took office in January of 1921 and died the next month. The bullet wound had reopened, taking his young life, and adding yet another name to the Powder River Gang's honor roll.

Croix de Guerre

AROUND THE TIME Peter returned from Seattle, another of Peter's army friends became quite taken with Aila. Most men were charmed by her. In addition to being beautiful, she was kind and animated. She had a spirit about her that drew others, even strangers. Her speech held a gentle note of enthusiasm that lifted the listener. This man's mother looked past the Hughes family's notorious reputation and saw a jewel. She liked very much the prospect of Aila Hughes as a daughter-in-law. Not only was Aila pretty and charming and kind, she seemed responsible and level-headed—good qualities for a wife and mother. The man's mother did all she could to encourage a romance between her son and Aila, and her son was certainly smitten.

Peter noticed.

He began to court Aila steadily and with a purpose. He employed every ounce of his charm and wit to captivate her. Being naturally loquacious and well-read, Peter made a fascinating conversationalist. And he was a gentleman, something Aila greatly appreciated and respected. They both enjoyed the life of the mind and cultivated a lively interest in the world around them and in the world at large, and they both had engaging personalities, so perfect together in so many ways. He took her dancing at the Winter Garden and ice skating at the Holland Rink. He said she was the prettiest girl in Butte and he was going to get her. When I asked her about him she replied with fervor, "He was the most *hand*some man I ever met, God love him!" Yet, Peter was more than a dandy, and she more than a beauty. Beauty is hollow if not undergirded by character—hers was. She stood fast on principle, and of those principles she was certain. And there was that intangible special something.

He asked her to marry him. She said yes.

Around that time, mine production ground to a halt. Nearly all the Butte mines shut down. Peter left town to find work.

I wonder if it was Grandma's idea not to marry in Butte.

Sarah stormed to the depot as soon as she found out. Seeing Aila was already gone, she accosted the sheriff.

My daughter has run off to marry that Irishman! You must go get her and bring her back!

There's no law against marrying an Irishman, replied Sheriff Duggan.

You must go get her and bring her back! I need her here!

How old is she, Mrs. Hughes?

She's not yet twenty.

How old, Mrs. Hughes?

She's only nineteen. It doesn't matter how old she is. It's your job to go get her and bring her back!

Nineteen is old enough, said Sheriff Duggan. She can do as she pleases.

Portrait Aila gave to Peter.
ZUBICK ART STUDIO, BUTTE, MONTANA

CHAPTER THIRTY-NINE

AILA STEPPED off the train in Pocatello and looked around. It was August 5 and terribly hot. Peter was waiting for her on the platform. They went to the courthouse and then to the rectory next door to St. Joseph's Church. Father Dolan greeted them warmly. He was young and very handsome. The three sat down. Father Dolan asked them several questions. Then he summoned his housekeeper, Mrs. Evans. A man named Mr. Leach also joined them. I don't know whether he was a friend of Peter's or someone Father Dolan invited. All stood. Father Dolan led Peter and Aila through their vows. Aila slipped off her left glove, Peter slipped on the ring. Then Father invited them into the dining room for dinner. After dinner, Peter and Aila thanked Father Dolan and walked back to the depot. They boarded the next train for Soda Springs and from there went to Conda.

Conda was still under construction at that time. The Anaconda Company had begun to mine phosphate there the year before and was building a town for the miners. The houses had four rooms and large yards; rent was twelve dollars a month. I think Peter and Aila lived in one of the temporary cabins. Peter had lived in the bunkhouse before Aila arrived.

Two weeks after they were married, Aila had her twentieth birthday. Peter would be twenty-six in September.

They stayed in Idaho for the rest of 1921 which turned out to be the worst year for the Butte mines since the 1893 panic, and 1921 was even worse than that. The mines shut down in April and remained down for the rest of the year. Only pumpmen were working at most of the mines. The rest of the state was still on hard times from the drought. Nationwide more than 600,000 veterans were out of work. This was a small "d" depression as opposed to the big "D" Depression yet to come. Whatever the historians and economists call it, it was awful. In Montana, it was particularly severe. Droves of men fled the state to find work. "There

Peter and Aila Thompson, newly married, Conda, Idaho, 1921.

Conda, Idaho, phosphate mine, September 1921. ABOVE LEFT: *Peter is the engine driver—with the hat.* ABOVE RIGHT: *Peter is on the left.*

were people going hungry because they didn't have jobs in Butte at that time," Aila said.

Though the economic trough was quite deep, thankfully it was short-lived, and by the end of the year, the economy was turning around. In January, the fires were started at the smelter in Anaconda, and soon the Butte mines would reopen. Peter collected his year-end bonus, and he and Aila went back to Butte.

As individuals, their immediate families were pleased to see them return, but as a married couple—no. Neither Sarah nor the Thompsons
were happy about this marriage. Sarah did not want Aila to marry at all,
and she did not consider Peter Thompson to be any prize. He was Irish
and he was Catholic and he had stolen her help. Peter and Sarah detested
one another and never kept that fact a secret. Had Rose Thompson known
of the marriage in advance, she would have disapproved because of Aila's
age. Rose did not approve of teenage weddings. Peter's immediate family
in Butte knew Sarah's reputation and assumed Aila must be the same.
And they knew the nature of some of the transactions conducted at 415
Kemper. The very idea that their family luminary, their beloved Peter,
had been taken away by a woman from such a disreputable family—it
was intolerable. Furthermore, she wasn't Catholic and she wasn't Irish;
however, I'm not sure how highly those two objections ranked since Peter's
sister Mary had married a non-Catholic non-Irishman.

As it is difficult for some
mothers to give up a son, it is
impossible for some sisters to
give up a brother. Mary was very
attached to Peter. She revered him
as would a younger of an elder
sibling, even though she was
older. Peter gladly assumed the
pedestal top position on which
Mary placed him. He could do
no wrong in her eyes and came
quickly to her aid whenever she
asked. Few women would have
been suitable for Peter in Mary's

Peter's sister Mary and her son, Gilbert, 1921.

eyes, though she did have one in mind—Nell Coughlin, the sister of Peter's
army friend Ray Coughlin. She was part of their group.

However, when Peter took Aila to meet his aunts and Uncle John, the
reception was different. They warmly welcomed Aila into the family. Aila
and Aunt B became instant friends and would remain so for the rest of
their lives. Aila quickly grew fond of the Gribbens and held them in high
esteem. They were "my uncle Johnny" and "my aunt B," not Peter's uncle
Johnny and Peter's aunt B.

Like the mother of that ex-soldier, Aunt B too looked beyond the Hughes family's sordid reputation to see not only Aila's physical beauty, but also her goodness. Aunt Bridget found beauty and goodness in the world and in those around her because she looked for it. Sometimes she had to look very hard.

As a little girl in Ireland, Bridget left school as soon as she mastered the three R's. Her teacher, seeing that she was a bright child, encouraged her to continue in school; however, by then Bridget's father was seriously ill and unable to work, and she needed to stay home and help her mother take care of him and their tiny farm.

Her first job away from home was as the babysitter for an infant and companion for the grandmother of a family who owned a hotel near Randalstown. The grandmother was a tippler who liked to stay up late and expected little Bridget, then all of ten, to stay up and keep her company. She would scold Bridget, calling her a sleepyhead, for nodding off as the tipsy grannie prattled on into the wee hours.

Bridget's next job was to cook and clean for the postmistress, Mrs. Marks. She was Scotch Presbyterian and according to Bridget, "just grand in every way." Bridget was awfully small, just a wisp of girl, and wasn't able to finish her chores. "Do what you can and leave the rest," said Mrs. Marks who always encouraged and never scolded young Bridget. When it became apparent that Bridget was too small to handle all the housework, Mrs. Marks hired Bridget's next older sister who turned out to be a very efficient housekeeper and could easily finish all the chores, leaving little for Bridget to do. Seeing this, Mrs. Marks decided that Bridget could deliver the telegrams for the post office. She rode a bicycle around the district delivering telegrams and was paid a whopping thirteen pounds a year on her majesty's service, a pound more than her sister earned for housekeeping.

Then Mrs. Marks died, and poor Bridget was heartbroken. She thought the world of Mrs. Marks. A new postmistress came, and she hired someone else to deliver the telegrams, so Bridget lost her friend and her job. After that, Bridget went to work for the Webbs as the governess for their children, the same family for whom her sisters worked. Bridget left the Webbs to take care of her mother when she fell sick. When Jane's health improved, Bridget took another job. A well-to-do family in Spring Hill named Conningham hired her at forty pounds a year to care for their children. One entire floor of their home was devoted to the nursery, and Bridget had a maid to wait on her and the children. Best of all, Bridget was allowed to use the family library—a privilege she relished.

The following year Jane Gribben died and John summoned his maiden sisters to Butte. Bridget was twenty-nine and she had a special beau. She didn't want to go, but she did as told.

While Uncle John Gribben was without a doubt the head of the extended Gribben/Thompson family in Butte, a paragon whose good opinion his nephews and nieces would strive to keep, Aunt B was its heart and soul. Her warmth and love drew her nieces and nephews and would be an enduring balm for little hearts broken by the premature deaths of their mothers.

Now that Peter and Aila were back in Butte, Aunt B decided to have a come-all-ye. Family parties were always at her house, at least in part because she had a piano. As soon as Peter and Aila arrived, Aunt B and Aunt Annie hurried over to greet them. They made every effort to make Aila feel welcome. Uncle John and his family were there, and he too was kind and gracious to Aila. Peter's sister Mary and her family were there. Mary had her hair in a net. She always wore it like that when she went to Aunt B's because she had bobbed it and didn't want Uncle John to know. Mary's friend Kathleen was there. She was always invited to Aunt B's parties. As soon as she arrived, she sat right down at the piano and began to play a lively tune. Peter launched into a furious horn pipe, dancing with "ice in the body and fire in the feet" as the Christian Brothers had taught him. Then Kathleen played a waltz and Peter and Aila danced. Then Kathleen took a respite from the piano to enjoy a cup of tea.

Kathleen's mother ran a boarding house. Sam Thompson lived there for awhile; Peter was living there when he left for the war. The old lady was a fierce Irishwoman. She fought constantly with the neighbors. She was always hollering about something, or so it seemed to them. She didn't want her pretty Kathleen to run off with some Irish miner, so she married her off to the butcher. If Kathleen had run off with some Irish miner, against her mother's wishes, that miner would have had Kathleen's brother to reckon with. He was a deputy sheriff and said to have shot twelve men in the line of duty, all in the back, all unarmed.

While Kathleen drank her tea, Uncle John asked Peter to give them a recitation, which he knew Peter was always happy to do. He definitely had a gift for it. He stood. Conversation quickly decrescendoed and then stopped. He began, from memory,

"THE CREMATION OF SAM MCGEE" by Robert Service

There are strange things done in the midnight sun
        By the men who moil for gold;
The Arctic trails have their secret tales
        That would make your blood run cold;
The Northern Lights have seen queer sights,
        But the queerest they ever did see
Was that night on the marge of Lake Lebarge
        I cremated Sam McGee.

Now Sam McGee was from Tennessee, where the cotton blooms
        and blows.
Why he left his home . . .

Peter continued to the end of the vivid, lyrical poem. It's a bit macabre. This poor soul dies in the frozen tundra, and per his last wish, his friend cremates his remains so finally he'll be warm. Peter had become a great fan of the Canadian poet whose works beg to be read aloud. Robert Burns was another favorite.

As the party continued into the evening, Peter and Uncle John and the other men made frequent visits to the bathroom to partake of the whiskey bottle stashed in the tank. The women chatted incessantly and drank tea. The children played and then sat down to eat their treat of bread and butter with sugar sprinkled on top. Aila sat off to the side sipping her tea, a bit intimidated by the clamorous assembly. Though in time she would grow close to individual members, Aunt B in particular, Aila would never feel part of this extended family of clannish, excitable Irish men and women. She would advise her daughters, "Marry someone from your own religion and culture."

Aunt B noticed her alienated guest and drew Aila into conversation with her and Annie. Inwardly, the two sisters were alike: kind, generous souls, witty and aware. Outwardly, they were as different as could be. Bridget was calm and cerebral; Annie was frisky and flighty. "I'm the one who sits with her feet on the oven door and lets the bread burn," Annie declared of herself. While working for the Webbs in Ireland, Annie would offer a quick retort whenever Mr. Webb arrived late for breakfast. "Breakfast was hot for them on time," she would say. Such words would never pass Bridget's lips.

In another corner of the room, a boisterous debate erupted among the men over Irish politics. Disagreement over the Anglo-Irish treaty had ignited a civil war in Ireland and that animosity had bubbled over into Butte. It was the all-or-nothing crowd against the let's-take-it-a-step-at-a-time-and-get-what-we-can-now contingent. Friends quit speaking to each other. A local priest refused to speak to Judge Lynch because of his acquiescence on the treaty. A few months hence, preparations for the Emmets' New Years Eve Ball would be interrupted when six sticks of dynamite were hurled into Hibernian Hall. No one was hurt. The culprits were believed to be an anti-treaty faction.

As for Peter, he had left the old soggy sod squarely behind him. He came to America to be an American. He fought in the American army, married an American girl, sang American songs—and still some Irish favorites, danced American dances—and still a hornpipe or jig. He disdained the keeping of a heavy brogue and pestered his sister to become an American citizen.

Somebody at the party mentioned that so-and-so was going back to Ireland for a visit. Another expressed a desire to go. Peter frowned.

"Don't you want to go back to Ireland?" the man asked.

"Why would I want to go back to Ireland?" Peter retorted. "All I ever got in Ireland was black bread and black tea."

The party broke up. Peter and Aila thanked Aunt B and said their goodbyes and walked home. Peter held up a few light poles along the way.

WE CHECK IN with our family in Belfast and find that after nine years of courtship, Peter's sister Nellie has finally consented to marry Jimmy Ledgerwood, or Jimmy has finally gotten around to asking. They married on a Friday during Lent. She just wanted to be different. Then he sailed away; he was a stoker in the merchant marine. Ten months later, he was dead. Nellie told me, "I was only married long enough to change my name." It needn't have stayed that way. Nellie was a beauty, and

Nellie Thompson Ledgerwood

Rose Gribben Thompson

delightful, always smiling. One evening while she was serving free dinners at a church charity, a priest walked by and said to her, "Ah, you've got those come-fetch-me eyes!" Nellie turned scarlet. She went right home and told her mother. A priest! Plenty of eligible men around Carntall Street noticed those eyes too, and after the appropriate period of mourning, they began to call on her.

"Good evening, Mrs. Thompson. I've come to see Nellie," announced one man.

"I wouldn't allow one of *my* sons to court some old widow woman!" Rose retorted.

"Mrs. Thompson," the man replied, "there are widows, and there are widows."

Another suitor met Nellie at the weekly whist game. He called on

Rose to ask, "Mrs. Thompson, how do you like the idea of me as a son-in-law?"

"Put on your coat and go from here and never come back!" Rose replied.

Whether it was due to her mother's sabotage or her own disinclination, the girl with the come-fetch-me eyes would never marry again.

Rose's other distraction around that time was twenty-year-old Pat, the seventh in her brood. Pat had joined the IRA. Rose did not approve. Sectarian fighting in Belfast was intensifying. Police looted Catholic pubs. Unionists drove two hundred Catholic families from their homes and destroyed the homes in the mixed blocks near the Thompsons. In the midst of all this, Pat was arrested. As far as I know, there were no specific charges. He would only say that "it was for my capers." Rose was in a state. Political prisoners either were not fed or not fed much, so Jenny, the next older than Pat, took food to him. She couldn't let anyone see her, because if her employer found out, she could lose her job. After the Anglo-Irish Treaty was signed, the British government released political prisoners. One was Pat. He was on the run immediately. He slept in a different house every night. Rose sent a telegram to Sam saying: *You must send for Pat. Next time they won't let him out.*

Sam sent the money and just in time. Belfast was a cauldron. The treaty did not bring peace. Civil war broke out between pro and anti-treaty factions. IRA military leader Michael Collins sent guns to the IRA in the north to help stave off the police and Ulster Volunteer Force. Sixty-one people were killed in Belfast that March.

Nellie had been skipped over in the family chain migration since she ran the household for Rose. Jenny was the next eldest at home, so it was her turn to go. Sam sent money for tickets for both Jenny and Pat. Rose got them on a ship as fast as she could. Only days after the two set sail, police attacked Catholics in their homes in Belfast.

Rose was in the kitchen when the door flew open. Policemen stormed into the house. Nellie ran in from the scullery when she heard the commotion.

"Where is Patrick Thompson?" demanded one of the policemen.

Rose didn't flinch. "He isn't here," she replied flatly. "When you find him, tell him to come home his dinner is *ready*."

I find this remarkable. Here's Pat, the red hot patriot in the Belfast IRA; nevertheless, when his mother said go, he went.

CHAPTER FORTY

PETER AND AILA rented a tiny house on Platinum Street, near Uncle John's. Peter's father lived with them and worked at the West Colusa.

During that first year back in Butte, Peter worked at the Tramway for a month, then at the East Colusa for six days, then at the Berkeley for two days, then back at the East Colusa for a month, then at the Anaconda for six weeks, then again at the East Colusa, and there he stayed for the remaining six months of the year. His favorite pastime—gambling—often depleted their finances. Scraping together enough money for food and rent taxed Aila's pecuniary skills which would become quite adept as the years passed. She returned to her job at Symon's.

In late May, ten months after they wed, their first child was born, a little girl. They named her Aila Rose. Aila delivered her at Sarah's house with a doctor attending. Try as she did, Aila could not nurse. She had no milk. The doctor and his wife had been unable to have a child. The doctor told Aila that he and his wife would like to adopt her baby. She declined. She would agonize over that decision for the rest of her life.

Peter walked into the room and picked up the baby and held her on his forearm. With her little head in his hand, her tiny feet barely reached his elbow. Peter was not a man of size. The baby was awfully small. He wanted a boy. He had a beautiful baby girl instead. He gazed in wonderment at the babe on his arm, and from that day forward, he never took another drink.

Pat and Jenny arrived in Butte a few days before Aila Rose was born. Since Pat was the only one of Peter's brothers in town for the baptism, he was her godfather. Patsy was her godmother.

Aila Rose with her godparents: Patsy Hughes and Pat Thompson.

Aila Rose's baptism, 1922. Above left: *Sarah holding Aila Rose, Aila, Patsy .
Hughes, Pat Thompson. The child in front is Peter's nephew Gilbert.*
Right: *Jenny holding Aila Rose; Gilbert, Aila.*

Denis and John were in the country and had been for two years. Denis
arrived in April of 1920; John arrived that June. When answering the battery of questions on Ellis
Island, both said they
planned to stay in this
country permanently.

Instead of going
straight to Butte, they
went to Boston first and
stayed with their cousin
John Stuart about whom
I know nothing. I don't
even know how he is re-
lated to us, nor how long
they stayed with him.
Eventually, they crossed
the country and joined the

Peter, Mary, Sam, Jenny, Pat, and young Gilbert.

family in Butte. They stayed a little while, left, and came back after Pat arrived, and when they did, the four Thompson brothers had a fine time tooling around the town together. The mines were up. There was "something doing" all the time. The town was lively as ever. In fact, there was a labor shortage.

John worked at the West Colusa for a few months. Denis worked for a rancher outside of town. When the rancher refused to pay what Denis thought he owed him, Denis grabbed the man by the throat and threatened to beat it out of him. John and Denis also worked as bellmen at the Thornton Hotel. Denis always collected a tip *before* he picked up the bags. John never expected a tip.

Denis was definitely the most spirited of the bunch. He was perpetually cheerful and burst out laughing at the least provocation. He would collapse in laughter at the vaudeville shows, so much so that a producer asked him to tour with the show. They'd pay him to sit in the audience and laugh. Paid to laugh—the very idea must have put Denis into side-splitting hysterics.

Though John stood head and shoulders above his brothers, he was by far the shyest of the lot. He was too shy to ask a girl to dance, so he'd have a drop of beer to get up his courage, maybe more than a drop, and then he was too ashamed to ask since he'd drunk the beer.

The four Thompson brothers in Butte: Peter, Denis, Pat, and John.

Sam and Denis Thompson
with young Gilbert

John and Peter.

Pat had no trouble finding work in Butte, thanks to Uncle John. He went to work at the West Colusa right away and remained there for a long time. Uncle John and his fellow Emmets were pleased to welcome the young patriot and quickly approved him for membership. However, there's no record of Pat paying dues, so I take it he didn't join the Emmets, though he did attend a few meetings right after he arrived and sang "Kevin Barry" for them and gave an impromptu speech.

But of the four brothers, each so different from the rest, everybody's favorite and the one they all looked up to was definitely Peter. So when John was cheated at cards, he went directly to Peter and Aila's and told Peter all about it.

Peter stood up. Where? he demanded.

John told him the name of the saloon. Peter put on his hat and coat and left. Denis followed him. They marched to the saloon. Peter demanded recompense. Receiving none, he challenged the accused to a fight and an all-out brawl erupted with Peter and Denis thrashing the guilty card players. Pat said Peter always threw the first punch and always won. Though an excellent boxer, at only five feet three inches tall Peter must have been considerably smaller than most of the men in the saloon. Being the only sober one in the place probably helped. Fights were a frequent occurrence for Peter. He was quick to take offense. He'd stand, fiercely challenge the offending party, and belt him. Peter even threatened to fight Uncle John one night. I don't know what that was about. Uncle John just laughed him off. "Calm down you young whelp," he said with a dismissive wave.

Once during an American Legion convention, a brawl broke out with Peter right in the middle of it. The deputy sheriff, the one who was Mary's friend Kathleen's brother, broke it up and threw the bunch of them in jail. Oh, was Peter mad. He was still spitting nails when he got home the next morning over being hauled off and locked up like that. Other than that time, as far as I know, he didn't get into trouble with the law for his fighting. Generally, police were not called to a saloon fight in Butte. If a man was knocked out in a fight, the others simply dragged him out of the way. Nobody called the police.

This night Peter came home with a few cuts and bruises. He sat down at the kitchen table and told Aila all about it. She was probably a bit unsettled at seeing her husband frequently battered and bruised like that. "We Irish fight too much," he muttered as she gently cleaned and nursed his wounds. In a few days, he'd be back at it.

One of the more colorful histories of Butte, *Copper Camp*, certainly bore out what Peter said about the Irish and fighting. There was the story about the Irishman and the Afghan tamale peddler. The Irishman accused the Afghan of putting goat meat in his tamales. The Afghan said, "By the beard of my father this is chicken," and he accused the Irish of lying like Hades. Then the Irishman cursed the Afghan's relatives from here to kingdom come and went on and on and on until the Afghan belted him. The Irishman retaliated and here came a big policeman—the bull—and grabbed the two of them and locked them up. When they appeared before Judge McGowan, the policeman said of the Afghan and his family, "They're in wrong all the time. They couldn't keep the peace if it was in a safe." The Irishman, ostensibly speaking on his own behalf, said he was walking down the street, minding his own business. He asked the Afghan, Is that chicken or horse meat in them tamales? "Then he calls me a jub- jub- balabo- karara, or something like that, which no decent man would take. So I makes a pass at him and miss, and he unwinds one to me map and then comes the bull and saves him from the undertaker, but don't worry judge, if you'll but let me at him, I'll knock him flatter than the decayed meat he pizens people with in his putrid tamales." Judge McGowan chuckled, fined the Afghan, suspended the fine, and gave the Irishman a warning.

Then there was the one about Mahoney of the Cabbage Patch. He forgot his claim ticket, so was denied his laundry, and then proceeded to trash the place to find his clean white shirt.

And there was the Chinaman justifying his opium den to a policeman: "Yung Lee sell dreams—very nice dreams . . . Much better than spend money for Irish whiskey and want to kill everybody. Much better dream— no hurt anybody."

As for our two recently arrived Irishmen, Denis and John didn't stay put in Butte. Denis went to New York and found a job in the merchant marine. At least once he managed to work on a ship bound for Belfast. "He looks like an American, so styled," his sisters exclaimed on seeing him.

I don't know where John went first. He wrote faithfully to his mother and never sent an empty letter; however, there was a stretch when Rose didn't hear from him. While playing cards in a saloon, one of his chums walked in and read aloud this notice from the newspaper: *Mrs. Sam Thompson of Belfast, Ireland. Would anyone knowing her son John Thompson please tell him to write to his mother.*

This was answered by profound embarrassment on John's part and hoots and chides from his fellow card players.

While in San Diego and running low on money, John saw an advertisement for the U.S. Marines: Join today $5, $1 per day pay. Soon he was bound for Shanghai.

As FOR PETER and Aila, they were thoroughly enjoying the wonderful new presence in their lives—their little daughter. Aila was overjoyed to be a mother, as was Peter to be a father. But that summer of 1923, as they enjoyed lovely family outings at the Columbia Gardens and Gregson Hot Springs and the idyllic scenes you see in the following pictures were playing out, quite another story was unfolding.

Peter, Aila Rose, and Aila. Aila wrote on the back:
"Don't we look happy. Katie, Peter, his brother, baby and I
spent the day, Aug 5, 1923, at Gregson. We had a glorious
time." August 5 was Aila and Peter's second wedding
anniversary. Gregson was Gregson Hot Springs near Butte.

Sarah with her first grandchild, Aila Rose. Columbia Gardens, 1923.

Sarah and Aila Rose
in the greenhouse at the Columbia
Gardens, 1923. Aila wrote on the back:
"I do not know whether you will like this
picture or not but the baby looks so sweet.
I want you to look at it just the same."
She must have sent it to her father.

Aila and Aila Rose in the
greenhouse. "My little daughter
and I look quite contented
do we not."

PART FIVE

The Merchant of Renova

CHAPTER FORTY-ONE

HE ISN'T HERE, and I don't know where he is, said Sarah defiantly, her black eyes shooting a glare at Sheriff Duggan as she shut the door. He had come to the house looking for Archie.

Sarah now lived on East Park Street with Archie, Patsy, and Bill and her star boarder, William Mitchell. He was a Cousin Jack and eight years younger than Sarah. She quite likely had other boarders too. Sarah kept as many boarders as she was able. She could always use the money, and most of all she enjoyed the company. She didn't like to be alone. One frequent boarder was a young drifter named Roy Walsh. He had lived with them at Kemper Street and was the same chronological age as Aila, though I think to Aila, Roy seemed much younger. He and Archie became friends.

Archie was now eighteen years old and had grown up to be a very striking young man. However, those good looks did nothing for his confidence. The physical and verbal beatings he endured from his mother had taken a toll on him, as they had on all the children except Bill. Being Sarah's favorite, Bill hadn't suffered the same treatment.

Archie should have graduated from high school that spring, but he didn't. Back in the fall of 1919 when Bill was awaiting trial for robbery and everybody was suing Sarah, Patsy and Archie should have been enrolled in school, but they were not. Patsy was twelve at the time and Archie was almost fifteen. Sarah did say that Archie had suffered from infantile paralysis (polio). This would account for his missing some school. However, he did recover, and there was no permanent paralysis. For whatever reason, after Aila graduated from high school, neither Archie or Patsy were ever again enrolled in the Butte schools.

Archie started working in the mines when he turned sixteen. He worked off and on in different mines for a few days at a time. During the

Archie holding Aila Rose.

1921 shutdown, he worked as an elevator boy in one of the dry goods stores—probably at Symon's thanks to his sister Aila.

Sarah chastened him time and time again to get money for her anyway he could. Aila's run off with that Irishman, she said. Your father's gone for good. You're a man now. You've got to get money for me.

As for Archie's pal Roy Walsh, life had already weathered his young face. Roy stood head and shoulders above Archie in height and sureness—whether that sureness was real or feigned is hard to say. Roy lived with the Hugheses off and on as far back as 1920, before Aila left to get married. "He was a nice boy," she said, then she added delicately, "He was slow." What she probably did not know was that this nice boy was an affable crime wave, an escaped convict on the run with two bullet holes in his leg. And of all boarders, he was one of the nice ones.

Roy was born in the Midwest in May of 1901. His mother left when he was two years old, and his grandmother took care of him and his baby sister. I don't know where his father was. Sometime later, his mother resurfaced and decided she wanted her son back but not her daughter. Roy and his mother then moved from place to place while she took up with this man, then that man, then that man. With every new face, she gave Roy a new last name. I don't know whether she ever married any of those men. Eventually, they ended up in Butte. While there, she or the authorities put Roy in the Orphans' Home in Twin Bridges. He was eight years old, so it was before Aila, Archie, and Patsy lived there. Six months later, his mother showed up with another new man. She took Roy out of the orphanage, and they moved to Seattle. Then one day, she didn't come home. Roy was nine years old. He lived by his wits and grew more wits to get by.

He worked on a ranch in western Washington and attended school until eighth grade. After that he worked various jobs—in a woolen mill earning $1.25 a day, driving a wagon, on a tugboat, and he logged. He said he was licensed as a first class steam engineer.

While living near Aberdeen and calling himself Albert Bell, two boys told him about a shack where he could find some money. He went to the place and took it. As he was leaving, the owner arrived and had Roy arrested for grand larceny. He was seventeen years old and this was already his third time in court. He waived his right to counsel, pled guilty, and was sentenced to one to fifteen years at the Washington State Reformatory at Monroe. He told the warden that his true name was Albert Mason.

A few months into his sentence, while working as a trusty on a farm, he escaped. He was captured two hours later. The months went by, and even though he had already escaped once, Roy managed to talk his way into again being allowed to work as a trusty outside the prison, this time doing electrical work. His minimum sentence date came and went. He wasn't released, he wasn't paroled, so he left.

The authorities in Monroe alerted sheriffs across the country and constables in Canada to be on the lookout for their fugitive. As those letters arrived and acknowledgments were returned, a young man calling himself Roy Walsh took up residence in Anna Hughes Boarding House at 415 Kemper Street in Butte, Montana. He stayed a few months, left, went to Missoula, was arrested for malicious mischief, pled guilty, served fifteen days in the county jail, and was released. He returned to Butte and again lived with the Hugheses, now on East Park Street.

Roy Walsh
BOULDER MONITOR, JULY 28, 1923

Archie became friends with this amiable boarder close to his age. He and Roy moved to Anaconda, and Archie worked in the smelter. Roy may have worked there too, but there were so many Walshes in Anaconda it's hard to say. If a person wanted to blend into the woodwork in Butte or Anaconda, Walsh was certainly a good name to pick.

They rented a small cabin in Anaconda, and shortly after they moved in, the landlord noticed an electric light burning inside. He was surprised to see it since the cabin wasn't wired for electricity when he rented it to them. Somehow without electrocuting himself, Roy managed to tap into the line and wire the house. He and Archie enjoyed free electric light until Montana Power found out.

They kept a large gasoline tank in the cabin. The sheriff found out and confiscated it. Somebody confiscated it back. Then automobiles began to collect around the cabin. The sheriff sent his deputies to investigate, but by then, Archie and Roy were long gone.

And now we come to that awful night in June (again, June). The year is 1923. Archie is eighteen, Roy is twenty-two. Mine production in Butte is increasing steadily. There are plenty of jobs. In fact, Archie just worked a couple of days at the St. Lawrence.

He and Roy surfaced at Sarah's during the night. She made breakfast for them.

"Stay here," she told Archie, "the sheriff already came looking for you. They're after you for stealing Cadillac car. If you go out, he'll find you."

"Mother, there's no time for stopping if they're after me," Archie replied. He and Roy finished their breakfast and left for their hide-out in Cedar Hill, a little spot in the mountains east of Butte. Archie drove the Cadillac he had stolen. Roy drove the Buick he had stolen.

They arrived at Cedar Hill shortly after dawn. It was a crisp June morning. They slept for awhile under the dense pine trees and then caucused about their next move.

What'll we do?

We'll go to Seattle and figure out something there. Maybe go to Canada.

If we go to Seattle now, they might catch us on the way, in Missoula or somewhere. Let's kill a week or two up the Madison until things cool down and then go.

All right. What'll we do for money?

Let's rob the store in Renova. There was a big doings out there last Sunday. Ol' Johnson must have plenty of money. We'll scare him with our guns and tie him and take the money and provisions and lay low until the sheriff quits looking for the Cadillac car. Then we'll leave for Seattle.

That was the plan.

After dark, they drove to Renova, each in the car he had stolen. Renova was a little whistle stop for trains hauling ore from Alder Gulch. There wasn't much to it. An old box car served as the depot. Across the tracks down a plank walk was the grocery and mercantile. There was a dance hall behind the store. Al Johnson had owned the store for years. He was fifty-four years old, a Spanish-American War veteran, and was divorced. His features–fair, blond, blue eyes—led neighbors to think he was Swedish. According to the newspaper, one of his daughters was married and the other lived with his ex-wife in San Francisco. Al lived alone in the back of the store.

Roy had worked on ranches along the Jefferson and made many purchases on credit at Al Johnson's store. Everybody bought on credit in those days in stores and saloons. The merchant kept track and the idea was to pay eventually, preferably monthly. Roy didn't. He and Al Johnson had words about it. Some said Roy threatened Al.

Archie arrived first. He parked the Cadillac near the loading platform and waited for Roy. A little while later, Roy pulled up and parked on the road along the main track. Archie stepped out of the car and walked over to the Buick.

"What took you?" he asked.

"I was trying to fix this flashlight but the bulb is burned out. Oh, well, Johnson might have some flashlights in there," Roy replied. Roy got out of the car and disconnected the tail lights. Then they walked to the Cadillac and he disconnected those tail lights. They climbed into the car and sat and waited for the store to close. As they waited, they tore masks from an old white shirt of Archie's.

After about half an hour, they got out of the car and walked toward the store. They were as conspicuous as could be wearing white masks and Archie in a red mackinaw, more the apparel of hunters not wanting to be shot than of burglars not wanting to be seen. They could see a man inside the store talking to Al Johnson. Al was seated on the counter. Roy didn't recognize the other man. I don't know whether Archie did. He was Fred D——, the convicted horse thief. He and his wife, Mildred, had been in prison at the same time as Arthur and Sarah.

It was raining lightly. Archie and Roy crouched down and hid in a ditch and watched the two men inside the store. Fred and Al seemed to have a lot to talk about. Archie and Roy waited and waited. Finally, Fred left. It was now around eleven o'clock at night. They saw Al Johnson slide off the counter and walk around to the cash register. They watched him count the money. Then he walked away. They couldn't see where he went, probably to the back of the store where he slept. They waited a few more minutes, then Roy whispered to Archie, "You go to the main door and I'll go to the side door, that way we'll get him whichever way he goes. You rob him because he'll recognize me. I'll tie him." Roy had decided that he didn't want to wear a mask after all, even though Al knew him.

Archie walked to the front door armed with a revolver. Roy crept around the side of the building armed with a 30-30 Marlin rifle. A light went on in the back of the store. Roy's eyes fixed on the lit window. Then he heard the door rattle. He stopped. Then he resumed walking stealthily between the store and the fence, all the while watching the lit window until—bang! He walked straight into a metal box. The butt of his rifle hit the box and made a loud hollow noise. It startled him. He jumped into

Al Johnson's store, Renova, Montana.
BUTTE MINER, FEBRUARY 14, 1925

the hop vines along the side of the store and crouched down. He was about five feet from the door.

Al Johnson opened the door and looked out. Then he stepped back, closed the door, and CRACK!

Archie bolted, Roy bolted, neither waiting to see whether the other was staying or running. Archie jumped in the Cadillac and took off for Butte. Roy ran straight into that same metal box, fell down, got up, leapt over the fence, ran to the Buick, and drove off.

The bullet had blasted through the screen door, through the wooden door, and into Al Johnson's throat, shattering his larynx. The tremendous force had knocked him to the floor. He lay there for a few moments, stunned and in horrible pain. Then he dragged himself to the telephone. He pulled himself up, turned the crank, and tried to speak. He couldn't. He was bleeding profusely. He clutched his bleeding neck and stumbled outside to the nearest neighbor's house. He knocked on their door, still clutching his bleeding neck. The neighbor Otto opened the door. It was dark and there was no light inside or out. From the way Al was stooped and couldn't seem to speak, Otto thought he was the drunken sheep-herder from across the river. "Get away from here," he scolded, "I don't want anything to do with you."

Otto's wife, standing behind him, said, "Dear, I believe that man is bleeding."

Otto then opened the screen door and stepped outside. He immediately recognized Al Johnson.

"What happened to you?" he gasped.

Able to make only a wooh, wooh sound, Al motioned toward his store. Otto tried to help him inside but Al pulled away and staggered home. Otto quickly dressed and he and his wife hurried to the store. They found Al lying on his bed. His clothes and the bed were saturated with blood. Several large pools of blood were coagulating on the floor. Now in the light, they could see the gaping wound in Al's throat. It was about the size of a man's fist. The jagged end of his windpipe was protruding from it and blood was gushing out.

"Can I do anything for you?" Otto asked.

Al gave no response.

"Is there anyone you want me to call?"

Al shook his head no.

"Shall I call Dr. Packard?" Otto asked.

Al nodded yes. Otto followed the trail of blood to the phone at the front of the store. The line was engaged. He tried again and again until he reached the operator.

I need Dr. Packard, he said.

Who is calling? she asked.

Otto Severtson. I need Dr. Packard right away.

What? I can't understand you.

Dr. Packard, I want to talk to Dr. Packard, in Whitehall.

Who?

I don't know whether Otto had a thick accent or they had a poor connection or what the problem was, but he had quite a time communicating with her. He persisted until finally she connected him to Dr. Packard.

While Otto was on the phone, his wife asked Al Johnson, "Who cut your throat?"

Al shook his head and pointed at the door.

Otto returned to the bedroom and then left to get another neighbor in case they needed help moving Al. He went to Sherman Shrauger's; he lived about seven hundred yards away. Sherman threw on some clothes and ran over to the store with Otto. He made a quick study of the scene and found the bullet holes in the doors.

"Did you see the holdup men?" he asked Al.

Al shook his head no.

"Did they get in?"

Al shook his head no.

"Did you try to call me on the phone?"

He nodded yes.

Sherman then called Sheriff John Mountjoy in Boulder.

Dr. Packard arrived. All this time, Al Johnson had been breathing through his shattered windpipe and sucking much blood into his lungs. His exposed tongue and trachea could be seen moving up and down with every tortured breath. Dr. Packard bolstered him up in bed. He was in shock. The doctor found the shape of a bullet under the skin on Al's shoulder. He bandaged his throat the best he could to control the bleeding while still allowing Al to breath.

"We have to get him to the hospital in Butte," he said. The men loaded Al into another neighbor's car and he sped off to the Murray Hospital.

By now, Archie had pulled into Butte. He parked the Cadillac several blocks away from home. He walked up the hill, into the house, and said to Sarah, "Mother, I'm here to stay," and he went to bed.

Roy had driven off in the other direction, toward the Madison. After he'd driven a ways, he turned around and drove back to Renova, thinking he might find Archie. He saw the lights of a car and thought it was Archie. He drove closer and saw three men with flashlights but no Archie, so he drove off, again heading east. After several miles, he approached the Lank Ranch. He remembered that Mr. Lank rented out a house on his property and it was usually vacant. Roy stopped to look. Sure enough, it was empty. Roy hid the car and stayed the night in the house.

Meanwhile in Boulder, some thirty miles to the north, Sheriff John Mountjoy dressed and prepared to leave for Renova. This newly elected sheriff of Jefferson County was a tall, reticent man with sculpted features. He was thirty-five years old, married with small children. As a child, he too had lived at the orphanage in Twin Bridges, though not as an inmate. His father had been the superintendent for several years. His father left that post the year before the Hughes children arrived, but he was still superintendent when

Roy Walsh lived there. By then, John was a grown man.

Sheriff Mountjoy woke Undersheriff Leslie Knight and told him to accompany him to Renova. It was still drizzling. The narrow dirt road through the Boulder Valley would be a morass of mud. They put chains on the car and set off.

They arrived at Renova around one thirty in the morning. They found Otto and his wife and Sherman and Fred D—— waiting for them outside Al Johnson's store. Sherman showed the sheriff the bullet holes in the door. Sheriff Mountjoy stooped down to examine them. He found two bullet holes about four feet from the floor: one in the screen door where the screen was fixed to the wood frame and another behind it in the wooden door. The hole in the

Sheriff John Montjoy
BOULDER MONITOR, JULY 28, 1923

wooden door was slightly higher than the hole in the screen door indicating the bullet had ranged upward. He opened the door and walked into the room. He stepped around the large pool of blood about five feet from the door and looked around. The rest of the floor was spattered with blood.

He then walked back outside and questioned the neighbors. Did any of you see what happened? No. Did any of you see any suspicious characters around here? Did any of you hear anything? One man thought he heard a shot but didn't think anything of it. No one else reported hearing a gunshot. Do any of you know who might have done this?

Then he turned to Fred D—— and asked, "Where were you when this happened?"

"I talked to Johnson this evening," replied Fred. "I left around eleven, went over to Jordan's ranch. About the time I got to the house, two cars came by going very fast, one car and then another following it right up. Didn't think anything of it."

"What kind of cars?" asked Sheriff Mountjoy.

"I didn't get a good look," said Fred. "One might have been a Buick. Don't know for sure. Big cars, about the size of a Buick." (That was a mighty good guess on a dark rainy night with no moon and no outdoor lights.)

"Which way were these cars going?" asked the sheriff.

"West, away from Renova," said Fred.

"I saw some tire tracks over there across the river," said Sherman gesturing.

Sheriff Mountjoy and Undersheriff Knight walked over and investigated. They found tracks for at least three cars leaving Renova. The tracks were fresh and headed west. They got in their car and followed the tracks as far as the turn off for Butte. Instead of continuing, they turned toward Whitehall and drove into town. Sheriff Mountjoy telephoned Silver Bow County Sheriff Larry Duggan in Butte and told him about the shooting and described the tread he was following. It was nearly daybreak. They waited for dawn and then resumed their search.

They followed the tracks to the outskirts of Butte. There the tracks disappeared into the mass of traffic. They went to Sheriff Duggan's office. He said he had been looking for a stolen Cadillac and it turned up during the night at the bottom of Wyoming Street. They investigated. Sure enough, the tread matched.

Sheriff Duggan said he had a pretty good idea who stole that car and led them to 516 East Park Street. Inside, they found Sarah making breakfast for Archie. They took Archie to the Silver Bow County jail for fingerprinting and questioning. According to the newspaper accounts, the conversation went something like this:

Where were you last night?

At home.

Did you steal that Cadillac?

Why, no, sir.

Were you in Renova last night?

No, sir.

Were you anywhere near there?

No, sir. I was home all night.

Was anybody with you? Who was with you?

I was home.

Did you steal that Mutch and Young truck and leave it in Cardwell a few weeks back?

Why, no, Sheriff. I don't know about any stolen car or truck.

Do you know Roy Walsh?

I haven't seen Roy Walsh for three weeks. I'd be happy to furnish you with information if I could, but I don't know where he is. I don't think he's in town.

For his part, Roy had slept undisturbed at the Lank place. In the morning, he rose and walked outside, probably contemplating where he might find some breakfast. Mr. Lank saw him. Knowing the house was supposed to be vacant, he walked toward Roy to find out what he was doing there. He hadn't heard about the shooting. Roy ran and hid. A little while later, Mr. Lank saw Roy again. He approached him and they spoke. Roy was garbed in a shirt and overalls and was half wearing, half carrying a sweater bundled under his arm. His feet were wet. They chatted about prospects for work in the valley. Roy mused that he might go to California to find work. After nearly an hour, the two concluded their conversation and parted company.

It was now around eleven o'clock in the morning. The lawmen in Butte were still interrogating Archie but getting nowhere. A deputy stepped into the room and said there was a long distance phone call for Sheriff Mountjoy. He stepped out and took the call. He came back and said he and Undersheriff Knight had to leave immediately. Sheriff Duggan then turned Archie over to the Silver Bow county attorney for questioning.

Sheriff Mountjoy and Les Knight drove back to Jefferson County, past Renova, to Jefferson Island. There they found a large, heavily armed posse of farmers and businessmen sweeping the countryside. Tempers and forefingers were on a hair trigger.

The posse searched abandoned buildings and then spread out on the high ground along the road. From this vantage point, they could view a wide expanse of the valley, a valley thick with gooseberry, scrub cedar, sage, quaking asp, and willows, a valley with countless hiding places.

One of the men, a fellow named Crane, found the Buick hidden in the brush near the river. He looked inside the car and found some clothes, bedding, a tent, a gallon of oil, a cup of grease, about a hundred feet of rope, some hack saw blades, and a 30-30 Marlin rifle. He took the bullets out of the rifle and put it back in the car. Then he sought out Sheriff Mountjoy and led him to the car. He told the sheriff about finding the rifle and that it was loaded. "It had one shell in the chamber and three in the magazine," he said and handed him the bullets.

By now, it was mid-afternoon. Another member of the posse ran up to Sheriff Mountjoy. He pointed to some brush and said he saw a man creeping through it. Sheriff Mountjoy summoned a few men and they painstakingly searched the two-acre patch of ten-foot-high brush for two hours, but they didn't find anybody.

While looking around in another spot, Undersheriff Les Knight spied a set of footprints. He followed them to a thick clump of chokecherry trees and wild roses. He saw the brush move slightly. He crept closer. He peered through the branches and saw what looked like a man lying in the gulch.

"COME OUT OF THERE," he yelled. The rest of the posse heard him and came running.

"COME OUT OF THERE!" he yelled again, this time with several expletives.

"DO YOU HAVE HIM?" yelled Sheriff Mountjoy.

"YEP," answered Knight. "I SAID COME OUT OF THERE!" More expletives.

Seeing the armed posse closing in on him and no way out, Roy hollered, "I'm coming out," and he stood up and climbed out of the damp gulch.

"Throw up your hands," said Undersheriff Knight. Roy didn't and walked toward him.

"I SAID THROW UP YOUR HANDS!" Roy momentarily raised his hands, then dropped them to his side, then tucked them into the bib of his overalls, all the while walking toward Les Knight.

"Why didn't you come out when I told you?" Les Knight scolded as he grabbed Roy's wrists and handcuffed him.

"I was afraid you were going to shoot me," Roy replied in a surly tone.

"Take some men and see if you can find a six-shooter," Sheriff Mountjoy told Les Knight. Then he turned to Roy and asked, "What's your name?"

"Mason."

"Aren't you Roy Walsh?"

"No, name's Mason."

"Do you know Roy Walsh?"

"No."

"Why don't you know Roy Walsh?"

"Oh, I know a Roy Walsh in Butte. There are several Roy Walsh's in Butte."

A man from Cardwell drove up and told Sheriff Mountjoy that there was a long distance phone call for him. He put Roy in his car and drove to Cardwell. He took the call, hung up, and went back to the car.

"Hughes confessed," he said to Roy. "You're lucky you didn't kill Johnson."

He started the car and drove off. Les Knight followed in the Buick. They stopped in Whitehall. A large crowd was milling in the street. The buzz was that two bandits had been caught but more were still at large. As Sheriff Mountjoy stepped out of the car with Roy, a man in the crowd called out, "Why that's Roy Walsh they have." Roy smiled and gestured hello to the man. This was a lot of attention for an abandoned boy.

Sheriff Mountjoy telephoned the Silver Bow and Madison County sheriffs and told them he had captured his fugitive. They could call off their searches. Then he put Roy back in the car and drove to Boulder.

"Where were you last night?" he asked Roy.

"I've been on the Madison for the past three weeks. I just came in to camp on the Lank place."

"Where on the Madison?"

"Around Cliff Lake and Henry's Lake."

"Who was you with?"

"Nobody."

"Where did you get that Buick?"

"I found it."

They rode on in silence. John Mountjoy was exhausted, having been up all night. As they topped a hill, they saw another car approach. Mountjoy and the other driver stopped their vehicles along side each other. The man in the other car was Mr. Fessenden, the editor of the *Jefferson Valley News*.

"I'm glad to see you got him," said Fessenden.

"Yep," replied Sheriff Mountjoy.

"Not much chance you got the wrong man. If he did it, he ought to hang," said Fessenden and he drove off.

When they arrived in Boulder, Sheriff Mountjoy locked Roy in the county jail and didn't see him again until the next day.

Meanwhile in Butte, Al Johnson sat in his hospital bed, propped up by pillows to ease his breathing, while dying a slow, painful death. The doctor had stitched his wound such that he could still breath; however, the damage was irreparable. Silver Bow Deputy County Attorney Emigh came to see him. With several written questions in hand, Mr. Emigh asked Al what happened. This was done in the presence of stenographer Flurry Sullivan and two others. Between tortured breaths, Al scratched yes or no next to each question.

"Do you know who shot you?"

No.

"Did you see them?"

Yes.

"You saw one man?"

Yes.

"You did not know him?"

No.

"Were they trying to hold you up?"

Yes.

"You were just bolting or unbolting the door?"

Yes.

"You heard a noise outside and went to investigate?"

Yes.

"Could you identify the man you did see if he was brought here?"

No.

And that was the end of the questions.

"Thank you, Mr. Johnson," said Emigh.

"You're welcome," Al mouthed. Emigh and Sullivan said goodbye and left.

Poor Al Johnson sat there wheezing and wheezing in agony. After nineteen tortured hours, he succumbed.

"How long before he dies and his name be forgotten?"—PSALM 41

CHAPTER FORTY-TWO

CORONER MURPHY announced that he would conduct an inquest. Nothing doing, said the county commissioners. There's no reason why Silver Bow County should bear the expense of an inquest for a crime that happened in Jefferson County.

There was no inquest.

Archie remained in the Silver Bow County jail in Butte and Roy in the Jefferson County jail in Boulder. They had not seen each other since they crept out of that ditch.

Two days after the shooting, Jefferson County's young new county attorney walked over to the jail to question Roy. Howard Johnson (no relation to Al) had been elected county attorney the previous fall, so he had been in office only a few months when the shooting happened. He was twenty-nine years old and was a very ambitious young man. Born in Wisconsin, he graduated from the Illinois State Normal School and then moved to Montana. He earned a bachelor of arts degree from the University of Montana in 1916 and a law degree in 1917. He then moved to Butte to begin his law practice. By this time, the country was at war. He tried to enlist, he wanted to be a pilot, but the army turned him down for medical reasons—an ingrown toenail or some such thing. He had the problem taken care of and tried again to enlist. This time the army took him and sent him to flight school in Texas after which he shipped off to France to complete his training. His French instructors spoke no English, he spoke no French, but he learned quickly and was commissioned a second lieutenant. Shortly after he finished his training, he and some other pilots were ordered to ferry several planes to another location. It was a type of plane he had never flown before. He was the last to take off, and before he did, he learned that all the other planes had experienced engine failure and crashed. He took off anyway, and sure enough, the engine went dead and the plane crashed. He spent the next sixteen months in army hospitals.

*County Attorney
Howard Johnson*
BOULDER MONITOR, JULY 28, 1923

He never was able to regain full use of his left arm, and he was left-handed. He taught himself to write and do everything right-handed and never let his injury slow him down.

In April of 1920, he was discharged from the army, returned to Butte and resumed his law practice. That fall, he was elected to the Montana House of Representatives as a Republican. He served one term and moved his law practice to Whitehall in Jefferson County. My guess is, this was a politically strategic move—he wanted to run for county attorney but didn't want to run against the incumbent in Silver Bow County. If that was his strategy, it worked. He ran for county attorney, was elected, and moved to Boulder, the county seat.

So in the course of five years, he finished law school, began his law practice, went to war, was seriously injured, spent over a year in the hospital, served a term in the State House, and was elected county attorney. This was definitely a young man with plans. In the midst of accomplishing all this, he found time to court a young woman from Butte. She too was a graduate of the University of Montana. They married in late May of 1923, one month before the shooting.

Now on the Thursday after the shooting, he, Sheriff Mountjoy, and Undersheriff Knight assembled at the jail to question Roy. County Attorney Johnson took notes.

"It will be better for you and all concerned if you tell the truth," advised Sheriff Mountjoy. "Where have you been?"

"Up on the Madison," said Roy. "I was there about three weeks."

"Where were you on the Madison?"

"Around Cliff Lake."

"Were you down near Renova on June 26, the night of the shooting?"

"No. I just came in from the Madison. I drove all night and got to the Lank place around two o'clock in the morning."

The interrogation continued. Roy maintained that he had just come up from the Madison. After I don't know how long, they gave up. As Sheriff Mountjoy was leaving, he turned toward Roy and said, "You're a pretty good liar."

Later that evening, Roy asked Les Knight, "How's Al Johnson doing?" He didn't tell him.

The authorities in Butte related the high points of Archie's confession to Sheriff Mountjoy and County Attorney Johnson. I never found Archie's confession, so I don't know what he said. It wasn't in the court files when I looked, not in Butte or Boulder.

On Saturday, June 30, the three men again questioned Roy.

"Tell us your story. Where were you on June 26, the night Al Johnson was shot?" asked Howard Johnson.

"I was on the Madison, drove all night, got to the Lank place around two o'clock," Roy said.

"What's this I hear about you and Hughes camping on Cedar Hill and being down to Race Track?" asked Sheriff Mountjoy.

"Were you at Race Track with Hughes?" asked Johnson.

"I haven't been there for quite a while," said Roy.

"Didn't you pull a car out of the mud between Race Track and Butte?" asked Mountjoy.

"I suppose I was there a few days," said Roy.

"Didn't you sell those people three gallons of gas?"

"I suppose I was there."

"How long?"

"About a week."

"Where were you June 26, the night of the shooting?"

"At Race Track."

"When did you leave Race Track?"

"Early in the morning."

"Where did you go?"

"Butte."

"Where in Butte?"

"Just Butte."

"Didn't you and Hughes have breakfast with Mrs. Hughes at four o'clock in the morning the day of the shooting?" asked Johnson.

"We stopped long enough to cook a sandwich. We didn't eat much breakfast."

"Did you know that the authorities were after Hughes for the stolen Cadillac?"

"Yes."

The interrogation continued, and bit by bit, Roy told all. Howard Johnson took notes which were later typed. In the end, he had a signed confession from Roy.

Later in the day, Roy asked Les Knight, "How's Al Johnson?"

He didn't tell him.

The next day was Sunday. Roy asked again, "How's Al Johnson?"

"He's dead."

Formal charges were drawn on Monday. That same day Archie and Roy appeared before Judge Lyman Bennett in the Jefferson County Courthouse in Boulder. He advised them of their right to counsel. Both said yes, they did want a lawyer and would get one right away. Judge Bennett said the arraignment would be continued the next morning at ten.

Later in the day, Roy wrote a letter and gave it to Les Knight and asked him to give it to his lawyer, John Elliott. Les Knight gave the letter to County Attorney Johnson who read it, copied it, and returned it to Les Knight who gave it to John Elliott when he arrived by train from Butte the next morning.

Jefferson County Courthouse, Boulder, Montana.
JEFFERSON COUNTY MUSEUM

John Elliott was from Pennsylvania, the son of an Irish father and Welsh mother. He had lived near Norris in Madison County for awhile and then moved to Butte. He was in his late thirties, married with young children. They lived on Galena Street. One of the men Bill robbed was H. J. Elliott who lived on Galena. I don't think it was the same man, though I don't know that for certain.

Sarah knew John Elliott. The year before this she had purchased one thousand shares, at ten cents a share, of the Montana Rex Mining Company. John Elliott was president of the company. Back then scores, probably hundreds, dabbled in mining, all hankering to be the next Marcus Daly, sure the next blast would unearth the big bonanza. Mining companies and mining stocks proliferated. Some were sincere attempts at a profitable business, some aspired to find enough geological promise to convince the ACM to buy them out for a hefty sum, others were worthless, and some, undoubtedly, scams.

Tuesday morning Archie and Roy again appeared before Judge Bennett, this time represented by their lawyer, John Elliott. They were charged with first degree murder, specifically:

> That on or about the 26th day of June, A.D. 1923, in the County of Jefferson, State of Montana, one Roy Walsh and one Arthur Hughes did wilfully, deliberately, unlawfully, feloniously, premeditatedly, and of their malice aforethought, shoot, kill and murder one Albert S. Johnson, a human being.

Both pled not guilty. John Elliott requested that bail be set. No bail, said Judge Bennett.

The next matter before the court was to decide what to do with Archie since the court understood him to be under eighteen. I was told that Archie was born September 13, 1904, in which case he was eighteen; however, I never found a birth certificate for Archie. Other records indicate that Archie believed he was born on that date. In any case, the court decided that Sheriff Mountjoy could hold Archie wherever he wanted to, in the Jefferson County jail or in another county jail.

After the arraignment, Howard Johnson spoke to reporters outside the courtroom. "I examined the scene of the murder," he reportedly said, "and after the examination I cannot give credence to that part of the statement made by Roy Walsh before Sheriff Mountjoy, Undersheriff Knight, and myself Saturday wherein he declares the shooting of Johnson was accidental. Facts in the case disprove any theory of accident. My examination of the scene of the fatal shooting revealed bullet holes in both the screen door and the inner door of the Johnson store. These holes are easily discernible. Therefore, the shooting could not have been an accident."

I must admit I have trouble following the county attorney's line of reasoning, assuming he was quoted correctly in the newspaper. If a person wanted to shoot someone, why do it when you can't see the person, that is, through a closed door with no window? And if Roy shot him deliberately, why didn't he rob him?

Talk of lynching buzzed through Jefferson and Madison Counties. Hang 'em and be done with it, was the oft-expressed sentiment. Sheriff Mountjoy heard the talk and decided to take Archie and Roy to the Silver Bow County jail in Butte for safekeeping. The jailer searched them when they arrived and found a piece of pipe tied to Roy's leg. He had pulled it from the plumbing in his cell in Boulder.

By this time, Howard Johnson had drawn the connection between his suspect and the desperado wanted by Washington State. He notified the authorities in Monroe.

As you might expect, there was considerable press coverage of all this. It was the first murder in Jefferson County in five years. Things were usually pretty quiet. The only serious crime County Attorney Johnson had dealt with before Al Johnson's murder was a rape case. It happened the month before, and there was no trial—the defendant pled guilty and was already in prison. Most crimes were Prohibition violations—possession or sale or manufacture of intoxicating liquors, and there weren't even many of those, and they were settled quickly with the defendants pleading guilty and paying a fine. Trials were rare. Now there would not only be a trial but a murder trial—that was big news. The day after the shooting a story came out in the newspaper describing what happened in vivid detail, the details of which only two people could have known—the assailant who had not yet been caught and the victim who could not speak. Archie read the papers and kept all the clippings. While in Boulder one day for a pretrial motion, he picked up the *Jefferson Valley News* and was very unhappy about what he read. He wrote to the editor, Mr. Fessenden, and told him so.

Boulder, Montana
July 16, 1923

Dear sir:

I am writing in regard to the prosecution your paper is carrying on against us at the present time.

I was well known in that part of the county for a long time and my name is being slashed enough with out no more prosecution from your paper. So I do not see that your paper has any right to stir the sentiment of the people.

God knows it is hard enough to goe through now as it is without any more heaped on to it.

I never killed or hurt any body in my life so lay off.

A. F. Hughes

Fessenden fired right back. No, he was not going to lay off. "It is time that public sentiment is stirred up against crime and criminals, just as it should be stirred up in favor of things that are good for the people and the community," he wrote. "In too many cases the criminal on trial is treated as a hero about to be decorated with a medal of honor."

The shooting was on Tuesday night, June 26. Al Johnson died the next day. Roy's confession was dated Saturday. Formal charges were drawn against Archie and Roy on Monday. They were arraigned on Tuesday. Six days later, the trial date was set for July 20. John Elliott requested separate trials. The court agreed and deemed Roy would be tried first. Four days later, the court issued subpoenas for prosecution witnesses. Another four days later, John Elliott moved for a continuance. He was trying to locate two material witnesses: John Doe and Richard Roe. He said they were eyewitnesses and their testimony was critical to waging a defense and he needed time to find them. He also said that Roy volunteered to take a scopolamin test, otherwise known as truth serum. A continuance was needed to allow time for the doctor to travel from Texas to administer the test.

No continuance, ruled Judge Bennett.

Sheriff Mountjoy brought Archie and Roy back to Boulder shortly before the trial was to begin and posted round-the-clock guards.

Less than one month after the shooting, the trial date arrived. The courthouse was abuzz with spectators and newspapermen and smack in the middle of all the excitement struck hurricane Sarah. Boulder hardly knew what hit it. Her imperious how-dare-you demeanor screamed story. The newspapermen flocked around her like a bunch of parched miners hovering over a bottle of whiskey.

"If Archie Hughes hangs, he has a brother in the British army to whom certain officials of Jefferson County will have to answer," Sarah proclaimed boldly. (I have no idea what she was talking about.) "Neither of those boys shot Johnson. Archie would have told me if they had. He would tell me anything and I would stick by him, right or wrong." (That I believe, if not out of motherly love, for the sheer drama of it.)

"Were your son and Roy Walsh in Renova the night Al Johnson was shot?" asked a reporter.

"Did they intend to rob him?" asked another.

"I know nothing about that," she declared. "When he came in the house I asked him what was the trouble and he said there had been some shooting at Renova. He told me that he heard the shots. I asked if he was mixed up in it and he said he was not. He has always been a truthful boy and I believe him." Then she said Archie had been afflicted with infantile paralysis as a boy, and Roy had been abandoned by his mother when he was only five years old.

"Your son and Walsh have also been accused of stealing automobiles," said one of the newspapermen.

"Well, what of it!" Sarah retorted. "Lots of people steal cars! There was a woman in Butte who induced both the boys to steal automobiles, and unless she comes through with money to help in my son's defense, I'm going to tell her name."

"Do you think your son will be found guilty?" asked a newspaperman.

"Why they couldn't hang a boy seventeen years old," she declared. "My boys never killed Johnson, but I know the man that did. Johnson helped send him to prison about ten years ago and he swore he would get him someday."

"Did you know Al Johnson, the man who was shot?"

"I knew him twenty years," she said.

The reporters had plenty of time with Sarah because the trial was delayed. It was supposed to have begun at 9:45 AM, but two civil cases were taking more time than expected. Finally, at 8:30 PM Friday evening, July 20, the case of the State of Montana versus Roy Walsh and Arthur Hughes came before Judge Lyman Bennett. Archie and Roy entered the courtroom manacled. Sarah sat close by listening and watching intently.

John Elliott moved for a change of venue. He had heard talk of lynching from several residents of the county and so had his driver. They both testified to this. Sheriff Mountjoy and County Attorney Johnson said they had heard the same talk but didn't think it was serious. They believed fair-minded jurors could be found in Jefferson County.

No change of venue, ruled Judge Bennett. They'll be tried right here in Jefferson County.

Judge Bennett then said that Archie would be tried in the next term of court which was in the fall. In the days leading up to the trial, Archie had

Judge Lyman Bennett.

become more and more rattled by the ordeal. This news of delay nearly undid him. A deputy took him outside. "Why don't they do something?" he said. "Why don't they take me out and hang me and be done with it?" The deputy took him back to the jail and locked him in his cell, and there he remained for the duration of Roy's trial.

The next morning, Saturday, the jury was selected—eleven farmers and one barber. Only one of them had known Al Johnson. John Elliott again requested a continuance. The eyewitnesses he sought were still at large.

No continuance, ruled Judge Bennett.

County Attorney Johnson then made his opening statement after which he called two witnesses. After he questioned them, he sat down, and the man seated next to him, James Kelly, rose to continue the prosecution's case. Johnson had hired James Kelly to assist him with the trial. Kelly had preceded Johnson as Jefferson County attorney and successfully tried a murder case while in office. He now lived in Dillon which is in another county. He was forty-five years old, the son of Irish immigrants, and was married with young children.

His first witness was Dr. McCarthy, the doctor who performed the autopsy. Dr. McCarthy said a soft-nosed bullet entered Al Johnson's throat at the front, drove through his neck, hit his chest bone, deflected off, punctured his lung, passed through his shoulder blade, and settled beneath the skin. He said Al's chest was pockmarked with splinters that impaled him when the bullet burst through the doors.

A civil engineer testified that he examined the gunshot holes in the doors and determined that the bullet had ranged upward. He calculated the trajectory and produced diagrams showing it. The bullet holes were about four feet from the bottom of the door. There was one step up from the ground to the door. Al Johnson was five feet nine or ten inches tall. Both Dr. Packard and Dr. McCarthy concluded that, for a bullet fired at an upward angle to travel through the neck into the chest cavity, Al must have been stooped, possibly locking the door, when he was shot.

Twelve prosecution witnesses testified that day. Judge Bennett admonished the jurors not to discuss the case with anyone. Court adjourned. County Attorney Johnson predicted the trial would be over on Monday.

Sheriff Mountjoy took the stand Monday morning. He recounted his investigation of the scene and how he apprehended Archie and Roy.

During cross examination by John Elliott, Sheriff Mountjoy said he had not advised the defendant, Roy Walsh, that anything he said could be used against him; however, the county attorney had so advised the defendant. As to when he first did this, the sheriff could not say.

Then a very confusing interchange took place, confusing on one side and deliberately so. John Elliott asked Sheriff Mountjoy about a particular conversation at the Silver Bow County jail on July 1, a few days after Archie and Roy were arraigned. He asked the sheriff whether he heard Howard Johnson tell him, John Elliott, attorney for the defendant, that he could not see the defendant until July 9. Sheriff Mountjoy responded, "I will say that I did not hear him tell you that, but I believe he refused to let you see Hughes."

County Attorney Johnson then took the stand. John Elliott asked him, "Did you refuse counsel for the defendants the right to interview them?"

Now came some deft lawyering from Mr. Kelly. The volley went from lawyer to judge to lawyer to judge . . . objection, further objection, sustained, objection, sustained, the defendant excepts to the ruling of the court, objection, sustained, the defendant excepts to the ruling of the court, objection, sustained. By that time, the jury was probably so confused, they forgot the original question, which was never answered anyway.

Howard Johnson stepped down and Roy took the stand.

"My name is R. W. Walsh. I am the defendant in this action. I was arrested on the twenty-seventh day of June at a place about two miles from Cardwell. I was arrested by Mr. Mountjoy or his deputy sheriff, Mr. Knight, and several others. I heard the testimony of Mr. Mountjoy as to statements he made to me. Mr. Mountjoy did not at any time advise me that I was entitled to counsel before making any statements."

"Did he at any time advise you as to making any confession or statements?" asked John Elliott.

"Why, yes, as to the truth," answered Roy.

"What if anything did he say at that time?"

"Do you mean when he arrested me?"

"When he asked you for those statements, about making any statements."

"Here at the county jail at Boulder, when he asked me my name on the way over from Cardwell to Whitehall, he did not at that time advise me that I was entitled to counsel before making statements," said Roy. "The first time that he asked me for any statements relative to this case was the first time he saw me at the time of the arrest. The next time he asked me for any statements was at Cardwell, and at that time he did not say anything only that it was lucky for me that I did not kill Johnson. After the time at Cardwell, the next time that he asked me any questions relative to this offense was at the county jail at Boulder. At that time he did not advise me that I was entitled to counsel before making any statements. The sheriff did not at any time advise me that anything I said would be used against me in the trial of this case."

"I will ask you if the sheriff advised you it would be better for you to tell what happened," asked John Elliott.

"When and where?" asked Roy.

"Any time he asked you for those statements."

"You mean of the shooting?"

"Any time he asked you anything relative to this matter."

"Not that I can remember," said Roy. "The only advice he ever gave me with reference to making any statements was to tell the truth."

"What did he say about telling the truth, what it would result in?" asked John Elliott.

"We object as being leading," said Kelly.

"It is leading," said Judge Bennett. "I am going to permit the question."

"Nothing against myself," said Roy.

"Do you understand the question?" asked Judge Bennett.

"I think I do," said Roy.

"You mean to say that the sheriff told you if you told the truth that nothing would happen to you?" asked the judge.

"He did not," said Roy. "His statement to me with reference to telling the truth was that it would be better for me if I would tell the truth. During those interviews the sheriff did not state any facts in relation to this case and then ask me what happened. During those interviews the sheriff notified me that somebody else had stated the facts in the case. He also told me where he got those facts and what those facts were reported to be. The facts as he related them connected me with this offense."

"Did you rely upon the statement of the sheriff in making the statements you did or any statements you made for the sheriff?" asked John Elliott.

"We object," said Kelly. "What statements is he referring to?"

"The objection is sustained," said Judge Bennett.

"The sheriff told me it would be better for me to tell the truth before I made any statements, and I relied upon that statement. The statements made by the other party did not have any influence on me in making the statement I did to the sheriff."

Everything stopped.

Judge Bennett sent the jury out of the courtroom. John Elliott vehemently objected to the admissibility of Roy's last statement. The lawyers sparred. Judge and spectators listened rapt. John Elliott used every legal argument he could to exclude Roy's testimony regarding making a statement. The defendant was coerced into signing a false affidavit, he said, Sheriff Mountjoy told him that he better tell the truth. The legal wrangling ended with Judge Bennett ruling that Roy's testimony stand. He ordered the jurors back into court.

James Kelly again called Sheriff Mountjoy to the stand. He recounted the conversations he had with Roy regarding Roy's whereabouts around the time of the shooting. This line of questioning formed the prelude to explain how a confession was secured from Roy.

"I offer in evidence State's Exhibit Number 18," said Kelly. It was the typed confession signed by Roy Walsh and notarized by County Attorney Johnson.

Judge Bennett looked at John Elliott. "Have you any objection other than your general objection?" he asked.

Elliott renewed his objection which was overruled. The mostly typed, partly handwritten confession was then read aloud in court.

> Roy Walsh, being first duly sworn, deposes and says: I am making this statement for the reason that you have told me of Hughes statement and since you seem to know most of the facts and will find out the rest of them anyway. Since you know about our camp on Cedar Hill I will tell you the rest . . .

The confession went on to describe the events leading up to Archie and Roy arriving at Al Johnson's store with the intention of robbing him.

> . . . Hughes stayed by the door that opens on the walk to the track. I went around to the other side of the store. Hughes was supposed to watch one side while I watched the other so that one of us would get Johnson whichever way he went. When I got there, and when I got around to the other side, Johnson was trying the middle door on that side, the one forward of his bedroom door. I heard him rattle the door knob. I ducked back and made a little noise. When I got up past the bedroom door I ran into a box by the fence. The fence was about eight feet from the store. The box was against the fence and had some tin strips on it. The box was at my left and the vines next to Johnson's bedroom door were at my right. I was trying to go between the vines and box. I hit the box with my gun and with my leg. Johnson opened the door and looked out. I crouched down by the vines with the gun in my right hand, started to beat it and the gun caught in something and went off. It probably caught in the vines or in the strings. After the gun went off, I went over the fence and ran . . . to the Buick. It may have been five minutes between the firing of the shot and the time I started the Buick car . . . When I got back to the Buick, I saw the tail light of an automobile going west along the main road to Whitehall. I know that it wasn't the Cadillac because I had disconnected the tail light. I started the Buick . . . As I went past the store I noticed the lights still on in Johnson's room. There was also a light in the house across the road.
>
> No promise has been made to me. I have made this statement not because of any promises that were made to me, and I am telling these things because I know that you would find them out anyway having learned about our camps and having got information from Hughes. I have not been threatened and am not making this statement or any part of it

under threats or promises, but make them of my own free will and because I think it will all be found out anyway. I did not know that Johnson had been hurt when I left. I know this statement may be used against me.

The last sentence was written by hand.

The Montana Penal Code said that murder "committed in the perpetration or attempt to perpetrate" robbery or other listed felonies was murder of the first degree and punishable by death or life in prison. The Code also said that "it is not necessary to allege that the acts of the accused were done deliberately to sustain a conviction of murder in the first degree." Instructions to the jury would state this quite plainly.

Roy sat smiling while his confession was read aloud, seemingly unconcerned about any dire consequences it might bring.

Court adjourned.

The next morning several newspapermen visited Roy at the jail. When asked whether he was worried about the confession, he said he had been in just as tight places six or eight times before and always got out of them.

Another reporter asked why he signed the confession. He said he signed it because he wanted the sheriff and county attorney to leave him alone. "When I get through here I suppose I'll have to go back to Butte and stand trial for the stealing of the automobiles," he said. "Of course they can't keep me here. They haven't anything on me."

As for the stolen car, Roy said the owner asked him to steal it so he could collect the insurance money.

One of the reporters reached for his cigarettes and offered Roy one. "Smoke?" he asked.

"Nope, don't use 'em," Roy said.

It was now close to 9:30AM. Les Knight unlocked the cell, handcuffed Roy, and escorted him across the street to the courthouse. The cortege of newspapermen followed.

Sheriff Mountjoy again took the stand. Referring to photographs, he described the scene in great detail. He said the bullet holes in the doors were jagged. He pointed to the box Roy had walked into and said, "In my opinion, taking the box as I found it on the night of the twenty-seventh of June, I do not think it would be possible for a man to bump into the box or bump a gun into the box and still have the gun in such a position that it would make the hole in the door as it did."

(Roy never said the gun went off when he bumped into the box. I don't know what the sheriff was getting at by saying that.)

"What has been his conduct as a prisoner?" Kelly asked.

"We object as incompetent, irrelevant and immaterial, not tending to prove or disprove any issue in this case," countered Elliott.

"The objection is sustained," said the judge. "You may make an offer of proof."

This Kelly did. Judge Bennet rejected it. Kelly offered another. Judge Bennett allowed him to proceed.

"Mr. Mountjoy, I will ask you, what was the conduct of the prisoner Walsh while in your custody with reference to any attempts to break jail?" asked Kelly.

"We object as leading," said Elliott.

"The objection is sustained."

The question was rephrased and objected to several more times with Kelly prevailing in the end.

"Well, he tore up the plumbing in there," said Sheriff Mountjoy. "He tore the toilet bowl altogether loose from where it was set in the soil pipe—"

"We object as incompetent, irrelevant and immaterial, not tending to prove or disprove any issue in this case."

"Overruled."

Sheriff Mountjoy continued, "He tore up a piece of pipe there that led into those cells, an old part of the plumbing that was not in use. He broke a piece off of it. He tore a strip of scrap iron off of one of the bunks and broke the chain that one of the bunks hung over, and conducted himself in such a manner that I thought he was breaking jail."

Judge Bennett instructed the jury to disregard the statement about breaking jail and admonished the sheriff to omit any of his own considerations regarding the case.

Kelly asked again about Roy's conduct in the jail.

"He and Hughes together have tried to spring the door on the cage over there," said the sheriff. He went on to say that Roy told him what kind of gun he had—a 30-30 rifle. As for Roy's confession, he said the county attorney took notes, and the typed confession did not include everything Roy said.

Court adjourned.

Court convened the next morning to news that one of the jurors was sick with influenza and his doctor had ordered rest. Judge Bennett recessed until 11:30AM. When the appointed hour arrived, the juror was still too sick. Court adjourned for the day. Reporters speculated that if the juror didn't recover soon, the judge may dismiss the case until the next term of court.

By Thursday morning, the sick juror had recovered somewhat. His doctor allowed him to sit for the trial as long as the judge recessed frequently, allowing him time to rest. The judge agreed and a cot was placed in the corridor for the sick man. The trial slowed but continued. As before, the lawyers objected incessantly to whatever the other one was doing.

During cross examination by John Elliott, Sheriff Mountjoy said he did not see Roy sign the confession.

He recounted in detail what Roy told him about the events leading up to the shooting. Referring to the rifle entered into evidence, he said, "The inside of the barrel was dirty as though it had been fired."

Les Knight testified that he had been present when County Attorney Johnson gave the typed confession to Roy to read. He said Roy asked that parts be stricken and changed, Johnson made some marks on the paper, then Roy signed the confession and swore it was the truth.

Mr. Locker, a former Jefferson County sheriff, testified that he examined the scene about three weeks after the shooting. "The bullet that made the holes came from towards the east . . . from the side," he explained. "A soft-nosed bullet is a bullet that is partly covered with metal, with a metal casing, and the point of it is pure lead exposed. When I speak of metal jacket, I mean the casing on the lead, around the lead. When a shell of that kind explodes the casing leaves the gun with the lead. As to . . . the marks around the hole on the inner door, I will say that when the bullet struck the screen door there it would cause it to what we call mushroom, that is, it would have a tendency to split the metal casing, and then when it hit the second door or object it would cause it to fly to pieces," and this accounted for the splinters around the bullet hole on the inner door.

He said he observed powder stains on the door indicating the gun was fired from about four inches away assuming high powered or smokeless powder was used.

A man named Smith testified next. He was one of the extra deputies hired to guard Archie and Roy. He said one of the prisoners offered him five hundred dollars to unlock their cell. He said he told them he didn't have a key. The prisoner asked the other prisoner, where's that key? The other prisoner produced a wire key and handed it to Smith. Smith said he pretended to try the lock. When asked which prisoner offered him the bribe, Smith said he didn't know.

Court adjourned for the evening.

The next morning, Friday, the prosecution rested. John Elliott requested permission to make a motion.

"Do you want the jury to leave for that?" asked Judge Bennett.

"Yes," replied Elliott.

Judge Bennet sent the jury out of the courtroom.

John Elliott then moved for a directed verdict of not guilty. He said testimony offered by witnesses did not support the confession; the prosecution failed to connect the defendant with the crime, failed to prove the confession to be a true statement of the defendant, failed to prove the defendant was at the scene of the crime, failed to show what kind of gun was used, and failed to prove that the gun taken from the defendant was the gun used in the crime.

I'm puzzled as to why John Elliott would say such a thing. No gun was taken from Roy. He was unarmed when arrested. The gun was found in the car. Not to play amateur lawyer here, but I would have thought that a defense attorney would try to disassociate his client from a firearm found in a car that did not belong to his client, a car his client was not in when apprehended.

"Do you want to argue the motion?" asked Judge Bennett.

"I just want to make it," said Elliott.

"The motion will be denied," said Judge Bennett. The jury returned to court and John Elliott began his case. He put Roy on the stand.

"My name is Roy W. Walsh, I am the defendant in this action. My business is that of a mechanical engineer and everything. I am twenty-two years of age. I was acquainted with Albert Johnson during his lifetime. I have known Mr. Johnson for about two years. I knew Mr. Johnson on or about the twenty-sixth day of June. I heard the testimony of Mr. Mountjoy, the sheriff of Jefferson County. I never acknowledged to Mr. Mounjoy that I was present at or near the store run by Mr. Johnson at Renova at that time. I made some statements to Mr. Mountjoy as to my whereabouts on or about the twenty-sixth day of June. I told Mr. Mountjoy that I was up on the Madison camping. I told Mr. Mountjoy how long I had been up on the

Madison. I told Mr. Mountjoy that I returned from the Madison on the night of the twenty-sixth. I told Mr. Mountjoy that I got back from the Madison something like two o'clock in the morning of the twenty-seventh of June or the night of the twenty-sixth of June."

"When did you first hear of the crime at Renova?" asked John Elliott.

"Well, I should judge about twelve o'clock that night—you mean I heard of the crime?" asked Roy.

"Yes."

"I didn't hear of the crime until after I was arrested," said Roy. "This information was given to me while I was in the county jail at Boulder. That information was given to me before I made the alleged statement to Mr. Mountjoy and Mr. Knight which they testified to . . . I heard that Mr. Johnson was dead about one or two days after I made the statement to Mr. Mountjoy, Mr. Knight, and the county attorney. I did not know this crime had been committed at the time I made those so called statements or answers."

"Did you make a confession to any one of the three of those, Mr. Johnson, Mr. Knight or Mr. Mountjoy?" asked John Elliott.

"Did I what?" asked Roy.

"Make a confession."

"Well, yes, according to the way they have it," said Roy. "I heard the testimony offered by Mr. Mountjoy and Mr. Knight. The statements made by them were not correct. There were some portions of the statements made by them that were correct. I should say that about one third of the statements made by them would be correct. As to the manner of making those statements, I will say that the questions were asked by Mr. Johnson and I answered them with yes or no. I heard the confession read by Mr. Johnson to the jury. As to just how the question was put to me that elicited the answer or statement that we got to Butte about three o'clock that morning from Race Track and had breakfast at Hughes, I will say that Mr. Johnson just asked me if Hughes and I did not camp at Race Track the night before, and I told him yes. The next question he asked me was if we did not camp on Cedar Hill and I told him yes. The manner I have just indicated is the way the most of this alleged confession was secured. I was not at Race Track at the time alleged in the confession. The night they have me at Race Track is the time I was on the Madison. I did camp on Cedar Hill a night at one time but not the night that they represent it. Mr. Johnson asked me if I was at Johnson's store on the night of the twenty-sixth and I told him I was. Mr. Johnson also asked me with reference to having a gun in my possession and I told him that I did. Mr. Johnson also asked me with reference to this gun being discharged down there and I told him that the gun caught on some vines or strings and it discharged the gun suddenly. Mr. Johnson did not exactly suggest this answer to me at that time. Mr. Johnson asked me how I came around to that door and whereabouts I was in those vines. I could not say whether I was present at the Johnson store at the time Mr. Johnson was shot or not. There were no shots fired there at the Johnson store while I was there that I heard. I was at the Johnson store on that night. I should judge it would be about twelve o'clock on that night when I was there at the Johnson store . . .

"As to whether I made this confession marked Exhibit Number 18 for the State to Mr. Johnson, Mr. Knight, and Mr. Mountjoy, I will say there are some statements there that I made. I never read that before, that is, to read the entire confession until yesterday here in the courtroom."

"Prior to that time did you see this confession?" asked Elliott.

"No, sir."

"Have you seen this confession?"

"Yes, I saw that confession here in the jail at Boulder. At the time I signed this confession I knew that I was signing with regard to a few of the statements therein contained, but I did not know that I was signing all of that. At the time I signed this paper I did not read it. At the time I signed this confession, Mr. Johnson read some of it to me. As to whether Mr. Johnson read all of it to me at that time, I will say that I do not think that he did. After Mr. Johnson had taken this statement, he notified me that it was a statement and that it would be used against me. Mr. Johnson told me that after I had told him those few statements. I did not swear to this statement. At the time I signed this statement, Mr. Johnson did not ask me if those were true statements I had made in the confession."

"State generally your acts on the night of June 26 say around about eight o'clock in the evening until twelve o'clock at night," said Elliott.

"You mean my presence in the county jail?" Roy asked.

"This was on the night of June 26," said Elliott.

"Well," said Roy, "on June 26, at night, Hughes and I went from Cedar Hill to Renova . . . We had intentions of holding Johnson up. . . " He went on to describe how they staked out the store. His description matched his confession until the part where he ran into the box. "Then I crossed the fence and went over to the Cadillac. I did not at this time know where Hughes was so I waited at the Cadillac car a short time, but Hughes did not show up so then I went on down to my car and got in my car and drove off. I did not at any time attempt to hold Mr. Johnson up. I went there with the intention of holding Johnson up, but after getting there and seeing the lay of the land, I changed my mind . . .

"I had a gun with me at the time I went up there. At the time I went around the store the gun was in my right hand. This gun was not discharged at any time during this trip that I know of. If the gun had been discharged I would have known it. I was not intoxicated at that time . . . I do not use liquor . . . After I got down to my car, the Buick car, I started the car up and drove out on the road and around in front of Renova and there I slowed up and looked for Hughes, but I could not see him, so I went on thinking Hughes would take the Cadillac and come to this camp of ours where they captured me. He knew about that as well as I did."

He said the reason he was hiding was he knew the authorities in Butte were looking for him because of the car.

Then out of the blue he mentioned Smith's testimony.

"You heard him testify as to an offer made by someone in the county jail at Boulder?' asked John Elliott.

"Offer made to who?" asked Roy.

"Smith," said Elliott.

"Did you hear Smith's testimony with reference to someone offering him five hundred dollars to let them out? This what you refer to is it not?" asked Judge Bennett.

"Yes," replied Elliott.

"I heard Mr. Smith's testimony with reference to that," said Roy.

"Did you make any such offer to Mr. Smith?" asked Elliott. "You understand the question?"

"I may know the man, but I don't exactly know the name," said Roy. "I did not offer anyone in the county jail of Jefferson County five hundred dollars for my release. As to whether anyone else made an offer to him of that kind, I will say there was none that I know of. I never gave him a wire for opening the lock. I heard Mr. Hughes talking something about that, but I was in the cell lying down at the time."

Johnson then began cross examination. He asked Roy to look at the signature on the confession. Roy said it was his signature. "Some of those interlineations in ink on that Exhibit Number 18 for the State were made at my suggestion," he said. "The statement with reference to the tail light of the Cadillac being out, and that made me recognize it, was made at my suggestion. The statement also with reference to hitting this box and ducking back in this vine was made at my suggestion, and also the statement about making the noise."

"When did you sign this statement?" asked Johnson.

"As to the time when I signed that statement, I will say that I think it was signed on the thirtieth of June, and as to the time of that day when it was signed, I will say that I think it was sometime in the afternoon."

"You have stated that during this conversation or at the end of the conversation with you on that day, but not until then, you were advised that whatever you said might be used against you. That was during the conversation at noon with three of us present," said Johnson.

"I remember you telling me that after I had given this statement, after the statement is made in there. I was not given that advice at an earlier interview to my knowledge."

Then Roy droned on and on and on about how he was on the Madison, how long he was on the Madison, which days he was on the Madison, then he went to Butte, then he went to Race Track, then back to Butte, then back to Race Track, then back to Butte, and when he left Butte, he had no intention of going to Cedar Hill, but he went there anyway.

"Who was with you?" asked Johnson.

"We object as incompetent, irrelevant, and immaterial," said Elliott.

"The objection is overruled," said Judge Bennett.

"The defendant exempts to the ruling of the court," said Elliott.

"Mr. Hughes was with me," said Roy.

Roy described how he and Archie drove to Renova, where they parked their cars, how they tore masks from an old shirt. "He fixed the masks for himself and I told him that I did not want any mask, that I didn't need any. I did not want to wear a mask because I was not the one that was supposed to go in and hold Johnson up."

Roy retold the story in exasperating detail about seeing the man in the store, how many minutes they waited, who walked to this side of the store, who walked to that side of the store, how he walked into the box, how far the box was from the vines, what kind of metal strips were hanging from the box. Throughout all this, he pointed to exactly what he was referring to on photographs taken at the scene. He used the same kind of wording and the same level of detail that previous witnesses had used, as if he was respectfully mimicking them, as if he wanted to be just like them.

"When he opened the door I saw him," Roy said, "but the light reflected on me and blinded me. I should judge that Mr. Johnson saw me because I was in plain sight. Johnson stood for a minute in the door, and I turned around and started to beat it. I was not exactly frightened at that time . . . I stayed in the vines for a minute and then I headed over for the fence . . . I went along the vines towards the front of the store. During most of this time Johnson was standing in the door. The door remained open until I got over the fence. I made some noise getting over the fence. During this time I was carrying my rifle in my right hand . . .

"I left Renova in the first place without finding out where Hughes was because I had given up the idea of holding up Johnson and I supposed Hughes would also give up the idea of holding Johnson up after seeing Johnson lock the front door after the man that was last in the store."

"Why didn't you see Hughes and talk the matter over with him?" asked Johnson.

Objection.

Overruled.

"What would be the necessity in talking anything over with Hughes at the time?" asked Roy.

"Did you know what Hughes would do when you left?" asked Johnson.

Objection.

He may answer yes or no.

"I did not," said Roy.

"Mr. Walsh, do you remember writing and delivering to Leslie Knight, the undersheriff, an unsealed letter on the morning of about the third of July?" asked Johnson.

Objection.

Sustained.

"We will make a written offer of proof," said Johnson. "We offer to prove that the defendant wrote a letter relating to the shooting of Johnson admitting he heard a shot while at the store."

Objection.

Overruled.

"I believe I did somewheres around that date," said Roy.

"Will you read this and state whether that is a copy of the letter?" asked Johnson.

"I did not write no letter stating the facts."

"Were you ever convicted of a felony?"

Objection.

Overruled.

"No. I think I understand what a felony is. As I understand it, grand larceny would be a felony."

CHAPTER FORTY-THREE

AND MERCIFULLY that was enough from Roy. Now came the defense's firearms witness, Mr. Everly. He insisted the bullet was too light to have come from a 30-30 Marlin rifle, the kind of rifle Roy admitted he was carrying. He said a 30-30 caliber bullet could be that light only if fired through metal in which case it would break into pieces.

He also said the bullet would not lose the steel jacket after passing through both doors, even if it hit a fleshy object, and there was no steel jacket on the bullet. (I've seen the bullet. It was flattened.) He said he did several experiments firing through a pine board and had extensive experience using soft-nosed bullets on big game and so knew the effect of firing through wood and through tissue.

Mr. Locker rebutted. He said when firing through several objects, the metal jacket sometimes does leave the lead bullet. Once after shooting a deer, he found the jacket near the ribs and the lead in another part of the animal.

Both Everly and Locker agreed that a 30-30 caliber bullet weighed 170 grains. This included the metal jacket, approximately 23 grains, and the lead, approximately 147 grains. Everly said the bullet recovered from Al Johnson's body weighed slightly over 119 grains, much too light to be a 30-30 caliber bullet.

Howard Johnson again called Undersheriff Les Knight to the stand. He testified that, on July 3, Roy gave him an open letter to give to John Elliott.

Johnson then took the stand and testified that he had read and copied the letter. He produced the copy and gave it to James Kelly.

"I will offer in evidence State's Exhibit Number 24, being a letter consisting of two pages," announced Kelly.

Judge Bennett looked at John Elliott. "Any objection?"

"We object to that on the ground that the letter itself is the best evidence," said Elliott.

"The objection is sustained."

"I now call upon counsel for the defense to produce the letter," said Kelly.

"Have you the letter here?" the judge asked John Elliott.

"I have, Your Honor."

"You may produce it."

"I object to the introduction of the letter or giving it up on the ground that it is a privileged communication between the defendant and myself."

"It now appearing that it can be produced, but that it is now outside of the reach of State's counsel, and defendant's counsel will not produce the same, I now again offer in evidence Exhibit Number 24 for the State," said Kelly.

"We again interpose the same objection," said Elliott.

"I am going to sustain the objection," said Judge Bennett. "The letter will not be admitted."

Though Roy's letter was kept out of the trial, it was given to reporters and printed that evening in the *Butte Daily Post*.

> Just before the shot was fired I was at the side of the store between the two side doors on the left hand side. Johnson opened the door which entered his bedroom, looked out and then closed it. I had my rifle on the ground, which I picked up, and started away. But I had not got over the fence when the shot was fired, which I believe was fired at me, because the concussion of the bullet when it passed over was very great, and I fell over the fence, got up and ran. As I neared the road a man ducked in the brush. I could not see very plain, but didn't shoot. I am sure it was the man who was last with Johnson that evening as we watched him come out of the store in the dark road toward the track and then stop and disappear.
>
> The rifle I had I know had not been shot for thirty days, as it was in my possession. I said (in the confession) that I stumbled and the gun went off, but it did not. That rifle I had was not shot that night, or neither did I have another gun of any kind.
>
> I left there with my car then, not knowing that anyone was hurt. The man that was last in the store with Johnson was the man that shot at me, I believe, as the gun I had was never fired that night, as I went with the intention of not even shooting the gun, just to run a bluff.
>
> Hughes did not say anything in the line of shooting anyone, or even shooting at them or shooting the gun at all. We were going to scare Johnson, jump on him and tie him with a rope and take what we wanted and leave, as I did not want to hurt him in any way. This is just as things happened that night.

John Elliott moved that a demonstration be staged for the jury to show the firing of a 30-30 rifle into pine boards.

Denied.

He moved that the jury be shown the scene of the tragedy.

Denied.

He again moved for a directed verdict of not guilty. He said the State failed to prove the defendant guilty of the crime charged, failed to show that the deceased was shot by any gun in the hands of the defendant, failed to show that the bullet hole in the door was made by a bullet from the defendant's gun, and failed to show that the lead taken from the body of the deceased, Albert Johnson, was from the defendant's gun. He referred to testimony by Mountjoy and Knight about how Roy approached Al Johnson's door. "Roy Walsh could not have fired the shot from that direction," Elliott declared. "Roy Walsh himself testified that he did not fire the shot."

Motion denied.

John Elliott then announced that Archie Hughes would not be called as a witness.

The defense rested.

It was now Friday evening. The lawyers presented their closing arguments. "The shooting was not accidental," boomed James Kelly. "There sits the biggest desperado in the state," and he pointed at Roy. "Any man who will plead guilty to stealing automobiles to escape a murder charge of which he is guilty is a criminal at heart. Gentlemen, it's the rope for him, and nothing less than the rope."

At that Roy was visibly startled. It was the first crack in his calm, carefree demeanor.

John Elliott reminded the jurors of testimony that claimed the bullet could not have been fired from Roy Walsh's gun. "The State has not proven that Roy Walsh killed Al Johnson," he declared. "Someone else could have fired the fatal shot. If the shot was fired from Roy Walsh's gun, it was accidental."

The lawyers then contested instructions to the jury. By 8:30PM, all disputes were settled. One of the instructions explained that if the jury determined that the defendant went to the premises of the deceased with the intention of robbing him with a loaded gun, it was not necessary for the State to prove that the killing was "wilful, deliberate, or premeditated" in order to sustain a conviction of murder in the first degree.

Court adjourned. The jury retired to the jury room and began deliberations.

Sheriff Mountjoy took Roy into the anteroom; they sat down and waited. The minutes dragged.

"Too bad we don't have some cards," said Sheriff Mountjoy.

"I'll make you a bet," said Roy. "I'll bet I can take these handcuffs off."

"You're on."

Roy pulled a key from his pocket and quickly unlocked the handcuffs. He had carved the key from a wooden spoon using a manicure file.

It was summer, and it was haying season—a short, critical window in the life of a Montana farmer. He had to cut his alfalfa, let it cure, gather it, store it, let it grow, cut it, let it cure, gather it, store it, let it grow, and do all this during Montana's notoriously short growing season. He counted on three crops to feed his stock through the winter and/or to sell as a cash crop. The previous year had been miserable for haying. It rained and rained and rained some more, ruining almost the entire first crop. Most of the rain is supposed to be done in June—before haying season. Mother Nature doesn't always cooperate. The alfalfa on most places was knee high by now. Some farmers had already cut their first crop and the hoppers were munching away on the second as fast as it grew.

And in the middle of all this, eleven farmers had to sit on a jury for some no-good troublemaker from Butte who shot a man and admitted it.

All were back in court at 11:20PM. Roy was again handcuffed, strain now visible on his face.

Judge Bennett asked the foreman if the jury had reached a verdict. Yes they had. The judge ordered the defendant to rise. He read the verdict and returned it to the foreman who read it aloud: "We, the jury, find the defendant, Roy Walsh, guilty of the crime of murder in the first degree and fix his punishment at death."

The clerk polled the jury. All concurred with the verdict. Judge Bennett set August 2 as the date to pronounce sentence. Court adjourned.

"Well," said Roy as he left the courthouse, "they didn't have much to say to me, did they."

"This is pretty serious, Roy," said Les Knight.

"The worst is yet to come," said Roy. "Ah, hell, these farmers out here do all their work with the rope."

Jurors told reporters that the first ballot was unanimous for the guilty verdict. As for the death penalty recommendation, two voted to leave the punishment to the judge. After an hour and a half of deliberation, all voted he be hanged.

Archie fell to pieces when he heard the news.

The next day County Attorney Johnson asked John Elliott to meet him at the sheriff's office. He told Les Knight to bring Archie. Sarah came with him. At the appointed time, Johnson walked into the office and went directly over to Archie and said, "This is your last chance! You can plead guilty to second degree murder or go to trial!" and he spun around and left.

"Don't let him scare you," said John Elliott, "this thing has just started."

"Don't plead guilty, Archie," said Sarah. "I got your brother off with a light sentence and I will do the same for you."

As THE DAYS passed, Archie vacillated back and forth as to whether or not he would accept the county attorney's offer. When alone or only with Roy, Archie was a wreck. His lapses into severe nervousness were so extreme that John Elliott considered an insanity defense for him. Visits from family members pacified him.

Archie asked to see Howard Johnson again. Undersheriff Knight handcuffed him to himself and took him to the county attorney's office. John Elliott went with them.

Referring to the plea offer, Archie asked Johnson, "Won't you give me until August 2, the day Walsh is sentenced?"

"NO!" he replied, "I'm giving you more of a chance than you gave Johnson!"

Archie fainted. Howard Johnson called a doctor. By the time the doctor arrived, he had come to. The doctor told Les Knight to take him back to his cell and put him to bed.

CHAPTER FORTY-FOUR

ON AUGUST 2, all assembled in the courtroom. Roy appeared indifferent to the proceedings. He said he was sure he would not hang. Judge Bennett asked if there was any reason why judgment should not be pronounced against him in accordance with the verdict. John Elliott moved for a new trial. He said he had found new evidence weighing heavily in Roy's behalf. Judge Bennett said the motion for a new trial would be heard on October 1 when he returned to Boulder. If after hearing it he deemed a new trial was not warranted, he would then and there pronounce sentence. Archie's trial would also be in October.

After they left the courtroom, John Elliott told reporters that if Judge Bennett denied his request for a new trial, he would take Roy's case to the state supreme court.

Archie and Roy returned to their cell in the Boulder jail. As time passed, I think Archie calmed down a bit. The two endeared themselves to their round-the-clock guards. Archie and Roy were amiable young men and were always polite and gracious to the girls who brought their meals. Outwardly, they gave the sheriff and his deputies no trouble. The two whiled away their days drawing pictures and writing poetry. Roy drew a picture of himself with a rope around his neck. Archie drew one of himself with Les Knight grasping his arm. The caption read: "Undersheriff Knight and Hughes an innocent man." He drew a sketch of Sheriff Mountjoy with the forlorn caption: "He never comes to see me." Roy drew a picture of a man standing under a tree with two heavily armed, scowling men. One said, "Lets get the job over with, I have to get home." The other replied, "No hurry, let's take our time, we have to get the crowd to help pull the rope."

From time to time, Sheriff Mountjoy took the pair for walks through town to give them exercise. During these walks, Archie and Roy were handcuffed together and closely guarded. One day Roy said, "I want to see the cemetery." Sheriff Mountjoy took them to see it.

While they were out walking, the deputies searched their cell. One time they found copper wire and a piece of carbon and burn marks on the cell bars.

A waitress from the Windsor Hotel brought them dinner each evening and returned later to retrieve the dinner basket. One evening as she was unloading the dirty dishes in the hotel kitchen, she found an envelope tucked under a plate. It was addressed to Mr. Bill Hughes, 516 East Park Street, Butte, Montana. The sender had written above the address: "Whoever finds this letter, please mail at once. Don't inquire, but just mail it. Yours most truly, and it will be appreciated." On the back was written: "Bring a dark tie, dark shirt and cap."

The waitress took the envelope to her boss. Her boss gave the letter to Sheriff Mountjoy who opened it, read it, and gave it to County Attorney Johnson who kept it as evidence for Archie's trial. It was also given to reporters and printed in the newspaper.

Boulder, Mont.
August 16, 1923

Say, Bill, will you go up town and buy some hack saw blades and put them in some kind of a package so that they cannot be found and send it to us and get Jack B—— to sign the package because they don't know him here. If you can get anyone to send it, do it and fix the hack saws in the package because I know you know just how to do it. Do this soon as you can. We are well and want to get out of here or we will be done for. Well, Bill, we will close, and you do this if you want to help us, and no one will know who done it. Say, if you can get someone to come to Boulder and be here at the jail at 2:00, when everything is safe, they can put them saws through the window to us. The window is always open and the guard is not here, and bring a long piece of wire about seven feet long and put the saws on the wire and it is easy then, remember and try your best.
Walsh and Art

Seeing their escape plan publicly foiled, and perhaps remembering that trip to the cemetery, Archie asked to see County Attorney Johnson again. He in turn summoned John Elliott.

"I've decided to plead guilty to second degree murder," Archie told the two attorneys.

"I cannot agree to that," said Elliott.

Despite Elliott's objection, Howard Johnson arranged for Archie to appear before Judge Bennett. John Elliott represented Archie at court but told the judge that he could not agree with his client's guilty plea. Judge Bennett said he would not accept Archie's plea if his lawyer disagreed. Archie dismissed John Elliott as his lawyer and stuck by his decision. Judge Bennett then appointed a retired judge, Judge Parker, to represent Archie. Judge Parker begged the court for mercy. "My client is but a youth of eighteen," he reminded the judge.

The minimum penalty for murder in the second degree was ten years in prison. "I'll bet he gives me from twenty to forty years," Archie joked to Howard Johnson. He was close. Bennett sentenced him to eighteen to thirty-six years.

As he was leaving the courthouse, a newspaperman asked Archie about his being allowed to plead guilty to second degree murder while his accomplice was set to hang.

"I never would have," Archie replied, "but he told me 'you better plead, Archie, you can't help me by staying here.' If Walsh killed Johnson then I'm guilty. I heard a shot that night but I don't know who fired it. If Walsh did, then I'm guilty, just as guilty as he."

Sheriff Mountjoy took Archie to Deer Lodge that afternoon. Before they left, Archie composed a lengthy poem and gave it to the reporter from the *Boulder Monitor* who printed it in the paper. Here is part of it:

THANK YOU

I am thanking you people of Boulder
   For the kindness shown to me,
When I was in jail in Boulder
   With trouble attached to me.
When I left the straight and narrow
   Many months ago,
I had no thought of killing
   No man's son, I know.
But all the friends have failed me,
   The friends I thought I had,
When I had plenty of money,
   And bribery was my fad,
Now I hope it does you justice,
   As it is true as gold
We buy and sell in the morning
   We barter and trade at noon,
We sell our breath to the dealer death
   For the golden coins of noon.

CHAPTER FORTY-FIVE

OCTOBER 1 CAME and went with no hearing because the court reporter was sick and hadn't finished transcribing the trial. October 13 was fixed as the new date for Roy's hearing. That day would not do, said John Elliott. He had a scheduling conflict. "Then it will be October 22," said Judge Bennett. "I wish it to be clearly understood that the case will be disposed of regardless of the circumstances on the morning of Monday, October 22."

On Saturday morning, October 20, Les Knight reported for work. He lived in the back of the jail; he was the jailer as well as the undersheriff. He called to Roy from the cage door and asked if he wanted some breakfast. Roy didn't respond. He knew that Roy hadn't eaten dinner the previous evening and had complained of feeling ill. Roy had been moody of late, some days laughing and joking with the guards, other days despondent and brooding. Les asked again if he wanted some breakfast. No response. He unlocked the door and entered the cell. He reached out to shake Roy awake, just as he had the night before to ask Roy if he wanted dinner, but this time, his hand flattened a fluffed bundle under the covers.

Heart pounding he ran next door to the sheriff's house and told him.

To get out of the jail, a prisoner had to pass through several locked doors, doors that were still locked when Les Knight reported for work that morning. Roy must have had help. Sheriff Mountjoy immediately arrested all three guards. Smith had been the guard on duty that night.

A posse assembled and combed the entire town and the surrounding area. They searched all day but found no trace of Roy. That's because Roy wasn't out there. He was still in the jail. He was in the attic.

That night he dropped into the vacant women's cell on the second floor and slept on the cot. In the morning, he climbed back into the attic and stayed there all day.

After dark, he cut a hole in the roof and climbed out. The Boulder jail was a two-story stone building. The sheriff's home adjoined the jail and it was one story. Roy climbed down onto the roof of the sheriff's house. It was still a long drop to the ground but not as long as from the roof of the jail. He scooted down off the roof while holding onto the edge. He was hanging from the roof by his arms, about to drop to the ground, when he heard the screen door swing shut. He looked down. It was Mrs. Mountjoy with her laundry basket. She walked to the clothes line, set down the basket, and proceeded to hang the wash. She picked up something from the basket, pinned it on the line, picked up something else, pinned it on the line, picked up something else, something else . . . All this time Roy was hanging from the roof. Finally she emptied the basket, picked it up, and went inside. Roy waited a moment to be sure she was staying inside. He was about to drop to the ground when he heard the screen door swing shut

Jefferson County Jail, Boulder, Montana.
The edge of the sheriff's house can be seen on the right.
JEFFERSON COUNTY MUSEUM

again. This time it was Sheriff Mountjoy with one of his sons. They stayed outside for a few minutes, then the sheriff ushered his son back inside.

Roy dropped to the ground and ran to a nearby barn and ducked into a corner. Through the darkness he saw a man enter, then another. They spoke briefly and left. Roy walked out of the barn toward the Masonic Hall thinking he'd find a car there to steal. He thought better of it and continued walking and walked right out of town.

He walked eight miles south to Basin. By the time he got there he was hungry. He went into a barn looking for food. He found a milk cow, milked her, and drank his fill. Then he continued south to Butte, about thirty miles away. The authorities there were already on the look-out for him. He waited until after dark and then slipped into the bustling town. He went directly to 516 East Park Street. Sarah fed him and probably gave him some provisions for the road. Then he walked another thirty miles south to Melrose. He traveled at night and hid and slept by day. In Melrose, he stole a car and drove further south through Dillon into Idaho. By this time, twelve days had passed since he escaped.

Meanwhile, Sheriff Mountjoy blanketed this country and Canada with pictures and a description of his fugitive: white male, age twenty-two, 6 feet 1½ inches tall, medium build, dark brown hair, hazel eyes, medium complexion, occupation machinist. The wanted poster offered a $250 reward for his capture, dead or alive.

Reports of sightings came quickly: at a house in Butte the Sunday after he escaped, there again Monday morning, in Rocker on Monday evening, Manhattan on Tuesday, Forsyth on Wednesday. Railroad detectives were told that he was heading east. The sighting near Rocker came from a little boy who said he saw a man crouching in a gulch. The description he gave matched Roy right down to his white tennis shoes. A man thought to be Roy was seen jumping from a freight train as it rolled into Belgrade. A man was spotted riding on the rods under a dining car near Forsyth. A telegram arrived from Las Vegas. A man who knew Roy said he saw him near there.

Sheriff Mountjoy followed every lead but all led to nothing.

Attention then turned to Smith. County Attorney Johnson charged him with helping Roy escape, specifically for "voluntarily permitting the escape of a prisoner while deputy sheriff." If convicted, Smith faced up to fourteen years in prison. There were lots of Smiths in the Boulder Valley and he wasn't related to any of them. One former Boulder woman told me, "He was just a fellow around town who never amounted to much." Judge Bennett probably thought five thousand dollars bail would keep him locked up. It didn't.

The week after Roy escaped Judge Bennett denied John Elliott's motion for a new trial, even though John Elliott didn't show up in court to present it. The judge fixed the date of execution for November 10. That date came and went with no Roy.

Around that time, a man calling himself Donald Stewart was arrested in San Diego for petty theft. He hired a lawyer to get him out of jail. He gave the car he was driving to the lawyer to cover the fifty-five dollar lawyer's fee and twenty-two dollar fine. He was released and promptly stole the car back. It was only then that the San Diego authorities made the connection between their thief and Montana's fugitive. The San Diego sheriff wired Sheriff Mountjoy, and he left immediately for California, but by then, Roy was long gone.

CHAPTER FORTY-SIX

PETER WAS ALWAYS singing or reciting poems or talking when he was in the house, never quiet, it was part of his energetic hyperness, he couldn't sit still, not even his vocal cords. One little ditty he used to sing was,

> Where is my father, where can he be,
> I'm so sad and lonesome, lonesome as can be,
> My father went and left me left me all alone,
> So if you see my father, please tell him to come home.

It's such a sad little song, especially for one whose father did go off and leave her, leave her all alone. Where was Aila's father? Portland. Her friend Rhea had found his address for her some time ago and she had been writing to him and sending him pictures.

"Peter, I'd like to live in a big town like Portland," she told her husband one day. "My father says he can get you a job there, a *good* job, if you'll stay." Peter didn't want to move to Portland, but Aila managed to prevail upon him, and he went. Through his Mason connections, Arthur found Peter a job and a place for them to live which he stocked with food. Once he was settled, Peter wrote to Aila and told her to come. She made sandwiches for Aila Rose and her to eat on the train. After she bought the train tickets, she had one dime. With the dime, she bought two half pints of milk for Aila Rose on the train, one for each day of the journey. She arrived in Portland penniless.

Arthur was working as a custodian at the First Congregational Church in downtown Portland. He either lived at the church or nearby. Aila and Peter rented the two

Patsy, Aila and Aila Rose, Peter's sister Mary and her son Gilbert, 1924.

housekeeping rooms he found for them across the park. Peter's job was on the waterfront across the river in St. John's and he did not like that long commute. "Aila, if you want me to keep this job, I'm not going to go all that way every day. We'll have to move," he said. So they moved to St. John's.

Around the time Aila and Peter moved to St. John's, a new family moved into the house across the street. They had young children, one a ten-year-old boy. The children were playing in the yard one day when another boy swaggered up with a knife and slashed the boy across the mouth and said he was going to cut the mouth of every —— kid in the neighborhood so they'd stop talking to him. The wounded boy was rushed to the hospital. His attacker was apprehended and put in "one of those homes where they keep boys," as Aila described it.

Aila, Aila Rose, and Peter

After that, Aila said under no circumstances would she go to work and leave Aila Rose with a sitter. They moved again though not far, still in St. John's. Their new home was one of several housekeeping rooms in a large house that had been a family home. Aila always enjoyed visiting and meeting new people and before long she met the other mothers in the neighborhood. Several worked in the woolen mill and each juggled babysitting arrangements. Aila proposed that she open a nursery school for the children. "I had the nursery school right at home," she said. "All you had to do was take care of the children properly and feed them properly, keep them clean, and do your job." She charged ten dollars a month for one child and fifteen dollars for two. Part of the arrangement was that the mothers had to take turns cooking dinner for all of them, which gave each woman several days when she didn't have to prepare that meal.

Aila found St. John's to be a pleasant little community. Spring came early, so it seemed to someone from Butte. Wild roses burst into bloom. Yards were lush with dense green grass and brilliant gardens—just compensation for the ever gray, ever rainy, damp climate. Peter worked steadily at the saw mill or ship building plant or as a longshoreman, wherever it was he worked on the wharf.

By this time, Arthur had been gone long enough for Sarah to obtain a divorce based on desertion. She began the proceedings on February 29. She must have had some kind of superstition about that. John Elliott took care of the legal paperwork. Three months later, on June 9, 1924, it was done.

"Am I through?" she asked the judge.

"You're through," he replied.

With a lady friend and John Elliott following closely on her heels, she left the courtroom and made a beeline for the clerk of court's office. En route, she spied a newspaperman in the corridor. She detoured long enough to sternly admonish him, "Don't put anything in the paper about my divorce until Thursday." She marched into the clerk's office and demanded a marriage license and told him to keep mum about it until Thursday. Then she left, rounded up her star boarder, William Mitchell, and married him.

Sarah and William Mitchell

Three weeks later, he dropped dead of tuberculosis.

CHAPTER FORTY-SEVEN

MEANWHILE, ROY DROVE into Mexico, then back to California, then back to Mexico, then back to California, then he headed east for hundreds of miles and turned north. By February he was in Missouri. A snow storm had left the roads muddy and he got stuck. He tried and tried to free his car and then gave up and set off on foot. He hopped on a freight train, rode awhile, and jumped off outside of Armstrong. By then he was pretty hungry. He stole some eggs from a henhouse. He spied a smokehouse, went in, and stole some meat. A little while later, the owner, who happened to be the constable, came along and noticed that some of his meat was missing. He looked around and found footprints in the snow and followed them. The footprints led to a barn. He looked inside and there was Roy. He had just made a fire and was about to cook the eggs. He looked up, saw the constable, and bolted. The constable chased him. The two men stumbled through the crusted snow until finally the constable caught Roy.

Roy told him that his name was Donald Stewart and that he had been traveling with his brother and a friend and their car got stuck in the mud and the other two had left him and gone to St. Louis.

The constable described his captive as a laborer who spoke broken English. He locked Roy alias Donald in the jail and went looking for the stuck car. He found it, and inside, he found a gun. He had intended to let Roy go but that made him change his mind.

Roy was charged with two counts of burglary and pled guilty. He wasn't too worried about it. All he did was steal some meat and eggs. He figured the judge would give him a light slap on the wrist, at most he'd spend a few days in the county jail and be on his way. He was in for quite a surprise. "You could have knocked me down with a feather when the judge gave me four years and then cut it to two," he said.

And off Roy went to the Missouri State Penitentiary.

THAT APRIL Smith's trial began in Boulder. Judge Bennett and County Attorney Johnson must have been quite surprised when he posted bond. You'd have to put up an entire quarter-section ranch to secure a five thousand dollar bond, and he didn't have one. In addition to posting a huge bond, this fellow who never amounted to much, and had no family in the area, and no visible assets to speak of, showed up in court with two high profile out-of-town lawyers: Matt Canning of Butte and James Kelly of Dillon, the same James Kelly who helped prosecute Roy.

James Kelly was the brother of the very well-connected Dan Kelly—the Anaconda Company lawyer with whom Burton Wheeler had so publically crossed swords during the 1918 wildcat strike in Butte. Prior to going to work for the Company, Dan had been the state attorney general and in that capacity was on the Board of Prison Commissioners when Sarah and Arthur were up for parole. He had also served in the State House as a Democrat from Butte and as Jefferson County attorney. Before all that, James and Dan practiced law together.

Smith's other lawyer, Matt Canning, was one of Butte's top criminal lawyers. His former law partner Burton Wheeler, now a U.S. senator, called him a "brilliant criminal lawyer." This tall, dark Irishman was the son of a prosperous County Mayo family. As a child, he was educated by private tutors before attending Maynooth College near Dublin. At age twenty-two, he immigrated to Butte and did a variety of jobs while studying the law at night. He began his law practice around 1905. He was now fifty-two years old, a widower with four grown children. One of Canning's more high profile cases was when he successfully defended that Rosebud County rancher charged with espionage during the war. And Canning, like James Kelly, had practiced on both sides of the criminal bar, having been Silver Bow County attorney.

In short, Smith's legal team had juice.

It raised a few eyebrows around Boulder.

The jurors were barely in place for Smith's trial when controversy erupted. One of the jurors had been eating dinner with several men when the subject of Roy's escape came up. The juror allegedly opined that Smith was not guilty, and if Mountjoy did not find Walsh, he surely would not be reelected sheriff. Howard Johnson petitioned to have the juror removed.

The day testimony was to begin those two clever legal minds hired to defend Smith filed a motion to dismiss. They called into question the wording of the statute. It said it was illegal to help a prisoner escape. It did not say from *legal* custody. On hearing the motion, Judge Bennett deemed a ruling by the state supreme court was necessary in order to ascertain the validity of the law as written. If the high court determined that the legislature intended to prohibit escape from *illegal* custody (a kidnap victim), which it had no power to do, the entire law could be invalid and no prosecution under it possible. Smith remained free.

WHILE ALL THIS was going on in Boulder, Roy alias Donald was working as a machinist in the Missouri prison twine factory, and every chance he got, he tried to convince the warden to send him outside the prison to do hard labor on a farm.

The constable who had arrested Roy offered to purchase his car. Roy told him that his lawyer in San Diego owned it and gave him the lawyer's name. The constable wrote to the lawyer. The lawyer immediately wired Sheriff Mountjoy telling him that the man who called himself Donald Stewart was in the Missouri penitentiary. He also requested the reward money. Sheriff Mountjoy contacted the authorities in Missouri. Photographs and fingerprints were sent across the country and compared. Sure enough, Missouri had his man. Six months after he escaped, the illusive Roy Walsh had been found.

When the news hit Boulder, it "set the entire Jefferson Valley agog."

Sheriff Mountjoy went to Helena to obtain an extradition request from Governor Dixon. Then he and Undersheriff Knight left for Missouri. The Missouri governor promptly signed away Montana's fugitive.

"Hello, Johnny," said Roy to Sheriff Mountjoy when he appeared at his cell.

"Hello, Roy," he replied dryly. A guard opened the cell door. Sheriff Mountjoy fixed an Oregon boot to Roy's ankle, handcuffed him, and fixed a chain between the boot and the handcuffs and led Roy out of the cellblock.

"The jig is up. I have not long to live," Roy said as he waved goodbye to his fellow inmates.

The train took them across the country to Butte. They stayed there overnight and would continue to Boulder by car the next morning. When

Sarah heard that Roy was in town, she hurried over to see him. She arrived just as he was getting into the car.

"I'll see you in Boulder," she said.

"I'll see you in hell," he scowled.

Once back in Boulder, Roy held court before a captive audience of Sheriff Mountjoy and his deputies, County Attorney Johnson, and newspapermen from the *Boulder Monitor*, the *Jefferson Valley News*, the *Butte Miner*, and the *Anaconda Standard*, all dying to know just how he pulled it off.

"When did you make your escape?" a reporter asked.

"Right after the new guard came on duty that night," Roy replied.

"How did you get out of the cell?"

The captured Roy Walsh. Sheriff Montjoy is on the left with the overcoat draped over his arm. Undersheriff Knight is on the right, leading Roy out of the Silver Bow County Jail in Butte. Unidentified man behind Roy.

BUTTE MINER, FEBRUARY 14, 1925

[ROY WAS CAPTURED IN MAY OF 1924; THE PICTURE APPEARED IN THE PAPER SEVERAL MONTHS LATER.]

"With a key."

"How did you get the key?"

"I made it."

"How did you know how to make a key that would work? You couldn't even see the lock since it was in a box."

That was easy. Roy explained that during a regular guarded walk in the corridor, he inserted a piece of wood into the lockbox to measure the length of the key. He said he knew instinctively that two teeth were false and the third and fifth teeth were beveled. From this knowledge, he carved a key.

"I don't believe you could carve a key," chided one of the newspapermen.

Roy took up the challenge. Using a pocket knife and some wire, he carved a key from a piece of wood. Then he stood up, reached in the lockbox, and unlocked the cell.

"How could you reach the lockbox from inside the cell?"

This, too, was no insurmountable challenge for the wily lad. He explained how he pulled one of the malleable steel strips from his bunk. Then he fashioned a spindle and windlass from odds and ends he found in his cell, fixed the spindle to the end of the steel, attached the key to the spindle, slipped this fishing pole like contraption through the cell bars and into the lockbox, inserted the key into the lock, pulled the string thereby turning the key, and click, the cell door opened. He locked it after he exited the cell. He also carved a key for the door to the corridor. He entered the corridor while the guard was conveniently outside. Then he walked upstairs to the second floor of the jail and climbed into the attic.

"Did you have any help?"

To that question, Roy was cagey. He tried to finagle a way to use this information as a way of getting a reprieve from his death sentence. While describing and demonstrating his escape, he changed his mind several times as to whether or not he had help. He said Smith had loaned him the key to the door to the corridor, he made a sketch of it, returned the key, and then carved a wooden key for that lock.

Roy also said he waited two days before leaving Boulder hoping to find the man he claimed shot Al Johnson. He said he didn't find him and complained bitterly that it was all Mrs. Sarah Hughes's fault. He said that man had gone to Anaconda because Mrs. Hughes had warned him, if Roy ever got out, he'd be after him.

"Would you like to say anything about the murder of Johnson?" asked a newspaperman.

"I didn't kill him. My gun didn't go off. That was the funny part of it. Someone else who wanted to make a reputation for himself did the firing."

"What do you mean, Roy? Who wanted to make a reputation for himself?"

"Oh, what's the use," said Roy shrugging his shoulders. "It's over now."

Roy still had to be formally sentenced; in short order, he appeared before Judge Bennett. John Elliott wasn't there because Roy had fired him. Judge Bennett said he would not sentence Roy without counsel and appointed the distinguished attorney James Murray of Butte to represent him. Murray prevailed upon Roy to retain John Elliott as his lawyer.

Elliott begged for clemency at the sentencing hearing. He beseeched Judge Bennet to reduce Roy's sentence to life in prison.

Judge Bennett listened carefully and then pronounced: "It is the judgment and sentence of this court that you, Roy Walsh, be punished by death by hanging June 16, 1924, between the hours of four o'clock in the morning and four o'clock in the afternoon of said day." And with a slam of the gavel, he closed the proceedings. The deputy took Roy back to his cell.

Roy spent his days in the jail as he had before: drawing pictures, writing poems, reading magazines. He carved keys to entertain the guards. One of the deputies showed him a padlock. Without examining it, Roy whittled a key from a bone using a razor blade and in five minutes he opened the lock.

He received a letter from Archie and apparently it included a picture. Roy was pleased to hear from him and wrote back.

May 5/24/24

Mr. Arthur Hughes

It's no dream;

You are sure looking fine and according to your letter you are not feeling so bad so they must take good care of you. I just received your letter today and as I was reading it I stumbled over most of the words and guessed the rest so this is my return answer.

Glad to hear that you have made good in the band and not much to do, but; I have got that beat.

I am taken care of like a prize wining stallion and I feel just like one. I get the best of every thing and nothing to worry about and what more could a fellow want.

You speak of me having too mutch nerve for my own good but why not die a man raher than a coward.

Of corse I am going to make the best out of it I can and if I do get a life sentense I am sure it wont be Jack Elliotts fault as the best he can do for me don't amount to mutch.

You ask some odd questions when you asked if I thought if I were out of the Union when I was in Missouri. I didn't think a thing about it; every thing looked so green that I couldn't see how I could be in the United States.

Well, just the same I had quite a trip and there was no grass growing under my feet either so you can see how I enjoyed it.

The Buick I had was a good one and a cheep one to, but I sat behind the wheel and listened to her purr and sing while I glansed over the country ahead and I don't think there was any moss gathered on the tires either.

I left Melrose about eleven oclock at night and was at Leadore Idaho at day break the next morning. I went through Idaho falls and Pocatello, down to Ogden and Saltlake Utah, through some of Arizona deserts and chiped a corner of Nevada and in to the State of Cal.

I first went to Los Angeles and then down to San Deigo and there I went in to the garage business with another fellow and made good of it for about six weeks and then I started east. Through the six weeks there I was over in old Mexico three different times but didn't see any thing to stay for so I came back.

Well after I started east I had the Buick in good trim and a camping outfit. I went through Arizona on in to New Mexico and about two thirds the length of Texas going through El Passo and Fort Worth in to Oaklahoma up across Kansis to Kansis City Mo. out in to middle of Missouri and then I was stopped by mud. I thought I was in the middle of hell and finely I knew it.

There was no mistake that ended my jorney but I was headed for Detroit Mich. Well my plan was to go to Detroit go to work till I got a stake and then hit the hills and work for farmers, and keep out of the way for a year or so figureing to go straight and I would be safe; but my plans were blowed up by some Missourians like Jim Carter, you know him.

. . . So here I am expecting any day to be my last but I havent give up yet and why holler before your hurt. Its all in a life time and experience is wonderfull; but I got to mutch to be good for my health and its acting like a dose of poison on me.

I have written my 'will,' in black and white and going to leave it for any one to read that wants to read it. Well I guess your getting tired of this bull so I will put the cork in the ink bottle, hoping this letter finds there and time to read it.

I send you my good luck and wish you some more and forteen dutchman whip one Irishman and I am the Irishman. Will see you in Hell so good bye good luck and dont get put in jail for there is no place like home. The sooner the beter.

Yours sincerely,
Roy William Walsh

OFO MR. JOHN W. MOUNTJOY
SHERIFF JEFFERSON COUNTY   BOULDER MONTANA

Frank Conly was no longer the prison warden. He had been accused of using his position for personal gain and was removed from his post. He was later acquitted. After he left, the prison went through several wardens in quick succession. Now M. W. Potter was the warden. He intercepted Roy's letter to Archie and sent a copy to someone in the governor's office with this cover letter:

> 5/25 1924
> Dear John: I am enclosing letter from Walsh (convicted murderer) which indicates no remorse for his crime. He is writing his partner Hughes who was implicated with him. Please read it to Gov Dixon as he will soon apply for Executive Clemency.
> He is no doubt a bad egg and should have his neck cracked by modern methods.
> Yours Truly,
> Warden

These days Deputy Johnny Williams had charge of Roy much of the time. Johnny Williams was married to John Mountjoy's sister Ruth. They met when Johnny was a young prospector. He used to pass by the Mountjoy ranch on his way to the blacksmith shop, and there would be Ruth feeding the chickens. Before long, "he was sharpening tools that weren't dull, and she was feeding chickens that weren't hungry." Johnny Williams was a strong, husky man and very likeable. Unlike many of his rural neighbors, he didn't hunt or fish. He couldn't bear to kill anything.

As the days passed, Roy endeared himself more and more to the citizens of Boulder. Al Johnson was long gone, it had been almost a year now; Archie was faraway in Deer Lodge; Roy was right there in Boulder, and a friendly, jovial fellow he was. He gave his captors no trouble. A small jail with a long-term, affable prisoner could almost seem like a boarding house after awhile and become downright chummy. The villain had become flesh and blood, and likeable flesh and blood at that. As time went by, it could be easy to forget what started all this.

As his execution date approached, worry began to invade Roy's calm demeanor. Then in early June, John Elliott filed an appeal to the Montana Supreme Court, and Roy's carefree spirit reemerged. Everybody told him that it could be months before the supreme court heard his case. Not wanting to afford Roy another chance to escape, Sheriff Mountjoy took him to the Montana State Prison in Deer Lodge for safe keeping. The day before they left, the hemp silk rope arrived.

County Attorney Johnson made another attempt to try Smith. He amended the charge to avoid double jeopardy, now charging Smith with "voluntarily permitting the escape of a prisoner in custody" while a deputy sheriff. Smith pled not guilty. His lawyers filed a demurrer saying the amended charge did not conform to the law, the facts did not constitute a public offense, and the court had no jurisdiction.

IN THE FALL, the Montana Supreme Court considered Roy's appeal. The ruling came down two days before Christmas. The court observed that, without the confession, the prosecution had no case against Roy Walsh; however, they found no reason to exclude the confession. The court ruled that it found no justification for a new trial. Roy's conviction and sentence stood. Those witnesses John Elliott claimed were vital to Roy's defense were never found or wouldn't talk. He had ten days in which to request another hearing.

CHAPTER FORTY-EIGHT

THE NEXT BOMBSHELL came by way of Deer Lodge.

"I did it," Archie announced to the world. "I shot Al Johnson. Roy Walsh didn't do it."

This sent Sheriff Mountjoy, County Attorney Johnson, a court reporter, and a gaggle of newspapermen scurrying to Deer Lodge.

"I went to the front of the store while Roy went to the side," he told them. "Then I went round to the side and saw Roy with his rifle pointed toward the bushes. Roy stepped backward and his rifle fired and Roy ran. Then I ran around to the door and shot Johnson with my six-shooter."

Right through a closed door.

"My, weren't you brave to stay when your friend ran away," said one of the men.

Then they interviewed Roy. "Tell us again what happened," said Howard Johnson.

"A shot came past my head," said Roy. "I don't know where it came from or who shot it. I ran away. I never fired my rifle."

It was a valiant try on Archie's part but nobody was buying it. Had he been able to convince the authorities that he shot Al Johnson, his sentence wouldn't have changed since he could not be tried again for the same crime. After interviewing the two of them separately, Howard Johnson issued this statement:

> Walsh is very stolid and hard, and Hughes is very nervous, so that it is impossible to imagine Walsh running and Hughes remaining after the shot was fired; even now Walsh betrays no nervousness.
>
> Although the steel jacket burst as the bullet spattered on hitting the door, the fragment taken from Johnson's body is heavier than the .38 caliber revolver bullet of any length or make . . . no credence can be placed on the story.

John Elliott filed a petition for another hearing with the Montana Supreme Court. He returned to the weight of the bullet arguing that it was too light to have come from Roy's 30-30 Marlin. In reviewing the application, the attorney general concluded that fragments of the bullet could have come off on impact; therefore the bullet weight argument was inconclusive. The petition was denied.

Meanwhile, Sheriff Mountjoy made arrangements to borrow the gallows from Butte, those being the more merciful trap door type which brought death much quicker than Boulder's old weight-operated gallows last used back in 1890.

In early January, Sheriff Mountjoy returned to Deer Lodge to retrieve Roy. As they left the prison, Roy handed the warden a written statement. It was another signed confession. The details of events leading up to Renova were almost identical to those in the confession used in court, except in this one, Roy said it was all Archie Hughes's idea. Archie wanted to rob the store, Roy didn't. Archie wanted to use guns, Roy didn't. Roy did as Archie wanted. Roy said there was another man around the store at the same time. He described how this other man and Archie walked around the store. "I just reached the other side and was in front of a door when Johnson opened it. The light shone through the door, so I stepped back by some vines and the shot was fired. As it was a surprise to me, I ran for my car. When I got there, I found all my ignition wires pulled out from the switch."

Sheriff Mountjoy and Roy stopped in Butte for lunch en route to Boulder. John Elliott came to see Roy at Sheriff Duggan's office. Roy told him there was a third man with them that night in Renova and he named the man. Roy said this third man and Archie robbed Al Johnson and those two were there when Al was shot, not Roy.

(When the neighbor Sherman Shrauger asked Al Johnson whether his assailants came into the store, he shook his head no. He was not robbed that night.)

John Elliott walked out of the sheriff's office with Roy and Sheriff Mountjoy. As Roy climbed into the car for the ride to Boulder, he said to Elliott, "You might as well put the rope around my neck and finish the job."

Back in Boulder, Sheriff Mountjoy locked Roy in his old cell. Roy stretched out on the familiar cot. The bang, bang, bang of carpenters hammering the scaffold sounded in the background.

Johnny Williams brought Roy a letter. It was from his aunt. He read it and asked for stationary and wrote this reply.

> Dear Aunt:-
>   I just received your welcome letter to-day and was mutch surprised to hear from you.
>   I did not want my trouble to be known around there so that is the reason why I did not try to locate you . . . The woman that took me from my Grandma is the cause of my being where I am today . . . I got in with a crooked family and they have framed up on me to this point . . . this woman who took me from Grandma was not my mother . . . She only took me to ruin my life . . . I have did wrong Aunt, but I am not guilty of murder and God knows that as well as myself.

He went on to say that he had never been sick a day in his life and had never used tobacco, alcohol, or drugs.

Roy's mother knew about his situation. His stepfather wrote to County Attorney Johnson. I never saw the letter, but it reportedly said Roy never had a chance. He had been on his own since he was eight or nine years old.

ON JANUARY 13, 1925, Deputy Johnny Williams handcuffed Roy to himself and with two guards took Roy to the courthouse across the street. Roy smiled to the crowd seated in the courtroom, there to witness the next chapter in his saga.

Roy chatted with Johnny Williams while they waited for the judge. He asked about the elderly man they had passed in the jail.

"His case hasn't come up yet," replied Johnny Williams. "He's a bootlegger. As it's his second offense, he'll probably be sent to the penitentiary."

"That isn't right," said Roy. "He's too old a man to go down there."

Judge Bennett entered. All stood, court was called to order, all sat. Judge Bennett ordered Roy to rise. He stood alone without counsel. Judge Bennett briefly summarized the case: the murder charge, the trial, the conviction, the escape, his capture, the supreme court appeal. When he finished he asked, "Roy Walsh, have you any legal cause why the judgment of the court should not be carried out?"

"Yes, I have," replied Roy coolly. "Your Honor, I feel that in justice, Arthur Hughes, who was my partner—," his voice broke—"we were there together at Renova. I don't see why he should get off with the sentence he got and I take the heavy end of it."

Judge Bennett listened and then replied, "The court came to the conclusion that the verdict of the jury in your case was a proper one."

He added that it was not his purpose to give a lecture on the punishment given to Roy Walsh or Arthur Hughes.

"There appearing no legal reason why the sentence should not be carried out, it is the order of the court to proceed with the execution on February 14 between the hours of one o'clock in the morning and one o'clock in the afternoon, and that you shall be hanged by the neck until you are dead."

Johnny Williams led Roy out of the courtroom, down the stairs, and across the snow covered street to the jail. Once inside, Roy spoke to the cortege of reporters that had followed him from the courthouse. When asked about what had just transpired, Roy said, "I'm ready. It's got to go one way or the other, but there never was a crime committed and an innocent man condemned but that the name of that man was cleared sooner or later . . . I don't know who killed Albert Johnson at Renova. If a bullet from my gun struck him, the gun was discharged accidentally. There are those who know about the Renova affair, but they say nothing, figuring if my neck is cracked everything will be fine and dandy. I was framed. Those I thought were friends conspired against me . . . The bullet taken out of Johnson did not weigh as much as the slug my gun carries.

"It isn't fair that Hughes gets off. He knows more about this than he's saying. He's too scared. I had no intention of harming Johnson. It was Hughes's suggestion that we rob him. I agreed to it but didn't believe Hughes would go through with it . . . I thought somebody was shooting at me and I also thought perhaps my gun had gone off accidentally, having caught in the vines . . ."

Then Roy complained bitterly about the man who furnished the guns for the holdup. "He double crossed me," he grumbled. He expressed ever more disdain for Archie. About Sarah, he griped, "I don't care if I ever see her. She never did me any good."

"Roy, have you given up hope?" asked a reporter.

"Nope. I'm not dead yet," he replied.

When the reporter mentioned the heavy guard placed on him, Roy said, "No, I won't try to escape again. I'm a little bit sore at myself. I had my chance once and I didn't make use of it. Now I'll stay and see 'er through."

Rumor had it John Elliott was absent from court that day because he had not received notice of the hearing. When asked by a reporter about his client's all but certain fate, he declared, "I still believe Walsh is inno-cent and I will make every effort to save him. I don't think that Walsh is a confirmed criminal. He doesn't smoke, drink, or gamble, and has no vi-cious habits. Furthermore, he is not lazy . . . I don't believe Walsh fired the shot that killed Johnson, and I don't believe Hughes knows who did. If Walsh were given a chance, he could make good. "

If he were *given* a chance? Roy said himself that he had a chance to make good and chose not to, even with a noose hanging over his head. I think for Roy it was always a game of cat and mouse. The idea of conse-quences was never real to him. And it was a lot of attention for an aban-doned boy, and judging from that letter he wrote to Archie, he thoroughly enjoyed it. A prize winning stallion indeed.

Back in the Boulder jail Roy turned into a real chatterbox. He spent his days visiting with the guards and deputies. None of them mentioned the looming event, but Roy spoke of it often. He joked to Johnny Will-iams, "I'll tell St. Peter all about the gallows."

The other prisoner, the elderly bootlegger, bored and looking for some-thing to do, told Deputy Williams that he was good at sawing wood. "Do you have any wood you need sawed?" he asked.

"Yes," Roy interjected, "go out there and saw that —— thing down."

Roy wrote to Governor Erickson. He said his lawyer had not been "true to his word" and had failed to prove his innocence. He said the holdup was all Mrs. Hughes's idea. He said he didn't want to use guns but Archie insisted. Before they left Cedar Hill, Archie put a rifle on the front seat of his car. "When getting out I had to push the rifle out ahead of me, so I took it with me." He said a bullet shot past his head. He ran to the car, the ignition wires had been pulled, Archie's car was still there. He accused John Elliott of furnishing Archie's gun. He said he was double crossed, to be the goat . . .

> I have did wrong and I know it, so I am willing to take my punish-ment for it because I know I have got it coming, but I have not did any-thing so bad, I don't believ, that I should hang. It don't seem justice that Hughes sould get the least punishment, and me get the extream penalty even if I had have fired the shot; because Hughes was there to commit crime as well as myself.
>
> I deserve good punishment for my acts and I am willing to except it, but I am praying that I can just have one more chance to make good and to prove myself a true citizen.

I am sure that your judgement will be true; so if I hang; Hughes should hang to; and if you don't hang Hughes for God sake don't hang me. I feel that this is justice, so please give me a chance to make good. I have been out in the world for myself since I was 8 years old, and not one to help me.

I am asking your mercy on my part, and hope that you will understand everything as I do. I will close with full trust and hope that you will have mercey on me.

I remain
Very Truly Yours
Roy W. Walsh

Governor John Erickson had just taken office that month, so Roy's case, an appeal for a reprieve from the death penalty which must be one of the most difficult decisions any governor makes, was one of the first decisions he had to make as governor. Erickson was quite familiar with the criminal justice system having been a county attorney and judge. He replied promptly to Roy's letter: "If you have any new evidence, not presented to the judge and jury, I will thoroughly examine it."

Now Montana's legislators were embroiled in the case. Representative Joffray of Jefferson County presented a bill requiring all legal executions be carried out at the state prison in Deer Lodge rather than in the county seat where the crime occurred. The citizens of Boulder did not want Roy Walsh executed in their town. The representative from Powell County, where Deer Lodge is located, and others fiercely debated against the bill. The scaffold would have to be erected in the prison yard, they argued, and even if enclosed, it would be demoralizing for the prisoners and depressing for the people of Deer Lodge every time there was an execution. The deterrent effect of capital punishment is better realized by having the executions carried out in the county where the crime was committed, they said. The more people aware of executions, the more will think twice before committing a heinous act.

The bill went down to defeat.

The newspapers said John Elliott circulated a petition far and wide asking the governor to commute Roy's sentence to life in prison. One report said the petition contained five hundred signatures from Butte alone. Rumor had it John Elliott even asked Morgan Johnson to sign it. He was Al Johnson's brother and had purchased the store in Renova and was now running it. I was curious to know who did sign it. I found no petition in the governor's files.

According to the newspaper, John Elliott did travel to Helena to make a personal plea for clemency to the governor. He brought his firearms witness with him. He insisted that the bullet was too light to have come from Roy's rifle, and that it was shot straight through the door, not from the side. Since Roy had been on the side of the house, he couldn't have fired the fatal shot.

He showed the governor drawings of a perpetual motion machine which he said Roy had designed. He said he had applied for a patent for it on Roy's behalf, and there was still a secret to the design that only Roy knew. He said it was but one example of what Roy could do. He pleaded with the governor to spare Roy's life and let him live the rest of his days in prison.

Scores of people from across the country wrote to the Montana governor on Roy's behalf. Letters and telegrams came from an insurance salesman in New Jersey, a woman in Seattle, a civil war veteran in Syracuse, and from men and women throughout Montana. The impassioned and often eloquent pleas poured forth:

> He is so young. Life in prison will give him time to reflect and save his soul. Many are victims of hereditary and environment . . .

> So many part and their children are thrown into the world . . .

> One juror told me Walsh's sentence would have been different had they known Archie Hughes would not stand trial.

> You and I have had the good fortune of having had good mothers and good fathers who reprimanded us when we needed it, and admonished us to always seek good company. Did Walsh? No, he was thrown to the care of a ruthless woman who has as much knowledge of God's laws as a dog would have.

> He should be punished for sins indulged while conscience slept . . . that conscience had never been awakened by the voice of love. Commute his sentence to life, the same as young Hughes.

If only such entreaties could be levied on behalf of the victim before the crime.

A Jefferson County commissioner wrote that he investigated the crime scene, and he was absolutely certain that the shot fired through the door and the shot that killed Al Johnson could not have been fired from the same weapon. (Where was he during the trial?)

One woman alleged there was a third member of the group, and it was unfair that he, an ex-convict who had threatened Al Johnson before witnesses, roam free. She named the fourth suspect as counsel for the defense. "Walsh unwittingly placed his life in the hands of a perfidious traitor," she fumed.

Yet another missive said Fred D—— had offered to spring the trap.

A letter came from lawyer James Murray of Butte. While he believed that Roy had been rightfully convicted, owing to his youth, his appearance and demeanor, and believing he never intended to kill, he urged Governor Erickson to commute Roy's sentence to life in prison.

Deputy Johnny Williams visited the governor to plead for clemency for Roy and he wrote to the governor twice. His lengthy first letter was strongly worded. He said he examined the crime scene, and he was about the same height as Al Johnson, and he could not get into a position where a bullet blasting through the door at an upward angle could enter the neck and drive into the chest cavity. He too believed someone else was involved and had not been brought to justice. Governor Erickson responded that he had heard nothing from the jurors. If any of them in hindsight believed the verdict unjust, they should write and tell him so. None did.

The resounding sentiment expressed in these letters and telegrams was: *Yes, this boy did wrong, but it isn't right that he pay with his life while his partner goes to prison. They are equally guilty. Either both should hang or both go to prison. There is good in this boy, let him live out his life in prison. The boy never had a chance. He fell in with bad company, that Hughes woman. The boy never had a chance, never had a chance because he fell in with the notorious Sarah Hughes.*

Well what of Aila Hughes? She was raised by the notorious Sarah Hughes. Couldn't it be said that she never had a chance? She made her chance. "There are set before you fire and water; to whichever you chose, stretch forth your hand." Aila, Archie, Roy, Bill, Arthur, Sarah—they all did the same. They chose. Aila chose differently.

Governor Erickson promptly responded to each letter with the assurance that he was giving the case every consideration. To one woman he wrote: "I shall be glad indeed if I can find some way to commute his sentence."

Others urged that he leave the case be. "The people of Silver Bow County would do well to attend to their own murderers," wrote one man. "The verdict of the jury should stand. Too many pardons have been handed out of late."

A girl came to the jail to visit Roy. She implored him to talk to Father Franchi or Reverend Smith. Please, Roy, please, what'll it hurt? Roy had declined all offers by clergymen to visit him. The girl persisted until he agreed to meet with the minister and the priest.

Roy's mood floated from joking to bitterness to joking. He cautioned the workmen outside pounding the final nails into the scaffold, "Better be careful up there or somebody is liable to get hurt on that thing."

Then he grumbled to Johnny Williams, "Mrs. Hughes tried to poison me when I went to her after I escaped. The robbery was her idea."

Later in the day Johnny Williams unlocked and entered his cell. "Another pie for you, Roy," he said. The women of Boulder were deluging him with cookies, cakes, pies. Friends from Butte sent candy. A woman in Butte sent him a rosary. He draped it over the corner of his cot, not knowing what it was for.

Johnny Williams's wife, Ruth, took their children to stay with her parents in Cardwell until it was over.

Father Franchi and Reverend Smith visited Roy. He wanted to talk about anything except what he was facing. Father Franchi encouraged him to be baptized. He said he would but then changed his mind.

The evening of Thursday, February 12, Roy played cards late into the night. Reverend Smith visited him again. He enjoined Roy to kneel and pray with him. They did for several minutes. Then Reverend Smith left. Shortly after midnight, a dog howled. "That's a sure sign somebody is going to die," said Roy and he stretched out on his cot and went to sleep.

The next morning, Friday, February 13, a newspaperman who had become a frequent visitor came to see Roy.

"Any news from the governor?" he asked.

"No," Roy replied, "but luck has been with me all along, I don't think it will desert me now."

Later in the morning his mood shifted. He told George, the guard, "I guess I'll be on the banks of the big river pretty soon. But maybe I can't get across."

"Can't you swim?" asked George.

"Sure, but maybe I'll forget how."

The telegram arrived at eleven o'clock that morning. Roy was taking a nap. Sheriff Mountjoy let him sleep. When he awoke, he handed it to him.

"If it's got to be, it's got to be. I'm ready," said Roy, and he read the telegram.

I have today denied the petition for commutation of sentence in the case of Roy Walsh.

J. E. Erickson
Governor

Roy spent the rest of the day writing letters and poems. He diligently finished his final statement in time for the newspaper deadline. It was a lengthy treatise, most of which was an ode to the horse. He closed it with this advice,

> . . . Remember, there is a God. You will meet him some day, though you never see nor hear Him now. And He wants you to have love and kindness in your heart for every faithful creature.
>
> This should be a lesson to all young fellows who are now free—don't think that you are in the crooked game too deep to quit. If you should be doing it or have done it, just drop all dishonesty and forget about it, because if you don't you will end up as I have . . .
>
> All young fellows who want help will get it from Dr. C. L. Clifford, minister at the Mountain View church. He will give help supreme and free.
>
> Good-bye, good luck to the world. I hope it will prosper and every living creature.

The Reverend C.L. Clifford was pastor of Mountain View Methodist Church in Butte. He was famous for delivering rousing, eloquent sermons. Extra chairs had to be brought in to accommodate the large crowds. He preached a sermon using Roy's situation as a stark lesson to deter young men from a life of crime. Roy heard about it and asked for a copy which the reverend sent. Roy liked the sermon and wrote to thank him. He signed the letter Albert Wallace Schoonover.

Roy received another letter from his aunt. She blamed Roy's mother for ruining his life. If he had never been taken away by his mother, none of this would have happened, she lamented. "Why didn't you write to us when she deserted you?" she implored. "We would have sent you money for the train." He wrote back and signed the letter Albert Schoonover.

He asked Johnny Williams to send for the barber. Then he wrote a letter to the girl who had visited him: "I shall always love you as a sister. I shall always remember you."

The barber arrived. He trimmed Roy's hair and shaved his beard. "Doll me up as pretty as possible," he quipped with a wink. "I want to make a good appearance. First impressions are so important."

He told Sheriff Mountjoy that he was leaving his last few dollars to him. Then he ate dinner and lay down for another nap.

He woke up later in the evening. Reverend Smith arrived, then Father Franchi, then the newspapermen. Roy reasserted his innocence. "I'm the goat," he said. "I've gone this far with it, I guess I can go the rest." Then he changed the subject.

Sheriff Mountjoy brought more visitors to his cell. Roy asked, "When's my party coming off, Johnny?"

"About two o'clock," said the sheriff.

"All right," said Roy.

John Elliott had said his goodbye to Roy that afternoon. He didn't stay to witness the execution.

It was now the middle of the night. A light snow fell on the dimly lit jail yard. The witnesses quietly assembled.

Roy was sitting in his cell, feet propped up on the table, eating an orange, when Sheriff Mountjoy came for him.

"Have you got everything done that you want, Roy?" Sheriff Mountjoy asked in his steady, quiet voice.

"I guess so, Johnny," Roy replied.

"Here are the doctors. They will give you something for your nerves. How are they?"

"They seem pretty good."

One of the doctors offered him a drug.

"To hell with that stuff," Roy said, "I don't need any."

He finished the orange, stood, and wiped his hands on a paper.

"Are you ready?" asked Sheriff Mountjoy.

"All ready and all right, I guess." Roy turned to the guard, shook his hand, and said, "Goodbye, George, and be good. Tell the girls many thanks for the pies and cakes they sent me."

Sheriff Mountjoy fixed straps around Roy's wrists and waist. They walked out of the jail, Roy between Sheriff Mountjoy and Deputy Johnny Williams followed by Sheriff Smith of Gallatin County and a Silver Bow County deputy. They crossed the yard to the scaffold and mounted the stairs. The pit beneath the scaffold was draped with canvas. Sheriff Mountjoy wrapped straps around Roy's knees and ankles. Johnny Williams bent down and tightened the straps around Roy's legs. Sheriff Smith examined the straps, then he and Johnny Williams walked down the stairs.

Sheriff Mountjoy asked Roy, "Do you want to say anything?"

"Well, gentlemen, I might as well say goodbye to you all," Roy said.

"I'm leaving you now and I don't wish any ill will to nobody and I hope that you and everybody else in this world prospers. I guess that's about all I got to say. Goodbye."

"Do you want to wear a mask?" Sheriff Mountjoy whispered.

"No," Roy replied.

John slipped the noose over Roy's head and adjusted the knot. Then he pressed a button on the scaffold. This signaled Johnny Williams who pulled the lever which sprang the trap.

The dogs howled.

CHAPTER FORTY-NINE

CLAIRE WAS A teenager then. She told me no one went to bed that night. "How could they?" she said. Her cousin George, the guard, witnessed the execution. "He came home white as a sheet," she said.

Her brother was a guard too. Roy offered to give him his shoes, but he didn't take them. He was superstitious about wearing a dead man's shoes.

Grandma maintained until her dying day that there was another man at Renova that night and he killed Al Johnson, not Roy Walsh. She said he was the Son of a Somebody from Butte and his name was kept out of it.

As I said before, Grandma was always very careful about what she said, and she was not prone to conjecture nor was she one to dramatize things. Her life was dramatic and traumatic enough, it needed no embellishment. She was a woman who dealt in facts and was very discerning, and in those cases where I have been able to uncover more of the story, the whole of it turned out to be more dramatic than what she said.

There is no question that Archie and Roy were there, they were armed, they were trying to rob Al Johnson, and he was killed in the process, and Grandma never made excuses for her brother's bad behavior. However, the facts do make one wonder if there was more to the story. This business about Smith—who put up his bond? Who paid his lawyers—two high profile, well-connected, out-of-town lawyers? Friends perhaps? If so, very generous, well-heeled friends. I can't help but wonder if Boulder's young county attorney felt a little blind-sided by all that.

It also strikes me as odd that Archie's confession was nowhere to be found.

And there's that ex-con loitering late into the night at Al Johnson's store.

If there was somebody else involved, and somebody connected with this Son of a Somebody told Roy keep your mouth shut and we'll get you out—it worked. He did get out. And then the fellow who allegedly helped him got some pretty high-powered help. Had Roy lain low and stayed out of trouble, chances are he never would have been caught. Both he and Smith would have gone free. Two months after Roy was hanged, the case against Smith was dismissed.

And as for John Elliott, you may have wondered if he was any relation to Tom Elliott, Sarah's handyman turned husband back in Forsyth. I wonder the same thing.

Mr. Fessenden wrote his final epitaph on the case in the next issue of the *Jefferson Valley News*:

> If life imprisonment meant "life imprisonment" there might be more in favor of that brand of punishment. But under the present law, a criminal who has killed a man in cold blood, with malice aforethought, with robbery as a purpose, knows that not one in a hundred are compelled to pay the supreme penalty. He also knows that a sentence to the state penitentiary means only a few years of incarceration and that if his record while so incarcerated is good he will, in all probability, be paroled after serving less than twenty years.

That was written in 1925. *Tous ça change, tous c'est la meme chose.* Everything changes and everything stays the same.

THREE YEARS LATER John Mountjoy was appointed secretary of state for Montana. His brother-in-law Johnny Williams succeeded him as Jefferson County sheriff and would remain in that post for twenty-eight years. Howard Johnson was appointed assistant U.S. district attorney and later became chief justice of the Montana Supreme Court.

As for Renova, the little whistle stop is gone now and, with it, the Johnson store. Cessation of mining in Alder Gulch obviated its only reason for being.

And as for Archie, he served his time, and he never got into trouble again.

PART SIX

Angel in the Whirlwind

CHAPTER FIFTY

BILL'S FINAL FORAY into lawlessness, as far as I know, came in the middle of all this. He went to Deer Lodge that summer, probably to visit Archie and Roy at the prison, and while there, he met a girl. I'll call her Lena. In early December, Lena appeared at Sarah's doorstep with a friend I'll call Anna Belle. The next day Bill and Lena were married; Miss Hamry, a spiritualist minister and friend of Sarah's, officiated. James Rigley stood up for Bill. Sarah was calling herself Ellen Rigley at the time, so I take it she and James Rigley were married, though I never found proof of said union.

A few days after Bill and Lena wed, Anna Belle married one of Bill's friends, a fellow named Herbert. The four newlyweds settled blissfully in Sarah's house until all was told in the newspaper about six weeks later. As it turned out, the girls were runaways from the children's home in Helena. They had snuck out of the home, took a taxi all the way to Alhambra, walked fifteen miles to Boulder, then took the train to Butte, and walked to 516 East Park Street. This somehow came to light when Anna Belle didn't come home one night and Herbert went looking for her and found her with Mose W—— in a room on Colorado Street.

Lena was only thirteen years old. Bill was twenty-six. What do we call him, a serial Svengali? As with his first illegal marriage, the only punishment he received was losing his wife.

The same day all this came out in the newspaper, Sarah found herself in Judge Lynch's court. No, not as a defendant, as a defense witness for a couple of career criminal defendants, Fred W—— and Willard B——, who stood accused of robbery. Mr. and Mrs. Mose W—— were also defense witnesses, and the defense lawyer, you guessed it, was John Elliott.

As FOR AILA and Peter, life went along smoothly and quietly in Portland. No more violent altercations occurred in the neighborhood. Their worst near disaster was when Aila Rose tumbled out of a first floor window. "Thankfully, the bush broke her fall," Aila said.

Aila liked Portland, and she was especially happy that Peter was working steadily. She enjoyed caring for the children in the nursery school. The extra income was a help. She enjoyed seeing her father.

Then Peter quit his job. Arthur found him another job, this one in the new Palmolive soap factory. He didn't like the smell. He came home one day and announced, "I'm on my way." He had quit his job and was returning to Butte. He picked up a few things and left. Aila was dumbfounded, and she was pregnant.

Now also distraught, she went to see her father. "Peter just quit and left for Butte. I didn't even know he was going until he came in the door and said I'm on my way and picked up a few things and away he was gone to Butte."

"Stay here, Aila," Arthur counseled. "You can't count on that Irishman."

She couldn't go anyway; she didn't have enough money. And she wasn't about to land in Butte without a penny to her name as she had in Portland. So she stayed and continued to run the nursery school and save money. Peter worked in the mines in Butte. He sent her money for a little while, soon it slowed to a trickle, and then it stopped. "Peter Thompson decided he wanted to start gambling again," she said, her voice drooping in sorrow. "He started gambling and he never sent me a penny for food for Aila Rose or me, so it's a good thing I did decide I couldn't depend on him for sure."

Peter wrote, begging her to come to Butte. "I'm so lonesome," he moaned. He didn't send her any money so she could come. She wrote back: "I'm not going to do what I did when I came here. When I came here you quit and went back to Butte and left me stranded. I'm not coming to Butte until I have enough money saved up to take care of the baby and myself."

Aila and Aila Rose
Portland, Oregon

A WOMAN'S ANSWER

Do you know you have asked for the costliest thing
    Ever made by the Hand above?
A woman's heart and a woman's life—
    And a woman's wonderful love?

Do you know you have asked for this priceless thing
    As a child might ask for a toy?
Demanding what others have died to win,
    With the reckless dash of a boy?

You have written my lesson of duty out—
    Man-like you have questioned me;
Now stand at the bar of a woman's soul
    Until I shall question thee.

You require your mutton shall always be hot,
    Your socks and shirts be whole;
I require your heart to be true as God's stars,
    And pure as heaven your soul.

You require a cook for your mutton and beef,
    I require a far greater thing;
A seamstress you're wanting for socks and shirts,
    I look for a man and a king.

A king for the beautiful realm called home,
    And a man that the Maker, God
Shall look upon as He did on the first
    And say, "It is very good."

I am young and fair, but the rose will fade
    From my soft young cheek one day—
Will you love me then 'mid the falling leaves
    As you did 'mong the blooms of May?

I require all things that are good and true,
    All things that a man should be;
If you give this all I will stake my life
    To be all you demand of me.

If you can not be this—a laundress and cook
    You can hire and have little to pay;
But a woman's heart and a woman's life
    Are not to be won that way.

                    —Mary T. Lathrap

When finally she had saved enough money and planned to go, the women whose children attended the nursery school banded together and offered to pay her considerably more if she would stay, but she wouldn't.

AILA DELIVERED their second child in November of 1925 at Sarah's house with a doctor attending. After freeing herself from the womb, the tiny baby lay limp and lifeless, not even a whimper.

It's a girl, said the doctor, but I'm afraid she's dead.

Sarah stood by in her usual no-nonsense, hands-on-hips pose, wearing her ever-present full apron over a floor length dress. Give me that child, she demanded, and without waiting, she scooped up the infant in a towel. She took her and I don't know what she did, massaged her or what, but soon the tiny arms and legs started to move. The baby let out a weak cry. She was awfully small, but she was fine. Sarah cleaned and swaddled her and handed her to Aila.

Aila named her second daughter Mavis Eleanor. She thought Mavis was the most beautiful name she had ever heard. She had a friend named Mavis. Eleanor was Sarah's *nom du jour* around that time.

In early January, Peter took the baby to St. Patrick's to be baptized. Naturally the family was there, but Aila wasn't. She was sick and unable to go.

When the priest asked the child's name, Peter said, Mavis Eleanor.

Mavis Eleanor! his sister Mary interjected. No one in our family has that name. You can't name her that! You must give her another name. Grace. You'll name her Grace, for my Aunt Grace, and Elizabeth for my Aunt Annie. You'll name her Grace Elizabeth.

So she was Grace Elizabeth.

THOUGH THE ROARING twenties were in full swing, the vibrant economy would not bring the Butte mines back to even pre-war levels. The bloom was gone from the

Aila Rose holding doll, Aila holding Grace. Winter of 1925–26.

Aila Rose and Sarah

mining boom, the industry was now fully mature, boom and bust had settled into a happy medium. In 1925, production slipped a little. The next year would see a slight increase. Work at individual mines fluctuated; however, all in all, even though the overall volume wasn't what it had been, the Butte mines hummed along steadily through the rest of the 1920s and wages remained stable.

On a typical day when he was working day shift, Peter got up in the morning, had his toast and tea, went to work with his lunch bucket tucked under his arm, worked an eight-hour shift at the mine, came home, read until dinner, ate dinner with Aila and the children, and then went out for the rest of the evening to a saloon to play cards. When he worked night shift, he ate

Peter's brother-in-law Gilbert, nephew Gilbert, friend Barney, and Peter

Aila Rose, Aila holding Grace, 1926

Aila Rose, Peter holding Grace

Aila, Grace, and Aila Rose on the lawn
at Columbia Gardens

Aila Rose and Grace on lawn
at Columbia Gardens

dinner with Aila and the children, went to work, came home, slept, got up, had his toast and tea, and then went out to play cards until dinnertime. His favorite haunt was the Board of Trade. It was open twenty-four hours a day like the rest of the saloons in Butte, and he didn't go there to drink, he went there to gamble. His favorite game was panguingue and he always played for money. There was gambling everywhere in Butte even though it was illegal. Even in the back of a supposed-to-be jewelry store you could gamble. A person could bet on all kinds of things, even solitaire. Saloons took bets on how many days it would or wouldn't rain in June.

Then there were days when Peter came home in the middle of his shift spitting nails. So-and-so did or said this or that, so I quit! He was a hot-head. He'd get in a spat with the boss and then quit or be fired. A friend of his once said to Aila, "If he's the same at home as he is in the mines, I don't know how you stand him."

Sometimes Peter got another job the next day, sometimes it took awhile. Plus there was the gambling. Aila couldn't do much to supplement their unpredictable income since she had a newborn and a toddler at home. All she could do was scrimp and save and stretch what little money she had for food and rent. Night after night, they ate macaroni and canned tomatoes for dinner. It was all she could afford. When Peter wasn't working, she couldn't afford meat. When he was working, she made stew. Peter didn't seem to mind, it suited him. However, the children were awfully small. And again, Aila had no milk for the baby. She always put Peter and the children first. She was probably malnourished. If only Peter could get a steady job, if only he would keep a steady job, she lamented to herself, and only to herself. Her face to the world and to the children said, all is well. That was what she tried to project; however, worry wore on her. This beautiful woman who before had always looked impeccable without a hair out of place, now rarely had a hair in place and looked worn and disheveled.

Peter came home one day and raided the jar in which Aila kept the grocery money. "Peter, I need that money to buy food for the children," she said.

"My father needs it," he replied and took the money.

Then one day the miracle Aila had long hoped for appeared on the horizon. Uncle John Gribben announced that he had arranged a job for Peter as a pumpman. This was a godsend. Pumpmen *always* worked, strike or no strike, copper market up or down, it didn't matter. The pumpmen had to work to keep the mines from flooding. It was one of the steadiest jobs in the mines. Aila was elated. Peter's sister-in-law was irate. Peter shouldn't get that job, she complained, he doesn't work anyway, my husband should get that job. She went on and on complaining until Peter grew tired of listening to her and capitulated. All right, he can have it, Peter said, and gave the job to his brother. Aila was hurt, disappointed, and the more she thought about it, furious.

CHAPTER FIFTY-ONE

AILA'S SISTER, Patsy, had grown up to be a quiet, somewhat timid, young woman. She was shy around strangers and a bit of a homebody. In photographs, she often looks as if she wished she wasn't there; one who wore glasses and was glad to have that barrier between her and the world. She lived with Sarah and Bill and their boarders on East Park Street. She worked as a clerk and sometimes babysat for Aila.

In October of 1926, Patsy married Carl Morgan. She was nineteen, and he was twenty-nine. They obtained the marriage license and were married before a judge the same day. Sarah stood up for Patsy, calling herself Mrs. Eleanor Mitchell, so I take it she sanctioned this marriage which is surprising considering the lengths she went to to try to stop Aila from getting married. Carl was born in West Virginia and was new to Butte. Morgan is a fairly common Welsh name, and West Virginia being coal mining country, it's a good guess his people were Welsh.

Carl and Patsy moved into a little place on East Platinum Street, and Carl worked in the mines. A few months after they married, they left Butte. As the story goes, Carl told Patsy that he would take her to California to be in pictures. I wonder if Patsy coaxed him into it. The train stopped in Salt Lake City. Carl got off the train and never got back on, at least that's how I heard the story. Grandma said Patsy married him to get away from their mother, which makes me wonder who ditched whom. Patsy got back on the train and kept going all the way to San Francisco. She stepped off the train and walked and walked until she saw a help-wanted sign for a waitress. She went in. The owner hired her, and years later, after she obtained a divorce, married her. She never returned to Butte. She never saw her mother again.

A couple of curious notes about Patsy's marriages. Both times she and her intended obtained their marriage license and were married the same

Patsy and Sarah Hughes

day (both times in October). The marriage license in Butte said she was a year older than she was (twenty instead of nineteen); the one in California said she was two years older (twenty-six instead of twenty-four). Under place of birth for her parents, the certificate in California says "unknown." As for her own place of birth, her license in Montana says Butte, her certificate in California says Wilkes-Barre. Neither say Rosebud County.

Around the time Patsy left Butte, Bill left. He never returned either, and he never saw their mother again.

PETER AND AILA and the children lived on South Dakota Street for awhile. Then they moved to a little house on John Street. Peter worked at the Bell Mine. Aila Rose attended kindergarten at St. John's School. The next year they moved to a small flat on Nevada Street. Sarah lived a few blocks away. Aila Rose attended first grade at the Monroe School.

Aila Rose came home from school one day to find her father there but not her mother. "Where is my mother?" she demanded. "She's run off with a soldier," said Peter from behind his newspaper. Aila Rose burst into tears and didn't stop crying until her mother came home.

Peter was home because he was out of work again. Aila did her best to juggle caring for her daughters while doing what she could to earn some income. When Grace was still a baby, she took a part-time job as a clerk at the Family Drug. Before that, she stretched curtains, took in laundry, cleaned houses, this in addition to keeping her own house which alone was an exhausting job in those days. She washed clothes, sheets, and towels in a tub with a clothes stomper, there being no washing machine. She made soap, to purchase it was too dear. She made all the children's clothes, including their coats. She wove straw hats for them. She soled their shoes. Every night she dropped into bed exhausted.

When Aila Rose and Grace were around five or six years old, she began to teach them how to help her with the household chores. She laid a board across two chairs in the kitchen and after she washed a dish she set it on the board, where it was low enough for the girls to reach, and they dried the dishes. She said, "You girls need to learn how to do this because I won't be around much longer." She was sure she wasn't long for this world. She had to teach the girls to be self-sufficient so when she dropped dead, sure to be any day, they could take care of themselves and their father.

Sometimes when Peter was not working and Aila was, he babysat Aila Rose and Grace. Come my little darlin's, he would say, I'll tell you a wee poem. They would climb onto his lap, one on each knee, and he would delight them with, "A bunch of the boys were whooping it up at the Malumet saloon . . . ," or he would launch into a perky jazz number, "*Saloon, saloon, saloon, it runs through my brain like a tune . . .*" He would tell them stories about his life as a boy in Ireland, only nice stories, of course. He taught them to say grace before and after meals in Gaelic.

Aila Rose and Grace knew their mother worked and other children's mothers did not. They knew sometimes their father was home when other fathers weren't, and usually he wasn't home at all, even when other fathers were. They didn't know why. Aila did her best to shield them from any unpleasantness. When she pleaded with Peter to find work, it was when the children were well out of earshot. To Aila Rose and Grace, their father was simply wonderful, and that's the way Aila wanted it.

One day when Peter was out of work, Ann Herzog, a friend of his sister Mary, told him there was a job available where she worked, at the Great Northern Railroad. Peter took the job. Aila was pleased. The railroad offered steady work.

When Christmas came, Peter took the girls to Mass. There was no money for presents. Aila bought an orange for the occasion, and on Christmas morning, she decoratively cut it into three pieces for Peter and the girls to have as a special treat with their breakfast of toast and tea and oatmeal. Then she crawled into bed and spent much of the day there.

SHORTLY AFTER THE Christmas of 1927, Uncle John's wife died. She was thirty-nine and Uncle John was fifty-eight. They had two young children. Everybody was feeling pretty low for Uncle John and the children. Aunt B decided the family needed some cheering up and announced a come-all-ye at her house.

Come my little darlin's, Peter said to Aila Rose and Grace as they readied to go to Aunt B's. Aila bundled them up in their coats, hats, boots, and mittens. Aila Rose and Grace scrambled onto the sled, and Peter pulled them through the snow-covered streets. Aila walked beside him. They chatted as they went. Party or no party, they visited Aunt B every week. She now lived on the Flat. Uncle John visited her every day. He had a car though he didn't drive. His son, Johnny, drove him wherever he wanted to go. Johnny started doing this around age nine.

It was always a joy for Aila to see Aunt B. The two women were kindred souls—gentle, intelligent women with difficult roads to hoe through life. The tiny house was already full of chatter when Peter

Aunt B

and Aila and the children arrived that day. Aila unbundled the girls and sent them to play with their cousins.

Aunt B made the tea and let it steep until it was "strong enough to trot a mouse across." Then she poured the tea and offered plenty of milk and sugar to go in it. Aila helped her butter slices of bread and then sprinkled them with sugar. They gave one to each of the children. This was their treat.

"Peter, give us a song," said Uncle John. Peter happily obliged with "I'll Take You Home Again Kathleen" or "The Maid of the Mill." Aunt B's daughter, Rosemary, provided the piano accompaniment. "Play this," Peter urged placing a sheet of music in front of her. "I can't," she said. "Sure you can," he said, "just try." She played, he sang.

> *Believe me, if all those endearing young charms,*
> *Which I gaze on so fondly today,*
> *Were to change by tomorrow, and fleet in my arms,*
> *Like fairy-gifts fading away, . . .*

Aila and the children listened rapt, mesmerized by his lyrical, tenor voice. Then Rosemary played a waltz. Peter danced with Aila Rose, then with Grace, they stood on his feet. Rosemary played a modern tune and Peter danced an impromptu soft shoe. He danced so light of foot it seemed invisible hands were holding him by the shoulders, helping him defy gravity. Then a recitation, then more tea, then another song, then another poem, then it was time to go home. Aila bundled Aila Rose and Grace into their coats, hats, boots, and mittens. They thanked and kissed Aunt B good-night. The girls boarded the sled, and Peter pulled them home.

In the summer, family gatherings moved to the Columbia Gardens. Sarah sometimes went with them. Peter's soccer league played there.

Their other hub of social activity was the American Legion. Peter played the bugle in the Legion drum corps, a responsibility he approached with utmost fastidiousness, as if preparing for an inspection by General Pershing himself. He would come home grumbling if he thought one of the men had not done his best in the parade. Aila belonged to the Ladies Auxiliary, and when the girls were old enough, they joined the Girls Auxiliary and marched in the drill team for Butte's frequent parades.

Peter was also a member of the Last Man's Club. It was a club within the Legion. They all chipped in to buy a bottle of cognac, and the last man alive was to open it and drink a toast to his departed brethren.

Aila thoroughly enjoyed going to Legion dances with Peter. Dancing was still her favorite pastime. The trouble was, other men wanted to dance with her too, and Peter didn't like that, so he quit taking her.

They sometimes went to the American Legion Hall just to visit. Aila enjoyed this immensely. All would be fine until one of the men said something like, remember when so-and-so did such and such in the war? Peter would stand and say, "Aila, we're away," and immediately, they left. He would not talk about the war and he would not remain in the presence of those who did. He said, "Any man who actually fought in a war wouldn't sit around and talk about it." It was too dreadful.

And then there were those who talked a good game but never saw any action. Peter didn't like that either, nor any kind of sham.

At night, after Peter came home from playing cards and the children were fast asleep, he and Aila would sit at the kitchen table and talk and drink tea. On occasion, when she felt the moment opportune, she would ask him about the war; in particular, she wanted to know more about how he saved that man's life in Flanders. At first he wouldn't say anything. Over time, he told her a little, but never much. He didn't want to talk about it. Perhaps Remarque put voice to Peter's reticence when he wrote in *All Quiet on the Western Front*: "A man cannot talk of such things . . . it is too dangerous for me to put these things into words. I am afraid they might then become gigantic and I be no longer able to master them."

IN MARCH OF 1928, Peter's brother John finished his four-year tour with the U.S. Marines and was honorably discharged. While traveling through the southwest en route to Butte, he came upon an Indian fortune teller who read the sand. She told him, "You've crossed a great body of water to get here. Then you crossed another body of water and crossed it again. You'll cross the first body of water once more and you'll never cross it again."

John continued north and made his way to Butte. Once there, he made the rounds visiting his siblings and aunts and uncles. He cut an impressive figure in that marine uniform, being so tall. He went to Peter and Aila's and scooped up Aila Rose and put her high on his shoulders. Then it was Grace's turn and up she went.

These days it was dark when Aila finished her shift at the Family Drug. Apparently it didn't bother Peter that Aila had to walk home in the dark,

John Thompson, second from right, with his fellow marines

but it bothered John. He didn't think she should walk home at night alone, so he met her at the store and walked her home each evening. She was touched by his thoughtfulness. She thought John was a real gentleman.

Peter's sister Jenny was married now, and she and her husband, Gordon, lived with Gordon's mother, Mrs. Reid. One night, Peter's brothers Pat and John and their two brothers-in-law borrowed Peter's car for a night on the town. Peter didn't go with them. They came back quite late. When only three of them returned with the car, Peter asked, "Where's Gordon?" The inebriated trio looked at each other puzzled.

Don't know, one of them said, we must have lost him.

Peter quizzed them as to where they had been. They had driven in and out of town, all over the place, so far as they could remember. It was a bitterly cold night. If they had left Gordon out of town somewhere he could be freezing to death. Peter took the car and went searching for him. Eventually he found Gordon and delivered him home safely to Jenny.

Around this time, Peter lost his job at the Great Northern Railroad. He got in a fight with the boss, and that was that.

Not long after he was fired, he came home from a night of cards and told Aila that he was going away.

You're going away? Where are you going? she asked stunned.

John and I are going to New York to get Denis, then we're going to go to Ireland to get my mother and bring her back, he replied. You and the children will live with Jenny. Gordon is going with us.

Can't Denis and John go by themselves? Why can't your father go get his wife? Why do you have to go? she asked.

I am going to go, he said.

(I was about to write, at least she wasn't pregnant this time, but I don't know that. She did miscarry twins, I don't know when.)

The day he was to leave, Aila found him rummaging through the kitchen. I know you have some money in here somewhere, he said tersely. He opened the cupboards, looked in jars. Where is it? he demanded.

Peter, you must leave me some money for food for the children, she implored.

Where is the money? he demanded.

She opened a drawer and pulled out a box. This is all I have, she said. He took it and left.

Aila cried and cried. How could he leave? Why would he leave? How long would he be gone? Why couldn't Denis and John go without him? They weren't married. They didn't have families.

Jenny Thompson Reid

Aila and the girls moved into Mrs. Reid's house on First Street. Aila worked full time at the Family Drug, Jenny worked at Gamer's, and Mrs. Reid babysat Aila Rose and Grace. Mrs. Reid was a kind, gentle woman. "Those poor, poor dears," she often lamented referring to the children.

Every evening when Aila came home from work, she took Aila Rose and Grace out for a walk. She told them about her day, only the nice things, of course. She would ask Aila Rose, "What did you learn at school today, dear?" and Aila Rose would tell her, and then she'd say, "Now teach Grace what you learned at school," and Aila Rose would explain to Grace what she had learned. They returned home and ate dinner with Jenny and Mrs. Reid. Aila helped with the dinner dishes. Then she read to Aila Rose and Grace and put them to bed. Then she washed, mended, and ironed their clothes. After an evening filled with such tasks, she fell into bed with the girls.

As for Peter, he and John and Gordon stopped in Detroit and worked there for awhile. Whether they had planned to do that or ran out of money and had to, I don't know. They worked in the Ford factory earning five dollars a day. They thought they were treated like animals, so they left. Gordon returned to Butte. Peter and John went on to New York.

They found their way to Denis's rooming house in Brooklyn. Denis burst with elation at the sight of his brothers. He went on and on about the glories of New York. This is the place, he told Peter. It has everything that's going. You must send for Aila and the children, you must. And you must meet Belle. She's the girl I'm going to marry. She's a marvelous girl, and he went on and on about the wonders of Belle.

Peter and John soon met her. She was a calm, retiring woman, quite the opposite of impetuous, gregarious Denis. She was nearly forty. Denis was thirty-one and had grown into a very handsome man. Their wedding date was set for October 3.

Belle, Denis, and Peter, Brooklyn, 1928

Peter up on the roof, Brooklyn, 1928

Around this time, Sarah moved out to Madison County, across the Divide, east of Butte. Perhaps this move had something to do with Mr. Rigley, the most mysterious of her husbands. I could find little about him and no one seems to have heard anything about him. I never found their marriage license or certificate. Years later she started calling herself Sarah Mitchell again, and then Sarah Rigley.

I don't know exactly where Sarah lived in Madison County, but around the same time she moved out there, John Elliott moved there. He lived about eleven miles outside of Norris. His wife and four children still lived in Butte. His wife filed for divorce, and they were divorced, but later reconciled.

One day Aila decided to drive out to see how her mother was faring in her new home. She took Grace with her. Aila Rose was in school.

Aila pulled up to the house and they went inside. Grace said hello to her grandmother, and Aila sent her outside to play in the backyard. Then she and Sarah sat down to tea. Aila told her mother that Peter had left.

Aila, Sarah clipped, he's gone home to Mother, he probably won't come back, and if he does he'll leave again, just like he did when you were in Portland, just like your father. You can't count on that no-good Irishman for anything. He's no good for you, Aila. Stay here with me. We'll manage—Grace!

Sarah jumped up and ran outside. Grace was standing on the edge of a small pond behind the house pelting the baby ducks with rocks. Sarah grabbed her by the arm and pried her little fingers from the pebbles. Those ducks are to be my dinner someday, she scolded.

Aila didn't move in with Sarah. She drove back to Butte and stayed at Mrs. Reid's and worked at the Family Drug. Every day she came home hoping to hear from Peter. She did. He wrote and asked her to send him money.

In September, Aila Rose began second grade at St. Joseph's School. This was her third school because they had moved so often. One day after school, she and Grace were playing with other children in the neighborhood and one of them was swinging a miner's lamp and let go of it and it flew right into Grace's forehead and cut it open. They scampered inside and Mrs. Reid cleaned up the wound. Then the girls went back outside and were playing on the curb in front of the house when they spied those familiar high button shoes striding toward them. They looked up. It was their father.

He looked sad.

A few days earlier Denis had been working as a painter at Pier 9 on the North River. The scaffolding on which he was standing, which was quite high, gave way and collapsed. He was killed instantly, only two weeks before his wedding.

The American consul broke the news to Rose in Belfast. "Was he your mainstay?" he asked.

"No," she said, "my husband is."

Belle asked that Denis be buried in New York, but Sam told Peter to bring the body to Butte, so he did. Belle wrote to Rose for years. She never married.

For some reason, John did not go back to Butte for Denis's funeral. He stayed in New York. Years later, he said it was because of a woman that he wouldn't go back to Butte.

John and Peter had a falling out in New York. No one seems to know why. I do know that John disapproved of how Peter treated Aila and the children. Whether that had anything to do with it, I don't know. I also don't know whether they ever reconciled. Five months after Denis died, John sailed to Belfast. He never returned to this country. He and Peter never saw each other again.

After Denis's funeral, Aila and Peter and the girls moved into the house next door to Mrs Reid. Peter found a job on the hill. Always he returned to the mines. It suited his temperament. He worked without anybody looking over his shoulder, and he enjoyed the comradery that inevitably develops between men engaged in dangerous work.

Peter was a curious conundrum—charming and argumentative, loquacious and impetuous, steady only in his mercurialness. Aila Rose and Grace cringed every time their parents began a game of pinochle with friends or relatives. Peter's legendary charm evaporated as soon as competition was introduced to the setting. He memorized all the cards played, and when his partner played the wrong card, he delivered anything from a sharp retort to a severe tongue lashing. As Aila watched him wind toward a tirade, she would gently tap him on the arm and say softly, "Now Peter." His siblings would never cross him; they took the abuse. However, his sister-in-law wouldn't. She shot right back. The list of couples willing to play cards with him quickly diminished.

In January of 1929, the authorities in Butte clamped down on gambling. It had been illegal in Montana since 1897. The clampdown didn't last long, but while it did, gambling didn't stop; it just moved from saloons to homes.

From the way Grandma told me this next story, I thought the card players this particular night were all men and they were at their house, though I don't know that for certain. For the sake of telling the story, we'll assume that was the case.

Peter and his chums were seated around the table engrossed in their card game. After several hands, one of the men folded his cards and stretched, evidently ready for an interlude. He called out to Aila, why don't you come tell my fortune? He coaxed and coaxed, the others chimed in, until finally, she acquiesced.

Now before some of my readers fall off their chairs in shock, it is important to remember that my grandmother was the offspring of a woman steeped in superstition. Sarah wouldn't get out of bed without reading the cards. And Grandma came of age during a time when spiritualism was seeing an upsurge in popularity. So it was in her home and in the culture. How much stock she put in any of it, I never asked.

I suppose superstition was born in ages past as an attempt to explain the unexplainable and control the uncontrollable. It persists as custom, entertainment, and I think to a large extent, wishful thinking. People remember and tell of the fortune or horoscope that came to pass and quickly forget the many that didn't.

There was plenty of superstition on Peter's side of the family too. Aunt B read tea leaves. Peter's siblings Martha, Jimmy, and Jenny read cards. "You'll have a change of doors and floors," Jenny once presaged for a nephew who moved often. Most of the time the fortunes were vague, nothing bad or untoward, sometimes a word of caution. It was something to pass the time, like a board game.

During the war, Rose would have someone read the cards to tell her where her sons were, and then she prayed the Rosary for their safety. It seems in her mind, knowing where they were, or believing she knew where they were, made the prayers more efficacious.

John could have drawn a pension for being injured in the war, but Rose wouldn't let him. "That hand will heal," she said. "You'll be able to use it again." She believed it was bad luck to profit from your misfortune.

Sam Thompson wouldn't see the new moon through a window. That was bad luck. If you saw the new moon first through a window and then you saw a corpse before the next new moon, somebody close to you would die. At every new moon, Sam would walk outside, walk around the block if necessary, look up at the new moon, and then turn his money over in his pocket for good luck. When he lived in Ireland, every May Day's Eve he would cut a branch from the hawthorn and place it above the door to keep the bad fairies out. I wonder what he did in Butte? Perhaps Butte was too cold for bad fairies. He never brought the hawthorn inside, mind you, that was sure to bring death. And he didn't eat meat the day after Christmas, that was to ensure an easy death.

In his later years after he returned to Belfast, Sam became more religious. He led the family Rosary every night and still he wouldn't see the new moon through a window. Every night he prayed "deliver us from evil" and every May Day's Eve he put the hawthorn above the door—just in case.

I saw Grandma tell fortunes a few times, only when asked, and she always seemed reluctant. She read tea leaves. After the person finished drinking his or her cup of tea, she would pick up the cup and turn it this way and that, carefully examining the placement of the leaves. Then she told you what it meant. She read cards—regular playing cards. First she removed the twos, threes, fours, fives, and sixes from the deck. Then she selected a card to represent the person whose fortune was being told: a jack for a man, a queen for a woman, the jack of clubs for a dark-haired light-skinned man, a red jack for a fair-haired man, and so on. She put the queen or jack face up on the table. It would be the center for what followed. Then she asked the person whose fortune she was reading to shuffle the cards and cut the deck into three piles away from himself. She picked up the middle stack and turned it over to see the card exposed on the bottom. Then she did the same with the other two piles and held these three piles fanned in her hand with only the bottom card from each stack showing. She explained what those three cards meant. Then she closed the deck and held it face down in her left hand. She picked up the top card, turned it over, and set it on the table, then another card, then another, until she came to a seven. The card after the seven she placed next to the queen or jack on the table. She continued to pull cards off the deck, and each time she came to a seven, she placed the following card next to the queen or jack. When she had gone through the entire deck, she asked the person to shuffle it again, cut it into three piles, and she repeated the process.

At this point there was a queen or jack on the table with a card at each of the four sides. The next cards she placed in between those four cards. She continued this process until she emptied the deck of all the cards except the sevens. She did all this slowly and methodically, pondering each new card placement as if deciphering some mysterious, ancient text. Then she would point to a card and say, this card next to that card means thus and so, or she would point to a card or group of cards and say, there's something here about a trip, or there's something here about a visitor— something brief and vague like that. She wore the same studied expression as the time she figured out what was wrong with the sewing machine. I was in the middle of making something and was at my wits end because the bobbin thread kept bunching up. The repairman came twice and couldn't fix it, so Mom asked Grandma to look at it. She had a knack for fixing things. She sat and pondered the machine for about an hour and then said, "It's something right here," and she pointed to the spindle. She pointed to the spindle in the same thoughtful way she pointed to the cards. Mom looked at the spindle and noticed that the spring was missing. Once found and put in place, the machine worked fine. Apparently, the repairman was in want of Celtic intuition, for I think that was what was at work, at least in part.

I think in Grandma's case, fortune telling was confused with intuition. She had keen intuition and she had premonitions. I suppose those are one and the same. Intuition is not the exclusive domain of women nor is everything that floats through a woman's mind intuition, and it isn't wishful thinking. Discernment can be difficult. Men call it their gut. You just know something. You don't know why you know, but you know. It's our interior compass. When followed, it keeps us from danger, joins the right people together in matrimony, directs us toward good decisions and away from bad ones. Some people do seem to be more intuitive than others. It's angelic knowledge. It's a gift, not something that can be turned on and off like a water faucet. "The wind blows where it will." Grandma knew things without the cards. I think it was merely a coincidence when cards or tea leaves were involved.

Now back to our story. Peter and his friends have been playing cards, and Aila is about to tell one of the men's fortune. She placed the appropriate jack on the table. Then she asked the man to shuffle the deck and cut it into three stacks. After he did so, she looked at the bottom cards and explained what they meant. Then slowly, carefully, she began to pull cards from the deck and place them on the table, making an array around the jack. She studied the placement of each card, absorbed in thought. When she finished placing the cards on the table, she pensively put her finger to her lips; then she gently tapped a card and said, "It says there's a fire. A large building on fire." She returned her finger to her lips. She remained pensive, still reading. Then one of the men burst out, so there's your fortune. The others laughed and conversation broke out all over the room.

Enough of that, said another man, deal the cards. They sat down to resume their game. Aila stood up to make room at the table.

"You better go home," she said to the man whose fortune she had read. "It says there's a big building on fire."

"Oh, you're just trying to break up our card game, aren't you, Aila," Peter joshed in his mocking tone.

"You really must go home," she reiterated. The man just laughed and scoffed at her.

"It won't work, Aila," said Peter. "We're going to keep playing cards no matter what your old superstitions tell you." The men laughed. One of them shuffled the cards and dealt. They picked up their cards and forgot all about fortune telling. The men played cards well into the wee hours.

The next day the man whose fortune she had told barged into the house. He accused her of all sorts of terrible things. His barn had burned down during the night.

Ever after, she was very reluctant to tell a fortune for anyone outside the family. A woman used to come to the house and plead with her to read her fortune. She politely refused. She didn't want to encourage her. Even for a family member she had to be coaxed and sometimes refused. She was afraid of what she might see, or she already knew.

CHAPTER FIFTY-TWO

ABOUT MIDWAY through the school year, Peter and Aila and the children moved again, this time into one of Uncle John's flats on Montana Street. Aila Rose attended St. Patrick's School. They stayed put long enough for her to continue there into third grade.

Peter came home one evening to find Aila Rose and Grace playing in an army pup tent on the balcony. He walked into the flat and asked Aila, "Where did that tent come from?"

"Oh, Bill Rundell was by this afternoon and set it up for Aila Rose and Grace to play in," she replied.

Bill Rundell was a friend of Peter's. He was never welcome in their home again.

At some point, the children's schooling became a source of disagreement. Aila Rose went to the Monroe School for first grade because a friend of Aila's was the teacher. Otherwise, Aila insisted that the children attend Catholic school. Peter didn't agree even though he wanted the children to be raised Catholic. I wonder if he objected because of the tuition.

When she told me about this, I asked, "Grandma, why did you insist the children go to Catholic school if you weren't Catholic?"

She replied purposefully, "Because when I got married I promised I would raise my children Catholic and I was going to do it the best way I knew how!"

Whenever I have told other family members that story, they all said the same thing: "Sounds like her." She promised. It was a matter of integrity.

I vividly remember that conversation. She spoke firmly, rapidly, and evenly, and concluded the sentence with an exclamation point in the form of a confidant nod of affirmation ending with her chin in the air. She had a dramatic way of ending a sentence when she was passionate about what she was saying, which was often, especially when principle was involved.

It had the effect of a crescendo without a change in volume. She never raised her voice. She was naturally theatrical. Her speech was charged with the appropriate level of emotion or enthusiasm, never placid, and she had an innate sense of timing.

NOW PETER was out of work again.

"Peter, you have got to get a job to feed these children!" Aila demanded.

"You get a job and feed them," he scowled and pushed her out of his way as he left for a night of cards.

Aila knew women who ruled their husbands with an iron rod. Some of those men needed it or they'd be at the bottle all the time. Had Aila been such a woman, she might have kept Peter working and away from the panguingue table, but Aila wasn't that kind of woman. She would stand unequivocally on principle, but she wouldn't rule Peter. That wasn't in her picture of wifely duties. The very notion of ruling another person wasn't in her at all.

By all accounts, Peter Thompson was the best uncle, the best brother, the best son, the best nephew, and the best friend. When his father needed him, he was there. When one of his sisters called, he went. His nephews and nieces adored him. It was in the combined role of husband, father, provider where the trouble lay—the role he chose. And he wanted to sire as many children as his father had: twelve.

One of his cousins used to speak of him with a sigh. He was a man of so much potential, so intelligent, interested in everything, never without a book. It was Butte's fault, she concluded, macho Butte. That's why Peter didn't live up to his potential—as if he had no will of his own and had no responsibility in the matter. It is beyond me how some women will make excuses for behavior in a man they would readily scorn in another woman. Peter lived life as he chose. It was not thrust on him.

IT WAS NOW Christmas Eve. Aila bought an orange. Peter took the children to Mass. On Christmas morning, Aila decoratively cut the orange into three pieces and gave them to Peter and the children as a treat with breakfast. Once they had eaten, she crawled under the covers and spent much of the day in bed.

She was sick and sad much of the time. She suffered terrible tooth-aches. There was no money to have anything done about them. She had probably never been to a dentist in her life, except maybe in the orphanage. She heated towels in the oven to use as compresses to relieve the excruciating pain. She was often plagued with respiratory ailments, bronchitis or pneumonia; it's hard to say which since she didn't go to the doctor. The constant worry must have aggravated her poor health. When they had to move, where would they live? When money was especially short, how would she feed the children? She paid the bills and learned to stretch every penny. She paid the premium on Peter's life insurance policy. His mother was the sole beneficiary. He refused to include his wife and children, even when Aila asked him about it. He said, "You'd just spend it on some other man." When their pecuniary problems became particularly dire, she quit paying it. About once a winter, the police would come to the house in the middle of the night, and Aila would go uptown and pay to get her mother out of jail. Peter didn't like that. Peter gave money to his father whenever he asked for it. And still Peter gambled, and when he was out of work, night after night, they ate macaroni and tomatoes for dinner. That's all she could afford. Aila was in knots worrying about tomorrow. She was married to a man who lived for the moment.

Now we come to 1931.

A mammoth ship does not stop on a dime, so we back up a little.

After the post-war depression was over, the 1920s were good years for the Butte mines. The first three quarters of 1929 were quite good. Production was up, wages were way up. The price of copper was unusually high. The mining companies couldn't find enough experienced miners to meet the demand. Peter was working at the Belmont.

Then at the end of October—the stock market crashed. The price of copper dropped precipitously and, with it, production. By the next year the price of copper dropped twenty-six percent; production plummeted down to half of what it had been in 1929. The price continued to drop and production continued to plummet into the next year, and the next, the Company began to shut down entire mines, production slowed even more until it sputtered, stalled, and all but stopped. The North Butte Company didn't hazard to quote profit and loss in their 1931 annual report. They

shut down their mines. As for the mighty Anaconda, their stock had been trading at $175 per
share before the crash; by 1932, it was down to
$3. But we aren't quite there yet. I suppose no
one knew how bad it would get nor how long
it would stay bad.

Peter

Despite their perpetual financial straits due
to Peter's gambling and on-again, off-again
working, Aila scrimped and saved and
scrimped and saved and saved and her thrift
paid off. By March of 1931 she had saved
enough money to put a down payment on a
house. This would remove one gigantic worry.
Every time they had to move, she worried that
they would be on the street with nowhere to go, and someone would take
her children away just as she had been taken away. She desperately wanted
to buy a house so her children would have a permanent roof over their
heads after she died, which she was sure would be any day.

They made a $200 down payment for a $1250 house on Reynolds Street.
Aila liked the darling little house. It had a nice yard and a lawn. The price
included some furniture. They would pay the rest in monthly installments
at ten percent interest. Miner's day's pay averaged $4.70 that year. Peter
was working as an attendant at Ray Coughlin's gas station earning $3.25
per day.

Earlier that same month, on March 3, the mercury climbed to an unheard of eighty degrees. Two days later, a blizzard swept through the
Rockies, paralyzing the town. A type for the times, perhaps.

Aila and Peter and the girls passed a pleasant spring and summer in
the little house on Reynolds Street. For awhile, Aila Rose and Grace entertained themselves by playing with a pet duck kept on a leash, at least
they thought it was a pet. One day it wasn't there anymore.

In the fall, Aila enrolled the girls at St. Ann's. Grace was in the first
grade, Aila Rose was in fourth.

One evening at dinner, Peter remarked, "The paper didn't list the price
of copper today. I wonder what it means."

Chapter Fifty-Three

COME MY LITTLE darlin's, said Peter hurriedly. We're going to see your aunt B.

Peter was ecstatic. He could barely stand still. He ushered Aila Rose and Grace outside to the car. They climbed into the back. He slid into the driver's seat and turned the key. Nothing. He tried again. Nothing. It was thirty below.

Stay right there and don't move, he told the girls. He ran in the house and rummaged through the kitchen. He found a crock of oil and a wad of cotton batting on a dish next to it. Aila had been saving that oil and cotton for the baby. Peter dabbed the cotton in the oil until it was saturated. It absorbed nearly all the oil. He lit the cotton with a match and crawled under the car. He moved the flame back and forth across the oil pan. Still holding the burning cotton, he crawled out from under the car and tried to start it. After a couple of tries, the engine turned over. He tossed the flaming swab into the snow and drove off to Aunt B's.

Once at the house, Peter leapt out of the car and dashed inside. Aunt B, I have a son! he exclaimed as he burst through the front door.

That's wonderful, love, said Aunt B.

Aunt Annie walked in from the kitchen. A boy is it? she said, clasping her hands in delight.

Yes, Aunt Annie, a boy! he said. Aunt B walked across the room to close the door. In his exuberance, Peter had left it open allowing arctic air to waft in. As she reached out to pull the storm door shut, she saw two little girls shivering in the backseat of the car.

Peter! You left those babies to freeze to death in that car! How could you do such a thing? she scolded and ran outside to rescue Aila Rose and Grace.

Peter and Aila named their son Samuel Arthur. Proudly holding his infant son on his arm, Peter said to Aila, "It's just as well that Aila Rose and Grace were not boys. They'd be old enough for the next war. Sammy will be too young for the next war and too old for the war after that."

Again, Aila couldn't nurse. She had no milk nor money with which to buy any. Each morning before the girls left for school, she had Aila Rose stir oatmeal through a strainer over and over until it was fine enough to pass through the nipple of the bottle. That was Sammy's formula.

Women from the American Legion Auxiliary visited shortly after Sammy was born. They gave Aila a baby layette. She was profoundly grateful. Peter bristled. He didn't like it that people knew they were on hard times. One of the women asked Aila, "Do you have milk for these children?"

"No, I don't," Aila replied.

The next day milk began to arrive at the front door.

Then the depths came—the struggling metals market completely collapsed. One dream shattered was the house on Reynolds Street. They lost it. Aila was crushed.

A dark blanket of gloom enveloped the entire country. Peter and thousands of Butte men lost their jobs. Sam Thompson had been employed at the West Colusa for years. He too lost his job. Citizens had priority for what jobs there were, and he never became one. Men who were able to keep jobs in the mines worked two weeks on, two weeks off, to spread the work out to more men. Peter's prospects for work were quite dismal; that is, until the next earthly angel of deliverance swept into their lives. Her name was Anne McDonnell.

Anne was Peter's cousin by marriage. She was Walter Breen's daughter from his first marriage. Anne's mother died when Anne was a little girl. Her paternal grandmother lived with them and raised Anne and her brother, William.

Anne skipped high school and, at age sixteen, took and passed the entrance exam for the Normal School at Dillon. The year was 1900. After she completed her course of study, she taught at a one room country school in Buffalo, Montana.

When she was twenty-four years old, her brother was killed in an accident at the smelter in Great Falls. The next year her grandmother died. Two years later, her father married Mary Gribben, Peter's aunt.

The following year Anne married Ed McDonnell, the son of a prominent family who owned a large spread in the middle of the state in Fergus County. Anne and Ed settled in a house on the family ranch until one

Anne Breen McDonnell
MONTANA HISTORICAL SOCIETY 86-1

day, he up and left. Thus ended her marriage. They never divorced. They had no children.

Anne stayed in Fergus County a while longer and then returned to Butte and lived with her aunt. When Mary Gribben Breen died, Anne moved in with her father and his two young children, Molly and Walter.

A friend of Anne's named Elizabeth had studied at Columbia, returned to Butte, and went to work as a librarian at the Butte library. Around

1922, the librarian at the state Historical Library in Helena recruited Elizabeth to organize their collection. She moved to Helena, and when she had their collection in shape, she told the librarian she was returning to Butte. He said he needed an assistant librarian, and since Elizabeth wouldn't stay and take the job, could she recommend someone else. She said yes and recommended Anne McDonnell. The librarian consulted Anne's in-laws and, upon their high words, gave Anne the job. Now in her late thirties, Anne took the job and moved to Helena.

A good part of her work involved assisting scholars in their research. She already knew the land. She could name every stream, every valley, every mountain. She soon became a compendium of Montana history and garnered profound respect within the historical community. Many authors expressed their indebtedness in print. K. Ross Toole wrote of Anne: "She has that rare ability to distinguish between the important and the unimportant. It is an ability that many a professional historian lacks."

Anne was a sober, no-nonsense woman, very bookish, and she adapted well to scholarly work. She did not suffer fools well, nor ineptitude. And there was always a twinge of sadness about her.

In July of 1929, Anne's father, Walter Breen, died. He left his younger children, Molly and Walter, financially secure; however, they were still minors, so Anne became their legal guardian. The problem was—Anne lived in Helena, and the children lived in Butte, and with Molly about to begin her last year of high school, it didn't make sense to move them just yet. Anne came up with the following solution. She made the very generous offer to Mary (Peter's sister) that she and her husband and two children could live in the Breen home in Meaderville rent free, and Anne would pay Mary a salary to do the housework and cook and look after Molly and young Walter, who were then seventeen and thirteen (almost fourteen). Mary agreed, and she and her family moved into the Breen home. This lasted about a year at which time Molly graduated from Girls Central and left for UCLA, and Mary's husband found a job in Utah and they moved there. Anne then enrolled young Walter at Mount St. Charles in Helena, and he boarded at the school.

AND NOW it is 1932, the Great Depression is on, and Peter is out of work. Anne finds him a job where she works, at the state capitol. So Peter and

Aila and the children pack up what little they have and move to Helena.

They rented a dreary little log house in Broadwater on the outskirts of town near Fort Harrison. It had no indoor plumbing. The pump was in the backyard. This was a giant leap back in time. Butte was a modern city with all the amenities of the day, and Aila was fastidious about personal cleanliness. Now having to use an outhouse with a baby and small children—it was disgusting. But there was a job for Peter, and for that, she was thankful. She would live with inconvenience and unpleasantness if it meant a roof over their heads and food on the table for her children.

Peter worked at his new job for two weeks and quit. He didn't like it. Anne was a bit peeved with him over that, but she found him another job. He worked at it for three weeks and quit. He didn't like that one either.

Now she was beyond peeved. She was absolutely livid. After work that day, this normally reserved though never reticent woman got on the bus and went out to Broadwater and stormed into the house.

What's this I hear about you quitting your job? she demanded of Peter.

I didn't like it, he replied.

YOU DIDN'T LIKE IT? she yelled. WHAT DO YOU MEAN YOU DIDN'T LIKE IT? I WENT OUT ON A LIMB TO GET YOU THAT JOB. A JOB IS A JOB. HOW COULD YOU DO THAT? YOU HAVE FIVE MOUTHS TO FEED, AND WHERE ARE YOU GOING TO GET A JOB WITH A DEPRESSION ON AND JOBS SO SCARCE? HOW COULD YOU DO THAT? YOU HAVE YOUR FAMILY TO THINK ABOUT. YOU SORRY EXCUSE FOR A MAN. YOU DIDN'T LIKE THE JOB—AS IF WE DON'T HAVE TO DO THINGS WE DON'T LIKE. CHILDREN DON'T LIKE TO GO HUNGRY!

Anne went on and on, upbraiding Peter. He didn't care what she thought or what she said. He didn't like the job, and he wasn't going to do it. She could stand there and yell at him all night for all he cared. To use one of his own expressions, he didn't give a tinker's damn.

Aila stood by in shock. Nobody spoke to Peter Thompson like this. Even the walls knew when Peter entered the room. He filled it. His blazing blue eyes said: I'm here world and I'm Peter Thompson and what have you got to say about it. He bewitched all he met. Family and friends venerated him, but not Anne McDonnell.

Aila became aware of Aila Rose and Grace hiding behind her, clutching her skirt, as Anne went on and on yelling at Peter. Aila ushered them into the bedroom and closed the door. They could still hear Anne lambasting their father.

Where things had been difficult before, now they were desperate. More than ever, Aila was a bundle of nerves. She taxed her creativity to stretch what little food she had into as many meals as possible. It was nearly gone. How would she feed the children? At least in Butte she could work at the Family Drug, or stretch curtains, or take in laundry, or clean houses. Here, they were out in the country with hardly any neighbors, and she had the baby to care for, so she couldn't go into Helena to find work, plus she didn't know anyone there, except Anne who had already tried to help them. She tortured herself with regret that she didn't let the doctor adopt Aila Rose. Then at least one of her children wouldn't go hungry. She wrote a note venting to herself, *"How could I have been so selfish? I loved my first-born so deeply—so strongly—so much—so desperately—but—for her own good, I should have let Dr. ——— adopt her—he wanted her so much—and I know now that he could and would have given her the things that she wanted and needed for happiness and all those things that make for a wonderful—well rounded and complete way of life."*

What Aila didn't know was that the doctor's wife had become a wretched alcoholic.

And then there was the rent. With Peter not working, how would they pay it? Aila was tormented with fear. If they couldn't pay the rent, they would be put out, and with nowhere to go, she feared someone would take her children away just as she had been taken away. It was enough to drive a person to do something desperate.

There was a knock at the door.

Mrs. Thompson? the visitor asked.

Yes, I am Mrs. Thompson, she said. Please come in, Father.

He stepped inside, smiled and introduced himself. He was Father Tougas, pastor of St. Helena's Cathedral. He was a slightly rotund man with dark hair and a jolly, pleasant face. Aila invited him to sit down. She sat down across from him perfectly poised, back straight, palms up resting one on the other in her lap. They exchanged pleasantries. Father Tougas asked how many children she had. She said she had three: Aila Rose turned ten in May, Grace was six, and Sammy, the baby, was seven months. He asked where her husband worked. She said he wasn't working right then.

"What do you have to feed the children?" he asked.

Father Tougas
DIOCESE OF HELENA ARCHIVES
XXVI25

The calm everything-is-fine demeanor she mustered for the children and the world cracked. "I don't know how I'm going to. feed the children, Father! I don't know what I'm going to do!"

He stood. "May I call on you again, Mrs. Thompson?" he asked.

"Yes, Father, you are welcome here anytime," she replied, probably embarrassed that she momentarily lost her composure before this stranger. His face was kind, though his manner quite direct. She didn't mind his directness. His presence was somehow comforting.

Later in the day, there was another knock at the door. It was Father Tougas again, and he was carrying a wooden grocery crate. "May I come in, Mrs. Thompson?" he asked.

"Yes, Father, of course."

He set the crate on the table. "I brought a few things—for the children," he explained. In the crate was a hefty beef roast, potatoes, carrots, onions, eggs, butter, flour, milk.

Thereafter he visited often, always bearing gifts of food or money.

"He saved our lives," Aila said. She never forgot.

JAMES GROVER TOUGAS was born on All Saints Eve, 1884, in Auburn, Massachusetts. He was the tenth and youngest child of John and Charlotte Tougas. His father was of French descent and Catholic. His mother had been Methodist but converted to Catholicism before he was born. When he was sixteen, James left home to enter the seminary in Montreal.

James studied diligently, and every day he prayed that his dream be fulfilled that he might join the *Péres Blancs* and go off to Africa to work in the missions for the rest of his life. As he matured and progressed in his studies, his superiors at the seminary concluded that he did indeed have all the qualities of a good missionary.

However after several years in Montreal, James was stricken with a respiratory ailment. It persisted. He opened the windows in his room thinking the fresh air would help, which it did somewhat. Despite his poor health, he managed to continue his studies. The illness lingered. Now a young man of twenty-four, his romantic dreams were tempered with enough realism to know that the foreign missions required men in robust health. In all likelihood, the *Péres Blancs* would never accept him.

One day he attended a lecture given by a visiting bishop, John Patrick Carroll of the Diocese of Helena, Montana. Bishop Carroll spoke of the far West as a land yet to be tamed, peopled with souls who longed to hear the Gospel and in need of the sacraments. As the bishop spoke, a spark ignited in the young man's soul. He needn't travel to foreign lands to be a missionary. There was mission territory in his own country, and the mountain air would be just the thing to restore his lungs. "The West is the place for me," he concluded.

He wrote to Bishop Carroll.

In 1911, James completed his studies and received a bachelor of canon law and sacred theology. He had to request a dispensation to become a priest because his mother was a convert. This was easily obtained; he was ordained and left for Helena.

His first assignment was to teach languages at Mount St. Charles. After five years, he became pastor at Augusta, west of Great Falls, and in 1918, he joined the army and sailed to France.

He was assigned to the 41st Division. They were a replacement division stationed at St. Aignan-Noyers. At the beginning of October, as the battle raged in the Argonne, he came down with the dreaded Spanish influenza. He was sick for two weeks. Once he recovered, he went back to work. He visited more than a thousand sick or wounded soldiers every day. He said Mass in the church and in the prison, anointed the dying, and buried the dead. He heard confessions everywhere—in the hospital, on the street, in the fields; soldiers stopped him anywhere. He walked and then ran along side a moving train giving one doughboy absolution as his train pulled out for the front.

Father Tougas also said Mass for the local French community. He said they were edified by the "religious attention of our boys." His French congregants were quite taken with him and begged him to stay after the war, but he wouldn't. He was very discouraged by the religious situation in France. He said it was even worse than before the war.

Father James Tougas, U.S. Army Chaplain
DIOCESE OF HELENA ARCHIVES XXV

After the armistice, a noblewoman whom Father Tougas had befriended, la Comptesse de la Roche Emont, arranged a private audience for him with Pope Benedict XV. During his military service, Father Tougas had heard confessions in French, German, Italian, and English, and he was absolutely appalled by the lack of religious upbringing he observed among Italian men. "Italians in the United States don't go to church because they aren't taught their religion," he complained. "Most men don't know a single prayer." He intended to make the Holy Father aware of this calamity.

He took the train to Rome and went to the Vatican at the appointed time. There he met a very tired, very beleaguered man. His European flock had just finished trying to annihilate each other. Deprivation and hunger reigned. Marxism was rearing its ugly head in Germany. Father Tougas didn't have the heart to burden the pontiff with complaints about the sorry state of religious instruction in Italy.

However, he did tell his bishop, and when he returned from the war, Bishop Carroll assigned him "pastor to the Italians in Meaderville."

Meaderville was part of Butte, and at that time, it fell within the boundaries of Holy Savior Parish in McQueen, which was Butte's Slavic neighborhood. Most of the parishioners at Holy Savior were Slovene or Croatian. Their native countries had been part of the Austro-Hungarian Empire which had been at war with Italy. Some say that's why the Italians wouldn't go to Mass there. Whether that was the case or not, Father Tougas would remove the excuse. He would build them their own church.

In addition to being the pastor in Meaderville, Father Tougas was responsible for mission parishes in Brown's Gulch and Trask, both outside of Butte. He lived at St. James Hospital and served as chaplain there. On top of all that, he was the city missionary. In this capacity, he attended juvenile court and tried to persuade the authorities to send Catholic children to the House of the Good Shepherd and St. Joseph's where they would receive Catholic religious instruction, rather than to the state institutions where they might not.

Within two years, Father Tougas had raised enough money to build a church in Meaderville. It would be called St. Helena's. The ACM donated the land. The Catholic Extension Society donated $3500. John Ryan, the president of the ACM and daily Mass attendee, gave $1000. Father Tougas gave $500 and Bishop Carroll gave $500. Father Tougas and the parishioners built the wood-frame church themselves. During construction, Father could be seen up on the roof, hammer in hand, barking orders in Italian. In no time the church was finished. (Though Meaderville is long gone, you can still see the little church today at the World Museum of Mining in Butte.)

During the next twelve months, Father Tougas completed construction of two more churches: St. Jude Thaddeus in Trask and St. Patrick's in Brown's Gulch.

Having built three churches in one year, plus saying Mass, hearing confessions, doing weddings and baptisms and funerals, visiting and anointing the sick, instructing converts, and visiting parishioners for three parishes not even in the same town, all the while serving as the city missionary and chaplain at the hospital, Bishop Carroll decided to reassign him. Father Tougas's new post would be as acting pastor of St. Helena's Cathedral in Helena. At least he didn't need to build a church for them.

Father Tougas dived into his new duties with his characteristic vigor and zeal. Though this was an established parish, he would seek out mission territory. He searched the highways and byways for the destitute and forgotten. A discreet network tipped him off to those in need. This included the sisters who taught in the school. Children who lived too far away to walk home for lunch brought their lunches to school. The sisters could tell by what a child brought for lunch that the family was on hard times. They discreetly told Father and he discreetly visited the parents and did what he could to meet their needs, be they corporal or spiritual.

He visited every patient in St. John's Hospital every morning—yes, every patient, every morning—except on his day off. Those on the floors above and below could hear his booming voice say, good morning, good morning, good morning, and knew Father Tougas was making his rounds. He and the other cathedral priests also said Mass at Fort Harrison.

Anne McDonnell began her job in Helena around the same time Father Tougas was assigned there. She lived at the YWCA and was a parishioner at the cathedral. She probably already knew Father Tougas since the Breens lived in Meaderville and were parishioners at St. Helena's. Anne and Father were around the same age and became friends. They often played bridge together with a professor from Mount St. Charles and a friend of Anne's named Bernice Boone, who was a distant relative of Daniel Boone.

Father Tougas was cheerful and stern, strict and kind. He chased the children off the cathedral lawn, and they loved and respected him, as did the adults, including his fellow priests. He commanded respect and got it. From what I have been able to glean, he was a man fulfilled and enjoyed the peace and contentment inherent therein.

He trained the altar boys to do everything exactly right—that was the only way to do anything. When they served a funeral, he gave each a quarter, which was a lot of money for a boy in those days. About once a year he took them fishing. While en route in his car, he would say to the boys, "Now we'll pray the Holy Rosary," which they did, possibly as much out of fear as obedience, praying for their own safe arrival, as Father sped down the dirt road with the gas pedal pressed flat against the floor.

One woman told me that Father Tougas used to come to her home to play cards. "He was a very competitive card player," she added. Her husband was Catholic; she was not. During one visit, Father Tougas turned to her and said, "It's time you came into the church." She agreed. "You did what Father Tougas said!" she told me. After that, he came to the house regularly to give her instruction. During part of that time the World Series was on, and as soon as he walked in the door, he would make a beeline for the radio, turn it on, and with one ear to the game, he quizzed her on the catechism.

During Advent one year, a young priest fresh from the seminary answered the rectory door and beheld a broad black woman, her cheeks heavily caked with purple rouge. She was the madame from the brothel. He was so stunned he nearly dropped of fright. She explained that Father Tougas had sent her to collect the presents for the Christmas party. Yes, he remembered all God's children. He went crazy with gifts at Christmastime, filling an entire room in the rectory. He bought presents for the prostitutes and for the men who were then called bums. His generosity led to the rumor that he was a man of means. I don't think that was the case. What he got, he gave. Even when he was alive, people said he was a saint.

And when he wasn't saving souls, he found solace fishing the upper Blackfoot.

CHAPTER FIFTY-FOUR

BY SOME MIRACLE, prompted by I wonder who, a job became available for Peter at Fort Harrison as an orderly in the hospital. It was steady work for the steadiest of all employers. Peter could work there until he retired and then receive a pension. Aila was immensely relieved.

As in Butte, Aila made sure that Aila Rose and Grace attended Mass every Sunday. The closest Mass was at Fort Harrison. It was an easy walk, about a mile away, but they didn't have to walk. Father Tougas, or whichever priest was saying Mass that day, picked them up en route.

When the school year began, Aila enrolled the girls at Kessler, the nearby country school. Grace was ready for second grade; however, the teacher decided she was too small and put her in first grade. The school was about a mile and a half from their house by road. There was a shortcut across the prairie made even shorter by cutting through a rancher's fenced pasture.

"You are not to go in that field," Peter sternly warned the girls. "There is a bull in there and if you go in there he'll come after you and trample you to death. You are not to go in there, if you do, I'll tear off your arm and beat you with the bloody hand! Now where are you not to go?"

"In the field with the bull," replied Aila Rose and Grace.

Peter left for work at the fort and the girls set off for school.

"I can beat him," said Grace, casting a defiant glance at the bull as she slipped under the barbed wire. The bull immediately saw the intruder and tore after her. Grace ran, the bull ran faster, all the while Aila Rose was screaming at the top of her lungs, sure any moment her little sister would be torn to pieces. The bull gained, Grace ran faster, the bull came closer; heart pounding, Grace dove under the fence just as the bull reared up in front of it.

By now, the family had adjusted to their new life in Broadwater and were enjoying a rare interlude of calm. It was broken by Archie. After nine years in prison, he was paroled and came to live with them.

This threw Aila into a state. Peter did not want him there either. And as a practical matter, they had no room for him. Peter arranged for him to sleep in the back of the saloon down the road.

Archie was by far the old-timer of those paroled that month—not in terms of age but in time served. The others had been in for only one or two years. Archie had spent his nine years in prison learning two trades: he learned to be a barber in the prison barber shop, and he took a course in bookkeeping. He wanted to have two ways to earn a living, so he could always find a job.

He found a job as a barber in Helena. Aila wrote to Governor Erickson on his behalf asking that his sentence be terminated. The Board of Prison Commissioners denied her request.

Peter and Aila and the children then moved from the dreary little log house into a dreary little shack, still in Broadwater, about two blocks away. It was a tiny narrow shack consisting of a kitchen and a bedroom. It had a sink with cold water. The toilet (outhouse) was outside; the workmen had just finished digging it.

"Aila Rose and Grace, be sure to keep the door latched on the outdoor toilet," Aila said.

They didn't.

"Aila Rose and Grace, keep on eye on Sammy. Don't let him in there by himself."

He was.

They were playing and forgot all about Sammy until they heard him cry. They looked around. Where is he? Then they saw the open, unlatched door.

They ran over to the outhouse. They could hear him but they couldn't see him. They stepped inside and peered into the hole. There was Sammy, at the bottom of the dirt hole, wailing at the top of his lungs. Aila Rose knelt down and leaned in. Arms flailing, she tried to grab him but couldn't reach. She ran inside and told her mother. Aila ran out screaming, terrified she'd find a frightful mass of broken bones. She tried to grab Sammy but she couldn't reach him either. A neighbor heard Aila scream and rushed over to see what was the matter. He reached in and managed to fish Sammy out. The child was no worse the wear. No broken bones, and thankfully it was a fresh hole, just dug and still clean.

Winter settled in for a good long stay. As in Butte, Aila hung the clothes, sheets, diapers, and towels outside on the line to dry. Everything on the line froze; the sheets, the clothes, the towels, all were dry but frozen solid. She had to let everything thaw inside before folding it. If she tried to fold a frozen diaper, or frozen anything, it would break.

Christmas came, and so did Father Tougas, bearing gifts, as he would every year they lived near Helena.

During one of his visits, he asked Aila, "Mrs. Thompson, do you want to become a Catholic?"

"Yes, Father, I do," she replied.

After that he came to the house regularly to give her instruction. He baptized her at St. Helena's and she received First Holy Communion. She was confirmed with Aila Rose that spring.

That May, her fourth child, my mom, was born at St. John's Hospital. Aila marveled at how big this baby was compared to her others, though I suspect the nurses and doctor thought she was tiny. She named her third daughter Patricia Ann and called her Patsy Ann. Anne McDonnell and her half brother, Walter, were Patsy Ann's godparents. Before the baptism, Anne came to the house and gave Aila Rose and Grace each a new dress. They were their first store-bought dresses and they were absolutely thrilled to get them.

Aila Rose completed fifth grade that June. The country school curriculum ended at fifth grade, so in the fall, she would attend the cathedral school in Helena. Children who attended country schools were tested before they went to school in town. Aila Rose took the test and scored best in the entire state. Even so, the teacher intended to fail her and keep her back. This brought out the education authorities to investigate why a teacher wanted to flunk the child with the highest score. Since Aila Rose had attended Catholic school before Kessler, from time to time out of habit she would call the teacher "Sister" which made the teacher absolutely furious. That may explain the teacher's ire and intention to flunk her, or perhaps the woman resented such a precocious child. Who knows. The uproar ended with Aila Rose advancing to the next grade.

PETER AND AILA and the children then moved into yet another dreary little shack in Broadwater, this one in between the first two. It also had no toilet inside, just an outhouse out back.

Late in the fall, a man came to the door with a telegram. Aila's heart must have skipped a beat. Telegrams usually meant bad news. She opened it.

> AILA
> PLEASE COME
> BERTHA

The day of Grace's First Communion. That's Grace trying to restrain Sammy. Aila Rose is holding Patsy Ann. Broadwater, near Helena.

Bertha was Mrs. Flomer. She owned the Family Drug, where Aila had worked in Butte. Her husband had been the pharmacist, and Mrs. Flomer worked in the store. They had been very kind to Aila, accommodating her schedule, so she could work for them. They knew she needed the money, plus they valued her as a good worker. Mrs. Flomer had been running the business by herself for at least a year now, ever since a man robbed the store and shot and killed Mr. Flomer. That happened in October of 1931, when Aila and Peter were still in Butte and Aila was expecting Sammy.

Why Mrs. Flomer needed Aila's help so urgently at this particular time, I don't know. Somehow Aila convinced Peter that she had to go. Aila Rose and Grace will help you, she assured him. I won't be gone long.

She hired a babysitter to look after Sammy and Patsy Ann while Aila Rose and Grace were at school. Then she packed a few things and boarded the bus for Butte.

Peter enjoyed rocking the children on his lap, telling them stories, reciting poems for them, singing them songs; but feeding them, cleaning them, getting them off to school, putting them to bed—this was a foreign language, one for which he had little aptitude nor interest in learning. He made a few vain attempts at cooking. The closest he had ever come to feeding himself was opening a can of rations. Aila Rose and Grace were eleven and seven, so at least they were big enough to change diapers and feed Patsy Ann and Sammy, sparing Peter those patience-demanding ordeals.

Every day after school, Aila Rose and Grace would walk to the bus stop and wait. The bus would stop. The door opened. They watched people step down, one by one. They saw a tiny woman, they drew a collective breath, no, she wasn't their mother. More men, more women, some children would step off the bus. The door would close. The bus drove away. Two simultaneous wails burst forth. They cried all the way home. Aila Rose would still be crying when Peter came home from work. "When is my mother coming home?" she implored. She was inconsolable. Every day they did this. Peter was beside himself. Aila Rose sobbed and sobbed at school. "What's the matter?" asked the nun. "My mother is *gone*," she cried. The seasons changed, months gathered into years—no, not really, it only seemed so to Aila Rose and Grace, and to Peter. Finally, after two interminable weeks, the girls walked to the bus stop, they waited, they watched, and their mother stepped off the bus. They ran to her and hugged her and all cried tears of jubilation. Probably the most relieved was Peter Thompson.

Sometime later, Aila Rose fell ill. She was awfully sick, too sick to go to school. Father Tougas brought a doctor to the house and visited more frequently. The children at school sent her games to occupy her convalescence. After a month or so, she was well enough to return to school.

She took the city bus into town to St. Helena's. It was several miles from their home. Children who lived close enough to walk went home for lunch. Those who lived too far away brought a sack lunch, but not Aila Rose, not for awhile anyway. By order of Father Tougas, she ate lunch at the rectory. As instructed, every day at lunchtime she knocked at the back door of the rectory. The housekeeper let her in. A place was already set for her at the small table in the kitchen next to the window. She sat down and the housekeeper served her a bowl of soup and crackers. This continued until Father Tougas was convinced that she had regained her strength and wouldn't have a relapse.

Anne continued to do what she could for Aila and the children. She was through helping Peter. He didn't need it anyway. He was working steadily and all were glad of that. Anne admired Aila for how she persevered with dignity and poise through the difficulties life had dealt her—living in miserable conditions, doing her best to care for and educate her children, and Aila so valued education. Even in that frigid, rundown shack, stacked safe from harm, there sat her treasured Harvard Classics and *The History of Nations*. She won the books in a contest while in school. Aila Rose was already devouring them. Aila carried those precious volumes with her every time they moved, and they had moved more than once a year her entire married life, which by then amounted to a dozen moves.

They moved once again but this time into no dreary little shack. They moved into regular *house*. It was a nice average size house in Kenwood, which was closer to Helena. It must have seemed massive compared to those three tiny shacks in Broadwater. It had a lovely fenced yard with a lawn, and best of all, it had a *bathroom*.

They even had enough money to subscribe to the newspaper. The paperboy delivered it on horseback at the same time every day, and every day Aila walked out to retrieve it and pet the horse. Grace always went with her.

One day after the boy rode off, Aila mused to herself, "Oh, I used to love to ride."

The next day when they went out to get the paper and pet the horse, Grace blurted out, "My mother would like to ride your horse!"

"Would you, Mrs. Thompson?" the boy asked.

"Oh, I would love to," she replied.

The paperboy dismounted and handed her the reins. Grace watched wide-eyed as her mother mounted the horse. She rode over to the skeet-shooting field across the street and sped the horse to a canter and rode round and round. Then she turned, spurred the horse and ran straight toward the irrigation ditch. Grace gasped. The horse leapt, and horse and rider sailed over the ditch. Grace was beside herself with excitement. Her mother was wonderful!

That evening Grace ran to the door as soon as she heard her father.

Oh, Father, Father! she exclaimed jumping up and down. Today when the paperboy came, he had a horse, a big white horse, and he let Mother ride the horse, and Mother rode the horse all through the field, and then the horse jumped over the ditch, with Mother on the horse, right over the ditch, oh, Father, it was wonderful, you should have seen it!

Peter canceled the paper.

ONE EVENING while drying the dinner dishes, a dish fell on the floor and broke. Before anyone else could pick it up, three-year-old Sammy grabbed it, gave it a jerky shake, and sliced the skin right above his eye. Aila nearly fainted. Peter attended to the cut. Aila ran to the neighbor's and called Father Tougas. He arrived promptly with a doctor.

The doctor examined, cleaned, and bandaged the wound. He held up his finger. "What's this?" he asked Sammy.

"Finger," Sammy replied. The doctor moved his finger and watched Sammy track it.

The doctor held up a dime. "What's this?"

"Dime," Sammy replied. The doctor gave him the dime and picked him up and handed him to Aila. He was fine.

By 1935, they had been living on the outskirts of Helena for close to three years. Peter was working steadily. Aila liked the house in Kenwood, my gosh, it had a *bathroom*, who wouldn't like it. Aila Rose and Grace were doing well in school. One evening after dinner, Aila was doing the dishes, Grace was helping her, Peter was sitting in the front room reading the paper, Sammy was playing at his feet. Aila put down the dish towel

BACK: *Aila Rose, Aila, Peter.* FRONT: *Patsy Ann, Grace. Helena, 1935.*

and walked to the bathroom door. Aila Rose had just given Patsy Ann a bath and was standing the two-year-old on the toilet to dry her.

"Aila Rose," Aila said, "we are going to have a baby."

Nonplused Aila Rose looked at her mother and asked, "Why do we need a baby? We've got one," and she resumed drying the one they already had.

Sometime before the blessed event, Peter announced that he had quit his job at the fort and was leaving for Butte. Aila was stunned.

She knew what this meant—Peter in and out of work, gambling in the saloons, moving from house to house, wondering how she would feed the children and pay the rent. She liked Butte, she was a convivial being to the core who enjoyed the excitement of city life, but much more she liked knowing there would be food on the table for her children and money to pay the rent. Here Peter had a steady job. Why not keep it? He could work at the fort until he retired and then receive a pension. And the Depression was still on. Why would any man in his right mind quit a job in the middle of the Depression? Especially a man with a wife and children to support and a baby on the way.

After the children were fast asleep, Aila told Peter that she did not want to go back to Butte. Here he had a steady job, and when he retired, he'd have a pension. How could he be sure he could find a job in Butte and keep it?

Peter moved back to Butte. He visited on Sundays.

Aila delivered their fifth child at St. John's Hospital, another girl. As with Patsy Ann, she was amazed by the size of her baby and very proud that she could produce such an infant.

Father Tougas stopped in to visit her while making his rounds at the hospital. "What are you going to name the child?" he asked.

"I'd like you to name her, Father," she said. "It's the only way I can thank you for all you've done for us."

He named her Mary.

Grace and Aila Rose in their store bought dresses. Cousins Patrick and Margaret are on the left. The baby is Mary.

While Aila was still convalescing in the hospital, Peter's brother and sister-in-law came to Helena and moved the children and the family belongings to Butte. Aila joined them with the baby when she was released from the hospital.

When Aila Rose saw her new little sister for the first time she asked, "What are you going to name the baby?"

"Mary," Aila said.

"Just Mary?" Aila Rose asked. "Aren't you going to give her a middle name?"

"You may give her a middle name, dear," said Aila.

Aila Rose remembered learning about St. Agnes in school.

"Agnes," she replied.

So she was Mary Agnes.

Mary was born in June. That October a severe earthquake struck Helena. St. John's Hospital was damaged beyond repair, as were the Kessler School and granite structures throughout the valley. The little log house that was their first home in Broadwater survived.

Chapter Fifty-five

Peter had rented a small house on Locust Street in Butte. It was aptly named. The place was full of bugs. Wide-eyed Patsy Ann watched her brave mother pluck furry monsters from the wall with a piece of newspaper and throw them in the fire. They had to have everything fumigated.

Soon after they were settled in Butte, Peter came home late after a night of cards—his old routine back in full swing. The children were fast asleep. He found Aila waiting up for him, sipping tea at the kitchen table. He sat down. She poured him a cup of tea. Then in her quiet, measured, firm tone, she said, "Peter, this has gone on long enough. You have five children now. You must work steady and support them."

As September drew near, the debate over sending the children to Catholic school reignited. Peter was adamant—they needn't go. Aila was equally adamant—they must go—when she got married she promised she would raise her children Catholic and she was going to do it the best way she knew how, which to her meant sending them to the experts—the nuns. Their pastor caught wind of this and came to the house and delivered a severe scolding: "You must send your children to Catholic school no matter what!"

Aila enrolled Aila Rose and Grace at St. Ann's.

Around the same time, news of a bonus for veterans of the World War resurfaced in the newspapers. It had been bandied about for years. Now it appeared imminent.

"Peter," Aila said, "that bonus money is going toward buying a house."

She looked around and found a nice house for sale on the West Side. It was the nicest part of town and a good neighborhood in which to raise children, and they could afford it.

Aila holding Mary, 1935

The picture of Peter that Aila kept in her wallet

No, that wouldn't do, Peter insisted, it was the house on the Flat, the one on Walnut Street, or no house at all.

On August 15, 1936, Aila bought the house on Walnut Street for one dollar. It cost $900. Peter used his war bonus to pay the $200 deposit. He mortgaged the $700 balance with the seller at six percent interest. Their monthly payment was $20. (Miner's day's pay was around $4.88 that year.) The deed was in Aila's name and her name only. The mortgage was in Peter's name. She owned the house, and he was obligated to pay for it.

THE HOUSE WAS in a typical Butte neighborhood. There was a bar across the street to the north, there was a bar across the street to the west, there was a bar across the alley, there were two grocery stores and a grade school within three blocks, and it was an easy walk to the closest Catholic church. It was also an easy walk to where Peter's father lived. Sam Thompson had lived with Jenny and her family for several years now. They still lived with Jenny's mother-in-law, Mrs. Reid. Mrs. Reid cooked and cleaned and babysat Jenny and Gordon's daughter while Jenny worked at Gamer's and Gordon worked on the hill. These days Sam left the house without a lunch bucket, meaning he wasn't working.

Each immigrant Thompson was supposed to send money for the next one until all came to America. The plan worked just fine until the chain broke. Even so, at one point I'm told the trunks were packed and Rose was ready to go with the rest of the children, but at the last minute, she changed her mind. No one seems to know why. Then one day twenty-one years had passed. Brigid, the youngest, was a preschooler when Sam left Ireland. Now she was a grown woman. The separation drew to a close in 1936 when Sam received a letter from Nellie saying: *If you want to see your wife alive you must come home at once.*

That convinced him.

He prepared to leave. He sold his half of the car to Peter. Peter's sister-in-law insisted that her husband should get Sam's share of the car. This time Peter didn't acquiesce.

Aunt B held a send-off party for Sam the night before he left. Everybody was there—Peter and Aila and the children; Mary, Jenny, and Pat and their families; Mrs. Reid; Aunt Annie and Uncle Hugh; Uncle John Gribben and his two adult children.

The next day all went to the depot to say their goodbyes. The huge clan huddled together on the platform for one final picture. Aila stood off to the side, feeling more spectator than participant. All took their turns

Farewell party for Sam at Aunt B's.
STANDING: *Mary; John Gribben's daughter, Jane; Pat; Aunt B; Aunt Annie; Ann Catherine—daughter of Jack Thompson who came on the ship with Peter; Aunt B's daughter, Rosemary; Barney Middlebrook—husband of the piano player Kathleen; Pat's wife, Katie; Uncle Hugh; Jack Thompson's wife, Mary; Jenny's husband, Gordon; Jack Thompson; Kathleen O'Keefe Middlebrook.*
SEATED: *Mrs. Reid, Jenny, Sam, Mrs. O'Keefe, Uncle John Gribben.*

Farewell to Sam.
STANDING: *Peter, Molly Breen, Jenny's daughter Martha, Jane, Walter Breen.*
SITTING: *Aunt B; Jenny; Mrs. Reid; Rosemary; Sam; Pat; Gordon;
Katie; Mary's daughter, Anne Jane; Mary.*

Pat, Jenny, Sam, Mary, and Peter.

Send off at the depot. Sam is in the middle with the tall hat. Grace, Patsy Ann and Sammy are in front on the left. At right front are Aila Rose, Peter holding Mary, Peter's sister Mary, and off to the side, Aila.

saying goodbye to Sam. When it was Peter's turn, he said to his father: "When you and I behind the veil are past, Oh, but the long, long while the world shall last." It's a verse from the *Rubáiyát* of Omar Khayyám. Seems a curious way to say goodbye to one's father. It continues: "Which of our coming and Departure heeds, As much as Ocean of a pebble-cast."

When Sam first arrived in Butte those twenty-one years ago, Aunt B told him, "Be sure to send the money to Rose through the bank." He did, and when he returned to Belfast, he carried with him a bundle of bank receipts proving he had sent money into the country and because he had, he qualified for a pension.

Sam found his wife in failing health though she was up and about. Forever the Victorian, Rose still wore her skirts to the ground with five or six petticoats underneath. She thought it improper for a lady's feet to show. (So did Sarah.)

John, Martha, and Jimmy were all married by this time; Nellie, Rosie, and Brigid were not and lived with Sam and Rose. Jimmy used to burst into the house as they sat down to tea and announce, "I'm going to sing you a song," and he'd sing them a song. Then he'd say, "Now I'm going to tell you a dirty joke," and he'd tell the joke and run off as abruptly as he arrived. After he left, Nellie would exclaim, "Our Jimmy! He's the picture of Denis!"

Brigid and Rosie Thompson

Martha holding John's son, Sam; Brigid and Rosie

Jimmy Thompson

Jimmy's chief interest in life was gambling, especially on the horses. "Our *purrr* Jimmy, he'd bet on two flies on the wall," said Brigid with a laugh. Jimmy never had any children. His first wife Eileen died of multiple sclerosis. He then married Kitty Kane, and when she contracted cancer of the throat, it looked certain he would be a widower again. However, later in life Jimmy suffered from edema and neglected to take his pills, for doing so would send him often to the bathroom and keep him from the bookies. Given the choice of doing what he wanted—going to the bookies—or living longer by taking his pills, he chose to do what he wanted. Kitty outlived him.

Two years after Sam returned to Belfast, his eldest grandson, Gilbert, won a writing contest and used the prize money to go to Europe. He traveled around the continent, visited relatives in Sweden, and whenever he ran out of money, stopped to work for awhile. In Paris, he rented an apartment near the Sorbonne with a wealthy Chinese man, or I should say, the man had been wealthy. His father had sent him to Europe to make the grand tour, but when the Sino-Japanese war started, he couldn't get any more money from his father in China, so he dismissed his servants and further economized by sharing an apartment with Gil. The two supplemented their spending money by playing the horses. The roommate devised a system: they never bet on the first race, started betting on the second race, always on the second favorite, and once they won they went home. They went every day. Apparently it worked pretty well.

Of course, Gil also went to Belfast. He was the only American grandchild Rose Thompson ever met. He went to see his great-granddad Thompson who was quite old, over ninety. He visited his uncle Denis Gribben (Rose's brother). Denis's wife was failing, and when Gil asked how she was, Denis said, "Oh, Gil, she couldn't pull a louse off a looking glass." She died soon after. The wake was at the house with the body laid out in the front room. After all had offered their respects and said a prayer, the men went to one part of the house and drank whiskey, and the women went to the kitchen and drank tea and told each other's fortune.

One day Nellie, Rosie, and Brigid took Gil on an excursion to Bangor. While walking along the beach, they came upon Foley's tent. Gil went in and had his fortune told. "You will marry a dark foreign kind of girl," Foley foretold. It proved to be a fortune remembered.

They returned to Belfast, and soon after, a policeman came to the door.

"Good morning, madame," he said to Rose. "Where's your good man?"

"He's yet to be born," she replied.

The policeman said he understood that she had an American grandson visiting. She said yes, she did. He said the American consul has asked the police to come 'round and tell all the Americans that their government wants them to go home at once on account of the war clouds gathering. Would she please tell her grandson? Yes she would.

She told Gil, and he went home.

BY THIS TIME, Rose was beginning to grow
dotty, as my Irish kin would say. She spent
her days sitting quietly in the chair next to
the window. Every day Sam would walk
downtown, bet a shilling on a soccer game,
come home, sit down in his chair, and
smoke his pipe. One day Rose dozed off
and awoke to see Sam sitting there, puffing
his pipe, and Nellie scurrying about the
room doing housework. Rose looked at
Sam, and then looked at Nellie, and said,
"Why are *you* with that old man? Why he's
as old as night, and you're as young as day.
And where did the wee 'un come from?"
and she gestured toward John's daughter.

Rosie and Rose

Rosie leaned over her mother and pointing to Sam said firmly, "That's
your husband."

Rose looked at her and laughed, she had a deep, hearty laugh. "My
husband?! You never saw my husband," she said. "That's an old man, and
he's a very, very *kind,* old man, but he's not my husband."

"Tell us what your husband is like," Sam said.

"My husband? My husband is young and tall and handsome with a
long ruddy face. 'Leave the gate open,' I'd say, 'Sam will be by.'"

Sam howled. "And I thought I was the one doing the chasing."

I'VE JUMPED AHEAD again. We return to 1936. War clouds are indeed gathering, yet see no evil is the order of the day.

The year wanes into 1937. Peter is standing at the mirror in the bathroom examining the gray streaks emerging along his temple. Hmmph, he
sighs, and shakes his head.

CHAPTER FIFTY-SIX

IN THE SPRING, the sad news arrived about John's wife. Peter's brother John met Annie shortly after he returned to Belfast. He courted her and they married and settled in a house near his mother and siblings. Their first child was a boy. They named him Sam. Their second child was a girl. John intended to name her after Nellie. Nellie thought naming a child after her was ridiculous and decided the baby should be named Mary. So she was Mary. John and Annie were expecting their third child when Annie became sick with cancer. She managed to hold on for the baby and delivered another girl, whom they named Rosaleen. Seeing that his wife was failing, John thought she should remain in the hospital, thinking she would get better care there, but Annie didn't want to stay in the hospital. She wanted to go home. She asked Nellie to ask Rose to tell John to take her home. They did and he did. The cancer wasted her away, she became frailer and frailer, so frail John could carry her in his arms like a small child, and six weeks after Rosaleen was born, she died.

PETER WAS NOW working at the Belmont. After his shift, he'd go home, stride into the house, into the kitchen, and greet Aila and the children. The delicious aroma of whatever Aila was cooking filled the room. No matter how simple, she managed to make it delicious. Her innate sense of style translated into flavor in her cooking. Nothing was plain, and now that Peter was working steadily, she could afford meat. Peter talked incessantly from the moment he walked in the house. He'd sit down with his newspaper, read a little then, "Aila, it says here that . . ." He'd read some more, "Aila, did you know that . . .," so even when he was reading, he was talking.

One day Grace bounded in the front door, and said to him, Look, Father, look! showing him the ring on her finger. Isn't it pretty? Grandma gave it to me.

Peter took the ring, left the house, went directly to Sarah's, and gave it back to her.

With Peter working steadily and keeping his gambling somewhat in check, Aila didn't have to work outside the home to make ends meet. She could devote all her energy to her family. She adored her children. Caring for them, educating them, protecting them, consumed her. She took them to the library every week. Every night she read to them. A favorite was the *Little Colonel* series. The children would listen rapt, laughing at the funny parts, crying at the sad parts, immersed in the escapades of the child heroine.

Though the children's essential needs were met, a roof over their heads and food on the table, Aila believed raising children entailed much more. She knew that their most enduring lessons came from how she and Peter conducted their lives and treated one another. Cross words were not spoken in front of the children, nor were adult worries, such as money, mentioned. She taught them right from wrong and good manners which Peter reinforced. She taught them good posture, how to sit, how to stand. She was determined to raise young ladies and a gentleman. She was particular that they spoke well and corrected their grammar. At dinnertime, she and Peter would ask Aila Rose and Grace what they learned in school that day, and they discussed current events. The younger three children weren't in school yet. Peter told them stories about the beautiful churches he had visited in France. They knew their father had fought in the war, but they heard none of the horrors. They knew about the *Croix de Guerre* from their mother. He never talked about it.

After dinner, Peter would quiz the girls on their spelling and their catechism. He taught them to memorize "Sam McGee" and "Dan McGrew" and the other lengthy poems he recited for them. He relished intellectual discourse and applied this pedagogically to his conversation with the girls. He would ask them about this or that, they answered, and he would round out their understanding of it, usually gently though not always, he did have a sharp edge. Once at the dinner table when his young nephew licked his knife, Peter reprimanded him sharply. "That's an ignorant thing to do," he said, which it was, but it was a rough way for a little child to hear it, and coming from his uncle Peter whom he adored, it really stung.

Aila sought to build a secure, peaceful world for the children. "Children don't ask to be born," she used to say. She was vigilant and had to be. There was a man in the vicinity, the husband of a woman she and Peter knew, who she made sure was never around the children alone. One didn't talk of such things, but everybody knew, and the women took steps to guard the children without alarming them.

June arrived. Aila Rose and Grace were out of school for the summer. The yard was finally bare of snow.

One day a commotion erupted in the backyard. Aila saw a boy shoot by followed closely by Grace wielding the clothes pole. The pole was so big and Grace so small that it must have looked like the pole was carrying her. Grace chased the boy way down the street until she ran out of breath. She walked home panting, still carrying the clothes pole. Aila was standing on the porch watching her.

Mother, that boy was being mean to Aila Rose! Grace blurted out, instinctively knowing an explanation was due. I imagine Grace then got a gentle talking to about how it wasn't lady-like to chase boys down the street with the clothes pole.

Peter walked in, said hello to everyone, and sat down in the front room. He called to Patsy Ann and Sammy. The four and five-year-olds obediently scurried to his side. He gave each a nickel and said, Now go across the street and buy me a pack of cigarettes. They ran out the door, down the steps, stopped dead at the street, looked both ways as strictly instructed by their mother, then dashed across the street to the saloon. They scurried up to the bar, grasped the edge, stepped onto the rail, and mounting their tallest tip toes tried to peer over the bar. Spying two sets of tiny fingers clutching the bar, the bartender leaned forward, and asked, What can I do for you?

A pack of cigarettes for my father, please, said Sammy in his most grown up voice. The bartender placed the cigarettes on the bar. Sammy pulled the nickel from his pocket and set it on the bar. Patsy Ann's eyes were fixed on something else.

Give me your nickel, Sammy said to Patsy Ann.

No, I want a candy bar, she said.

Patsy, give me your nickel.

No! I want a candy bar.

Patsy, Sammy said growing cross, we're supposed to buy cigarettes for Father. Now give me the nickel.

No!

Ahhh, Sammy grimaced and turned around exasperated. Girls! He stomped back across the street. Patsy Ann remained firmly planted at the bar, dreaming of her candy bar.

Sammy returned with their father. Patsy Ann, give me the nickel, Peter said. She did as told. Peter bought his cigarettes and the three walked back across the street. You little spalpeen, he said to Patsy Ann, and playfully swatted her on the bottom with his newspaper all the way home.

The year before Aila and Peter and the children returned to Butte the miners went on strike. It was violent and it was long—four and a half months. When it was over, the miners had a five-day week and a union, ending twenty years of open shop. Return of the union meant return of Miner's Union Day, and now it was Miners' Union Day 1937. They went to the parade, and a fine parade it was. Then Peter and Aila and the children joined the rest of the extended family at the Columbia Gardens for a picnic and, of course, the miners' competitions. Peter played the patient in the first-aid competition as he had the year before. Afterwards, the children frolicked on the swings and monkey bars, the adults visited, all had a grand time on the beautiful lush lawn adorned with magnificent flower arrays.

Pipefitters Union parading.
BUTTE-SILVER BOW PUBLIC ARCHIVES PH01851D

First-aid competition, Columbia Gardens.
BUTTE-SILVER BOW PUBLIC ARCHIVES PH01854

The next big event was the Fourth of July, which lasted three days. No snow was forecast, only thunderstorms. On the fifth of July, Peter emerged from the bedroom decked in his American Legion uniform and sat down to brush his shoes. Aila walked to the back door and called the children. They scampered in. She washed the little ones' hands and faces and dusted off the clothes that only moments ago had been presentable. Aila Rose and Grace descended the stairs sporting their drill team uniforms. Together they left for the parade.

The men in the drum corps were aligned according to height with the tallest in front. The buglers marched behind the drummers. Peter was a bugler and among the shortest men, so he marched in the last row. Aila Rose and Grace marched in the drill team. Aila and the little ones watched from the sidelines. Butte really knew how to put on a parade. The entire town turned out.

After the parade, there was a mass exodus up the hill to the Columbia Gardens. The adults sat on blankets laid out on the lush, green lawn while the children frolicked on the brightly painted cowboy swings, slides, monkey bars, and other amusements. One looked like a giant umbrella frame. The children grasped the bottom ring, ran as fast as they could, then lifted their feet and spun round and round.

BACK: *Peter and Aila Rose.* FRONT: *Mary, Sammy, Patsy Ann, summer 1937*

IN THE FALL, Aila Rose began her second year at Girls Central. It was an all girls Catholic high school run by the Sisters of Charity. Most of the teachers were nuns. The students studied Latin, history, mathematics, religion, science, and English. Home economics was not in the curriculum. Grace continued at St. Ann's. She was in the sixth grade. The little ones were still at home.

About once a month, or more, Peter would come home battered and bruised after a night of cards which had ended in a brawl. "We Irish fight too much," he muttered as Aila dressed his wounds. Then she made a pot of tea, and they sat and talked.

Unfortunately what had looked to be an improving economic picture was not to last the year. The economy again sputtered and stalled. Copper buying stopped. Mine production was curtailed. The Second World War would rescue the red metal, but that was still a few years off. The Great Depression was still on.

Despite the grim economic conditions, Peter kept his job and worked steadily on the hill. These days, he was working at the Tramway Mine. Aila wished he had stayed at the Belmont. She wished he would work anywhere but the Tramway and told him so. She had a bad feeling about it.

One day he came home in the middle of his shift white as a ghost. What happened? Aila asked. He said he went to inspect a drift, and as he turned the corner, he came face to face with a human skeleton imbedded in the wall of the mine. It shook him to the core.

Now he was working night shift at the Tramway. This particular evening he sat down to dinner grumbling about the greenhorn he was training on the motor. Then he changed the subject and asked the girls what they had learned at school that day. Aila Rose said her teacher had assigned a project and she needed pictures for it. After dinner, Peter laid

Trolley tram motor on the 1500 level of the Tramway Mine.
© WORLD MUSEUM OF MINING #2979

The Tramway shaft looking up to the surface.
© WORLD MUSEUM OF MINING #2641

out his newspaper on the table and opened it to the colorful rotogravure in the center. "There are the pictures you need, Aila Rose," he said.

A car honked. Peter walked into the kitchen and picked up his lunch bucket. Aila dried her hands on her apron and said to him, "Peter, don't let that man drive that motor today," referring to the greenhorn.

"Aila, what do mean don't let him drive that motor?" he said

"I mean it, Peter. It will be trouble for you. Don't let him drive the motor for *three* days. Something is going to happen in that mine today, I just know it."

"You're always going by those old superstitions of yours," he said, "nothing will happen."

"Oh, yes, something will happen," she said. "Don't let him drive that motor for *three* days."

He scoffed at her.

"Then don't go to work today," she said. "I tell you, Peter, I know something is going to happen to somebody down in that mine today!"

"Aila," he said, "you're always hollerin' at me to go to work when I'm not working, and now I'm working and you want me to stay home."

"Yes," she said, "but when I want you to stay home it's because I know something is *wrong*!"

In fact, there had been days when he came home and said something happened just as she had predicted, and he should have listened to her and stayed home. But I suppose he forgot all about that.

He said goodbye and left.

Later in the evening, Aila Rose and Grace went up to their room. They slept upstairs in the big open room on the second floor. The chimney passed through the middle keeping it toasty warm. It was now late October and below freezing at night. Aila got the little ones ready for bed. They slept in the big bedroom in the back of the house. Aila read to them, and then heard their prayers, and tucked them in. Then she finished the ironing and fell into bed in the small bedroom off the kitchen.

The men from the Company came during the night. Either they brought Sarah with them or Aila asked them to go get her.

Aila returned before the children were up. She started breakfast. The little ones woke up and crept sleepy-eyed into the kitchen.

Sammy and Patsy Ann, come get dressed, she said, and ushered them back into the bedroom. She picked up Mary and Mary's clothes and walked into the kitchen. She pulled a chair over in front of the oven and stood Mary on it and began to dress her. Sarah walked in from the small bedroom. She looked at Aila with a silent expression that asked, Well? Aila shook her head and continued to dress Mary. Aila Rose walked down the stairs into the kitchen just as this unspoken conversation was taking place. Aila stopped what she was doing and turned to her and said, "Aila Rose, your father has been in an accident. He's in the hospital."

Aila finished dressing Mary. Then she fed the children and sent Aila

Rose and Grace to school and returned to the hospital. Sarah stayed with the little ones.

Peter had been working as swamper on the motor that night on the 2800-foot level of the Tramway. He told his partner, this greenhorn whom he was training, that he would walk ahead to move the cars out of the way. The greenhorn was supposed to wait until Peter was safely clear of the tracks before he drove the motor through. He started the motor, drove along, drove through a split curtain at a bulkhead, kept going until he heard Peter yell, "—— Help me I'm hurt!" He didn't even know he had hit him. He stopped the motor and ran back to where Peter was lying on the side of the tunnel. Peter had been crushed between the bulkhead and the motor. The partner found the shift boss and told him what happened. The shift boss came immediately with three men. They put Peter on a stretcher and covered him with a blanket. He was in shock but conscious. They hurried him to the waiting cage. Once above ground, they loaded him into the waiting ambulance.

Though the students at Girls Central were not allowed to leave during school hours, at lunchtime Aila Rose snuck out and went to the hospital. From outside the room, Peter could be heard yelling at Aila, "This is all your fault! You made me work! This wouldn't have happened if you hadn't made me work!" Then more softly, Aila could be heard saying, "Peter, be careful you'll hurt yourself." Aila Rose walked into the room. Peter was in a pelvic sling. His left femur was broken and his pelvis was crushed. The nurse saw Aila Rose and quickly ushered her out. She fainted. The nurse put her in a chair.

When she came to, the nurse asked her, "Have you had any lunch?"

"No," she said. The nurse sent her back to school.

Peter rallied the next morning, but by afternoon, he slipped out of consciousness and never awoke. Two days later, during the night, he died. It was October 31, All Saints Eve, the anniversary of the day he saved that man's life in Flanders. He was forty-two.

AILA SAT IN the front room of the house, not moving, not speaking, catatonic as it were, paralyzed by shock and sorrow. Aunt B sat beside her, holding her hand. Peter's brother Pat walked to the back bedroom. The five children were asleep in the bed. He gently shook Aila Rose awake.

He gathered her up in his arms, and held her on his lap, and told her. She got up and walked into the front room. She looked at her mother. Aila didn't move, didn't react, said nothing. Aunt B extended her arms. Aila Rose went to her and Aunt B embraced her.

Throughout the day, a steady stream of family and friends filled the house. The neighbor stood at her gate and watched. All who entered looked at her and shook their heads.

"He'll be waked here at the house," someone said.

"No," said Aila. Not with the little ones. She left the room. Aila Rose and Grace found her later. She was in the closet crying.

Neighborhood children knocked at the front door. They didn't know what had happened. It was Halloween and they wanted to know if Aila Rose and Grace could come out and play.

Why don't I take the children to a movie, someone offered, and did.

John Gribben bought a coat for Aila to wear to the funeral.

The wake was at Daly-Shea. Family and friends gathered to pray the Rosary. The next morning the American Legion drum and bugle corp marched with the hearse from Daly-Shea to St. Ann's. After the solemn requiem Mass, the cortege of hearse and drum corps and mourners processed slowly to Holy Cross Cemetery, the drummers beating a sorrowful refrain. The family car was behind the drum corps, so for three miles, there before them, Aila and the children could see the empty spot where Peter had marched.

The procession slowly turned into the cemetery. The large crowd of silent mourners massed at the grave site around the flag-draped casket. Father said the prayers and gave the blessing. The honor guard lifted the flag from the casket, pulled it taut, carefully folded it, and presented it to Aila. The casket was then slowly lowered into the grave. The riflemen raised their rifles, took aim at the sky, and fired. Aila screamed and fainted. They fired the second volley, the third.

The bugler sounded Taps.

American Legion leading the funeral procession to St. Ann's.

Leaving Peter's funeral, St. Ann's Church.
Aila is walking to the left with Pat. Grace is behind them.
SMITHERS, BUTTE, MONTANA

Processing to Holy Cross Cemetery.

The three volleys

*Aila, Pat, Aila Rose,
and Mary*

CHAPTER FIFTY-SEVEN

SAM THOMPSON had just walked in from his brother Peter's funeral when he heard the news.

Rosie dropped to her knees beside Rose. "Oh, Ma," she said, "all the praying you did for those sons of yours and they came out of the war. Now look how quickly they were taken away!"

"Yes," said Rose, "but at least I know where their bodies are."

AILA WAS THIRTY-SIX years old. Night after night, she retreated to her room, closed the door, and cried. During the day, she held herself together by sheer force of will. She was overwrought with sorrow and worry. She had $250. That's it. Peter had no life insurance. Social security had just started, but it didn't include widows and dependent children. The Depression was still on. She had five children to support, three of them preschool. She was terrified that she would lose the house and they'd be on the street with nowhere to go and someone would take her children away just as she had been taken away.

I asked Mom and my aunts, "Did anyone help Grandma after Peter died? Was anyone even in a position to help?" In separate conversations, two of my aunts said the same thing: "They could have not hurt." Auntie Mary added, "Our Lord taught us to help the widows and orphans, not to steal from them."

A man from the Company came to the house. He explained to Aila that she was due money because of the accident. She listened numbly. He asked whether she would like to have all of it right now or in monthly payments. Her first thought was the house—to have it paid for would eliminate her greatest worry. And she still owed a considerable sum to the funeral parlor. The Company paid for a standard funeral, but when she was making the funeral arrangements somebody insisted that Peter be buried in the most expensive casket and left Aila to pay for it. Even with the settlement, she knew she had to get a job. She couldn't afford to be sick so she better get her teeth fixed. She asked the man if she could take part of the money right away and get the rest monthly. He said he would arrange the payments any way she liked.

Within a month, she received the partial lump sum and paid off the house. Her home was now secure. The house was in her name and her name only. No one else could lay claim to

Patsy, Mary, and Sammy, taken shortly after Peter died

it. Had the house been in Peter's name with no will, there's no telling what could have happened. Now it was hers. Her dream of a permanent roof for her children had been realized. All she had to do was keep up with the taxes.

She paid the funeral parlor bill and put the rest of the partial lump sum in the bank. The remainder of the settlement she would receive in monthly payments of $83. That was roughly two-thirds of what Peter had been earning. Those payments would continue until Mary entered first grade.

Aila was very private about her personal business, but everyone knew if a man was killed in the mines, there would be a settlement for the family. Soon after she received the money from the Company, a couple appeared at her door. Aila was at the next door neighbor's when they arrived. Seeing who the visitors were, the neighbor cautioned, "Aila, those people are not your friends." Aila walked back to the house and did the polite thing—she invited them in.

This was a married couple in which the wife ruled the husband with an iron rod. Her work was easy. He was known around the neighborhood and in the mine by his wife's maiden name. We'll call her Atrocia.

Years earlier, shortly after Atrocia and her husband were married, Peter's quick mind discovered her dark secret. He confronted her with it one evening. I wonder if the husband even knew before then. It suffices to say, Peter and Atrocia were never friends. He tolerated her, and she him, because of the husband.

Atrocia kept quite busy attending society and church functions, leaving her children to be raised by a variety of babysitters. Though she watched Aila struggle to keep body and soul together, when Atrocia's children outgrew clothes that would fit Aila's children, those clothes went to the church. Oh, you donate such beautiful things, the women would say. Her charity was strictly for strangers and for show. When one of Aila's daughters happened to be playing with her children at her house and the dinner hour arrived, Atrocia would send Aila's daughter to sit on the porch while the family ate. Her own mother scolded her, "How can you be so mean to a little child?" As a little girl, Atrocia had been one of the poor little neighborhood children who could always count on a bowl of soup from Mrs. Hughes. She often spoke of how kind Mrs. Hughes had been to feed her when she was a hungry little girl, that same Mrs. Hughes whose granddaughter she would not feed and sent to sit on the porch.

When Aila ran off to marry Peter, she had to leave some of her books behind, which must have been heart breaking for her; she so valued books. Sarah gave the books to Atrocia, probably out of spite. Atrocia didn't read much, but she was one of those persons who likes to have things. Aila had written her name in the books, so there was no mistake as to their ownership. Some years after Peter died, Atrocia tired of having those books around the house, but instead of asking Aila if she would like them back, she gave the books to the Salvation Army.

And now she has learned that Aila has received a settlement from the Company, and as soon as she does, she marches her husband directly to Walnut Street and demands that Aila "loan" them some of that money. They wanted to build an addition to their house, and Atrocia's brother wanted money to start a business. You'll have plenty of money, she told Aila. You can do without some of it right now.

Aila said she couldn't afford to loan money to anyone. Atrocia insisted that she could and she bullied and insisted and bullied and insisted and bullied and bullied and bullied poor Aila until she wore her down. Grace was sitting on the steps, out of sight, listening to all this, and when she heard these repeated demands for money, she burst into the room crying, "Don't hurt my mother! Don't hurt my mother!"

Aila was emotionally in ruins after Peter died. She was easy prey. She could barely think straight. She couldn't muster the strength to throw Atrocia out of the house, and Atrocia wasn't about to leave until she accomplished her mission, which she did.

Aila never saw a dime of that money returned.

Stealing from widows.

Sarah was still living with Aila and the children. She had been there since the night of the accident. Aila allowed her to stay under the condition that she not bring any of her friends over. Aila didn't want Sarah's friends around the children and she didn't want her children to witness their grandmother's legendary drunken parties. Sarah's stay came to an abrupt end when Aila walked into the house and found Sarah beating four-year-old Patsy Ann and the house full of drunks. She ordered the drunks out of the house and told Sarah that she couldn't live there anymore. "Children don't ask to be born," she said.

Winter settled in and laid his thick, icy blanket over the town. Aila was taking the children somewhere in the car. She had the right of way and pulled into the intersection. The other driver tried to stop at the stop sign but couldn't. The car slid on the ice and hit Aila and the children broadside. Sammy was cut perilously close to his eye and required stitches. Aila and the girls were badly bruised. Atrocia's brother came as soon as he heard about the accident, the one to whom Aila had "loaned" money for his business. He said he'd fix the car right away. He took the car and she never saw it again.

Stealing from widows.

Others did try to help. This day, three of Aila's friends came to see her. They were Helen Davis, Bertha Flomer, and Rhea La Londe.

The women sat down in the front room. Aila served tea. They asked how she was getting along, how were the children coping. Then one spoke for the three. She said they knew, with Peter gone, Aila would have to work to support herself and the children. Aila Rose and Grace were big enough to fend for themselves after school until she got home from work. As for the little ones, she proposed that Aila send them to the Paul Clark Home.

Aila with Sammy, Mary, and Patsy Ann at their house on Walnut Street

They could stay there during the week, they would be well-fed and cared for, and they could come home and stay with her on the weekends. That way Aila could work during the week and not worry about them. She said the three of them had agreed to pay for the children to live there.

It was a very generous offer—so many decisions. Thoughts of the orphanage came back. She could not fathom being separated from her children. She graciously thanked the women, but said no thank you, she'd keep the children at home. She'd manage somehow.

She went to the dentist to see what could be done about her teeth. One evening little Patsy Ann climbed into bed with her. By morning the pillow was soaked with blood. "It's all right, dear," she comforted Patsy. "I had a tooth pulled, that's all." She had to have all of them pulled.

She took a job working part time in the fabric department at Penny's. She worked on commission. She was a skilled seamstress, so well-suited to the job. She sent Sammy, Patsy Ann, and Mary to nursery school while she was at work. This would do for now while the children were small and she was still receiving a monthly check from the Company. However for the long term, she resolved to find something else. Her path was clear. She had five children to feed, clothe, and educate, and they depended on her and her alone. She said, "I made up my mind I was going to work every day for the rest of my life regardless of everything. I had my family to raise."

They needed towels, so she put a set on lay-away at Penny's. Finally, she paid for them in full and took them home. When it came time that they needed to be washed, she washed the towels and hung them outside on the clothes line to dry. The next morning they were gone. About a week later, the towels appeared on the neighbor's line.

Stealing from widows.

Peter's military headstone arrived and was put in place at his grave in the Thompson family plot. While standing there, it occurred to Aila that

Denis had no headstone. She wrote to the War Department and asked about getting one. They referred her to the British government. She never did receive a British military marker for Denis; however, there is now a headstone at Denis's grave. It's rose granite. My guess is, she bought it, probably years later when she could afford it. She probably thought it's what Peter would have wanted her to do.

At some point, she applied for and received a veteran's widow and dependents pension. A man from the American Legion told her she was eligible. She received a small monthly pension for each child which would continue until he or she left school. The widow's portion was means tested. Aila easily qualified, though not for long. And she told no one, not another living soul, about getting this money. She kept it a strict secret. She didn't need anybody else coming around demanding money from her.

A man from the Legion wrote to the army on her behalf about getting a certificate representing the *Croix de Guerre*. Through the army, she received the beautiful certificate from the French government. It was quite impressive. She had it framed and hung it prominently in the front room. (Rose had the original in Belfast.)

Visits with Aunt B remained part of her ritual and were a comfort to both women. She always brought the children with her. The youngest, Mary, said she loved to sit and listen to her mother and Aunt B talk. When asked what they talked about, she said, "Oh, I don't know, they didn't gossip. They just talked. I loved to listen." Aunt B would read the tea leaves in Aila's cup. It would be something like, "Oh, Aila, you're going to receive a letter, an *important* letter."

Even years later, Aunt B would remark wistfully, "I still miss Peter when I read a book. I don't have him to talk to about it."

After a nice visit over cups of tea and bread and butter with sugar sprinkled on top, Aila and the children would thank Aunt B, say goodbye, and walk home. This day was in winter. A frigid gale "strong enough to blow the

Aunt B

horns off a goat," as Aunt Annie used to say, pushed and froze them all the way home. They rushed shivering into the house. Aila quickly closed the door and hurried the children over to the stove. She peeled coats, hats, and mittens from the little ones saying expressively as she did, "The north wind doth blow, and we shall have snow, and what will poor robin do then?" and she cast the back of her hand against her forehead. "He'll sit in the barn, to keep himself warm, and hide his head under his wing, poor thing." And they scurried off and she started dinner.

After dinner, Aila Rose and Grace said goodnight and went upstairs to their room. Aila ushered the little ones to the back bedroom and helped them into their pajamas. Then she sat down on the bed and read to them. Then she heard their prayers, tucked them in, and kissed them goodnight.

In May, Anne McDonnell came to town, and she and Walter took the children out for ice cream for Patsy Ann's birthday.

THREE YEARS after Peter died, Aila Rose graduated from Girls Central and entered nursing school. The school was at St. James Hospital and was run by the Sisters of Charity. The students lived at the hospital and were sequestered all but half an hour a day. Tuition for the entire three-year program was due soon after enrollment. When the bill came due, Aila went

Sammy's First Communion. Aila Rose and Grace; Patsy, Sammy, and Mary, 1939

to see Aila Rose at the hospital. "Aila Rose," she said, "are you sure you are going to stay? Because if you aren't, I won't pay Sister." Despite severe homesickness, Aila Rose was determined. She always wanted to be a nurse. "Yes, Mother," she said, "I am going to stay." Aila couldn't afford to pay the full amount up front as required, so she worked out a payment plan with the very stern Sister John Marie. Then she had a telephone installed in the house just in case one of the sisters or Aila Rose needed to reach her.

In the spring, a neighbor from down the street, a tall, ponderous woman, came to the house complaining that Sammy had been playing ball and broke her window. Aila apologized and said she would pay to have it fixed. She scraped together the money and paid for the window. The woman came back another day and complained again that Sammy had broken her window. Aila paid for it.

A few weeks later Aila was standing at the sink washing dishes when suddenly the tall, ponderous woman appeared at the back door, which was next to the sink. "Mrs. Thompson!" she boomed, "Sammy's broken my window *again!*" and she glared down at Aila from her towering height. Aila lifted the cast iron frying pan she was washing, looked up at the woman, and said sternly, "Sammy is at camp!" The woman ran off and never accused Sammy again.

More stealing from widows.

Aila returned to her dishes. A little while later Mary pattered into the kitchen. "Mama," she said.

"Yes, dear."

"Would you help me cut out paper dolls?"

"I'll give you a penny for each one you can cut out in the lines," Aila said, and Mary learned she could do it herself without hearing no, I'm too busy.

After Sammy returned from camp, Aila took him with her to Twin Bridges. They went by train. Her going there had something to do with someone she had known at the orphanage who was now on hard times or sick. She took steps to help. I wish I knew the rest.

CHAPTER FIFTY-EIGHT

IT IS EARLY morning. In Helena, Father Tougas has risen and turned on the radio and turned it up quite loudly so he can hear the war news wherever he is in the rectory. In doing so, he wakes up the entire house.

Father has diabetes. This is a good day. On his day off, he locks himself in his room. After a day of thorough rest, he is reinvigorated for the next six, every minute of which he will fill. He will die spent.

Aila has been up for two hours. The children are waking to the delicious smell of pop-overs puffing in the oven, forming crisp outer crusts while the moist insides fill with air. They emerge from their bedrooms to find their mother, as usual, looking impeccable, her hair perfectly coifed, her dress neat and appropriate, and wearing those fashionable high-heeled open-toed pumps with barely a hint of toe showing.

A few hours pass and the air-raid siren sounds in Belfast. All scurry to the coal-hole, all but Nellie. She puts on the kettle. God forbid they endure an air raid without a cup of tea.

When the all clear sounds, Brigid asks her, "What are you going to do now?"

"I think I'll go up and go to bed," says Nellie.

"Me, too," says Brigid.

Neighbors search high and low for the Thompson sisters. They are nowhere to be found, presumed buried in the rubble.

The next day the postman exclaims to Nellie, "Did you hear? Whitehouse Mill was bombed last night!"

"Good riddance!" she says.

The first time the air-raid siren blew, the only thing Rosie grabbed when she ran for shelter was Peter's *Croix de Guerre* certificate which hung prominently above the mantle. Shortly after the Blitz began, Sam and Rose and Rosie and John's children evacuated to the old McDonald/

Rose at Magheralane during the war. John's son, Sam, is in the foreground.

Gribben home in Magheralane. Nellie and Brigid stayed in Belfast. "If the bomb's for me the bomb's for me," Nellie said with a shrug. Brigid agreed. Nellie would live to be ninety-seven. Brigid is still with us as I write; she is over ninety.

John also remained in Belfast and worked as an ambulance attendant during the war. "He visited his sisters *every* day and night," Brigid said. Around the neighborhood, he was known as "the marine."

Nellie; Sam; John; Rose; Brigid; Rosie; Brigid's husband, James. The children are John's—Rosaleen, Sam, and Mary. This was taken around 1941. Rose passed away in 1943.

AILA WAS NOW contemplating her next move. The monthly checks from the Company would end soon. The part-time job at Penny's would no longer do. She resolved to find something else. "I had a man's job to do and I needed a man's job to do it!" she said. She said this not out of competition but *survival*. Her children depended on her and her alone. She had been thrust into the role of sole provider, and she needed a provider's job to do it.

On Saturday, as was her habit, she took the children uptown to the library. Aila visited for a few minutes with her friend who ran the children's section. The children disappeared into the stacks; each found a book and sat down to read. Aila walked to the reference section and began her research. This became a regular component of their Saturday ritual. After much study and thoughtful consideration, she concluded the job for her was that of postal clerk. Whether the mines were up or down, the post office was always going. It was a stable, steady job, and when she retired, she would receive a pension. It spelled *security*, something she had never known.

Mary, Sammy, and Patsy Ann

She took the civil service exam and achieved a near perfect score, extra points were added for being a veteran's widow. She received a temporary appointment as substitute clerk. As a substitute, she would have to work on short notice at all hours, which was difficult with small children at home. Nevertheless, she was determined to do it. Once she had proven her abilities and demonstrated that she was a hard worker, she should have a good chance at a permanent appointment as regular clerk, with regular pay and regular hours.

When a position became available, the boss, who was a married man, told her she couldn't have the job because she was a woman. However, he would reconsider if she would . . . "go out with him." She was appalled. Of course, she would do no such thing. She refused, and the job went to someone else. She kept working there, sure that if she worked hard and did a good job, she would get an appointment. Her married boss frequently reminded her how easy it could be . . . She bristled at the indignity. She would not give in. She was single-minded in her determination to get the job honestly and she would not be diverted by a predatory reprobate. She was convinced that this was the best job for her, it was secure, she needed it for her children, and she was going to get it.

And every Tuesday evening after work she left the post office and walked next door to St. Mary's and made the novena to Our Lady of Perpetual Help.

Again a position became available, again she was propositioned, again she said no, and was passed over for the job.

She kept praying.

Some of the men at the post office were resentful toward her. She thought it was because they didn't want a woman to work there. Once she came home after a day of abuse and scowled, "They can push a mouse against a brick wall but they can't push it through!" I wonder if part of the reason they were resentful and gave her a hard time was because she was a hard worker. The lazy are often resentful of the hard working— they don't want to be shown up. Aila was a diligent worker and very bright. Some of her co-workers were not. She said some days the men threw entire bags of mail into the fire. They just couldn't be bothered with it. She glanced down at one bag about to be burned and spied a familiar name. It was an envelope addressed to Aunt B. She picked it up and delivered it to her. It was money from some stock.

Other men at the post office were kind to her, were conscientious, were gentlemen, were not married, and were smitten with her.

Since she was a substitute, she worked wherever she was needed, usually at the main post office in the Federal Building across the street from the ruins of the blown-up Miners' Union Hall. Sometimes she worked at the P.O. Newstand. The man who ran the newstand gave her out-of-date magazines with the covers torn off that otherwise would have been thrown out. As a result, she and the children read a wide variety of magazines, whichever he gave her that week. Regarding news magazines, she said, "You must read several to get a balanced view."

The big news, of course, was the war. The mines were booming. Miners were exempt from the draft. The United States had been in the war for over a year now, the war for which Aila Rose and Grace were old enough had they been boys and for which Sammy was too young.

Aila traded ration coupons to get what she needed. She traded cigarette coupons for butter, coffee coupons for sugar or for shoes for the children. She never had enough money to spend all her ration coupons.

Aila Rose was now midway through her third year of nursing school. One day while in the midst of performing her hospital duties, Sister John Marie sent for her. Aila Rose held her breath, anticipating a severe scolding that always ended with, "If it weren't for your little mother, I'd put you out!" Instead, Sister said sternly, "Your grandmother is in the hospital and you are not to see her."

I don't know why Sarah was in the hospital. Since Sister John Marie forbade Aila Rose from seeing her, no doubt at Aila's request, I wonder if it had something to do with her drinking.

After James Rigley departed from Sarah's life, and possibly from this life for all I know, Sarah went through a succession of men. It seemed every time Aila and the children saw her, she was with a new man. Not long after her hospital stay, she settled on one. He was either a bit dim or in a perpetual drunken fog. Everybody called him Denny though his name was Daniel—Daniel Sheehan. He was from County Kerry. His brogue was so thick that the children could understand almost nothing he said, so possibly he was saying Danny but it sounded like Denny.

Sarah married Denny on August 6, 1943. She was sixty-eight and he was sixty-five. He had been married before and was divorced. One day that November Sarah must have been feeling lone and lorn, or bored, for she marched to the courthouse and filed a complaint against Denny. She claimed that they had never cohabited, and he secretly never intended to live with her nor consummate the marriage. Therefore their marriage was a fraud and should be annulled. They must have patched things up because she didn't go through with it.

They lived in what was left of the Cabbage Patch. Much of the Cabbage Patch had been destroyed by this time. On that score, Aila had a strong opinion, "Some would-be goody, goody politicians or somebody cleaned out the Cabbage Patch and you see the Silver Bow Homes there now. It was history that they destroyed. Every nationality, they say, on the globe was represented in the Cabbage Patch. It was like a small town by itself!"

Sarah and Denny's little gray shack together with several others formed a horseshoe. In the center of the horseshoe, amidst the dirt and weeds, sat three outhouses. Sarah and Denny's shack had a dirt floor except for the kitchen which had a plank floor. Even in a house with a dirt floor, Sarah adorned the tables with her embroidered handiwork. Her home always smelled faintly of goose grease and the inhabitants of whiskey. As always, she kept herself stitched and starched and her house neat and clean, she was up to date with happenings around Butte and around the world, and much of the time she was drunk.

In her sober moments, she never sat with an empty lap; she crocheted or embroidered, rocking in the rocker, singing Welsh hymns, and everywhere she lived, she kept a garden.

Aila took the children to visit their grandmother from time to time. Before they went in, she would lean down and speaking directly to each child, delivered firm instructions: "You are to sit quietly in the chair and you are not to move." They entered and did as told. Sarah would sit and embroider while she and Aila chatted. Her revolver was always lying out on the table. After a brief visit, Aila would turn to the children and say, "Children, we are going now," and off they went.

Grace and Mary were the only two who ever visited Sarah on their own. One Sunday morning after Mass Mary walked up the hill to Sarah's and found her grandmother sprawled on an armchair holding her head. Denny poured a shot of whiskey and gave it to Sarah. "Your grannie is sick. This will make her feel better," he explained. When Mary returned home, she told her mother, "Mama, I hope I'm never so sick I have to drink whiskey for breakfast."

During one summer Patsy Ann took piano lessons and Mary took tap dancing lessons. Patsy Ann didn't like to go over to Sarah's. She didn't like that whiskey smell. Mary didn't mind it and sometimes stopped in to see her grandmother on her way home. One day she walked in to find Sarah sewing. Her feet peddled the treadle so rapidly they were nearly a blur. "Go pick dandelion leaves for me," she said glancing at Mary. "Pick only the young tender ones." Sarah would use the leaves to make dandelion wine. After Mary completed her chore, Sarah took her by the hand, and they walked up the street past Big Ethel's brothel to the C.O.D., one of Butte's roughest bars, where as advertised, there was "something doing every minute," which usually meant a fight. My dad told me the C.O.D. was so rough that he and his friends wouldn't go there. It was one of Sarah's favorite haunts. Sarah and Mary sat down at the bar. Sarah had a shot of whiskey. Mary had a shot glass full of pop. "Why don't you dance for us?" one of the men asked, seeing Mary's tap shoes. So she put on her shoes and gladly performed. The old men threw coins.

By now, Sammy, Patsy Ann, and Mary were all enrolled at St. Ann's School. It was close enough to walk, about a mile away. When winter weather was especially fierce, Aila told them, "Try to go to school. If it's too bad by the time you get to Grand Avenue, come back." They never did. During one terrible blizzard, while walking home they found their mother walking to meet them. It seems surviving the trek to school still counted as one of the smaller securities.

Though Aila was proficient at stretching every penny and found a use, a reuse, and another reuse for everything, her income was meager. As a substitute, she didn't always have full-time work. Children get sick and unexpected bills arise. Sammy and Mary had to have their tonsils out. Patsy Ann had her tonsils and appendix out. Aila made every tuition payment, though not always on time. When Father handed out the report cards he would bellow at the Thompson children, "You don't pay on time and you don't even pay the full amount!" (They had a family discount.) The children were mortified.

Grace used to say, "When I die, if I see him, I'll know I went to the wrong place."

Sammy, on the other hand, saw an opportunity. "Sister, I couldn't finish my assignment because my mother is a poor widow and she has to go to work and I have to do all the work around the house. My sisters don't do anything."

Mary overheard him and retorted, "No, he doesn't! He doesn't do anything! Patsy does it!"

That priest was transferred, and a new pastor was assigned to the parish, an Irishman named Father O'Connor. One of his first acts was to do away with tuition.

The next year Patsy Ann was in the fifth grade and Sammy was in sixth. The two grades were combined, so brother and sister were in the same classroom. One day the door flew open and in burst Father O'Connor. Sister stopped talking, all scrambled to their feet and intoned, "Good *morrrning, Faaa*ther."

"Good morning, Sister. Good morning, children," he said cheerily. "You may be seated, children. Sister, what are the children learning today?"

"American history, Father," she replied.

"American history is it?" said the Irish immigrant. "Do you children know the names of all the presidents? Well, it's time you learned," and

*Grace, Sammy, Mary, and Patsy Ann with
a stray dog Sammy brought home.*

while saying this, he ushered Sammy to the front of the room. "Now the hardest to remember are those between Jackson and Lincoln. Jackson, Van Buren, Harrison, Tyler, POLK," and with a wide swing he gave Sammy a playful poke. Sammy giggled and the class giggled. "Taylor, Fillmore, PIERCE, Buchanan" and with another wide, playful swing, he pierced Sammy. Sammy giggled, relishing his moment in the spotlight, the class giggled, especially Patsy Ann, and ever after she remembered the names of the presidents, and her brother being Polked and Pierced.

On a typical day, Aila came home from work, walked briskly through the front room and into the kitchen where the girls were starting dinner. She greeted them, shed her coat, hat, and gloves, put on her apron, and launched into dinner preparations.

"How was school?" she asked.

"Mama, Sister was mean to me today," said Mary.

"Oh, she must not have been feeling well," Aila said gently. "You must always respect the habit, dear."

Aila looked over at Patsy. She looked a little blue. Aila started singing, "*Where is my Patsy, where can she be, . . .*" and Patsy brightened.

"Mother, when can I stop wearing these long stockings?" she asked.

"When the snow is gone from the mountains, dear."

Aila invited Mrs. Flomer to dinner every Sunday. She never called her Bertha, always Mrs. Flomer; she was old enough to be her mother. Aside from seeing a dear friend, it was also an opportunity to teach the children how to entertain a guest. She usually made pot roast with carrots, onions, and potatoes. She always served a salad and bread and butter with dinner and had fresh fruit in the house. She was a great believer in balanced nutrition as the prevention of many ills.

When Aila bought a banana, she would cut it on the bias and give each child a piece. She didn't do anything in a plain way, everything had style, even a cut up banana. "It looked so fancy," Mary said. "Other kids mothers' just handed them a banana. I thought, those poor kids, their mother doesn't make it look special." Years later she realized that her mother cut the banana because she could afford only one. "We didn't know we were poor," she said laughing.

One day a woman came to the house to see Aila. She told her that she was very upset with her husband, she had had it with him, and she was leaving. Aila put on the kettle and made a pot of tea. The two sat down at the kitchen table. The

Mrs. Flomer

woman complained and complained about her husband. Aila sat and listened, not agreeing, not disagreeing, just listening and sipping her tea. After an hour or so, Aila said gently, "All right, dear, it's time for you to go home now," and the woman went home, back to her husband, and that was that.

When Christmas came around, Aila was able to buy or make a little something for the children. It didn't really matter what it was, she made it look special. One Christmas Patsy Ann and Mary awoke to find teddy bears emerging from tissue paper stuffed in their stockings. They were delighted.

Aila and the children went to Christmas Mass at St. Ann's and then came home for breakfast. For a special treat, each child got an entire half an orange with breakfast. Aila scalloped the edge of each orange half, cut out the fruit and piled it back into the decorative orange basket and sprinkled the top with coconut. This they feasted on with their usual scone or biscuit or pop-over, fresh from the oven, and bacon and eggs and tea with milk and sugar.

One Christmas when she took the children to see Sarah, Aila found her mother uncharacteristically subdued, her usual imperiousness nowhere to be seen. Sarah said one of the priests from St. Mary's had stopped in and brought her a basket of food. And to think all those years I didn't like the Catholics, she said, and here this priest brought me this food, and you, Aila, you're the only one who ever helped me, and after the way I treated you. I tried to cut off my nose to spite my face.

She seemed quite humbled.

CHAPTER FIFTY-NINE

DESPITE THE indignities she suffered at work and the odd last minute hours, Aila enjoyed working at the post office. She often worked as the postal savings clerk. She was so tiny she had to stand on a box to reach the window. She was quick with figures and dispatched her duties with ease. She could add columns of numbers in her head and be correct to the penny. At the grocery store, she would have her check written for the exact amount before the clerk totaled her purchase.

What she liked most about her job was waiting on people. She thoroughly enjoyed the constant interaction. She would greet her customers with a warm cheery smile and visit with them while she conducted their

Aila at work at the post office

business. How are you? she would ask. How is your son in the army? Where is he stationed? How is your daughter? Is she over her scarlet fever?

When men from the Company came to her window, she would ask, what's new at the Company? And they would tell her—including things that were not yet public. As a result, she knew about changes affecting the town long before they were announced in the newspaper. The most dramatic changes were years later after the war. "A man from the Company came in today and said they're going to change to a new method of mining," she told her miner son-in-law. "Oh, they'll never do that," he said. Well, they did, and you can see that new method today—a gigantic open pit that gobbled up a vast chunk of the town.

A man from the Company told her about plans to close the Columbia Gardens long before it was announced. She was incensed.

A Chinese man came to her window one day very distraught. "What's the matter?" she asked. He frantically explained that he had misplaced a very large amount of cash. "Look in the bottom of your duffel bag," she told him. He went home and looked and there it was. He came back and told her, "Thank you, thank you, Mrs. Thompson, thank you. It was right where you said it was. How did you know that?"

Yet, some days her more difficult fellow employees made life unbearable. Plus, her degenerate boss still propositioned her. It disgusted and humiliated her. Even without those burdens, her schedule was exhausting: working odd hours, plus laundry, mending, sewing, cooking, cleaning. No matter how busy she was, she attended the children's school activities as though that particular event was the only thing in the world of concern to her. She repaired whatever needed fixing around the house—electrical wiring, carpentry, anything. When she needed book shelves, she built them. On extremely cold nights, which meant pretty much every night all winter, she would sit bundled in one of her heavy quilts, watching the pipes, worried they'd freeze. She'd nap, get up, turn on the water, let it run a little, then nap, get up, turn on the water, let it run a little, and she would do that all night. Even when she wasn't watching the pipes, she survived on only four to six hours of sleep. When there was no one to wait on at her window at the post office, sometimes she momentarily dozed off standing up.

One day it must have been altogether too much. I found a paper towel among her papers on which she had written,

Sometimes
Unless one has work
to do,
There is very little use
to go on living.

It was her children who kept her going. She knew they needed her.

And then she came home to find the piano in pieces all over the living room floor. Sammy wanted to see how it worked so he took it apart. She walked past the mess, into her bedroom, closed the door, and cried.

Opportunities landed at her doorstep. She was offered the postmistress job in Moses Lake. She fretted and fretted, should she take it? Grace was convinced. She called Aila Rose at nursing school. "You must talk to Mother," she urged. "You must tell her to take that job in Moses Lake!"

A friend of Aila's had moved to Washington DC to work for an insurance company. She wrote to Aila again and again, come to Washington, I'll get you a job, I found you a job, I have a place for you to live, pack up the children and come.

Aila thought and fretted. She owned her home. She managed to scrape together enough money for Grace to attend Girls Central and for Aila Rose's nursing school. Despite the hardships, her life was more stable than it had ever been. Washington DC and Moses Lake were two giant unknowns. Why upset the apple cart, as she would say. She had already endured enough upheaval to last several lifetimes. And her mother was in Butte. There was no one else to look after her. Aila turned down the offers and remained in Butte, still confident that one day she would get her permanent appointment as regular clerk.

She was now in her early forties. She finally had enough income to buy some decent clothes. Though she could never afford to spend much, she knew how to wear what she could afford. One woman said of her, "She always looked like she just stepped out of a fashion magazine." She did have an elegant air about her. She preferred severe cuts and high-heeled open-toe pumps; she usually wore jewelry, and *always* a hat and gloves. She would go to the glove counter at Hennessy's. The clerk would put a pillow or cloth on the counter and Aila would put her elbow on it with her forearm straight up. The clerk would then pull gloves onto her hand until they found the perfect fit. The hats she wore her entire life, long after the milliners all but disappeared. Everything about her was appropriate—her attire, her remarks, her conduct.

Easter Sunday. BACK: *Grace, Aila, cousins Margaret and Patrick, Aila Rose.*
FRONT: *Patsy Ann and Mary.*

She aged ten years overnight when Peter died. The sorrow and worry had worn on her physically, but over time, slowly, the bloom returned. She again raised her flag. Gentlemen came calling.

She had lots of gentlemen friends, and they all wanted to marry her. She enjoyed having escorts to take her to lunch, and for rides, and mostly to take her dancing. Her favorites were the schottische and the polka. Once when she was in her mid eighties I asked, "What's the schottische?" and she jumped up and started doing it.

When a man started to include her children in their outings, a marriage proposal was imminent. Even after Sammy threw up in his car, that one was undeterred. He proposed. She said no.

Another suitor took Aila and the children out for ice cream. All through the outing, Sammy kept tormenting Patsy Ann. Finally, in retaliation she retorted, "You egotistical, arrogant male!" The suitor had a good laugh over hearing those big bold words from such a little girl. He proposed. Aila said no.

She dated a couple of the nice men at the post office. She met another gentleman friend at the Pioneer Club. His name was Al. He took her dancing for their first date. They danced one dance and then he escorted her off the dance floor and they sat down. The music started up again.

"Well, Al, aren't you going to dance another dance with me? This is a schottische coming up," she said.

"No," he replied, "one dance is enough for me."

"If you aren't going to dance with me, I'm going to dance," she said.

"Nobody else will dance with you, you're with me."

"Oh, yes, they will!"

"No, they won't! I won't let you dance."

"Al, will you dance this dance with me?"

"No, now sit here."

She stood up. She walked a few steps toward the dance floor, and before she got there, a partner whisked her out to dance. She said, "I didn't care who he was as long as he was a good dancer."

Al wanted to marry her too. She said no.

Another man coaxed and coaxed her to marry him and said if she wouldn't, he'd marry somebody else, which he did. Then he called her on the phone, moaning that it was all a big mistake, he shouldn't have married this woman. Aila told him never to call her again and hung up. "He goes off and marries somebody else and now he wants to cry on my shoulder about it."

Grace was after her to marry one man in particular because Grace was convinced that he was a millionaire and money would solve everything. He was a wealthy rancher, how wealthy I don't know. Aila used to go to the Sunday dances at Borden's in Whitehall, so perhaps she met him out there. An old ranch hand who frequents that establishment today still remembers her. "She was a beauty," he said. "If I'd 'a had money, I'd have married her." The wealthy rancher did propose. She said no. She told him and the others that she had to raise her family first. She wouldn't remarry as long as she had children at home.

The children were never around these beaus long enough to become attached. They were hardly around them at all. Aila didn't have her dates pick her up at the house; she met them uptown wherever they were going. So the heartbreak of Aila's refusal of marriage was felt only by the suitor, never by the children.

A very kind, very resourceful man who was a widower and whom she had known for years asked her to marry him. He was the same age as her father. He didn't court her though he was quite fond of her, and she thought the world of him. Even so, she declined. She said years later, meaning no disrespect, "All I needed was an old man to take care of."

Even with all these beaus, Aila kept Peter's memory alive for the children. She told them about the family in Ireland, most of whom she had never met. She taught them the names of all those aunts and uncles and cousins. She told them about their father saving that man's life in the war and being decorated for it. Peter's portrait and the *Croix de Guerre* certificate hung prominently in the front room. All the other tangible memories of him—his medals, his army uniform, his gas mask, the burial flag—she kept as treasured artifacts safely stowed in her cedar chest. She kept him alive as a flesh and blood person. Never did she turn him into a myth. She told the facts. It was up to the listener to draw conclusions. She praised him, "He was a marvel of medicine. He saved that man's life. He should have been a doctor, " and she said flatly, "He worked when he wanted." Then she'd say something about the war, what he'd endured, how horrible it must have been . . . perhaps that's why . . . and every year she had a Mass said for him on the anniversary of his death.

As for Peter's sisters, they kept him firmly fixed atop a lofty perch, even Rosie who was only four when he immigrated and barely knew him.

Mom said, as a child, everyone she met who knew her father sang his praises. She thought they were being kind to a little girl who had lost her daddy, but from what I've been able to glean, I think it was more than that. Peter had a way of making an indelible, endearing impression on people, and it didn't go away after he was gone.

XXI

Ah, my Beloved, fill the Cup that clears
To-day of past Regrets and future Fears:
   To-morrow!—Why, To-morrow I may be
Myself with Yesterday's Sev'n thousand Years.

XXII

For some we loved, the loveliest and the best
That from his Vintage rolling Time hath prest,
   Have drunk their Cup a Round or two before,
And one by one crept silently to rest.

XXIII

And we that now make merry in the Room
They left, and Summer dresses in new Bloom,
    Ourselves must we beneath the Couch of Earth
Descend—ourselves to make a Couch—for whom?

XXIV

Ah, make the most of what we yet may spend,
Before we too into the Dust descend;
    Dust into Dust, and under Dust, to lie,
Sans wine, sans Song, sans Singer, and—sans End!

—*Rubáiyát* of Omar Khayyám

EVERY FRIDAY evening after work, Aila had Sammy, Patsy Ann, and Mary meet her uptown, and she took them out for orange floats and to see a movie. She always insisted that they sit in the back row near the exit in case there was a fire.

"Always be a lady," she told the girls.

"Stand up straight, dear."

"Eat what you want and leave the rest."

"Nothing on the floor but feet and furniture."

"Never do anything to hurt another person's feelings."

And when one of the children asked, "Mother, why can't I ____? Everybody else does," Aila would rejoin, "Who's everybody? If everybody jumped off a cliff would you want to do that too?"

On matters of principle, she was steadfast. Where principle was not involved, she was a softie. And whatever one did, whether it be work or school or simple chores, all she asked was that they do their best.

THE WAR ENDED, summer waned into fall, October approached. Every year, Aila looked on the coming of that month with fear and trepidation, certain she would die. "She was dying all my life," Mom said. Every year, October came and went, and she didn't die.

"Let your acquaintances be many, but one in a thousand your confidant," advised an ancient sage. Aila certainly followed that advice. She was intensely private. By now, she had worked at the post office for three years, all the while enduring those humiliating, disgusting overtures from her boss. She must have been terribly beleaguered this particular day because, after all this time, she finally confided to her friend Rhea the conditions her boss imposed for giving her a permanent appointment.

Rhea told her boss, who was Senator James Murray. Aila's boss was replaced. On his first day, the new man gave Aila an appointment as regular clerk—with no strings attached. It was during the month of October.

THE FOLLOWING SPRING Monsignor Tougas asked the bishop for permission to apply for the job of full-time chaplain at the veterans' hospital at Fort Harrison. This would be in addition to his duties as pastor of the cathedral. He intended to give part of the chaplain's salary to St. Helena's School and the rest to Carroll College. The bishop gave his permission and Monsignor took the job. A few days later he collapsed in the stairwell while making his rounds at St. John's Hospital. He was admitted as a patient and died in his sleep. He was sixty-one.

That other bulwark, John Gribben, passed away two years earlier.

PHOTO FACING PAGE: *Daughters of Isabella state convention, Immaculate Conception Church, Butte. Aila is in the fourth row back, third from the right, wearing a dark hat. The men in front are, left to right: Father Leonard Spraycar, Father James Dowdall, Bishop Joseph Gilmore, the next three are unidentified. The Daughters of Isabella is a charitable and social organization of Catholic women.*

CHAPTER SIXTY

BILL NOW LIVED in California and worked as a mechanic. Shortly after the Second World War, his home was robbed and all his tools stolen. He built a new house. Everything in it was hidden. When you walked in, all you saw were walls. Touch this one here, and a door opened to the bedroom. Touch this one there, and a cupboard opened revealing a stove. He had a walnut grove for awhile. Later he moved to Oakland where he met a widow named Elsa and became her star boarder. As the story goes, this woman's emotionally fragile adult son would have been traumatized had his mother remarried, so she and Bill lived together unmarried.

By now, Aila's sister, Patsy, was married and had two daughters with one more on the way. They lived in San Francisco. Bill visited them sporadically. They never knew when he was coming, he just appeared. Over pots of tea, he talked about books he had read and told the girls the sanitized story of his life. They were never sure what to believe from Bill, so it

Patsy

Patsy and her husband, John

may have been a fictionalized version as well. When the girls asked him about the rest of the family, he wouldn't tell them anything. He just said, "Every family has skeletons."

Yes, and he was certainly one of them.

SARAH SEEMED more settled now that she and Denny were married. They lived on the Anaconda Road for awhile and on East Woolman and probably other places in between. Now they lived in the Hesperus Lode, a remnant of the Cabbage Patch. I couldn't believe it when I read that address—the *Hesperus*, a shipwreck—what a metaphor for Sarah's life.

And still about once a winter the police would call, and Aila would go uptown and pay the fine to get her mother out of jail. "Please be careful, Mother," she would say. "Be careful," Sarah would scoff, "I'll dance on your grave."

In contrast, Aila was now enjoying grandmotherhood. Aila Rose had married after she finished nurse's training, and on April 16, 1947, she delivered her second child, another boy. The happiness of his arrival was tempered with much worry. He was having trouble breathing and he couldn't keep food down.

Aila Rose and her baby were still in the hospital the following Tuesday afternoon, April 22, and all were quite worried about the little guy.

Aila holding her first grandchild, Kenny, 1946

Sarah was feeling lone and lorn and out of sorts that day. Whether it was because of the baby or some other reason, I don't know. To cheer herself up, she went to the saloon where her friend Lillian worked and visited with her for awhile. She left and went back several times, and when Lillian got off work, the two went out. First they went to the Silver King Tavern and then to the Golden Gate rooming house. Sarah was looking for someone there. They left the Golden Gate around eight o'clock in the evening and started to cross East Park in the middle of the block. Sarah stepped out into the street from between two parked cars. Lillian tried to grab her, the driver didn't see her, the car hit her, and she was knocked to the ground. The driver stopped and jumped out and ran into a store to call for help. A policeman arrived almost immediately. The driver told him that he had called for an ambulance. The policeman, seeing that Sarah was unconscious and a pool of blood was forming under her head, said we can't wait, and he loaded Sarah and Lillian into his squad car. With siren blaring, he raced off to the hospital and took Sarah to the emergency room. Lillian didn't appear to be hurt. He said he would take her home and asked where she lived. She didn't seem to know where she lived, so he left her in the jail for the night.

Aila rushed uptown to the hospital as soon as she received the call. Sarah was still unconscious. She had a cerebral hemorrhage and a fractured skull and broken leg. When the doctor examined her the next afternoon, her pupils didn't react to anything, not to light, not to movement. She never awoke. She died two days after the accident. She was seventy-one.

By the time Aila reached her mother's house in the Cabbage Patch, it had been completely looted.

Aila had no portrait of her beloved grandmother Ann Thomas. If she had, it certainly would have been framed and prominently displayed in her home. I have to assume that such pictures were among what she wanted to retrieve from Sarah's but were gone.

All the tension of Aila's life flowed out in tears when Sarah died. She said, "It felt like a five hundred pound weight had been lifted from my shoulders." She had kept these stories I have told you bottled up inside all this time. Years later, after hearing the stories about Sarah beating her and the rest, one of her daughters said, "You must have hated your mother." Aila stiffened. "I *loved* her," she said, "she was my *mother*!"

Aila wrote to Archie and Patsy and Bill to ask for help with Sarah's funeral and burial expenses. Bill refused flat out. He said, "What did she ever do for me?" Archie helped with the cemetery expenses.

When Archie left Helena some fifteen years earlier, he went to Chicago where he met a sweet, quiet, Jewish girl named June. They married in Yuma, Arizona, and then moved to San Francisco. They lived in the same apartment building as Patsy and her family, and Archie worked as a bookkeeper.

Archie and June Hughes
STILLMAN, HOLLYWOOD

To Patsy's daughters, Bill was the serious one, but Uncle Archie was full of fun. Archie and June later moved to southern California and lived in Pasadena for awhile and in Santa Monica. They had no children. During the war they saved and saved to pay the ransom, or bribe, to get June's brother out of a concentration camp in Germany. They sent the money but learned later that he was already dead.

Archie

Archie and June used to celebrate their wedding anniversaries in style, Archie looking dashing in his tuxedo and June so lovely in her satin evening gown. Patsy's daughters said he had the looks and presence of a movie star. But despite his good looks and well-groomed veneer and years of earning an honest living, that dark cloud from his past would never leave him. Crimes are like lies—they have no legs. He wrote this letter to Governor Ayers in 1940 when he was thirty-six years old:

> Your Excellency:
>
> Accept my deep thanks for your past generosity and if it be possible for you to accept this humble petition it will clear away the last obstacle in my life.
>
> Although you kindly granted me complete reinstatement of my citizenship the past conviction is still a bar to me in many ways. California electoral laws still forbid me a great many opportunities. Also, the federal government's rulings with their own employees and the employees of many firms holding government contracts. Although nearly every prominent official in the bay area has recommended me to many firms they cannot overcome that conviction.
>
> The people who have written the letters enclosed in this missive are all aware of my position so there is no letter that has not been written willingly.
>
> I humbly pray that you can grant me freedom from that mistake. If it be possible for you to do so, I swear to you that no action of mine will ever cause you to regret your leniency.
>
> Thanking you deeply for any possible courtesy.
>
> Very Truly Yours,
> Arthur F. Hughes

The governor replied: ". . . there is no possible way in which your conviction can be stricken from the records."

Chapter Sixty-one

On the first business day of every month, Denny Sheehan walked to Walnut Street in his suit and bowler hat, swinging his walking stick like a London banker. He knocked, Aila invited him in, they sat down at the corner of the dining room table. He pulled an envelope from his inside breast pocket and, from it, a check. She handed him a pen. He marked his elegant X on the back of the check. Aila countersigned it. Then she put the check back in the envelope and sent Sammy to the saloon across the street to cash it. Sammy returned and handed her the envelope full of money. Aila counted out six dollars and said to Denny, "That's for rent." She counted out a few more and said, "That's for food." She gave the pennies to Sammy. The rest she left in the envelope and wrote *Denny* across the front in her immense, exquisite script.

"You keep the rest of the money for yourself," he said.

"No, thank you, Denny," she said, "it's your money. It will be here for you when you need it."

Denny put the money Aila had given him in his pocket, stood, doffed his hat, bid her goodbye, and left. He'd be back when he needed more. She gave him only what he needed in the short term because she worried that he could be easily taken advantage of, or robbed, or would drink it all.

Aila, standing in the yard of her house on Walnut Street

Now it was two years since Sarah passed away and new life was coming into the family at a steady clip. Both

Sammy in Peter's uniform

Aila Rose and Grace were married and had five children between the two of them. Sammy had left home to join the navy. Patsy Ann and Mary were in high school. They could fend for themselves for a few days, and Aila could afford to buy a train ticket to visit her father, so she did.

Arthur married Eunice about a year after Aila and Peter left Portland. She was a widow with several grown children. For years she and Arthur lived in her home on Albina Street, and Arthur worked as a custodian at the auditorium. He visited Patsy and her family in San Francisco at least once. He never returned to Butte.

When Aila visited, he and Eunice were living in Fairview, a tiny town east of Portland near Gresham. Arthur was retired and his health was failing. He had diabetes and had already lost a foot.

The year after she visited her father Aila received a telegram from Eunice saying he had died. She returned for the funeral. Shortly after, a check for five hundred dollars arrived in the mail. "He didn't send me anything for my children when I needed it, and now I don't need it," she said with a shrug. I don't know whether she ever cashed it.

That was a brief departure from her usual remarks about her father. She usually spoke of him as a paragon. My father could do this, my father could do that, always singing his praises. Her adult daughters were not convinced. One said, "I don't think too well of a man who goes off and leaves his children." "Oh, but we were old enough to take care of ourselves by then," she replied, referring to when he left them in Butte. She was old enough, but Archie and Patsy weren't. She probably thought it was up to her to take care of them.

Another daughter said, "How could he go off and leave his children with a crazy woman?"

She didn't respond.

When she told me about her father leaving, I had the impression that she didn't blame him because her mother was so difficult, but no matter how difficult Sarah was, he didn't just leave her, he left his own children. Some childhood idols are forever cast in bronze even after a plethora of facts demand that the hero be melted down to flesh and blood. She said she wanted to hold on to a good memory from her childhood and she chose him. In her twilight years, the bronze melted.

THE YEAR AFTER Arthur died Aila's daughter Patsy Ann graduated from Girls Central and went away to college. A few weeks into the school year she received a letter from her eldest nephew, Kenny. He was seven years old and had just learned to write.

> Dear Aunt Pat,
>
> How are you.
> Uncle Sam's ship was bombed.
>
> > Love,
> > Kenny

She was naturally very shook up to hear this and worried about Sam. Then she learned that the bombing to which little Kenny referred happened several months ago, and she already knew about it and knew that Sam was all right. (This was the Korean War.)

After Patsy Ann graduated from college, she and Aila went to California to visit Patsy and Archie. It was the first time Aila had seen her sister in twenty years. She planned to go again the next year. Shortly before she was to leave, she received a telegram from Patsy's husband saying she had died. It was quite a shock. She went but for the funeral instead. Before Patsy passed away, she became a Catholic, just as Hector had.

The next year Archie came to Butte to visit Aila. He looked ill. When asked, he said he was fine. The fact was his health had deteriorated since being in a serious automobile accident while driving in fog near Bakersfield.

Patsy

Archie and June with an unidentified friend on the left

While in Butte, he bought Aila a beautiful blue coat at Hennessy's. She hung it in the closet and there she left it. "When I could have used the help when my children were small he didn't help me. Now he wants to help me and I don't need it," she said.

NOW HER DOCTOR ordered surgery. She decided to have it done at a famous clinic in the Midwest. Before she left, she wrote this letter and filed it away in her impeccably organized papers.

Butte, Mont.
March 1, 1958

To my five wonderful children, —
a letter, —

to my handsome son,
and to my four beautiful daughters, —
all of you are doing very well with your lives, — doing
the jobs that come along, taking care of all your responsibilities,

and living good lives in every way. If all
the peoples on earth lived as my children are living,
there would be no wars, because there would be no
greed, hate and jealousy to prompt such conditions.
And so when I am gone, do not cry, I am so very tired,
that I shall be glad to go.

As a wife, I was a total flop, —
as a mother, I have been a failure, — —
and as a good Catholic and everything else that I should
have been, I was lukewarm, ——but for all my
failures, I love all my children with a greater love
than they realize, — and so in parting, — I hope and
pray for the best that this life can offer for all
my children and their families.

                    Mother

She was fifty-six years old
when she wrote that.

She survived the surgery
though she had a terrible reaction to the anesthesia. As for
the doctors, she said, "They're
all butchers."

Aila, age 50

PART OF A FAMILY PORTRAIT / LAURETTA, BUTTE, MONTANA

LATER THAT SAME year the last
of her daughters married. All
had left the nest. She had no
more children at home. Peter
had been gone twenty years.
One of those suitors came back
and renewed his proposal.

"Now will you marry me?" he asked.

"No," she said.

And still, she wore her wedding ring and kept Peter's picture in her
wallet and his ring in her purse.

Chapter Sixty-two

By the time I was old enough to call her Grandma T, Archie had passed away and Bill was roaming through California in a makeshift motor home reading Steinbeck and doing odd jobs.

As a little girl, I thought we called her Grandma T because she drank tea. She loved her tea. She let it steep until every bit of flavor leached from the leaves. Then she filled a china cup two-thirds full, never a mug mind you, added a heaping teaspoon of sugar or a couple of sugar cubes and topped it with half and half. This was her most sublime beverage, often accompanied by a piece of toast slathered with butter—and I do mean slathered. Even toward the end when she lost interest in eating, she always finished her tea, sitting in that flawless posture.

Her intuition rescued a granddaughter from disaster. I was utterly amazed when she told me the story. "Grandma, how did you do that?" I asked. She answered brightly, "Oh, anybody can. Just close your eyes and say a Hail Mary," and she tossed her head back and closed her eyes.

She told that same granddaughter, "You're the fifth child and fourth daughter of the fifth child and fourth daughter—think about that." Neither my cousin nor I know what it means.

When Grandma told me about being offered the job in Washington, I said, "But if you had taken it, then Mom wouldn't have met Dad and I wouldn't have been born."

"No. Everything would have happened just as it did," she replied confidently.

As for Portland, she said, "I was a fool not to stay, and yet I think God must have meant for me to come back and have the rest of my family."

I'm glad she did.

Cataracts urged her into retirement after twenty-five years at the post office. Still, every day she got dressed, donned her hat and gloves, and

Grandma T
LAURETTA, BUTTE, MONTANA

went uptown. She went for a walk every day no matter how icy it was. "I think the fresh air is good for me, no matter how cold it is," she said. She bought records to teach herself Welsh. "If you didn't learn something it was a wasted day," she used to say. Gentlemen friends still took her dancing. Even after she was gone, one man, though never a suitor, every time he saw one of her daughters, after a polite, "Hello, how are you?" said, "Your mother was the most *beautiful* woman I ever met."

It seems those endearing young charms never faded.

She traveled—to Yellowstone, to Glacier. She never stayed long, she enjoyed the going. On one senior citizen trip, some of the ladies got a bit tipsy at lunch and accidently sat on their boxes of cherries. Grandma was disgusted. "I'm not going anywhere with those *old* people anymore," she said.

Most trips were to visit her daughters and their families. Sometimes she stayed only one day—just long enough to see that everybody was fine. She was always in a hurry to get back to that house, that old house she didn't want, built on an old placer claim, the house with the dirt yard and no railing on the ice-covered steps, the house that was her home for fifty years and became her security. She worried that the pipes would freeze. She had to get home and watch them.

The house was always tidy and organized "with a place for everything and everything in its place." She was never one to decorate. She'd rather cook or sew or read, but mostly she'd rather be out and about.

She didn't like to fly. I suppose it's no wonder. The first airplane she saw back in Forsyth crashed. Daughter Patsy Ann (my mom) worked as a stewardess for a small airline and her plane crashed. No one was hurt but it ended the company. When passenger train service went by the wayside, Grandma resorted to the air. I remember waiting for her with Mom at the airport one day. The airport was small. There was no jet way. An airline employee helped Grandma off the plane. She slipped her hand in his arm, and I could see her chatting away with him as they walked crossed the tarmac. As they neared the gate, I heard her say in a comforting tone, "You're a nice young man." He was beaming.

During a doctor visit while in her seventies, the doctor told her, "Well, Mrs. Thompson, you have to expect a few aches and pains when you get old."

She left the appointment and got in the car in a huff. "I'll never go back to him again," she told Aila Rose.

"Why not?"

"He said I was old!"

I remember her saying, "I'm as *old* as the hills," but by that time, she was over eighty. I suppose that's when "old" set in.

The doctor also told her, when she was "old," that she had the heart and lungs of a thirty-five-year-old. Even so, she continued to be plagued by bouts of bronchitis and pneumonia; it's hard to say which since she was reluctant to go to the doctor. She was diagnosed with tuberculosis;

however, Mom and my aunts think she was mis-diagnosed. The medicine was hard on her stomach. That's probably what caused her ulcer.

One time she was in the hospital for something, I don't remember what. She decided she was fine, got up at four o'clock in the morning, as was her habit, got dressed, called a cab, and started to leave. The woman in the next bed asked where she was going. She said she felt fine and was going home. The woman told her, if the doctor doesn't discharge you, the insurance won't pay for your stay in the hospital.

That did it. She stayed.

I remember as a small child going to Ben Franklin's Five and Dime with her and sitting at the counter. I remember having lunch at Gamer's. The customers made their own change at the cash register. Grandma visited with Carl, the owner, or whoever was working. She knew somebody

Grandma T

everywhere she went. But then, that's the way it is in Butte. Even outside her beloved town, nobody was a stranger. She had a way of endearing people.

I remember stopping at her house in the afternoon. She and Mom would visit while my brother and I played quietly. Then at four o'clock, BOOM! The house shook. They were blasting in the mine.

I remember a treat of bread and butter with sugar sprinkled on top. I remember her hats and gloves. I remember perusing the contents of her closet floor. The heels of her open-toe pumps looked as high as the shoe was long. Everything was wonderful, happy, and well-ordered in the world of Grandma T, so it appeared to this grandchild. It would be years before I learned about her life. The effects of what she had endured did not mar her countenance nor her disposition. One never knows what's behind a face, even a face you think you know. I remember asking if she'd like to watch a TV program with us. "No, thank you, dear," she replied, "I've seen enough sadness in my life."

I remember her purse being so heavy. I think she carried about fifty dollars in quarters in it. She could use it as a weapon if need be. She always felt the need to be able to physically protect herself.

I remember the way she addressed birthday cards to my brother when he was little—to *Master Jeff*, written in that huge, exquisite script.

As for Peter, she said matter-of-factly (after I was grown), "He worked when he wanted," and in a hearty tone, "He was the most *hand*some man I ever met, God love him!" A hearty "God love him!" frequently came into remarks about Peter.

She told me quite plainly, "I do not have a sense of humor." Life had been painfully serious business for her, and she saw it for what it was, not as she wished it to be. And she was not one to skim the surface of life; she felt and understood its joys and sorrows deeply.

I remember her eightieth birthday party. She was sitting between two grown grandsons while opening her gifts. The two bantered back and forth in their usual repartee. The rest of us laughed. Grandma wore an uncomfortable smile. I think teasing was a foreign language to her, she being a person who said what she meant and meant what she said. Though a bright smile was her most frequent expression, laughter did not come easily. She expressed it judiciously and softly. She did have a sense of fun and imagination. When she did something as simple as arrange stuffed animals on a bed, no longer were they mere toys, they had personality. Her favorite funny story was the one about the IRS agent investigating cattle guards in

Montana. He couldn't find any record of them paying taxes. He wanted to know who these cattle guards were and where they lived and how much money they made so he could collect taxes from them. She thought that was so funny. (A cattle guard is a metal grate on the road.)

I remember walking into the kitchen to say goodnight to her and Mom and being amazed to see Grandma T in

Grandma T at her eightieth birthday party

her chenille bathrobe with long hair down to her elbows. She always wore it up in a bun so it never occurred to me that it was so long. It looked like strands of fine silk, a beautiful brown—no gray.

She used to accompany Aila Rose to the hair dresser. The woman would ask, "Mrs. Thompson, won't you let me wash your hair for you?"

"No, thank you, dear," she would say. Then one day when she was well into her eighties, she told the hair dresser, "Cut it off." So she cut it off, and it turned gray.

Whenever she sat down to eat at home, she always set an extra place in case someone dropped in. She wanted them to feel welcome. And quite often someone did drop in.

I remember her warm joyous smile. I remember her greeting—three quick kisses on the cheek, one kiss insufficient to express her delight, followed by a heartfelt, "Hello, my darling." She had a way of making each of us feel that we were her special someone. I think that's because we were.

She carefully and thoughtfully chose her words. Often after asking her a question, I could see her jaw moving back and forth in her closed mouth as she contemplated what to say. "Think three times before you speak," she used to say.

"Grandma, how do you like my hair?" asked a granddaughter.

"Well, dear, I've seen it look prettier," was her frank yet delicate response.

She had a gentleness and a daintiness about her and also fierce determination. There was nothing lukewarm about her. As for right and wrong, she was unequivocal and did not mince words. I learned much about life from her and Mom over cups of tea at the kitchen table. Those conversations are precious pearls to me. Their clarity of thought was, and is, a blessing in this murky age.

"God made it that it takes two to make a baby because it takes two to raise one!" Grandma T used to say. She knew that the hard way. She couldn't understand women who wanted to have children but not raise them.

When a man complained about the Lady of the Rockies, a huge statue of the Mother of God in honor of all mothers set atop the Continental Divide overlooking Butte, she retorted, "Where do you think you came from, a rock?"

As for nostalgia, all she had to say was, "There was nothing good about the good old days."

She grew gravely serious when talking about politics. She looked on politicians with a heavy dose of cynicism and suspicion. She thought most of them were either lining their pockets or wanting to show everybody who's boss. On the subject of income taxes, she said, "They're punishing the producers." The Constitution didn't allow it when she was born.

And whenever someone asked for whom she voted, she always said, "The best one," but never who that was.

About Peter's accident, she said confidently, "He wasn't supposed to be there. He wasn't supposed to die," then forlornly with a sigh, "He was just starting to grow up." I asked her more about the accident, how long did he live, was he in a coma. She cried. One day, well into her twilight years, she remarked wistfully to Aila Rose, "I still miss your father every day," and he'd been gone fifty years. She told one of my cousins, "Peter Thompson stole my heart the day I met him. I'll love him 'till the day I die."

While going through Grandma T's effects to write this book, I puzzled over why she kept that particular picture of Peter in her wallet all those fifty years. He was a good looking man and it wasn't a terribly good picture of him. I don't think he ever smiled for a picture. I studied and studied it wondering, of all the photographs she had of him, why this one? Guessing at his age, it would not have been the last photograph taken of him. I'd say he's in his thirties. He's standing in the street, facing to the side, his head is turned toward the camera. It looks as if he was walking away, someone called to him, he turned, and the photographer snapped his picture. He is wearing his hat and coat, his hands are stuffed in his pants pockets, something is tucked under his arm. I looked closer at the picture. Then it struck me. That thing under his arm is his *lunch bucket*. He was going to *work*. That's how she wanted to remember him.

Work was paramount to her. It meant *survival*. In her best of all possible worlds, Peter would have lived, worked steadily, not gambled too much, and she could have devoted all her time and energy to raising her children. But things didn't work out that way. Putting a best of all possible light on things, referring to her life after Peter died, she said, "I'm glad I had to work hard. I didn't have time to pity myself or get into mischief." It seems every time I chatted with Grandma T on the phone, to my question, "How is everybody?" invariably, her reply was, "*Ev-ery-bo-dy* is working." That was the ultimate—everybody who needed a job, had a job. It was right up there with being a lady.

> Dearest ——;—
> Your letter made my world a better place to live in, and if I was well enough to travel,—your grandmother would be on her way to visit a most special granddaughter;—but time & health forces one to change & change again, plans carefully made;— but I am grateful to feel as good as I do—& I have learned to adjust to changing conditions as— to tire more easily as one gets older—but, as to being wiser,—I wonder.
> I am delighted that things are going along nicely, you have a very important place in this great big & wonderful world,—may the best of everything that you strive for,—be yours as time goes by;—it is a strange world,—we have control over so many things,—yet Father Time goes along paying little attention to anything else . . .
> Everyone here well—busy. Weather wonderful for October.
> Best of wishes, my darling, and may all your dreams come true,—and all your plans work out in very special ways.
> All my love
> Grandma T

I can still hear the cadence of her speech when I read that.

THE YEAR GRANDMA T turned eighty a newspaper reporter asked if she could interview her about her life. Grandma just shrugged and said, "Oh, it's something nobody would be interested in." I spoke with the reporter while researching this book. Even though I was asking about an interview she had done twenty years earlier, she remembered Grandma T right away. "Oh," she said, "I remember her with the little bun and her hair was still black and she didn't dye it. She was one of my favorite memories of all the people I interviewed!" She said after the story ran, Grandma made a point to go see her and tell her how wonderful it was. Knowing Grandma T, I've no doubt she was animated and cheerful throughout the interview, and she probably wasn't thinking about the fire, or the orphanage, or where "place to place" was, or her brothers' misdeeds, nor did she mention any of it to the reporter. But even without knowing the whole of it, the reporter recognized that this tiny delightful woman had hoed a very difficult road through life. "How did you do it?" she asked.

"With God's help," Grandma replied. "Work, pray, work, pray. I'm still praying. Hope I have brains enough to keep on praying as long as I live!"

And through it all, every hardship, every disappointment, every tragedy, always and forever, she was a lady.

CHAPTER SIXTY-THREE

THE PHILOSOPHER William James wrote, "It is a common habit to blame life upon environment. Environment modifies life but does not govern life. The soul is stronger than its surroundings."

Indeed, hers was.

She was tried in the crucible, tested and not found wanting—in character, where it matters; a ship continually tossed, but with firm ballast, so never sunk.

Her life was a purgation, though in the span of eternity, it was just one night in a bad inn.

She was ninety-one when Our Lord took her home. She had earned her rest.

ACKNOWLEDGMENTS

THANK YOU to so many, first and foremost to Grandma T for leading an impeccable life, deserving of a telling. Thanks especially to Mom and Dad for their encouragement and help. My naturally literary Mom handed down so many clever turns of phrase in her everyday speech. I have Dad to thank for how I began the book, the hardest part for so many writers, made easy for me thanks to him.

Heartfelt thanks go to Aunt Aila and to Auntie Mary and Uncle Ed for telling me their stories, for their patience with my endless questions and hunt for pictures, and for their warm hospitality during my frequent and lengthy visits. And thanks to Aunt Aila and Auntie Mary for recording Grandma as she talked about her life and for saving those tapes and giving me copies.

Thanks also to Uncle Sam, Aunt Brigid, Archie's sister-in-law, Ellie, and to first cousins, first cousins once removed, second cousins, cousins galore on two continents and cousins' spouses for passing on their stories and memories and pictures to me and for their warm hospitality as well.

Special thanks to Ellen Crain and her staff at the Butte-Silver Bow Public Archives and to Brian Shovers and the staff at the Montana Historical Society Library and to Jodie Foley and the staff at the Montana Historical Society Archives. Theirs were the holdings I mined the most frequently and the deepest and the staffs made the already fun work much easier and so pleasant.

Thanks to Liz Cole, Sharon Borla, and rest of the staff at the Rosebud County Clerk of Court Office. Little did I know what a treasure hunt I was sending Liz on when I called that day, sending her down into the bowels of the courthouse, and what a treasure trove she and Sharon found. Thanks also to Liz for making me so welcome during both trips to Forsyth.

Thanks to Christopher Sims at Flanders Field American Military Cemetery for answering my many questions and providing invaluable hard-to-find sources about the war and for his patience with my endless questions.

Thanks to John Slonaker at the U.S. Army Military History Institute for guiding me through their many resources, and for referring me to James Controvich, and to Mr. Controvich for sending me the 362nd Regimental History. Thanks also to the families of veterans and others who donated their papers to be archived. A seemingly insignificant slip of paper can be a treasure to a researcher.

Thanks to Mitch Yockelson at the National Archives and Records Administration. During my week at the Archives, Mitch found materials for which I would not have known to ask and was a tremendous help, especially in filling out Colonel Parker's character, and what a character he was.

Thanks to Whit Longley, Dorothy Spannagel, Esther Dean, and Mignon Tadsen of Rosebud County; Henry Lockwood, Bill Hanley, and Rossellia Templeton for telling me about the orphanage; Reverend George Johnson at the First Welsh Presbyterian Church in Wilkes-Barre; Mair Faulkner at Llandovery Heritage; Richard Morgan of the Glamorgan Record Office; Honora Nerz at North Carolina State University; Mary Anne Hansen at Montana State University; Marilyn Craft of the Jefferson County Clerk of Court Office; Ardella Berzel at the Bureau of Land Management in Billings; and Colonel Ray Read at the Office of Military Affairs for the Montana National Guard.

Thanks to Father Darragh, Paula House, and Sister Dolores of the Diocese of Helena, and Father Bud Sullivan, Father Fenlon, Father Plummer, Jim Higgins, and Margaret Rachac for helping me fill out Father Tougas's background.

Thanks to Claire Maierle for telling me about those dark days in Boulder at the time of the execution. Thanks to Terry Badger at the Washington State Archives. Mr. Badger did yeoman's work digging up Roy Walsh's records. It was a challenge because Roy had used so many aliases, but Terry kept at it and found the records for me, and it turned out the state of Washington kept copious records on inmates, so those records were a big help.

Thanks to Ellen Rae Thiel for providing pictures of Boulder and putting me in touch with Al Johnson's family.

Thanks to Dr. Gary Telgenhoff of the Clark County Coroner's office for answering my questions regarding the Granite Mountain Fire victims and about Arthur digging up poor John Kiernan.

Thanks to archivists at Radcliffe and Bryn Mawr; Rosebud County Sheriff Tim Fulton for giving me Sheriff Moses's picture; Dave Walter for giving me

Judge Crum's picture; Rosebud County Librarian Cheryl Heser; Rosebud County Coroner Robert Beals; Stella Shiue and the rest of the staff at Clark County interlibrary loan; Al Hooper; Inez Shifty; Sylvia Baltezar Giachino for telling me her stories about growing up in the shadow of my great-grandmother; John Shea for answering my Butte mining questions; Cheryl McDonnell and Megaera Ausman with the U.S. Postal Service for answering my government pension questions; Dick Rennie for telling me about the old Boulder jail; Miguel Monteverde for answering my many military questions; Andrea McCormick who interviewed Grandma for the *Montana Standard*; and Marcia Gibson for digging up that old test eighth grade test.

Special thanks to the descendants of people in the story who were not my relatives for indulging my many questions: Colleen Llewelyn, Carter Williams, Wanda Bartholow—all descendants of Johnnie and Ruth Williams; John Mountjoy's son Jim; Howard Johnson's son Keith, and Al Johnson's great-grand niece Roberta Barrows.

Thanks to William Lake who was a very alert 107-year-old when we met and the only surviving member of the 91st Division from the First World War. And as for my introduction to Mr. Lake, I thank General Moffett of the 91st Division whom I met while visiting Flanders Field American Military Cemetery for Memorial Day 2002.

Thanks to Colonel Mollica of the 91st for providing the Captain St. John Whitney letters and the text of an interview with William Lake, and to Major Martin and Sergeant Hudson for sending me archived material about the 91st.

Thanks to the staffs at the Butte-Silver Bow County Courthouse, the Luzerne County Courthouse, the Fergus County Courthouse, the Madison County Courthouse, the Missoula County Courthouse, the Custer County Courthouse, the Wyoming Valley Historical Society, the Aberdare library, the Rosebud County Superintendent of Schools, the National Archives, the State Law Library of Montana, the U.S. Army Center of Military History, the Anaconda Historical Museum, the Fort Lewis Military Museum, the Oregon History Center, the Missouri Archives, the Soda Springs Chamber of Commerce, San Francisco Superior Court, the California State Archives, the Nevada State Archives, the Idaho State Historical Society, the New York Public Library, the New York Historical Society, the U.S. Military Personnel Center, the Pennsylvania State Archives, the U.K. Public Record Office, U.S.

District Court in Butte, the Seamen's Church Institute, the Twin Bridges Library, the University of Nevada Las Vegas Library, the Las Vegas Sahara West Library, the LDS Family History Centers in Las Vegas and Salt Lake, the Miles City Library, the Montana Department of Livestock, the Montana Department of Public Health, and the Montana Tech Library; and to so many other people who were so kind to answer my questions.

For help in collecting pictures from public collections, I thank Susan Mattson at the World Museum of Mining; Judy Strand and Ellen Crain at the Butte-Silver Bow Public Archives; Katie Curey and the rest of the staff at the Montana Historical Society Photo Archives; Holly Reed and the staff at the National Archives and Records Administration Still Pictures Collection; General Moffett of the 91st Division; Alan Archambault at Fort Lewis; Christopher Sims at Flanders Field; and Clif Hyatt of the U.S. Army Military History Institute.

Special thanks to Mom, Dad, Aunt Aila, and Uncle Ed for reading and commenting on early drafts of the manuscript; to my brother, Jeff, for his helpful, insightful, unbridled comments on the close-to-done (or I thought it was) manuscript; and to Patty Baugh, Ellen Brubeck, Cheryl Byrne, Marion Connell, Donna Levin, and Ellen Suess for reading and commenting on various chapters.

Most special thanks go to Mom and Dad for their encouragement throughout the research, the writing, the rewriting, the hunting for pictures, and especially to Mom who patiently edited and edited for me over and over again.

And I thank Bill and Carolyn McSpadden and Weymouth Symmes for their help in bringing this to publication.

To all, again, I thank you.

Thanks and acknowledgment to the following for permission to reprint from copyrighted material, archived letters and photographs, and portraits:

The excerpt from *Testament of Youth* by Vera Brittain is included by permission of Mark Bostridge and Rebecca Williams, Vera Brittain's literary executors.

Letters from the Montana Governors' Papers, MC-35, are included by permission of the Montana Historical Society Archives.

Portraits by Lauretta are included by permission of Lauretta Bonfiglio.

The photograph taken after Peter Thompson's funeral in front of St. Ann's is included by permission of C. Owen Smithers, Jr.

Photographs from the Butte-Silver Bow Public Archives, the Montana Historical Society, the World Museum of Mining, and the Diocese of Helena are included with permission.

NOTES

The following notes provide sources for quotes. Unless noted otherwise, quotes by and with relatives and their acquaintances were spoken to me, or repeated to me, or recorded on tape, or written by the person quoted. Unless noted otherwise, quotes by Father Tougas were told to me by his former parishioners, one of whom was my grandmother. Where I knew a conversation took place, but could not be sure of the exact words, quotation marks were not used. In some cases, an exact quote was available, but in the interest of brevity, I chose to summarize rather than quote. In such cases, quotation marks were not used.

The names of some of the towns in Flanders have Flemish and French spellings. Because the French spellings were used in the First World War literature, I used those. The spellings of some Flemish names have changed since the war. I used the First World War era spellings.

PART ONE, CHAPTER 1
"to drink beer like water": Jones, *Wales in America*, p. 205.
"the first mistaken impulse . . .": Dickens, Charles, *David Copperfield*, p. 747. Referring to her husband, Annie says, "I should be thankful to him for having saved me from the first mistaken impulse of my undisciplined heart."

PART ONE, CHAPTER 2
"Good land cheap . . .": *Forsyth Times Journal*, July 14, 1905.
"We couldn't believe how they came in and just plopped down like that": Mignon Tadsen, interviewed in Forsyth, Montana, July 27, 2000.
"And we'll all go to meet her . . .": Song "She'll be Coming Round the Mountain," lyricist unknown.
"It is argued . . .": Steinbeck, *East of Eden*, p. 12.

PART ONE, CHAPTER 3
Sheriff Moses, the boys, Aila Hughes, Tom Elliott, Sarah Hughes, and inquest dialogue: Transcript of Rosebud County Inquest, verdict rendered March 8, 1913, transcript filed March 22, 1913.
Quotes implicating Sarah in the fire: Motion and affidavit filed by County Attorney Henry V. Beeman, April 8, 1913, Rosebud County Case No. 177.
"On Bridal Trip are Arrested . . .": *Forsyth Times Journal*, April 3, 1913, p. 1.

PART ONE, CHAPTER 4
"I'll lock you up too if I catch you . . .": Letter from Sarah Hughes Elliott to Tom Elliott, Rosebud County Case No. 177.

PART ONE, CHAPTER 5
"The children are destitute . . .": Orphanage records for Aila, Sarah Patricia, and Arthur Hughes.
Philosophy behind how orphanage was run: Montana Governors' Papers, MC-35, Box 247, Folder 247-4; Montana State Orphans' Home Records RS-95, Box 5, Folder 5-11; paper written by G. H. Davey, president of the Board of Trustees, 1935; Montana Historical Society Archives.

PART ONE, CHAPTERS 6, 7, AND 8
Dialogue: Transcript of depositions taken in New York, September 1913, Arthur D. Strahl Commissioner, Rosebud County Case No. 177.

PART ONE, CHAPTER 9
Dialogue: Letter from Parker, Davis, Wagner & Walton to Henry V. Beeman, County Attorney, Forsyth, Montana, October 4, 1913, printed in the *Forsyth Times Journal*, October 9, 1913, p. 1.

PART ONE, CHAPTER 10
Telegrams: *Forsyth Times Journal*, October 9, 1913, p. 1.
"'Dead' Man is here . . .": *New York Times*, October 4, 1913, p. 8.
"He wouldn't stay dead . . .": *World*, October 4, 1913, p. 8.
"When the facts are made public . . . ": *Forsyth Times Journal*, October 2, 1913, p. 1.
"Arthur F. Hughes Located and . . .": *Forsyth Times Journal*, October 9, 1913, p. 1.
"Nothing doing, Arthur, no home . . .": Quoted in the *Forsyth Times Journal*, October 16, 1913, p. 4.
Judge Crum speaking to Arthur Hughes in court: Quoted in the *Forsyth Times Journal*, October 16, 1913, p. 1.
"Hubs sit side by side": *Butte Miner*, November 2, 1913, p. 1.
Sarah Hughes and Crum dialogue: Trial minutes, Rosebud County Case No. 189.

PART ONE, CHAPTER 11
Burgess/Moses altercation dialogue: Quoted in the *Forsyth Times Journal*, May 21, 1914, p. 1, 4, 6; and May 28, 1914, p. 1, 4, 6, 7.
Moses shot through the back of the neck: This information came from one of the newspaper articles noted above. To confirm this, I looked for the inquest transcript, thinking a doctor would have examined the body and testified. The Rosebud County index lists an inquest, but the transcript could not be found.
"quarrelsome" and "overzealous:" Custer County court records for the Burgess case, depositions taken May 18, 1914.

PART ONE CHAPTER 12
"Idleness is the curse . . ." and subsequent quotes: State Board of Charities and Reform Report, December 15, 1924, Montana Governors' Papers, MC-35, Box 53, Folder 8, Montana Historical Society Archives.
Frank Conly's writings about penal theory and his correspondence: Nineteenth Annual Report of the Montana State Prison for the Year Ending November 30, 1914; Montana State Prison Records, RS-197, Volume 15; Montana News Association insert, January 2, 1917 or 1918, Prison Vertical File; Montana Historical Society Archives and Library.
Board of Prison Commissioners meeting minutes: Montana State Prison Records, RS-197, Montana Historical Society Archives.

PART ONE, CHAPTER 13
Letter from Rickman to Shobe, August 12, 1914: Orphanage records for Aila, Sarah Patricia, and Arthur Hughes.

PART TWO, CHAPTER 14
"simply an outpost . . .": Quoted in Malone, *The Battle for Butte: Mining and Politics on the Northern Frontier, 1864–1906*, p. 58.

"Grant will encircle Lee's forces . . .": *New York Tribune*, quoted in James, *Butte's Memory Book*; and in Marcosson, *Anaconda*.

"San Francisco and other insignificant . . .": From the *Butte Weekly Miner*, quoted in Malone, *The Battle for Butte: Mining and Politics on the Northern Frontier, 1864–1906*, p. 23.

By 1905, Butte had the largest payroll . . . America: Emmons, *Encyclopedia of the American West*, p. 214.

"We'll send the old man to the Senate . . ": Quoted in Malone, *The Battle for Butte: Mining and Politics on the Northern Frontier, 1864–1906*, p.113.

"moral leper" and "well-paid harlot": Ibid, p.118.

"The kind of bill most frequently introduced . . .": Political cartoon from the *St. Paul Dispatch*, quoted in Malone, Roeder, and Lang, *Montana: A History of Two Centuries*, p. 221.

"I never bought a man who wasn't for sale": Quoted in Malone, *The Battle for Butte: Mining and Politics on the Northern Frontier, 1864–1906*, p.113.

"blackmailer" and a "thief": Quoted in Malone, *The Battle for Butte: Mining and Politics on the Northern Frontier, 1864–1906*, p. 148.

"able to make the mighty Standard Oil . . .": Howard, *Montana High, Wide and Handsome*, p. 69.

an Irishman named the town . . . saloon: Emmons, *The Butte Irish*, p. 19.

PART TWO, CHAPTER 18

"Fellow workers, in the name . . .": Quoted in Toole, *Twentieth Century Montana: A State of Extremes*, p. 134.

"Here Lies the Remains of 36 Years . . .": Quoted in Emmons, *The Butte Irish*, p. 282.

"The union faction whose doings . . .": Glasser, U.S. Department of Justice report.

"cowardly and dastardly": Quoted in Calvert, *The Gibraltar: Socialism and Labor in Butte, Montana, 1895–1920*, p. 43.

PART TWO, CHAPTER 19

"The thermometer's done fell up to zero!": Rice, *Mrs Wiggs of the Cabbage Patch*, p. 3.

PART THREE, CHAPTER 21

"Just when people . . .": 1 Thessalonians 5:3. The extended text, verses 1 through 4, reads: "As regards specific times and moments, brothers, we do not need to write you; you know very well that the day of the Lord is coming like a thief in the night. Just when people are saying, 'Peace and security,' ruin will fall on them with the suddenness of pains overtaking a woman in labor, and there will be no escape. You are not in the dark, brothers, that the day should catch you off guard, like a thief." *The New American Bible*.

"so long as he (Daly) ran the Anaconda . . .": Malone, *The Battle for Butte: Mining and Politics on the Northern Frontier, 1864–1906*, p. 157.

"We have come here to pay you a visit . . .": Quoted in the *Butte Daily Post*, June 29, 1914.

Britain's ambassador . . . at sea: Keegan, *The First World War*, p. 56.

"Austrian guns fire . . .": *Butte Daily Post*, July 29, 1914, p. 1.

"The war will not end until Germany . . .": *Madison Monitor*, November 21, 1914.

The year before the war began . . .: Description of a cartoon in the *Madisonian*, June 27, 1913, p.7.

John Gribben and Jeremiah Lynch quotes about the war: Robert Emmet Literary Association meeting minutes, 1911; September 17, 1914; September 24, 1914; February 18, 1915; June 10, 1915; Minute Books, Butte-Silver Bow Public Archives.

PART THREE, CHAPTER 23

"They will not even come because . . .": Quoted in Keegan, *The First World War*, p. 372.
Wilson quotes: Quoted in Dudley, *World War I, Opposing Viewpoints*, p. 86–91.
"Is a life lost by the destruction of a vessel . . .": Ibid, p. 96.
"I want to stand by my country . . .": Quoted in Harries, *The Last Days of Innocence: America at War, 1917–1918*, p. 72.

PART THREE, CHAPTER 24

"U.S. IS AT WAR WITH GERMANY": *Butte Miner*, April 6, 1917, p. 1.

PART THREE, CHAPTER 25

Ancient Order of Hibernian members speaking about the war: Ancient Order of Hibernians meeting minutes, April 18, 1917; May 30, 1917; June 13, 1917; Collection #OC 012, Butte-Silver Bow Public Archives.
"There is no reason . . .": *Butte Miner*, April 8, 1917, p. 5, quoting an unidentified editor in an unidentified newspaper.
"Every drop of patriotism . . .": Quoted in the *Butte Miner*, April 8, 1917, p. 5.
"It does matter if you are blind, deaf, dumb . . .": *Butte Daily Post*, June 4, 1917, p. 9.
"Why not enter a trade . . .": *Butte Miner*, June 6, 1917.
"riveted the chains of slavery . . .": Quoted in the Jordan Chronology, p. 12, Butte-Silver Bow Public Archives. Source cited is the *Butte Bulletin*, June 4, 5, 1917
"Kill the cops": Quoted in the *Butte Daily Post*, June 6, 1917.
"I don't know, maybe five feet . . .": Quoted in the *Butte Miner*, June 7, 1917, p. 7.
"Oh, I've been married for four years . . .": Ibid.
"DISASTER . . . MANY LOST": *Butte Miner*, June 9, p. 1
"Say, mister, I can't read that . . .": Quoted in the *Anaconda Standard*, June 11, 1917, p. 9.
"almost super human effort": Harrington, *Department of Interior, Bureau of Mines Bulletin 188, Lessons from the Granite Mountain Shaft Fire, Butte, Montana*.

PART THREE, CHAPTER 26

"If the IWWs start things in Butte . . .": Quoted in the *Butte Daily Post*, June 12, 1917, p. 3.
"no time to talk of wages . . .": Quoted in the *Butte Miner*, June 14, 1917.
"enemy agents and the IWW": *Forsyth Democrat*, July 10, 1919.
Frank Little quotes: *Butte Miner*, August 6, 1917.
"Others take notice . . .": Quoted in Toole, *Twentieth Century Montana: A State of Extremes*, p. 149.

PART THREE, CHAPTER 27

Dos Passos quote: Dos Passos, introduction to *First Encounter*.
"simply one continual watch . . .": Remarque, *All Quiet on the Western Front*, p. 273.
"No human courage could face such a peril . . .": Quoted in Fries and West, *Chemical Warfare*, p. 11–12.
Sassoon quotes about gas: Sassoon, *Memoirs of an Infantry Officer*, p.11.
"a sunlit picture of Hell": Quoted in Marshall, *The American Heritage History of World War I*, p. 196.
"If unconscious heroism is the virtue . . .": Quoted in Dawson, *The Good Soldier, A Selection of Soldiers' Letters, 1914–1918*, p. 39.

"Out of the light you . . .": Graves, *Good-bye to All That*, p. 113.

"Every position must be held to the last man . . .": Quoted in Harries, *The Last Days of Innocence: America at War, 1917–1918*, p. 231.

"we should be coming to the trenches . . .": Sassoon, *Memoirs of an Infantry Officer*, p.22.

"permanent human wrecks": from "War Costs at a Glance" by Charles F. Horne, Ph.D, quoted in Straubing, *The Last Magnificent War, Rare Journalistic and Eyewitness Accounts of World War I*, p. 402.

"It's too big to comprehend . . .": *Forsyth Times Journal*, December 3, 1914, p. 6.

PART THREE, CHAPTER 28

"And we won't come back 'till it's over . . .": Song "Over There" by George M. Cohan. Quoted in Meldrum and Madsen, *History of the 362nd.*, p. 8.

"it is a nice day and the ocean is full of salt water": Whitney, *Letters to His Family . . .*, letter of July 8, 1918.

"The Yanks are coming!": Quoted in Meldrum and Madsen, *History of the 362nd.*, p. 10.

"A cattle car here . . .": Letter from Private O. J. Swanes, July 20, 1918, Box 94-202-1, Fort Lewis Museum Archives.

"Everything seems so old and ancient . . .": Letter from R. A. Barrett, Co. E, 316 Supply Train, September 18, 1918, Box 98-160-1, Fort Lewis Museum Archives.

"tin hats" . . . "wearing the kitchen stove" . . .: Whitney, *Letters to His Family . . .*, letter of August 25, 1918.

"You see, we think the French . . .": Gibbons, *"And They Thought We Wouldn't Fight."*

"Mademoiselle from Armentières . . .": Song "Mademoiselle from Armentières," lyrics attributed to Edward Rowland, 1915.

"We don't want the bacon . . .": Title and lyricist unknown. Quoted by Kendloss Jacobsen in veterans' survey, 181st Brigade Box, U.S. Army Military History Institute Archives.

"What? Never heard of the Powder River?" . . . "Why it's the greatest little body of water . . .": Quoted in the *Butte Miner*, May 25, 1919, p. 15.

"nowhere . . . and end in much the same fashion": Burt, *Powder River Let 'Er Buck*.

"Wild and wooly, full of fleas . . .": Quoted in Shore, *Montana in the Wars*, p. 68.

"an artist with a machine gun"; Description on photograph 56637 of Colonel John H. Parker, 111-SC National Archives and Records Administration.

PART THREE, CHAPTER 29

"I had to wait to let a large contingent of troops . . .": Brittain, *Testament of Youth*, p. 420–421.

"Personnel must be called excellent . . .": from German communique of June 17, 1918, quoted in American Battle Monuments Commission, *American Armies and Battlefields in Europe*, p. 31.

"The nationals of no country . . .": Pershing, *My Experiences in the World War, Vol. 2.*

"As usual, the American soldier . . ." Ibid.

"self reliant infantry": Ibid.

"dagger pointed at the heart . . .": Expression used by the Germans, quoted in Gibbons, *"And They Thought We Wouldn't Fight."*

PART THREE, CHAPTER 30

"Two hours of rain will produce . . .": Letter from R. A. Barrett, Company E, 316th Supply Train, October 31, 1918, Box 98-160-1, Fort Lewis Museum Archives.

"No American officer . . .": Field order No. 9, 362nd Regiment.

"hold their manhoods cheap": Shakespeare, *Henry V*.

"Here I am in France . . .": Quoted in Gibbons, *"And They Thought We Wouldn't Fight,"* p. 209, and in Genthe, *American War Narratives 1917–1918, A Study and Bibliography.*

PART THREE, CHAPTERS 31 AND 32

Battle sequence quotes, orders, and messages, unless noted otherwise: 181st Brigade Box, U.S. Army Military History Institute Archives; Meldrum and Madsen, *History of the 362nd*; "Narrative of the Operations of the 362nd Infantry and 181st Brigade of the 91st Division, Meuse Argonne, 26 to 29 September" by John H. Parker, U.S. Army, Retired, RS 117, Box 255, last folder, and letter from George P. Dykes (former Sergeant Major, Second Battalion, 362nd Regiment) to John C. Burgard, September 24, 1928, RG 117, Box 247, 2nd Folder, National Archives and Records Administration.

"all the horrors . . .": Churchill, *World Crisis*, p. 4.

"Not tho' the soldier knew . . ." and "Cannon to the right of them, . . .": Tennyson, Alfred, Lord, "The Charge of the Light Brigade."

"The order came to advance . . .": Clerc, Lieutenant E. L., 148th Infantry Liaison Officer with the 362nd, 181st Brigade Box, U.S. Army Military History Institute Archives; and in Meldrum and Madsen, *History of the 362nd.*

"Gee whiz, this war is getting . . .": Quoted in the *Butte Miner* May 25, 1919, p. 15.

Interchange between Casement and Irish soldiers at Limburg prison camp: Part quoted in Denman, *Ireland's Unknown Soldiers: The 16th (Irish) Division in the Great War, 1914–1918*, p. 142; part quoted in Gilbert, *The First World War, A Complete History*, p. 114.

"just locked horns . . .": Whitney, *Letters to His Family . . .* , letter of October 20, 1918.

"no Regiment of any Division or any service at any time . . .": General Order No. 15, October 25, 1918, forwarding message from Colonel John Henry Parker, RG-391, Box 4153, National Archives and Records Administration.

"their gallant conduct . . .": General Order No. 16, October 26, 1918, memorandum from General J. B. McDonald, RG-391, Box 4153, National Archives and Records Administration.

"tonic effect": 91st Division Publication Committee, *The Story of the 91st Division*, p. 57.

"running like jack rabbits": Lt Charles Lembke, Company G, 364th Infantry, field message, October 31, 1918, Box 94-203-1, Fort Lewis Museum Archives.

PART THREE, CHAPTER 33

Letter from Sister Mary Monica dated November 21, 1918: RG-120, Box 124, National Archives and Records Administration.

"The people here are certainly . . .": Whitney, *Letters to His Family . . .* , letter of November 12, 1918.

Sign posts: 600 *Days' Service, A History of the 361st Infantry Regiment of the United States Army*, p. 179. (The 361st was with the 362nd Regiment in the 181st Brigade.)

"If waiting made us sick . . .": Letter by [couldn't make out name, possibly McGraw], March 15, 1919, Box 92-002-1, Fort Lewis Museum Archives.

"I did not see in the whole regiment . . ."; "Report of Operations of the 362nd Infantry During the Offensive 25 to 29 Sept" by Colonel John H. Parker (written while in hospital in Bordeaux), 181st Brigade Box, U.S. Army Military History Institute Archives.

"They that had fought so well . . .": Tennyson, Alfred, Lord, "The Charge of the Light Brigade."

PART FOUR, CHAPTER 34

"USS *Tampa* is Sunk, Fearful struggle on the West Front . . .": headlines from the *Anaconda Standard, Butte Daily Post,* and *Butte Miner*, October 1918.

Interchange between Felkner Haynes and Judge Crum: Quoted in Walter, "The Tragedy of Judge C. L. Crum," p. 59–60, quotes from Judge Crum.

"that this was a rich man's war to carry out a . . .": Judge Charles L. Crum Articles of Impeachment, LR15, Box 1, Folder 4, Montana Historical Society Archives.

"Receiving the benefits and blessing . . .": Quoted in the *Anaconda Standard*, September 19, 1918, p. 7.

Wheeler and Kelly quotes: *Anaconda Standard*, October 3, 1918, p. 5.

PART FOUR, CHAPTER 35

"I wouldn't have missed the experience . . .": Quoted in the *Butte Daily Post*, March 16, 1919.

"Bride's Father Starts Action . . .": *Butte Miner*, June 12, 1919, p. 5.

Quotes about Sarah's legal travails: Dougherty vs. Hughes and Simeon vs. Klenze, Silver Bow County Court records.

Robbery quotes: *Butte Miner*, August 19, 1919, p. 1.

PART FOUR, CHAPTER 36

"What a man thinks of himself . . .": Thoreau, *Walden*, p. 7.

PART FOUR, CHAPTER 37

"I don't see why it is that a bunch . . .": Quoted in the *Anaconda Standard*, April 22, 1920, p. 1.

"Look out for that man . . .": Glasser, U.S. Department of Justice report.

"Everybody suspects everybody now . . .": Quoted in Calvert, *The Gibraltar: Socialism and Labor in Butte, Montana, 1895–1920*, p. 124.

PART FOUR, CHAPTER 38

"A very small cat . . .": Poem "The Proud Cat," author unknown. Aunt Brigid can still recite it from memory.

"The Philosophy of Life . . .": Author unknown.

PART FOUR, CHAPTER 40

"By the beard of my father . . ." and following quotes: Writer's Program, *Copper Camp*, p. 95.

"Yung Lee sell dreams . . .": Ibid, p. 112, with accent removed.

PART FIVE, CHAPTER 41

Dialogue, except for Aila: Roy Walsh's confession and the trial transcript, State Law Library of Montana and Jefferson County Court records. Though the transcripts for the other trials in this book were destroyed, Roy's case was appealed to the Montana Supreme Court; the Supreme Court records included a copy of the trial transcript.

PART FIVE, CHAPTER 42

Dialogue: Ibid, unless noted otherwise.

"I examined the scene of the murder . . .": Quoted in the *Boulder Monitor*, July 7, 1923, p. 1.

Archie's letter and Mr. Fessenden's reply: *Jefferson Valley News*, July 26, 1923.

Sarah Hughes and reporters: Quoted in the *Boulder Monitor*, July 28, 1923, p. 1. *Butte Daily Post*, July 20, 1923, p. 7.

"Why don't they do something . . .": Quoted in the *Butte Daily Post*, July 24, 1923, p. 2.
Roy Walsh and reporters: Quoted in the *Butte Daily Post*, July 24, 1923, p. 1.

PART FIVE, CHAPTER 43
Trial dialogue: Trial transcript, State Law Library of Montana.
Roy Walsh's letter to John Elliott, "Just before the shot was fired . . .": Printed in the *Butte Daily Post*, July 27, 1923, p. 12.

PART FIVE, CHAPTER 44
Cartoon captions, letter to Bill Hughes, poem by Archie Hughes: Printed in the *Boulder Monitor*, July, August, September, October 1923; and *Butte Daily Post*, August 1923.

PART FIVE, CHAPTER 45
"Then it will be . . . I wish it to be clearly understood that the case . . .": Quoted in the *Boulder Monitor*, October 20, 1923, p. 1.

PART FIVE, CHAPTER 46
Sarah Hughes and judge: Quoted in the *Butte Miner*, June 10, 1924, p. 7.

PART FIVE, CHAPTER 47
"You could have knocked me down . . .": Quoted in the *Butte Miner*, February 14, 1925, p. 2.
"brilliant criminal lawyer": Wheeler, *Yankee from the West*, p. 69.
"set the entire Jefferson Valley agog": *Boulder Monitor*, May 10, 1924, p. 1.
"The jig is up . . .": Quoted in the *Boulder Monitor*, May 10, 1924, p. 1.
Roy Walsh and Sarah Hughes: Quoted in the *Butte Miner*, June 10, 1924, p. 7.
Roy Walsh and reporters: Quoted in the *Boulder Monitor*, May 24, 1924, p. 1 and 4.
"It is the judgment and sentence of this court . . .": Jefferson County Court records.
Letter from Roy Walsh to Archie Hughes, May 24, 1924, and letter from Warden Potter, May 25, 1924: Montana Governors' Papers, MC-35, Box 258, Folder 4, Montana Historical Society Archives.
"he was sharpening tools . . .": Carter Williams, son of John and Ruth, in a telephone conversation on January 4, 2001.

PART FIVE, CHAPTER 48
Archie Hughes, Roy Walsh, Howard Johnson at the Montana State Prison in Deer Lodge: Quoted in the *Boulder Monitor*, January 3, 1925, p.1.
"You might as well put the rope . . .": Quoted in the *Butte Miner*, January 12, 1925, p. 1.
Letter from Roy Walsh to his aunt dated January 3, 1925: Montana Governors' Papers, MC-35, Box 258, Folder 4, Montana Historical Society Archives.
Courtroom dialogue, conversations in the Boulder jail, statements by John Elliott, Roy Walsh's final statement: Quoted in the *Boulder Monitor*, January 17, 1925, p. 1, January 31, 1925, p. 1, February 21, 1925, p. 1, 8 ; *Butte Daily Post*, January 13, 1925, p. 1, January 14, 1925, p. 1, February 13, 1925, p. 14; *Butte Miner*, January 14, 1925, p. 1, February 13, 1925, p. 1, February 14, 1925, p. 1,3, February 15, 1925.
Letter from Roy Walsh to Governor Erickson, undated, received January 22, 1925, and Governor Erickson's response: Montana Governors' Papers, MC-35, Box 258, Folder 4, Montana Historical Society Archives.
Letters dated June 9, 1924, January 14, 1925, February 4, 1925, February 5, 1925,

February 7, 1925, to the Montana governor about Roy Walsh and the governor's responses: Montana Governors' Papers, MC-35, Box 258, Folder 4, Montana Historical Society Archives.

"There are set before you fire and water . . .": Sirach 15:16, *The New American Bible*.

Telegram from Governor Erickson dated February 13, 1925: Montana Governors' Papers, MC-35, Box 258, Folder 4, Montana Historical Society Archives.

Letter from Roy Walsh's aunt dated January 27, 1925: Montana Governors' Papers, MC-35, Box 258, Folder 4, Montana Historical Society Archives.

PART FIVE, CHAPTER 49

"If life imprisonment meant 'life imprisonment' . . .": *Jefferson Valley News*, February 19, 1925.

PART SIX, CHAPTER 51

"A bunch of the boys were . . .": Poem "The Shooting of Dan McGrew" by Robert Service, *The Best of Robert Service*.

"Saloon, saloon, saloon, it runs . . .": Song "Saloon," lyricist unknown.

"Believe me if all those endearing young charms . . .": Song with lyrics based on a poem by Thomas Moore, found in Felleman, *The Best Loved Poems of the American People*.

"A man cannot talk of such things . . .": Remarque, *All Quiet on the Western Front*, p. 165.

"The wind blows . . .": John 3:8. Complete passage is, "The wind blows where it will, you hear the sound it makes but you do not know where it comes from or where it goes. So it is with everyone begotten of the Spirit." *The New American Bible*.

PART SIX, CHAPTER 53

"She has that rare ability . . .": Tribute K. Ross Toole wrote about Anne McDonnell when she retired in 1953, *Montana Post, Official Newsletter of the Montana Historical Society*, February/March 1978, p. 3.

Quotes by Father Tougas: Letters from Father Tougas to Bishop Carroll, March 31, 1908; January 6, 1919; and March 5, 1919.

"Pastor to the Italians in Meaderville": Letter from Bishop Carroll to Father Tougas, August 28, 1919.

PART SIX, CHAPTER 55

Peter quoting the *Rubáiyát* of Omar Khayyám: Aunt Brigid, Peter's sister, told me this. The following verse was found in Fitzgerald's translation.

PART SIX, CHAPTER 56

"Help me I'm hurt": Inquest over the death of Peter Thompson, Silver Bow County records.

PART SIX, CHAPTER 57

"The north wind doth blow . . .": Title and author unknown.

PART SIX, CHAPTER 59

Passage from the *Rubáiyát* of Omar Khayyám: Grandma (Aila) had torn the pages with these verses from a small booklet and used them as a bookmark in a book of poems we had given her. She had marked these particular verses with large asterisks. It is a compilation of the third, fourth, and fifth versions translated by Fitzgerald.

"Let your acquaintants be many . . .": Sirach 6:6, *The New American Bible*.

PART SIX, CHAPTER 60
Letter from Arthur (Archie) Hughes to Governor Ayers dated July 28, 1940, and governor's response dated August 23, 1940: Montana Governors' Papers, MC-35, Box 283, Folder 7, Montana Historical Society Archives.

PART SIX, CHAPTER 62
Conversation with reporter: *Montana Standard*, October 14, 1981, p.18.

BIBLIOGRAPHY

In addition to the following, I drew heavily from archived material, letters, memoirs, meeting minutes, oral histories, etc., and from city, county, state, and U.S. government records as well as British public records. The places that house those records and the people who worked there and helped me are noted in my acknowledgments. I also relied heavily on personal interviews with family, friends of the family, and others.

BUTTE

Anaconda Standard, Anaconda, Montana newspaper.

Bradley, Omar N.; Clay Blair. *A General's Life.* New York: Simon & Schuster, 1983.

Butte Daily Post, Butte, Montana newspaper.

Butte Miner, Butte, Montana newspaper.

Calvert, Jerry W. *The Gibraltar: Socialism and Labor in Butte, Montana, 1895–1920.* Helena: Montana Historical Society Press, 1988.

Cole, Ronald H.; Clayton D. Laurie. *The Role of Federal Military Forces in Domestic Disorders, 1877–1945.* Washington DC: Center of Military History, United States Army, 1997.

Economists at the Department of Commerce and the Department of Interior. *Minerals Yearbook,* volumes for years 1934 to 1937. Government Printing Office.

Geologist in Charge, Division of Mineral Resources [different names for different years]. *Mineral Resources of the US, Part 1, Metals,* volumes for years 1914 to 1933. Government Printing Office.

Glasser, Abraham. U.S. Department of Justice report on labor trouble in Butte, 1917 to 1920. Butte-Silver Bow Public Archives.

Hammett, Dashiell. *Nightmare Town, Stories by Dashiell Hammett.* Edited by Kirby McCauly, Martin Greenberg, and Ed Gorman. New York: Alfred A. Knopf, 1999. [I used the introduction for biographical data on Hammett. The introduction is by William F. Nolan.]

Harrington, Daniel. *Department of Interior, Bureau of Mines Bulletin. 188, Lessons from the Granite Mountain Shaft Fire, Butte, Montana.* US Government Printing Office, 1922.

Ingalls, W. R.; James Douglas; J. R. Finlay; J. Parke Channing; John Hays Hammond; *Department of Interior Bureau of Mines Bulletin No. 75, Rules and Regulations for Metal Mines.* Government Printing Office, 1915.

James, Don. *Butte's Memory Book.* Caldwell, Idaho: The Caxton Printers Ltd., 1975.

Malone, Michael P. *The Battle for Butte: Mining and Politics on the Northern Frontier, 1864–1906.* Seattle and London: University of Washington Press, 1981.

Marcosson, Isaac F. *Anaconda.* New York: Dodd, Mead and Company, 1957.

Montana Standard, Butte, Montana newspaper.

Murphy, Mary. *Mining Cultures: Men, Women and Leisure in Butte, 1914–41.* Urbana and Chicago: University of Illinois Press, 1997.

Rice, Alice Hegan. *Mrs. Wiggs of the Cabbage Patch.* New York: Grossett & Dunlap, 1901.

Shovers, Brian. "Miners, Managers and Machines: Industrial Accidents and Occupational Disease in the Butte Underground, 1880–1920." Thesis, Montana State University, April 1987.

Sketches of Old Butte. Author unknown. Butte-Silver Bow Public Archives.

State of Montana Department of Labor and Industry Reports.

State of Montana Industrial Accident Board Reports.

Wheeler, Burton K.; with Paul F. Healy. *Yankee from the West*. Garden City, New York: Doubleday & Company, 1962.

Workers of the Writers' Program of the Work Projects Administration in the State of Montana. *Copper Camp, Stories of the World's Greatest Mining Town, Butte, Montana*. New York: Hastings House, 1943.

HOMESTEADING AND ROSEBUD COUNTY

Forsyth Times-Journal, Forsyth, Montana newspaper.

Raban, Jonathan. *Bad Land, An American Romance*. New York: Pantheon Books, 1996.

Rosebud County Bicentennial Committee. *They Came and They Stayed, History of Rosebud County*. Billings: Printed by Western Printing and Lithography, 1977.

Spannagel, Dorothy Tait; Janet Spannagel Guptill. *Trials and Triumphs*. Jordan, Montana: 1994.

Vichorek, Daniel N. *Montana's Homestead Era*. Number Fifteen, Montana Geographic Series. Helena: Montana Magazine, 1987. [This is a book published by Montana Magazine. It is not an article in the magazine.]

IRISH

Bardon, Jonathan. *A History of Ulster*. Belfast: Blackstaff Press, 1992.

Cohen, Marilyn, Edited by. *The Warp of Ulster's Past*. New York: St. Martin's Press, 1997.

Commager, Henry Steele, arranged for one volume. *Churchill's History of the English Speaking Peoples*. New York; Avenel, New Jersey: Wings Books, 1994.

Crawford, W. H. *The Irish Linen Industry*. Ulster Folk and Transport Museum, 1987, p. 33–34.

Emmons, David M. *The Butte Irish*. Urbana and Chicago: University of Illinois Press, 1990.

Foster, R. F. *Modern Ireland, 1600–1972*. London: Penguin Books, 1989.

Linen: Continuity and Change. Ulster Folk and Transport Museum, 1988, p. 15, 26, 35–42.

Maguire, W.A. *Up in Arms: The 1798 Rebellion in Ireland*. Belfast: Trustees of the Ulster Museum, 1998.

Seagrott, Margaret. *A Basic Textile Book*. New York: Van Nostrand Reinhold, 1975, p. 17–19.

Wiltke, Carl. *The Irish in America*. New York: Teachers College Press, 1968. [pamphlet]

Woulfe, Reverend Patrick, collected and edited with explanatory notes. *Irish Names and Surnames*. Kansas City, Missouri: Irish Family Journal, 1992.

MISCELLANEOUS

Armstrong Herald, Armstrong, Howard County, Missouri newspaper.

Barry, John M. *The Great Influenza*. New York: Viking, 2004.

Editors of Time-Life Books, text by Wheeler, Keith. *The Old West: The Railroaders*. New York: Time-Life Books, 1973.

Crosby, Alfred W. *American's Forgotten Pandemic, The Influenza of 1918*. Cambridge: Cambridge University Press, 1989.

Encarta Encyclopedia, 1997.

Encyclopedia of New York City. New Haven and London: Yale University, 1995.

Encyclopedia of the American West. New York: Simon and Schuster Macmillan, 1996.

Felleman, Hazel, selected by. *The Best Loved Poems of the American People*. Garden City, New York: Doubleday & Company, 1936.

Glad, Betty. *Charles Evans Hughes and Illusions of Innocence*. Urbana and London: University of Illinois Press, 1966.

Gordon, John Steele. *The Business of America*. New York: Walker & Company, 2001.

Jefferson Valley News, Whitehall, Montana newspaper, 1923–1925.

King, Moses. *Kings Handbook of New York City 1893*. Boston: Moses King, 1893. Reissued New York City: Benjamin Blom Inc., 1972.

Kolata, Gina. *Flu, The Story of the Great Influenza Pandemic of 1918 and the Search for the Virus That Caused It*. New York: Farrar, Straus and Giroux, 1999.

New American Bible. Nashville, Camden, New York: Thomas Nelson, Publishers, 1971.

New York Times.

Rousmaniere, Leah Robinson. *Anchored Within the Vail: A Pictorial History of the Seamen's Church Institute*. New York: The Seamen's Church Institute, 1995.

Rubáiyát of Omar Khayyám. Rendered into English verse by Edward Fitzgerald. Garden City, New York: Doubleday & Company, Inc., 1952. [I also used Walter J. Black publishers for verses after Peter died.]

Ruiz, Mario. *100 Years of the Automobile, 1886 to 1986*. New York: Gallery Books, 1985.

Service, Robert. *The Best of Robert Service*. New York: Perigee Books, 1907.

Steinbeck, John. *East of Eden*. New York: The Viking Press, 1952.

Stern, Robert A. M.; Gregory Gilmartin; John Montague Massengale. *New York 1900 Metropolitan Architecture*. Rizzoli International Publications, 1983.

Thoreau, Henry David. *Walden*. 1854.

World, New York City newspaper.

World Book Encyclopedia.

World Book Medical Encyclopedia. Chicago: World Book, Inc., 1988.

Montana

Adams, Ramon F. *Cowboy Lingo*. Boston: Houghton Mifflin Company, 1936, p. 20–23.

Adams, Ramon F. *Western Words, A Dictionary of the American West*. Norman: University of Oklahoma Press, 1968.

Annual and Biennial Reports of the Montana State Prison.

Burt, Struthers. *Powder River Let 'Er Buck*. New York and Toronto: Farrar & Rinehart, 1938.

Butler, Anne M. *Gendered Justice in the American West, Women Prisoners in Men's Penitentiaries*. Urbana and Chicago: University of Illinois Press, 1997.

Butler, Anne M.; Ona Siporin. *Uncommon Common Women*. Logan, Utah: Utah State University Press, 1996.

Dodd, Donald B., compiled by. *Historical Statistics of the States of the United States, Two Centuries of the Census, 1790–1990*. Westport, Connecticut; London: Greenwood Press, 1993.

Edgerton, Keith. "Power and Punishment in the Rocky Mountain West: The Montana Prison, 1871–1921." Dissertation, Washington State University, 1994.

Flaherty, Cornelia M. *Go with Haste into the Mountains, A History of the Diocese of Helena*. [No publisher nor date listed.]

Galen, Albert, Attorney General, compiled and prepared by, adopted by the State Board of Prison Commissioners. "Laws, Rules and Regulations Relating to the Government and Management of the State Prison." Montana: Compiled on the 3rd day of Sept 1908.

Great Falls Tribune, Great Falls, Montana newspaper.

Gutfeld, Arnon. *Montana's Agony, Years of War and Hysteria, 1917–1921*. Gainsville: University Presses of Florida, 1979.

Helena Independent and *The Independent Record*, Helena, Montana, newpaper.

Howard, Joseph Kinsey. *Montana High, Wide and Handsome*. Lincoln and London: University of Nebraska Press, 1943.

Kent, Philip. *Montana State Prison History*. Pamphlet prepared for Powell County Museum and Arts Foundation, 1979.

Madisonian, Virginia City, Madison County, Montana newspaper.

Madison Monitor, Twin Bridges, Madison County, Montana newspaper.

Malone, Michael P.; Richard. B. Roeder; William L. Lang. *Montana, A History of Two Centuries*. Seattle and London: University of Washington Press, 1976.

Raymer, Robert George, M.A. *Montana, The Land and the People*. Chicago and New York: The Lewis Publishing Company, 1930.

Silver State, Deer Lodge, Montana newspaper.

Toole, K. Ross. *Twentieth Century Montana: A State of Extremes*. Norman and London: University of Oklahoma Press, 1972.

Walter, Dave. "The Tragedy of Judge Crum." *Montana*, November–December 1990, p. 56–63.

PORTLAND

Bicentennial Committee. *St. Johns History*. Oregon History Center.

Paulsen. *Portland Neighborhood Histories*. Bound essays [no publisher, no date]. Oregon History Center.

Snyder, Eugene. *Portland Names and Neighborhoods*. Portland: Binford & Mort, 1979.

WALES/WELSH AND WILKES-BARRE

American National Biography, Volume 11.

Crowther, M.A. *The Workhouse System, 1834–1929*. Athens, Georgia: The University of Georgia Press, 1981.

Hartman, Edward George. *Americans from Wales*. Boston: Christopher Publishing House, 1967, p. 61–101.

Hartman, Edward George. *The Welsh of Wilkes-Barre and the Wyoming Valley*. Wilkes-Barre: St. David's Society of Wyoming Valley, 1985 [pamphlet].

Jones, Gareth Elwyn. *Modern Wales, A Concise History*. Cambridge: Cambridge University Press, 1984.

Jones, William D. *Wales in America, Scranton and the Welsh, 1860–1920*. University of Wales Press, University of Scranton Press, 1993.

Llewellyn, Richard. *How Green Was My Valley*. New York: Simon & Schuster Inc., 1939.

Longmate, Norman. *The Workhouse*. New York: St. Martin's Press, 1974.

Miller, Donald L. *The Kingdom of Coal*. Philadelphia: University of Pennsylvania Press, 1985.

Owen, Trefor M. *The Customs and Traditions of Wales*. Cardiff: University of Wales Press, 1991.

Phillips, Edward. *History of Wilkes-Barre and Luzerne County*.

Roberts, Peter, PhD. *Anthracite Coal Communities*. New York: The MacMillan Company, 1904.

Rousn, Trevor; Edwin Jones. *Old Brynmawr, Nantyglo and Blaina in Photographs*.

Thomas, Malcolm. *Brynmawr, Beaufort and Blaina, Volumes 1 and 2*. Abertillery, Gwent: Old Bakehouse Publishers.

Wilkes-Barre Record, Wilkes-Barre, Pennsylvania newspaper.

Wilkes-Barre Record Almanacs.

Zbiek, Dr. Paul J. *Luzerne County History of the People and Culture*. Charlestown, MA: Strategic Publications, 1994.

WORLD WAR I

Abbeke, W. "The First Months: The Campaign of the Belgian Army in 1914." *Stand To! The Journal of the Western Front Association*, Spring 1990.

American Battle Monuments Commission. *91st Division, Summary of Operations in the World War*. Washington: United States Government Printing Office, 1944.

American Battle Monuments Commission, prepared by. *American Armies and Battlefields in Europe*. U.S. Government Printing Office, 1938.

American Legion. *Silver Bow County in the World War*. 1919.

Angell, Norman. *The Great Illusion, A Study of the Relation of Military Power to National Advantage*. New York and London: G. P. Putnam's Sons, 1910.

Barnes, Harry Elmer. *Genesis of the World War*. New York: Alfred A. Knopf, 1926.

Black, Jeremy, Edited by. *Atlas of World History*. London, New York, Sydney: Dorling Kindersley Publishing, 2000.

Brittain, Vera. *Testament of Youth*. New York: Penguin Books, 1933.

Brown, Frederic J. *Chemical Warfare: Gas, A Study of Restraints*. Princeton, New Jersey: Princeton University Press, 1968.

Burg, David F.; L. Edward Purcell. *Almanac of World War I*. Lexington: University Press of Kentucky, 1998.

Carroll, Andrew, compiled/edited. *War Letters*. New York: Scribner, 2001.

Center of Military History, United States Army. *American Armies and Battlefields in Europe*. Washington DC: U.S. Government Printing Office, 1995.

Center of Military History. *The Army Lineage Book*, Volume II, Infantry. U.S. Government Printing Office, 1953.

Churchill, Winston. *World Crisis*. New York: Charles Scribner's Sons, 1931.

Clark, Birge. *World War I Memoirs of Birge Clark*. Self published, revised 1971.

Clodfelter, Michael. *Warfare and Armed Conflicts, A Statistical Reference*. Jefferson, North Carolina and London: McFarland & Company, Inc. Publishers, 1992.

Coffman, Edward M. *The War to End all Wars, The American Military Experience in World War I*. Madison: The University of Wisconsin Press, 1986.

Collier's Photographic History of the European War. New York: P. F. Collier & Son, 1916.

Croddy, Eric. *Chemical and Biological Warfare, A Comprehensive Survey for the Concerned Citizen*. New York: Copernicus Books, 2002.

Dawson, N. P. *The Good Soldier, A Selection of Soldiers' Letters, 1914–1918*. New York: The MacMillan Company, 1918.

Denman, Terence. *Ireland's Unknown Soldiers: The 16th (Irish) Division in the Great War, 1914–1918*. Dublin: Irish Academic Press, 1992.

Dos Passos, John. *First Encounter*. New York: Philosophical Library [no date]. [I used the introduction which was written April 26, 1945. The book was written twenty-five years earlier.]

Dudley, William, Book Editor. *World War I, Opposing Viewpoints*. San Diego, California: Greenhaven Press, Inc., 1998.

Editors of American Heritage, narrative by S. L. A. Marshall. *The American Heritage History of World War I*. [No city listed]: American Heritage Publishing Co., Inc., Simon and Schuster, 1964.

Esposito, Colonel Vincent J. *The West Point Atlas of American Wars, Volume II, 1900 to 1953*. New York: Frederick A. Praeger, Publishers, 1959.

Fries, Amos A.; Clarence J. West. *Chemical Warfare*. New York: McGraw-Hill Book Company, Inc., 1921.

Gail, W.W., edited. *Yellowstone County Montana in the World War*. Billings: War Book Publishing Company, 1919, p. 2–3.

Genthe, Charles V. *American War Narratives 1917–1918, A Study and Bibliography*. New York: David Lewis, 1969.

Gibbons, Floyd. *"And They Thought We Wouldn't Fight."* New York: George H. Doran Company, 1918.

Gilbert, Martin. *Atlas of World War I, The Complete History*, 2nd Edition. New York: Oxford University Press, 1994.

Gilbert, Martin. *The First World War, A Complete History*. New York: Henry Holt and Company, 1994.

Graves, Robert. *Good-bye to All That*. Garden City, New York: Doubleday & Company, Inc., 1929.

Gudmundsson, Bruce I. *Storm Troop Tactics, Innovation in the German Army, 1914–1918*. New York; Westport, Connecticut; London: Praeger, 1989.

Harries, Meirion and Susie. *The Last Days of Innocence: America at War, 1917–1918*. New York: Random House, 1997.

Haythornthwaite, Philip J. *The World War One Source Book*. London: Arms and Armour Press, 1992.

Johnson, Paul. *Modern Times*. New York: Harper & Row, 1983.

Keegan, John. *The First World War*. New York: Alfred A. Knopf, 1999.

Kennedy, David M. *Over Here, The First World War and American Society*. New York, Oxford: Oxford University Press, 1980.

Lawson, Don. *The United States in World War I*. New York: Scholastic Book Services, 1963.

Livesey, Anthony. *The Historical Atlas of World War I*. New York: Henry Holt Company, 1994.

McMaster, John Bach. *The United States in the World War*. New York, London: D. Appleton & Co., 1918.

Meldrum, T. Ben; Axel A. Madsen. *A History of the 362nd*. [No city listed]: The 362nd Infantry Association [no date].

Mustard, Helen M., translated by. *Medieval Epics, The Nibelungenlied*. New York: The Modern Library, 1963.

91st Division Publication Committee, San Mateo, California. *The Story of the 91st Division*. San Francisco: Press of H. S. Crocker Co., Inc., 1919.

Pages of Glory and History: The 91st Division in Argonne and Flanders. Paris, New York, San Francisco: City of Paris.

Parsons, I. M., edited by. *Men Who March Away, Poems of the First World War*. New York: The Viking Press, 1965.

Pershing, John J. *My Experiences in the World War* New York: Frederick A. Stokes Company, 1931.

Preston, Diana. *Lusitania, An Epic Tragedy*. New York: Walker & Company, 2002.

Remarque, Erich Maria; translated by A. W. Wheen. *All Quiet on the Western Front*. New York: Little, Brown and Company, 1929.

Sassoon, Siegfried. *Collected Poems, 1908–1956*. London, Boston: Faber and Faber, 1947.

Sassoon Siegfried. *Memoirs of an Infantry Officer*. London: Faber and Faber, 1930, p. 1–94.

Shore, Chester, compiled by. *Montana in the Wars*. Miles City: American Legion of Montana, 1977, p. 62F–75.

600 Days' Service, A History of the 361st Infantry Regiment of the United States Army. [no city, no date]

Stand To! The Journal of the Western Front Association, several articles.

Straubing, Harold Elk, edited by. *The Last Magnificent War, Rare Journalistic and Eyewitness Accounts of World War I*. New York: Paragon House, 1989.

Tuchman, Barbara. *The Guns of August*. New York: Bantam [first published by Macmillian], 1962.

U.S. Army War College. *Order of Battle of the US Land Forces in the World War, American Expeditionary Forces*. US Government Printing Office, 1931.

Vaughan, Edwin Campion. *Some Desperate Glory*. New York: Henry Holt and Company, 1981.

Whitney, Arthur St. John. *Letters to His Family 1917–1919 while on Active Duty, World War I, in the Grizzlies Artillery Regiment (Second California Field Artillery, California Militia) and the 91st Division, 348th Machine Gun Battalion*.

Winter, Jay; Blaine Baggett. *The Great War and the Shaping of the 20th Century*. New York: Penguin Studio, 1996.

Young, Brigadier Peter, Editor in Chief. *The Marshal Cavendish Illustrated Encyclopedia of WWI*, Volume 10. New York, London, Toronto: Marshal Cavendish, 1986.